PIMLICO

819

EDWARD BURRA

Jane Stevenson is the author of two collections of novellas, *Several Deceptions* and *Good Women*, and four novels, *London Bridges*, *Astraea*, *The Pretender* and *Empress of the Last Days*. She is Reader in English at the University of Aberdeen.

Also by Jane Stevenson

Several Deceptions
London Bridges
Astraea
The Pretender
The Empress of the Last Days
Good Women

EDWARD BURRA

Twentieth-Century Eye

JANE STEVENSON

PIMLICO

Published by Pimlico 2008

4 6 8 10 9 7 5 3

Copyright © Jane Stevenson 2007

Jane Stevenson has asserted her right under
the Copyright, Designs and Patents Act, 1988 to
be identified as the author of this work.

First published in Great Britain in 2007 by
Jonathan Cape

Pimlico
Random House, 20 Vauxhall Bridge Road
London SW1V 2SA

www.randomhouse.co.uk

Addresses for companies within The Random House Group Limited
can be found at: www.randomhouse.co.uk/offices.htm

The Random House Group Limited Reg. No. 954009

A CIP catalogue record for this book is available from the British Library

ISBN 9780099501664

The Random House Group Limited supports the Forest Stewardship
Council® (FSC®), the leading international forest-certification organisation. Our
books carrying the FSC label are printed on FSC®-certified paper. FSC is the only
forest-certification scheme supported by the leading environmental organisations,
including Greenpeace. Our paper procurement policy can be found at
www.randomhouse.co.uk/environment

Printed and bound by CPI Group (UK) Ltd, Croydon, CR0 4YY

www.randomhouse.co.uk

CONTENTS

For my oldest friends –
not forgetting the one I married

LIST OF ILLUSTRATIONS

Burra's family and his circle as young adults

1. Henry Curteis Burra, Edward Burra's father*

2. Ermyntrude (Trudy) Burra (extreme left, in profile), Edward Burra's mother, with unidentified family members*

3. Formal photograph of Burra aged about five (Copied from the Burra Archive with permission of Rye Art Gallery)

4. Snapshot of Burra with his sister Anne as children at Camber Sands (Copied from the Burra Archive with permission of Rye Art Gallery)

5. Springfield Lodge, Burra's home from his birth to the mid-Fifties (Courtesy of Jane Stevenson)

6. View from behind Springfield Lodge, Playden (Courtesy of Jane Stevenson)

7. Burra's drawing of his nanny, Miss Isabella McCallum, c. 1924 (Estate of the artist, c/o Lefevre Fine Art Ltd)

8. Burra's drawing of his youngest sister, Betsy, c. 1924 (Estate of the artist, c/o Lefevre Fine Art Ltd)

9. Billy Chappell aged 16 or 17 (Estate of the artist, c/o Lefevre Fine Art Ltd)

10. Billy Chappell at 18*

11. Billy Chappell in the 'Creole Boy' costume from the ballet *Rio Grande* (designed by Burra)*

12. Burra in his studio, photographed by Barbara Ker-Seymer*

13. 'Birdie' Rushbury in the early Twenties, drawing by Burra's Royal College tutor, Randolph Schwabe (Courtesy of the Schwabe Estate)

14. Anne Burra, photographed by Barbara Ker-Seymer (Courtesy of Max Ker-Seymer)

15. Clover Pritchard (Courtesy of Edward Pertinez)

All captions marked * are courtesy of the Barbara Ker-Seymer Estate, c/o Tate Images.

PREFACE

I can guess what Burra would have said, in his whisky-roughened Edwardian drawl, if he had heard that someone was writing his biography. 'What can they know of *may layfe*?' He didn't care for being questioned.

Burra: 'I don't know what all this personality has to do with it exactly but I suppose you have to have that . . . You must have personalities.'
Interviewer: 'Do you think that's wrong?'
Burra: 'I don't know whether it's wrong. But I was never really interested.'

As far as Burra was concerned, it was only painting that mattered. He gave his life to creating artworks of extraordinary authenticity and originality. When he was at home, he slept five or six hours a night, gave his fragile, arthritic body and its environment the absolute minimum of necessary attention, and otherwise painted, read and, very usefully from my point of view, wrote letters. Painting was the way he kept his nightmares at bay; the only real reason why he didn't drink himself into the grave at the double (as he put it). His likes and dislikes, his experiences, do not in any real sense explain his art, let alone explain it away, they only give it a context.

But although the paintings are all that he cared about himself, they are not the only reason to find Edward Burra interesting. Apart from being charming, original, funny, gallant and sardonic, he was staggeringly observant. Since his originality of mind and spirit had never been submitted to the psychological strait-jacket imposed by public schools and Oxbridge, his vision was his own, almost entirely unencumbered by any externally imposed sense of what 'one ought' to do, or see, or be.

His disciplined routine was regularly broken. Once a fortnight or so, he ventured out of his self-imposed seclusion and went to London to stay with one or other of his friends for two or three days. Almost every year, except during the war, he travelled, as far afield as Morocco and Mexico on occasion, but also in Spain, America (mostly Harlem, the lower East Side of New York, and Boston), the South of France and Paris, and Italy, as well as within Britain. Thus he alternated his work as a painter with gathering the experience that fuelled it.

Crucially, his was an era of reliable postal services, so there is an enormous mass of correspondence surviving from his seventy-one years of life. Living as he did in Rye in Sussex, on the south coast of England, the network of beloved friends whom he saw in London and abroad had to be maintained. One thing he always found time for was writing letters. Some of his friends were painters, but others were poets, writers, dancers, lesbian socialites, photographers, nightclub owners, business-people, film directors and men about town. His changing perceptions, his witness to what was going on in the arts in his time, are consequently recorded in countless letters, many of which were preserved by his friends because they were sharply funny and worth keeping.

Burra, like his contemporary Christopher Isherwood, was 'a camera'; and since his life took him on a zigzag course through much of what is enduringly important in twentieth-century English (and American) culture, the letters give a snapshot collage of the world of twentieth-century art, ballet and literature, as observed by an alert, cool, sceptical and uniquely irreverent intelligence. No-one was spared his mockery, least of all himself. Though he respected real achievement in others, he was reliably acid about anything he considered facile or bogus and, above all, about emotional exhibitionism.

His painting is an important reflection of the changing moods of the last century. His earliest work, as Andrew Causey, who catalogued Burra's paintings, says, is about human energy and popular style; an aspect and witness of the Twenties' cultural revolution which makes the First World War so definitive a watershed. Though he hugely enjoyed the vitality of people who either lived for pleasure or in the service of the pleasure of others, he retained a detachment from their concerns. He was as resistant to the seductions of sex and fame as Savonarola, but unlike the Florentine reformer, he had a sense of humour. He preferred to celebrate the vanities rather than to toss them onto bonfires; but he did not lose sight of the fact that they were vanities. He was linked with the surrealists, for want of any better way to place him, but it might be truer to say that he was a magic realist before such a concept had been invented.

As the Thirties progressed, in tune with the darkening mood of the time, Burra's art became overtly tragic. Following the example of Goya, whom he admired profoundly, he painted both the horrors of war and the corruption wrought in young men by turning them into soldiers. From 1935, the year before the Spanish Civil War broke out, much of his work had a new seriousness, though with elements of terrible comedy. In the Fifties, he turned away from the human form (though never entirely) to concentrate on landscapes of luminous serenity and weirdly powerful flower pieces; in the Sixties and Seventies, he was one of the first artists to protest at the ravaging of the English countryside that went along with the creation of the new motorways; to perceive the real costs of you've-never-had-it-so-good.

The process by which experience and emotion turn into marks on paper is one which the painter him- or herself cannot describe in words. Burra was no more able to answer a question such as 'but what is it *about*?' than any other painter of his time – when Melvyn Bragg asked it of Francis Bacon, the latter said, 'You tell me'; when John Rothenstein, who was writing a book on Burra at the time, asked it of his subject, he said, 'Bring a psychiatrist and we'll find out.' He distrusted and disliked intellectualising, but his instinctive response to his times was backed up by an unusual amount of knowledge and a very finely developed critical intelligence. He was extremely well read, he studied old-master painting very seriously both through books and by visiting the great galleries, and he had a sharp, analytic mind. He detested talking about 'Fart', as about anything that was really close to his heart, but everything he said on the subject was interesting.

Burra was an observer, not a voyeur. He engaged fully with mass culture, and expressed this through his art; he loved the pop music of his day, jazz and the blues, he loved pop culture, while at the same time he responded sharply and discriminatingly to the avant-garde. But he did not feel that anyone, or anything, was entitled to automatic reverence. Not only did he not suffer fools gladly, he barely suffered them at all. He refused to make time for timewasters, and he detested earnestness. The half-hour documentary which was made about him in 1972 bored and irritated him beyond measure.

Well if you want to know dearie I thought the whole thing was deadly. I particularly dislike talking about 'Art' or 'myself' & being questioned. Nobody ever gets very Far. They should have learned that by this time youd think.

Burra was profoundly private, to the point of being secretive. Even Billy Chappell, to whom this letter was written, is warned off very clearly: Burra is saying, fifty-one years of friendship do not entitle you, let alone the world at large, to try and climb into my head. 'Edward's personality,' Chappell explained, 'his nature, was full of barriers and barricades. Those who were fairly intimate with him learnt never to attempt to overthrow them. Anything he felt strongly about – such as his work – he would not discuss.'

   And yet here I am, trying to climb into Burra's head. The interest of the letters lies not only in what they reveal about his time; but also, in a sense, what they don't reveal about the writer. When I was first thinking about Burra, I came across a comment on Dickens in a letter by George Bernard Shaw:

There is a curious contrast between Dickens's sentimental indiscretions concerning his marriage and his sorrows and quarrels, and his impenetrable reserve about himself as displayed in his published correspondence. He writes to his family about waiters, about hotels, about screeching tumblers of hot brandy and water, and about the seasick man in the next berth, but never one really intimate word, never a real confession of his soul. David Copperfield is a failure as an autobiography because when he comes to deal with the grown-up David, you find he has not the slightest intention of telling you the truth – or indeed anything – about himself. Even the child David is more remarkable for the reserves than for the revelations: he falls back on fiction at every turn.

This is as true of Burra as it is of Dickens. 'A camera' is a good metaphor for Burra, not least because the one thing a camera won't show you is the person behind the viewfinder. But there are ways round even the most obstructive observer. Shaw continues, on Dickens, 'Clennam and Pip are the real autobiographies.' Similarly, Burra's statements about what he truly felt and believed are many. They are the paintings, which are beyond any possible doubt sincere, though not easy to interpret. Using the trajectory plotted by the letters, with their observations and omissions, what Burra read and saw, and to some extent the reactions of his contemporaries, Burra can be coaxed into revealing something of himself.

From time to time, as I worked on this biography, I spent intensive weeks in the archives of Tate Britain, wading through the hundreds and hundreds of grubby letters which are the principal evidence for Burra's personal world, and scribbling down transcriptions as fast as my hand could move, in a state of such concentration that the hours passed by unnoticed, an experience which, as it developed, began to feel more and more like eavesdropping on a fifty-year-long conversation between Burra and his group of lifelong friends. Between one day and the next on one such visit, I received a message, as Burra might have put it, 'from the Other Sayde' – as biographers often do, in one way or another. I was sitting at my desk; and the phone rang. I picked it up; and Ed's unmistakable voice enquired, without preamble, 'Well, dearie. Having fun?' I was so startled I woke up. But in a way, this whole book is the answer to his question. Yes, Ed. I had wonderful fun. It's been such a pleasure trying to get to know you.

I

RYE

IT was a placidly monumental, foursquare house, with wide eaves and green shutters. English children still draw square houses, a door in the middle, windows either side, a central chimney with spiralling smoke, though very few now live in anything of the kind. For the first two or three years, a child's world is his parents' house and garden. Edward Burra grew up in a square house, designed, it would seem, to produce normality, conformity and absence of introspection; yet he became one of the twentieth century's most original painters. But the deep springs of his art and his personality were nourished by the life which was led in that square place.

Burra was born in 1905, the second son of wealthy upper-middle-class parents (his older brother, Henry, died in infancy), and the house was called Springfield Lodge. It was a white stucco box with a mansard roof, four bays wide, three storeys high, from the very beginning of Victoria's reign. The drive was, and is, closed in on either side by over-scale, twenty-foot hedges, one of laurel, the other of rhododendron, brooded over by wellingtonias and monkey-puzzles, and curved so that the house is all but invisible from the road. From the point of view of Master Edward, the household baby, the drive was a dark-green tunnel, leading to the unknown.

These gardens, a small child's world, were actually on a very considerable scale (eleven acres), divided by walls into sub-areas, and tended with Edwardian thoroughness by two gardeners. There was a vast cedar of Lebanon, its huge armlike branches sweeping down almost to the ground (Burra later drew it, and it eventually blew down). White marble gleamed from the deep shadows of mature shrubberies; a small Greek temple and a variety of other statuary, including an elaborate group of a neoclassical lady in a chiton communing with a very English terrier, which marked the end of a vista. There was also a tidily railed round pond, and on the edge of the garden proper, a corrugated-iron drill shed put up in 1880 by Burra's grandfather for the use of the Rye Volunteers, which became the children's wet-weather playroom, and was known to them as the Velodrome Buffalo. Other areas grew vegetables for the kitchen and dahlias for the house; there were borders, an orchard and greenhouses. Springfield had a staff of eight. Apart from the gardeners, there was a cook, two housemaids, a parlourmaid, a handyman/gamekeeper and a Scottish nanny.

Stumping towards a border in 1907 or so, Edward traversed smooth, emerald lawn towards an explosion of colour. When you are two, you look up at a peony. The flower is surprisingly heavy, and if you take one in your hand, it is like grasping a crimson satin football. Oriental poppies are flaming vermilion, the thin, gleaming petals contrasting with the sooty frill of stamens. They open tantalisingly, the rough, slightly hairy olive-green oval bud splitting along a seam to disclose something crumpled, wet-looking, red. Such a temptation to help it along. 'Don't touch, Master Edward. You'll spoil it.' Later in the year there were dahlias, huge, quilled and cool-textured, but often containing earwigs. Iris, green swords and lolling velvet tongues; old roses, blowsy, pink and scented, Fantin-Latour, Souvenir de Malmaison. Even the dark, shiny-leaved rhododendron hedge exploded with enormous freckled magenta mops in late spring. As an adult, Burra painted flowers with hallucinatory intensity. They seem to be coming out to meet you, or trying to suck you in; he liked to paint them head-on, so you are looking down their throats. The colours and shapes of flowers were in the deep layers of Burra's mind, part of what formed him as an artist. John Rothenstein noted his interest in the garden and its plants when he visited the house in 1942, long before Burra began his sequence of flower-paintings.

A visitor who came to the house a hundred years ago saw tweed coats and caps hanging up in the hall, fishing-tackle and tennis rackets leaning against the wall, spaniels fussing out to welcome the guest. In the Twenties, more surprisingly, he would have been greeted by an elkhound, which belonged to Burra's sister. The house's interior was high Victorian; comfortable and orderly; with marble fireplaces, over-stuffed chairs, bibelots on cluttered overmantels, and well-polished furniture. Much of the furnishings dated to the era of Burra's grand-parents; nothing was changed merely because it had become a little shabby, or for the sake of change. By the Twenties, the décor looked distinctly old-fashioned. A visitor remembered 'everything crumbling away a little bit. Lovely grand old curtains faded at the edges.' The overall effect was goldenish, 'a perfectly English look, coloured blond, pale brown, faded blue'. There were Victorian watercolours in the drawing-room, and a model of the Taj Mahal under a glass dome. There was a stuffed barn owl on the mantelpiece, which Burra subsequently appropriated. Heavily varnished landscapes 'the colour of old violins' in heavy gold frames hung on the walls of the hall and staircase (which, incidentally, was a beautifully curving mahogany spiral, the house's sole moment of architectural distinction).

Burra drew a few of Springfield's interiors by way of technical exer-cises when he was in his teens, with a clear preference for views through a window or involving a mirror, but visually, the house left no direct impression on him. The environments he chose to inhabit as an inde-pendent adult suggest total indifference to any of the considerations which governed Springfield as a whole; his aesthetic, if it can be so called, was that of the dog-basket; fetid strata of papers, letters, maga-zines, books, scratched Bakelite 78s and occasional fossilised food items, welded together with cigarette ash.

Burra was born nine years before the First World War, thus into the sunset of lives supported on personal capital, though at the time, as has so often been said, the Edwardian era seemed a long, golden afternoon. The founder of the family, financially speaking, was Edward Jeremiah Curteis (1762–1835), of Windmill Hill, Worthing, who made so much money from banking that his own extensive brood and his many grand-children did not have to work for a living unless they chose to. His granddaughter, Frances Curteis, made a very suitable match with Edward's grandfather, the scion of an old-established Westmorland family with roots trailing back as far as the fourteenth century.

Burras first appear in the historical record as small independent farmers living near Maulds Meaburn, King's Meaburn and Crosby Ravensworth. In the course of the eighteenth century, Robert Burra, who was born at Crosby Ravensworth in 1742, moved south to Carshalton to become a partner in a merchant house. His eldest son returned to Westmorland, but his youngest, William (Edward Burra's great-grandfather), joined his father's firm and married a daughter of another banking family, Miss Pomfret of Tenterden. Their son Henry was sent out to the East India Company, but when his mother died in 1862, he came home again, entered the Rye Old Bank (then called Pomfret & Curteis) and married Frances Curteis. Subsequently, he became a successful banker and Mayor of Rye. He bought Springfield Lodge in 1867.

His oldest son, Henry Curteis Burra (1870–1958), Edward's father, was one of the two sons and four daughters born before Frances died, worn out, at only thirty, when her oldest son, Henry Curteis, was four. Henry Burra's unmarried sister-in-law, Mary Curteis, came to live with him to look after the orphan children. Once they could manage without her, she settled nearby at The Hooks, Playden, where she died in 1922. Henry Burra himself died in 1886, when his son was a schoolboy of sixteen; so the house was presumably shut up for some years until Henry Curteis Burra was ready to become a householder.

Henry Curteis Burra was educated at Charterhouse and Magdalen College, Oxford. Thereafter he became, briefly, a barrister, but on his marriage to Ermyntrude Robertson-Luxford (known as Trudy), he was in a position to live magnificently on his share of the family money. He threw up his practice and took his new bride to the house he had grown up in. He became a JP, took an active part in local affairs and sat on endless committees, but never again did he work for money.

My own gallery-going began in the mid-Seventies. I could very well have crossed paths with Edward Burra, who died in 1976. I find it a strange thought that the small, wispy-haired, hopelessly scruffy old man that he had become by then had been born into a milieu which would have been completely recognisable to Jane Austen: the cultivated, provincial upper middle class.

The wife Henry Burra chose was the delicate, wilful, much-indulged daughter of two Scots, John Robertson-Luxford of Coiscraig on Loch Rannoch, in Perthshire, and Cecilia Walker of Dalry. They had moved to Sussex in 1875 when John Robertson-Luxford inherited Higham House, Robertsbridge, from an uncle. But for all that Burra's maternal grandparents had settled in the south, his Scottish connections were not unimportant. Trudy Robertson-Luxford, who had been born in George Street, Edinburgh, maintained contact with relatives who remained in Scotland after her father had taken the family to Sussex. She instilled a love of Scotland in both Burra and his sisters, and Cecilia, her own mother, was an important person in their lives. Her children did not get on with their grandfather, whom they found repressive.

When Edward and Anne Burra were growing up, East Sussex was full of their relatives. Curteises, Burras, Pomfrets and their connections ramified through the county. Half the grand houses of Playden were owned by relatives; when Aunt Mary Curteis (who had looked after the children when they were young) died, Henry Curteis Burra's only unmarried sister, Denise Burra (Aunt Denny), moved into her house, The Hooks, just opposite. The other three married, respectively, the architect Reginald Blomfield; a soldier, Major Herbert Neve; and a teacher, Francis Hammond Brodrick. The Brodrick children, Billy and Frankie, used to come to Aunt Denny's for the holidays. Billy was born in 1904, Frankie in 1907, so they were much of an age with Edward and Anne (born in 1905 and 1909 respectively). They were very close to Edward and Anne as children, and the foursome regularly played and biked about Sussex together. Edward and Anne were also close to their Robertson-Luxford relations – Trudy had both a brother James and a sister Audrey, and Audrey's children, Lawrence and Sheila Rich, were very good friends of Edward and Anne's.

Henry and Trudy Burra's household was cultivated, even arty. The house was full of books, many of them about painting. 'The library at Springfield . . . overflowed down every passage and into the loos.' Both Edward's father and his grandfather painted for pleasure, and his intensely musical mother had studied singing both in London and at a finishing school in Dresden. She was passionately devoted to opera throughout her life, and managed at least to transmit a profound love of music to her son, though his taste was principally for jazz and blues rather than for classical composers (he did, however, go to concerts of classical music, as his diaries and letters bear witness; he seems to have liked Verdi and, above all, a number of French composers; Emmanuel Chabrier in particular, but also Ravel and Debussy).

Though Burra's parents were convention personified in many ways, there were clear strands of resemblance between both of them and Burra himself. Billy Chappell, a frequent visitor to Springfield from the Twenties through to the Fifties, concluded:

Physically, Ed resembled each of them; and his character was an amalgam of theirs. His beautiful manners; his kindness; his generosity and compassion; even, probably, his talent (Dah was an amateur painter of no mean ability) came from his father. His charm; his obstinacy; his great capacity for enjoyment; his sharp wits and his sense of style came from his mother.

He remembered Trudy Burra as tiny and always immaculately turned out, but also as very funny, with a waspish sense of humour. She was very sociable and played a lot of bridge, and she would 'go to tea parties and come back and be wicked'. Henry Burra (Dah) was a gentler character altogether, and less communicative, though they were a very united couple.

Some key shibboleths of the pre-war world of his parents never deserted Burra. Courtesy, consideration for others, always writing thank-you letters, loyalty. Also, living within your income, never touching your capital, leaving your money within the family. He died worth £272,000, which in Seventies' money was no mean sum, but his late letters are hymns to frugality: 'half a pound of shin [beef] stewed up with carrots onions turnip Bisto & some Knorr powder very non U Im sure'; and he was horrified by an American friend's profligacy with heating and lighting. Even given the post-war Labour governments' frankly declared war on inherited income, the scale of his estate represents the tail-end of Burra family money more accurately than it does Burra's own earning capacity.

Burra's background was of rocklike solidity, which it is hard now even to imagine, both financially and personally. His parents were deeply fond of one another, and of their children. There was plenty of money; but no waste, ostentation or extravagance. Nothing was bought without due consideration, except possibly books, and the household's only other extravagances were travel and the opera. They did not, for example, run a car. As a family, they were self-sufficient and pleased with one another's company. They socialised with relatives and with other people of their own kind; they did not care tuppence about fashion. They did not long to join the Smart Set, to hobnob with aristocrats or to be, or to seem, anything whatsoever other than exactly what they were.

Similarly, they were not at all concerned about style. Burra mentions, for example, that the Christmas decorations in 1926 came from the International Stores. They were profoundly, and quite unselfconsciously,

snobbish. When Aunt Audrey (Trudy Burra's sister) came for that
Christmas lunch in 1926, she held forth on the subject of C.B. Cochran's
Blackbirds, the first revue of black American artistes to play in London,
which Burra and his friends adored. As Burra told it – he never learned
either to spell or to punctuate – she said:

'Oh realy we didn't care for black birds realy these people have no sense of humour
we never laughed <u>once</u> why they hardly said <u>anything</u> and there were no jokes . . .
there was too much charleston and as for that creature with large feet[1] I thought
I was on the beech at Margate' . . . so I ses 'oh yes & the <u>audience</u> so common
such people I don't know where they came from', so she ses 'yes very suburban,
I was so busy showing them <u>I</u> wasn't suburban I may have missed some of the
things.'

Burra found much to mock in the older generation's attitudes. But while
many of his beliefs and habits were profoundly divergent from those of
his parents, they were entirely successful in passing on to him their
confidence in themselves and their total indifference to what anybody
else might think.

Among the happy accidents of Burra's childhood was his nanny.
When Trudy Burra had her children, she turned to her own childhood
nurse for help, Miss Isabella McCallum, a formidable little Scotswoman
with a distinct moustache, a long nose and grey hair. The relationship
between Burra and Nana was a good one. She had a a gift for story-
telling, and a penchant for disasters that fed Burra's Gothic streak.
Burra's sister Anne recalled her récits of the collapse of the Tay Bridge
and the sinking of the *Titanic* – with which she had a personal connection, since her brother, a carpenter, had helped to build it. She also read
with the children: Edward, and Anne, who was four years younger. Anne
recalls their reading Scott, Burns, Stevenson, the cornerstones of
Scottish literary identity, as well as Dickens. Other books Nana chose
had more Gothic tendencies; they read Harrison Ainsworth's shiver-
provoking *The Tower of London*, and Burra liked a book about French
history with a gruesome illustration of Ravillac, who murdered Henri
IV, being executed by being torn apart by four horses. Anne couldn't

---

[1] The tiny and exquisite Florence Mills. Her pure, high voice defied description, but was usually
likened to a bird or a bell.

bear to look at it; Burra used to try and make her; probably ordinary small-boy ghoulishness, but also a foretaste of a lifelong attempt to look steadily at horror.

Anne Ritchie's affectionate memoir of the happy childhood she shared with her brother does not mention music-halls and their songs, but Burra's passionate enjoyment of such things later in life suggests that the taste goes back to his childhood. It was certainly well in evidence by his twenties. Like his mother, he could sing, and enjoyed doing so (falsetto), and he had an extensive repertory of music-hall numbers. He painted an affectionate portrait of the music-hall comedienne Nellie Wallace in 1934/5, caught in the process of putting over her act; and through the Twenties and Thirties he regularly reported on visits to the panto in Rye and Hastings, often made together with his family, and he was a frequent visitor to the Chelsea Palace variety theatre in the King's Road.

Burra's contemporary Osbert Lancaster, who was similarly the product of a solid upper-middle-class background, and a successful designer for the ballet, made these thought-provoking comments on the life of a privileged child before the First World War:

The popular music of the Edwardian era played an important rôle in the national life ... In the strictly stratified social world of my childhood they seemed to me in my bourgeois pram to be the one thing enjoyed in common by the whistling errand-boy and the ladies I occasionally observed ... as they emerged from the glittering Paradise of *The Devonshire Arms* ... and the world of which the pillars were Kate and my father.

Nana may have had a jollier side, but in any case, she was not the only significant influence on the Burra children. In a household such as Springfield, with eight servants, the children of the house were inevitably profoundly involved with its inner life, because they spent a great deal of time below stairs. They knew much about the house and its inhabitants which their parents did not; and they lived in it in a different way. They were exposed to whatever aspects of the popular press suited the taste of the servants' hall, whether *Photoplay*, *The Watchtower* or the *News of the World*. The images which Burra reached for in later life suggests that *Peg's Paper* is likely to have been part of Springfield kitchen reading: a cartoon that he drew in the Twenties of a maharajah, a half-nude showgirl and a sinister lesbian in a harem setting is identified as a *Peg's Paper* illustration.[2] Similarly, he observed in 1927, following a barbed remark from a friend, 'Well dear I'me sorry I'me not as good as the Tatler but London Life and the World Pictorial News flavoured with the police gazette is more my line.' These publications might have entered the upstairs world of Springfield, but they are far more likely to have been read in the servants' hall.

It is easy to overlook the real importance of these experiences, since there is no equivalent in young children's lives today. But in a stable household such as Springfield, where servants might well work for decades, or even for a lifetime, the servants' hall was often a gallery of strong personalities, their foibles and interests a source of fascination to pre-school-age children who so often sat unheeded, soaking up the gossip. Agatha Christie, who had a similar background, commented, 'One of the things I think I should notice most, if I were a child nowadays, would be the absence of servants. To a child, they were the most colourful part of daily life. Nurses supplied platitudes; servants supplied drama, entertainment, and all kinds of unspecified but interesting knowledge. Far from being slaves they were frequently tyrants.'

Upstairs, also, there were certainly images in the house which helped to form Burra's taste. He mentioned to Rothenstein that among the first artists he remembered liking were Caran d'Ache and Doré. His father had perhaps hung onto *Picture Magazine* (a late-Victorian precursor of comics) from his own childhood, since it had strip-cartoons by Caran d'Ache, but in any case the house was full of cartoons and caricatures. 'The library ... had books of drawings by Caran d'Ache, Hogarth, Steinlen, Rowlandson, Gilroy [Gillray], Constantin Guys and Sem. Edward looked at them again and again.' Where Gustave Doré is most likely to have entered his consciousness is via his visionary steel-engraved illustrations to the Bible and *Paradise Lost*: Burra's familiarity with Doré suggests parental sharing of material from their own library. Sunday afternoons, Mother sitting with a small child and a big book with thick pages, which whisper as you turn them. The Springfield library ensured that Burra became familiar with a great deal of art that was deeply unfashionable by

[2] 'I enclose the most beautiful still of the month posed by Lionel & Gloria Entitled "Don't sit goggling at me I tell you a scorpions run up me & wont come down".'

the time he went to art school – he remained fond of the pre-Raphaelites throughout his life, and never brought himself to endorse the modernist rejection of the concept of 'telling a story' through painting.

As Burra moved out of babyhood, he would have become more conscious of the world outside Springfield, due to the routine of taking the air. Upper-middle-class children of his generation were taken out in perambulators, which were often enormous affairs designed to admit several children and a goodly number of casual purchases; deep-bodied chariots of black and chrome, well-sprung and suspended over four wheels. Sitting in a pram was completely unlike the experience of riding in a buggy, not only because one sat unconfined by straps in the tank-like depths of the body, bouncing gently on the springs, but also because one progressed, as in a gondola, with one's back to the direction of travel. Osbert Lancaster observes that, 'for sheer pleasure few methods of progression, one comes gradually to realise, can compare with the perambulator. The motion is agreeable, the range of vision extensive, and one has always before one's eyes the rewarding spectacle of a grown-up maintaining prolonged physical exertion.'

Springfield Lodge was in Playden, a pleasant residential district about a mile out of town at the top of Rye Hill, looking down on Rye proper. All other directions look out over a long, misty pastoral vista of copses and rolling chalkland. Playden even now consists almost entirely of a double row of gentlemen's residences, set well back from the road in spacious grounds, together with a couple of highly respectable hotels and a medieval church. The impression it gives is overwhelmingly leafy; vast, mature trees nodding from behind high walls, handsome iron gates, hedges, with only a distant hint of roofs glimpsed down well-maintained gravel drives.

The drive of Springfield Lodge does not open onto a pavement. There is none on that side of the road, and only a narrow, uneven one on the other. The well-heeled residents of Playden were expected to approach by horse or by carriage, and later by motor-car. It is not an easy place to get about as a pedestrian. If Nana took Burra, and later, after his sister Anne was born, the two children together, out for an airing in the pram, she is unlikely to have taken them much further than the church. Going down into Rye would have meant the prospect of pushing them back up the hill again. Sooner or later, though, he became aware that the town existed.

Before the First World War, Rye was a maddeningly picturesque little town on the south coast, as, on the whole, it still is. It was built on a low sandstone hill on the edge of Romney Marsh, its streets winding up to St Mary's Church at the top, in a coastal area of East Sussex which is otherwise more or less flat. The street-plan is a little cramped, since the town was more or less confined within a magnificent set of medieval walls and gates. As these fortifications suggest, Rye was a very important place in the Middle Ages. It was one of the Cinque Ports, a group of towns looking out on the Channel which were granted by Edward the Confessor the right to keep all legal fees assigned in court cases, in exchange for producing ships and sailors for coastal defence. This peculiar privilege brought the Cinque Ports a great deal of wealth.

In the case of Rye, the medieval period has left relatively little in the way of visible structures except the principal church, the walls and a splendid fourteenth-century bastion known as the Ypres Tower. The harbour silted up in the late sixteenth century, destroying Rye's significance as a port, after which it became a quiet country town, though since it kept its privileges, it remained an extremely prosperous one. Visually, it is an early-eighteenth-century townscape of steep, cobbled streets, with a certain amount of timber-framed quaintness to add texture to the trim houses of red brick with white paintwork.

Burra's start in life must at first have seemed one attended exclusively by good fairies. The only real shadow was his dead older brother, Henry. Burra himself will only have come to know about this shadow sibling as he got older, but it will have affected him, whether he knew it or not. There is a particular emotional investment in a second child when the first-born has died; an extra protectiveness towards the fragile newcomer. But his parents were interesting and attractive people; fond of each other, and with affection and money to spare; and it was a lively house with many visitors. Four years after Burra was born, he acquired a sister, Anne (and subsequently a second, Elizabeth, usually called Betsy, ten years his junior, born when he was at prep school). He was good friends with both.

However, by the time Anne was old enough to sit up and look about her, it was obvious that whatever anyone may ever have hopefully surmised about 'late developers', all was not well with Master Edward, to an extent which must have made his parents begin to fear for him. Unlike Anne, who was a sturdy and active child, and in adult life a passionate tennis-player, he was an undersized, pixieish, waiflike little creature who tired quickly and did not find it easy to run. Edward was

physically very like his mother to look at; and she had long been diagnosed as a victim of pernicious anaemia. It eventually became clear that
along with her looks and small stature, he had inherited her fragility.
Precociously communicative, affectionate and intelligent, he was also
that ominous being, a delicate child.

Any hopes that he might grow out of it were soon dashed. He was
still a very little boy when he began to complain of stiffness and sore-
ness in his hands and feet, the first symptoms of early-onset rheumatoid arthritis. The joints of his fingers and toes, and also his knees and
ankles, were visibly beginning to deform before he was ten. Even in
photographs of Burra at five or six, his knees look oddly large.

It was also apparent that, in some measure, he had inherited his mother's
anaemic tendencies. There is a syndrome called Still's Disease, identified
in 1897, which links juvenile arthritis with anaemia and an enlarged spleen,
and since the various treatments meted out to Burra suggest that arthritis
was thought of as his principal problem, he may have been diagnosed as
a victim of this. But in fact, in addition to the arthritis, he suffered from
a blood condition called spherocytosis, which was the real explanation for
why he tired so quickly. 'Pernicious anaemia' is now defined as a specific
type of anaemia caused by failure to absorb vitamin B_{12}, but since B_{12} was
not even isolated until 1948, the term was probably more of a catch-all
before the First World War. The condition is hereditary, so his mother's
'pernicious anaemia' was probably also spherocytosis.

Sufferers from spherocytosis have red blood cells that are smaller,
more globular and more fragile than normal ones, which are discus-
shaped. They tend to get trapped in the spleen, which makes it swell,
and this causes anaemia, because the bone marrow has to produce an
abnormal quantity of red cells to replace those destroyed in their passage
through the spleen. Thus if red-cell production is interrupted – as it
is, for instance, for the duration of an ordinary viral illness such as a
cold – anaemia can quickly become profound. None of this was diagnosed when Burra was a child, but by the time he was old enough to
write letters, he suffered mysterious collapses, which was probably also
the case in his childhood. 'I went to bed the other day I felt so ill I
dont know what it was I feel a bit better now having lived on boiled
eggs and tea for the last day or 2.' As Burra got older, any kind of stress
could bring on an anaemic crisis, often accompanied by jaundice,
extreme nausea and physical collapse.

In his childhood, though, arthritis was the problem that his family knew about. By his late teens, he found it difficult to stand for any length of time and, well into his twenties, though he referred to Nana irreverently as Mrs Marsuple,[3] he habitually went up to her room to talk to her in the evenings, and as they chatted, she would massage whichever joints were worst at the time, hands, legs or feet. Thus, for all Burra's detachment and independence of spirit, they remained child and carer. He will also have been aware from an early age that he was embarked on a life which would give him chronic pain as a daily companion, and it was assumed, and stated in his hearing, that he would not make old bones. Arthritic pain can be managed now, up to a point. There was very little that could be done for the child Burra in the years before the First World War except to give him aspirin.

There are many sides to the status of a delicate child. Victim and tyrant are two of them. Burra was a nice little boy on the whole, quaint, bright, loving and beloved; his parents and Nana were sensible people. But from early childhood, he experienced episodes of fevers and skin-rashes, waking up with red, sore, inflamed joints; periods of remission, apparent normality; the ordinary frustrations of childhood exacerbated by weakness and pain. For all his kindness and thoughtfulness, traits that were well developed in him, the adult Burra had volcanic depths of anger roiling in the depths of his personality, which came out in his painting. In his babyhood, he was therefore presumably liable to something spectacular in the way of fits of black, screaming rage and distress.

There is a peculiarly adult misery which comes over anyone who finds themselves staring into the enraged, red, smeary face of a young child in pain who cannot be helped and will not be comforted. Doubly so when the child is your own, and his anguish is caused by hereditary disease. The patterns of Burra's life suggest that, however irrationally, his mother must have blamed herself to some extent; must have felt, if not precisely in a position of apology towards her adored son, at least determined to make it up to him. That, since much would necessarily be denied him, including long life, he should be allowed to be himself to the top of his bent, whatever the cost.

This is not to say that the senior Burras were silly about the boy. Snobbery aside, they seem to have been a rather sensible pair. They

[3] After the fearsome duenna in Aubrey Beardsley's pornographic novella, *Under the Hill*.

took him to a specialist in children's arthritis, and sent him to Bath
(which is still a centre for arthritis management) for treatment in the
warm thermal waters, which he quite enjoyed, though it was completely
ineffectual. But they also took what must have been a difficult decision.
His first educator was a governess, Sophie Forbes, but when he was old
enough to go to prep school, they sent him to Northaw Place at Potters
Bar, Hertfordshire, despite the fact that the First World War had just
broken out, which must surely have added to the anxieties of sending
a delicate child away from home. Northaw Place was a feeder school
for Haileybury public school, which was nearby, but was able to prepare
students for other schools if so required. The Burras wanted their son
prepared for the Eton Common Entrance. It was a small school, which
went into new premises in 1905, so its pleasant, well-mannered building
in extensive leafy grounds was still fairly new when Burra went there.

His father, at least, was determined that, if possible, his son would
have a normal life. The few messages to Burra from his father which
survive are signed 'Yrs H.C.B.', suggesting the formality of father–son
relations typical of Henry Burra's generation, and the contents also
suggest a desire that the child should meet expectations. One postcard
written when his son was eight says, 'I hope you are better & a good
little boy'; another from when he was nine demands, 'Écrivez moi une
carte postale à Bigorre en Francais! H.C.B.', which indicates that he
started French very young (he also started Latin with Miss Forbes).

Though formal, Henry Burra was not a distant or unaffectionate
parent. Anne remembered that he had to go to Lewes every Tuesday
because he served on the East Sussex County Council, and he invariably brought back sweets and biscuits for the children from a special
shop. When one or other was at school, the sweets were sent, unfail-
ingly, by post. He would also collaborate with his young son on projects, such as making new scenery for the children's toy theatre. But
Burra's mother was still writing to him as 'Dearest Snooks' when he
was twenty-two, and signed her letters off 'best love from M'; a warmth
that is absent in Henry Burra's communications with his son.[4]

One of Burra's predecessors at Northaw Place was Clement Attlee

---

[4] Snooks as a pet name may derive from 'Baby Snooks', an *enfant terrible* played by an American
comedienne called Fanny Brice, who first developed the character as a vaudeville act in 1912.

(subsequently Prime Minister from 1945 to 1951). Attlee's story suggests the kind of life Burra might have been expected to have. He went up to Oxford to read law, though it didn't interest him, since it was assumed by both himself and his father that he would follow in the paternal footsteps. Eventually he rebelled sufficiently to move over to history, the only subject that he really enjoyed, and subsequently entered politics. As this narrative suggests, the mores of the time endorsed upper-middle-class fathers' rights to put considerable pressure on their sons to conform; and schools cooperated with this venture by 'moulding' boys, an enterprise that pre-First World War culture perceived as entirely legitimate.

In consequence, many of Burra's contemporaries remember their prep schools as some species of concentration-camp populated by sadists and madmen. However, Northaw Place was clearly not like that. Burra, though he was puny, unathletic, self-willed and odd, fitted in perfectly adequately.

17 October 1915

Dear Daddie

We heard the Zepps on Wednesday night and the windows shook. How exiting for Tunbridge Wells Ma says they dropped some bombs there. I don't know where I am in Form this week whitch is horrid. Love from Edward

P.S. I am third and please tell Nana to send me my tortch.

The 'tortch' appears in several letters, as do reports on his reading; on the one hand, struggling dutifully through *Westward Ho!* for English, on the other, devouring thrillers: a book called *In White Raiment*, William de Queux's *The Band of Black* and *The Temptress* (he continued to be fond of de Queux for the rest of his life; 'he's really a terribly bad writer! But you cannot put them down'), which suggests that the torch was for reading under the bedclothes in time-honoured style. He wanted to be normal; it was not his temperament that prevented him from fitting in. He reported cheerfully, 'there is a magnet crase now it was ships last Christmas term'. He learned to play the piano, cheered on the football team in season, did well in Latin (he was always good at languages), worried about his maths, which was – and continued to be – abysmal, didn't worry about his spelling, though the letters suggest he should have, but on the whole bobbled along near the top of the class. Somehow that comes as a surprise, given his chronic nonconformity in later life, but he was bright, and a reader. It also speaks well for the school. Burra made no friends there that he bothered to remember or keep in touch with, but this is not necessarily because he was shunned or bullied. Equally possibly, it was because school life exists almost entirely in the present, and a child who was yo-yoing in and out of the sickbay would have found it hard to build relationships.

Another lesson which he certainly learned, because it was a central virtue of his caste, and he exhibited it to a very marked degree, was stoicism. To an extent now hard to conceive, an upper-class Englishman born before the First World War was trained to keep misery, physical or mental, to himself. The teenaged G.K. Chesterton, tortured by his teeth and ears, scribbled a little poem:

> Though pain be stark and bitter
> And days in darkness creep
> Not to that depth I sink me
> That asks the world to weep.

The only thing that Burra would have quarrelled with in this heartfelt doggerel was the impulse to write it down. Before he was out of his teens, his health, or lack of it, became part of his secret life, mentioned as seldom as possible, and never discussed. He learned not to complain, but two pathetic, undated letters written from the sickbay towards the end of his time at Northaw Place, when he was about twelve, express his boredom and unhappiness.

Dearest Daddie

I hope you have got my letter by this time. I shall have been up here 2 weeks tomorrow & at this rate of going I shall be up here for the rest of this term. I'me sure I could get better far quicker at home . . . I shall die if I have to stay in this room another day . . .

Dearest Mummie

I have been up here 2 weeks on Saterday & at this rate of going I shall be up all the term I am getting awfully tired of this room Sister says she wishes that I would be sent home as she is getting sick tired of me. I am longing to see Betsie again she must be getting quite big . . . I am in bed with a horrible little boy called Levy . . . I shall commit suicide if I stay in this room much longer.

The repetition between the two letters and unchildish phraseology suggest a remark of the school doctor's which has struck him to the heart (also, reading between the lines, it sounds as if the matron was beginning to worry about being responsible for him). This *cri de coeur* may or may not have been directly answered, but ultimately the whole enterprise of easing Burra into the life expected of an upper-middle-class boy had to be abandoned. These letters come from only one of many visits to the Northaw Place sickbay, and finally, just before Eton Common Entrance, he went down with pneumonia and had to be brought home. That was the end of his formal education.

Thus, as John Rothenstein observed, Burra was not shaped (or deformed) by the public-school experience which, for many men of his generation and social class, was the apogee of their lives. Cyril Connolly, reflecting on the phenomenon, famously formulated his 'Theory of Permanent Adolescence', which stated that 'the experiences undergone by boys at the great public schools, their glories and disappointments, are so intense as to dominate their lives and arrest their development'. For that generation, there is abundant evidence that this perception contains a substantial measure of truth. Burra, by contrast, had the great privilege and good fortune of avoiding the whole business, and educating himself. As Rothenstein says, 'the early ending of his formal education allowed him to read, in place of classics and mathematics, the books required to enrich his visual imagination'.

Apart from reading whatever took his fancy, Burra had some lessons with the local curate; he went to an art class in Rye run by a lady called Miss Bradley, and when he was in London (staying with his grandparents, who had a house in town as well as their principal house at Robertsbridge), he had lessons with an elderly Frenchwoman who read French newspapers with him. However informal this instruction may have been, he was sufficiently bright and self-disciplined to make real use of it, since his French was good enough for him to read in that language with pleasure throughout his life. But he completely escaped the secondary purpose of the public schools, the process of being trained in conformity.

A result of another, more problematic, kind was that he retained the child's – or upper-class woman of the time's – belief that he need not trouble to understand, or think about, money, finance, taxes; aspects of life that pertained only to the responsible adult male: the householder, or future householder. When Henry Burra died, neither Burra nor his mother had any more notion of the financial basis of their life than if they had been domestic pets.

It is probably true to say that Burra's health problems won him his freedom. His vocation to art was obvious; but if he had been normally fit, it is probable, though not certain, that pressure would have been put on him to go into a 'proper' profession and (like his father) to paint on the side, as an amateur. As things were, since he was condemned to going through life as an invalid, he was also able to go to art school.

Thus in 1918, when Burra was thirteen, rather than being flung out of his family on the centripetal trajectory of Eton, Oxford and a suitable career, the experience of a normal upper-class boy of his generation, he was wound back into the life of his childhood home. It was accepted in the family that he was going to follow his own bent. He thus had both more, and less, freedom than his contemporaries. On the one hand, he was free to do what he wanted, but on the other, he was condemned to live within the family support system, since he was not strong enough to spend long, concentrated days painting and to look after himself as well. He habitually painted till he was exhausted, then spent much of the rest of his time reading. When he went to art school in London – the subject of the next chapter – he lived with his grandparents. One of Burra's earliest surviving paintings, from when he was seventeen, shows the window of a big Victorian house. Inside is a young man alone, passively seated in an armchair. Outside, girls and boys are running and playing in an idyllic garden, while a balloon-seller hands out her bright wares. He already knew that his life would be that of an onlooker.

Burra's Ma was not a Freudian carnivore. If she had ever had tendencies that way, an impulse to hover protectively/devouringly over her delicate child, Burra must have realised intuitively in his early teens that he would have to fight her for the right to autonomy since, on a purely physical level, he could not escape from her care. It is worth pausing for a moment to contemplate a contemporary queer, artistic, 'delicate child' of wealthy parents, Stephen Tennant (born 1906), who was actually in very much better shape, physically, than Burra. But his mother's determination to keep him in cotton-wool, which he was unable to resist, ensured that he ended up as nothing better than a fribbling amateur, partygoer and celebrity. An instinctive awareness of the possibility of being engulfed caused Burra to build a stronger and higher wall around his core self than most children. His personality was secret and intransigent, and he could be quite extraordinarily obstinate. A friend who knew him from sixteen onwards remembered the way he used to dig his heels in. 'It's no good asking,' he would declare, 'I'm not going to do it.'

His mother and father, for their part, were intelligent enough to perceive that the mutual difficulty between themselves and their son was situational rather than personal, and, as a result, they were amazingly forbearing towards him. Burra treated his parents with a certain coldness, and guarded his privacy. Several friends observed that he was far fonder of them than he ever allowed himself to show in any overt way, but this apparent detachment does not seem to have deceived the parents, either. Both Burra and his sister Anne, though they were to prove themselves the most loyal of children in the long term, habitually kept their parents at arm's length as teenagers, and were stern with any tendency to fuss. As a friend later commented:

Anne was able to turn a routine visit to the tennis club into a secret mission for MI5.

'Where have you been?' her mother might enquire mildly. 'Did you see anyone? What did you do?' In return, Anne offered the solid negatives 'Nowhere', 'Nobody', and 'Nothing.'

Edward carried the process a good deal further . . . any morning he might meander down the garden. He could have been merely walking to Rye to buy cigarettes, going to Hastings for the day, or to London for the weekend . . . he left as always, apparently empty-handed, for if his usual morsel of luggage (much the same for a weekend or a six-month visit) were needed, it would have been hidden beforehand in a convenient pick-up spot, and taking the back way through the fields to the station he walked, as it were, into limbo, leaving behind him dead silence.

Perhaps surprisingly, the Burras accepted this treatment; it was exceptionally ruthless, considering that it was meted out to parents who by that time had already lost two of their four children. Burra in general was quite considerate; so it suggests that maintaining at least an illusion of autonomy and emotional independence was hugely important to him, and that his parents understood this.

The Burra parents trusted their children to an unusual extent, and let them go their own way. Looking back, with some degree of surprise, Anne commented, 'Our parents must have had absolute faith in Edward's common sense, as we were allowed to go out together when I was really very small – seven or eight, I suppose . . . he would take me to the sea at Camber where we always played by a tidal creek which was shallow at low tide but deeper than me when the tide was high.'

Sending children to boarding-school at the age of eight is not the only aspect of upper-class Edwardian parenting which seems now to belong to a lost world. The Burras' sublime faith that Edward and Anne would never do anything really stupid is easily paralleled. In that classic of Twenties' children's literature, *Swallows and Amazons* (based on life), a group of children is given permission to boat unsupervised about Lake Windermere with this trenchant telegram from their father: 'Better drowned than duffers if not duffers won't drown.'

Importantly, this parental faith in their offspring's powers of judgement was maintained when the Burra children were in their later teens and twenties. As a result, the senior Burras' relationship with the children was a benign one, and mutual loyalty within the family seems never to have wavered.

The information embargo imposed by Burra and Anne may in fact have made life easier on both sides, since it ensured that very real and fundamental differences in outlook between family members could coexist without strain. Many of the things Burra did, and the places he went to in order to do them, would have dismayed his parents. They really did prefer not to know; which in some families would have been a statement of indifference towards the child's welfare, or at least, read as such by the child. This was not so with the Burras, at least in part because a relationship of mutual trust was established so early and so completely.

Nothing in Burra's work suggests the compulsive need to create and blow up a Queen-Kong-like mummy-monster which afflicted so many of his male contemporaries, gay and straight alike, and for all his sharp tongue, he never wrote slightingly of either parent, or of his sisters. He was sufficiently sure of himself to achieve deep and enduring friendships with women, which, given the difficulties of his life, was a considerable achievement; his mother's as well as his own.

When his formal education in art was complete, Burra came back to Springfield, and remained based in Rye for the rest of his life. It says something for his scale of priorities that he could never be bothered to move out of 'Tinkerbell Towne', as he often called it, even after his parents had given up Springfield, though he had never been charmed by it, and liked raffish Brighton and even scruffy Hastings, just down the coast, very much better. He was very rigorous about what mattered – essentially painting, hanging out with his friends, reading and travelling – and what did not. He could not bear to waste time. Moving to Brighton would have been time- and energy-consuming, and disliking Rye was not sufficiently important for him to bother with doing anything about it.

Rye had had a certain interest for literary figures in the pre-war period – Henry James lived at Rye, in Lamb House, and Rudyard Kipling, Stephen Crane, Virginia Woolf, Katherine Mansfield, Ford Madox Ford and Joseph Conrad all lived in the vicinity – but in the decade after the First World War it was distinctly sedate. James's tenure of Lamb House had been superseded by that of E.F. Benson, waspish chronicler/satirist of the upper echelons of Rye society. The Burras were the sort of people Benson's heroine Lucia would unhesitatingly have asked to 'Mallards' and honoured with her signature party dish, lobster à la Riseholme. She would have considered them rather a catch. Benson himself would certainly have been known to the Burras, since, like Dah, he was deeply involved in local politics (he became Mayor of Rye in 1934, so they would have met on many a committee).

It is interesting, therefore, that the first of Benson's series of mock-heroic social comedies set in Rye, lightly disguised as 'Tilling' (*Mapp and Lucia*), was published in 1922, the year after Burra started at art school; his style already precociously formed. The only character who disturbs the social and cultural consensus of bourgeois society in Tilling is Irene Coles, first introduced as follows: 'suffragette, post-impressionist artist (who painted from the nude, both male and female), the socialist and Germanophil, all incarnate in one frame . . . the bitterest part of it all was that if Miss Coles was amused at anybody, and she undoubtedly was, she was amused at Miss Mapp'. 'Quaint Irene' as she is generally referred to, is thus a fairly generalised caricature of the Modern Artist, but she has some Burra-esque features. Irene's insouciance and social confidence suggest Burra, who quite clearly did not give a damn what the Miss Mapps/Bensons of his world thought about him; her broadly hinted-at lesbianism suggests Burra's already well-developed campness. Burra and his friends read the Mapp and Lucia books, since several letters exchanged between them in the mid-Twenties sign off with Lucia's signature 'au reservoir' for 'au revoir'.

Benson, though he mocks Miss Mapp and her acquaintance, mocks from within, and is broadly on their side. But he is aware, as they are not, that the post-war world is changing; and his account of Quaint Irene suggests that he had some acquaintance with modernity and found it little to his taste. Burra did not normally join his parents when they entertained, preferring to eat in the kitchen with the servants, but if Benson ever encountered the Burras' peculiar son and heir, he would have recognised him as a threatening visitant from a parallel world. The terrifying distance between modernism (in all the arts) in the 1920s and the aesthetic world inhabited by members of the provincial bourgeoisie is brought to a clear focus in an episode in *Mapp and Lucia* that describes the annual exhibition of the Art Society of which Miss Mapp was president:

Miss Mapp had sent in half a dozen water-colours, the Treasurer a study in still life of a teacup, an orange and a wallflower, the Secretary a pastel portrait of the King of Italy, whom she had seen at a distance in Rome last Spring . . . but quaint Irene had sent some at which Miss Mapp felt lines must be drawn . . . there was one, harmless but insane, that purported to be Tilling Church by moonlight: a bright green pinnacle all crooked (she supposed it was a pinnacle) rose up against a strip of purple sky and the whole rest of the canvas was black. There was the back of somebody with no clothes on lying on an emerald-green sofa: and, worst of all, there was a picture called 'Women Wrestlers', from which Miss Mapp hurriedly averted her eyes.

Burra's confident use of colour was a feature of his art from the beginning; so were louche subjects (were the 'Women Wrestlers' really wrestlers, or lesbians in action?). So was landscape, treated in a boldly individual fashion. He actually exhibited at the Rye Art Society in 1926; and his reaction to the other pictures sounds strangely like the voice of Quaint Irene commenting on Miss Mapp.

I have also visited the show of the Rye local artists. Oh dear you should see it No. 1 is old Mill at Twinkleton no 2 is moonlight and old tinned Salmon & no 3 is 'Church of Santa Maria del Tomato Assisi'. I have sent a dreadful little thing I did at the Chelsea P my dear very sweet so as not to infuriate Mr Revel.[5]

But as the Twenties progressed, Rye's resemblance to Tilling began to recede, and more congenial company appeared. One of the first indications of this is that Paul Nash moved into the area (to Winchelsea, only three miles distant). Nash was, as a matter of habit, kindly and fostering towards young artists, and Burra made friends with him in 1925. 'I went to see P last week in great trepidation & was met with the greatest charm he showed me all his wood engravings and some lovely stuffs he's had printed.'

Burra's trepidation was due to being only twenty and completely unknown, while Nash was thirty-six, an established artist, famous for his wartime paintings (he had been an official war artist, and the creator of some defining images of the Western Front, particularly the great *Menin Road*), as well as for his landscapes. But Nash saw the power of Burra's work; and the friendship was to be an important one in many respects, especially after Nash moved to Rye, as he did in December 1930. Burra saw Nash at least once a week in the late Twenties and early Thirties. Another aspect of Nash, his fascination with American cartoonists, suggests that the friendship can only have encouraged Burra's already-existing interest in integrating macabre and surreal aspects of popular culture with high art.

Nash, though, had a conventional side that Burra found less congenial, which was due to his having been born in 1889 rather than 1905. And Burra was not attracted to Margaret Nash, who was about the same age as her husband, and 'arty', in the conventional, or post-William-Morris, English sense. That is, her personal taste was formed by what was avant-garde *before* the First World War, from Burra's point of view, practically out of the Ark.

I went to see Paul N again to day and Mrs N was there too it was so funny we went to tea across the way to some jolly people called Buchanan who live in an old 13 cent farm house ... the B's are a mass of rare homespun exquisite old rugs

[5] Mr Revel was the head of Chelsea Polytechnic, where Burra was then a student.

bamboo whistles and morris dancing.[6] my dear Madame Nash said Edward must come to the dancing too its <u>such</u> fun we do 'widdy come toddy' and 'Parsons fuddle' & 'fuck a chickabiddy' & 'flummox a bubby nit in the navel' and all the old dances you know I don't know if Paul takes up the dancing as he ought he said my dear <u>must</u> you? when Mrs N executed a few steps of the dear old Elizabethan farragado 'Maiden heds Bung ho' to the pipeing notes of a bamboo rigadon bought by Mrs Buchanan for 20 pesetas in Palermo . . .

Nash was, at times, quietly appalled by the way his wife carried on (though profoundly dependent on her, he was persistently and determinedly unfaithful). She and her friends liked to perform Elizabethan music as well as dancing rigadoons: one of them, Alice Dalglish, asked Nash what he thought after they had, in their opinion, done rather well by a tricky madrigal, only to be told politely but firmly, 'Well, I'd describe it as a pleasant din.' Burra's encounter with Mrs Nash is a clear indication of the profoundly different strands coexisting in the creative arts in the Twenties – some individuals, Nash being one, moved between them, while others did not.

Not the least of Nash's gifts to Burra is that he introduced Burra to the American modernist poet Conrad Aiken, a friend and coeval of T.S. Eliot who came to live in Jeakes' House, Rye, in 1924. Aiken, settling in, reported to a friend at home, 'Paul Nash, artist, is nice, and ditto his wife, and another wild young artist, Burra, is amusing . . .' Aiken enjoyed Rye as, probably, only a foreigner could, certainly much more than Burra did. Viewing it as an outsider, he perceived it as an endless pageant: 'the variety of [Rye's] characters, whether well known, or simply encountered by chance in the narrow streets, was as extravagant as that in any Elizabethan play'. He loved Jeakes' House, archaic and inconvenient (it dated to 1689), and the picturesqueness of Rye's winding, cobbled streets. Burra did not. He positively disliked quaint old houses where one 'couldnt walk a step without falling over a dormer window or something', and he found Rye completely charmless.

Burra's attitude towards housing was firmly utilitarian, and if he had any views beyond that, he probably shared the belligerent

---

[6] Colonel Bertram Buchanan and his wife Kathleen: the house was called Oxenbridge Farm. Iden Cottage, where the Nashes were then living, belonged to them.

modernism of Paul Nash, who in 1931 launched a passionate assault on English country-house taste: 'Just as the modern Italian has revolted against the idea that his country is nothing but a museum, so we should be ashamed to be regarded by the Americans as a charming old-world village. They do not respect our modernity because we have no pride in it ourselves.'

Despite the fact that Aiken was sentimental about Rye precisely because it was quaint and antique, the friendship that developed between Aiken and Burra from 1931 onwards was a seminal one in Burra's life. Through Aiken, he gained an insight into American culture he would not otherwise have had.

Aiken, very well read and a formidable drinker, broadened Burra's world considerably, not least because the Gothic aspects of his sensibility resonated with Burra's own concerns. Aiken himself had monstrous, or Gothic, aspects; he was profoundly misogynist, devious, manipulative, and haunted by a variety of demons. But Burra was sufficiently sure of himself to be at ease with monsters, even with an alcoholic and somewhat predatory Prospero. The aspect of Aiken which perhaps linked them most closely was his uncompromising devotion to his art. 'He made no effort to polish his image; he forbade the reprinting of one of his most popular early poems because he detested it. He was known to pay a price for sticking to writing, and writing only what he believed in.' No mean tribute from an ex-wife.

Aiken's perceptions of Rye are interestingly opposed to those of Burra, who simply found it dull and bourgeois. Though he loved the town, it had for him a Gothic and grotesque aspect, as if it was just a little too good to be true.

If the town itself was quite magically situated on its little hill, in the triangle formed by the three 'baby rivers', and looked, when seen against the sunset, like a ship setting gallantly out to sea, out to the channel, it also had the singular power of attracting to itself the most diverse company of human beings that surely was ever gathered in any place so tiny. It looked so innocent, so tender, so humble and true in the evening light ... The window-curtains stirred as one passed, stirred and were still again, and one was aware of the watchful eyes behind them ... it bore a sinister resemblance to that dark little town, in a story of Algernon Blackwood's, which was haunted by cats; where, every night, as soon as the moon was up and its golden swale of light on the vast marsh, the inhabitants all came

out on the walls in the form of cats. It would not have been in the least surprising
to find this so at [Rye] – there was undoubtedly a sense of evil in it, and this had
been repeatedly drawn on . . .

In complete opposition to the invincible cosiness of Benson's perceptions, Aiken reminds one that Rye was the chosen home of Henry James,
the master of horror latent beneath a civilised surface; Aiken sees weird-
ness and obsession where Benson sees silliness and snobbery. He and
Burra were therefore drawn to one another by the fact that the skull
beneath the skin interested them both.

It says something for the profound cultivation of the Springfield
household, as well as for Burra himself, that despite his almost total
lack of formal education, he could hold his own in conversation with a
sophisticated, Harvard-educated modernist poet. From small beginnings, the acquaintance ripened into intense mutual interest: Clarissa
Aiken (the second of the three wives that Aiken brought in succession
to Jeakes' House), who had little verbal dexterity of her own and was
wary of Burra, describes him, rather sourly, as her husband's 'court
jester'. He 'kept up Conrad's spirits at weekly dinners with us by
satirising Rye's characters in his falsetto drawl and cockney accent. I
did not join in the merriment, afraid of being the next target.' Joan
Aiken, one of Aiken's three children from his first marriage, remembered listening to her father and Burra talking:

The conversation at supper whipped back and forth, lots of jokes, lots of argument, Ed's voice high, light, weary and nasal, Conrad's much lower, gritty and
snuffly.

Aiken mentions an evening in 1939 when he and Burra 'chewed the
fat on the usual round of topics, art, poetry, america, Boston, Gordon
[Bassett], Jane [Aiken], Portugal, Mexico, Malcolm [Lowry], Svanna
[*sic*], New Orleans, Cuba, and back to Rye in time for him to leave at
11.30'. Aiken (himself born in Savannah, Georgia, though his roots were
in New England and his principal American home was Boston) shared
Burra's fascination with the south of both Europe and America. He
gave Burra a kind of intellectual companionship which he had not previously experienced, and vastly extended his knowledge of literature; it
was Aiken, for example, who interested Burra in Elizabethan revenge

tragedy, as well as insisting that he read modernist poetry such as that of his own close friend T.S. Eliot.

In any case, Burra always read very widely, and habitually picked up new writing as it came out. In 1925 he noted, 'Ime reading a book by D.H. Lawrence which is so full of guts and maleness and femaleness it gives me the fidgets.' Lawrence, with his weirdly prescriptive sense of what people could and should be like, would have written Burra off as an inadequate male, like Clifford Chatterley; Burra was patently unamused by such masculinist posturing. But he was far more interested by other modernist writers. Wyndham Lewis impressed him hugely, and Burra bought everything he wrote as it appeared.

But in the Twenties and Thirties the Tillingesque features of Rye continued to be very much part of its overall texture, though those who clung to the certainties represented by E.F. Benson must have felt as if they were standing on a sandcastle with the tide coming in. Aiken was not chagrined, but delighted by an episode that could have come straight out of *Mapp and Lucia*. Rumours were rife that his wife Mary (no. 3) had left him, and when he called in at his favourite pub (the Ship), he heard the following, which he promptly sent Mary in a letter, certain that she would be amused rather than mortified:

Tony, all beaming and bristling had a piece of gossip ready for me, ABOUT US . . . I'm afraid I really screamed with delight, and Tony had actually been rather afraid to tell me. It seems, par exemple, that Mrs Rood's bringing of the rhododendrons was a piece of scouting, pure and simple – for on her way back she darted into the Moretons' kitchen, hissed quickly to Mabel 'it's *all right*! She's coming back next week!' and darted out again . . .

Unfortunately for Mrs Rood and those like her, they were no longer acknowledged social arbiters, or only so within a subsection of the Rye community. From the viewpoint of Burra and the Aikens, what Tillingites thought about them was neither here nor there.

Local gossip must also have been busy with an even more scandalous addition to the scene: Radclyffe Hall, who settled at 4 High Street, Rye, with her lover, Una, Lady Troubridge ('that astonishing pair – and extremely entertaining too – who could be heard almost any morning bawling out the wretched little tailor in the High Street, or flinging back at him, all publicly, a badly made pair of breeches'). Both Hall and

Lady Una were flamboyant figures, old-fashioned, cross-dressing, short-haired sapphists; the sort of women Burra sketched in the margins of his early letters.

Burra, who was friendly with a good many lesbians, was delighted to see the ladies about: they were on visiting terms with Paul and Margaret Nash, so he would have encountered them socially. He also avidly collected gossip from a masseuse called Miss Wadcot who treated him and also visited Miss Hall: 'Miss W is very funny about les fillettes.' In 1928, he wrote to a friend, 'the antiente town is getting a regular Montparnasse I am thinking of opening a branch of the fétiche [a lesbian nightclub in Paris] with old world beams and lanterns Im sure it would pay hand over fist I am just going to hire Sheila Kaye-Smith as hostess at my fétiche branch she is so popular here'.

Thus, as Burra moved up his twenties, Rye local society was developing a distinct arty stratum. In addition to the figures already mentioned, the novelist Sheila Kaye-Smith (who, despite Burra's vile aspersions, was a novelist of rural life, and not that kind of girl at all), the painters John Banting, Edward Wadsworth and Robert McKechnie and the art critic Anthony Bertram came to the town. 'Sooner or later, everyone was sure to turn up.' The Quaint Irenes, if they had not won precisely, had at least fought Tilling to a draw.

The curious thing about the life of Springfield was that the two sides of Rye existed in it simultaneously. Burra's parents, though far better informed and more genuinely cultivated than Benson's caricatures, were people of precisely that type. Burra's sister Anne, once she had returned from her Florentine finishing school, led the life of John Betjeman's Miss Joan Hunter Dunn, playing lawn tennis and going to dances with a gaggle of impeccably conventional cousins and suitable young men. 'Anne is having her beau to stay next week for the Grand Tournament such a jolly ruddy faced Cambridge Laddy,' Burra remarked drily. He never ran down his family, even to his closest friends, but he refused to involve himself with haut-bourgeois social life.

Sometimes the tone of his letters sharpens to outright mockery – of the friends, though never of Anne herself.

We are having a jolly lot of young people to stay soon which will be so twee I am preparing a bottle of vitriol to take if it all becomes too much to bear my dear such

an array of dainty gowns trimmed with swansdown and attractive boat shaped neck-
lines by the score also nice low heeled novelty gold shoes for misses by Peter Yapp
of Sloane Street & some jolly fellows too 1 in the Worcester Regmt & one or 2
from topholeski old Eton etc Im getting my Old Borstalian tie out of the jolly old
tie press given me by aunty macassar.

Burra's relationship with his sister is worth pausing on, since it
was to be one of the most important of his life. Superficially, Anne
seemed to be completely conventional, and it might appear that brother
and sister had absolutely nothing in common (she bewildered some of
his friends, he couldn't stand hers). In fact, though they were absolutely
divergent in their habits of life, they were extremely congruous in their
habits of mind: observant, sardonic, practical, unsentimental, sceptical
and little given to sympathy. Anne, as a dutiful unmarried daughter in
her twenties, accompanied her mother to Bordighera for a little rest-
cure, but a letter to her brother suggests that she did so with a certain
detachment: 'Mummy got quite annoyed because twice in one week the
party ended at 6 AM or thereabouts. Peggy came over the other day . . .
I wish she would come here as I've no one to be really mad with as
Larry and Jean play tennis too much and anyway Larry is convention
itself.' She, by implication, was not.

Another of the letters in which Burra chronicles one of his sister's
friends' visits is interesting: 'We have such a jolly deb staying here with
Anne eats us out of house and home my dear and before she came her
mama wrote my mama a long letter saying all the things the jolly girlie
wasnt to do such as go out with young people in a car as it was so
dangerous . . . also other intime little details about the dear girlies
periods you know you can't be too careful.' Quite obviously, the Burras
were united in thinking that this kind of fussing was ridiculous; but it
is also worth observing that Anne discussed the letter with him; it was
not every girl in the Twenties who would have talked about menstrua-
tion with her brother.

Later letters make it clear that Anne was very independent in her
attitudes, for all that she conscientiously performed the duties of a pillar
of county society. Brother and sister understood each other very well
indeed. A letter which Burra sent her shortly after she arrived at her
finishing school in Florence offers a further hint of the texture of their
relationship:

Betsy is going to do riding at Miss Ansells in breeches and a jockey cap what she will look like I cant think Mummy has gone to London what she is doing there I cant think. what do you <u>think</u>! Miss Kay Cooper went mad and tore all Miss Murphys clothes off in Season Lane they must have taken a great deal of tearing for they havent been off for years after which Kay-C rushed home and locked Miss Bernard in the lav and discovering the cooks young man in the kitchen picked up a dish full of bloaters and threw them at his head then she went to evening service and shot at Mr Shaw with an airgun causing a panic in the audience which consisted of about 3 she has since been captured.

The letter starts with genuine news, and segues into fantasy purely for the fun of it. The whole thing is a sort of practical joke; it is about the moment of recognition when his sister, reading it, moves from a shocked/avid 'no!!!' to a dawning realisation that he is teasing – somewhere around line four.

However, despite the essential sympathy of brother and sister, the differences were important ones. In Springfield in the late Twenties, 'romance' signified Anne's virginal flirtations with vacant undergraduates. 'Anne has been to a jolly dance at Woolwich with a boy called Teddy Colville whether his trousers slipped we have not heard to see his face you'd think vertue reigned supreme.' As late as 1934, a girl could put the south coast in a spin simply by appearing in high summer wearing open sandals displaying painted toenails: 'as for Clovers toes!' Burra reported, 'every clergyman who passed we heard say "girls of that type – mutter mutter mutter" we never got as far as hearing about girls of that type'. At the same time, the letters Burra was sending and receiving from London detailed the adventures of two of his closest friends who were actively homosexual, and a third who was not only, as the phrase then went, a Kept Woman, but also dancing in a chorus line.

But, just as in the larger world of Rye, the bridge-playing and tea-drinking vicars, captains, colonels and widows celebrated by Benson were in fact forced to coexist with artists, adulterers, homosexuals and murderers, so, within the safe and orderly world of an extensive bourgeois household, Burra created an oasis of anarchy. Aiken evokes Springfield as:

That Victorian house on the hill, outside [Rye], with the beautiful sloping gardens, and the little rococo Greek temple under the trees, and that unbelievable chaos of a workroom, where he painted (with spit!) the brilliant panels of water-colour, patiently pasting each to the last, until, with the completion of the final corner, the great vision opened its translunar and as if death-stilled infinitudes of vista, and of motionless violence in vista, for super-human, and subhuman, joys and despairs, or loves and hates.

In his teens and twenties, Burra used the billiard room on the ground floor, near the kitchen, as his studio; the floor littered with records, books and magazines, the walls with sketches, images and postcards, though when John Rothenstein visited him in 1945, he had constructed a precisely similar lair at the top of the house among the servants' bedrooms:

The walls are covered with vast numbers of photographs of Greek sculptures, paintings by Tiepolo, Signorelli, Magnasco and the Spanish masters, and with pictures clipped from newspapers – English, French, Spanish, Italian – of dramatic incidents and vivid poses. One of these shows the face of a leper, close up. Covering the floor, the wireless, the gramophone, and the chairs are many hundreds of books and magazines: there are novels in several languages, South American picture papers, Victorian scrap-books, and volumes of Elizabethan poetry and drama.

Whichever room Burra worked in (as well as using at least two at Springfield, he established similar spaces in other houses, as, for instance, when he was staying with the Aikens in Boston), they were all fundamentally the same. He never put anything away, on the grounds that it wasted time, you'd just have to get it out again. Books, magazines, postcards piled up around him, and underneath him; he habitually adjusted the height of his chair relative to the table by adding or subtracting from the heap of magazines he sat on. If he was working in oil, as he sometimes did in his teens and twenties, the pile was relatively low, and the canvas was propped on his knees. With a watercolour, he perched himself higher, laid the paper flat on the table and leaned over it.

A friend recalled, many years later, Burra saying, 'The only time I don't feel any pain is when I'm working. I become completely unaware.' Pain, humdrum and continuous, shadowed Burra's life. But when he began to draw or paint, the focus of his awareness dwindled down to a single small, intensely observed point. He saw the area of paper he was working on, and nothing else. His hand, sometimes swollen into a little red bear's paw with delicate claws, sometimes thin and bony with big, chalky knuckles, accommodated his pencil or a surprisingly small sable brush. Familiar motions, familiar pains. His consciousness tuned out the noises of the household – hushed, in any case, in a big house with well-fitting doors. If he put a record on the gramophone, as he often did, he perhaps heard Billie Holiday's catlike wailing for a time as he was sinking into his trance of concentration, but he was not necessarily aware of the end of the record, the stylus lifting off and the arm clunking back to its rest. A cigarette dangled from his bottom lip, which he sometimes got around to lighting; the rhythms of lighting a cigarette and drawing in the smoke were as automatic as breathing.

Awareness of his body and its position in space drifted away from him. The eyes saw; the brain clicked through uncountable numbers of simultaneous decisions: about the direction of the line currently in progress, the area under construction, the picture as a whole; while in the responsive fingers, the complex musculature of the hand and wrist adjusted in constant, minute movements to achieve the effect he was aiming for. His whole will, his conscious intelligence, and much of his unconscious as well, was bent on the tiny, travelling spot where his pencil or his brush actually touched the paper.

This is true of all painters to some extent, but in Burra it took an extreme form because of his rheumatic condition. He said himself, 'Painting is of course a sort of drug', and he painted compulsively. When he was drawing, his feet and hands did not hurt, because he was no longer aware of them. His work was not merely his vocation, it was also his most effective painkiller. It took him out of his body, in effect, a place where he didn't much want to be.

II

LONDON

BURRA'S early development took place within almost exaggeratedly secure confines. But the world beyond insinuated its presence. Sometimes blatantly, in the children's film matinées at the Rye cinema, which, his sister recalled, 'we . . . could not bear ever to miss because of the serials'. Serials such as *The Perils of Pauline* (1914, twenty episodes), *The Exploits of Elaine* (1914, forty episodes, followed by *The New Exploits of Elaine* in 1915) and the *Hazards of Helen* (1914–17, 119 episodes), the original cliff-hangers. Like Bollywood musicals, the serials addressed sex and cognate issues only through the medium of a highly abstract code. While the most iconic of Pearl White's perils in the role of Pauline was being tied to a railway track in front of an oncoming train, some serials hinted at murkier worlds. Episodes of *The Exploits of Elaine*, which also starred Miss White, include 'The Vampire', 'The Blood Crystals' and 'The Devil Worshippers'.

And more discreetly, like smoke curling under a door, a consciousness of what was then called 'the seamy side of life' crept even into a house such as Springfield. A principal route was the reading material in the servants' hall, periodicals such as *London Life*, *The World Pictorial News* and *The Police Gazette*. The discourse of these papers soaked deeply into Burra's mind because he had heard them discussed over his head before he could read.

The sensational press of the 1900s, like the films, operated to a great extent in code. 'White slavery' meant organised prostitution, with the particular implication that innocent English virgins might be beguiled, or even kidnapped in tea-shops and suchlike places of legitimate resort, drugged and sold wholesale to South American brothels. Other forms

of unmentionable crime such as paedophilia and sodomy were tackled
with similarly relishing euphemy. Also, of course, there were sensational
sex cases – such as the Russell divorce in 1924, in which the pregnant
Lady Russell claimed (successfully) that she was a virgin and that the
marriage had never been consummated, while England boggled – and
murders. Wives were drowned in their baths, dismembered bodies found
in trunks in left-luggage offices. While coy about details, the sensational
papers created a pure, abstract glamour of crime and vice, and offered
plenty of room for the imagination.

Young children were generally a tolerated presence in the servants'
halls of Edwardian England. Master Edward, silent lest anyone realised
he was listening, must have avidly absorbed these narratives of inner-
city darkness. The more that the calm and orderly world of 'upstairs'
implied, in its solidity and propriety, that none of these things existed,
the more the child's mind was engaged by the knowledge that they did.
His fascination with the infinitely exciting world which the picture-
papers opened up for him is evidenced from very early in his life.

Burra's childhood imagination was possessed by inner cities. From
the time when he was seven or so, he and his sister would spend part
of most days building a town. She recalled:

I was only allowed to arrange the suburbs which were composed from six very
ornate Russian houses and a box of a few simple English village homes made of
cardboard. Edward would build the rest of the town and cram it with terrible tenements and glamorous theatres and cinemas.

Anne also recalls that they used to darken the room, once the town was
constructed to their satisfaction, and bomb it: this sounds like a wartime
variation on an established game. The First World War came close to
home for the children who lived through it, due to the Zeppelin raids;
Burra experienced these when he was away at school (a Zeppelin actually came down near Northaw Place). The experience was evidently
frightening enough to require exorcism through acting it out, though
at the time, characteristically, he reported it as thrilling:

The Zepp raid on the North of London was most exciting. We got up in our
pyjamas about 10 o'clock on Sunday evening and stayed from then onwards to
about 3 o'clock on Monday morning with intervals in the cellar. The cellar here

is most appallingly dirty and damp. This morning we went out and collected bits of aluminium and canvas and burnt silk, the burnt silk smells horrid ... Miss Lloyd the mistress who used to teach me arithmetic saw it come down in flames I wish I could go and see it but we can't ...

Dah, an inveterate smoker (as was Burra himself in adult life), collaborated pleasantly with the more Gothic aspect of his son's imagination by giving the children his old Gold Flake boxes, which Edward and Anne turned into houses with cut-out windows and doors: they would then put lighted spills inside, and wait for the flames to come shooting out of the openings, just like a story in the papers: THREE LIVES LOST IN TENEMENT BLAZE!!! One of the more permanent items of the Springfield townscape (as opposed to the Gold Flake boxes) survived to be memorialised by Burra's friend Billy Chappell: a rectangular piece of driftwood, which the child Edward had carefully decorated with rectangular windows, its sides and top framed by bold lettering: GIN; and less insistently, STOUT, ALE, LEMONS. Chappell also saw a theatre, which had started life as part of a box of pictorial wooden blocks: when the original pictures had abraded away, it became, with the aid of black and red ink, the PHOENIX THEATRE and BAR. Two posters drawn on stamp-paper have been added: 2.30, *What Fools Men* with Jay Gliezen and Krista Lubin, and G. Dilly as Widow Twankey. This city of the mind was served by trams, since a model tramcar, also surviving from the toybox, was given destinations by Edward: Dog Island via Concordia Square and Kremlin, or Bindi via Fan Tan Street and Luna Street.

A more elaborate game of the same kind was also played communally, but on a more equal footing than big brother–little sister. The Burra family always spent part of the holidays with Trudy Burra's Robertson-Luxford parents at Higham House, Robertsbridge, in East Sussex. Two cousins, Lawrence and Sheila Rich, the children of Trudy Burra's sister Audrey, also came to see their grandparents, and while the two little girls played games of their own, Edward and Lawrence used to build an elaborate town, which Anne described as 'resembling Monte Carlo', on an island in the middle of a shallow ornamental pond. Crucial to this game was a pair of small, nude china dolls, which Edward made clothes for out of coloured wax. They were the Dilly Sisters (named, presumably, after a well-known sister act, the Dolly Sisters, Hungarian-born American entertainers, a far more wholesome pair) and, through them, Edward and Lawrence led a private and exciting life.

A letter survives from 1917/18 (when the boys were twelve or so) from Lawrence to his cousin:

Dear Edward I am coming over on the sixth when Mummie is playing in the tournament at Rye so don't go out. Gladys & Phylis can meet
  Lots of Love
  Lawrence

It is absolutely clear that Edward and his cousin Lawrence *were* Gladys and Phyllis Dilly (interchangeably), and that the game was far too important to be left to the specific *mise en scène* of the pond at Higham House. The envelope was addressed to:

  Miss Phylis Dilly
  c/o E.J. Burra Esq
  Flat 9
  Liberty Buildings
  Lower Tartan Street
  GEV. N.W.

A letter from Gladys – i.e. Edward – written from Flat 8, Soho Block, Tivoli Alley, San Sebastian (all interesting reference points: Soho crossed with southern Europe) may not be a reply, but certainly represents his side of the correspondence:

Darlin Sis
  Thank u so much for your letter to the paper. I henclose a photer of self signed which u can ang up in the flat – Will yer send me one of you. Sara tore yer photer up in a fit of rage because I didn't payer . . .

Edward's attempt at the discourse of the underworld obeys the rules of 'Comic Cockney', misplaced aitches and (slightly more subtly) the demotic English tendency to be imprecise about the last vowel in a word (represented here in 'yer', and 'photer').

The sources for this imaginary world include the highly stylised images of vice and low-life in the children's matinées at the Rye cinema, children's comics such as *Chips* and *Comic Cuts* and sensational newsprint aimed at adults: on the back of an envelope, Edward/Gladys has a drawing of a mascara-and-lipstick bedizened harpy in a hat, with the legend, 'Don't you think our new cook is a jolly girl? We found the advertisement in the Police Gazette.'

The child Edward, though not without wit, does not show any very marked degree of sophistication or insight in his invention. But the Dilly Sisters are important. Unlike his cousin, who, by 1930, was described by Anne as 'convention itself', Edward found that Gladys and Phyllis became permanent denizens of his imagination. Far from putting away childish things as he moved into his teens, he moved into the life of his inventions, which got deeper, more serious and more elaborate as he read more and his perceptions became more sophisticated. Cities with cinemas, theatres, tarts, layabouts and working people, and GIN ... When he went to London, at sixteen, he had already invented it.

But there is another important point; he remembered it. It was not put away with the box of toys in the attic. The phantasmagoria of popular journalism never lost their charm for him. If Burra had gone to Eton, one of the things he would have learned, in the process of being groomed to become a leader of men, would have been to be ashamed of having tastes in common with his nanny and the cook. He would have undergone the brutal training in conformity which boys give to one another, and would have learned to distance himself from 'the lower orders' (and women), to look back with humorous condescension at the things that fascinated his infant self, before he had learned proper discrimination. Very unusually, Burra was in the position of having enough education genuinely to enjoy and appreciate abstruse high-modernist literature in two languages (and later also in a third, Spanish) without ever having learned to cut himself off from his childish likings. This is something rather more fundamental than merely not being a snob.

However, when the sixteen-year-old Burra went to art school, he took his highly original and unusually unified set of perceptions to a London that was very stratified. He was staying with his Robertson-Luxford grandparents at 31 Elvaston Place, South Kensington, where he had been born. Elvaston Place was part of the Harrington Estate, a large area of South Kensington owned and developed by the Stanhopes, Viscounts Petersham and Earls of Harrington. Like many of the roads in the Estate, its name is associated with the Stanhopes, in this case with their country house, Elvaston Castle in Derbyshire. It is a street of clifflike five-storey mid-Victorian town-houses in pale brick, which swooped up and down the social scale in the course of Burra's lifetime. In 1921, Elvaston Place was much as it had been before the First World War, 'the very model, mirror and protoplast of residential respectability', according to Nicholas Bentley. In the years after the Second World War, such houses became untenable as private dwellings, and were turned into flats or hotels. In the 1950s, no. 31 became the Divan Hotel, allegedly one of the best-run brothels in London, and according to the singer Al Stewart, Elvaston Place in the Sixties was a bedsitter-land of absentee landlords, one-bar electric fires and peeling wallpaper. By the time of Burra's death in the Seventies, the street was climbing back towards plutocracy, the houses returning one by one to single occupancy, equipped with batteries of labour-saving devices, steel shutters and burglar alarms.

Burra might quite have liked it in its mid-century manifestation, but in the Twenties his grandparents' house still ran on archaic, ample lines and, like his own home, breathed solid, settled respectability. Burra often mentions his grandmother in letters to friends, but not his grandfather, with whom he did not get on; John Robertson-Luxford appears in the correspondence only after his wife's death: 'Nothing will induce me to stay a minute with that horrible old man,' Burra declared – though he did. It is probable that his grandfather spent most of his time at Higham House, while his grandmother moved to London to make a home for him during term-time.

The life lived at Elvaston Place was one of quiet, elderly routine. A charming and atmospheric drawing which Burra made in 1924 shows his grandmother, stately as a galleon in a tea-gown and string of pearls, with her several chins propped in her hands, smilingly contemplating a jigsaw puzzle; the drawing suggests both the decorous dullness of her evenings and the fact that he loved her. They got on very well together: Burra's letters from his grandmother, like those from his mother, address him as 'dearest Snooks'; they contain trivia, along with a great deal of affection.

At the beginning of 1921, Burra enrolled as a student at the Chelsea College of Art, then in Manresa Road, a shortish bus-ride from South Kensington. He turned up with his satchel, small, pale and self-possessed, looking about fourteen, though in fact he was only two months short of his sixteenth birthday. The College, unlike the Royal College of Art or the Slade, was not actually a school of fine art at that time. It was a faculty of the South-Western Polytechnic, hence its being prepared to take students of sixth-form age. However, most of the other students turned out to be eighteen to twenty, or even older. Inevitably, he gravitated towards the only other male of his own age in the class, a beautifully made boy, with the straight back of a natural athlete, a faunlike face and slanting turquoise eyes. His name was William (Billy) Chappell, and he actually *was* fourteen – because he had been unhappy at school, his mother had lied about his age and browbeaten the Principal into taking him.

Chappell's background was very different from that of his new friend. He had grown up in a fatherless home. His mother, a divorced ex-repertory actress called Edith Blair-Staples, had been brought up in Ceylon and India, because her father was in the regular army. Something of a rebel, she went on the stage, and married twice, choosing, on both occasions, a fellow-actor, but her second husband deserted her when the youngest of her four children was still a baby. When Burra met Chappell, she was struggling to bring up her son, his sisters Dorothea and Honor (known as Thea and Donie) and his half-sister Hermina, with the assistance of her mother, in a rented house, 35 Darnton Road, Balham, SW13. A long way from South Kensington, both literally and metaphorically. She had been forced to give up the stage after her second husband left her, because her mother was past running a large household and coping with the children, and thus she could no longer tour. She reverted to her maiden name, took up journalism and worked immensely hard to keep her family by writing fashion and society columns for a weekly called *The World*, and chatty little pieces for anything else that came along. The household ran on a shoestring, bohemian, hospitable and beset with financial emergencies.

One of the first things that Burra will have observed, with the ineluctable caste-consciousness of a boy of his generation and background, is that Chappell, the semi-educated product of Balham Grammar School and a household of overworked women, was, compared with himself, 'common'. He will also have come rapidly to the conclusion that Chappell's talent for drawing was extremely limited (however, he had other gifts, which became obvious later). But Burra did not care if people were common or not, as long as they were interesting, and

Chappell was a link into a world which he already inhabited imagina-
tively: the backstage world of sequinned shoes, marabou boas and darned
stockings. One of his new friend's sisters gave dancing-lessons, another
became a chorus girl. Lives very different from that of his own sister
at her boarding-school in Eastbourne.

To a boy who went home each night to the dull comfort of Elvaston
Place, Chappell's background, for all its financial poverty, was strangely
glamorous. The converse, of course, was also true. Billy Chappell was
dreamy and diffident, a worshipper in search of a hero; very conscious
of his déclassé origins. A revealing letter which he wrote in 1924 shows
his awareness of his odd position with respect to the class system:

We have a trying uncle here. His son my cousin is at Public School and going to
Oxford has his 1st Eleven colours a thing never known before for a boy of his age
(16) does Latin poetry dreadful snappy

    oh I feel quite the poor wee gutter child.

He was seventeen himself when he wrote this. His mother's brother
had pursued a more conventional path, and was a tea-planter in Ceylon,
who sent his son to school in England. Thus Patrick, the son, often
joined Edith Chappell's hospitable household in the vacations. Although
Chappell and his cousin got on very well, Patrick clearly gave him the
destabilising sense that if his mother's life had turned out differently,
he would have been going to Eton and Oxford, not Balham Grammar
and Chelsea Poly. Because of his own social uncertainty, he was fascinated by Burra's precocious assurance, both personally and as an artist,
by his inventiveness and his sharp tongue, as well as by his indifference
to his social position. The pair were soon as thick as thieves. Mutually
fascinated, they plunged into an intense, exclusive teenage friendship
which, unlike most of its kind, lasted the rest of their lives.

The world into which Chappell's family drew Burra was one that
possessed its own language. In the Twenties, the theatre was still a
distinct subculture. Chorus boys and girls were miserably poor. By way
of compensation, they were smart dressers and smart talkers; sharing a
language of catchphrases and snappy comebacks larded with the slang
peculiar to the entertainment world, Polari. This constantly evolving
and centuries-old dialect was a mixture of pidgin Italian – as the term
Polari (*parlare* is Italian for 'to talk') itself suggests – backslang, such

as ecaf (shortened to eek) for face, a smidgin of Romany, thieves' cant, cockney rhyming slang and invention. 'Trolling' for walking (or cruising), and 'barnet' for hair (rhyming slang; Barnet Fair: hair), are two Polari coinages which made it out of theatreland into English popular culture more generally. Polari was a language created by and for outlaws, designed to facilitate sex and chicanery and to confuse outsiders; by the mid-twentieth century it became the argot of the homosexual community. But in 1920 it still belonged to the theatre, and Chappell introduced Burra to the world that used it.

Burra's own gift for language was notorious in his circle, and was honed by this competitive environment. His own peculiar argot was not Polari (or not often, though he used the odd phrase – 'Oh her hubbie was such a jealosy box ...'). It was an inspired mixture of gossip-columnist and the diction of sensational newspapers and trashy novels; a mélange of essentially feminine verbal styles. He was much given to adopting a feminine persona: 'I knew the hideous secret for months you know dear but wouldnt give another girl away we must keep a bold front against those hateful men.' He also had a music-hall comic's gift for deflation. Like that of his contemporary P.G. Wodehouse, his style gains a lot of its impact by offering a mock-epic commentary on the familiar and mundane. Gossip became virtually an art form. By his late twenties he had learned the effectiveness of speaking seldom, but devastatingly, and in later life he spoke slowly and deliberately. In his teens, he probably chattered like the rest.

Because the majority of students, chorines and artists' models were virtually penniless, their principal recreation was mooching around and talking about each other, fuelled by nothing more exciting than milky tea and beans on toast. Burra and his friends used to meet at the Samovar in St Martin's Lane, or the Tea Kettle in Rupert Street, the favourite haunt of the chorus boys and girls (who included Chappell's sister), and hang about, 'talking nonsense by the hour ... What we liked to do was sit in tearooms and gossip about our friends and run them down.'

We were very juvenile. We didn't do very serious work and we used to cut classes and go to the cinema half the time and we'd sit for hours in tea shops ... we didn't have any night life because we all had to be home ... we used to sit in Lyons Corner House later on till about 4 o'clock in the morning, because it's very cheap and then we could have porridge and tea and vegetable cutlets which cost fourpence halfpenny, we couldn't afford to have much more than that.

Burra and his friends spoke of each other as if they were a gang of sluts, whores and apaches. But as Chappell observed many years later, looking back at his and his friends' teenage years, they were far less practically experienced than they tried to make out. Like Edward and Lawrence pretending to be the Dilly Sisters, their chatter was misleading. Theatreland was a time-honoured cruising-ground for men looking for semi-professional sex, and drugs and prostitution were undoubtedly aspects of the world that chorines such as Donie inhabited (Chappell recounted, for example, how his sister 'was out with a party and a man in it spent hours trying to persuade her to go home with him . . . if you will come home for the night says he I will give you £500 – Ho No dear says she I don't do it you know – I'll give you 20£ for <u>five minutes</u> says the creature. I thought that seemed a good price I should have gone').

But the boys and girls from the art college were not so much participants as fascinated spectators. Chappell subsequently confessed to Frederick Ashton that he had never ventured beyond masturbation between the ages of twelve and twenty. Despite the cheap remark about his sister's admirer, he was romantic and a little puritanical at seventeen, though he would rather have died than admit it. The group's frenzied gossip and speculation came nowhere near actualisation till they were into their later twenties. With the exception of the waifish Burra, the clique were all extremely attractive, but despite their intense theoretical interest in sex, they lingered in the prolonged latency period of Edwardian youth for a surprisingly long time: Billy seems finally to have lost his virginity in 1928.

The actual innocence of Burra and his friends makes a suggestive contrast with Anthony Powell's evocation of 'the typical Twenties party'. Such an occasion, as Powell remembered it, involved the same world that was observed by Burra's gang. There was a good deal of inversion ('hostesses were for some reason often well-to-do lesbians') and a fair amount of sex. To Powell, ex-public school and Oxford, a significant part of the point of going to such dos was that, unlike the debutantes' dances, 'girls expected to have passes made at them, and were well able to look after themselves'. Powell paints what is essentially a consumer's eye view of bohemia, which assumes the availability of 'girls' from that milieu, and their capacity to take responsibility for the risks they would undergo (it should be remembered that although Marie Stopes opened Britain's first birth-control clinic in 1921, this was for married women only: any flapper who dared to present herself would have been chased out with shrieks of affronted virtue).

Painters would be more in evidence than writers. There would be occasional musicians; architects; photographers; in the theatrical contingent, the Ballet likely to outnumber the Legitimate. The girls, largely drawn from the all-inclusive (one avoids the word all-embracing) vocation of model – both artist's model, and one who 'modelled' clothes . . . usually showed an altogether exceptional standard of looks . . . the age of most of those present would be well under thirty; a few probably in their forties; then perhaps a steep rise to comparatively ancient figures, long established in High Bohemia.

In Powell and Burra's generation, most of the English writers perceived as enjoying any real significance, with Lawrence and Joyce as the great exceptions, came from professional families and were educated in the single-sex environments of the public schools and Oxford or Cambridge; men such as Auden, Isherwood, Spender and Waugh. This created problems of its own when they came into contact with other people, especially women. The writer Goronwy Rees described Twenties' Oxonians robustly as young men living in a state of 'sexual infantilism . . . under such conditions what men love and admire most is formed in the male image'. For many of them, when they finally emerged into the real world, women were either invisible or incomprehensible. It seemed obvious to Powell that 'artists' inhabited one category, 'possibly available girls' another: the notion that girls might be anything other than hangers-on does not seem to have struck him. He certainly seems to have had no idea that a smooth young siren with kohl round her eyes, an Eton crop and a line in sexy repartee might be considerably less experienced than she made out.

One of the interesting things about Burra and Chappell is that they didn't think like that at all. Chappell was born and bred as the only boy in a matriarchy; and in a sense, so was Burra. Since Eton and Oxbridge had had to be abandoned due to his health, his world was shaped to a very unusual extent by his mother, nanny, grandmother and sisters (though unlike Chappell, he still had his father as a benign, somewhat silent, presence). Even as teenagers, Burra and Chappell both knew infinitely more about women as people than fell to the lot of most young men of their time who made any mark on the arts. Once their tight little duo expanded to include others, nearly all the new friends they acquired were girls, as silly and virginal as themselves, and for all their gossip and unspeakable innuendos, they stuck together like a group of stunt parachutists holding hands in free fall.

The first girl to be admitted to Chappell and Burra's exclusive society was a fellow student called Barbara (Baba, later Bar) Ker-Seymer whom they annexed in the autumn of 1921. She had arrived at the college at the same time as they had, a dowdy little figure dressed just like her mother. Six months later she sprang out of her chrysalis, shingled her hair, chopped the bottoms off her skirts and reinvented herself as a flapper. When Chappell fell into conversation with this metamorphosed creature, he discovered that she shared his and Burra's passion for films. There were two King's Road cinemas in the Twenties, the King's Pictures Playhouse and Chelsea's House of Enchantments, which had a continuous showing of silent films. Burra was an addict. His diaries and letters are full of accounts of films he has seen, with a very marked preference for schlock. One of his and Chappell's great amusements as teenagers was seizing upon and memorising particularly dreadful silent-film subtitles ('familiarity bred in Costa a terrible dead contempt' was one he cherished) and declaiming them to each other in the Springfield drill hall between shrieks of laughter. He was also a great reader of *Photoplay*, one of the first celebrity magazines, devoted to filmstar lifestyles and gossip.[1] Looking back, Bar said:

We spoke the same language, we liked the same artists, we liked the same books. We were cinema-mad and great ballet fans. We would queue for five hours for Ballets Russes tickets in the gallery. We were what you might call birds of a feather, and yet we all came from different nests.

Bar Ker-Seymer's nest more closely resembled Chappell's than Burra's at a casual glance, though appearances were to some extent deceptive.

---

[1] By 1918 the editors could boast a circulation figure of 204,434. The popularity of the magazine was fuelled by the public's ever-increasing interest in the private lives of celebrities. It is credited, if that is the *mot juste*, with inventing the concept of celebrity media.

Her family background was upper-class, from the more creative and enterprising end of the Victorian *grande bourgeoisie*. One grandmother, Gertrude Clay Ker-Seymer, had been a friend of both Edward VII and Sir Arthur Sullivan (of Gilbert & Sullivan), who dedicated the tune of 'Onward, Christian Soldiers' to her. She also wrote and published a number of novels. The other grandmother, Caroline Creyke, was an even more remarkable character. She was a passionate huntress, and wrote a book called *Sporting Sketches*, published under a pseudonym in 1891. It is worth observing that her enthusiasm for strenuous field sports was distinctly counter-cultural in her own time, and that contemporary reaction to her book was quite hostile. The *Leeds Mercury*, for example, commented drily, 'The book is adorned with pictures which represent this characteristic product of the nineteenth century . . . crouching on the rocks alone to pot a seal, or floating downstream on her back in a waterproof boat, with a rifle over her shoulder and two huge dogs sitting on her, and in other graceful and feminine attitudes.' It was, at any rate, healthy: she lived to 101, dying only in 1946.[2] Bar Ker-Seymer inherited something of her spirit, as also of her looks and her actual interests, since these included painting, journalism and photography as well as shooting and fishing.

Caroline Creyke's third daughter Diana, Bar's mother, 'painted, sang, & was clever & amusing & dressed well', according to her sister. She married Horace Vere Clay Ker-Seymer, who, like Henry Curteis Burra, had been brought up to live on inherited income (Bar's birth certificate gives his profession merely as 'of independent means'). But he became addicted to cards, and gambled away his fortune. He lost the family home, so the story went, 'in one hand of poker at Whites', and Diana and her two daughters (Manon, the elder, and Barbara) went to stay with Grandmama Caroline in her Park Lane mansion for a time. There was enough money around to send Barbara to a suitable boarding-school. A letter that Barbara wrote to a friend much later suggests that her relationship with her father was an affectionate one: 'Every time I read your address I think of my childhood and school. That's where I was. My father and I used to go to the White Rock Pavillion to the Fol de Rols and then on the Pier to listen to the Band on Sundays!'

[2] She said to Barbara three years before her death, 'I have a word of advice for you. Never grow to be ninety-eight. It's deadly dull.'

However, the actual relations between her parents were less successful. Gambling puts an enormous strain on a marriage, but in any case, Diana's preferences were lesbian, and she periodically retreated abroad with a girlfriend. Barbara long remembered this interchange between her parents:

> 'I've done my painful duty for seven years!'
> 'But if you go off to Italy, what am I to do?'
> 'Do what other men do. Go to clubs.'

By the time Barbara left school, she, her mother and sister were living in West Kensington (perceived at the time as one of the areas of London 'where the fly-blown respectability of the lower middle class clings to its dreary outposts against the slums'). Like Chappell's mother, Diana Ker-Seymer was in exile from the world she had been brought up to inhabit, but unlike Edith Chappell, she did not have a profession to fall back on. She sought consolation in the theories of Mary Baker Eddy and become a Christian Scientist, which meant that Barbara was supposed to overcome her ailments by the power of prayer. Since she had trouble with abscesses in her ears as a child, failure to treat them caused long-term damage which made her deaf in later life.

For all the unglamorousness of her immediate milieu, Barbara was very well connected. For example, she knew that quintessential Twenties' figure, Brian Howard, from childhood, and was one of the very few of his friends whom his alarming mother Lura approved of. Another family friend was the great actress, Mrs Patrick Campbell. Poverty is relative: while Mrs Ker-Seymer thought of herself as 'poor', in comparison with the life she had been born to, Bar was presented at court as a debutante, ostrich-feathers and all, in the company of Meraud Guinness ('I do think a bunch of feathers stuck on the back will improve any face,' Burra remarked).

A third recruit to Burra's gang, who came to Chelsea in the following year, was also a girl, Clover Pritchard. Her background was as pukka as Bar's and Burra's – her father had been a colonel in the Indian Army (she was born in India), and her parents were impeccably conventional people who sent her to Roedean and retired to High Salvington, which bore roughly the same relationship to Worthing as Playden did to Rye. Highly intelligent, and a natural rebel, she refused to go to university, and insisted on art school. She and Burra first met in the life-class, because, like most of the students in that foggy November, she was coughing – but perhaps louder, more persistently or more annoyingly, since she suddenly heard an acid voice declaring, 'She needs some Veno's Lightning Cough Cure.' It was typical of Burra's verbal style to be absolutely specific about such things. She turned to see a small, pale boy sitting behind an easel and glowering at her (as she later discovered, his feet were already gnarled to the extent that he could not work standing up).

From this unpromising beginning, they rapidly became friends. Looking back, she thought that he might have been attracted by her personal style: 'Chelsea Poly was under the influence of Augustus John. Raggle-taggle gypsies were all the go . . . I think he liked me because I tried my best to look and behave as if I were thirty, and dressed in black when I was seventeen.' Burra always liked beautiful clothes, even though he never bothered himself about looking after them, while Bar Ker-Seymer and Chappell were, in their different ways, stylish, aiming at the sleek and chic rather than the bohemian look. Henry Moore, a few years older, remembered Burra and his circle looking extraordinarily sophisticated in what was a comparatively unsophisticated context. They all had a passion for shoes (new acquisitions are frequently sketched in letters), which ideally came from Peter Yapp of Sloane Street, or at least looked as if they did. On a continental jaunt, Burra considered the elegant mock-croc shoes available in Cassis, and rejected them: 'You know dear I like everything to be real you know realy good.'

What a smart girl was wearing in 1920 was a dress or suit which de-emphasised the waist (though the waistline had not yet plummeted southwards as it was to do later in the decade) and which was carefully cut, often on the bias, with a calf-length skirt. It was a chic, tailored style which created a sleek, narrow, tubular silhouette, crisp and urban rather than overtly sexy. The mode had the enormous advantage, from the viewpoint of girls who had more style than money, that the construction was relatively simple, and consequently tended to elide the difference between the moderately rich and the moderately poor, as long as the clothes were chosen with care, which had not been true of pre-war fashions. Underneath their low-waisted frocks, the young and slender such as Bar and Clover, rather than donning a defensive armour of corsetry, were beginning to favour directoire knickers and brassieres (which were seamed so as to flatten the breasts), and dealt with their silk stockings by rolling them down to the knee, where they were secured with garters.

Matters were somewhat other with men's clothes. 'Good' was instantly distinguishable from 'cheap', because gentleman's clothes were made of exquisitely high-quality fabrics, and built to last. The sort of Clyde-built garments that Burra bought, or had bought for him at his father's tailors, were constructed with the utmost refinement. A good Twenties' overcoat was made of Crombie cloth with a silk-satin lining, but the side-pockets were lined with silk velvet, to comfort cold hands. My husband has one, made for his grandfather in 1922, which went through eighty winters before it began to show outward symptoms of wear. It cost twenty guineas, a lot of money. Chappell, from a genuinely impoverished home, was deeply conscious that his own wardrobe did not measure up, and was delighted when Burra passed on some old clothes to him in 1929, particularly by a coat. 'Dearest Ed you are lady bountiful and no mistake. Thank you very much the various gifts are terribly acceptable and Im so pleased to have come in to your coat as my old chinchilla was giving way rapidly.'

Burra had an educated eye for clothes; his drawings and paintings not only chronicle passing fashion, but use clothes to offer subtle clues to the wearer's identity. He enjoyed describing Anne's posh friends' dowdily expensive fashion disasters, especially to Bar, to whom he reported with dark glee on one unfortunate girl's evening frocks (with drawings): 'this evening she has on her dinkie cyclamen "crêpe tomato" with boat shaped neck and around the bottom roses à la poached egs to tone yesterday we had on our black crêpe noir carried out with daring decolté censored with pastel gauze embroidered with peagreen ribbon à la serpent'. His own clothes were unusually colourful for a man of his generation. On a couple of occasions, he was caught out by a funeral without either a sober suit or a plain white shirt to his name; he mentions shirts of sky blue, mauve stripes, chocolate brown, all of which were fairly outré in the Twenties.

The principal point in the year at which the Chelsea students emerged into the view of London arts people was the Chelsea Arts Club Ball, held at the Royal Albert Hall. Far from typical of day-to-day life at the art school, it was one of the annual fixtures of high bohemia, where the more painterly end of Bloomsbury mixed it with the lower orders, and Nina Hamnett might be found being sick on a boxer, to the disgust of the lesbian speedboat racer, 'Joe' Carstairs. Everyone wore outrageous costumes at the Arts Club Ball, sometimes to the point of getting themselves arrested, but even there, Chappell and Bar managed to make themselves conspicuous, by dressing identically: they both owned pairs of white matelot trousers, and improvised tops for them year by year. At the Ball of 1928, when they were twenty and twenty-two respectively, they went as 'drowned sailors with open work net tops', decorated with real seaweed, collected by Burra (with, as he added pointedly, in a letter to Bar, 'some nice cockle shells covered with barnacles so they will keep the boys at bay'). The costume was a revealing one, but they must have danced primarily with each other, since otherwise the effect would have been lost. In effect, they were using one another as chaperons just in case anyone got the wrong idea.

But were they being drowned sailors in general, or had they been reading *The Waste Land* – were they, that is, Phlebas the Phoenician, a fortnight dead (and friend)? If they were in fact being arty and literary, which seems highly likely, Burra was determined that they shouldn't get above themselves; thereafter, one of his many nicknames for Chappell was Fishnet Annie.

Burra himself did not go to the Ball, in that or any other year. He couldn't stand up for long enough, let alone dance. While Billy and Bar were busy annoying the likes of Anthony Powell, he was at the panto – *Cinderella* – in Hastings, with his family, and enjoying it very much in his own ironic style ('it was a perfect dream the principal boy would act through thick and thin even singing "when I saw Sally coming down our Alley" didn't stop her').

The foursome became inseparable, and obnoxious on principle. Chappell summed up this phase of the friends' lives:

Each buttressing the others' egos, the quartet was quite formidably self-sufficient and almost unsupportable: noisy, over-pleased with themselves, determined, above all, to shock. Their antics were regarded by most of the female students with amused tolerance. Not so by the men (predominantly a cloddish lot) who were overtly suspicious and hostile: an attitude returned a hundredfold by its recipients.

The curriculum at Chelsea was primarily vocational, focused on commercial art, illustration, textiles, etching, lithography and architecture. It did not start teaching sculpture until the Thirties, or painting until after the Second World War. Most of the students were preparing themselves for jobs involving art, rather than for a future as artists. They were therefore, from the clique's point of view, a dismally bourgeois bunch. Teenagers setting out to be irritating generally succeed, but there was a little more to the mutual hostility than that. Burra writes with the disdain that comes readily to a seventeen-year-old:

> God rot the tea club.
> & may L and his foul sluttish friends
> fall and break their necks.
> > Bugger them.
> and T and his friend
> are stupid oafs
> > not worth bothering
> > over by sensible
> members of the human
> race – annoy everyone as
> much as possible dear & my
> blessings gang with you.
> Messages, Messages.
> > xx Ed xx

This implies the flavours of wind-up that were practised, aside from ineffable contempt; the cod Scots of 'my blessings gang with you' suggests silly voices, and 'dear' (not a normal mode of address between boys at the time) that campness was already a well-developed routine. The friends developed a common voice, supercilious and exaggerated, an assumed accent known at the time as 'Mayfair cockney' (Burra's voice in old age reminded George Melly of 'an elderly but game Edwardian tart propositioning from the shadows' – by that time, his natural light tenor had been roughened by whisky and cigarettes). In surviving interview footage, Burra's diction is markedly camp, though with a very definite upper-class intonation (rather like Francis Bacon's voice); Chappell's is similar. The boys were doubtless suspected of being lovers, a queasy thought to most men of the time, though to be thus regarded would have delighted Burra and Chappell.

The girls were equally annoying in a different way, especially to those men who regarded women as consumables. Clover was exotically beautiful, with her bobbed hair curled over one eye, high cheekbones and a cleft chin, a sexy minx in the style of Betty Boop, who perversely preferred going about with a pair of pansies to going out with suitable young men. Bar was a good-looking flapper in the fashionable, androgynous mode of the time, flat-chested, short-haired and 'boyish', with small, neat features. Like Burra, she was renowned for her sharp tongue. Though she was in some ways diffident and lacking in self-confidence, no-one would have guessed it from her offhand manner. She struck a subsequent boyfriend (Goronwy Rees) as birdlike, with a high clear voice, and she was nothing like as spinsterish as this makes her sound – in later years, she was remarkably successful in attracting lovers. The pair of them were precisely the sort of dreadful modern girl that moralists were wringing their hands about. 'To hear them talk theoretically was most impressive. They were terribly at ease upon the Zion of sex, abounding in inhibitions, dream symbolism, complexes, sadism, repressions, masochism, Lesbianism, sodomy, etcetera.' It is worth noting that they were also modern in another key respect; they belonged to the first cohort of women to have the vote at twenty-one.

The quartet have obvious points in common: they were all, even Billy Chappell, the children of gentlefolk. Like most of the 'Chelsea Set' of the Sixties, though they were reacting strongly against their parents' values (with the exception of Chappell, the son of a woman who had been a similar sort of rebel in her own day), they had a confidence and address which stemmed from their upper-middle-class origins, and made good use of it. Within the foursome itself, Burra was perceived by all four as the genius; he and Bar as the principal wits. Bumble, a slightly later recruit, said, '[Ed] always made you feel you were being pompous. I don't think any of us was as funny as him or as sharp rather more than funny.'

The mutual dynamics were complex. Bar thought, in retrospect, that Burra 'wrote most frivolously to me, he revealed himself more to Billy, and wrote about literature to . . . Clover who was cleverer than the rest of us'. Any two might unite to be nasty about an absent third, quarrel, make up again. While it might be assumed that the social dynamics of a Twenties' teenage coterie would ensure that the boys were the acknowledged centre, with the girls as hangers-on, this was not the case.

Chappell had a naturally subaltern personality. He was the youngest of the four, queeny, lacking in self-confidence and his penchant for bustling around and looking after people was already observable (not least by Burra, who often referred to him later in life as Mrs Chappell, or Nurse Chappell).

Also, whatever they may have seen fit to imply, he and Burra were not lovers. In his art-school days, Chappell was still a virgin, and obtuse to his own sexual identity. His attraction to – and for – Burra was clearly not physical. Burra wrote with complete detachment about Chappell's romances; to Bar, for example: 'mind you watch out and see Billy doesn't go out too much with Emile or someone will be carrying within them the burden of their fault' (a phrase which almost certainly derives from a silent-film subtitle). Chappell was blessed with startling good looks, as his photographs make clear, but Burra's portrait of his best friend suggests that he was not susceptible to them. He makes Chappell look dull and bovine, which he was not. And though Burra's pallid, curiously wizened little face was not without charm, particularly when he smiled, for all his venomous gift for gossip, he was an essentially sexless creature. Anthony Powell recalls the revue actress Hermione Baddeley cross-questioning Burra on the topic at a party:

'Have you ever loved a man?'
'No.'
'Have you ever loved a woman?'
'No.'
'Not even your mother?'
There was a short pause while Burra considered the matter. A conclusion was
    reached.
'No.'

This is obvious nonsense, in that Burra was self-evidently a man of profound personal loyalties; these, however, he presumably did not consider to be any of Miss Baddeley's business, especially given her rhetorical unfairness in switching the ground from an enquiry about his sexual life, which was a suitable subject for smart party conversation in the Twenties, to one about his emotional life, which was not. However, he had not the slightest trace of masculine vanity, and was perfectly happy to be perceived as asexual. On another occasion, an equally intrusive questioner asked him if he had ever had an erection, and he admitted only to a very slight one, experienced while watching a Mae West film. One does not have to take this absolutely literally (it is an answer obviously intended to fend off further enquiry). What can certainly be said, on the evidence of his paintings as well as his letters, is that Burra's sensibility was camp, and in some early paintings, queer to the point of misogyny – *Marriage à la Mode* (1928/9), for example, in which the joke is definitely against the swooning, bosomy bride and her weeping walrus of a mother, since the priest is patently in the process of organising an assignation with a far-from-unwilling bridegroom. But that may have been as far as it went.

It is severely doubtful whether, even in his teens and twenties, Burra had the physical stamina for much in the way of a sex-life. He was disabled from normal experience in two ways. Firstly, by his anaemic constitution, which meant that his body was like a machine running on a nearly-flat battery; he had a very limited amount of energy with which to get himself through a day. Secondly, he lived with chronic rheumatic pain in his limbs, and above all in his hands and feet. Even as an adolescent, he spent much of his time in a state of almost continuous depletion and, at least some of the time, also in discomfort which modified intermittently into pain. At twenty-four, he wrote in a letter, 'Just been to Paris qui remue Josephine B's piece tonight I stood dearie so my feet are much in evidence.' This suggests that all his friends were quite aware that although this was not normally to be mentioned, he could not stand for two hours or so without suffering for it. Clover Pritchard, looking back, thought that he lived in almost continual pain.

However, one of the saddest things in the Burra archive is a tiny scrap of evidence that, at twenty-five, he was still having to work on his self-sufficiency. About a dozen pocket diaries survive from various years, the earliest of which is for 1929. One thing they reveal is that through the Twenties and Thirties he was in the habit of telling his fortune from time to time with a pack of playing cards, particularly at the New Year. A fortune recorded in the 'notes' page for January 1929 runs:

My wish ~~affair~~ ♥
Unexpected prosp or GL [prosperity or good luck]
Some disapointment visit of Doc D may by miss rep [misrepresentation] try to estrange me from someone who likes me very much & P [the person?] from me

There would be many visits from the doctor in 1929, and a certain amount of prosperity and good luck. But if his secret wish, censored by scoring out the word, was for an affair of the heart, then it did not happen.

Burra's shyly expressed desire for 'someone who likes me very much' was, at best, only a wistful hope. It is hard, and perhaps impossible, for someone living with Burra's degree of handicap to experience rapturous physicality; or even to think in terms of the body as a site of self-expression and intense pleasure. The only kind of physical experiences to which Burra could easily abandon himself were drinking and drug-taking; unsurprisingly, both alcohol and, later, cannabis became important to him. He was not by any means an alcoholic. He enjoyed getting drunk; Chappell recalled that when he was drunk, Burra would 'giggle an awful lot', but when he started getting hangovers that prevented him from working, he reined back. He was similarly self-disciplined about cannabis, because it interfered with painting: 'I love to be stoned,' he wrote, 'it quite prevents one from doing any work so I can rarely be really stoned.'

Further, if he felt like that about cannabis, it is most unlikely that he ever experimented with other fashionable drugs of the Twenties, such as cocaine, morphine, heroin or Veronal, though all of these were readily available among nightclub dancers and the London party-going set, and some quite good friends of his were heroin addicts. Burra's own drug was painting. He was not in any ordinary sense an addictive person-ality, he was tough and stoic, and seldom took even prescription drugs other than aspirin. Whatever the potential temptation of opiates for a man who lived with chronic pain, he was not prepared to fuzz his perceptions for the sake of mere personal comfort.

Logistical considerations aside, Burra may have had significant diffi-culties with love as well as with sex. Even for an upper-class male born in 1905, Burra was extraordinarily private. While he had a vast capacity for friendship and loyalty, he would have needed to lower his defences to surrender himself to a partner, and this he was almost certainly incap-able of. Several times in his life he made serious errors of judgement because he underestimated, or failed to perceive, the way that love and attendant anxiety had set one of his friends off balance emotionally, suggesting that he had no idea what this felt like.

This aspect of his character may, once again, be related to the miser-ably finite amount of energy at his disposal: he needed all his energy and integrity for his painting. Though it might not have struck anyone who was listening to him dispensing scabrous gossip in the Tea Kettle; he had embarked on his career as a painter in something of the spirit of a monastic vocation; a private dedication of his will and energy to his art.

However, most people outside the group would have seen his preoccupations as worrying to the point of being decadent. Another thing besides a shared attitude of generalised defiance and a shared taste for gossip, films and ballet which linked Burra and his friends was a devotion to jazz and the blues. It was not easy music to get hold of at the time, but American imports could be bought at Levy's in Aldgate, which was a regular port of call for all of the friends, or at Keith Prowse, a firm which had started as a music publishing company, but also sold records (it later became Keith Prowse Music). Burra, Chappell, Bar and Clover all collected records, swopped, recommended and discussed them. Just as they liked to see themselves as bigger and badder than they were, they liked this music of desperate lives, with its narratives of survival, poverty and violence. A contemporary, Hubert Nicholson, who shared Burra's musical tastes, recalled the sheer excitement of his first encounter with imported American discs:

I . . . had never heard anything like the terrific strident, hard, highly organised machine jazz of Red Nichols and His Five Pennies, Miff Mole's Molers, Venuti's Blues Four, Rollini's Goofus Washboards, to say nothing of the negro bands. Even the titles of the new music were different . . . Hot jazz was a thing apart, and after I had my ear attuned to it I could never again care two hoots for 'sweet society' playing or the commercial product of ordinary English bands.

What Burra particularly liked and commented on were songs by big, tough women who belted out the blues. He seems to have enjoyed their assertiveness and sexual aggression, so antithetic to the notions of femininity put forward in his own culture. He had a great liking for the East Side Jewish singer, Sophie Tucker (a taste he shared with W.H. Auden and Cecil Day Lewis), and was particularly taken by 'I Guess He Will Tonight', a song in which Miss Tucker announces her intention of getting her way with a shy boyfriend, by force if necessary. Ida Cox was another favourite. Very popular in the Twenties, Miss Cox made about a hundred recordings between 1923 and 1940 with some of the best jazz musicians then working as her accompanists. She also wrote blues songs, which were recorded by other singers such as Bessie Smith (most famously, 'Nobody Knows You When You're Down and Out'). Burra particularly liked 'Four Day Creep', which Ida Cox wrote and recorded in 1939 with her All Star Band, and quoted it with relish.

... And I'm gonna buy me a bulldog to watch my man while he sleeps
I'm gonna buy me a bulldog to watch my man while he sleeps
Men are so doggone crooked, afraid he might make a four day creep ...

Another verse of the same song suggests something of the toughness of her approach.

And I'm a big fat mama, got the meat shakin' on my bones
I'm a big fat mama, got the meat shakin' on my bones
And every time I shake, some skinny gal loses her home

Burra's feeling about fat women in the superabundant flesh was tinged with ambivalence, but viewed thus, from a safe distance, he enjoyed the brutal clarity and drive of Ida Cox. He saw Bessie Smith herself in performance in Harlem, and was impressed, perhaps a little intimidated:

die Ruth Baldwin yellow and blow for 24 hours with a bicycle pump and pour into a long wine coloured dress with paillette short sleeves and you have Smith.

Lines and half-lines from blues songs are quoted all over letters to his friends, common reference points. 'Hot lips like pips' ... 'Ime ½ alive and hes driving me mad hes only human if hes to be had I must have Nils Asther ...' – from 'Louisville Lou' and 'I Must Have That Man' respectively (the last with reference to a glamour photo of Nils Asther on a postcard).

He also liked big-band sound: 'If you want to get a glorious record get Doing the new Lowdown & Digga Digga Doo by Duke Ellingtons wonder orch: on the Parlophone Ive never heard anything so lovely both have vocal chorusus I play nothing else.' Nat King Cole is also mentioned, and he loved Cab Calloway; it was black bands that he liked, for the most part.

Burra's records ended up, like most of the contents of his studio, in the Tate, from which it is clear that, though he prized them, he didn't look after them. They lay about amid the detritus without their paper sleeves, and took their chance. The poet Paul Farley, contemplating the remains of Burra's record collection, observed:

these ten-inch bakelite records, hundreds of them, are among the most punished playing surfaces I've ever seen. Some must have spent years sliding around the artist's studio floor. Cab Calloway, Pearl Bailey, Louis Armstrong, all are pitted and flecked with pigment. My Hi De Ho Man by Lil Armstrong looks as though an eclipsing bite has been taken from it.

Part of the attraction of 'hot jazz' is that to middlebrow consensus culture, it was decadent and horrifying, 'nigger music'. A reason in itself, apart from its intrinsic attractions, for the avant-garde young to love it. As Burra, Chappell, Ker-Seymer and Pritchard (there was a fad for using surnames at the Poly, though in their letters they addressed one another as Eddie, Billy, Baba and Clo) sloped about Chelsea, talking in loud, high-pitched voices and hoping to be overheard, they could be comfortably aware that nearly everything they discussed was liable to annoy or disturb respectable adults.

They were being Twenties' people, self-consciously so. That is to say, they were cool; in reaction against the moral earnestness of the pre-war generation. Both Chappell and Bar tried to explain this at various points during the interviews they gave to the makers of a documentary on Burra in the Seventies. 'We were all so used to hearing people sitting round and discussing art in hushed, earnest tones – it was all a question of higher values. And I think really our attitudes were a reaction,' said Chappell. 'We were much less solemn than people now are, we were very, very frivolous, or apparently very, very frivolous,' said Bar. Burra himself summed up his attitude: 'I'm serious about my work but I don't spread seriousness around it's such a bore.' That last clause is pure Twenties; being boring was the ultimate social sin, linked with other crimes such as pomposity and earnestness.

But it is important to recognise that sexual transgressiveness (actual or theoretic), the devil's music and bohemian chic were only part of the story of Chelsea art school as Burra experienced it. In the same sense in which one can assert that 'the Sixties' as a cultural phenomenon did not begin until 1963/4, the Twenties started slowly. T.S. Eliot, looking back, suggested that modernism did not really get under way until 1926.

At Chelsea, Burra and his friends were highly self-conscious about iden-
tifying themselves as part of something that was still very new indeed.
Orwell, from the vantage-point of 1940, perceived the prevailing mass
culture of the early Twenties as one of cheeriness and manliness, dominated by men such as J.C. Squire, influential editor of the *London
Mercury*, and popular authors such as Hugh Walpole and John Buchan.
The majority of Chelsea students were highly conservative, practically
oriented and orthodox in their inclinations: for all that the female
students were dressing as 'Augustus John' gypsies, conventionality ran
deep. Barbara commented much later:

We called normal men 'He-men'. They were a special brand that you don't see
nowadays, unless you watch old black and white films. They had moustaches and
were interested in cricket and thought it cissy to like art. It worried me terribly
because I didn't think I'd ever be able to get married. I couldn't stand any one of
them.

By 1925, the gap between youth/avant-garde culture and a powerful
middle-of-the-road consensus that the war had changed nothing fundamental and things were 'getting back to normal' had widened to the
extent of becoming a war in its own right. Going out of one's way to
offend representatives of the older generation was perceived by not a
few intellectuals as a species of duty: Betjeman, Waugh and the Sitwells,
for example, were all rude to their fathers on principle. Orwell observes
that 'at that time there was, among the young, a curious hatred of "old
men" . . . every accepted institution, from Scott's novels to the House
of Lords, was derided because "old men" were in favour of it'. Burra,
though not rude (his war-cry was the relatively mild 'for God's sake,
don't FUSS'), excluded his parents from his inner life with polite firm-
ness, and refused to answer any questions about, for example, where he
was going. A story which circulated widely is that he disappeared one
afternoon telling his mother that he was just going into the garden, only
to return six months later, having in the interval been to America, which
has a kernel of truth (it is discussed in a later chapter).

However, Chelsea seems to have done surprisingly well by Burra. The
curriculum suited him perfectly: he wrote to Chappell in the summer of
1925 that he was actually thinking of going back to Chelsea for the next
year; 'I should like to draw all day without stopping.' Chelsea concen-

trated on drawing above all, precisely because it was *not* a fine-art school, but training future draughtsmen and illustrators. It therefore gave him a daily life-class (the cornerstone of his art, since so much of it, in the first half of his life, was based on the human body), and he also made measured architectural drawings, a piece of technical training that was evident for ever after in his confident treatment of buildings. He also did illustration about once a week, and drew outside the school. Though his oeuvre suggests that he had absolutely no interest in animals for their own sake (apart from birds and perhaps cats), there is a sketchbook of animal studies which were probably done in the Natural History Museum as a student assignment. But he was several times asked to produce illustrations in his life, and was always very pleased to get these commissions.

Drawing was the centre of his life, one of the few subjects on which he was never prepared to mock. John Aiken, Conrad's son, observed, 'He was a wonderful draughtsman, as a result of a rigorously self-imposed apprenticeship; and had a mild but dismissive contempt for those contemporaries (among whom, good friend that he was, he numbered Paul Nash) who could not draw'. Burra intensely disliked talking about art, but there is every reason to think that he shared Michael Ayrton's passionate conviction that drawing is of the first importance.

The process of drawing is before all else the process of putting the visual intelligence into action, the very mechanics of taking visual thought. Unlike painting and sculpture it is the process by which the artist makes clear to *himself*, and not to the spectator, what he is doing . . . Drawing makes more precise and delicate demands on the intellect than does the physically more generous art of painting.

The artists Burra most admired (Tiepolo and Goya among them) tended to be the ones who could draw like angels. His own drawing technique was highly individual; he had a wonderful sense of line, and some of his drawings, influenced by artists such as Georg Grosz and Aubrey Beardsley, depend above all on fluid line set off with occasional patches of black (a technique which he borrowed from Beardsley). But his most formal drawings are quite different. They are utterly disciplined, and based on broad outlines composed of clustered pen hatchings, like engravings.

Burra's drawing as a teenager impressed everyone; Chappell's did not. He (rashly) illustrated his own books later in life, revealing a wide streak of mimsy sentimentality and an uncertain grasp of anatomy. 'I'm not at all sure painting is his milieu he photographs well it's a bad sign,' judged a contemporary, Florence Rushbury (as quoted back at Chappell by Burra). Clover and Bar were both modestly competent: Clover sometimes illustrated her letters, charmingly, while one of Bar's sketchbooks (now in the Tate), a memento of a beach holiday some time in the late Fifties, shows her as a vigorous and confident draughtswoman. However, neither woman was committed to a career in art, and Bar's recollections are quite clear: Burra was seen within the group of friends, within Chelsea more generally, and by their instructors, as infinitely the most talented and original of the four.   ʌ

There were a lot of serious students at the Poly doing rather dreary paintings . . . Billy and I were at the stage of doing crinolined medieval ladies and knights jousting and I remember Edward doing a picture of two hideous old crones hitting each other with carpet beaters.

Chappell commented much later on the tremendous energy of Burra's early paintings, most of which have been lost.

Burra established a basic style in the course of his teens which developed in various ways in the course of his life, but which he never really abandoned. Michael Rothenstein, the eight-years-younger brother of John, was briefly friendly with Burra at Chelsea. He is a valuable witness to Burra's early development, since they both liked to paint in watercolour.

We would sit side by side at a big table, working away at these water colours. He laid wash over the surface of the paper, really like an ant, inch by inch . . . he worked so minutely. He would draw out an area, quite carefully, with a hardish line, and then he'd fill it in with his water colour, with small brushes, and he always used white with his water colour, so the technique which he later developed that was so remarkable, of a sort of deep gouache technique was already appearing . . . his fingers were already getting crooked and the joints were swelling. And I noticed whenever he did a tree, he had sort of knotted branches with swollen joints, just like his own fingers.

In social terms, though the loathsome quartet were sufficient unto themselves, they received more support from the adult world than they were prepared to acknowledge. Florence (known as 'Birdie') Rushbury was important in the early lives of Burra and Chappell. She was in a somewhat separate category from the other students due to the fact that she was a mature student (born 1896) and married; moreover, her husband Henry Rushbury was a tutor at the Royal College of Art and a Royal Academician. Birdie was talented, kindly, frivolous and longing for amusement, which her husband was not always able to provide. He worked abroad a good deal, and if she went with him, she could not easily fill in the time while he was painting, because if she wandered off on her own, local men tended to jump to conclusions about the kind of entertainment she was looking for. The Rushburys came to a joint decision that he would have to go abroad alone at least some of the time, and so she joined the Chelsea school to give some shape to her days. Burra and Chappell were exactly what she wanted: amusing, affectionate and absolutely safe.

Chappell was particularly useful, since he could act as her escort and take her to parties, which Burra could not, or at least, would not. Chappell reported, for example, in December 1924 (when he was still only seventeen), that he 'went with the Rushbury to the Slade Dance and afterwards to a studio off Charlotte St – very sinister – we were at the studio till 4 am oh Ed realy it was so drunk everyone was drunk except me. It was like wasted Flaming youth – there were couples embracing passionately under the Grand piano . . . Even Rush herself (hush never a word mention) was drefful put out by gin & soda.' Burra was told all about it, and promptly doubled the fun by reflecting them back to themselves in the terms of contemporary sensational journalism: 'I hear you have been luring my innocent William into the nighthaunts of London crool crool leprous white Circe thus to tear the veil from the eyes of innocence . . . its women as you as puts orange peel neath virtues foot am daily expecting a vivid rendering of all that happened & more besides.'

They gave one another a great deal of entertainment. Birdie repaid them by insisting on taking the boys to that bastion of all that Burra most scorned about Chelsea, the Tea Club, to the dismay of its habitués. More importantly, after Burra had left Chelsea, she and her husband were prevailed upon to take them to Paris in 1925 (a story that will wait for a later chapter).

III

MOVING ON

BURRA spent only two years at Chelsea. In 1923, when he was old enough, he transferred to the Royal College of Art (which admitted students at eighteen), where he could work more directly on painting. He and another of the most distinguished watercolourists of his generation, Eric Ravilious, found themselves side by side at the entrance scholarship exam: Ravilious was surprised to observe that Burra made no attempt to draw the life-model, but spent the entire day drawing a single eye, in meticulous detail, in the middle of his very large piece of paper.

Of the two schools, Chelsea seems to have been the more important to him, because of the solid grounding in drawing he got there, but the Royal College was significant for other reasons. While at Chelsea, where he and Michael Rothenstein were fellow-students, he had visited the Rothenstein household; at the Royal College, he came directly under the eye of Michael's father, Sir William, who was then President of the College, and Michael's much older brother, John, who later became Director of the Tate and one of Burra's principal champions. His principal teachers were Randolph Schwabe, interested both in drawing and in theatre-design, and Raymond Coxon, who was a very close friend of Henry Moore. John Rothenstein was initially less impressed with Burra's work than with the force of his personality.

In those days he was a silent, pale boy, who put me in mind of a machine which had almost run down, so near did his small reserve of energy seem to exhaustion . . . There was something most bizarre in the contrast between the sedate existence of this delicate, home-loving schoolboy, and the products of his imagination: nocturnal street encounters in the red-light districts of Continental cities, scenes in the tough water-side joints and in the sailors' brothels of Mediterranean ports.

Burra's drawing at this stage still showed some *fin de siècle* influence, from Beardsley in particular, as well as from the more recent work of Georg Grosz. Rothenstein comments austerely:

The small figure compositions to which he gave the greater part of his time seemed to me to afford less evidence of exceptional talent; they had the same exquisite finish as the nudes, but they were a belated and sterile flowering of *art nouveau*, a deft but arbitrary blend of the mannerisms from Aubrey Beardsley, Walter Crane, Caran d'Ache and Edmund Dulac.

He liked Burra's academic drawing much better. What this suggests is that it took some time for Burra's technical ability and the powerful individuality of his imagination to reach an accommodation with each other – not unreasonably, since he was at this point only eighteen.

However, another result of the Royal College experience was an enlargement of Burra's circle of intimate friends. Three important new additions at this time were Lucy Norton, Doris Langley Levy and Irene Hodgkins. Lucy Norton's background was like that of Burra himself, wealthy and established, but unlike the Burras, who were not in the least smart, she had connections with the Bloomsbury set. She was born at Kentwell Hall, Suffolk; but her mother died when she was six, and she was brought up by two considerably older sisters at Lancaster Gate. She was very close to her older brother Harry, whose friends included Maynard Keynes and Lytton Strachey – the latter introduced both Nortons to the ballet, a passion that she shared with her art-school friends.

Lucy was talented, but did not have Burra's discipline. She studied under Paul Nash at the Royal College, who said of her (as redacted by Burra), 'he thought . . . Lu had a charming invention but she is realy so social I dont know if she'l do anything realy'. 'Social' in this context means not 'sociable', but 'concerned to maintain her place in good society'. A good few of Bar's letters from the late Twenties comment acidly on Lucy's tendency to pull strings, her desire to distance herself from mere art-school acquaintances, and indeed, on the Nash connection: 'she took three books full of her life drawings to Dottie & Paul

Nash, who raved over them and said "what line! What expression! so this, so that!" etc etc. that girl is getting a bit beyond herself'. She did some illustration work for the Fanfrolico Press, and worked as a scene-painter, but in the end Nash's intuition that it wouldn't come to much was proved correct.

Meanwhile, Bar and Burra became increasingly sceptical. They particularly disliked Lucy's airs, since both of them felt, in the terms of that class-conscious generation, that they were quite as good as she was. Billy, on the other hand – less secure, and coming from as impov-erished a background as he did – was much more inclined to go along with her pretensions. He was somewhat dazzled by someone so obvi-ously privileged, who, in 1927, even acquired a car! 'I went out in Lady Nortons new car yesterday such an advanced model full of gadgets of every kind it is very comfortable,' he reported excitedly. Bar was catty: 'Billy has once more succumbed to the hypnotic influence of Queen Nortons £.s.d. and has quite deserted his old pals. Clover said he was so grand at the Strauss concert that she hardly dared speak to him.'

Lucy made a modest reputation as an artist in her twenties, and had an exhibition at the Redfern Gallery in 1927. Burra, who had not yet had an exhibition himself, was, on the one hand, consumed with envy; on the other, contemptuous of her methods of self-advancement. But the exhibition was not a success. Nash enjoyed 'fixing', was rather apt to see the best in handsome young women, and was also not indifferent to Lucy's connections. As a result, he talked her up well beyond her merits. The exhibition showed up the limitations of her talent to an embarrassing extent, and Burra and Bar were inclined to feel it served her right. The latter lost no time in circulating Rex Nan Kivell's comment, 'They are not such bad little things, but she can't etch, and her drawing is nothing to be proud of', which she repeated to Burra and Chappell, both of whom were gleeful.

Even if this did not get back to Lucy directly, she was clearly aware that the exhibition had caused her to lose face rather than gain it. The experience led her to retreat from trying to make her mark as an artist, though she continued to earn money working as a theatrical scene-painter. Much later, through her brother Harry's literary connections, she finally discovered her real gift, which was as a translator. She found the perfect subject, the *Memoirs* of Saint-Simon, a witty, caustic and penetrating record of politics, chicanery, intrigue, gossip and love-affairs at the court of Louis XIV, which allowed her to transmute her own gift for society into art. Unlike most of Burra's friendships, this one did not last, but in the Twenties her connections helped to involve the group with both the literary world and the world of ballet.

Doris Langley Levy entered the group as a friend, first of all, of Bar's, because she lived with Bar and her mother for a time. She was South African by origin, and her own father and mother were respectively a writer and newspaper editor, and a theatrical designer. Though she did not go to university, she studied Latin and Greek with her father and was the most intellectual of the new recruits to Burra's coterie. A sophisticated writer and scholar, when she and Burra became friends in 1925, she had just sent to press a translation of the ancient Greek love-poet Anacreon; later, in 1928 – more in tune with the concerns of the clique – she wrote an elegant, tongue-in-cheek advice manual, *The Technique of the Love Affair*, which was a considerable hit. It is written as a dialogue between 'Cypria' (a girl who knows what she wants and knows how to get it) and naïve and sentimental 'Saccharissa', in which Cypria dispenses advice on the conduct of an affair. Dorothy Parker commented in the *New Yorker*, '[it] makes, I am bitterly afraid, considerable sense. If only it had been placed in my hands years ago, maybe I could have been successful instead of just successive'.

It is worth observing that Burra's circle seems to have been absolutely free of that endemic vice of English culture in the Twenties, anti-Semitism. While Burra wrote fantastically of the villainous inhabitants of his semi-imaginary underworld from time to time, never at any time did he add the words 'Jew' 'or yid' to these pen-portraits – as so many contemporary writers, from John Buchan to T.S. Eliot, did without scruple, indeed without thought. In the Thirties, Burra in Harlem ends a letter enthusing about America, 'Ime thinking of becoming a naturalised Jewish citizen (Hitler is mud in New York).' In strong contrast to their public-school intellectual contemporaries, the group did not, apparently, find Jewishness a focus of anxiety in any way.

A third new recruit to this eclectic group was a startling beauty, Irene Rose Hodgkins (usually known as Hodgkins, though intermittently referred to as Georgiana, probably from a perceived resemblance to the eighteenth-century beauty, Georgiana Duchess of Devonshire). She came from Eastbourne, where she went to the Art College and won a scholarship to the Royal College. She was the daughter of an off-course bookmaker. She was potentially very talented as a painter, but distracted by the number of men who fell at her feet. She, Lucy Norton and a boyfriend, a charming, melancholic bisexual called Basil Taylor, took a studio in Peel Street together in 1926. Taylor turns up in a good few letters of 1926–7, mostly getting up to no good at parties, but he did not really establish himself as a member of the clique in his own right. He faded out of the picture after the flat-share fell apart, and committed suicide in 1935.

Hodgkins painted a little, modelled a little, and in 1926 tried her luck as a chorine, to Burra's delight.

What is this you say about Hodgekins going into the Hotel Metropole caberet when I read your letter dear you could have knocked me down with a feather as they say what does she do if you please step dancing clog or double shuffle tango paso doble or simple ballroom? does she sing or does she simply appear as Nadia Hodgekins the uncrowned empress of Eastbourne in dimond soup plates and tinted ostrich feathers more news I beg dear . . .

She then managed a step up – via, Bar guessed unkindly, her friend-ship with Lucy, Lucy's work as a scene-painter and Nigel Playfair's casting couch.

Do you mean to say you hadnt heard of Miss Hodgkins affaire with Nigel Playfair, well, well, you are behind the times. Lucy I suppose is so busy painting scenes for the 'Bourgeous Gentleman' that she has no time to post her little friends with the latest choice tit-bits.

Nigel Playfair was manager of the Lyric, Hammersmith, and also a devisor, director and playwright. Hodgkins duly appeared in Playfair's *Midnight Follies* the following month, by which time she and Bar were not on speaking terms (quarrelling and making up was a great feature of the group's interactions). Burra was equally snide: 'I am so glad that Irene is in something just a bit highbrow for I don't think it nice for any refined girl to go into a thing like Palladium Pleasures or Rack and Ruin or any of those sorts of things.'

He affected to be shocked, and perhaps was, to discover that by the end of the year she had embarked on an active sex-life. One of the friends she made at the College was a girl called Susan (Susie) Salaman,

the daughter of a wealthy, aesthetic and hospitable Jewish family which
had been involved with the arts in England since the mid-nineteenth
century. She and Lucy (and Billy) were quite often invited to stay with
Susie's parents in their house near Horsham. There she met a Salaman
cousin, Denis Cohen, who ran the Cresset Press, and who fell in love
with her. 'My <u>dear</u>,' wrote Burra, 'havent you <u>heard</u> that dreadful
Hodgekins nothing but a monster goes to bed twice nightly with a
hippopotamus no wonder she looks tired out!' Lucy was certainly
shocked, indeed prurient: 'allways so interested in Georgiana like a ~~boa
constrictor~~ a rabbit being fascinated by a boa constrictor' – as in their
different ways, were they all – and Hodgkins became increasingly
annoyed by the lot of them.[1] But they all got over it: Bar and Hodgkins
kissed and made up in January. 'By the way,' Bar wrote, 'Ive had such
a reunion with Miss Hodgkins, theres no holding us we're almost bosoms
again.'[2]

The enlarged circle gave enhanced gossip opportunities: whenever
one of the friends called on another, they cruised about the room looking
for letters, read any they could find, then rushed off to tax the writer
with his or her crimes. 'Barbara spends her time going round picking
me over with people, the viper,' Chappell complained, but so did he,
and so did they all. Many letters beg the recipient to keep them under
lock and key: 'do not let this fall in wrong hands . . .', and there could
be awkward moments; Bar on one occasion was reduced to whisking a
particularly scandalous communication from Burra up into the leg of
her knickers on the sudden arrival of Basil Taylor, whence, unfortunately, it descended at a critical moment.[3] 'Well dear, what have you done
now?!!!' wrote Burra from Paris.

Your directoires should never have disgorged their dread secret I suppose the
Taylor is about to start a libel action and will never speak to me again . . . when
I read your letter my dear walking down the R Vaugirard and saw its <u>contents</u> I
walked under 1 bus fell into the metropolitain walked through a plate glass window

---

[1] His slip of the pen suggests that on the whole he thought Lucy, who had a strong personality
and a weakness for food, more like a boa constrictor than a rabbit.

[2] Shorthand for 'bosom friends'.

[3] Directoire knickers had elasticated legs reaching to mid-thigh; Bar was not the first or the last
girl of her time to use a knicker-leg as a temporary cache.

and got off with a sister of mercy I will never recover from the shock why didn't you swallow it in the purée during dinner <u>and</u> my dear as for B being a B[ugger] for years we have been wondering why he had that <u>worn</u> look we charitably put it down to whiskey I dont believe its true for why hasnt he ruined Billy, a nice healthy strong lad allways to hand and short of money into the bargain. Well dear dont send me any more letters like that for the flesh is frail and brandy is such a price.

In mid-1927, Hodgkins was set up in a little house, 31 Godfrey Street, Chelsea, by Denis Cohen. Since he was much older and richer than they were, he was not exactly one of the gang, but they all liked him; Chappell remembered him as a kind and sensitive man. Hodgkins was thus the first of the group officially to become a Fallen Woman, and probably, in actual fact, the first to lose her virginity. Burra, half admiring, half mocking, affected to believe she had gone into business as a prostitute: 'Have you heard anything of Tearsheet Hodgekins lately I want to know her address so as to send her a congratulatory card on getting into new premises just to hope trade will be good you know . . . I hope Queen H will ask us to tea I'me dieing to see the inside of the <u>cocotterie</u> I'll have to give her a gilt Buddha to put in the all.' Why a gilt Buddha in the hall should be a mark of the kept woman remains a mystery.

Hodgkin's connection with Denis Cohen had some repercussions for Burra himself: Bar tipped him off in 1928, 'Dennis is in search of <u>new</u> artists to illustrate his books.' Burra subsequently drew a book of cartoons, his *ABC of the Theatre*, for the Cresset Press, which was published in 1932 and earned him £50.

Once Burra's formal education in art was over, he went back to Springfield, where he was to live for the next three decades. Once a fortnight or so, he would descend on London to catch up with what he called 'our world'. Hence the vast collection of Burra letters. Since the friends were no longer meeting every day, they took care to keep each other up to date with the news, and Burra, marooned in Rye, acted to a great extent as Gossip Grand Central, with Billy, Bar and Clover as his most regular correspondents. He must have spent part of every day of his adult life writing letters. When in London, he sometimes stayed at Elvaston Place, sometimes with the Ker-Seymers at Gledstanes Road, or in Balham with the Chappell ménage, once in a while with Lucy

Norton. Occasional vague thoughts about renting some kind of pied-
à-terre, perhaps with Chappell or Hodgkins, came to nothing.

He came to realise that it actually suited him best to spend two or
three concentrated days with his friends, then retreat to Rye and recu-
perate. 'He didn't like to see people *too much*. It exhausted him,' said
Chappell later. 'He liked to spend a *bit* of time with his friends, on his
own terms, and run away.' He was happiest of all in the bohemian and
welcoming household at Balham, and he and Mrs Chappell became very
fond of each other. In June 1927, when he hadn't seen her for a while,
he sent down a hamper of produce (roses, new peas and gooseberries)
from the Springfield garden, an act of thoughtfulness which touched
her deeply.

Bar continued at the Royal College for a year after Burra left. Her
earliest surviving letter to him, written just after the first day of term,
suggests the intolerance of these youthful style queens. 'Dearest Ed,
your timely document has saved my life. I arrived at the college this
morning, in company with all the worlds drabbest drabbies I've never
seen such a display of spectacles and rabbit teeth and a few pimply
chaps . . .'

The following year she moved on to the Slade, which was not quite
such a howling wilderness. She made an interesting new friend quite
quickly, Beatrice Dawson, whom she introduced to the coterie in 1927.
Chappell recollected, 'She was a plump, attractive and amiable character, very short sighted and given to falling over a good deal. Bumble
– as she was known to her intimates – had a strong personality, much
more positive than her nickname implies.' The tendency to fall over
things was presumably to do with the short sight: women in the Twenties
and Thirties were often reluctant to wear glasses (then desperately
unflattering) for reasons of vanity; and contact lenses had not yet been
invented.

Bar and Bumble rapidly became 'bosoms'. In 1927, when Billy
brought Bar a copy of *Ulysses*, which the heroic Sylvia Beach had just
produced in Paris, they read it together: '. . . oh my dear never have I
read such a cess pool as "Ulysses" ho! reely words fail me, I adored it,
though I do think the last chapter was a bit unnecessary, in parts. Billy
brought it to the slade wrapped up in miles of their brown paper and
Bumble and I smuggled it into Little Antique still in its miles of wrapping and there we sat absorbed the whole of one morning we kept letting

out shrieks of laughter.[4] They were twenty-two, and not quite as sophisticated as they thought.

Apart from the routine of work, gossip and writing, Burra weath-
ered two major personal tragedies in his twenties. The first was the
death of his grandmother, of whom he was fond. This occurred in 1927,
when he was twenty-two, and was not unheralded. She went into a
nursing-home in October for an operation on her liver, which was
evidently not a success, since she died at the end of November. His
letter to Bar Ker-Seymer is one of the few in which uncensored emotion
breaks the surface. It opens with an uncharacteristic admission. 'Dear
Ba Ba. How are you getting on dear old thing? I am not getting on so
well.' He found the funeral a deeply disturbing experience.

My dear never do I go to another funeral I thought I should collapse at any moment
I never thought they dug graves so deep they let the coffin in with ropes and realy
I thought when is it going to arrive? all I can say is dearie you may be afraid of
lifts but youl be much more afraid of graves when your time comes going down
such a long way.

Burra was supposed 'not to make old bones'; his parents had resigned
themselves to the possibility of losing him at an early age, and he had
nearly died of rheumatic fever a couple of years previous to this letter.
But his grandmother's funeral seems to have brought him up against
the reality of death in a stark enough way for him to apply the notion
to himself, and he was clearly horrified. Burra is for once letting down
his defences, and asking obliquely for comfort. Paul Nash, when he first
collapsed with asthma and realised that his life was likely to be short,
became overwhelmingly terrified by death and spoke of his anxieties to
a variety of people, including the American writer and cartoonist James
Thurber, and Burra. Burra did not, but this letter implicitly suggests
that he endured periods of private anguish and fear. He was notably
kind and supportive to Nash, while never admitting that he shared any
of his feelings.

The second tragedy, a couple of years later, was infinitely less to be
expected. As we know, Burra's youngest sister Betsy, the last of the

[4] Drawing from casts of antique sculpture was a central point of the Slade curriculum: Little
Antique was the smaller of the two rooms full of plaster casts.

Burra children, was born while he was at his prep school – she was ten years his junior. She seems to have been very like Burra himself, though without the health problems, a small, thin, odd and charming child, of considerable intelligence, with a sharp sense of humour and a gift for drawing. He kept a handful of her letters to him; one, written from school when she was eleven, shows her developing gift for fantasy.

Dear Ed I got the note book and the films you sent me have you got your fond mother yet she has gone to America or where ever you get diamonds to smugle she hollosw out a hole in her wooden leg to put them in this is Miss Haines in a temper [drawing of her headmistress] I cant right much more Best love Betsy

The letter ends with four drawings, three ghoulish schoolmarms and 'Mother', vigorous caricatures. Most of her letters have drawings: another letter (in which, again, Trudy Burra is afflicted with a wooden leg) is decorated with six different hats, captioned 'Fashionable hats belonging to mother'; a third, with a well-observed group of ladies performing 'Thining Exerxcies'.

Burra loved Betsy dearly. His own letters from school show that even when she was a baby, he was devoted to her, and as she got older the attachment strengthened because their sense of humour was so similar, and also because she liked to draw people more than anything (as Burra did himself, at that time). He used to work over her drawings, which amused them both. They read *Chips* and *Comic Cuts* together, and he took her to the cinema – he also drew her several times. He genuinely enjoyed spending time with her. When she was at school in Eastbourne, he visited her two or three times every term to take her out for a picnic or to a film, which is a great deal more than most elder brothers would have done.

But Betsy died in August 1929, when she was only twelve, of meningitis. Apart from her intrinsic lovableness – like many late-born children, she was the adored pet of the whole family – she was the second child that Ma and Dah had lost, which must have made the whole appalling situation even worse. Meningitis was more cruel even than an accident, or a prolonged affliction such as cancer. In the first case, the grief and shock would have hit the family all at once; in the second, there would have been time gradually to absorb the tragedy. As it was, the family was forced to watch their darling die over two agonising weeks, as she rambled in delirium, knowing that absolutely nothing could be done for her.

Burra wrote to Chappell – who was in Glasgow at the time – with the news. It is worth quoting the letter from the beginning, for what it says and does not say.

Well dear

So nice to hear from ye as we say in Glesgie if Marsuple [Burra's Scots nanny] knew you were in Glesgie Im sure she would introduce you to some really nice friends. We are having <u>an awful time</u> as Betsy developed a headache last Sunday and on last Sunday week a specialist was sent for & it appears she has meningitis & apparently can only live a fortnight I can hardly write it mother is in a dreadful state and has fits of sobbing Such merry times have been going on at Thornsdale what with dashing nude into the river and Brenda Dean Paul walking about in Lido trowsers the whole village is in an uproar (if you can believe the Nashs) . . .

Burra's prose style and general mode of speech, camp irony, was designed to deflect emotion; to set up a context in which the expression of strong feeling would inevitably seem un-cool, essentially a defensive strategy. The letter to which this is a reply was a lengthy and headlong scrawl of vacuous theatre gossip: 'I did get a letter from you either in Blackpool or just before we went but I don't think I answered it. Well dearie this Tour seems to go on for ever and I don't like it much . . . have you heard the latest dirt about Headley Briggs my dear . . .'

Burra is left with the problem of bridging the gap. He does little more than allude to his sister, and veers immediately off into a Tillingesque story about the Nash household, and their friend Lady Brenda Dean Paul (actress, pianist, junkie and, a few years later, England's first celebrity addict, even then a somewhat exhibitionist figure), who went for a nude dip in the River Rother and created a predictable imbroglio. There is then a bit of ballet chat about the death of Diaghilev, before he touches momentarily upon his inexpressible grief: 'Just got back from a jolly day in town where I bought Artistes materials anything anything to get away from the atmosphere of this house everywhere I look I see a reminder some little book or something and its too awful I got a record at Foyles Victor (9d) of Downhearted Blues . . . I darent play the phono for fear of making a noise . . .' What this suggests, among other things, is that he does not altogether trust Chappell; since their relationship is shallow, silly and fun, he is not sure that it can accommodate genuine tragedy.

Bar, on the other hand, happened to be passing through Rye with a friend en route for the Isle of Wight when Betsy was taken ill, and was rather hoping to be invited to stay at Springfield. She sent a telegram to Springfield hinting as much, but when they got to Rye, they dropped in on Nash first of all, who warned them that Betsy was ill. So she wrote a sensible, unaffected letter full of concern, dropping the 'well, dearie' act completely and apologising for having proposed herself at an unsuitable time. 'I'm so sorry to hear about your little sister, I do hope she is better now write at once to me here and tell me how she is getting on . . . [Nash] told us about your sister so that's why we didn't call, though we passed your house three times. I wanted to ring up, but thought perhaps I'd better not.'

In response, Burra is far more candid than he felt he could be to Chappell; in fact, painfully honest. He cannot entirely discard his habitual facetiousness, but it is a thin veneer over obvious distress.

Well dearie

& did you find a cottie anywhere about Rye? I hear you visited the Nashs & did you find Twit ruling the roost We are in red in dutch and what you will as Betsy died last Monday afternoon at 5.15 I did hope to the very last she would recover but on Monday morning when I went to see her she was babbling as usual about everything from My Ohio home to killing the neighbours but her colour!! greenish with a mauve flush I thought to myself she must die tonight poor little thing it was so pathetic one day in the midst of her rambling she said to mother 'oh Ime beyond repair.' Lifes but a tear and a joke and I had just been plotting to go to Toulon with Sophie as she wrote and said she was going down to make sketches & would I come too so I wrote back and said yes but of course poor B began to get so bad I couldn't have gone and now shes croaked.

Mother wants to go away for a fortnight so I felt I had to go with her so we're going to Scotland if you please so expect a daintie post card of Robert Burns sitting on Annies lorrie bound in tartan . . . the funeral is tomorrow I dread it what Ime supposed to wear I cant think the nearest mourning Ive got is a pair of shoes Tan with orange flavour a greyish suit with stripe and a nice sky blue shirt or perhaps mauve stripes or chocolate brown I realy think its too awful mother has refused flatly to go at all it would only upset her again and shes been in a state enough as it is. my dear you've no idea how lovely B looked layed out holding a bouquet of nasturtiums quite lovely with a subtle smile such a lovely colour & her eyes looked heavily made up & immense long eyelashes realy she looked beautiful.

Well dear I hope you enjoy this merry letter but I daresay after weve had a go at the scotch we'll feel more hearty au revore Tot
believe me
I feel
her death
very much

The last sentence is written in the margin, an afterthought, offsetting the flat brutality of 'now shes croaked'. He sat by her bed all that night, keeping watch over her body. And, probably, memorising her small, wax-white face, since one of his lifelong gifts was a photographic memory.

Chappell replied to the letter quoted earlier, aghast, in infinitely more conventional terms. For all his ditsy manner, he was loyal, affectionate and deeply fond of Betsy, whom he knew well. Burra then wrote more seriously, an episode which deepened their friendship. But he refused, then or ever again, to share his sorrow. He never mentioned Betsy again, and so it is difficult to know what her death meant to him, since the subject was thereupon closed. But it would be an enormous mistake to assume that silence implies it meant nothing. One reasonable guess is that this tragic and appalling death may have strengthened his aversion to emotional dependence of any kind.

Other things were happening as well at this time. The reason why Billy Chappell was in Glasgow in 1929 is that 'Fate, the ringmaster, had cracked his whip' (a catchphrase they both liked, lifted from a silent-film subtitle). His life had taken an unexpected turn, which was to bring Burra a significant breakthrough into a completely different world, of great importance to his life and oeuvre. Burra and his friends had always been mad about ballet, which was in any case practically a defining taste for the Twenties' avant-garde. Lucy Norton, whose brother was a friend of Maynard Keynes (married to the dancer Lydia Lopokova), was instrumental in getting her friends out of the upper circle and giving them the entrée backstage. In 1924, Chappell found himself more or less literally shanghaied by Marie Rambert, to whom Lucy had introduced him. As Chappell explains in an autobiographical fragment printed in *Fifty*

Years of the Ballet Rambert, having looked him up and down over the tea-table, Rambert began talking him into becoming a dancer.

Though he could do a very respectable Charleston and Black Bottom (the flappers' signature dances), and he had always loved to dance, Chappell was totally untrained in classical ballet. But he was athletic, long-legged, broad-shouldered and gracefully proportioned; and at that point, male classical dancers in England were as rare as hens' teeth. He was also still only seventeen, since he had gone to college so early, thus young enough to start from zero. Rambert persuaded him to take early-morning barres with her at the studio before her first pupils arrived. He did so (Chappell seems always to have had elements of the boy who couldn't say no), though he became increasingly sulky and reluctant. Ballet at close quarters was, to say the least of it, disheartening.

I approached the inevitable church hall . . . there were always puddles on the paths leading to those grim Gothic doors opening onto windowless caverns, lit by glowing white electric bulbs; and giving out a wave of overpowering C of E perfume; a scent of dust and damp: mildew and mice . . . I decided almost immediately it was not my idea of what the ballet was about.

What won him over was Frederick Ashton: Chappell and his chorus-girl sister had gone to a matinée performance given by Rambert students, in which Ashton somehow twisted his ankle. Chappell, though he had stopped going to classes, still felt sufficiently part of the family to nip backstage and commiserate. There he found Ashton, his bad leg propped up on a chair, in his Harlequin costume and full make-up, a spectacle glamorous enough to give Chappell second thoughts. 'Perhaps I would, after all, go back . . .'

He and Ashton, the only two boys in a studio full of girls, both gay (though Chappell was, at this time, still unaware of his own sexuality, or his attractiveness), naturally gravitated towards one another. In the mid-Twenties their respective coteries therefore amalgamated to some extent, which produced two important new relationships for Burra (as well as for Ashton, who became very close to Bar for some years, and to Doris Langley Moore for a lifetime). Ashton's particular women friends were the Polish painter Sophie Fedorovitch and the socialite Olivia Wyndham. Sophie had escaped from Russia at the time of the revolution and had, for a time, supported herself by driving a taxi in

Paris. As a follower of the influential guru Georges Ivanovitch Gurdjieff, she was drawn towards Quakerlike frugality, but she was also as poor as she was proud. When she first came to London, she lived in a single room on the Embankment where, for some time, she slept in a reclining chair since she could not afford to buy a bed.

Post-Gurdjieff, she returned to London in the mid-Twenties and shared a flat (13a Market Street) in Shepherd Market with Bumble Dawson, who became, for a time, Olivia Wyndham's secretary, a role subsequently taken over by Bar Ker-Seymer. Shepherd Market (W1) is between Mayfair and Piccadilly, but in the Twenties it was a run-down district of little shops, pubs and patrolling ladies of the night. The novelist Anthony Powell also lived there at this time (at 9 Shepherd Market), and he and Bumble became good friends, while Sophie also became close to Lucy Norton.

Sophie was gifted as a painter, but was not first-rate, and Bumble, though she was a painter of real talent, had given up the idea of making a career as a fine-artist, and had started working as a designer/costumer/props maker. Sophie began to see that her own gift lay in that direction. In 1926 Ashton asked her to design the décor for his first venture into choreography, *A Tragedy of Fashion*, which launched her on her career as one of the most distinguished designers in the history of English ballet. The flavour of the Sophie–Bumble ménage is suggested by an undated letter Burra wrote to Bar:

I also visited the 2 cinderellas of Shepherds Market no sooner had little prince Bartholin & myself got in the house when in came Sophia Bunny Roger[5] and boy and we all started to talk of the cinema Sophie curled up & went off to sleep nestling in a packing case covered by 3 sheets of talc & ½ made celophane hats a few sheets of the NY evening graphic and 2 or 3 licquorice all sorts & gramo-phone records as a pillow.[6]

Sophie's arrangement with Bumble was fairly short-lived due in part to the latter woman's devotion to cats – Sophie's standards of personal

[5] Birger Bartholin, was a Danish dancer of good family (often called 'the Baron'), of whom Burra was particularly fond, and Neil 'Bunny' Roger was a noted gay beauty and dandy who was also very much part of the friends' social circle.

[6] These sound like the accessories for Ashton's ballet *Les Masques* (1933), designed by Sophie, which included transparent hats and muffs made by Bumble.

comfort were not high, but she drew the line at having a mother cat give birth in her bed. It didn't help that the flat was over a butcher's shop; Burra reported to Bar: 'Sophie says what with the hot weather the cat & the butcher underneath the air in the Shepherd Market love nest is very thick indeed.' Subsequently she moved to Redcliffe Gardens in Earls Court.

Sophie was small, shy, gruff and dignified, with cropped hair and a somewhat masculine personal style; she associated a good deal with lesbians, though the only lover she owned up to was male, Captain Mordaunt Goodliffe. Chappell describes her as 'quiet, calm and deliberate, with a low murmuring voice, and an eye just as observant and critical, only a little more mocking than Mim's [Marie Rambert's]'. Burra and Sophie became very close friends. They appreciated one another's sense of humour: 'my dear I adore her she used to enrage Lucy by saying oh you know Ime not a woman at all HA HA HA I said we dont like that remark Sophie in a voice of hauteur.' Though their personal styles were very different, her almost minimalist, very fastidious work as a designer, and her concentration on expressiveness through colour, perhaps had some influence on Burra's own design work later on.

Olivia Wyndham, on the other hand, was Sophie's polar opposite in many ways, though not all: both women were generous to a fault and incapable of a mean action. But Olivia, rather than being a penurious nun of the arts, was the product of a wealthy family which had long been a nexus of society, art and politics, of conspicuously higher social status than the Burras. Her grandparents' house, Clouds, designed by Philip Webb and decorated by William Morris, Frederick Leighton and Edward Burne-Jones, was one of the civilised and leisured venues where the great house-parties so central to late-Victorian political and social life took place. It was the meeting-place of the Souls, a group of aesthetically minded aristocrats who represented much of what was forward-looking in late-nineteenth-century England.

Olivia was partly brought up at Clouds: her father, a younger son and career soldier, did not have a home of his own in England. Her grandfather died in 1911; Olivia's uncle, the heir, died in 1913; and his only son, 'Perf', was killed at the battle of the Aisne in 1914. It was then discovered that Perf had made a will which passed over his uncle

Guy, Olivia's father, in favour of the latter's son, Dick (as he was known), hoping to avoid death duties. A fire damaged the house that Guy was renting in 1915, so he and his wife and daughter moved to Clouds (Olivia was then eighteen) and stayed there for five years. Olivia was not offered training for any sort of career because she was a girl, but during the First World War she joined the Voluntary Aid Detachment and served in France as a nurse, while the house itself became a convalescent home.

When he became owner of Clouds, Dick was still on active service, but in 1918, once he was in a position to take up his inheritance, he found himself faced with the ownership and upkeep of a vast mansion, annuities to three separate widows and innumerable other fixed outlays, at a time of increased taxation and collapsing agricultural prices. In 1924, he let the house, and subsequently sold it.

Though after the war Olivia was living on an allowance from her father, who was not himself particularly wealthy, she had been brought up to spend money. She became one of the queens of lesbian London, among the most notorious party-girls of a party-giving decade, a hostess who offered cocaine as well as alcohol[7] and who turned up at Norman Hartnell's notorious Circus Party in 1928 as a snake-charmer, with real snakes twined round her arms and neck. (It is hard to think of the Queen's couturier, creator of a thousand inoffensive coat-and-dress ensembles, giving that sort of party in his wild youth.)

Olivia's family had long been patrons of modern art and, to some extent, creative people themselves. Her brother Dick was a painter, and Olivia herself became a photographer. She worked for a time with the avant-garde American photographer Curtis Moffat, himself influenced by Man Ray, who was married to the 'poet-actress-adventuress' Iris Tree. Like Moffat, Olivia was very well connected, and used her connections ruthlessly. Bar commented, 'She was invited to a lot of parties where the press were barred but she was allowed to take photographs as she was a friend of the various hosts.' Among her subjects was the beloved mascot and alter ego of the extraordinary Marion ('Joe') Carstairs (a cross-dressing lesbian oil millionairess who drove fast cars and raced speedboats), an eleven-inch-high

---

[7] Then illegal: possession of cocaine was criminalised in 1916 under an addition to the Defence of the Realm Act (Regulation 40b). This legislation did not cover heroin, morphine or cannabis.

boy doll called Lord Tod Wadley. She created a dummy magazine spread of Wadley in his various costumes, which Carstairs cherished; and she also photographed the Queen of Spain (to whom she was connected by marriage), Cecil Beaton and Brenda Dean Paul, among many others.

Olivia also solved Bar's difficulty over the impossibility of tolerating a 'He-man' in her life by the simple expedient of seducing her. And Ashton and Bar also became very close, and remained intimate friends through the rest of the Twenties and Thirties.

Burra and his friends thus became part of the world Evelyn Waugh represents in *Vile Bodies*. Few of them had any money, but on the other hand, they were young, amusing and good-looking; so they were welcome guests at many a party, and once in a while someone else would pay for them to eat in Rudolf Stulik's Restaurant de la Tour Eiffel, a great meeting-place for the avant-garde, which had been a haunt of painters for a decade, along with celebrities of the time such as Tom Driberg, Evelyn Waugh, Brian Howard and Brenda Dean Paul. Well-heeled and sympathetic grown-ups such as Susie Salaman's father or Denis Cohen would take the whole lot of them out on occasion. Olivia often took Bar to the Tour Eiffel, and Chappell and Bar became – and remained – very friendly with Bunny Roger.

But though the Tour Eiffel has been described as 'part of the cultural archaeology of the twentieth century', it was not so much the restaurants as the parties of the Twenties that became legendary. 'Masked parties, Savage parties, Victorian parties, Greek parties, Wild West parties, Russian parties, Circus parties, parties where one had to dress as somebody else, almost naked parties in St John's Wood . . .' Bar's and Chappell's letters chronicle parties where the men necked with one another on the sofa, or took off all their clothes and danced; one where Bumble, tottering into the garden to be sick, fell over Cedric Morris writhing on the gravel of the carriage-sweep with, to her astonishment, a woman.

Homosexuality was a dominant idiom in London smart circles in the Twenties, despite, or perhaps to some extent because of, male homosexuality being illegal. The public school–Oxbridge nexus naturally produced a good few men who were aware of a homosexual orientation from an early age, and since some of them were strong personalities and leaders of fashion, they set a tone – Bunny Roger, Brian Howard,

Harold Acton and Stephen Tennant were among the more conspicuous male beauties, dandies and celebrities of that generation.

As far as women were concerned, society in the wider sense was so concerned to prevent 'respectable' women from spending time alone with men (thus, for example, Lucy Norton, who unlike Burra's other women friends, was concerned about her reputation, went to complex lengths never to be alone with her friend Gerald Reitlinger in his house, even calling upon Burra himself as a chaperon: 'As no one was at Thornsdale but J [i.e. Jerry/Gerald] & "Daintie" the last resort was had in,' he wrote on one occasion). By contrast, nothing whatsoever prevented young women from spending time, and sharing beds, with their female friends. In 1921, a Tory MP proposed that a clause covering 'Acts of Gross Indecency by Females', be added to the existing law proscribing male homosexuality. The House of Lords, however, decided that the minor gain of controlling existing lesbianism had to be offset against the dire possibilities raised by informing women in general that such a thing was possible. The Lord Chancellor was of the opinion that 999 out of a thousand women 'have never even heard a whisper of these practices', in which he was probably correct.

Burra and his friends were far from unusual in arriving at art college having barely heard that there was such a thing as homosexuality, male or female, but they rapidly became better informed. At a party that Lucy and Chappell went to together in 1926, 'one of the young men at the party came up to L and said tell me is that youth all that he looks? Realy sir what can you mean his teeth are his own and his legs are no sham ones I can vouch for that ha ha says Lucy so the creature said ho reely if you don't understand I cant tell you!' Similarly, Burra was chastely obtuse to veiled hints for a surprisingly long time: 'Of course says Birdie in Lesbia a friendship between women is not complete without things we wot not of, I dont suppose I wotted either,' wrote Burra in 1927. But by 1929, he wotted all right. Most of his friends, of either gender, were queer. He wrote to Bar in that year (using the convention that gay boys are referred to as women, and, which is now uncommon, lesbians as men):

Are you going to be the only gentleman at the widow Lloyds party which our old tart of a Chappell is going to? I am longing to hear about it as Ive no doubt we shall in the News of the World the police having raided it just as our Freddie

[Ashton] trips out of a giant champagne glass (dressed only in a black sequin widows veil gloves & shoes) on the dining room table.

Burra himself seldom went to the parties, he tended just to hear all about them. Party-going requires a fair amount of physical stamina. A term of the time for a cocktail party was 'a stand up and shout'. No fun for someone who found standing difficult, and disliked being in a crowd. His friend John Banting recalled much later, 'Ed was rather quiet at the parties.' As he got a little older and his personality matured, he began to avoid any kind of social event that called for making random conversation at high volume with semi-strangers. His own social life preferentially took place seated, and in bars and clubs, though he was avid for gossip and delighted in passing it on. 'Did B tell you of the matelot party empress N [Lucy Norton] took him to? Did I say matelot party, matelots is not what I've heard it called. oh dear no. my dear I read all about it in the Weekly dispatch everyone attacked everyone else and mounds of young men writhed in heaps in every corner. However our B was not naughty with another fellow however gorgeous it may be, tho' he did dance with a lovely ammerican.' This was the much-chronicled 'Sailor Party', which the guests were supposed to attend dressed as matelots, which was held in Gerald Reitlinger's London house and described by Chappell himself as 'Bugger Heaven and no mistake.'[8]

Chappell and Bar also both ended up at one of the era's more notorious fiascos, Brian Howard's Great Urban Dionysia, which demanded authentic ancient Greek dress. The doubtless much-sought-after role of Sappho went to Viva King, one of the first society ladies to parade a black boyfriend. Olivia Wyndham had a starring role as Athena, or would have done, had the party not fallen flat. Unfortunately, it had needed so much preparation that it couldn't possibly live up to its own expectations. Chappell was there as a gatecrasher:

I had been at Olivias and dressed them both I stitched Olivia into her clothes and she looked ever so dignified by the time we had finished and then Barbara said why not take Billy as your electrician & Olivia said that's a lovely idea – so I went

[8] A phrase of Bar's: 'She says as men look much nicer semi nude than women she is going to have a male cabaret with a chorus of gladiators in gold sequin tunics . . . and call the show Bugger Heaven.'

you would have died we were ever so professional Olivia called me Chappell and I said Miss Wyndham very respectfully and held all the lights and told Tilly Losch and David Tennant what to do with their hands . . . people seemed to think it was rather twee to talk to the electrician who wouldn't have looked at me twice if I had been in a dainty Greek costume as a guest.

Chappell, because of his curious background, was rather happier to be patronised by celebs than his friends thought reasonable. His abject response to condescending attention from the 'A' list annoyed Burra and Bar immensely ('desgusting I call it silly nancy boy,' said Burra). They had the last word when they issued an invitation of their own, for his twentieth birthday, in the mouth of one of Burra's personas of the time, a frightful society hag called 'Lady Bureaux'.

Lady Aimée Bureaux & the Lady Maclaren

Request the Presence of Mr Chappell at their 'Less than 20' party
<u>Don't</u> bring less than 20 (bottles)
<u>Don't</u> stay less than 20 (minutes)
<u>Don't come</u> more than 20 (times)
& don't be more than 20 (years)
c'est la jeunesse qui coûte[9] dear guest of honour

By the end of the Twenties, Burra's personal circle of friends had come together – surprisingly few were added after that, though some dropped out. What is truly remarkable is that the core members of this group, none of whom seem ever to have been lovers in any permutation, were mutually involved for more than fifty years. They quarrelled, sometimes fiercely, fell out and made up; Bar and Clover so fundamentally at one point that they did not speak for a decade. But they were part of one another's lives, alongside their various marriages, relationships and children, from adolescence to old age. It was partly Burra himself who brought that about. He could not be entirely independent. He needed help to live the life he wanted; people to stay with, or go on holiday with, and all who took a share in caring for him also kept in touch with one another.

---

[9] It's youth that counts.

Bar's induction into the world of Twenties' lesbianism was not without incident. Her mother began to smell a rat in September 1928, and, despite her own sapphic tendencies, she was less than sympathetic. Bar commented philosophically, 'My dear I have been ordered out of the house since "The Well of Loneliness" was found accidentally left lying on the piano, I'm in coventry now & my bed sitting room has been confiscated so that I have to sleep in the box room . . .' Late 1928 was not a good moment for coming out. *The Well of Loneliness*, just then published, had made it explicitly clear that at least some 'boyish' girls were sexually attracted to each other, something which society at large had contrived, up to that point, to overlook. In April 1929, 'Colonel Barker' (born Lilias Arkell–Smith) added fuel to the general panic over the masculinisation of English maidenhood when she was tried for the somewhat esoteric crime of causing a false entry to be made in the marriage register (as 'bachelor' rather than 'spinster'), and was described by the judge as 'an unprincipled, mendacious, and unscrupulous adventuress'. Birdie Rushbury wrote to Billy, who was dancing in Milan, 'and to think you are missing the Captain Barker case . . . !' They must all have been fascinated.

Bar was still living with her mother for most of 1929, but her pocket diary for that year has Olivia's name on almost every page. In February, she wrote to Burra, 'I'm having three jolly days in the country at Capt Dick Wyndham's cottage with Olivia (hes in Vienna) & by the way I'm supposed to be staying with the Nash's I don't know what he'll say when he hears I've used his name but I knew I shouldn't be allowed to stay away with Olivia.' Burra, delighted, wrote back: 'yes dear I shant forget to tell Paul who he has been having to stay with him last week "oh what a tangled web we weave when we first practice to decieve"'. By August, writing to Burra from Olivia's maisonette, 19 King's Road, Sloane Square, Bar had moved on to saying vaguely, 'I must go home, I seem to have quite lost the ability.'

Soon after that she stopped trying, broke with her mother and moved permanently into 19 King's Road, which became Burra's new favourite place to stay in London. Given Olivia's diligent promiscuity, drunkenness and drug-taking, this cannot have been a wholly easy life. 'She had no taste at all,' Bar recalled. 'Sometimes a great butch lady would arrive at the door and Olivia would send me up to cower in the dark while she showed our empty bedroom to the irate visitor.'

Burra, evidently delighted, told Chappell all about it:

I saw dainty Bubbles Ker-Seymer last week her last remaining bonnet is over the mill my dear she's fully launched in the demi-monde . . . Well old sport Miss Wyndham had a cocktail party last Friday . . . from what I hear in my radio grammes they all went down like ninepins (and it was suspected that aphrodisiac had been added to the cocktails) except Lucie Norton . . .

Both Ashton and Burra were welcome guests in lesbian bohemia. Bar and Olivia's circle of friends included Ruth Baldwin, an American woman who made Olivia look like a debutante. 'Ruth took drugs. She drank – she replaced her kitchen with a bar.' She was a big girl, tall as well as hefty, known to some as 'Fatty', and completely out of control. She was the principal lover of Joe Carstairs, with whom she shared a house, 5 Mulberry Walk, off the King's Road, which made them near neighbours of Olivia and Bar. Evelyn Waugh in his diary records a party given by Olivia Wyndham and Ruth Baldwin on a Thames steamer. He didn't enjoy it. 'It was not enough of an orgy. Masses of little lesbian tarts and joyboys. Only one fight . . . poor old Hat [Brian Howard] looking like a tragedy queen . . .' Bar and Chappell were probably among the lesbians and joyboys; Frederick Ashton certainly was.

Burra thought Ruth was a hoot. As he told Chappell after a night spent at 19 King's Road:

Babs went out with the Girlies after supper so I leant out of the window & played the gramophone till about 1.30 when staggered to Bed about ½ an hour afterwards a loud crashing was heard which was Ruth Baldwin and Babs dropping in Ruth was quite drunk & kept rushing at B and biting her however after a bit more crashing & screams they went off I dropped off Ruth Baldwin is my beau ideal I think I like them fat I cant resist anyone that goes about with an airoplane in dimonds where there ought to be a tie.

He also liked Joe Carstairs, unsurprisingly; since she was a dandy, an eccentric, faintly grotesque and completely unselfconscious, a 'monster', in his terms.

Barbara's relationship with Olivia was a significant one in other than sexual terms. Olivia, as Cecil Beaton observed acidly, was completely incompetent as a photographer. She 'was never mistress of her camera, a huge concertina affair . . . the technical aspects were always a bafflement to her: mechanism had a sure way of defying her'. She had an eye for an interesting composition, and even Beaton admitted that 'she produced some beautiful "Mrs Camerons"' (that is, good pictures produced by the method of 'point and hope for the best'), including some of Beaton himself, now in the National Portrait Gallery. But apart from being hopelessly untechnical and accident-prone, she was often too drunk to focus the camera. Barbara succeeded Bumble as her assistant. 'My job was to stay up all night after the parties developing and printing the films in order to take them round to the *Tatler*, *Sketch* and *Bystander*, etc.' She then started covering for Olivia to the extent of taking the actual pictures, and discovered that she had a genuine talent for photography.

Subsequently, Olivia went to America, and Bar opened a studio of her own, a thirty-shillings-a-week room above Asprey's the jewellers on Bond Street. The décor was utterly of its time: it had black walls, a black ceiling, three full-length curtains, one black, one grey, one white; there were paintings by the surrealist John Banting, a good friend of both Burra and Sophie Fedorovitch, and, inevitably, a gramophone. She emerged as one of the foremost women photographers of her generation – 'a sharply radical portraitist of a new English avant-garde'. Her style as a photographer was considerably influenced by German expressionism, and perhaps also by Burra.

But if Burra influenced Bar, it is also true that Bar influenced Burra or, perhaps more accurately, the use of unusual perspectives and foreshortening which she discovered in avant-garde German photography and used herself was directly influential on Burra as a painter. Paul Nash noticed this as early as 1932:

Burra's extraordinary fantasies, perhaps the most original in imagination of any contemporary English artist, owe something to his keen appreciation of the aesthetic of modern photography. In his passion for solid individual shapes rounded and stippled to a high degree of finish with intense concentration on high lights, in a peculiar insistence on isolated objects such as the furniture of cafés, or upon bottles, baskets and napkins . . . or again in his use of foreshortening and other dramas of perspective; in the sum of these characteristics, he seems to have employed, with persuasive intelligence, suggestions which photography may well have supplied.

In *The Café*, for example, Burra's principal focus is on an individual sitting at a table, smiling slyly; but a disproportionate amount of the foreground is taken up by a cloth cap which conceals his interlocutor's head (such caps were the mark of an apache, a Parisian gangster). This is what someone standing immediately behind the nearer sitter's right shoulder would see, what a camera would see. There is just such a photograph, dated 1932, in one of Barbara Ker-Seymer's albums. It is not a way of presenting the couple which would have occurred to a painter in any previous generation.

Nash's article also singles out Bar as one of the most interesting professional photographers in London. That may have been to do with his personal affection for her, but she was certainly successful. The people she met at Olivia's parties were highly image-conscious leaders of fashion; where they went, others followed; and they liked her work. Another friend who was very helpful was Brian Howard, a dedicated partygoer and member of the smart set whom she had known from childhood:

Brian at one time announced that he was going to be my partner, as being a professional photographer was an excellent way of introducing himself to the more 'difficult' people, as failing all else they always succumbed to having themselves photographed . . . it ended up by Brian making a tremendous business of posing, arranging the lighting etc. and his 'assistant' (me) taking the actual photographs! Unfortunately he got fired with the bug, and decided to become very modern, hence the metal tubing, chicken wire and rope etc. he insisted on wrapping all the clients in . . . I was allowed to take my more normal portraits, but Brian invariably turned up for the proof showing, and intimidated the wretched clients into at least taking some of the horrors.

She photographed Nancy Cunard against tiger-skin in one session and corrugated iron in another (the tiger-skin photograph became iconic, and was therefore subsequently attributed to Cecil Beaton, which, characteristically, Bar found funny rather than annoying). She worked on commission for *Harper's Bazaar* from 1931, and experimented with bold shadowing, 'making her subjects appear as creatures from the demi-monde', just as she and Burra habitually represented themselves and their friends as whores and sluts in their correspondence. Another avant-garde photographer whom she became personally close to around this time was Len Lye, later a documentary film-maker, who remained a friend throughout her life and was also a friend of Burra's.

But Bar's casual, socially-oriented introduction to professional photography may perhaps explain why she felt a little fraudulent and tended to be dismissive of the value of her own work, though her work was admired by other photographers, up to and including Man Ray. Val Williams observes, 'Non-serious amateurism, laced with talent, wit and energy, was the true stuff of the twenties.' But detachment, distrust and self-doubt seem to have been significant aspects of Bar's personality, though not the whole of it. Another friend and fellow-photographer, Humphrey Spender, commented, 'It seemed to me that "Bar" always stood outside the events of her life and observed things with marvellous wit and sympathy and perception, and sometimes just a touch of very enjoyable malice.'

In 1930, Bar became involved with an American journalist called Marty Mann, both as business partner and lover (it was she who suggested opening the studio). It is not clear who effected the introduction – Marty was a friend of Joe Carstairs, and probably of Olivia Wyndham – but in any case, the world of upper-class lesbian socialites was a relatively small one. Marty arrived in London in the course of 1930, but by the end of that year she had run out of money and needed a job. In that December, or perhaps January 1931, Bar wrote to Burra, 'How about coming up to London & spending a week with your old pals at no. 19? Sophie [Fedorovitch] is in London, & Marty is the photographer now & takes still lives all day, so I can't go near the camera.' With Marty, she experimented with portrait studies in very bold close-up in the early Thirties, following the example of the German photographer Lerski and the American Curtis Moffat, making massive images, 'at least 5 times life size', according to Ed. Another development which may spring from Marty's connections with Condé Nast (she was writing for one of their magazines, called *Town & Country*), or from Irene Hodgkins's eventual marriage to Alfred Varley, is that Bar started working as a fashion photographer for the Varley Colman Prentice agency in the Thirties. Advertising photography also became an important part of her business over time, as Burra observed in 1938 ('Miss Ker-S seems very busy photographing Miss Modern washing her panties in Trex').

Marty Mann was another wild character; and, like Olivia, an alcoholic.

Her friend Forbes Cheston gave her the sobriquet 'Temeraire' (taken, by association of ideas, from Turner's painting, *The Fighting Temeraire*). She was 'a tough American woman of distinctly Lesbian appearance . . . she was apt, when in her cups, to become belligerent and would have taken on and probably defeated Joe Louis. When sober, she was a sagacious and amusing companion, with a raffish insight into other people's foibles.' She had considerable ability as a journalist, photographer and organiser, despite her problem with alcohol. Burra was fond of her; and she of him. They corresponded throughout the early Thirties, and she did what she could to advance his profile in America: 'have just heard from Dame Marty Mann this morning with letter from Condé I had hoped for a full page rotogravure supplement entirely devoted to me but owing to the present business conditions in Ammerica it couldn't be. so tiresome.' To Marty herself, he wrote lightly, 'Am so sorry about Condé but I somehow felt there wouldn't be quite enough Vanitie about my fayre!' – suggesting that he was genuinely concerned about her feelings.

Unfortunately, Marty was losing her battle with the bottle in the early Thirties. As Cheston implies by his choice of sobriquet for her, she became increasingly obnoxious when drunk, and slid gradually towards being drunk all the time. After two or three years both her relationships with Bar, personal and professional, came to an end. Dolly Wilde, Oscar's sad and gallant lesbian niece, wrote out of deep experience to Bar, 'I feel it best if you do put M out of your mind as her attitude shows so little imagination & kindness that I feel she is no longer the M you know' – a conclusion that many partners of alcoholics have reached.

Marty sold her share of the studio and tried her hand at managing a sixteenth-century inn at Broadway in the Cotswolds, but her life went from bad to worse. By the beginning of 1936 she was spending her days huddled in a deckchair in Hyde Park, drinking herself comatose: Bar would visit her at intervals to check up and plead with her to stop. Later that year she went home, joined Alcoholics Anonymous, pulled herself together and started a new life as Director of the National Council on Alcoholism. Marty thus dropped out of Burra's world (though she reconnected with Bar in the Fifties, when both were middle-aged and happily settled with other women: 'I thought more than once of a question you asked me very long ago,' she wrote, after a visit in 1956. 'And after all these years the answer is Yes – I do like you, more than anyone').[10]

Even without Marty, the new web of connections in which Burra lived through his friends ramified in various directions in the late Twenties and early Thirties. Ashton, of course, was involved professionally with Constant Lambert, who wrote most of the new music for the new English ballet; this, for example, led to an evening in 1929 in which Chappell and Burra found themselves at a party given by Lambert and the novelist Anthony Powell in Tavistock Square at which Evelyn Waugh began publicly breaking up with his first wife, and subsequently to a friendship of sorts between Burra and Powell (also a friend of Bumble's), which was renewed some years later in Toulon.

Meanwhile, some of Burra's other friends moved on. Burra and Chappell at twenty-odd remained passively content to be looked after by their respective families. Burra was not looking for a lover, and as late as mid-1927 Chappell (he was twenty that year) remained obstinately innocent: 'Thanks for your interesting letter,' Burra wrote to Bar, 'and pray dear from whom did you hear that our little Pox has been had? I must try and find out. Our dear red Lett asked him if he had been f——d? NO says our primrose well then come to Paris for the week end with me what you want is a big strong man' (Lett was Arthur Lett-Haines, the lover of Cedric Morris). Chappell finally acquired a boyfriend in 1928, and Bar promptly dished the dirt:

well at last I've seen Billy's new piece the Widow Lloyd he's such a creature, so killing about Billy but of course I can't tell you in a letter, & anyway if I do it will all get back to Billy I suppose, & then what will happen I'd like to know? I danced with him quite a lot & had some very interesting conversation with him, I also gave him some very good advice about Billy so we really got on famously (I thought) I hear on good authority that Billy has been had at last I tasked him with it but he flatly denied it but of course frankly I don't believe it, after last Wednesday night. I'm sure I'll never get it out of Billy for years and years, have you succeeded in getting him to admit it?

---

[10] A sentiment which by then was not reciprocated. Bar in middle age thought Marty 'quite the most boring woman Ive ever met, but I must say she has guts'.

John Davies Knatchbull Lloyd was, like Olivia Wyndham, a contact-point between Burra's circle and the Bright Young People: he was from Montgomeryshire, and an alumnus of Winchester and Trinity College, Oxford, where the arty/intellectual Hypocrites' Club had christened him 'the Widow' on account of a then-available shaving-lotion called 'The Widow Lloyd's Euxesis'. He periodically played up to the name by dressing up as a Victorian old lady. His fellow-Hypocrites included Harold Acton, Evelyn Waugh, Robert Byron and Oliver Messel, and his appearance in Chappell's life is an indication of the way that avant-garde products of the London art schools mingled with avant-garde ex-Oxbridge. The liaison also suggests that Billy had come a long way from Balham, and confirms that his mother was 'a lady' fallen on hard times. Since he was not by any possible computation rough trade, he was evidently managing to pass in a set particularly sensitive (and antagonistic) to symptoms of non-U in speech and manners. He and Ashton were regular guests at the parties Morris and Lett threw for the Bloomsbury group. However, Chappell continued to use his mother's flat as his London base until the mid-Thirties, when he finally flew the coop and took a house with the actor Anthony (Tony) Hankey in Queen's Gate Mews, South Kensington.

All the girls in Burra's circle, not just Bar, had launched themselves into independent life long since. Doris Langley Levy married a wool merchant, Robert Sugden Moore, in 1926, and moved to a large house in the environs of Harrogate. Lucy Norton's first gesture of independence from her overbearing older sisters was running off to Paris with Burra in 1927, and thereafter, having taken a studio with Hodgkins and Basil Taylor, she stood on her right to live as she pleased. She remained, however, notably more careful of her reputation than the rest of the coterie, who passed a variety of barbed remarks about her desire to be Hon. and rebel simultaneously. Hodgkins, by contrast, ensconced herself in Godfrey Street with Denis Cohen, while Clover Pritchard got engaged to a handsome Hungarian count, Adam de Nagy. In May 1928 she married him and vanished from her friends' ken for some years. It was subsequently discovered that he had made her virtually a prisoner on his lonely estate at Jakfalva, outside Budapest, forbade her to correspond and intercepted her letters. As Chappell comments (he and Burra enjoyed the somewhat out-of-date romantic novels of 'Ouida'), she, in effect, moved temporarily out of real life and became a creature out of fiction: 'she had become identical with the heroine of *Moths*: icily beautiful, desperately unhappy. Driving, wrapped in sables, in a sleigh through a winter-struck landscape.'

Meanwhile, what Burra himself did, then and in all the subsequent decades of his life, was stay at home with his parents and paint. When he was in his teens and twenties, his father gave him an annual allowance, which, according to Clarissa Aiken, was £400. That was a perfectly reasonable young professional's salary – Virginia Woolf's prescription for independence (in her book published in 1929) was a room of one's own and five hundred a year. Burra certainly never acted as if he had a disposable income on such a scale, so Clarissa probably exaggerated the amount out of envy, since the Aikens were permanently broke. But even if they did not go so far as to make him potentially independent, Burra's parents were supportive and very undemanding. A letter which his mother wrote in the course of his first visit to Paris (in 1925) suggests that they were bending over backwards to be cooperative – it is worth noting that it was only when he wrote to them that they acquired his Paris address.

Dearest Snooks

I was very pleased to hear from you at last and to glean an address. Paris sounds delightful how I wish I was with you, no doubt if your money does come to an end we could let you have a little more to come home with – if you want to come home. I heard from Christine yesterday who tells me that Thea Davidson you knew her at Bordighera and children have gone to Paris for 3 months and are all living en pension in Passy an entirely French spot quite cheap, the children are going to day schools and Thea is going to do a little work in a studio. Christine and I thought that if you would like to stay on you could go to her pension and she would take a friendly interest in your health as well as being a very nice unconventional clever person for you to talk with in odd moments.

The artistic Mrs Davidson was of course totally unacceptable. Apart from being a friend of his mother's, she was living in a highly respectable area of Paris, and such an arrangement would clash with undisclosed agendas such as spending half the night in gay *boîtes* on the rue de Lappe. In any case, arty ladies were anathema to Burra. But this letter could hardly be fairer. Trudy Burra had genuine reason to worry about her son's health, and her suggestion is most scrupulously couched in terms of an offer that *could* be refused.

Burra's freedom to paint, think and explore without much in the way of restraint other than his lack of physical energy resulted in work that was so original as to be puzzling to his contemporaries, partly because of its powerfully unique style and lush colour-sense, and partly on account of his subject matter. In the Twenties, his paintings tended to start from a particular individual or scene that caught his imagination. 'This afternoon I saw 2 of the most dissipated men I ever saw in the Café they gave me the shivers they had 2 Jolly girlies with them but my dear I don't feel they will be jolly long one mans face looked like a cross between a crossword puzzle and Clapham junction . . .' Such encounters gave shape to other impressions, which he got from reading crime fiction. As Causey puts it, with respect to the various Burra paintings in which shabby and furtive individuals do deals in cafés:

a feeling that the covers are being lifted on some petty criminal underworld relates to his enthusiasm for the *fantaisiste* circle of French novelists . . . [Francis] Carco's novels about gangsters, prostitutes and drug-dealers have a realism involving a precise knowledge of criminal habits and conventions . . . the approach to the criminal underworld as a source of entertainment and a freedom from moralising were shared by Blaise Cendrars' slightly later reporting on criminal society in Paris and Marseilles in *Panorama de la Pègre* (1935).

Burra was interested in evil, though he felt no desire to moralise about it. However, he was perfectly clear in his own mind that there was such a thing. He read extensively in decadent literature. The Comte de Lautréamont's *Les Chants de Maldoror*, the narrative of an unrelentingly evil character called Maldoror who has forsaken God and mankind, was a favourite of Burra's (it was loved by all the surrealists, particularly André Breton), but he was also very fond of J.K. Huysmans, not only the decadent novels *A rebours* and *Là-Bas*, but his life of the emaciated, gangrenous fourteenth-century saint, Lidwina of Schiedam, which is recounted pang by pang. Burra seems also to have looked at the French 'decadent' painters of the *fin de siècle*; Burra's *Medusa*, with its curious river of hanged men, suggests some familiarity with 1890s painters such as Léon Frédéric and Jean Delville.

Similarly, Burra studied both the explorations of the demonic in the 'Gothic' writers of the English eighteenth century and those undertaken by painters of the same period. In addition to being interested in

John Martin, Blake and Fuseli, he knew *The Monk* and *Melmoth the Wanderer* particularly well, and referred to them in his correspondence (for example, 'last night was a blizzard with a howling NE gale which sounded like Melmoth being thrown over the cliff by demons when his pact with the devil ran out').

But some people attracted Burra for other reasons: '. . . there was such an Ammerican sailor in the dress cercle he was so delightful I didn't know what to do I enjoyed him as much as the ballet'. Burra drew him in this letter: a fresh-faced boy with an expression of amiable incomprehension. He often painted sailors, whom he liked because of the strong association between sailors and the buying and selling of casual sex, but also because sailors ashore are, by definition, just passing through. Burra was intensely interested in the things sex makes people do, and the delusions, delusiveness and dark comedy of the mating game in all its aspects enchanted him, but in addition his paintings often include a detached observer who functions as an intermediary between the principal picture-plane and the viewer. For this purpose also, sailors came in handy.

Burra's sensibility was camp; but campness is not necessarily either trivial or trivialising. He disliked any form of pomposity, but he was wholly serious as an artist. Campness in Burra is the spirit defined by Christopher Isherwood: 'You can't camp about something you don't take seriously. You're not making fun of it, you're making fun out of it. You're expressing what is basically serious to you in terms of fun and artifice and elegance. Baroque art is largely camp about religion. The ballet is camp about love.' What Burra was camp about was modernity, human interrelations and mass culture.

Burra's uncondescending fascination with the preoccupations of ordinary people was distinctly unusual at a time when most of his literate contemporaries, faced with a member of the working classes, were inclined to bleat, 'but what can one say to these people?' Orwell observed brutally, 'The real reason why a European of bourgeois upbringing . . . cannot without a hard effort think of a working man as his equal . . . *the lower classes smell.*' This was true. The poor were not referred to as 'the great unwashed' for nothing. A significant proportion of the urban population still lived in tenements with no water laid on, where every drop used had to be carried up from an outside standpipe (though pre-war standards of cleanliness even among the middle-class intellegentsia in England were surprisingly primitive; in 1937, the film-maker Humphrey Jennings changed his clothes once a week, on Mondays). But working-class smelliness would not have bothered Burra: he himself was notably careless about washing, and the very fastidious Paul Nash was reduced to pleading with him, '[I hope] you are having baths every day & changing your shirts often you know it is horrid not to & I am sure you would be much healthier if you did. Please Edward dear for my sake pay attention to this.'

Despite his attitude to personal hygiene, Burra was nicely brought up; his family perhaps even on the paranoid side of conservative – his grandmother was terrified of 'the lower orders' (as he observed during the General Strike in 1926), but he seems to have had no trouble whatever with the notion of the dignity (or indignity) of mankind in general. As Causey observes:

Burra's primary interest was human energy and style . . . Burra liked life on the margins and wherever he saw natural vitality unawed by social conventions; at the top and bottom of his social hierarchy are the dandy and the tramp, both displaced types far from the centre of everyday acceptability. The world of entertainment with its uninhibited physical display, which fostered illusions and compensated for people's inner emptiness, had a special attraction for him . . . Burra's art in the twenties is not a simple statement of what he saw; his point of view is hard to determine because he was both a participant and a critic, he enjoyed the bohemian world and at the same time ridiculed it.

Lacking physical energy himself, he was awed by the sheer busyness that other people put into the business of living. What is so interesting about his images of avid consumption, or avid existence, is that they have no element of the contemptuous (the traditional upper-middle-class reaction), nor do they suggest a sexual agenda. Not a few upper-class Englishmen of Burra's generation took refuge from the frigidities and rigidities of their early training by making sexual contact with men or women of the lower orders; Burra did not, but he did respond strongly to the vitality of urban popular culture.

For all but the most avant-garde (or the sexually motivated), the primary mode for dealing with working-class people in the art of the Twenties was to treat them as a faceless, blobby mass called 'the workers'. Samuel Hynes, a specialist in the writers of the Twenties and Thirties, has pointed out the fundamental inability of the intelligentsia in that era to take the working classes seriously, as witnessed by their response to the General Strike, in which even people such as Christopher Isherwood, whose instincts were strongly leftist, were happy to act as strike-breakers. 'Most of us didn't even know why the men had struck,' he confessed, looking back. 'I didn't know myself.' Burra, as it happened, was abroad (in Florence) for the duration of the Strike, but his friends automatically sided with authority: 'we all volenteered but nothing came of it,' said Bar. But Burra somehow developed a perception that this was an inadequate response to the world they were all living in.

Burra did not take a stance on the rights or wrongs of the proletariat, in the mode of his contemporary George Orwell, since politics was one of the many things for which he had no energy to spare. However, he had a far clearer apprehension than most of his educated coevals that they were human: while Orwell, for example in *The Road to Wigan Pier*, sees working people either as squalid, insectile sub-humans, 'blackbeetles', or – particularly the miners – as romanticised demigods, Burra had far more of a sense of common ground. As his godson Edward Pertinez put it, 'he treated everybody with equal contempt' – the stress is on 'equal'. His instincts were egalitarian, but he was practically rather than ideologially or politically minded; in a letter to Aiken written during the war, taking issue with a variety of intellectuals bemoaning the fall of civilisation, he commented, 'I fly in a rage because everyone cant have water H&C [hot and cold].'

However, since Burra was personally imprisoned in a body which caused nothing but trouble, and which he as far as possible ignored, there were moods in which he loathed the whole of humanity. His occasionally evidenced sense of people as appetitive meat in motion, sometimes expressed in his letters and savage little caricatures, is almost Swiftian. Not unusually, the people he finds it hardest to tolerate are the ones nearest at hand: the denizens of the Rye Tennis Club and suchlike Tillingesque locations. 'Rye is hateful now full of abominations with raw necks and sports nets you cant imagine such gawpingoafish lumps of raw beefy FLESH flesh and butchers meat how I hate people.' Burra had a tiny appetite, though he enjoyed food; he was small, slim and slight, generally a little repelled – though intermittently fascinated – by the large and fleshy.

But the heavily painted woman devouring a sandwich at a lunch counter whom he painted in 1930 is observed not condescendingly, but as a fellow-human satisfying a simple need. The code of feminine daintiness that Burra so often mocked in his discourse makes this image of a working girl stuffing food into her mouth an extremely unusual approach to representation of the female body in 1930. Clover identified the subject positively as a tart: 'typically French . . . Soho tarts were mostly French around 1930 and dressed and made up just like that'. Bar pinpointed the venue as the Continental Snack Bar in Shaftesbury Avenue, which 'was very handy for ladies on the game to have a sit down and a cup of tea in their rest periods'. Women, particularly prostitutes, were persistently eroticised, etherialised, reified or abstracted in the art and imagery of the period. Burra enjoyed the rhetoric of 'sin flaunting with a painted grin', but it is not what he represents in this wholly unromantic picture. Similarly, in another early painting, *Les Folies de Bellville*, Burra's danseuses have masklike faces. They shove their groins at the viewer with impersonal energy and vigour, wearing rictuslike lipsticked grins and very little else; but he could hardly be clearer that they are just doing a job. If one doesn't find chorines either sexually threatening or alluring, the whole business of representation shifts into a different key. Burra's asexuality allows him to see that hopping about in a costume the size of a postage stamp is a damn-fool way of making a living.

In a decade in which writers insistently posed the question: what are we to *do*? – in which art, and the practice of art, became more and more politicised – Burra was absolutely certain that he knew the answer with respect to himself. There were so few things that he could do, after all. As the prisoner of his fragile body and depleted energy, his role was to observe; to celebrate the human and individual in a world increasingly dominated by abstractions. 'What other artist,' commented John Rothenstein, 'can portray so exactly, for example, the exuberant cut and fibrous texture of cheap clothes?' Burra's images could hardly be further from the anonymous, aggressively de-individualised masses of Soviet 'proletarian art'. His work is absolutely un-ideal and individualistic; harking back to the French recorders of the urban scene, notably Théophile Steinlen – indeed, Clover subsequently said, 'if it hadn't been for Steinlen, Ed would never have become interested in low life Paris subjects'. Steinlen's *Dans la vie* was in the library at Springfield, with its images of bars and dances, sailors and pick-ups. But Burra's own images of working people are painted with an imaginative identification and sympathy which sets him apart from this journalistic tradition, and aligns him with the art of the Left.

However, what people such as the Sunday painters of Rye thought of as 'Art' was the representation either of individuals remarkable for wealth or beauty, or of a rural landscape that was, for most people, vanishing into the past. In 1927, a middle-aged lesbian couple invited Burra for a weekend visit under some illusions about what his being an 'artist' meant, an invitation that he rashly accepted, out of politeness or curiosity.[11] The encounter that ensued illustrates the gap which had opened up between the avant-garde and conventional opinion:

Don't you adore that pointing to a small water colour of the Virgin M nursing an allenburys progressive baby with a gas ring going off round its head seated on a toadstool in a bluebell wood. I kept wondering what ever would happen when my pictures were displayed & I couldn't get out of showing them, so they said on seeing my pictures Oh futurist I suppose, of course I don't understand them at all but I am very old fashioned but you paint so neatly & such lovely detail I think it such a pity you don't paint artistic things . . . it doesnt seem right that you should be painting such things at your age by that time I got the giggles I didn't know where to look the half of the time.

Burra evidently realised that there was no point in trying to explain, and probably could not have done even if he had wanted to, but the purposes and preoccupations of art were necessarily changing because society was undergoing a major transformation. In the early twentieth century, the mass of the population began to transfer itself ineluctably from the country to the cities, a process that was first observable in Britain. While this was not explicitly recognised at the time, intellectuals and artists were subliminally aware of it, since one of the central preoccupations of modernist art in the Twenties was coming to terms with cities.

High modernism has a lot to say about the urban working class and popular culture. Imagery taken from contemporary life is a strong

[11] They seem to have been Catholic and to have lived in an old house in the vicinity, but Burra makes it clear that at least one was a big-game hunter, so they were not Radclyffe Hall and Lady Troubridge.

feature of avant-garde art of the Twenties and Thirties (causing tradi-
tionalists, such as the good ladies who had Burra to stay, to complain
that young people seemed to be rolling in the gutters for the fun of it).
That archetypic modernist novel, James Joyce's *Ulysses*, is a celebration
of the merely human and specific in an urban context. Leopold Bloom
does not exist in the heroic squalor of dire poverty, but at the level of
humdrum 'rubbing along' which had always been considered beyond
the province of serious art.

It is also interesting that in the 'Nausicäa' section of *Ulysses*, Joyce
engages directly with popular culture: Gertie McDowell's perceptions
are shaped by the women's magazines that she reads. The language she
possesses acts as a system of filters between reality – the fact that she
is about to start her period, her erotic impulses – and her inability to
comprehend or even acknowledge these essential facts about herself.
Burra similarly read *Peg's Paper* and *Photoplay* and allowed them to
shape his discourse, though as he used them, the disjunction between
what the words said and the realities they described was comic rather
than tragic, since the disjunction was, for him, something to be
consciously played with.

The most influential poem of the Twenties, T.S. Eliot's *The Waste
Land*, begins with a perception of the urban masses as a grey, fleeting
multitude, a crowd flowing over London Bridge, but moves on, in a
subsequent section, to a sharply observed vignette: a working-class
woman talking about her friend's husband coming home from the war;
later, there is a portrait of a typist in a bedsit, home from work, receiving
her lover as the last of the day's chores. At midday, she might very well
have bolted a hasty sandwich in the Continental Snack Bar alongside
Burra's tart. Burra's Twenties' paintings focus on such people, though
he preferred to portray them at play rather than at work, sitting at café
tables or on balconies; dancing, gossiping, quarrelling, spilling off a tram
or listening to jazz. He is interested in the ways they interact, in details,
in the particular. His painting in this decade draws on the quondam
Vorticists, Wyndham Lewis and William Roberts, both of whom were
satirists and interested in working people (he went to William Roberts's
first solo exhibition in 1923, which impressed him greatly, and was
always interested in Wyndham Lewis, both as a writer and as a painter,
throughout his life).

'Burra's concept of modern life was a Romantic one, a Whitmanesque brotherhood of races and types; and his approach was sensuous rather than intellectual, evoking the whole feel of the city street, not just its visual aspect,' Causey commented. In 1945, Rothenstein remarked on the strangeness and newness of this as a project:

Artists are continually enlarging our conception of the beautiful, by including in its canon subjects from which preceding generations averted their gaze. (It was not so long ago that all but the most ceremonious aspects of contemporary life were held to be unworthy of the attention of the practitioner of 'High Art'.) It has remained for Burra to create, out of the flashy decoration of the *boîte*, a new rococo which has a copious and exotic grandeur, and the deliquescent fantasy which belongs to dreams.

Nash called Burra the modern Hogarth, a perception with some truth at this time, though Burra was far less of a moralist than Hogarth. In the Thirties his friendship with Nash himself, among other things, would lead him in quite different directions.

IV

FINISHING SCHOOLS

THERE were two kinds of 'abroad' in Burra's life. One was parentally sponsored, the other was going off with his friends. They overlap to some extent, but in the narrative of Burra's life there is a case for distinguishing them as different kinds of experience.

Travels with his parents came first. The Burra family took visits abroad for granted; but within a particular compass. There were places one might go for one's health, and places one went for art, uplift or education; the rest of the world, unless one had commercial, military or other interests of a particular kind, one could manage perfectly well without. Burra's parents thus took it as axiomatic that since he was a painter, he must go to Paris. They did not necessarily feel the same way about his visiting New York or Mexico.

Health

Trudy Burra was a great believer in health tourism, and was herself a regular visitor to spas both at home and abroad. She took her son to Bath for treatment when he was still a child: not only had it been England's traditional centre for convalescence for more than a hundred years, but from about 1900 the mineral-rich water from the natural springs at Bath was marketed as 'Sulis Water' and touted as offering relief from rheumatic disease. Ineffectively, in Burra's case; but there was still a repertory of other possibilities for her to try.

By the Twenties, Switzerland had also become a place strongly associated with convalescence. The notion that clear, thin mountain air benefited weak lungs generally and tuberculosis in particular led to a proliferation of clinics, and something of a national specialism in the provision of healthcare facilities more generally. The peculiar benefits of Swiss air were advertised as early as the 1880s by Johanna Spyri's hugely popular children's book, *Heidi*, in which a pale, fragile city child is given health and a new lease of life by a sojourn in the Alps: 'Is that round-faced, healthy-looking child my poor little, white, sickly Clara?' cries the ex-invalid's delighted grandmother, in the final pages.

The possibly beneficial effects of healthy mountain air on poor little, white, sickly Burra were hopefully tried in 1920, when he was fifteen, to no particularly good end. Unlike the fictional Clara, he drew no new strength from the experience of Alpine life. Though it was his first experience of foreign travel, Switzerland seems to have made little or no impression on him. His dreams of 'abroad' centred on southern port towns baking under a white-hot sun, infested with prostitutes and matelots, and scented with garlic, fish and raw sewage.

But the Burras were not prepared to give up. Switzerland, pure and bracing, hadn't helped, but perhaps mild, constant warmth might be the thing that would pull him round. Many a delicate child has become a reasonably healthy adult. The next place to try was obvious. Like Bath and Switzerland, Bordighera, the most hygienic town on the Italian Riviera, was strongly associated with rest-cures and convalescent regimes, due to its mild climate. It was 'frequented mainly by convalescents and tourists', according to Baedeker, the bible of the English abroad. It became popular with the English in the later nineteenth century; Edward Lear and George MacDonald, for example, both lived there in their old age. Though it was the chosen retirement home of Margherita of Savoy, Italy's Queen Mother, who died there in 1926, it was very much a little England; a middle-class England, of pottering walks, tea and afternoon calls. There were beautiful gardens, in various styles. 'Bordighera is famous for its floriculture (roses, carnations, anemones, etc.) . . . and for its date-palms.' Wintering on the Riviera was particularly attractive to northerners, so all along the coast late-nineteenth-century developers supplemented the native flora with semi-tropical evergreens: palms, mimosa, succulents, to give all-year-round displays. But the palms were older; they had been 'the special glory of Bordighera' since the sixteenth century, when an enterprising local had been given the monopoly of providing Rome with leaves for Palm Sunday. They lined the streets, providing welcome shade and rustling in the breeze off the sea.

Baedeker's Guide to Northern Italy, the essential source of information for people such as the senior Burras who were planning a trip abroad, includes this soothing information. Bordighera boasted no fewer than seventeen hotels and pensions largely patronised by the English, including the Grand Hôtel des Îles Britanniques, the Hôtel de Londres and the Hôtel d'Angleterre. Besides the hotels, there were eleven resident doctors, an English church and a British vice-consul. Between them, they must have ensured that the essential desiderata of respectable English travellers were supplied (proper religion, drains and tea, not necessarily in that order).

Burra's mother decided to take him to Bordighera in March 1925, since he had been working very hard and had not been well – she decided to go by sea, rather curiously, given that she was a martyr to seasickness and getting to Bordighera meant sailing the Atlantic coast of Europe and entering the Mediterranean at the Straits of Gibraltar. 'The sea will be choppy and Mama will be sick it don't need a choppy sea to upset our Mama tho on viewing the round pond she has been known to heave,' Burra commented.[1] It is hard to see why she decided on running the gauntlet of the Bay of Biscay in the season of equinoctial storms, unless perhaps she thought her boy would benefit from the sea air.

They booked into the Hôtel du Cap, the most expensive hotel in Bordighera. Trudy Burra was probably hoping that a gentle, convalescent holiday in the sun would ease the long-term health problems that afflicted them both. It might have done so. Rheumatoid arthritis is an autoimmune disorder; that is, the immune system begins to attack healthy cells and tissues, resulting in redness, heat, pain and swelling. Since such conditions are affected by the patient's overall physical state, Burra might genuinely have benefited from a general increase in health and vitality. Furthermore, Bordighera was well supplied with therapeutic baths, masseurs and so forth to provide soothing palliative treatment for Burra's sore joints.

Though the senior Burras were surely aware that Bordighera was not precisely the epicentre of their son's notion of the South, they may also have hoped that he would enjoy the experience as a painter, since the

---

[1] The Round Pond in Kensington Gardens, toy-boat sailing venue for nicely brought-up little Londoners for many generations.

beauty of the Ligurian coastline was universally acknowledged. A contemporary travel book makes the point:

When the sick people arrive from the cold, bleak North and look for the first time on the rich colouring of this southern shore, how great must be their sense of joy over the wonderful change wrought by a few hours' railway travelling! Grey or leaden skies have changed to blue: such a blue as is only to be seen in sunny countries ... Walking along the Cornice towards Bordighera, we were never more impressed than by the beauty of our palm-bordered way, and the exquisite blue of the tideless sea: cerulean near at hand, where it beats on rocky bays and creeks, but an intenser and intenser blue in the distance up to the point where the white foam edges the beaches.

In the Twenties, battalions of Sunday painters sat on little portable stools set in shady corners, looking out to sea and diligently punishing the cerulean, azure and Chinese white in their paintboxes. But not Burra. The weather was against him; when they arrived, it was as grey and leaden as that of Rye, rainy and discouraging, as Italy can be in the spring. He spent mornings in his room, working on drawings out of his imagination; and for entertainment, he and his mother took tea in the Café de Paris, and on one occasion went to Monte Carlo in a chara-banc (it poured the whole time). From his account, Trudy, at least, was enjoying herself, but Burra was anxious about his work, low-spirited and short of energy.

In terms of Burra's personal agendas, Bordighera was too hygienic and organised and not in itself very exciting, but at least it was the South. There were palm trees and bougainvillea, and stucco villas with balconies. Drinking absinthe with whores and matelots might have to wait till he was able to get away on his own, but meantime, even in Bordighera, there were things to enjoy. The concept of the Riviera more generally had a certain glamour as a rich people's frisking-ground; an association with the *jeunesse dorée*, open-topped cars and the carefree, moneyed lives of Dornford Yates's Berry & Co. If it wasn't louche, there was at least some faint hope that it might be mondaine. Perhaps there might be carefree, godlike beauties in sports kit vaulting athletically over the doors of their Hispano-Suizas or Humber Super Snipes ... In fact, he saw none, but he did at least observe, and draw, fashionable Frenchwomen in the Café de Paris, drinking vermouth and wearing smart hats and mascara, delighting in the contrast they made with the English ladies in their horrible cardigans.

But when he and his mother had been there a bit over a week, just as the weather began to improve, he went down with a sore throat, and was confined to bed, with the scent of lemon-blossom drifting in through the hotel windows. It must have been like school all over again; the minute he started finding his feet, he was swept off to the San. Intensely frustrating, until he became too ill to care.

He had developed rheumatic fever, a potentially fatal condition which generally appears within three to five weeks of an untreated strepto-coccal throat infection; probably the illness that had prompted his mother to take him abroad in the first place, and also the reason for his anxiety and low spirits. The symptoms, apart from fever, include painful inflammation of one or more of the larger joints: as the symptoms become less severe in one joint, they tend to start up in another, though sometimes several joints are affected at the same time. In Burra's case, his knees and ankles seem to have got the worst of it, though his spine was also involved. The disease often causes permanent damage, and can also affect the valves of the heart. It may have affected Burra's, making him still more prone to exhaustion. The fact that, in later life, his feet and ankles swelled if he had to stand for any length of time may suggest that the action of his heart was slightly impaired (though he never speaks of breathlessness as a problem, film-footage of Burra in his late sixties suggests that he became a bit wheezy).

There is no actual cure for rheumatic fever even now, though today it can easily be prevented by prompt and thorough treatment of a 'strep throat' with antibiotics. But 1925 was three years before the discovery of penicillin, so no help was available. Rather than giving him the hoped-for boost, the Bordighera episode represents a further downward step in his overall health. He was very seriously ill throughout the whole of April and May, and needed professional nursing, as he told Birdie Rushbury:

I had a nurse at Bawdi she was a scream I don't know what I would have done without her, she had been at the college!!! And had no more idea of art than an illegitimate kipper therefor sensibly took to nursing now we know where the distressed debitants go to. She had meant to be an <u>art teacher</u> no wonder Englands what it is but I liked her very much she was a pearl and used to sing to me 'Jesus wants me for a <u>sun</u>beam to shine for him this dayee, he wants me to shine ever brightlee, at home, at school, at playee' I love such homely simple tunes don't you they radiate true British Spirit.[2]

The Burras tended to be economical travellers in normal circumstances, but he was still barely able to walk when his mother eventually decided she must get him home. Returning by sea was out of the question; she bundled him up in all the clothes he possessed, heaved him, shuffling, bent double and wearing bedroom slippers, onto a train at Ventimiglia and took him to Nice to catch the Blue Train, for maximum ease and comfort on their return journey. This was the new, smart way of travelling between Paris and the Côte d'Azur. Launched on 8 December 1922, it consisted of connecting luxury compartments for eighty first-class passengers, with no second-class accommodation at all. Not only was it, like the Orient Express, a train strongly associated with the *beau monde* in general, but the previous summer Bronislava Nijinska had premiered a modern-dress ballet, *Le Train Bleu*, with a plot by Jean Cocteau, costumes by Coco Chanel and a drop-curtain by Picasso. This was designed to showcase the beauty and talent of Anton Dolin, and played at the Coliseum in London in November, where it was well received, and Billy Chappell promptly developed a crush on Dolin.

Burra wrote to Chappell from Springfield when he got home. Characteristically, he does not discuss his illness; but focuses on the extent to which the Riviera had failed to live up to its propaganda (Chappell, who was still only sixteen, had never been out of England at this point of his life).

We came back from Bawdi in the Blue train which is sposed to be ever so mondaine but all I saw was ancient invalids and a couple with a baby that looked as if it came off Margate Sands there were a few mondaines though to lighten the gloom . . . Bawdi is <u>not</u> mondaine and is just a wee bit inclined to be scabby but the native population are too beautiful and wear such exotic garments speshly the men.

---

[2] A song by Nellie Talbot of Missouri, set to music by Edwin O. Excell in 1900, and widely adopted by English Sunday-school teachers.

He sounds tired and sad. Later in the letter he notes in passing, 'I still hobble and cant do this and that and I want to see Delysia.' Alice Delysia, one of the great ladies of the French music-hall, was then starring with Ernest Thesiger in C.B. Cochran's revue *On with the Dance*, devised by Noël Coward, at the London Pavilion. Naturally, Burra was dying to see her. But he was stuck in Rye, almost unable to move, and the only thing on in the local cinema was Cecil B. de Mille's *The Ten Commandments*. A grim prospect.

His parents then sent him to Bath, as he had feared they might: 'I cant walk properly yet nor scarcely do anything for myself but I am better than I was and maybe I shall have to go and drink drefful water.'[3] This was even grimmer, since he was crippled, and surrounded by crumbling elderly gentlewomen – and unfortunately he found himself stuck at Miss Godolphin's convalescent home in Pulteney Street for several weeks 'in an odour of <u>extreme gentility</u>', since his mother had contrived to catch typhoid from unpasteurised cream shortly after their return, and Springfield was quarantined. An alarming letter she wrote, once she was allowed to communicate, asks, 'How are you old man do you feel quite supple now your feet and hands I mean and I hope your back gets straight again.' The feet and hands were never to recover, but at least his spine must have straightened out, since his posture in adult life was reasonably good.

Education

However, things were looking up. It was possible for Burra to endure the lonely boredom of Bath, since he fervently hoped to be well enough to go to Paris. As well as having a well-established habit of going abroad for one's health, the Burras regarded education abroad as wholly appropriate. His mother had herself gone to finishing school abroad – since she was very musical, it was Dresden she went to, to study opera.

Burra's sister Anne preceded him abroad. When she was sent to a finishing school in Florence in 1925 to study art, Burra expected to miss her badly. 'Anna departs for Italia on the 25th or something for years it seems she wont be seen again before next summer. its vewy sad

---

[3] According to Dickens, Bath mineral water has 'a very strong flavour of warm flat-irons' (*Pickwick Papers*), as Burra well knew, having experienced it before.

that families should be so separated I think pwaps we may go to Florence some time . . .' Burra's faux-naïf use of baby-talk defocuses attention from the emotional content of what he is saying. He does mean it – they were a very close-knit family – but he does not want to hear any more about it. Baby-talk was considered quite chic in the Twenties; E.F. Benson's Lucia, for instance, resorts to baby-talk on a regular basis, and so did many actual women of the time (like much of Burra's verbal repertoire, it definitely belonged to a female, or camp, mode of discourse).

However, Florence in 1925 was not quite what it had been; the city was falling under the control of Benito Mussolini and his Fascists; and it was less and less possible even for well-chaperoned teenage brides of art to live only for the Uffizi, unaware of what was going on around them.

My sister is having such a rollicking time in Florence what with fascisti officers and only the other day a perfect brute pinched her on the ——

A drawing follows: hand pinching bottom; the front end of the figure, typically, is coiling round to cock a snoot at the pincher, and the drawing is signed 'Gino Severini 1925'. This links back into another aspect of Burra's life; Severini was a modernist sculptor with a certain reputation in England, since he had had a one-man exhibition there in the early Twenties. Severini wrote a book, *Du Cubisme au Classicisme* (1921), which argued for a reinvention of the rigorous, mathematical structuring employed by painters such as Uccello and Piero della Francesca in the context of modernism; an argument that Burra evidently took seriously, as the rigorous structuring of Twenties' paintings such as *The Two Sisters* bears witness.

The family did indeed visit Anne in Florence. Burra wrote to his sister, who shared his faintly sceptical attitude towards their parents, 'I returned from London yesterday and found Mama in bed looking ever so well she may not be able to go on Sun but we are coming. Such a fuss as Dah will be in no doubt we shall fuss into the Berlin express instead of the Rome . . .' What Burra particularly liked in the Uffizi were the Botticellis. Where the art of Botticelli connects most obviously with that of Burra is in its linearity; like Burra, Botticelli is a draughtsman who paints. The flatness, and the meticulous all-over diapering of patterned surfaces which characterises much of Botticelli's work, may also have interested Burra, since again it had something in common with his own approach to making pictures.

Paris

Just as Florence was the place to go for art appreciation, so Paris was the place for practising artists. Burra could assume from an early stage of his life that his own education abroad would be in France, since in the mid-Twenties, Paris was the undisputed world capital of aesthetic innovation. This was something that his parents completely accepted and encouraged. Since he was good at drawing, they encouraged him to work on his French from the age of eight, if not earlier, with the result that Burra had a fully literary command of French by the time he was twenty, and read French literature with pleasure and interest. He liked the Unanimists, particularly Jules Romains, a group of poets who were interested in crowds and urban life, and he liked Blaise Cendrars for his use of imagery from the streets, dance halls, circus and cinema. He was also attracted by Baudelaire, whom he frequently quotes.

Before the First World War, Paris-based painters such as Matisse, Cézanne and Braque had been the first begetters of a style of painting that was perceived in all advanced circles as a genuine reflection of modernity. Post-war, Paris was still the place to be. Influenced by such Francophile critics as Roger Fry and Clive Bell, young English modernists grew up in the shadow of what was happening in France.

This is certainly the case with Burra. In so far as Burra's work relates to any movement at all, it is connected with surrealism, and that meant Paris: where André Breton, Louis Aragon and Paul Éluard began publishing proto-surrealist statements in the Dada magazine, *Littérature* (founded in 1919), and identified themselves as a separate movement in 1924 with a review of their own, *La Révolution surréaliste*. In the early Twenties, English artists interested in surrealism were entirely dependent on manifestos and reproductions in French periodicals. Surrealism did not officially cross the Channel until the International Surrealist Exhibition was staged in London in 1936.

The ideas which the nascent surrealist movement held in common were a belief in the significance of dreams and the random selection of images. They also strongly believed that the roots of creative impulse were in the subconscious, and, unlike the Dadaists, they were concerned to make constructive statements about society. Burra was intensely interested by these principles, since he was a dedicated irrationalist who painted in what was virtually a trance state, tended to let his pictures develop apparently of their own accord (normally from right to left, bottom to top, rather curiously, though he was not left-handed) and was something of a social satirist.

Another aspect of surrealism that increased its attraction for Burra was its connection with pop culture, particularly film. As Frederick Brown puts it, 'At war with bourgeois culture, the surrealists-to-be . . . inhabited an Underworld before taking up residence in the Unconscious.' They were fascinated by crime, and above all by figures from cult movie serials. They liked *The Perils of Pauline*, but above all they liked the rather more counter-cultural French serials, especially the Napoleonic anti-hero Fantômas, perpetrator of fantastic, indeed surreal, crimes (1913–14), and Musidora's character Irma Vep in *Les Vampires* (1915–16). Whereas Pauline was, notionally, the 'goodie', both Fantômas and Irma Vep were figures of extravagant evil. Irma Vep ('vampire' anagrammatised) was the ultimate seductive assassin, eyes darkly ringed with kohl, pearl-handled revolver concealed in her corsage. She was protean, liable to turn up anywhere, slinking in a black cat-suit, pretending to be a financier's secretary, disguised as a housemaid or singing apache songs in a low dive. Fantômas's outrages include substituting sulphuric acid for perfume in the dispensers of a Parisian department store, and hanging a rebellious henchman upside down as the clapper of a huge bell, so that as he smashes from side to side he rains blood, sapphires and diamonds on the street far below. His daughter Hélène, an opium-smoker with a death's-head tattoo, and a frequent cross-dresser, seems to have slithered fully formed from Burra's own imagination. Fantômas and his world were reference points for surrealist artists who include Juan Gris, René Magritte and Blaise Cendrars, among others.

These Gaumont serials did not come over to England. It was American shows such as *The Perils of Pauline* that nourished Burra's childhood imagination, but his private created world of the Dilly Sisters, the Phoenix Theatre and Bar, Tivoli Buildings, Lower Tartan Street, show that he, like Breton and Aragon, had sensed a basic linkage of the underworld with the unconscious from his earliest years.

Meanwhile, back in the real world, the surrealists' particular meeting place in the mid-Twenties was the Café Cyrano in the Place Blanche, where they met daily at noon, and again in the evening. Max Ernst (whose painting had a perceptible influence on that of Burra, particularly in the late Twenties) was another member of the group, and so was the English socialite and apostle of black culture, Nancy Cunard, who became Aragon's lover in 1926.

Towards the end of 1925, the ever-patient Dah allowed Burra to go to Paris, under the chaperonage of Florence and Henry Rushbury. The Rushburys went to Paris some time in the summer, around the time when Burra went to Bordighera and collapsed with rheumatic fever. He says in a letter to Chappell, 'I have again heard from the Rushbury . . . she said she would ask me for a sejour when they had got a studio and if there was a room which would be ever so nice but I shall still probably be tottering and impotent.' He was desperate to go, and she wrote to him again, very affectionately, in Bath, to assure him that he had not been forgotten; explaining that they were having trouble finding somewhere suitable: 'Studios meublés [furnished] do materialise but studios propres avec cabinets civilisées [nice studios with proper lavatories] don't.' In the end, they moved not to a studio, but to a better hotel in the rue de la Grande Chaumière, and asked him over.

He was still not at all fit, but the whole of his will was fixed on going. As an act of kindness to all parties, Dah paid for Chappell to go too, throwing the latter into social panic: 'You do write me lovely news Eddie. It is very very nice of your papa but do you think I should let him? I don't know what to do about it. It is overwhelming . . . should I write to him or what. Do write by return and tell me properly as I don't know what to do at all.'

Birdie was not quite what Dah Burra would ideally have envisaged as a chaperone. While she was deeply attached to her husband, and not looking for sexual adventure, she was dismally bored from day to day. Her problem was that an attractive and vivacious young woman running about Paris on her own was apt to find adventures whether she wanted them or not. In addition to being a magnet for artists, Paris was a haven for the sexually experimental of both genders and all persuasions. The wealthy American lesbian, Natalie Barney, observed around this time that it 'has always seemed to me the only city where you can live and express yourself as you please'. This could, of course, create problems for those such as Birdie who basically wanted to watch from the sidelines.

She wrote plaintively to Burra in July, 'I have been back in Paris a fortnight – but Heavens above what ennui! L'illustrissimo Enrico works from nine o'c till 7.30 in these impossible streets, and all day for hours and hours I have just nothing at all to do. I have looked at pictures till I loathe every one that was ever painted ...' The solution, obviously, was to become a fag-hag. Thus, once the boys turned up, rather than trying to keep them under control, she took them with her to *boîtes* and louche parties, where a good time was had by all.

The hotel they all ended up in was on the boulevard de Montparnasse, the centre of artists' Paris. The many bars and cafés up and down the road each had their regulars, quite a few of whom were more or less famous and surrounded by a seething mass of models, *flâneurs*, wannabes, and romantics of all descriptions, many of them American. The Café du Dôme, 'by all odds the most interesting place in all Paris', stood at the meeting-point of the boulevard du Montparnasse and the boulevard Raspail; in 1925, habitués included Kiki, the Queen of Montparnasse, and her lover Man Ray, Americans such as Ernest Hemingway and Robert McAlmond, the enormously successful Japanese painter Foujita, the poet Anna de Noailles and many another. Burra was initially suspicious ('the café du dome is so awful & so crowded with all the artists the very sight of it drives me to be a sausage maker'), but it rapidly became one of his favourite places. A letter he wrote in 1931 begins with a paraphrase of an English nursery rhyme: 'Well dear hear am I little jumping Joan when nobodys with me Ime allways in the Dôme.'[4] Many of his letters over the years are datelined from the Dôme, and not a few are on its paper; he must have used it regularly as a place to sit and catch up with correspondence.

Another great favourite of his throughout the Twenties and Thirties, which he may have discovered on this first visit, since it opened in 1925, was the Select, 99 boulevard du Montparnasse. The owners, M. and Mme Jalbert, made no particular effort to attract artists; the bar's principal claim to consideration was that it was the first in Montparnasse to stay open all night. Madame, a masterful lady with a high, shelflike

---

[4] 'Here am I, little jumping Joan; when nobody's with me, then I'm all alone.'

bosom, presided in fingerless gloves, while Monsieur made Welsh rarebit, the house speciality. In the first couple of years, the habitués tended to be American writers and would-be writers, though as time went on it acquired a good many gay customers; and was adopted by the ballet crowd.

Burra, though he did not lack belief in himself, was too young and too English to barge in on the surrealists at the Café Cyrano and try to impress them. However, one important encounter which happened around this time, and which did link him with the Café Cyrano set, was with John Banting, who was twenty-three in 1925. Banting, whom the painter Julian Trevelyan described as 'the eternal outsider', became a lifelong friend of Burra's. He was a distinctly glamorous figure: though he was balding from his twenties, his neatly shaped head, high cheek-bones, slanting eyes and full mouth ensured that his lack of hair, like his broken nose, merely lent an intriguingly rough edge to his good looks. He knew Paris well, since he had first gone there as a student in 1922. From 1925 he had a studio in Fitzroy Street in London, where he was in contact with the Bloomsbury group of painters (this would also have located him in circles that overlapped with those of the Rushburys), and was one of the few thoroughgoing English surrealists. He was homosexual (bisexual in earlier life), and this, together with his surrealist interests, made Paris more congenial to him than London. He seems to have met Burra at some studio party or other, since they clearly became friends around this time.

Another fact about Banting that may be relevant to his relationship with Burra was his friendship with Nancy Cunard (they were so close that she later described him as 'my sort of Irish brother'). Like Nancy, he was considerably more of a political animal than Burra. He shared Nancy's passionate opposition to racial prejudice and her predisposi-tion towards interest and sympathy with black people, and he was very much a man of the Left. He may have introduced Burra to these ideas, as well as acting as a bridge between Burra and the surrealist move-ment, and introducing him to Nancy Cunard, whom Burra could well also have met through Olivia Wyndham.

A variety of Burra's interests in adult life show an affiliation with the surrealists. For both Breton and Aragon, the streets of the metropolis were locales for encountering the marvellous and the *inconnu*. Burra, simi-larly, was much given to walking in London (also in other great cities,

Paris, New York, Madrid and Barcelona), keeping his eyes open, receptive to the weirdnesses of urban life, which was the central subject of his painting before the war. Most surrealists and many Dadaists were avid collectors of the debris of popular culture, such as nineteenth-century pulp fiction and erotic postcards. Burra similarly liked both; and just as Duchamp and others prowled Paris's flea-market, he rummaged in junk shops, particularly when he was with Bumble, who shared his weakness for tat and junk jewellery. He also collected found objects on occasion, a favourite surrealist game. Bar wrote in the Sixties, 'We went down to Billy's little cottage on Romney Marsh and scavenged about on Dymchurch Beach for "objets Trouvee". Ed is very good at this and comes up with some objets which are very strange indeed.'

Apart from involving himself with contemporaries, soaking up current ideas and seeing what was new, one thing that Burra certainly did in Paris, as he had done in Florence, was to study great paintings. This would have been encouraged by the Rushburys, but in any case, there were aspects of doctrinaire modernism which Burra had no time for at all. Above all, those theorists of modern art who rejected the importance of drawing, which was the centre of Burra's art and, indeed, life. Moreover, 'among the younger artists and their supporters in the years immediately before the war, distaste for the art of the Renaissance was virtually an item of faith'. Not so Burra. Despite the fact that galleries were a genuine physical problem for him, because he found it so difficult to stand, he was a gallery-goer, and took Severini's *Du Cubisme au classicisme* seriously. He explored the Louvre in depth; and came away with, among other things, a renewed respect for the baroque.

However, if Paris was on one level, an education in fine art, it was also a visual feast in other respects, especially for anyone with a taste for pop culture, which had always been an important aspect of Burra's aesthetic. The *folies* delighted him. Cognate with, but more elaborate than, English music-hall, they had a style all of their own: elaborate, spectacular and very expensive. By the mid-Twenties, the costume of the Parisian revue star had evolved into a bizarrely stylised, cut-away version of eighteenth-century court dress: a towering headdress crowning a slender, all-but-naked torso, and a paniered skirt with a sweeping train, cut away at the front so as to frame the legs; as drawn, for example, in 'R for Revue' in Burra's illustrations to Humbert Wolfe's *ABC of the Theatre*. One of Mistinguett's headdresses weighed more than fifteen pounds; another outfit had a twenty-one-foot ostrich-feather train. The star was set off by prancing lines of chorines and a flock of adoring young men. The Folies-Bergère had sixteen showgirls, ten boys and sixteen nudes, besides the English Tiller Girls who supplied the row of long, mechanically kicking legs that were an essential aspect of the whole phenomenon. It was a world of feathers, sequins and rhinestones, a glittering spectacle as magnificent as it was preposterous; it is not surprising that Burra couldn't resist it. On a later Paris trip, in May 1929, Burra went to the Folies so often that, as he comments, he found he was starting to recognise the chorus boys and girls if he saw them in the street.

In this, he was in touch with French avant-garde opinion. French intellectuals took the music-hall rather more seriously than did the English intelligentsia: there was more of a tradition of looking to popular culture to reinvigorate high art than there was in London, and also of overlap. Jean Cocteau, for one, argued for the music-hall, the circus and jazz as the most fertile of contemporary influences on art, music and literature alike; and emphasised this by himself creating a circus-ballet called *Le Boeuf sur le toit* in 1920. The Paris music-hall entered its golden age in the Twenties, with stars such as Mistinguett heading the bill.

But, even more importantly for Burra, he first visited Paris in the year of the arrival of the *Revue nègre*, starring Josephine Baker, at the Théâtre des Champs-Elysées. The first black jazz band arrived in Paris in 1917, brought by the music-hall star Gaby Deslys who had spent the initial years of the First World War in America, and provoked a wave of enthusiasm for *négritude* in avant-garde circles. Blaise Cendrars, for instance, wrote an *Anthologie nègre*, and Poulenc composed a *Rhapsodie nègre*. Caroline Dudley, a Chicago society woman who was the backer and organiser of the *Revue nègre*, was thus fairly sure by 1925 that it was worth bringing a whole show across.

In the late autumn, Paul Colin's poster was all over Paris. It showed two huge-lipped, caricature 'coons' framing a perkily posed, dinky little girl in a tiny white dress, giving small hint of what was in store. Nonetheless, jazz was fashionable, and when the Americans opened on 2 October, it was to a packed auditorium. 'Chic Paris had not turned out in such numbers for any performance since the Ballets Russes before the war.' Cocteau was there, and so was practically every opinion-former in the arts. The *Revue* was a smash. The run was extended and extended, and they eventually played through till December. It was the biggest aesthetic shock that Paris had had since Diaghilev, and as with the Russian ballet, the excitement was embodied, above all, in the person of its star.

The *Revue nègre* eventually went home, but Josephine Baker received an invitation to join the Folies-Bergère the next season as star of the show, an offer she accepted. She opened in *La Folie du jour* in 1926, appearing in a costume consisting only of a circle of plush bananas round her hips, a garment, if it can so be called, which was for ever after irretrievably associated with her, though she never wore it again. She had entered on her stupendous career as the black queen of Parisian revue, and did not return to America, even to visit, until 1935.

La Joséphine had an infectious grin, slicked-down patent-leather hair and a beautiful body, but it was the way she moved that electrified her Parisian audience. Unlike those of Nijinsky, some of Baker's perform-ances have been captured on film. This jerky antique footage reveals the dancer's consummate skill and artistry, the preternatural speed with which she could vibrate her buttocks, and the apparently boneless flex-ibility of her legs and torso, but cannot convey the effect that all this had on an audience of 1925. Josephine Baker doing the Charleston has the edgy quality of more modern street performance such as break-dancing: fast, reckless and apparently improvised, and to Paris, it was both alien and exciting. Her bottom, like Presley's pelvis thirty years later, was perceived as a menace to civilisation; and adored or execrated on that basis. To one commentator, there was 'a wild splendour and magnificent animality. Certain of Miss Baker's poses . . . had the compelling potency of the finest examples of Negro sculpture.' To another, sourer observer, the *Revue nègre* 'makes us revert to the ape in less time than it took us to descend from it.'

Burra, of course, was among the adorers; as were many contempo-rary artists and writers, notably Alexander Calder, who made a sculp-ture of her; Nancy Cunard, and e.e. cummings, who described her as a 'tall, vital, incomparably fluid nightmare'. Burra and Chappell were bowled over by the *Revue nègre*. It would have been a magnet for them in any case because of the music, but it turned out to be a revelation in other respects as well. Thereafter, Burra's work shows his fascination not only with black music, but with black visual aesthetics.

An interest in black culture was common among modernists, and surrealists in particular. Picasso, among others, had been turning to African art, particularly masks, for inspiration since the first decade of the century, and African motifs were strongly influential on Twenties Art Deco. But most contemporary commentators on Josephine Baker, and black art more generally, perceived it as interchangeably 'African' and 'naïve'; as if Baker's dancing, Gabon masks, jazz, Yoruba textiles (and indeed, child art) were all versions of the same thing. Harold Acton once overheard Nancy Cunard, who really should have known better, exhorting her lover Henry Crowder to 'be more *African*'. 'But I *ain't* African,' he protested, with remarkable restraint. 'I'm American.'

Burra's interest in black culture was not based on an illusion of primitivism of this kind. He thought he was looking at a distinctive sense of style and a way of inhabiting the landscape that was urban and American; it was inner-city chic, not imaginary jungle-drums that interested him. Later, he followed it home to Harlem; but in an early painting such as *Market Day* (1926), in which two tough-looking black sailors wearing blue jeans and reserved expressions shoulder their way through a largely black crowd, he shows that he did not need to go to New York to observe precisely what cool and street-smartness looked like. Burra collected postcards of Baker, of which there were many. Though he never drew or painted Baker as such, a picture of 1929, *The Tea Shop*, includes a waitress, nude but for high heels and a wreath of leaves round her hips, who has Baker's smile and hair, and moves like her – and her leaf-skirt is reminiscent of Baker's famous skirt of bananas. The basic concept of this picture may well have been suggested by an eight-minute comic film starring Baker, *Le Pompier des Folies-Bergères* (*The Fireman of the Folies-Bergère*) (1928), in which a drunken fireman in a café hallucinates that all the decorously clad women around him suddenly metamorphose into nude chorus girls.[5]

When Burra returned to Paris in January 1927 with Lucy Norton, they were unchaperoned and able to be a little more adventurous. From Lucy's point of view, going off with a male friend was a major step: having got there, she got cold feet, and worked herself into a state about the fact that she and Burra had rooms in the same hotel – 'You know what will people think when we live next door & Vanessa Bell sees me here and if ever Duncan came up what a tongue the creature has all Bloomsbury would

---

[5] Years later, in 1973, Burra wrote, 'I had another Fan letter from a lady at Lea on Sea who said shed never heard of me & knew nothing of "Fart" & had gone to the Tate & seen the show & she would never be able to enter a Tea shop again she was in fits over the Topless waitresses! . . . I have a very odd public I must say.'

know . . . in the evening we met Sophy Fedorovitch at the Select & when the reputation was mentioned she had a fit of giggles so I said I refuse to leave Paris New York so here I am and entend to remain.'

Even for Burra, it must have been important, since it was the first time he had really had to manage for himself for any length of time. The Hôtel Paris New York turned out to be a *maison de passe* – not a brothel, but a place where the management were indifferent to whether their clients occupied their rooms singly or not. The sounds of nocturnal merriment and slamming doors mystified Burra and Lucy, innocent as they were, until eventually the penny dropped. Burra considered it excellent value:

. . . you should see the suite I have run into for a mere 30 francs I have a lovely private lavabo wash basin and bath and a hall ¼ in by 2 ins also a sitting room with 2 beds in curtained alcove . . . unfortunately the lavabo door wont shut and swings open with a crash at the most inoportune moments however away with prudery I say, I never was prudish . . . Ive got a lovely view of the infants hospital from my casement my dear I can see full into the mortuary all the little coffins in rows decorated with sham wreaths made of tin makes your heart bleed to see them I don't wonder my suite was so cheap regular morgue I look out on.

Burra and Lucy were inevitably believed to be lovers. He wrote from the Café du Dôme, 'havent yet got over the looks the chamber maid gave me as she brought in the breakfast my dear as much as to say is she under the bed or in the wardrobe?' He rather enjoyed this, though it is clear that he was not to the slightest degree physically attracted to bossy and buxom Lucy. Billy, enduring an endless round of rehearsals at the time, wrote enviously in January, 'of <u>course</u> they think you and Lucy are lovers. Poor fools what imaginations they must have.' He added unkindly, 'Hold Lucy back from the patisseries, they have been the undoing of better women than she.'

Burra was unsuccessful in standing between Lucy and French gâteaux; his subsequent letters issue ironic regular reports on her frantic alternation between dieting and self-indulgence (she favoured that time-honoured method of dieting, having a virtuous salad, and then suddenly giving way and going on to devour all the things you wanted to eat in the first place).

Lucy had a job painting scenery for Bronislava Nijinska, so during the day she was kept busy, while Burra did his own work, but they spent their evenings in cafés, cinemas and dance-halls, sometimes together, sometimes apart. She had a great deal more energy than he did. 'Lucy went twice to Le Boeuf sur le Toit from all I could see of the place it ought to be called Les Vaches sous le toit . . . I did not go as I was feeling quite worn out & couldn't bear the thought of being up till 5 in the morning.' Apart from Lucy, Burra saw a good deal of Sophie Fedorovitch (who also became very friendly with Lucy herself), John Banting, Olivia Wyndham, and of two couples: Rupert Doone and Robert Medley, and Cedric Morris and Arthur Lett-Haines – he and Chappell had already met Morris and Lett (as the latter was known), in 1925. 'When we were in Paris with the Rushburys we saw dear Let dancing with Morris, did I say dancing more like rapine my dear such twists and turns and wriggling and writhing I never knew. Then danced with Billy and worked hard for a response but as he said afterwards to Birdie "the boy is no good"'.

Medley, Morris and Lett-Haines were all painters, though not in styles that would greatly have interested Burra. Rupert Doone, a dancer, had been the lover of Jean Cocteau in 1923, and appeared in Cocteau's *Roméo et Juliette*, though his uncontrollable temper led to his being dismissed from the company. He met Medley in 1926, and went back to Paris with him. This concatenation of talent increased Burra's involvement with the world of ballet, and also with that of overtly gay men; as he remarked to Bar, 'I am beginning to fear for my vertue here this place is so manly it quite reminds me of the days when me and Aunty Maisy had a little flat in Sodom.'[6]

It is also worth noticing that Doone gave Burra a link with Cocteau, with whom Burra had been very impressed since 1926, when *Parade*, the ballet that Cocteau and Picasso designed for Diaghilev, was revived in London, or even before. Writing to Chappell, he mentioned his admiration for Cocteau as an artist, and also for his involvement with music and poetry. Cocteau was also the instigator (though not the manager) of the nightclub Le Boeuf sur le Toit, spoken of in a 1925 guidebook as 'the work of Jean Cocteau, its godfather . . . at the Boeuf one encounters the artistic trend of the moment, the literary trend of the moment, and, briefly, the trend of the moment, whatever it may be'. Burra made

[6] 'Aunty Maisy' was a mythical personage, related to the Dilly Sisters of Burra's childhood, who appears as a running gag in many letters from 1925 to 1927, especially those exchanged between Burra and Bar. She was a fearsome hag with a complicated sex-life, who kept on having triplets.

a painting of it, one of his many paintings of *boîtes*, bars, pubs, cafés and dives in various parts of the world, a sort of homage.

Cocteau and Burra had a certain amount in common. Both had been delicate and precocious children who never really left home; both permitted a wealthy, haut-bourgeois parental lifestyle to give shape and context to their own plunges into anarchy. Both were intensely interested in popular arts such as the music-hall and the circus, and involved with integrating popular and high art. Cocteau's drawing, linear and precise, had a discernible influence on Burra's own. Causey comments, 'Perhaps more than any other single figure it was Cocteau who was responsible for Burra's change from the port scenes of the mid-twenties, which had been crowded to the point of confusion, to the elusive and decadent art he was practising by the end of the decade.'

One painting in which the various flavours that Burra was extracting from French culture come together is *Minuit Chanson* (1931). He wrote to Paul Nash:

my new occupation is going to the Boulevard Clichy to Minuit Chanson which is glorious. You put bits in the slot and listen to gramophone records. The clientele is enough to frighten you a bit what with listening with one ear and looking at the intrigues going on elsewhere. I quite forsake Montparnasse for the Place Pigalle. The people are glorious. Such tarts all crumbling and all sexes and colours.

The whole point of the Minuit Chanson was to pick up what was new and hot; Burra, presumably, was chasing jazz imports. His painting shows the customers wandering in and out, cheaply but fashionably dressed. The central figure is a black dude looking thoughtful, as if, perhaps, he is trying to remember the name of a song; other clientele include several tarty boys and girls, a sailor, and a figure whose deranged stare out of a cadaverous face strongly suggests James Joyce, doubtless intentionally: Joyce was a highly recognisable figure around Montparnasse, and Burra was well aware of *Ulysses*, though it seems that he didn't actually read it until many years later (he mentions having done so in a letter of 1945). But he admired Wyndham Lewis, who mocks Joyce (and Sylvia Beach) in *Childermass* (1929). Admiration or mockery, or both, might have led him to represent Joyce soaking up popular culture. Paris was the place where extremes met, after all. It became an essential recourse throughout his life.

V

ART AND CRAFT

BURRA'S technique was markedly idiosyncratic; his chosen medium, watercolour, was unfashionable. How was he to establish himself as a professional artist? The Wall Street Crash brought in the Great Depression in 1929, when Burra was twenty-four. Life is seldom easy for highly original painters, but it was a particularly tough time in which to launch oneself on a career as a producer of luxury items.

In the late nineteenth century, the most successful English contemporary artists were extraordinarily well rewarded. G.F. Watts and William Holman Hunt could demand more than £5,000 for new work (at a time when an early Renaissance painting could be bought for £100). After the First World War, that massive nineteenth-century confidence in the value of the contemporary evaporated. Artists who were members of the Royal Academy, such as Augustus John, still made money, though nothing like as much, but as Paul Nash pointed out, 'Art' as defined by the Royal Academy and 'Modern Art' inhabited different conceptual spaces in the public mind.

Modern Art was a singularly ill-rewarded activity, and Burra's instincts, subject matter, associates and style all put him in the modernist camp, which was no easy option. Modernism sat uneasily with the strongly established English tendency to respect tradition and, domestically, to enjoy antique furniture, old rugs and old pictures. It is taken for granted now that a mix of old and new in interior decoration is perfectly acceptable, but it took some time for this principle to become established: Osbert Lancaster dates the eclectic style which he identifies as 'Vogue Regency' to the late Thirties (Colefax and Fowler, perhaps its leading proponent, was founded in 1934). Before then, modern art was seldom seen outside modernist interiors, of which there were relatively few. Nash himself, in a moment of depression, moaned, 'Boy, it's tough to be Modern!'

From Burra's point of view, the art world existed entirely in London. There was a separate involvement with, and a surprisingly vigorous market for, avant-garde art in Glasgow and Edinburgh (more so than in contemporary England), but the English and Scottish art establishments did not really intercommunicate, let alone make common cause. Despite his family's Scottish connections, he had nothing to do with it. And within England, modernism was metropolitan.

One of the crucial reference points and hang-outs for young English artists interwar was a commercial bookshop: Zwemmer's on Charing Cross Road, a dismally ugly thoroughfare which forms an axis between the British Museum in Bloomsbury and the National Gallery in Trafalgar Square and was the centre of the London book-trade in the Twenties and Thirties. Its residential tenements, with retail units on the ground floor, sold 'highbrow culture and lowbrow sex . . . the most polymorphously perversely human, humane, humanist area of London'.

The biggest of the Charing Cross Road bookshops was Foyle's, but most of its shops were small independent concerns. Marks & Co., at no. 84, celebrated by Helene Hanff, was one such. There were several shops dealing in stock of special interest to Burra, such as no. 75, where from 1910 onwards Cyril Beaumont sold books on the ballet. Another concern which might have attracted him, since he was a reader of *The Anarchist*, was the Bomb Shop, no. 66, owned by the embattled F.R. Henderson.

Henderson was short, rotund, brusque in manner, with bristling white hair, pointed beard and scarlet tie; his was the only socialist bookshop in the West End. An open-style shop – unusual then – it had been designed and decorated in red and gold and emblazoned with the names of past rebels, by socialist painter Walter Crane. Its defiant name, red doors and window frames, and display of socialist and anarchist publications, incited upper-class louts and their toadies to heave an occasional brick through the full-length plate glass door and windows, to daub blue and white paint on to the red, and sometimes to break in at night and wreck the interior.

Another reason why Henderson's stock might have interested Burra is that he was connected with the Vorticists before the First World War, and in 1919 published David Bomberg's book of lithographs, *Russian Ballet*.

However, the most important establishment on Charing Cross Road for Burra, as for British artists generally, was Zwemmer's at no. 78. The original shop was founded before the war by Richard Jäschke, who was more a scholar than a businessman, as an outlet for foreign books. A German by birth, he found himself awkwardly positioned during the First World War, since he had rashly taken a fourteen-year lease on his premises in 1915. Afraid that his business would go to rack and ruin if he was interned as an enemy alien, he hired an ambitious young Dutchman, Anton Zwemmer (the Netherlands were neutral) as his manager in 1916. Jäschke was indeed interned, but in his absence Zwemmer made good, and Jäschke, even after his release, was happy to leave the principal responsibility in his hands. Zwemmer bought Jäschke out, by mutual agreement, in 1923.

Zwemmer did not share Jäschke's linguistic interests: subtly, the stock began to change. The shop remained somewhere to go for foreign books, but in Zwemmer's hands, the focus was increasingly on art. Roger Fry's post-Impressionist exhibitions of 1910 and 1912 created considerable interest in modern art among the educated, but thereafter, due to the First World War, information became hard to come by. Edwardian London was less philistine than it is sometimes represented as, but the press remained stiffly conservative, and created what amounted to an information blackout. The directors of the Leicester Galleries identified this as a serious problem in a discussion which they initiated in the *Morning Post* in 1921.

The determined neglect of modern art on the part of the daily press in recent years is one of the greatest difficulties that artists have to contend with.

Nash, similarly, complained in the *Week-End Review* of 'the gradual dwindling of interest in all matters known as "art", as shown by the English daily Press'.

Zwemmer's singular contribution to English culture was that he had faith that a public for reading and learning about modern art *was* out there, a faith that, it turned out, was amply justified. Hard-headed man of business though he was, he was extremely tolerant of youthful would-be customers who browsed for hours, getting their education standing up, reading books they could not afford to buy: 'that liberty to browse along the shelves which is still the only way to teach oneself the history of art'.

Every aspiring young artist learned his trade by propping up the bookshelves in Mr Zwemmer's shop in the Charing Cross Road. It was the centre for the dispersal of artistic fashion.

The other area where Zwemmer's was unique was in the breadth of its stock of high-quality reproductions, which made his shop a principal conduit for foreign influence on British artists. This was immensely important to Burra, who, for a dedicated modernist, was unusually interested in the art of the past. John Rothenstein, who visited his studio, testified to the vast numbers of 'paintings by Tiepolo, Signorelli, Magnasco and the Spanish masters' that Burra had lying about, or pinned to the walls – the bulk of these prints would have come from Zwemmer's. The shop also stocked foreign art journals – by 1936, Zwemmer advertised subscriptions to eleven English, eleven French, thirteen German, four Italian, two Austrian and two Dutch magazines, forty-three in all, and actively promoted the magazines that he handled. Burra browsed these also. The shop had a special atmosphere, recalled by Nigel Halliday:

No. 78 Charing Cross Road was small and the air was touched with the distinctive smell of concentrated books, which seemed to fill every available space. Bookcases lined the walls, and others were freestanding on the shop floor. Glass-topped display cabinets contained the more valuable or delicate items, while a table by the till displayed the latest foreign magazines. Partly because of its limited size, Zwemmer's always seemed to be full. This added to the feeling of the shop as a popular attraction . . . a considerable amount of stock, particularly second-hand, was therefore consigned to the cellar.

The interactiveness of book-selling, publishing and picture-dealing is a strong feature of the interwar arts scene. Zwemmer distributed Wyndham Lewis's writings, but also dealt in his paintings and manuscripts. Galleries such as the Adelphi published artists' works, and so did at least one of Zwemmer's neighbours, Henderson of the Bomb Shop. Conversely, Zwemmer's was invited to provide a bookstall at the notorious *International Surrealist Exhibition* of 1936 in the New Burlington Galleries in London, and published the resulting *Bulletin*.

Painters inform themselves by buying art books and periodicals as well as by looking at paintings, but they also need to sell. Galleries are the essential interface between artists and their clients, and the galleries that were prepared to present modern art to potential buyers were a relatively small group in the Twenties. The Leicester Galleries and the Independent Gallery were among the first actively to promote modern European art. The Leicester, under the guidance of Oliver Brown, mounted London's first one-man exhibition of Matisse in 1919, and of Picasso in 1921, showed Cézanne in 1925 and Van Gogh the following year. What was more to the point, as the Twenties progressed, they began showing English painters as well.

Zwemmer opened a gallery of his own in 1929, which brought in work by foreign artists, but also mounted shows by English modernists. Another very important venue for English artists was the Mayor Gallery. Freddy Mayor was a pivotal figure in the battle to get modern art onto upper-class English walls. He was a man who knew everybody, 'not only in the artistic world but also among the young socialites of the day, and was a highly amusing adjunct to any house party'. He opened his first gallery in January 1925 and in that year showed English paintings by Paul Nash, Mark Gertler and William Roberts. The Mayor Gallery became the home for Unit One, which will be discussed later. Wyndham Lewis wrote to Zwemmer as late as 1935, 'Yours and the Mayor Gallery [are] the only two places where the more radical forms of experiment are consistently encouraged.'

Other galleries that were supporting the cause of English modernism when Burra was coming to maturity were the Adelphi, opened by the art critic Frank Rutter in 1919, which showed British modernists such as David Bomberg, Edward Wadsworth and Ben Nicholson; the Redfern Gallery, run by Rex Nan Kivell; and the Warren Gallery. Dorothy Warren was remarkably adventurous – one of her exhibitions of 1928 was of the paintings of Stanley Spencer's *femme fatale*, Patricia Preece, and her lover Dorothy Hepworth, and the following year she caused a furore by exhibiting D.H. Lawrence's erotic watercolours.

The Lefevre Gallery, then in King Street, St James's, and Arthur Tooth & Sons in New Bond Street were established dealers who were also involved with the selling of modern art. Both, however, were international businesses with offices in Paris and New York, and therefore relatively conservative. They went where the visionaries had demonstrated that the market already existed: when modernists started to sell, they picked up on the trend.

By the time he was twenty-one, Burra was trying to define himself as an artist. The Chelsea College of Art aimed at producing professionals; people with a clear sense of the commercial value of their work. Happily, he was not in the position of having to starve for his art. His money was jealously hoarded to pay for the things he really cared about: books, paint and paper and, above all, travel. He was supposed to dress himself out of his allowance, and although in his teens he had been a dandy, as a young adult he owned almost no clothes. He badly wanted to earn. The first thing he needed, therefore, was for a gallery to take a chance on him.

Burra's first commission was from Birdie Rushbury, a watercolour called *Hop-pickers who have lost their mothers*, for which she paid him fifteen shillings and sixpence.[1] His first public debut, however, was in a show of the work of students from the Royal College of Art at Rex Nan Kivell's Redfern Gallery in 1924: an anonymous reviewer, in a newspaper clipping in one of Burra's scrapbooks (from an unidentified paper), took note of 'decorations with a Mexican flavour by Mr E. Burra'. He even sold something, since he complained in a subsequent letter to Birdie that it was a very long time before he got his money, and also about his unwelcome discovery that commercial galleries take a commission.

His first really significant appearance was three years later, in December 1927, at the New English Art Club. This was probably the result of pressure on the Club from Paul Nash, who had been showing there since about 1911, since 'New' was something of a misnomer by 1927. The Club had been founded by the Young Turks of 1886 to defend Impressionism against the fuddy-duddies of the Royal Academy. The most significant artists to exhibit there in Burra's time were Augustus John and Stanley Spencer.

In any case, the Club accepted pictures from both Burra and Bumble. Though she subsequently took another direction, Bumble was the most able and serious painter among the friends, after Burra himself. She

[1] It was last sold by Sotheby's (Hong Kong) for £74,000 on 2 June 2004.

received the accolade of being admitted by Henry Tonks into his painting class at the Slade, and he thought very well of the work she did for him. Burra found his first experience of proper exhibiting somewhat deflating.

Bumble and me had such a time leaving our pictures at the New English we roamed about in a thick fog and finaly arrived at what looked like a charming new block of residential flats in course of erection a creature flew out and shouted out 'pictures' in a furious voice so we said yes and he grabbed our pictures and stuck them against some scaffolding so by now they are built into the wall securely I should say never to be discovered till 1999 I havent heard a word about mine so I fear the worst.

However, the exhibition was not unimportant. Another of Burra's supporters, Hugh Blaker, wrote a letter of encouragement in January 1928: 'You are not forgotten! Brown & Phillips of the Leicester Galleries are only waiting a vacant date. They like your work in the N.E.A.C. very much.'[2]

Another thing that this initial exposure reveals is the senior Burras' fierce pride in their son, which helps to explain why they put up with so much from him. He was too bashful to go to the private view, but 'Mother and Father went & Mother said "yours killed all the other water colours so they hung it in the roof and all you could see was feet".' Years later, when the Aikens organised a summer exhibition at Rye for various artist friends in the working men's club next door to Jeakes' House, 'Mrs Burra took umbrage at the gallery director for refusing to put her son's sixth painting in the balcony, a Laura Knight watercolour preempting it . . . as Ed's mother struck off Laura's name, her husband announced loud and clear, "I really detest some of her work," then smirked, saying blandly to me, "I hope you haven't been listening, Mrs Aiken."' As the account makes clear, Clarissa Aiken disliked all three Burras, and was personally fond of Laura Knight, whom she admired, but what comes through her anecdote above all is the parents' protectiveness and loyalty.

[2] Hugh Blaker, painter, curator and dealer, was an indefatigable supporter of avant-garde young artists: he bought three of Burra's paintings in 1927, and tried to interest the Leicester Galleries in his work.

At the same time as he was exhibiting at the New English, Burra was becoming guardedly hopeful that he might have an exhibition of his own:

A strange old person called Mrs Dew Smith who knows dear Dotty Warren said to me not long ago you know I realy think you ought to have a show at Miss Warrens Galleries she is so interested in young artistes so I ses there are young artistes and young artistes and I am one of the other artistes, my dear it seems Dew S saw Dot the other day and said I know such a clever young artiste named Edward Burra do you know anything of him. 'Ive heard a great deal about Edward Burra' says Dot & what she has heard I should very much like to know.

Nothing actually came of this, perhaps because Oliver Brown at the Leicester already had him under consideration; Burra complained, 'My pics may be shown to Dottie when I have got them out of the Leicester Gallerys clutches Im sure they must have been mouldering there at least 6 weeks.' It was very wearing from Burra's point of view: Hugh Blaker had introduced him to the Leicester in August 1927, and yet the months were drifting by as if nobody thought it mattered.

Rex Nan Kivell was also showing renewed interest in Burra by the autumn of 1928. 'If the Leicester galleries dont like my interesting little drawings,' Burra wrote to Nash, 'Basil [Taylor] tells me the Redfern galleries would like to see them, so I have 2 strings to my bow one string is not quite such a string as the other string but you cant have everything.' Paul Nash also put Burra in contact with Freddy Mayor, who took some paintings and exhibited them in mixed shows, where they didn't sell.

As it turned out, Oliver Brown at the Leicester was the first person to make a real commitment to Burra's work. 'My dear,' Burra wrote excitedly to Bar from Paris in October 1928 (fifteen months after the initial contact), 'what do you think arrived on Saterday a great typewritten letter from the Leicester Galleries saying "Paul Nash tells me you have some more interesting drawings, I should like to see them soon, as we might be able to show them in the course of a few months."'

Both Hugh Blaker (who subsequently wrote the catalogue essay) and Henry Rushbury were involved in talking up Burra to the Leicester, but it was Nash who did the negotiating. It was also Nash and not Burra who worried about the details, after Burra was accepted. 'I am doing a show with "Ethelbert W a modern landscape painter" as Mr B[rown] put it in a letter so theres a treat Paul asked B about it and B said well we couldn't put him with Henry Lamb as the people coming to see Henry L would all be carried off rigid & doubled with a stricture at the sight of my frivolitys.' The show finally went up in April 1929, without the support of either Ethelbert White or Henry Lamb, and did very well for a debut. The Leicester shifted a total of fourteen of Burra's thirty-three pictures and drawings, at prices ranging from £10.10.0 to £26.5.0,[3] and the total came to £228.18.0, which meant that minus the gallery's third, and the framing and mounting costs (which are carried by the artist), Burra got £144.7.0, which was encouraging, at least, though as his major earning for that year, it suggested he had some way to go if he was to consider himself a professional artist. On the other hand, a *Portrait* he sold that summer through the Rye Art Club made, in that amateur context, all of three guineas. He needed a gallery.

Burra was happy to consider anything at that point that would help to establish him as a professional artist. 'Lucy [Norton] was so charming & said Someone asked me for a list of the best English illustrators so I gave your name in. I know you havent done any illustrations but you can send some of your drawings & pretend they belong to books.' He was at a loss how to start selling. 'Its awful the poverty that strikes everyone when they see my work.' When he exhibited with the London Group (a cooperative society of modernist artists, founded in 1915) in October of the same year, someone offered him twelve guineas for an oil painting called *Grog*, now lost, or unidentifiable as such.

I wrote back and said 15 gns was the lowest I could consider well they wrote back & said (through Miss Brinton sec) I am afraid I cannot spend more than 12 gins at present but hope Mr Burra will make it possible for me to possess one of his works . . . I just wrote back to Brinton to say yes after all 12 gins is better than nothing about £9–10s that is deducting frame & percentage. Mr Brown [of the Leicester] would have a fit if he knew but Ill do anything for money.

---

[3] Pictures were priced in guineas – that is, units of £1 1s.

However, for all his interest in money, his notions about it were primitive. He was cautious about spending because he never really grasped the idea of money, and only believed in the stuff if he could see it. Once it had vanished into a bank, it had vanished, as far as he was concerned. Chappell said much later: '[He] only really understood cash. He much preferred the idea of £100 in crisp bank notes to a far larger sum in the form of a cheque. He had no belief in banks, bank statements, deposit accounts or cheques. As far as he was concerned, they were all abstractions.' This was confirmed by Barbara Roett, who knew him in the last twenty years of his life and told me, 'Ed was very unrealistic about money. Anyone who offered him a tenner could have anything.' Even late in life, he still liked cash; when he was knocked over, dead drunk, in 1974, he turned out to have £1,900 on him in twenty-pound notes.

Part of the legend of Burra is that he was reclusive, allergic to publicity and indifferent to his commercial standing. This goes back to John Rothenstein's book: 'He is as nearly indifferent as an artist can reasonably be to the public's opinion of his work. This indifference is due, I believe, not to any sense of superiority, but to the realisation that, on account of the frailty of his health, his strength is barely sufficient for him to do his work, and he has no superabundance to spare for the politics of art, or for dispensable personal relations.' There is certainly a sort of truth here. Burra did have to husband his strength. However, far from being reclusive, as several of his friends pointed out again and again, he was highly social, though only within certain parameters.

Another part of the story is that he never went to his own private views. But Burra did in fact go to the private view of his first one-man exhibition at the Leicester, since his diary entry for 10 April runs: 'Went to private view which was so gay had tea with Lucy Paul & M at Gunters'.[4] However, he seems never to have done it again. The problem was probably that private views were particularly acute versions of a type of social occasion he had trouble with at any time. He liked talking with old friends, and he liked talking to total strangers. But he had a lifelong problem with the middle ground; that is, talking to people who knew who he was, but only in a superficial way, and who consequently

---

[4] Gunter's was an extremely elegant tea-shop in Berkeley Square, which had been there since the end of the eighteenth century and was famous for its ice-cream.

asked superficial questions. Thus he never much enjoyed parties, and came actively to detest them. The prospect of being asked again and again, 'How do you get your ideas?', 'Why do you paint such strange things?' was more than he could stand.

Another legend for which Rothenstein is responsible is that Burra's pictures didn't have names, only arbitrary labels, since Burra told him as much. 'He did not give them titles until their exhibition was planned. "Then somebody comes along, stamps them with my signature with a rubber stamp, and presses me to invent titles for them."' The truth is stranger than that, and reveals Burra's determined defence of his privacy. His pocket diaries make it clear that pictures might well have names from the beginning (his diary entry for 22 May 1929 is 'Started Dollys Party'), but he didn't tell anyone what they were. They went on exhibition with made-up names: thus he deliberately withheld an important clue to his own sense of what his work was about.

It would certainly be a mistake to assume with Rothenstein that this 'indifference', or rather Burra's refusal to come out and meet the buying public, meant that he was not interested in selling his work. His letters reveal that he was keenly interested, but ineffectual. When he went to Charlestown to stay with the Aikens in 1937, he took twenty-five finished pictures with him. 'We've got fifteen of them up in our queer cellar-salon,' Aiken wrote, 'and thanks to a judicious gossip-campaign, People of Importance have been coming to see them. We hope to sell some of them, and also to move the whole lot into Boston presently for a real show at a real gallery.' In this they were successful; Burra subsequently had a one-man show at the Springfield Museum of Art, Massachusetts, in May, and sold several paintings as a result.

At Chelsea, Burra had studied illustration as well as drawing, and he made repeated, unsuccessful attempts to establish himself as a commercial artist, which probably failed because he found it hard to stay within the parameters of a commission, and 'not liking being told what to think' could be a problem. As early as December 1927 he writes, 'I'me so busy doing a cover design for The Buggers own Bumper Joybook . . .' Given the way Burra writes, this appellation could cover just about anything, but there is a meticulously executed single black-and-white illustration for Ronald Firbank's *Concerning the Eccentricities of Cardinal Pirelli* from around then; an illustration to the book as a whole rather than to any particular episode. *Pirelli*,

Firbank's last book, was privately published in 1926, and then by Duckworth in London in 1929 as part of their limited, special first collected edition. Burra read *Pirelli* in December 1927 and enjoyed it immensely, but this is the only occasion on which he responded to an author he liked by producing a highly finished drawing. However, if Gerald Duckworth commissioned the drawing as a book-jacket, it was evidently not bought or used (the jacket that was used was plain dark-blue paper with a border). It was perverse of Burra to put a minor character, La Adonira, a matador's mistress, centre-stage and to consign the Cardinal to the background. In 1931, Paul Nash proposed to Cassell (the publisher) that Burra illustrate a de luxe edition of Conrad Aiken's long poem *John Deth*, which resulted in a remarkable watercolour (a response to, rather than an illustration of, *John Deth*), but the project did not come off because of the Depression.

Burra went on to do further commercial work – much more than might appear, since much of it went unused. As early as 1922 he designed a poster for the Olympia Horse Show, and in 1928 he was commissioned by Crawfords to do advertising designs for motor-cars, which were ultimately rejected, partly because he drew the wrong sort of wheels. He made advertising designs both for Shell-Mex and for London Transport in 1934, which again went unused, though both companies were unusually committed to using noted contemporary artists as designers, and were happy to accept highly idiosyncratic work. It is not clear what went wrong. Jack Beddington, the advertising manager of Shell, commissioned artwork from many avant-garde English artists, including Burra's Unit One co-workers Paul Nash, John Armstrong and Tristram Hillier, thus, in turning their lorries into mobile art galleries, firmly associating themselves with modernity.

Similarly, the visionary Frank Pick, the traffic development officer for the new London Underground, was passionately committed to the principle of the civilising effects of good design. He not only made the Underground's visual presence in London, from lettering to architecture, a splendid affirmation of modern-movement principles, but decided to use the Underground as, literally, a platform for bringing art to the people, and commissioned both extensively and intelligently (a commitment which London Transport, unlike Shell, maintains to this day). Burra, it is clear, approached LT, and not vice versa. A friendly note survives, from the publicity officer: 'Thank you for your postcard.

I shall be glad to have a talk when you are back in England. Would you send me a card when you are ready to come along?'

Burra's design for the Underground was related to Covent Garden, and featured both the then-characteristic sight of a market porter with a stack of wicker baskets on his head, juxtaposed with an advancing corps de ballet, associating the two principal attractions of the area. It is hard to see why this was rejected (which it apparently was, since the original artwork remained in Burra's possession); the design is charming. There is no surviving trace of his work for Shell.

Paul Nash also talked a textile firm (perhaps his own principal textile client, Cresta Silks, run by Tom Heron) into giving Burra some work: he wrote in 1933, when Burra was in America, 'the textile merchants have agreed to pay you £10 but want your Pimento design in exchange. I have it here but its not finished; shall I say you will finish it for them when you get back?' This seems to have been Burra's only venture into this area of design work.

A letter from the Beauty Editor of *Vogue*, which Burra kept, suggests that he also considered working for them – he was, of course, immensely interested in clothes, though his satirical impulse militated against successful fashion work: 'We are going to have a little exhibition here of the work of artists and photographers who might do work for *Vogue*,' the Beauty Editor wrote. 'Mrs Garland has suggested your name and I am wondering whether you would care to let us have some specimens for the Editor and other heads of departments to see. The exhibition will not be held till after May 20th and we should only need to have your exhibits for a day or two, when they will be returned to you safely.'[5] Madge Garland may first have heard of him via Lucy Norton, who was friendly with her: she spent her summer holiday in 1927 at Varengeville in Normandy with Garland and her lover, Dody Todd, who edited British *Vogue*. Similarly, Marty Mann tried to interest Condé Nast in Burra's work, without success. Typically, when she reported her failure, his response was, 'You may keep the drawings if you want them dearie.'

A certain amount of his book illustration did actually reach print throughout his career. The first actually known to have been used is one in which artwork and text have equal status, Humbert Woolf's *ABC of the Theatre* (published by Denis Cohen's Cresset Press in 1932).

[5] Madge Garland, fashion journalist, writer and teacher.

These illustrations are a set of sophisticated caricatures of theatre personalities with large heads and small bodies (the tradition in which David Levine now works), and they reveal that Burra, when he wished, could achieve an extraordinarily effective likeness.

He produced a frontispiece illustration at the request of his friend Desmond Ryan for a sub-Pope invective by Anthony Powell, which was printed by Ryan (who, Powell says somewhat darkly, 'possessed control over a small printing press') as a wedding-present in 1934. Burra's own contribution is less in the spirit of Pope than of Ronald Searle. According to David Gascoyne, Burra also had a Firbank commission from Desmond Ryan, who wanted to bring out a limited edition of *The Artificial Princess*, illustrated by Burra. This was a book that Firbank had not published in his lifetime, but which survived in a publishable form. Unfortunately, this project seems to have been pre-empted. It was the Centaur Press that brought out a limited edition (in 1934), illustrated not by Burra, but with three semi-erotic plates after drawings by Hugh Easton. According to the agreement between Duckworth and the Centaur Press, the latter's sixty-copy edition was to be issued subsequent to Duckworth's trade edition, which it was, just: both were published in May 1934, a few days apart. Between them, they presumably put a firm stopper on Ryan's endeavour.

Another illustration project that went adrift was a design for the jacket of Salvador de Madariaga's *Heart of Jade*, which occupied him in December 1942, and was again not used, which did not surprise him: 'It remains to be seen chicks if they take anything *I* do I cant believe they will I always seem to <u>frighten</u> people . . . need I tell you my Jade wasn't quite "the thing" so Ime getting 3 gins [guineas] I quite well knew from the first what would happen. I never can think what makes them try in the first place.' Nash wrote to him about this, in terms which suggest that even as late as the Forties he continued to act as Burra's adviser on professional issues. 'I'm terribly shocked to hear about the foul behaviour of Collins don't tell me they got out of paying for the "roughs" because they just cant get away with that. I'd love to see the designs don't you think someone else could use them?'

However, Burra did get a few illustrations published in the Forties: a colour-lithograph frontispiece for C.F. Ramuz's *The Triumph of Death*, which Routledge published in 1946 (though the seven additional illustrations that he also produced were not used), and in 1948 cover art for

Poe's *The Tell-Tale Heart*, and a series of drawings in Laurie Lee's *The Voyage of Magellan*, both published by John Lehmann (who also published some Burra drawings in his *Penguin New Writing* series in 1947).

In the same year, Burra undertook his biggest illustrations commission for Paul Elek, a popular edition of Mark Twain's *Huckleberry Finn*. This was a more successful series of drawings, though Burra always had difficulty in subordinating his own concepts to those of an author (and, he remembered resentfully, he had trouble in getting paid: it was one of the occasions where he did his own negotiating, and came bitterly to regret it, since he forgot to sort out the ultimate ownership of the drawings). His last-known work in this field was for the *Oxford Illustrated Old Testament* in 1966: his Judith drawing was published, but his work on Daniel and Zachariah never appeared, because he lost it.

I also heard a plaint from the Oxford Press about illustrations to Zachariah & Daniel or the seven deadly children which, as I hadnt heard a word for months I thought they didn't want. (they took the ones I did for Judith & payd me for them) of course I couldn't find the drawings for Z & D Ide done. I realy thought Ide go off my head & began tearing about in heaps of rubbish. Finaly I ran them to earth in my bedroom under a pile of old shirts & sweaters that hadn't been moved for I don't know how long realy by the special intervention of the 7 deadly children otherwise they would have been there another 6 months.

The 'three holy children' did not intervene soon enough: it was too late for the drawings to be used.[6]

The idea, often repeated by journalists, that Burra was ignored by the art world because he was reclusive and eccentric is hard to substantiate. His work was shown on at least fifty separate occasions during his lifetime: twenty-five times in one-man exhibitions, mostly in London, but also in Manchester, Hamburg, Paris and Amsterdam; and in America, in New York, Springfield, Massachusetts, Boston and Providence, Rhode Island. It was exhibited in some of the prestigious private galleries in London: the Leicester, the Redfern, Zwemmer's, the Lefevre, the Mayor and Arthur Tooth & Sons, as well as by the Arts Council, the Tate and

---

[6] His Bible drawings are reproduced in the Sotheby's *Works from the Estate of Edward Burra* catalogue (2002), labelled 'Costume Sketches for "Miracle in the Gorbals"', which would have made him laugh.

the Hayward. There have been more than a dozen exhibitions since his death.

Rothenstein's 1945 Penguin states, 'from time to time he contributes (generally under mild protest) to exhibitions, and he has held three one-man shows . . .' But this exposure was certainly not happening without Burra's cooperation, let alone his knowledge and consent, in the way that Rothenstein implies. For example, Burra actively tried to establish his own presence in America, without success, on his first visit, in 1933:

Have been to 2 gallerys – Levys – I was too 'literary' in subject dearie Constance [Askew] said if only youd come from across the channel it would have been quite a different story however Levy gave me an intro to John Becker (Beckers Gallery) and he likes them very much and said I should redecorate the new Bar at the Yale Club I feel everyone will get up and say it ought to be an ammerican artist to do a job like that.

'Levys' is the Julien Levy Gallery, 602 Park Avenue, then the most influential modernist gallery in New York; Levy put on the first surrealist exhibition America had seen, in 1932. The shows that went up in 1933 were of works by Lee Miller, Mina Loy, Pavel Tchelitchew, Henri Cartier-Bresson, Serge Lifar's Russian Ballet collection and Salvador Dalí; all either home-grown talent or substantially formed by Paris. There is real point to Mrs Askew's comment. Similarly, nothing seems to have come of the contact with Becker's, who were, then as now, at 520 Madison Avenue. Burra's first American break came when he impressed Alfred Barr of the Museum of Modern Art in New York, and his work was included in the *Fantastic Art, Dada, Surrealism* exhibition of 1936, following on which he had a one-man show in May 1937 at the Springfield Museum of Art, Massachusetts. Back in England, in 1935, he was in dialogue with the Brook Street Art Gallery, though again to no effect.

It is worth asking how well John Rothenstein understood Burra. He admired him enormously; he was Burra's indefatigable champion, bought his work for the Tate, wrote the catalogue essay for Burra's retrospective, and did more to establish his reputation than anybody. But the portrait that he draws in the Penguin Modern Painters *Edward Burra* and recycles in the Tate retrospective catalogue is a curious one. It is as if Rothenstein is selective about the aspects of Burra that he wishes to see. The reader is told that Burra's favourite composer is Berlioz; though his friends are unanimous that he listened to almost nothing but imported jazz and other forms of pop music (and the classical music concerts he chose to attend and noted in his diary suggest that Verdi and Emmanuel Chabrier were his favourite classical composers). Burra himself had mixed feelings about Rothenstein; he was conscious of how much he owed him, but embarrassed by his earnestness, and perhaps also by his imperceptiveness. Later in life, he often referred to Rothenstein as 'the nutty professor', but on one occasion added, 'I know Ime very ungrateful.'

Rothenstein writes of Burra's debts to a variety of painters, but does not mention that his workroom was littered with copies of *Photoplay* and postcards of Josephine Baker and the Dolly Sisters. His perception that Burra was indifferent to selling his work may well be similarly obtuse. The buttoned-up, upper-middle-class aspect of Burra's personality may have made him reluctant to discuss his professional aspirations with Rothenstein, but inarticulacy does not imply indifference. Talking to close friends such as the Aikens or Bar, he reveals a quite different attitude. It is perfectly clear that he was eager to sell his work, though Rothenstein is right to say that he was not often concerned about what art critics had to say about it (but he could be hurt by them: he was particularly thin-skinned about anyone representing him as 'a disabled painter').

As must already be clear, the most crucial single individual in the early days of Burra's establishing himself commercially was Paul Nash, whom he met in the summer of 1925, when he was twenty. Nash was sixteen years Burra's senior, an interesting difference of age – half a generation – which often permits tranquil and productive friendships, or support without rivalry. Though their art had relatively little in common, Burra admired Nash and respected him. He trusted Nash as a mentor at the time when he was finding his feet in the professional art world; relied on him to make the contact with gallery-owners which he was too bashful to do himself; and even took Nash's advice when it was offered.

For example, he let Nash talk him into learning how to make woodcuts. This was potentially a very useful skill, especially for a young artist with a training in book-illustration. One purely practical aspect of print-making is that it enables a painter to extend his market downwards and sell some modestly priced work without compromising the amount charged for originals. Mastery of block-cutting also opens up new possibilities for hand-press book-illustration commissions. Nash, who had been working on wood for ten years and was a member of the Society of Wood-Engravers, offered to teach Burra how to do it in February 1928.

While he was concerned to help Burra develop his place in the market, Nash was also interested in developing his art. Nash himself was an awkward painter with rather limited technical skill; he distrusted painterliness, which Burra loved; Burra commented (with respect to Banting's views, though it also applies to Nash), 'you mustnt enjoy the actual peenting of the peenting one <u>bit</u> none of that morbid delectation in pigment'.

To Nash, Burra's apparently effortless fluency was suspect, a sort of rhetorical glibness. Speaking of woodcuts, he used the revealing phrase 'the dangerous seduction of skilfulness'. He may have hoped that Burra, working in a slower, more recalcitrant medium, would focus his attention more on the formal aspects of design which interested Nash himself, and on what he was trying to communicate, rather than on the beguiling surface.

Burra's nine prentice pieces are charming, but they are basically line drawings in negative: only *Cup Bearer* shows any sign that he was starting to grapple with the particular problem of an effective woodcut, which is balancing white and black. It cannot be said that either of Nash's aims was achieved, and the experience was not repeated. Cutting blocks was completely unsuitable for Burra's delicate, strengthless hands. Wood-engraving does not need a great deal of physical force, but the right hand has to hold the graver locked in place, while the left manipulates the block. A technical manual advises:

The tool has to be held in such a way that none of the fingers nor the thumb is underneath it. The handle rests in the lower part of the hand, the fourth finger in the groove of the inner part of the handle and the third finger by its side; these two fingers touch the handle and keep it in position within the hand. Following the third and fourth, the two forefingers rest on the outer side of the blade while the thumb, extending beyond the fingers almost to the point, is on the inside. The thumb is the only part of the right hand that touches the block.

The position would not have been easy for Burra's warped fingers to sustain, even in his twenties. Another problem, as Bar observed affectionately, was scale. 'I'm sure nothing short of dragging the front door off its hinges will provide a large enough block for your sort of picture.'

The few woodcuts he achieved were exhibited at the 1929 Society of Wood-Engravers' exhibition at the Redfern Gallery. They had attracted the attention of Robert Gibbings of the Golden Cockerel Press, probably thanks to Nash, who had liked them enough to show them to the Director of the Redfern, Rex Nan Kivell. Gibbings, a producer of fine illustrated books, evidently thought Burra a talent worth encouraging, so he might indeed have developed commercially in that direction if his hands had let him. Nan Kivell also thought enough of the woodcuts to hang on to a set for himself.

Even though the engraving experiment turned out to be a mild fiasco, Burra and Nash worked together on collages at the end of the Twenties (for example, the joint work *Rough on Rats*), which, since the choice of images was associative, was a favourite game among the surrealists. 'We never bother to paint in this part now we just stick on things instead,' Burra wrote to Bar in 1929. 'I have such a twee one started of 2 ladys walking along with pieces of motor engine for heads & a table at the side made of anita paiges legs with a drawn in top and a dishful of heads reposing on it its fascinating' (it ended up called *Eruption of Vesuvius*). Both paintings and collages of Burra's survive from this period that portray humanoid figures, but substitute something, often mechanical, for their heads. The collection of studio bric-à-brac now in the Tate includes a turn-of-the-century fashion magazine, *The Queen – The Lady's Newspaper and Court Chronicle*, probably rifled from his grandmother's house, with portions of stately, full-bosomed dames cut out here and there; they ended up in a collage of ladylike centaurs, which is now in the Edinburgh Museum of Modern Art. Burra set store by his collages, at least at this early period of his life, perhaps because they are the most conventionally weird of his productions, and therefore a bridge between his own work and that of the surrealist movement. Also in the late Twenties he began painting humanised birds, or animated, birdlike creatures, which have something in common with Max Ernst's Loplop (and these 'bird folk', as he called them, recur throughout his painting life).

Nash had a well-developed sense of the importance of promoting one's work. 'I always say you can't expect publicity unless you see to it yourself.' He was conscious of the political dimension to success, and succeeded in conveying to Burra his own conviction that joining some kind of movement was an important aspect of becoming an established professional artist. But Burra had no instincts for how to do it. He made a maladroit attempt to join the 'Seven and Five' group, and Sophie Fedorovitch had to write to him to say that there was no way his work could just be added to the forthcoming exhibition at short notice.[7] 'I was late to ask you to send some work for the 7 & 5 show – but I am certain there was very little chance of your being accepted as a lot of members work [had] to be thrown out.' He needed to do what other young artists did: meet people, make himself known, be seen around, write little articles, before proposing himself.

He did conquer his basic shyness and make the attempt, to a far greater extent than Rothenstein was aware of. Surprisingly, he even apparently edited some kind of art review in 1930 – the evidence for this is a letter from Sir William Rothenstein (then Principal of the Royal College of Art, and John Rothenstein's father). 'Many thanks for sending me the review edited by young Burra. I am always interested in his development, ever since he left the College I have looked out for his work. There are too many people who pretend, or make up as artists but Burra is a thoroughly genuine "eccentric" & has a touch of real genius, I think.' The review seems to have vanished without trace, probably in a single number: little reviews came and went like mushrooms in the interwar art world (and much of the evidence for their existence vanished in the wartime paper-salvage drive). There is nothing whatever to suggest that Burra had either the organisational or journalistic ability to succeed with such a project. He had a way with words, but he had no interest at all in writing as a craft.

Organisation; journalism; caballing with opinion-formers: like illustration and commercial art, these were intensely useful skills for a young artist, but Burra came swiftly to realise that he possessed none of them. He was at least spared the pressure of needing to earn a living,

[7] The Seven and Five Society was first formed in London in 1919, but it was hijacked by a group of advanced modernists led by Ben Nicholson in the early Thirties and renamed the Seven and Five Abstract Group in 1935, in which year it held the first all-abstract exhibition in Britain, at the Zwemmer Gallery.

but the problem of getting himself recognised was just as real for him as for anyone else. All that he could really do was pursue his own, strongly individual vision, and hope for the best. Thus he was deeply grateful to Nash for doing the work on his behalf which he knew he had no talent for himself. If coming out as a surrealist was the price of Nash's help, Burra was perfectly happy to be steered in that direction, and to cooperate with Nash's efforts.

Nash exerted himself substantially on Burra's behalf. In addition to talking him up to gallery owners, he also advertised his work to journalists. For example, Burra's first exhibition received welcome publicity from Eleanor Smith's chat column in the *Dispatch*, after Nash had given her lunch, deployed his considerable charm and urged her to go and see it. She also contacted Burra himself; and in Chappell's view, he failed to make the most of it: 'Why you ever said you were 24 I can't think. You could easily have got away with 20 or less.' Nash put considerable effort into keeping good communications with the papers, on behalf of himself, his protégés and modern art in general. He wrote any number of little articles and gave interviews: 'I sacrificed myself on the altar of the Daily Mirror (see Monday 19th) . . .'

In talking to Eleanor Smith, he was doing for Burra something that the younger man could not do for himself. Burra was very bad at soundbites. The most coherent statement he ever made about his painting is 'If you do it you do it and if people like it they like it and if they don't they don't and that's the end of that.' His lifelong policy of never explaining anything to anyone if he could help it made him a terrible interviewee, and he had no idea how to get a point across. On the odd occasions on which he came into contact with journalists early in his career, he bewildered them a great deal more than he charmed them. When M.J. Rosenau interviewed him for the *Boston Herald*, the result was a fiasco: not only did Burra fail to make himself understood (the headline was 'Just Bad Feeling, Surrealist Says in Explaining Grotesque Creations'), he ended up thrusting one of his paintings upon the mystified Rosenau out of sheer embarrassment.

As well as dealing with journalists on his behalf, Nash can be glimpsed pushing Burra into alignment with suitable contemporaries in a letter Burra wrote to Bar in 1931: 'Dearie can I come on Monday instead of Fri? As bonny Edward Wadsworth is coming over to the N[ash]s with someone who is writing an article about the exhibition at Brussels &

they want to see some work so I must stay – so tiresome.' Wadsworth was an established painter of Nash's generation whose work had points of contact with Burra's: he liked tempera rather than watercolour, but his work around 1930 was meticulously finished and brightly coloured, based on objects for the most part, but abstractly handled. He did not consider himself a surrealist; but as with Burra himself, surrealism offered a convenient way of giving his work some kind of context. Burra did recognise points of contact between his own art and that of the surrealists, but after an initial burst of enthusiasm, he became increasingly wary. 'I didn't like being told what to think, dearie,' he told George Melly, much later.

The implication that being identified with surrealism might represent a strait-jacket rather than an infinitely free space is directly corroborated by the contemporary critical response. Burra is represented – by one work in each – in Herbert Read's 1933 *Art Now* (and also in the accompanying *Art Now* exhibition in the Mayor Gallery), in *Fantastic Art, Dada, Surrealism*, the New York Museum of Modern Art (MOMA) exhibition of 1936, and in Herbert Read's 1936 anthology of writings and artwork, which is simply called *Surrealism*. Three different pictures have been chosen for these three publications, but they are strongly similar, and notably uncharacteristic of Burra's work more generally. All three portray a pair of oversized, abstract female figures with tiny heads and bodies composed of large, geometric shapes, posed in a garden in front of a building. These figures recall Giorgio de Chirico and Max Ernst, among others; they are poorly individualised, attired without reference to current fashion, and without any of the tokens of social, sexual and class identity which Burra delighted in. But they were very well received: Alfred Barr of MOMA wrote, 'There are, I think, a few of your paintings in America, but none, in my opinion, as good as the "Hostesses",' and asked to borrow it for the MOMA exhibition. The letter was sent to Paul Nash, who was asked to forward it: it came, revealingly, accompanied by a note from Margaret Nash, warning, 'Barr is a very important chap' (her underlining).

But it becomes clear from Burra's letters that these pictures are exactly what they look like, his most perfunctory work, because they were painted against the clock in order to put together enough paintings for his second one-man exhibition in June 1932. He wrote to Bar at the beginning of January that year:

Thank you for your letter dearie & invitation which I cant accept till the beginning of March at least as I am having to do more than 15 paintings between now and the end of February. Ho Hum I am working all the morning and all the afternoon till darkness falls I have developed a special type of Pompeian Beauty Panel that I can do ever so quickly if you or Marty want to come for a week end do come as you can allways watch me working so restfull.

He was, by his own account, thus producing one of these pictures every four days. Even if this was not literally true, this group of paintings shows signs of haste: they are decidedly less finished-looking than most of his work either before or after. What Herbert Read and Alfred Barr perceived as 'real' modern art is actually Burra's least engaged and least characteristic work.

But Burra was well aware of critical expectations, and of his professional need to meet them. He was a modern artist, and he could not afford to jeopardise the support of those better at art politics than he was himself. One result of this was the 'Pompeian Beauty Panels'; another was his involvement with Unit One.

Unit One was Nash's idea. He created the group in 1934, and invited Burra to join it. It sprang from his sense that it was essential to create a unified, identifiable modern movement in English art if anyone, at home or abroad, was going to pay attention to what was going on. He wrote to *The Times*, announcing its creation: 'though as persons, each artist is a *unit*, in the social structure, they must, to the extent of their common interests, be *one*'. The group was to stand for 'the expression of a truly contemporary spirit, for that thing which is recognised as peculiarly of today in painting, sculpture and architecture'. Burra's French experience will have confirmed Nash's conviction that real painters happened in groups and movements; that to join Unit One was a necessary phase in his development and, indeed, of his establishment as a commercially successful artist.

An early step towards the formation of Unit One was the exhibition which the very well-established gallery of Arthur Tooth & Sons held in October 1931: *Recent Developments in British Painting*. This showed new work by Paul Nash, John Armstrong, Edward Wadsworth, Ben Nicholson and Burra, all of whom subsequently became members of Unit One. After a certain amount of discussion, the new group was identified as the sculptors Henry Moore and Barbara Hepworth, the painters Paul Nash, Ben Nicholson, John Armstrong, John Bigge, Frances Hodgkins, Edward Burra and Edward Wadsworth, and two architects: Wells Coates and Colin Lucas. Frances Hodgkins (rather older than most of the members) resigned soon after and was replaced by Tristram Hillier, a painter whom Burra had met in Paris, who was something of a protégé of Edward Wadsworth. There was thus a considerable overlap with the personnel of the 'Seven and Five' group which Burra had tried to join a few years earlier. John Armstrong was a somewhat derivative surrealist; while both Wadsworth and Bigge liked to paint machinery in ways that were not precisely surrealist, but had a dreamlike and mysterious quality which linked their work with that of painters such as de Chirico (Hillier's pictures were rather similar; his, like theirs, are hard-edged, clear images whose surrealism consists of strange collocations, a pylon on a beach, for example). All of them had a concern with design and structure, a tendency towards quiet, well-mannered colour and towards essentially static images. They sometimes painted landscapes; when they did, these were rural, or seascapes, and for the most part devoid of human figures.

Burra had, inevitably, failed to keep up with what was happening, and was thus caught napping. 'My Inertia received a rude jolt the other morning,' he wrote in 1934. 'UNIT 1 has suddenly got up from its age long sleep and I had a letter from Douglas Cooper saying there was going to be an exhibition and he wanted 5 new pictures . . . realy I have none all my new pictures you can tell what they are so they are no good so have busily started a snake coming out of a sort of vegetable marrow with a storm at the back it might be anything so will do nicely . . .' The paintings he was doing at the time were his Harlem street-scenes, now among his best-known work, but his title to recognition within Unit One depended on being identified as a surrealist, and for that specific purpose they were quite useless.

Thus Unit One, unfortunately, enforced a sort of conformity with which Burra was not comfortable. Though he and Nash developed their interest in surrealism together, in the course of a summer holiday in 1929 that will be discussed in the next chapter, and Burra also had concerns in common with John Armstrong, in the early Thirties, he was more interested in painting hustlers, ladies of the night and music-hall artistes than anything else. His work was thus far too narrative to fit with Unit

One's agendas, as Osbert Lancaster observed in a crisp and extremely perceptive review. His use of colour was stronger and bolder than any of the other Unit One artists, and his interest in the human comedy pointed in a different direction entirely. An occasional picture, such as *South West Wind* (c.1932), which depicts abandoned machinery on a beach, suggests that he made some attempt to align himself with Wadsworth, Bigge and Hillier, though even here, typically, human presence, and movement, are suggested by a line of washing fluttering in a lively breeze.

The pictures he finally exhibited with Unit One were *Serpent's Eggs* (the viper coming out of a marrow), two of his high-speed 'Pompeian Beauty Panels' (*The Three* and *Surrealist Composition*), his *John Deth* picture and a very strange picture, *Still Life with Figures in a Glass*, which seems more serious in its intentions than any of the 'Pompeian Beauty Panels'. The tiny figures in the glass are homunculi, suggesting that Burra's interest in magic and alchemy, which was very evident in the Sixties and Seventies, was lifelong. The *Surrealist Composition* and another picture painted around this time, *Wheels*, are directly influenced by Nash. Both feature a detached doorway opening onto a scene distinct from that of the surrounding picturescape, an effect Nash developed as early as 1931 (in, for example, *Opening*) and returned to periodically in his later work – in *Surrealist Composition*, the opening is even onto a yacht at sea handled in a very Nashean manner.

The complexities of Burra's relationship with Nash are suggested by a very curious painting, most probably painted in about 1937/8, which is somewhere between a homage to, and a joke about, Nash's work. It is called *Sea Urchins*, and shows three sweet chestnuts, still in their spiky outer coats, on the hard sand of a beach with distant cliffs behind. It is thus a visual pun, and a bringing-together of the themes of three of Nash's paintings, *Equivalents for the Megaliths* of 1934 (mathematical cubes and cylinders set out on rolling farmland) and two 1937 paintings, *Environment of Two Objects* (a damaged doorknob and a doll's head, both found on a beach) and *Voyages of the Fungus*.

Abstract art reifies. Burra, though his art was not naturalistic – indeed, considerably less naturalistic than that of Wadsworth, Hillier and Bigge – was very much concerned with specifics in the late Twenties and early Thirties: the fashions of the moment, actual things. While in retrospect he seems an inappropriate addition to Unit One, it is easy to see why he joined. However, despite repeated nagging, he failed to fill out the biographical questionnaire that Herbert Read had asked all the contributors to complete, or to write a personal statement, in keeping with his general reluctance to try and explain himself in any way at all, which suggests that his real enthusiasm for the group was very limited. In the end, Douglas Cooper and Herbert Read had to write something on his behalf, and Nash was genuinely annoyed with him: 'you never heard what I've got to say about you letting us down over your bit of writing you old tripe pouch . . . but you will one day'. Predictably, once the book appeared, he didn't care for it. He wrote to Nash, rather pettishly considering how unhelpful he had been, 'The Unit I Book Realy Ive never laughed so much in my life . . . PS the picture of my "studio" is the oddest thing to look at one would think I painted nothing but photos of Greta Garbo and gramaphone records & rather out of focus too that gives it a mysterious glammer.'

The early Thirties were, in general, a great period for insisting that one should stand up and be counted. Burra was even seduced into making a political gesture, of sorts. Surrealism was a movement of the Left, and in October 1934, Artists International staged an exhibition on 'The Social Theme' of revolutionary proletarian art, which was intended to tour the Ukraine, White Russia, the Causasian and Middle Asian Republics and Leningrad. Suggested subjects began with 'working class subjects of all kinds . . . strikes, elections, demonstrations, meetings, etc. showing definite working class activity'. Burra, surely the poshest revolutionary proletarian in history, was warmly invited to contribute by Pearl Binder, one of the organisers, though there is no evidence that he did.[8] If he offered her something, his images of members of the proletariat having fun seem not to have been quite what they had in mind.

However, the manifesto states, 'Today, when the capitalist system and the socialists are fighting for world survival, we feel that the place of the artist is at the side of the working classes. In this class struggle, we use our experience as an expression and as a weapon making our first steps towards a new socialist art.' The signatories include Henry Moore, Paul Nash, Eric Gill – and Edward Burra.

Burra was also involved with one of the turning-points in English art, the *International Surrealist Exhibition* of 1936, at the New Burlington

[8] She was an artist, married to Jack Driberg, a massively unorthodox anthropologist and old Africa hand, brother of the more famous Tom.

Galleries. It was surrealism's great year (as well as the London exhibition, MOMA put on *Fantastic Art, Dada, Surrealism*, in which Burra
was represented, and in Paris there was a special number of *Cahiers
d'Art*, and a surrealist exhibition at the gallery of Charles Ratton). It
was an important moment in twentieth-century art. The English organising committee included Paul Nash and Herbert Read. Salvador Dalí,
Paul Éluard and André Breton, among others, came to London and
gave lectures; the exhibition was opened to an audience of about two
thousand, and was visited by about a thousand people a day. Most of
the journalists, and a significant number of the intelligentsia, treated it
as a huge joke. 'The press, unable to appreciate the significance of a
movement of such unfamiliar features, prepared an armour of mockery,
sneers and insults.' It didn't help that Dalí lectured in a diving suit (and
nearly suffocated himself), while a young woman wandered about with
her head encased in a cage of roses. Some wag attached a bloater to one
of the paintings, to make it more surreal. But ultimately, the joke was
on the scoffers. Surrealism was established as a defining aspect of twentieth-century culture.

The *International Surrealist Bulletin* no. 4, which reported on all this,
emphasised the Socialist character of the movement.

Among artists and intellectuals especially, there is a tradition of individualism
. . . moral, ideological, and political irresponsibility is assumed to be the proper
basis of English art. Those of us who have overcome these difficulties in ourselves
have done so because we realise that the situation is acute; because we see that
religion is once more re-establishing its hold upon the life of the country, and
because the movement of our government towards Fascism threatens to put a
stop to all creative activity.

There was an explicit political agenda. 'The validity of theory must be
tested in the field of activity; and the object of philosophy is not to
interpret the world but transform it. Beginning from such a standpoint,
the Surrealist is naturally a Marxian Socialist.'

Burra's *Wheels* is illustrated in the *Bulletin*, but unfortunately, by
1936, Burra was no longer all that interested, and he was certainly not
a Marxist. He dutifully appended his name to the *Bulletin*, along with
Nash, Henry Moore, Herbert Read et al., but surrealism, for Burra,
was about taking a walk around the unvisited corners of his own mind.

He was profoundly an individualist, and this collectivising agenda was not to his taste. What was more, at the time he was trying to digest his reactions to Spain and to the imminent, and plainly unavoidable, Spanish Civil War, including the discovery in himself of some kind of religious feeling. What he put into the actual exhibition were a 'Pompeian Beauty' – *The Three* – which had already had an airing at the Unit One show, *Wheels* (1933–4), probably on the advice of Paul Nash, to whom he had given both pictures (they were the only Burras that Nash owned), and *John Deth*, which had also been shown with Unit One. With the 'Pompeian Beauty Panels', Burra had successfully demonstrated that if he painted pick 'n' mix motifs from the collective unconscious – motifs, that is to say, identified as such by the surrealists of the Twenties – he could command both an audience and critical respect. This did not, on the whole, increase his personal respect for the opinions of critics.

Burra's work continued to be associated with the international surrealist movement in the years immediately following the London show. He was represented in the surrealist section of the Artists International Association exhibition, *Unity of Artists for Peace, Democracy and Cultural Development*, in 1937; in 1938, he exhibited in the *International Surrealist Exhibition* at the Galerie des Beaux-Arts in Paris; and in 1940, he was included in *Surrealism Today* at the Zwemmer Gallery. What his inclusion primarily shows is the high regard in which his work was held internationally, and the force of inertia: both his own, and that of the critical establishment. But the fact that he had drifted off in a different direction was increasingly apparent.

Fortunately for Burra, he acquired a dealer in the mid-Thirties, somewhat serendipitously, who took over where Nash left off. When Bumble acquired a place of her own, it was a flat over a butcher's in Shepherd Market, 13a Market Street, in the middle of the tarts' quarter. Burra's 1932 painting, *Saturday Market*, of a négligée-clad lady of the night picking her way through an early morning market, may evoke this milieu (though the Home & Colonial shop front that is portrayed was in Rye). When her first flatmate, Sophie Fedorovitch, got tired of the cats and the smell of the butcher's shop underneath and moved out, Gerald Corcoran moved in. He was half Irish, half Hungarian, tall, handsome and elegant, and at that time a member of the Household Cavalry.

Corcoran was one of the series of attractive, very masculine men who charmed and fascinated Burra at various times in his life: Chappell, reminiscing late in his life, was emphatic that he was an extremely glamorous figure. Bumble at this time was working sporadically as a designer and props-maker in both theatre and film, but she persuaded Corcoran to leave the army and start a business with her making costume-jewellery, belts and handbags. She was a good businesswoman, and this concern flourished into the mid-Thirties; Burra remarked in 1934 that 'the great Dawson Corcoran button consortium is ataining gigantesque proportions with two immense workrooms & 23 employees!'

On the side, Gerald Corcoran began to concern himself with furthering Burra's career. His first purchase was *Dancing Cows* (1929), for which he gave the artist a fiver. In the Thirties, he moved away from the costume and props business, and began working for Matthiesen's gallery in Bond Street, but he continued to act as Burra's agent and try and place his work. He sold pictures to the Tate on Burra's behalf through Matthiesen, and planned a one-man exhibition for Burra at Matthiesen in 1938, which fell through. Bumble herself was instrumental in getting two exhibitions of Burra's work on at Rex Nan Kivell's Redfern Gallery in the Forties.

After his war service, Corcoran returned to civilian life to find that his job at Matthiesen had been given to a German, and for a couple of years dealt privately from his home in Pont Street (in the work of Burra, among others). In 1949, A.J. Macneil Reid approached him to join Alex Reid and Lefevre and revive the business after the war, in which he was successful. He eventually became its chairman and owner. In 1952, Corcoran gave Burra his first one-man show at the Lefevre, which was a success, and thereafter the gallery became Burra's regular dealers, showing his work more or less in alternate years from 1952 to 1980 – to Christopher Neve, 'those ... shows in Bruton Street that used to leave the world looking booby-trapped for months'.

Burra thus achieved a professional safe harbour in the end, though it took him until his late forties. The Leicester had given him two exhibitions in 1929 and 1932, and gave him two more after the war (1947 and 1949), and in the years in between he showed some work somewhere nearly every year, but the bitterness he showed late in life in the context of his Tate retrospective suggests that he was infinitely more anxious, angry and depressed about lack of recognition through his thirties and forties than he was prepared to share with any of his friends at the time. Understandably so, given that this is a not untypical response to the Leicester show of 1932: 'Mr Burra is good fun but the total effect of his exhibition upon a reflective person is rather pathetic.'

The relationship with Corcoran, later with the Lefevre Gallery, had its price, which was exclusivity. There is a rather sad letter from Rex Nan Kivell in 1947 – before Corcoran joined the Lefevre – 'I was so sorry about Gerald Corcoran collecting all your work as we were always having people looking at them . . . Cheque for final balance enclosed at last, £15.00 minus ⅓ £10.' Nan Kivell had been one of the first dealers to back Burra, indeed had given him his first ever airing back in 1924, and had been a faithful supporter of him in difficult times. But that was not good enough; there was no permanent commitment, and Burra was sick of struggling with galleries. In the final analysis, the Redfern never made him much money. He also seems to have been under the impression that Nan Kivell cheated him, as suggested by a letter he wrote to Bar in 1944: 'I was informed they made 200£ almost out of that Gorbals at the Redfern but I havent seen any of it.'

His relationship with the Corcorans took the pressure off him entirely. Their efforts (Bumble's as well as Gerald's) helped him to establish a following. After 1940, he refused to toe anybody's line: the only category anyone ever tried to include him in after that was 'Modern British Painter'. But when he eventually started selling through the Lefevre, they ensured that he earned enough – indeed, more than enough. For the rest of his career he painted what he liked, secure in the knowledge that it was up to Gerald Corcoran, and later his son, Desmond, to put his work over to potential buyers.

After the Lefevre took him on, Burra was completely relieved of the strain of trying to explain himself, keep track of paintings, deal with framers, keep accounts, negotiate, write business letters and cultivate contacts, tasks he hated, performed incompetently and relinquished gratefully and completely. 'Gerald and Desmond knew exactly how to handle him,' said Chappell, which has a slight innuendo of exploitation, but in fact the relationship was one of genuine benefit on both sides. 'They did all the things he didn't like,' Chappell added. In 1970, when John Banting was sounding off about parasitic dealers, Burra took him up sharply and said he owed a great deal to Gerald Corcoran's gifts as a salesman.

Moreover, Burra retained his freedom. He still had the right to sell pictures from his house if he wanted to, without involving the Lefevre (which was generous on their part), and quite often exercised it in favour of old friends – though not without grumbling, since he was conscientious about producing a sufficient number of paintings every two years to make a decent exhibition. 'Bar says she wants to buy that picture of Falmouth for 500£ the day before. Gerald rang up and enquired about getting the pictures framed – I am trying to collect enough paintings and I don't want to sell it & would like to <u>exhibit</u> it – it being one of the Best ones – & it's a terrible struggle getting enough – otherwise I would be pleased to sell it to her.' If his friends went off with the best ones as they were finished, he had to work harder, or at least faster.

The story of Burra's professional life thus represents a huge measure of talent combined with a significant measure of luck. It is absolutely characteristic of him that his career as a painter was consolidated through his circle of personal friends. Paul Nash died in 1946. If Gerald Corcoran had not moved in with Bumble and gradually made himself responsible for Burra's career, Burra would not have stopped painting, but with nobody to push him, it is perfectly possible that discouragement and poor health would have caused him to paint almost entirely for himself in later life.

VI

THE WARM SOUTH

TRAVELLING was intensely important to Burra, as to most modernists of his generation. When he was only twenty-two, and Hugh Blaker amazed him by giving him forty pounds for three of his paintings, the first substantial sum he had ever earned, his immediate reaction was: 'I think of going to Toulon Nice Valencure Cassis Cannes and Marsailles.' It was important to him, also, that he should do so unquestioned, and he successfully imposed upon his family his view that this was reasonable behaviour. 'One couldn't ask him where he was going because he'd gone before you knew he'd gone,' said Anne, in interview. 'He never said when he was going to go away . . . it was very sensible, because there would have been a fuss and people would have said where are you going and hope you enjoy it and all this sort of thing. I was at ordinary school, and he would suddenly say "I'm going to" – well, he usually didn't even say, he just disappeared, and I knew what he was doing. He used to send splendid postcards and write to me every so often.'

'Where are you going, Ed?' his mother might enquire, if she caught him on his way out.

'I'm going to see a friend.'

In Rye? In London? In Paris? In New York? There was no way of knowing.

Burra's independent travels began in January 1927, when he went to Paris with Lucy Norton (discussed in Chapter IV). After some weeks, his father finally managed to glean an address for him from one of the gang, and wrote to enquire about what he was doing. The response was firm. 'Do not fuss. I am still here and mean to remain till L returns then I might come back for a week after which I might go to Marseilles for a little I don't suppose it's very expensive.'

In fact, he was home sooner, and for longer than he had intended. He had to come back in the third week of March because he was in agonies with a wisdom tooth, and preferred to go to his own dentist. He had terrible trouble with his teeth: as he wrote to Birdie soon after his return, 'there is no known type of stopping that is not in my mouth in fact I go round to the young dentists who learn them off. Also such a thrill my dear one of them is to have a celluloid top so I mustnt speak any firey language for fear of it going off.'

He thus ended up spending the summer in England, but the adventure he had really been longing for began in September of the same year, when he finally made it to the South with Billy Chappell, who had spent most of 1926 dancing in cabarets and frantically saving up. They went to Cassis and Marseilles together by train, third-class, by the longest, cheapest route; many, many hours of hard wooden seats.

The French Riviera, which Burra had momentarily visited when catching the Blue Train home in 1925, was the smart South of France. Cassis and Marseilles were not, though Cassis turned out to be a bit more bourgeois than the boys perhaps hoped. When the painter Tristram Hillier was first there in the early Twenties, he found it 'a pleasant little port, frequented in summer by a few painters and writers, and as yet undiscovered by the bands of tourists who were to make of it, some years later, a seething inferno.' A letter that Burra wrote to Bar from Cassis suggests that by 1927 the transformation was well under way.

If you could see the jolly men bathing at the bathing beach everyone skilfully undresses on the plage in full view of everyone prizes are given to those who manage to undress and not show the organs only this morning it was won by the celebrated poet of the advance guard William Chappell . . . the Grand Rue where we get our jolly marin ware and linen trousers the guide book says is a veritable ghetto of houses of ilfame my dear I stares into every window hoping for a thrill but all I see is little Georgette having her nappy changed by loving mothers hands.

The Cassis that Burra knew was much frequented, and colonised, by artists. André Derain spent time there. Roland Penrose and Jean (Yanko) Varda built a studio in Villa les Mimosas, a crumbling twenty-room mansion that overflowed with indigent artists, and was also frequently visited by Picasso, Braque and Miró. Bloomsbury liked Cassis as well: Roger Fry, Duncan Grant, and Clive and Vanessa Bell had a jointly owned cottage at Fontereuse, and Hillier also had a rather more downmarket cottage there, shared with a girlfriend. As Burra saw it, 'Everyone walks about with drawing books and canvasses the canvasses look a bit futurist you know you cant tell if it's the old manse at twilight or death at the festival.' All the visitors wore white, rope-soled espadrilles and white trousers, dark jerseys and hankies round their necks. Burra and Chappell made haste to acquire the uniform. 'Billy has come out in a lovely toilette of linen trowzers bathing shoes a pull over & red kerchief and a jolly béret, bought at Elli's hat shop Marseilles, oh you know old men have young ideas when they see Bill.'

Marseilles, on the other hand, was anything but twee. It was what Burra had dreamed of. 'I hear you are going to Marseilles,' wrote Bar. 'It seems very queer to me but I suppose you know what your about. What will you find to do there except go to the bad?' Marseilles was, and is, the second-largest city in France, an ancient and complex place with a history going back beyond even the Romans to the Greeks. Since it was a major port, it received wave after wave of immigrants in the nineteenth century, and had a complex and mixed-race community (*Banjo*, published in 1929, about an expatriate African-American musician and beach-bum in Marseilles, was based on the author Claude McKay's own experience there; Burra read it the same year, with interest). The variety of human types fascinated Burra, as they fascinated many others. Tristram Hillier was also in Marseilles around this time.

from a café table at the Cannebière one could watch a flowing stream of colour and hear a babel of tongues; chocolate coloured negroes, Chinese and swarthy Greeks, blonde sailors from the fjords of Norway, priests like shabby crows in their flapping soutanes, proud Spahis in vermilion cloaks, prostitutes, beggars and deformities of every kind. Thence one could wander along the *Quai du Vieux Port* and lunch at Basso's off a *salade de mer* or a *bouillabaisse* reeking of saffron and garlic . . . on the further side of the port stood the tall decaying houses, like rows of rotten teeth, which hid the strange labyrinth of the *Quartier Privée*; a world of stinking alleys and cavernous doorways leading into the eternal twilight of dim courtyards or foul tenements that housed the very dregs of human corruption. It was a kingdom of whores, thieves and murderers who were left very much to themselves . . . I loved this quarter in which I never suffered greater injury than a picked pocket or the embarrassment of ribald laughter when I refused invitations to beds upon which, in full view of the street, were enacted every form of sexual indulgence and perversion. There was here a sense of mystery, suffering, despair and passion, whether of lust, love or hate, and such an abandonment of the soul that it bordered on the heroic.

Doubtless there were also babies and humdrum domesticity; Hillier was far more of a romantic than Burra. Other people Burra saw there who made a strong impression on him were men with the noseless, caved-in faces of terminal syphilitics (in those pre-antibiotic days, by no means unfamiliar in such an environment). He made a careful drawing of a group of men with the terrible, mirthless grins of those who have lost their upper lips to rodent ulcers, and returned to these fearful visages in a number of serious paintings many years later.

The enjoyment that Twenties aesthetes derived from observing sexy Mediterranean decadence is confirmed by Constant Lambert, in a letter which he wrote from Marseilles in May 1930, to Anthony Powell:

As I write I am surrounded by so many negros and dwarfs that I can hardly believe I am not in the heart of old Bloomsbury . . . All the female whores look like Greta and all the male ones like Brian Howard. There is an exact replica of —— who dances a solo charleston outside one of the homosexual bars – a cosy place whose principal attraction is a monkey that picks pockets and a boy with only one leg and one arm.

The Vieille Ville of Marseilles in the Twenties was genuinely rough: crime, as well as prostitution, flourished there. Tall buildings leaned together, with washing festooned between them; while a good few of the houses were connected at cellar level by smugglers' tunnels which led down to the shore. The likes of Lambert and Hillier seem by and large to have escaped with nothing worse than picked pockets or the odd sexually transmitted disease. The landscape of urban poverty was significantly safer for aesthetic tourists in the Twenties than it was to become, because drugs and drug-addicts were not yet a sizeable problem. However, Burra left the Vielle Ville alone for the most part, though he paid at least one visit, chaperoned by Bar, who wanted to take photographs, as she recalled many years later:

Ed and I went up to the red light district in Marseilles, where the elderly (to us) tarts sat on wooden chairs outside their bedrooms which opened onto the street concealed by bead curtains. We were going to photograph them but one saw us and rushed after us calling out in French, 'You'll have to pay money for that', but Ed and I flew down a side street and escaped.

He found more entertainment in the ships' chandlers and cafés of the Vieux Port, which was subsequently bombed flat by the Germans in the course of the Second World War. His *Dockside Café, Marseilles* (1929) lovingly records its zinc-topped tables and curly light-fittings.

Rothenstein's view of the young Burra and his work (quoted at the beginning of Chapter III), had been extremely persuasive, since after all he had known the painter since 1923. In his book on Burra, he suggested that the painter's imagination seethed with invented encounters in sailors' brothels, and had done so long before he actually visited the Mediterranean; but this seems simply not to be the case. Rothenstein was fascinated and somewhat shocked by Burra's work, and seems to have found things in it which do not objectively appear to be there. If Burra's surviving paintings, painstakingly catalogued by Andrew Causey, are brought into witness, only one painting from the period before he began to travel, *The Taverna* (1924), unequivocally depicts an imagined southern scene. After his first visit to Paris in 1925, Burra painted French flea-markets, cafés and bars, but these related to his actual experience. He began an imaginary Spanish *Fiesta* in 1925–6, but left it unfinished. As these two titles suggest, it was places of public, not private, entertainment that interested him; when he paints prostitutes, they are among the other customers in places of general resort, such as cafés, not in brothels, and they are fully, if elaborately, dressed.

Burra's Marseilles images are principally of sailors hanging around in cheap bars drinking and idly chatting to the barmaid or to one another. They are animated scenes, but they involve neither lust nor violence, let alone suffering, despair and passion. Some allied images of hands with cards, dice, knives, revolvers hint at the possibility of violence, but never realise it, while similarly some images suggest negotiations which might conceivably precede sex, but do not approach towards consummation. Edward Wadsworth, Burra's fellow-Unit One member, made more than a dozen drawings and at least one painting of the Vieille Ville of Marseilles in 1924, with its narrow, medieval streets and distinctive festoons of laundry (reminding one that the practicalities of running a bordello include providing inordinate quantities of bed linen), from which it is absolutely clear that Burra did not. One might have thought that Burra would at least have liked the ornate signs, as Wadsworth clearly did: 'Au Flamboyant', 'Rebecca', 'Madeline'; but he ignored them.

A place that Burra discovered with his friends on a subsequent visit was Toulon, which was also much liked by artists because it was cheap. Chappell and most of the rest of the gang were extremely poor; and Burra, though he was not, was extremely cautious with his money. Getting away to the South as a group could only be done on a shoe-string; hence third-class rail tickets, and avoiding places where rich tourists put the prices up. Stella Bowen, who joined Josette and Juan Gris there in 1925, analysed Toulon's particular appeal:

Toulon was not concerned with the tourist trade. There was no casino, no prom-enade, and no fashionable cocktail bar. The social life of the town circled round the officers of the navy whose slender purses and civilised requirements kept ameni-ties high and prices low. The merchandise in the shops was cheap and attractive and as Josette said when she met us on our arrival, 'il y a cinq cinémas et deux dancings. Ca fait juste la semaine!'[1]

It was not a pleasure-town in the sense that Saint-Tropez or Monaco were – places which existed entirely for tourists – it was the French equivalent of Portsmouth. Apart from the vast naval dockyards, there was a small inner harbour, a row of cafés along the *rade*, separate from the business quarter, and a paddle-steamer, which puffed and threshed its way several times a day between this roadstead and a beach called Les Sablettes. The town's naval bias, however, gave it certain advantages of its own. The Hôtel du Port et des Négociants on quai Cronstadt was basic, but very cheap (about four shillings a night), and convenient for both the cafés and the paddle-steamer. And there were other attractions:

Toulon was a great naval port and thus a centre for opium, brought back by colo-nial officers and sold openly in purple tins. It was also a staid middle-class town where beach pyjamas were frowned on and a man who bared his chest on the beach was likely to be arrested.

---

[1] 'There are five cinemas and two dance-halls. That does the week!'

Burra did not take opium. Adventurous though he was in some ways, he did not pursue pleasures that might jeopardise his painting. However, Cocteau and his circle were partial both to opium and to chasing sailors, and both these ends were easily achievable from a base in Toulon, which thus acquired a certain reputation among French intellectuals. The area was also beautiful, in its own way. Paul Nash observed, 'Nothing can be pleasanter than sitting on the Rade in the sun slowly enlarging ones liver with too much coffee and gazing out into the port ... All the country is a wild tangle of pink marble, scented bushes and pine trees, with Napoleon's old fort on top.'

Most of Burra's personal clique converged on the Hôtel du Port, recommended to them by Constant Lambert, in September 1928. Apart from Burra himself, the party consisted of Chappell, Bar Ker-Seymer, Irene Hodgkins, Bumble Dawson, Frederick Ashton and Sophie Fedorovitch. Some other English visitors arrived independently, a couple of ex-Oxford Bright Young People and celebrated beauties Bunny Roger and Brian Howard (the latter a childhood friend of Bar Ker-Seymer), along with a fellow-Oxonian, the novelist Anthony Powell, whom Chappell and Ashton knew slightly and Bumble knew quite well.

One of the purposes of the trip was to say a sort of goodbye to Hodgkins. She had been Denis Cohen's mistress since late in 1927, but he became so profoundly attached to her that he asked her to marry him. She had agreed to convert to Judaism and to undergo instruction. The idea was that he would come out and join them when he was free of his work commitments, and take her back to London with him to be transformed into Mrs Cohen. Though Burra and his friends liked Denis Cohen immensely, and he liked them, he was so much older, wealthier and more respectable than they were that once Hodgkins became his wife and the mistress of an orderly and prosperous Jewish household, she would no longer quite be the girl they had known.

For most of the party, one of the principal entertainments of their holiday was pursuing the latest fashion, sunbathing, invented around 1920, which had the great advantage of being almost free. Like most styles, it rapidly established its own aristocracy. 'The boys who had turned the deepest mahogany walked among those people with paler skins, like kings among their courtiers.' Thus Stephen Spender. They surrendered happily to the sun and the pleasure of doing absolutely nothing. Since local mores did not permit wandering about half dressed, they took the paddle-steamer to the beach at Les Sablettes where they could lie about in bathing costumes. Often enough, Chappell didn't even leave the hotel, but lay naked on the floor in the patch of blazing sunlight by the open window, trying to match his pale bottom to his deeply tanned back. Bunny Roger, as Chappell later recalled, craftily stayed in the shade: 'Everybody else was black and he was *so* white he looked absolutely magical . . . Ed loved that. He loved anyone who made what he called "a stylish sensation".'

In the evenings, all of them would dress up and rendezvous at an agreed meeting-point, either Raymond's Bar overlooking the place de Puget, which had a mouldering eighteenth-century fountain with entwined dolphins, for which Burra was later to find a use, or the Café de la Rade, patronised by Cocteau and his protégé Jean Desbordes (though the English contingent were shy about approaching the great man). They often went on to visit the *bal-musette* where the sailors danced. The flavour of these encounters is recalled by Sibylle Bedford.

A girl must either accept to dance with everyone who asked her or not get up at all. The band was two accordions and the tunes were chaloupés and javas valsées, penetrating, jerky, fast, and they were danced with extreme devotion and virtu-osity. The dancers did not speak. The place smelt of caporal tobacco and hot light bulbs. There were a few wooden tables and benches and those who occupied them drank diabolo, white wine clouded with crème de menthe. The men against the wall drank little or nothing, and the most serious devotees danced chiefly with each other.

The group was fascinated by the fact that Cocteau was also a guest at their hotel. In 1930, when he was to be found cavorting about the town with a tattooed sailor known as Pas-de-Chance, he chose the Hôtel de la Rade, which was rather more luxurious, but in 1928 he was at the Hôtel du Port, where he and his entourage spent the days smoking opium in shuttered rooms. Bar Ker-Seymer gained the entrée because Cocteau loved being photographed, but since she had no flash and the room was in near-darkness, it was a waste of her time – moreover, she was disappointed to find that Cocteau and company were virtually unconscious. Detaching herself from Cocteau's monkey, which was bent on destroying her camera, she tiptoed out. She managed to photograph him the following year, and he was immensely pleased with the results:

Desbordes wrote to her, 'Les photographes sont <u>spendides</u> jamais Cocteau n'en a eu de si bonnes.'[2]

Burra, meanwhile, worked during the day in a dark back bedroom overlooking the tramlines, and went out drinking with the gang at night. Powell's autobiography suggests that he was impressed both by Burra's industry and by his unusual working methods.

Burra never sunbathed (then the rage), his skin retaining its constitutional tint of parchment, appropriate to the air of having just stepped out of a Cruickshank engraving. Like the rest of the party, Burra was in his mid-twenties, but seemed prematurely old; truer perhaps to say that he resembled a prisoner just brought out into the sunlight after years of confinement in a pitch-dark subterranean dungeon. He spoke rarely, but always with devastating aptness.

Burra, something of a reproach to myself, spent a great deal of time at Toulon working. His method – anyway in those days – was one of the most unusual I have ever observed in a painter. He would sit in a hotel bedroom on a rickety hotel chair at an equally rickety hotel table – possibly even a dressing table – dozens of extraneous objects round about him (including the remains of petit déjuner) while he executed his pictures. What was always an immensely complicated design would be begun in the bottom right-hand corner of a large square of paper; from that angle moving in a diagonal sweep upward and leftward across the surface of the sheet, until the whole was covered with an intricate pattern of background and figures. If not large enough, the first piece of paper would be tacked on to a second one – in fact would almost certainly be joined to several more – the final work made up of perhaps three or four of these attached sections.

This glimpse of Burra in action suggests some interesting things about his work at this time; that he liked to work very big from early in his career, even if he couldn't get paper large enough, and that the picture was going straight from his head onto paper, which testifies to the genuine connection between his oeuvre and that of the surrealists. It also confirms the technical point that he worked with virtually dry pigment – only thus would it have been possible for him to work with watercolour across jointed paper.

At the end of the last week of September, the little group of friends was unexpectedly augmented. Tristram Hillier, one of Burra's Unit

[2] 'The photographs are *splendid*; Cocteau has never had such good ones.'

One confrères, together with Hillier's great friend the painter and mosaicist Jean Varda, put in at Toulon in Varda's little lateen-rigged boat, *Lou Cat*, which they had sailed over from Cassis. Cassis is no great distance from Toulon, but according to Hillier's recollection, they were caught in a storm and ended up running before the wind for a matter of days. There is a strongly nautical flavour to English modernism. Hillier's passion for boats was shared by another Unit One member, Edward Wadsworth, and also by Christopher Wood, among others. This chance encounter was to have unexpected consequences. As Hillier recounts it:

there stood a group of old friends who had seen our arrival from their table outside the café and now called us to join their party . . . caked with salt spray, bearded and deeply burned by the sun and wind of several days at sea, with bare feet and no more clothing than a dirty singlet and a pair of patched cotton trousers, we must have presented an odd contrast to our elegant companions . . . a couple of writers, a painter whom I had known in Paris, a ballet dancer and two or three young women, of whom one was so astonishingly beautiful that I could not refrain from gazing at her in wonder . . .

He and Varda swarmed up the harbour ladder, and joined Burra and friends at the Café de la Rade on the quay. Chappell afterwards recalled the sudden apparition of a glamorous blond pirate, blue eyes blazing from a deeply tanned face, with a light-blue hankie wound turban-fashion round his head. After dinner, everyone except Burra, who did not dance because of his arthritic feet, went off to the *bal-musette*. Powell, who wasn't getting anywhere with any of the girls, got bored after a while and went home (apart from Hodge, they included Enid Firminger, Powell's 'Dark Lady', so perhaps he could not stand watching her ignoring him and having fun with the sailors). The rest of the group made a romantic night of it, 'dancing to the music of accordions, strolling along moonlit quays, drinking at little zinc bars in the company of sailors and their sweethearts'. The next day Hillier and Varda took themselves off in *Lou Cat*, and in the afternoon Denis Cohen arrived by train. The friends, naturally, left Cohen and Irene to themselves, but the following morning, when Powell went out to find some breakfast, he saw Cohen sitting alone at a café table.

'I'm leaving tomorrow,' he said. 'Hodge isn't coming with me. She's going off to live with this fellow who came over from Cassis the other night.'

This was the sort of wildly romantic bad behaviour that normally delighted Burra. Unfortunately, everyone who might have prompted him to seize his pen and write, 'well dearie, you could have knocked me down with a feather as they say!' was in Toulon with him (except Clover, who was incommunicado in Hungary). Doubtless they all had plenty to say at the time, but it has left no trace.

Hodgkins's story continued to be a romantic one. She and Hillier stayed in Paris for a few months, but when she fell pregnant they moved to an eighteenth-century farmhouse in Gascony attached to a huge fourteenth-century ruin, the Château de Mansencôme, which cost all of £200. She was not completely cut off from her old friends there – Doris Langley Moore visited late in her pregnancy, and persuaded her to marry Hillier for the sake of the child (children, as it turned out, twin boys).

After a year or so, Hillier, uninspired by the landscape of the Gers and longing for the sea, let the castle, and they migrated back to Provence, to Martigues, where they found that the South African poet Roy Campbell was their new neighbour: 'Tall and slim, clothed in a singlet and blue cotton trousers, he might have been a fisherman but for his face. He stared through me with the largest grey eyes I have ever seen, set slightly aslant and giving him an indefinable air of wildness.' As this suggests, Hillier both espoused Hemingwayesque masculinity and was highly susceptible to masculine glamour in others. It was a generation in which poets had a tendency to mythicise themselves and each other; to see themselves as larger than life; and Campbell, very right-wing and pro-Franco, was one of the most extreme. Similarly, Hillier was relatively unusual among painters in being a romantic man of action, and he found Campbell highly congenial: they set about being wild together.

Hodgkins met up with a group of her friends in Toulon in 1931 (Bar and Marty Mann, Sophie and Fred were there together). Burra was not there at the time – but he enquired of Bar: 'Did Madame H bring the kiddies? I'me dieing to see the kids.' He went out to join them a little later, but by then, Hodgkins had gone. Subsequently, he made a pilgrimage to Martigues in the early autumn of 1933 to visit her, and was less than enthusiastic about what he found there. He had a deadly diagnostic eye for anything bogus, and evidently detected an element of macho self-regard in the Hillier style:

In the restaurant were two men who looked so artistic they must be English who I took no more notice of. ½ an hour later I turned round & there was Hodgekins so of course Ide been staring at Birdie [Tristram] Hillier without knowing who it was she hasn't changed at all swathed in backless cotton dresses & eating ice cream cones just the same only thinner and better looking . . .

Hillier introduced Burra to Roy Campbell, who was playing *poète maudit* with a will. Burra was underwhelmed: 'We met some people in a bar a poet called Roy Campbell roaring drunk apparently theyre allways getting drunk.' The testosterone-enriched atmosphere failed to amuse or impress him.

He was far more interested in Hodgkins; and worried about her. The Hemingway style is not compatible with much consideration of the interests and welfare of women and children, so he was relieved to see her well and happy, and delighted by the twins, who were called Jonathan and Benjamin. As quoted by Burra, she sounded very contented. 'You need never go home to see your friends says Hodge they all trickle here sooner or later. The twins [then four] are a dream & live in a pen tended by a french maid. I feel tempted to go over to Toulon in the bus for old times sake just to see how many monsters I can recognise.'

Burra's real fondness for small children had been in evidence since the birth of his sister Betsy. Many of his friends were not of the marrying kind, but he was devoted to Phyl and Gerald Corcoran's son Desmond, for whom he drew cowboys in a special book (since lost); to Clover's son Edward, who was his godson; and was later fond of, and understanding of, Max, the late-born son of Bar Ker-Seymer.

Sadly, Hodgkins was not as happy as she seemed. The romantic marriage was already on its last legs at the time of Burra's visit. She was sick of Hillier's self-absorption and the benders with Roy Campbell. She asked Hillier for a divorce in 1935, and subsequently married Colonel Alfred Varley, one of the three founders of the advertising agency, Colman, Prentis and Varley. Burra's letters reveal that in 1936 Burra was in dialogue with them about design work – abortively – 'I sent Varley & Prentis a drawing from Paris but Ime certain it never arrived & now of course its too late somebody must have opened it mistaking it for a filthy French

picture.' Even if the connection did not come to much, it is further
evidence that the friends looked after one another.

Hodgkins got back in touch with Bar as well (who also did work for
Colman, Prentis and Varley). In Bar's photo album for 1936 there is a
series of idyllic photographs of Jonathan and Benjamin, and the little
girls (Pansy and Buttercup) who came along later, taken at Hodgkins's
home, Hoptons Farm, near Folkestone. But this attempt at happiness
was as illusory as the romance with Hillier, though for quite other
reasons; she succumbed to cancer in her late thirties, at the beginning
of the war. Meanwhile, Denis Cohen married an American, Kathryn
Hamill, a woman of similar physical type. When he met her, she was
starring in the Ziegfeld Follies, but she was also a designer: the initials
in the *ABC of the Theatre* for which Burra did the drawings are her
work.[3]

Burra himself returned to Toulon in 1929, the year after Hodgkins
threw her bonnet over the windmill, in somewhat more respectable
company. Paul Nash and his wife wanted to spend some time in the
South, but they were at that time much involved with a woman called
Ruth Clark, known to her friends as Twit, a relative of Margaret Nash,
who had shared a flat with her before her marriage.

Ruth was recovering from an operation on her ear, which had nearly
killed her. Burra and his clique thought her a bit of a bore even when
she was in flourishing health (Burra's response to her mastoid operation was the less-than-sympathetic 'not content with a bandage, she has
a crêpe de chine veil draped round she looks like Toots Pounds in
mothers of the world at the least shock she bursts into tears').[4] Ruth's
capacity for being tiresome was somewhat enhanced by the fact that she
was convalescent, and the Nashes decided that two plus one would, in
the circumstances, be uncomfortable. 'To make an even number we took
along Edward Burra, a young painter who lives at Rye, an eccentric
talented delicate creature, extremely amusing,' said Nash.

From Burra's point of view, on the one hand, yes, it was Toulon and
the South. On the other, the Nashes were considerably older than Burra,
and did things, therefore, in a middle-aged way. The fact that Burra

---

[3] She subsequently decided to leave the stage, and after a brief stint as Aneurin Bevan's secretary,
enrolled at Newnham College, Cambridge, to study medicine and became a doctor.

[4] Toots Pounds was a particularly kitsch star of the London Palladium.

went along is an indication of his respect for Nash and his desire to please him and spend time with him, but he found it wearing. Reporting to Chappell, he commented, 'Hey dey here we are in Toulon If you could have seen the fuss with which we left Paris having loaded about 7 suitcases 3 hat boxes and a napsack onto a taxi with string . . . [we] got the train alright having bought bars of chocolate sandwiches Evian wine & biscuits I sat gapeing realy we might have been going to Vancouver.' Bar got a similar report. 'Yew should see the luggage we travel 50 rucksacks a kettle & 90 suitcases. It turns me grey.' Burra himself was famous for travelling with a toothbrush, a change of socks and his paints. Nash himself, once it was all over, said, 'jamais plus, jamais plus, my dear Percy, will I go abroad in a circus', suggesting that it was Ruth and Margaret who were responsible for the fuss.

Burra found the Nashes trying company, despite his gratitude to, and affection for, Paul. Margaret Nash was not exactly his sort of person. She was two years older than her husband, and before her marriage she had been an organiser in the field of women's suffrage and social welfare: Burra had no objections to either, but he was not attracted to organisers. He commented on an early visit when he had evidently been glad to find Paul at home by himself, 'Mrs N was not at the cot to eye us through her lorgnette', suggesting a certain mutual lack of sympathy (though he came to like her more as he got older).

The trip was not a success. Ruth and Margaret didn't like the Hôtel du Port, and Nash grumbled, 'Toulon is quite famous for bad or indifferent cooking, unless you can afford more than you ought to have to pay, so it became rather a bore hunting hungrily up and down smelly streets for new cheap restaurants that weren't too nasty', though he added, 'I enjoyed Toulon as much as any part of the trip.' Equally, Margaret and Ruth did not enjoy the sailors' bars; Ruth regretted the time 'wasted in cafés in this glorious country', but for Burra, the cafés were quite a bit of the point of being there. They shifted over to Tamaris – more rural, which the women liked and the men did not. Nash put his foot down when a goat got in and ate some of his oil-paints, so then they went to Nice, where they found the address they had turned out to be that of a stupendously genteel, Bordighera-style hotel where Burra swore he would not spend more than a single night, though the Nashes rather took to it. The ladies seem to have done a good deal of complaining, and Burra ended up saying that he wished he had gone to Marseilles, exasperating Nash still further.

Another problem was that after Ruth Clarke went home because she had to start a new job, Burra was slightly superfluous. Ruth wrote much later, 'I remember Paul telling me afterwards rather ruefully that instead of their little time *à deux* Edward had stuck on to them, and much as they enjoyed Ed's companionship it wasn't quite what they had in mind.' Nash clearly felt that Burra should have realised he would want to be alone with his wife; Burra, however, who had never been half of a couple, realised no such thing, and the Nashes were too polite to drop anything more than the most veiled of hints.

The trip, however, did no lasting harm to relations between Burra and Nash. It was also very important to the art of both men. Burra had been drawn to surrealist art and writings since his first visit to Paris in 1925, but Margaret Nash notes in her memoir that it was during this 1929 trip that Nash himself began thinking seriously about surrealism: 'Paul ... became really interested in an aspect of Surrealist painting, namely, the release of the dream.' They met Ernst and Picasso in Paris, and they also saw paintings by de Chirico and Ernst, among others, in the Galerie Léonce Rosenberg in Paris, a valuable exposure to international surrealism for them both. As they travelled, the pair had fruitful conversations about their work, above all, its relationship to dreams and the unconscious. Two early Burra paintings, *Revolver Dream* and *Opium Dream*, seem, from their titles, to have originated from this surrealist preoccupation.

Burra visited the South of France again several times, but the period in which it is important to his painting is the late Twenties. There are several paintings set in Toulon, or depicting beaches, balconies, cafés and encounters in southern cities. The Hôtel du Port's attractive iron balconies appear in *Toulon* (1927) and *Balcony, Toulon* (1929), and the view from his back bedroom produced a study of the no. 27 tram. The sorrow-in-sunlight of holiday romance in *On the Shore* also alludes to Toulon life: a deeply tanned naked lady in a hat waves what seems a melancholy farewell to a departing steamer, while keeping hold of a black matelot by way of consolation.

VII

BALLET

BURRA'S involvement with the ballet was, if anything, overdetermined. He, Chappell, Bar, Lucy Norton and their other friends had been passionate balletomanes and queuers for seats in the upper circle since their art-school days. When he was seventeen, Billy Chappell had a crush on Anton Dolin, the rising English star of the Ballets Russes: 'Dolin sent me a photograph a lovely one the one they have outside like this and a letter to say he thought the drawing very clever & why didn't I ring up?' (an invitation that he did not have the nerve to accept). Susie Salaman, a great friend of Billy's who had been at the Royal College of Art with Burra in 1925, was a designer and choreographer by 1929, working for Marie Rambert.

More generally, an interest in ballet was a defining taste for interwar aesthetes. Several of the painters Burra knew – Robert Medley, Paul Nash and John Banting, among others – were interested in dance, while Rupert Doone, Medley's partner, was actually a dancer. Furthermore, Diaghilev had introduced the principle of co-opting distinguished artists into working for ballet alongside professional designers – such as Picasso, who designed *Parade* for him in 1917 – which sharpened the artists' interest. Besides Burra himself, other modernists of his circle, such as his Unit One confrères Paul Nash and John Armstrong, together with John Banting and Christopher Wood, would all design English ballets in the Twenties and Thirties.

But the development that sealed Burra's personal involvement with the ballet was that Marie Rambert talked Billy Chappell into becoming her pupil in 1926. Only a year later, he danced professionally for the first time, in the dances Frederick Ashton arranged for the Purcell Opera Company's revival of *The Fairy Queen*. In early summer of 1927, both Chappell and

Ashton were employed as dancers with the Royal Opera at Covent Garden, on the princely salary (negotiated by Ashton) of £5 per performance. The following year Ashton's ballet, *Leda and the Swan*, premiered in June 1928 to celebrate the opening of Rambert's new studio in Ladbroke Road, and Chappell and Harold Turner were male Naiads to Ashton's Zeus. As Chappell recollected, 'It became Mim's [Rambert's] showpiece. We did it everywhere. There was no grand charity matinée at which we weren't doing *Leda*.'

In October 1928, after the Toulon holiday which had ended so dramatically with the sudden departure of Hodgkins, swept off by Tristram Hillier, Chappell and Burra went to Paris to meet with Frederick Ashton, who had told them he would be there. He had borrowed £5 from Sophie Fedorovitch, gone over to Paris and got himself accepted by Bronislava Nijinska as a member of a company that she was gathering under the backing of, and as a vehicle for, the wealthy and wildly eccentric Ida Rubinstein.

Rubinstein was beautiful as well as rich, though since she was born in 1885, by 1928 she was not exactly a *jeune fille en fleur*. She was, by Russian standards, barely trained, but her angular, extraordinary beauty and her tremendous stage presence were sufficiently remarkable for Diaghilev to recruit her as his Cleopatra in the ballet of the same name in 1909, a production in which she was required to mime rather than dance, as was also the case with her second starring role for him, the sultaness Zobeida in *Schéhérazade* (1910). She amply justified his choice. According to a Russian critic, 'Elle a la souplesse du serpent et la plasticité de la femme; ses danses offrent la grâce voluptueuse et stéréotypée de l'Orient, grâce pleine de mollesse et de la pudeur d'une passion impulsive.'[1] Unfortunately, as time went on, she became possessed by the idea that she could actually dance, which was not the case, and in 1928, when she was forty-three and, as Chappell put it, 'thin, frail and brittle as blown glass', she decided to start a ballet company as a showcase for her own performances.

When Burra and Chappell eventually caught up with Ashton, who had moved from the address he had given them to the (even cheaper) Hôtel St George, it was to find that Ashton, completely surrounded by Poles,

[1] 'She has the suppleness of a serpent, and the fluidity of a woman; her dances present the stereotypic voluptuous grace of the East, a grace full of softness and the shame of an impulsive passion.'

Lithuanians, Russians and Czechs, was not only delighted to see them, but anxious to talk Chappell into the company. And Nijinska, to Chappell's astonishment and stark terror, agreed to accept him. He didn't know at the time that Nijinska – aware of, and sympathetic to, Ashton's loneliness – had told him privately that if he brought her an English-speaking friend who could dance, she would take him on. She had already noted his extraordinary potential and wanted to ensure that he was happy enough for it to flower. Thus Chappell was swept off into the terrifying company of a really first-rate artistic director and choreographer, who had not only danced with the Ballets Russes, but was the sister of the legendary Nijinsky. As he recalled it, he had been a somewhat lackadaisical student up to that point – 'I'd not done very much. I hadn't really concentrated.' Now he had no choice but to learn as fast as he could: Nijinska was a martinet. Ashton, incandescent with enthusiasm, wrote to Rambert, 'her efficiency is overwhelming & her knowledge & vitality something quite super-human & inspiring. She gives a brilliant class, very difficult & never dull.' He, of course, was as driven as she was. Chappell, by contrast, cowered at the back, hoping that the storms would break over someone else. On one occasion she lost her temper completely and threw all the music at him.

Burra was delighted by Chappell's success in an area absolutely antithetic to anything he could achieve himself. He found that he enjoyed the ballet world: the fraying tempers, the urgency of it all, just as he revelled in the dramatic lives of Bar's friends among the London lesbian community. He stayed on, fascinated, to watch, and reported to Bar:

We are all in the pink rehearsing till 12 midnight daily so you may imagine our tempers are a little off instead of Faith hope & charity its vinegar vitriol and acrimony. As for bonny old Ida! Oh Fi Madame will have to have a special arrangement of invisible ropes to keep her for more than 3 seconds on her battered points. Billie says she's just like Beatrice Lillie in her famous skit on Les Sylphides. Also ma chere about 6 goods trains will be required to travel the scenery as it is all real staircases & real columns and real marble and real gilt & everything real but poor old Ida.

Though she spent a fortune on sets and costumes, Madame Rubinstein was trying to shave her wages bill, so Ashton and Chappell had almost no money. They had 1,000 francs a month during rehearsals (about £20), with a promise of 1,300 when performances started. Together with Burra, they removed to the Hôtel Saint Brieuc, which was very cheap indeed. The two dancers shared a bed, for reasons of sheer poverty (any possibility of further developments was removed by the fact that they were barely on speaking terms), and tried to ensure they spent less than twenty-five francs a day on food – not easy, when hard exercise left them permanently ravenous. Burra observed, 'What our Ballerina will look like at the end of the run I dread to think all his suits are on the go and the seat of his overcoat is like a mirror.'

Burra made no attempt to paint rehearsal scenes, apart from an occasional sketch (there are several drawings of boy dancers, which probably date to this trip), but simply enjoyed the drama from the sidelines. He also bailed Chappell out financially to some extent, since he told Bar: 'The only person who hasn't payed for Freddie yet is me & you know Ime so mean and what with keeping Mistress Billy Ive nothing to spare.' He probably bought Chappell some clothes, since he mentioned that the latter was going about looking 'very fanciful and Montparnassian'. So did Chappell's boyfriend, John Lloyd, who had also come out to visit: 'someone told him how a friend of theirs had fallen in love with me on sight . . . this had such an effect on John he immediately went out and bought me a blue oilskin with a luggage strap round the neck and a black silk hankie with white spots and a knitted tie at 40 francs . . . and he paid for all my meals on the train and gave me 200 francs at the station so your old tart did quite well,' Chappell reported smugly.

Socially, things began to look up after Burra and Chappell arrived. The faithful Sophie Fedorovitch also came to Paris, and settled down just across the boulevard Montparnasse. Two more English dancers joined the company, Robert Medley's partner Rupert Doone and Joyce Berry, as did some English-speaking foreigners. Burra and his friends congregated at Select, a Montparnasse café terrasse establishment which was acquiring an increasingly gay clientele. It was liked by Doone and Medley, along with the painters Cedric Morris and Arthur Lett-Haines, whom Burra and Chappell had known since 1925. Burra commented, 'Jolly Carline [one of a family of artists, Burra couldn't remember which one] saw Billy, Rupert & Freddy in the Select last night so Billys reputation will be quite gone what there was of it.'

Burra always enjoyed Sophie's company, but he was also particularly attracted to two other members of the troupe, a new American recruit,

Arthur Mahoney, who joined in October 1928, and a Dane, Birger Bartholin. Mahoney's appearance enraptured him.

There is the sweetest little Ammerican creature in the company so Ammerican from Boston Mass he wears a large Diamond ring and produces boxes of aniseed & black currant gums and says 'aave a caandeee' he is a little protegée of Ruperts I believe . . . realy if I was Billy I should cultivate such a treasure.

Doone may have advanced Mahoney's career as a dancer, but he was not, as this letter might seem to imply, his protector in any other sense, since Mahoney was inveterately heterosexual.

However, though the evidence is of the vaguest and most inferential, in so far as there is the faintest hint that Burra's forlorn dream of 'someone who likes me very much', recorded in his 1929 diary, relates to anyone in particular, Arthur Mahoney is a good candidate. Julie Kavanagh, Frederick Ashton's biographer, sums up: 'He was not only wonderful looking – blue-eyed, with striking Native American features, and a virile, muscular physique – but he possessed an intriguingly adventurous past.' Mahoney had started off in Boston, as a choirboy at St Paul's Cathedral, but when his voice broke, he ran away from home and went west to become a cowboy. Subsequently, looking through magazines in a drugstore, he saw a picture of Nijinsky and decided to become a dancer – and turned out to be immensely talented. He was much loved in the company (even Ashton liked him) and very entertaining; he enjoyed jazz and had an extensive record collection, which will have endeared him to Burra, and he made a third with Chappell and Ashton in impromptu revues.

Arthur & Billie open in pullman porter suits and Freddie comes on later whilst theyre singing the hot number and does his german Jazz dressed in an ostrich feather tail a diamonte bust boddice & top hat holding an imitation tin saxophone.

Some people are erotically drawn to the familiar, others to the exotic. Burra seems to have been one of the latter (a proclivity he had in common with Clover). He was, quite clearly, unmoved by Chappell or Ashton. Mahoney, on the other hand, was American, delightful, full of energy, affectionate, highly sexed and cheerfully priapic. And straight. Mahoney was perhaps the last person on the planet likely to interest himself in Burra's fragile, enervated body and hesitant sexual impulses, but that sort of consideration has never stopped anyone having a crush.

Barbara Roett, who knew Burra well for more than twenty years, suggested to me that he was susceptible to magnificence. At various times she observed the way he was attracted towards one or another large and splendid man, exuberant and physically expressive, the sort of man who sweeps you into a hug and lifts you slightly off your feet without even noticing your weight. Perhaps not so much an erotic yearning, as a more diffused responsiveness to unselfconscious virility – though it had to be unselfconscious. Burra disliked posturing 'He-men' on the Tristram Hillier model, and, perhaps for that reason, all the men he had strong feelings about were straight.

In his fifties Burra was clearly not looking for anything beyond a hug and a kiss. It may be that as a young man in his twenties, he dreamed of something more, but no-one will ever know. Chappell, asked if Burra had ever been in love, said, 'You'd never have known. He would never have said so.' His manner was actively designed to discourage anyone from trying to guess at his feelings, and even in lesser matters he would have gone a long way to avoid running the gauntlet of Chappell and Ashton's mockery. The evidence for such a crush even existing is fragile, but Mahoney was certainly the type of man that Burra was later drawn to.

Burra and Mahoney met in the summer of 1928, and Burra's 1929 diary opens in a state of profound depression (which does not escape into the correspondence with his friends). This is the moment when he confessed to his diary, 'My wish ~~affair~~ ♥'. What gives a pointer that the 'wish' might have focused on Mahoney in particular is the entry for 1 January: 'Worked drivelled about . . . wish I could go to Ammerica tried to go to Hastings but hadn't the force.' The only personal contact with American he had had in 1928 was with Mahoney. Later entries in January confirm his mood: 20 January, 'ennui ennui ennui'; 22nd, 'oh to be off somewhere'; 31st, 'oh Im stifleing'. It is not much to go on, but it shows that something was making him very unhappy at the beginning of that year.

Early in the May of 1929, Burra went back to Paris to see how the Ida Rubinstein company was getting along. His own efforts during the visit were concentrated on two quite conventional, more or less naturalistic, somewhat cubist-influenced companion oil portraits of Ashton and Chappell, the only two such that he is known to have made. Burra was pleased with the Ashton portrait, and wrote to Bar, 'If it ends as

its begun my dear it will be a triumph for Artiste & model its so like
yet lovely Freddies delighted Ive given him such a daintie bouche &
huge grey eyes like a gazelles.' But as the painting progressed, Ashton
complained that it made him look sulky (it probably did, since at the
time he was), and after a period of being nagged about making him
look more agreeable, Burra slapped a layer of black paint over the
whole thing, to Ashton's chagrin, and painted something else on top.
The portrait of Billy, though competent as a painting, was not, Bar
thought, a good likeness – in her view, John Banting's was much better.
All the same, Chappell kept it all his life, and hung it in his dining
room.

What is equally to the point, Burra saw a great deal of Arthur
Mahoney, as the diary indicates, and noted in a letter to Bar, 'am
becoming addicted to aniseed lifesavers' (which Mahoney was handing
out). He went to the ballet with Mahoney, and often to Select with him,
and to the Dodges, who were friends of Mahoney's. In that diary, and
such subsequent diaries as survive, Mahoney's often-changing addresses
are regularly recorded. Burra kept a handful of letters in Mahoney's
illegible masculine scrawl; and went to lengths to get in contact with
Mahoney when he himself eventually visited New York. There are thus
indications of more, and stronger, feelings than the circumstances of
their acquaintance would suggest. After 1929, Mahoney worked in the
Americas. To keep any kind of contact, Burra had to work quite hard,
and yet Mahoney was not a wit, in the sense that, say, Conrad Aiken
was a wit and a letter-writer of genius. But Burra wanted to know what
happened to him, and took care that he did.

Another of Rubinstein's dancers of whom he became very fond was
the Dane Birger Bartholin, whom he also went around with a good deal.
Bartholin was, like Burra, a young man of good family, known to some
of his English acquaintances as 'the Baron'. He originally trained as a
painter (he worked in an Impressionist manner, and while he was not
strongly original, he was more than competent). His interest in the
visual arts obviously gave him common ground with Burra. Chappell
describes Bartholin fondly: 'He was a neat, elegant dancer from
Copenhagen, with a nature of pure gold.' Bar was not so keen on him;
Burra wrote defensively to her, 'I adore him whatever you say he was
hysterics & shows miles of gum' – that is, he was one of those people
whose upper lip skins right back when they laugh.

Bartholin was notably less poor than his colleagues in the Ballets Ida Rubinstein. He had an apartment in Montparnasse, and his family regularly sent him money, with which he was generous: he was greatly impressed with Ashton's waspish wit, and happy to subsidise him ('Fred used to bully him unmercifully as he always did when he had someone he liked absolutely under his thumb,' said Chappell, in an interview he gave much later to Julie Kavanagh). Bartholin and Burra spent some time in Paris together in May 1929; since Burra says, of mutual friends of himself and Chappell, 'Bartholin and me asked them to dinner yesterday . . .' he was possibly staying with the dancer. He was again going about with Bartholin and Sophie Fedorovitch in Paris in 1931, and renewed the acquaintance in London in the spring of 1932.

But Bartholin seems to have left London owing his friends money, since Bar wrote in 1935 (from Madrid), 'I got a shock when studying the pictures outside the Alhambra to see a large smiling fuzz of the Baron Bartholin, he is here with the Fokine Co! I've not seen him in the flesh & I don't suppose we'll any of us get our money back.' Little is heard of him in the correspondence after the Thirties, though Burra's diaries note his various addresses in Denmark, where he enjoyed a distinguished career as a dancer, impresario, teacher and choreographer of the Danish ballet. Sophie Fedorovitch worked with him periodically, which meant that although Burra never visited Denmark, he had news of Bartholin from time to time, and they occasionally met when Bartholin passed through London, even as late as the Seventies.

Meanwhile back in 1929, Burra met his ballet friends in the Select most nights, and he, Ashton, Sophie and Chappell also enjoyed visiting the overtly gay bars on the rue de Lappe: far more down and dirty institutions than the cafés of Montparnasse, since they catered primarily to a local and working-class clientele. 'The loveliest thing about the dancing in the Rue de Lappe is that one sees the <u>toughest</u> creatures in check caps and mufflers with <u>heavily</u> painted faces dancing together,' observed Chappell. A Canadian poetaster called John Glassco similarly saw 'heavy men with the muscles of coal-heavers, rouged, powdered and lipsticked', and found himself being 'waltzed around the floor by a coal-black Negro of ferocious appearance who never uttered a word'.

Burra had a wonderful time there. 'We went to the Rue de Lappe on Sunday me & Billy danced a beautiful tango my dear you shold have seen it and as for Freddie he was surrounded by doubtful Spaniards who terrified him into paying for all there drinks they also took all Sophies cigarettes when she was doing a can can with Billy . . . I have done a drawing of the scene on the strength of it.'

This is the only known instance of the adult Burra dancing; he must have been feeling remarkably well – though he did have an instinct to dance. Chappell says that when they were teenagers, mucking about in the echoing corrugated-iron drill hall at Springfield where they went in wet weather, Burra would sometimes improvise a *zapateado*, stamping and windmilling his skinny arms (and, because of the corrugated iron, 'producing a thunderous response from the sounding board of the roof', which must have been part of the point). By his twenties, his feet were too damaged for him to do much jumping around.

Another place the friends of 1929 all liked was the Bal Nègre on the rue Blomet, near Montparnasse, but over in the 15th arrondissement. Joan Miró had his studio in the rue Blomet, and a number of French surrealists of the mid-Twenties worked there, but the draw for the ballet crowd was that the Hôtel Jeanne d'Arc, also on that street, was a flophouse for black workers from the French colonies. The Bal Nègre was their bar. It was a great place to go to watch, rather than to listen, since musically the flavour was French-Antilles Creole rather than the US jazz/blues which fascinated modernists, but the dancing was wonderful. Their particular dance was the Biguine (as it was then spelt): 'two short gliding steps resulting in a supple swaying of the hips form its essential principle. The Biguine differs from the "blues", characterised by a swaying of the whole body, and from the "Charleston", which is nothing more than a rhythmic exercise.' Sophie Fedorovitch was enchanted with it, and often went to watch.

But sociability, gossip opportunities and even hopeless passion only take you so far. By the third week of October, the company was gearing up for its European tour, and Burra decided to go home. While it was one thing to cheer from the sidelines of the Hôtel Saint Brieuc, it was another actually to follow Ida Rubinstein about from city to city on what promised, in any case, to be a nightmare tour. 'The real truth is the pace was getting too hot for me by far,' he confessed to Bar. Leaving aside the possibility that his emotions were painfully involved, he did not have the energy to cope indefinitely with the storms generated by a group of extremely fit and volatile young people working under unremitting pressure. Doone had a filthy temper, and he and Ashton quarrelled all the time, due to

Doone's resentment of Ashton's pretensions as a choreographer, while Ashton and Chappell were also at war due to Ashton's resentment of Chappell's sexual success. Chappell was by that point making up for being a late starter, and had become the 'undisputed queen' of Select. Burra commented, rather wearily, 'If Fred & Billy are going to share a room on tour for the sake of economy it will be no economy as after 10 minutes they'll be clawing off the taps of the washbasin to ram up each other's bums.'

The tour turned out to be exasperating for all concerned. After months of gruelling work, it was depressing to find their efforts ruined by their *soi-disant* star. 'All the work we did building up for her entrances would sag right down,' Ashton recalled. '*On* would come this poor old thing and everything would collapse.' Osbert Sitwell said, 'the effect was that an amateur, upon whom the spotlight had happened to fall, had strolled into the middle of a performance of professionals'. The tour was run entirely according to Madame Rubinstein's whims. She suffered severely from stage-fright, and when she decided she simply could not go on, she would cancel the engagement without warning, leaving the dancers stranded in a cheap hotel till she had regained her nervous tone. Dancers deserted right and left; Chappell wrote to Burra in a panic, 'now everyone has left I have been put into the front of a pas de quatre in the Bach Ballet. It is far too difficult for me . . .' He returned sadder and wiser perhaps, but certainly a better dancer, and committed to a dance career.

In his own writings, Chappell is invariably modest about his abilities as a dancer, and inclined to put his professional career down to the sheer shortage of men in his day. But though he was never a virtuoso, he had real gifts. Mary Clarke, historian of the Sadler's Wells Ballet, described him on the one hand as 'a limited dancer', but added, '[he] was so good in the parts that really suited him that they have ever since been associated with his name'. He created nearly forty roles between 1930 and 1939, and his dreamy, diffident, lyrical temperament led Marie Rambert to choose him to recreate two of Nijinsky's most famous roles, *Le Spectre de la rose* and the Faun in *L'après-midi d'un faune*. The male dancer in *Spectre* is supposed literally to represent the ghost of a perfume – that of the rose which the young girl had worn on her ball-dress. Since he was not noted for elevation, Chappell cannot have made much of the famous final moment in *Spectre*, when Nijinsky, with his unique talent for jumping, seemed, as he leaped off stage, actually to hang in the air; but he could certainly have conveyed the bizarre, dreamily romantic flavour of the piece as a whole. And he was wonderful in *L'après-midi*. Peter Brinson observes:

As the faun he moved with an astonishing grace and indolent sensuality which has stayed in my mind. When she showed me the film Marie Rambert said it was Chappell's self-confessed indolence and sense of style which led her to choose him for so difficult a re-creation.

With Chappell thus signed up for a life in ballet, Burra, thereafter, was an eager participant in the ups and downs of a career in a world that was, at that time, running absolutely on a shoestring. Ida Rubinstein was not the only impresario to leave her dancers on the verge of starvation. The £5 per performance Ashton got out of Covent Garden in 1927 was the exception: the rule was more Ballet Rambert's tariff of 3s. 6d. for boys and 2s. 6d. for girls (as an index of what this meant, a cheap lunch at the Express Dairy cost between 10½d. and 1s. 3d.).

Burra commiserated with Chappell when things went wrong, congratulated when things went right, and sent news of ballet events round the rest of their circle. He enjoyed getting involved:

Did I tell you of Sophie & me picking corn to compose a suitable bouquet for Sockolova in Sacre last Monday week? Sophie insisted on having corn so having climbed over a high hedge full of brambles we picked an imense sheaf of corn & staggered back with it looking like a bit of old Russia as Gerry [Reitlinger] said such a useful bouquet as with a little grinding & kneading you could make ever such an economical pudding with it.

He was perhaps a little less pleased that Marie Rambert encouraged Chappell to combine his art-school and ballet training by designing sets and costumes, which Burra longed to do himself. Chappell's first venture as a designer was *Leda and the Swan*, for the Ballet Rambert, choreographed by Frederick Ashton, in 1928. His next was *Capriol Suite*, also for the Ballet Rambert, inspired by Thoinot Arbeau's 1588 treatise on dance, *Orchésographie*, which Cyril Beaumont had translated in 1925, re-interpreted by the composer Peter Warlock (real name Michael Heseltine). This was, to some extent, a recreation of sixteenth-century dance, carefully researched, and therefore unusually intellectual for a ballet of its

Henry Curteis Burra,
Edward Burra's father.

Ermyntrude (Trudy) Burra
(extreme left, in profile),
Edward Burra's mother, with
unidentified family members.

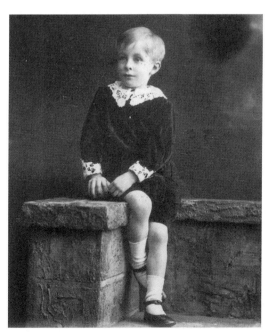

Studio photograph of Burra
aged about five.

Snapshot of Burra with his sister Anne
as children at Camber Sands near Rye.

Springfield Lodge, Playden, Burra's home from his birth to the mid-Fifties.

Burra's personal landscape: the view from the hill behind Springfield Lodge.

Burra's drawing of his nanny, Miss Isabel McCallum (c. 1924).

Burra's drawing of his youngest sister, Betsy, when she was nine (c. 1924).

Billy Chappell aged 16 or 17.

Chappell at 18.

Billy Chappell in the 'Creole Boy' costume from the ballet *Rio Grande* (designed by Burra), 1932, photographed by Barbara Ker-Seymer.

Burra in his studio, photographed by Barbara Ker-Seymer.

'Birdie' Rushbury in the early Twenties, dressed as
an Augustus John gypsy, by Burra's Royal College
tutor, Randolph Schwabe.

Anne Burra, photographed
by Barbara Ker-Seymer (c. 1930).

Barbara Ker-Seymer in 1925.

Clover Pritchard.

Burra and Clover looking out of the window of Bar's flat, 4 Church Street, May 1935.

Bumble Dawson (c. 1930).

Gerald Corcoran (c. 1930).

John Banting, early Thirties.

Doris Langley Moore in fancy dress (c. 1930).

time. Chappell's part in the enterprise was not unduly glamorous; far from permitting him to revel with the brocade and pearls that might be naturally associated with an 'Elizabethan' ballet, Rambert led him firmly to John Barker's bargain basement where they bought beige linen at 6d. a yard and pink linen at 2s. 6d.

Burra's concern, after seeing this ballet, that Chappell should not, thereby, see fit to give himself airs is evidenced by a 'fan letter' which he sent, written on the shocking-pink paper that he frequently used.

Dear Mr Chappell

Nite after nite I have admired yr legs they certinly r yr trump card. When you come on as a nun I can hardly stay still and in 'Vitriol Suit' by that wonderful Frederick Ashton you are a dream especially wen yr shoes fly off showing a beautiful foot.

May I hope for a photo?? most other stars (Gertie Gitana, Scot & Waley etc)[2] have sent me ones. believe me you do not guess at what you bring to my life. Thanking you in anticipation from

Your 'shadow Fan'

P.S.

I am an other & sent one of my little booklets for even dancers have kiddies.

Burra almost invariably referred to this ballet as *Vitriol Suite* thereafter (the Cinderella-like shoe loss did occur, but only once). It may be worth noticing that 'shadow Fan' has literary pretensions. Burra may be hinting that Chappell should stick to his trade, and not encroach on Burra's own domain.

Chappell's work as a designer was, at its best, charming but never challenging; suited to ballets with a sentimental, nineteenth-century feel, such as Ashton's *Les Patineurs*, for which he designed treillage suggesting an early Victorian public park and very becoming period skating-costumes. The ballet has remained in the Royal Ballet's repertory, and 'there has been no attempt to improve on designs that always seemed just right'. His designs for *Les Rendezvous* (a ballet that was, to a great extent, his conception) have similarly remained classic; though other of his designs have since been dropped as fussy or clichéd. His work tended to be a little bit too sugary.

[2] The former a music-hall star whose most famous song was 'Nellie Dean', the latter a black tapdancing minstrel duo who did a comic radio show for the BBC from 1927; their characters were called Pussyfoot and Cuthbert. Chappell is being warned not to get above himself.

Burra was somewhat jealous, and beginning to wonder what he himself could do with a ballet. As early as 1929 he had had hopes of doing stage work. He wrote excitedly in his diary for 3 and 4 January:

Mr Cochran rang up!!! You could have bowled me over with a toothpick. Mr Gwernts to see my work all I can say is I hope something will come of it however I dont expect anything & wont be disapoint. I hop the Leicester will give up my portfolio ... Got Portfolio out of Leicester without a murmur. Mr 'Corker' so charming and says he is so sorry not to have seen my work before he aranged all the scenery for the 1929 revue but will give me something in next (I hope).

Mr Cochran is the entrepreneur C.B. Cochran, who staged many of the revues Burra and his friends loved most, particularly the successive 'Blackbirds', which showcased black American artists.

Cochran never came through, which is much to be regretted, but the Camargo Society, which the distinguished Russian dancer Lydia Lopokova and a number of associates founded in 1929 to foster the creation of new ballets, had its eye on Burra from its inception. The Society's minutes show that when they were planning their first season at the beginning of 1930, there were thoughts of a ballet based on part of César Franck's unperformed opera, *Hulda* (goodness knows why, since it has a blood-stained Wagnerian plot in which Hulda, abducted by enemy Aslaks, avenges her slaughtered family). Arnold Haskell, a founder member of the Society, was asked whether he thought Burra would be suitable as a designer, but, perhaps fortunately, the project was quietly dropped.

In 1932, Anthony Tudor choreographed *Lysistrata* for the Ballet Rambert (it received its first performance in March that year): Chappell is named as the designer, and the costumes that resulted could be described as Bakst-and-water, a *réchauffé* of elements from the great Russian designer's *Daphnis and Chloë* and *L'Après-midi d'un faune*. But mysteriously, there is a surviving costume drawing for *Lysistrata* which could have come from no other hand than Burra's, much more modernist in conception. Burra was always more interested in the work itself than in being recognised; he may, perhaps, have tried out some ideas as a result of discussion with Chappell.

In the same year, he finally got a chance to try his hand at set-design. Lopokova had been so struck by Constant Lambert's jazz-influenced piece for chorus and orchestra, *Rio Grande* (1927), that she bought the rights to it for the Camargo Society in 1930. The Society was not itself a ballet troupe, but drew as necessary on dancers and other personnel from the Ballet Rambert and Ninette de Valois's Vic-Wells Ballet, and she leaned on Ashton to choreograph it for her, over his protests that he had too much to do for Mim already. 'It is absolutely nonsense,' she told him, 'you must do it.' Her bullying was combined with a tempting offer of double the money, a whole £20, not £10. They kissed and made up, and he got to work.

The direction Ashton decided to take (somewhat against the grain of the poem by Sacheverell Sitwell that was the point of origin of the piece) was to draw on his memories of Toulon holidays, and create a dockside scene of sailors, tarts, stokers and riff-raff. Lydia Lopokova was Queen of the Port, Walter Gore her Sailor, while Alicia Markova and Billy Chappell were a Creole Girl and Boy. It was almost inevitable, therefore, that he should ask Burra to design it. Burra, delighted, painted a backcloth based on the dolphin fountain at Raymond's Bar in Toulon, smothered in creepers, further ornamented by a nude statue (the nude was later suppressed by the straitlaced Lilian Bayliss, manager of the Old Vic, who, as it were, activated the fountain and disappeared her under flowing water). He also created a frontcloth, which, sadly, does not survive even in a photograph, since it was a great success. Ashton remembered:

The buzz of surprise in the audience . . . when the curtain rose on the front cloth of Rio Grande, showing a row of houses in the brothel quarter of a southern sea port; the shutters open to reveal in every window the most wonderfully outrageous tarts. It produced the same kind of buzz – slightly startled, half affronted, half delighted – that greeted Picasso's front cloth for *Le Train Bleu* at the Coliseum in the nineteen twenties.

Burra's costume designs were also very effective. They were unusually sexy; sufficiently so that some of the ballet mothers took their daughters out of the cast. Ashton was particularly pleased with Chappell's Creole Boy costume: white trousers and singlet, but with the neck and armholes outlined in silver sequins; dramatic against tanned (or fake-tanned) skin. '[Burra] had a gift for this kind of heightening of reality, which produced a strong theatrical effect. When the dancers carefully followed the make-up and the hair styles – both clearly delineated in his costume drawings – the result was not only splendidly unusual but acutely realistic; again the same *heightened* reality.' He was the first designer in Ashton's experience to use sequins with cotton. However, Cyril Beaumont was shocked by the Tarts' 'skin-tight bodices, dresses about six inches long at the front, bare thighs and stockinged legs', which was not at all what anyone was used to in an English ballet in 1932. Some of the girls also had what Lopokova delicately described as 'a big flower sticking out in a little place'.

Lopokova's own costume seems to have been derived from Olga Baclanova's outfit in Josef von Sternberg's 1928 film *The Docks of New York*, which amused Burra so much he drew it in a letter to Chappell ('Baclanova is a rare old gem of the streets too in a blouse & skirt a protruding tum (& bum)'). The designer, Hans Dreier, had produced a masterpiece of atmospheric seediness (though of course in black and white), and Burra evidently learned a good deal from it.

One of *Rio Grande*'s other claims to historical importance is that, as chance would have it, it was one of the first ballets ever seen by a solemn thirteen-year-old then called Peggy Hookham, recently arrived in London from Singapore. When it was revived three years later, in 1935, she was dancing in it. The first named role of Margot Fonteyn (as she became) was Markova's original part of the Creole Girl. Innocent as she was, she made a precocious success of projecting zestful sexiness, partly from innate ability, but also because she had a terrific crush on Billy Chappell, the first man who is known to have attracted her.

Burra's next design opportunity came when he was asked to do *Barabau* for the Vic-Wells Ballet. The first *Barabau*, to music by Vittorio Rieti, had been choreographed by George Balanchine in 1925 for Diaghilev with designs by Utrillo; and was a hit in Diaghilev's Coliseum season of that year. It was always a successful ballet for him, but because the music was partly supplied by a chorus, it was expensive to stage and dropped out of the repertory for that reason. The Vic-Wells version of 1936 was choreographed by Ninette de Valois as a satiric comedy, with political overtones. Barabau is the hero of an Italian nursery rhyme:

> Barabau, Barabau, why did you die?
> You'd wine in your cellar, your bread was not dry,
> And salad you grew in your garden near by:
> Barabau, Barabau, why did you die?

In 1936, Mussolini's Fascisti were worrying the English public a great deal – it was the year of the Axis pact between Mussolini and Hitler. In de Valois's ballet, Barabau entertains his friends with food and wine, a group of Fascist soldiers arrive and Barabau is killed. The important female role was a friend of Barabau's, who fiercely resists the military tyranny of the Fascist Sergeant. Ashton danced the part of the Sergeant, Ninette de Valois herself was the Peasant Woman, Harold Turner, Barabau. Arnold Haskell judged, '*Barabau* is the most successful of her *bouffes*; here she has preserved the Italian village atmosphere and made splendid play with her company of Fascists, and the laughs come because she has been true to life.' The ballet was successful enough to be revived early in the Second World War as a response to the times, at which point Ashton exaggerated his part so as to make it a broad caricature of Mussolini, which was well received. But it did not outlast its Thirties context. However, Burra produced some very bold designs for it; the peasants were effective, but it was the soldiers who gave him most scope for camp invention.

There were a couple of abortive ballet-projects in the Thirties. He and Ashton played with the idea of an 'opium' ballet, which went far enough for Burra to complete a drop-curtain design: a mass of huge red poppies and sinister insects framing a vista of dreamy addicts, leaning, as much as anything, on his studies of the actual flowers. Oriental poppies were, as they still are, common plants for the herbaceous border; there were almost certainly some at Springfield. Burra also did an opium-den painting around the same time. Since he had never seen an opium den, it is patently based on descriptions in authoritative guides such as the Fu Manchu and Fantômas books, or illustrations in sensational journals such as the *Illustrated Police News*, which gave a full page to 'A West-End Opium Den' on 2 January 1919.

It is worth observing that, in the Thirties, Burra was successful in establishing himself as a designer. Despite his general waywardness and frequent debility, he was completely professional and reliable. However, his work was too individual for him to be considered a general designer. He was only called upon when someone was projecting a show which was manifestly connected with his known interests. But, having designed successfully for both Ashton and de Valois, he was involved with a number of subsequent projects which came to fruition in the Forties and Fifties. These, since they belong to very different moments, will be discussed in context.

VIII

SPAIN

Burra fell in love with the idea of Spain years before he went there. He was excited in his twenties by Spanish art in the Louvre and other major collections, and in particular by the work of painters from the sixteenth through to the eighteenth centuries, El Greco, Zurbarán, Ribera and Goya. Back home at Springfield, his reading also included the writings of Sacheverell Sitwell, which introduced him to the intensely dramatic architecture and sculpture of the Jesuit baroque churches of Mexico, and books on Spanish baroque sculpture.

But, following on from his interest in Spanish art, he also became attracted to Spanish literary culture. Clover was also interested, so they started teaching themselves the language in 1932, from Hugo's *Spanish Simplified* (Who has taken the ink? The man has an axe. Has the servant given a chair to the gentleman?, etc.). Burra was serious about learning languages. Among the notes in his pocketbooks are random lists of words in Spanish – and also in Italian – often with English equivalents; these are clearly the result of going through a chapter of a book he intended to read, noting unfamiliar words and looking them up in a dictionary before actually applying himself to the text. These notes suggest that he never made much headway with Italian, a language, and culture, that interested him less, but that his Spanish became quite sophisticated.

With Hugo behind them, Burra and Clover began avidly reading Spanish poetry, both pre-modern and contemporary: Federico García Lorca, Rafael Alberti, the Machado brothers, Francisco de Quevedo and Luis de Góngora, starting with Góngora, perhaps the most gratuitously baroque of all seventeenth-century poets. Burra seized upon a line of Góngora's, 'a mis soledades voy, de mis soledades vengo' ('to my solitudes I go, from my solitudes I come'), and habitually quoted it when anyone was unwise enough to ask him about his movements. He also acquired a personal motto, from the Andalusian poet Juan Ramon Jiminez, 'la minoria siempre' ('always join the minority'), a principle that he showed no hesitation in living up to. This love-affair with Spain and its culture was an important part of his relationship with Clover and Conrad Aiken, who were both Hispanophile and Hispanophone, though other close friends, such as Bar and Chappell, did not share it (Chappell, for all that his was a travelling life, never really liked 'abroad': he was suspicious of foreign food, and preferred by far to stay in England).

In the years running up to the Civil War, when Burra was first there, an encounter with Spain was an extraordinarily intense experience. Visitors found Spanish lives, manners and entertainments of the Twenties and early Thirties apparently untouched by external influences. According to temperament, they perceived it either as archaic or timeless. But another point, too, is acutely made by Gertrude Bone, who was a regular visitor to Spain with her husband, the artist Muirhead Bone, in the interwar period: 'The sensation which goes with one all the time through modern Spain [is] that one is seeing the last of things.' Her loving recollections of an almost medieval society are balanced against her perception of 'an impatience of backwardness and old fashions manifest in all parts of the country . . . it is evident that even such recent scenes as are described in the present volume have been witnessed for the last time by the Spaniard himself.'

Conrad Aiken, who was there in 1926, summed up old Spain trenchantly:

Spain: stinks. Hokusai colouring: red soil, grassless, planted for miles with olive orchards and cork trees. Hard slaty mountains, bare and sharp. Aridity. Buzzards, vultures, eagles, and orioles. Red goats, red pigs, red sheep, all in one herd, tended by a boy with a stick. Goats with protracted bifurcated udders which drag on the ground. White houses with flat roofs, barred windows; cactus, prickly pear, and aloes. Open drains in the street frequently. Children wear no drawers and use the streets (preferably adjacent to a wall) for all purposes.

The Spanish countryside struck visitors as extraordinarily spacious and bare. 'Ashen and orange fields . . . economy of landscape . . . the accent

of black on tawny and bronze.' Tristram Hillier similarly loved the light
and the landscape.

The translucent light of the south is comparable to that of Greece, which so deeply
fascinated me, with the addition of a dramatic quality, both noble and cruel, with
which the landscape as well as the people are invested . . . a land set apart from
all others, but one pre-eminently to inspire a painter.

Burra responded strongly to this combination of dry, sparse beauty with
squalor; and also to the cultural life of Spain, both popular and literary.

His first visit to Spain was in 1933, two years after Spain became a
republic. Aiken, whom Burra had got to know a couple of years earlier
in Rye, sailed for Spain in April of that year with his then-wife Clarissa
(whom he usually referred to as Jerry because she was of German extrac-
tion), and the younger writer Malcolm Lowry. According to a later letter
to Kempton Taylor, in which Aiken detailed his chronic money worries,
'My trip to Spain, if that's what you're thinking of, wasn't a holiday by
a damned sight – I was in charge of a dipsomaniac, and was paid for
it.' The dipsomaniac was Malcolm Lowry. It was Lowry's long-suffering
father, who gave Aiken $100 a month as teacher-therapist to his wayward
son, who was doing the paying.

Aiken was by any normal standards an extremely heavy drinker
(Lowry's future wife, Jan Gabrial, described him bitterly as a 'bottle-
a-day bard with full blown sexual neuroses'), but he was functional;
indeed, he could get a great deal done in a day. Lowry, on the other
hand, was an alcoholic in the sense that drink was rapidly paralysing
his ability to achieve anything at all. The book that made him famous,
Under the Volcano, is essentially about alcoholism and its effects on
the personality. His relationship with Aiken, twenty years his senior,
was complex. Profoundly moved and impressed by Aiken's semi-autobiographical novel, *Blue Voyage*, the twenty-year-old Lowry had
attached himself to the older man as tutee, or perhaps sorcerer's
apprentice, in 1929. Aiken, deeply flattered by this hero-worship from
a genuinely talented youngster, and sufficiently short of money that
the dole from Lowry's father (which, when he was in England, translated into about five guineas a week) was a real inducement, took him
on as a son in art. Four days after their first meeting they got so
drunk together they ended up having a wrestling-match at one in the

morning in which Aiken fell and fractured his skull – this might have served as a warning to both men that they were bringing out the worst in each other, but it did not. Aiken remained more or less *in loco parentis* to Lowry for some years (some might say, with the emphasis on 'loco'). He took Lowry to Rye with him in August 1930, and Lowry was also there in 1931, around the time when Aiken got to know Burra.

Lowry was charming, insecure and difficult. His quasi-father-and-son relationship with Aiken was one of terrific oedipal tension, fuelled by prodigious quantities of alcohol and punctuated by mutual accusations of plagiarism. Unfortunately for Lowry, in the game of more *maudit* than thou, Aiken was an easy winner. Lowry was damaged by a cold and indifferent mother, and by the suicide of a Cambridge friend in which he was possibly implicated. Aiken, however, at the age of nine, had witnessed his own father killing first his mother, then himself.

Burra's relationship with Aiken, on the other hand, was constructed on quite different principles. He had been delighted in 1931 to meet someone living within walking distance with whom he could talk seriously about modern literature, about America and, indeed, about Spain, since Aiken had studied Spanish at Harvard. Burra was deeply interested by, and even fond of, Aiken, whom he regarded as a close friend, but there was absolutely none of the upwelling of irrational feeling that characterised Aiken's relationship with Lowry, and vice versa. Predictably, therefore, Lowry disliked him.

Their mutual situation made this inevitable, but beyond that, Burra had a lifelong distaste for posturing, particularly the macho variety; he was an acknowledged master of the lightning put-down, and Lowry was far too fragile to have any capacity to laugh at himself, especially that particular summer, since Aiken had just taken on a second young genius, much of an age with Lowry: Edward Doro, the son of a Californian banker, and a would-be poet.[1]

Aiken encouraged the two young writers to strive for his attention. Burra was also young; but he was a painter, a métier that Aiken could

---

[1] Doro did in fact go on to produce a number of slim volumes of verse. Burra bought or was given a copy of the first, *Alms for Oblivion*, and thought it worth keeping, since it was among the books in his house when he died. He and Doro became rather good friends, and stayed in touch through the Thirties. However, though he was clearly a much more agreeable person than Lowry, Doro's impact on the world of letters was negligible.

not influence in any way. Furthermore, his disabilities made him seem ageless, like a changeling, and the confidence of his class and background, combined with his justifiable faith in his own abilities, put him in a different bracket from Lowry and Doro, who were Aiken's disciples. If Aiken ever tried on him the destabilising manipulations to which he subjected Lowry, Burra shrugged them off, and bore no grudge.

Aiken enjoyed Burra's company, but Clarissa felt sorry for Lowry, and distrusted Burra, who dined with them weekly, for his capacity to tease. Burra's observation, made to mutual friends, that although the Aikens kept complaining about poverty he noticed there was always plenty to drink, got back to her, and she was disinclined to forgive him for it. Or for his lack of sympathy when Aiken had trouble with his teeth: when the older man railed at fate, roaring and swigging whisky, Burra suggested acidly that he might be cutting new ones. He had absolutely no tolerance for self-pity, to which Aiken was sometimes prone.

However, the Aikens were, as so often, broke in 1933, and Clarissa's doctor had ordered her to have a holiday. Conrad wanted to go back to Spain, and Burra wanted to see Granada; so they decided to go together. Burra had a very strong preference for travelling with a companion, or in a group of friends, probably because, for good reason, he was afraid of being ill, helpless and alone in a cheap hotel, and on that basis would have been good-tempered about paying slightly more than his share, if necessary. He was, however, not unduly optimistic about this particular adventure, which was first mooted in October 1932. 'A daintie "colony" is forming to go to Spain in January as we have found a pension at about 3/- per day the "colony" will be down each others throats in 2 ticks I may add.'

The Aikens and Lowry eventually sailed from Tilbury to Gibraltar in April 1933, went by train to Ronda, and thence to Granada, where Aiken had booked two rooms at the Pension Carmona near the Alhambra. This was a white stucco building which had had quite a few artist patrons, including Manuel de Falla, Herbert Read and, rather earlier, John Singer Sargent, and it was near to the Generalife gardens and the Alhambra. The proprietors approved of Aiken, who both spoke Spanish and was known to be a poet. Clarissa describes it thus:

Weather permitting, we ate al fresco, enclosed by flowering bushes and fruit trees, a fountain and a well. Pomegranate petals dropped into our omelet, soup, or *olla podrida*, delicious fare. All this for twelve pesetas a day. The smell of olive oil and saffron blended with musk and urine.

Lowry, however, was thrown by Spain from the start. He was, like Hamlet, fat and scant of breath, and the heat made him pour with sweat. He was not at all interested in the art or the architecture, in history or natural beauty. He observed the grotesque poverty; the cripples lying in the white dust, their faces swarming with flies.

A legless man on a stool used the stool for legs, & his heart went out to them. If I could reach them – their hearts! Only those who are low, down, down, only those who really suffer ... the heat, the dust, the terrible heat, the suffering ...

But it is questionable what he meant by 'reach'; since he was more than disconcerted to find that the Spanish street-people were observing him right back, quite as if they had equal rights as human beings, and, moreover, that they were not at all impressed by him. The name that followed him around was *cochinito* ('little porker').

Even more disconcertingly, an English couple coincided, quite by chance, with Aiken's party at the Villa Carmona: I.A. Richards and his wife Dorothea (née Pilley). Apart from the fact that they were old friends of Aiken's, sophisticated, much travelled and well read, this was particularly discomfiting, since Richards had been Lowry's examiner for his final Cambridge examinations, in which he had achieved a somewhat abject Third. Dorothea, though neither an academic nor a writer, was also a considerable personality in her own right: a climber with extensive experience in the Alps, Pyrenees and Dolomites. Neither of them was pleased to be thrown into the company of a boorish and delinquent ex-student about whom Richards, at least, knew much, none of it greatly to his credit.

Then Burra arrived: 'a travel-weary, shabby figure in a dusty green hat and dragging a stuffed laundry bag, his only luggage. "I took the wrong train from Barcelona and got lost", he said in his languid voice. "But then I wound up in Almeria, a spot so beautiful I wouldn't have missed it for the world."' Almería is the hottest corner of Spain, an extraordinary desert, semi-lunar landscape of sandstone cones and dried-up riverbeds. The city is at the foot of a mountain, with a Moorish military fort at the summit, of which little but walls and towers survive. The 'laundry bag' was in fact a sailor's duffel-bag, Burra's favourite travelling-kit.

He and Lowry shared a room for economy's sake, where Burra, as always, worked throughout the day. Aiken recorded lightly fictionalised memories of the holiday in his semi-autobiographical novel *Ushant* (I have replaced Aiken's sobriquets with the real names; his other significant departure from the facts is to imply that the quartet had a room each):

Lowry and Burra and Aiken and Clarissa all had balcony rooms round the blossoming patio, and its sprawling pomegranate, at Granada, and where, at almost any hour of the day or night, one could see, protruding from beneath Burra's bed, Lowry's feet, as he there thrummed away – four years later – on that very taropatch; while Burra, on a broken-legged table, glued his papers together, and smoked, and painted.[2]

This is substantially the same picture that Anthony Powell gave of Burra in Toulon; some kind of surface, however rickety, was appropriated, and Burra then painted there doggedly for much of the day, smoking incessantly (Gauloise for preference), and pasting together sheets of paper as he needed them. It stands for all Burra's sojourns in cheap hotels in various parts of the world.

Burra's relationship with Aiken continued on its previous footing; he made himself entertaining. Clarissa remembered him singing old music-hall songs in a jaunty falsetto, which amused Aiken, though not Lowry. Aiken, who was rather tired of his protégé, suggested shortly after Burra's arrival that Lowry show him the town. Without enthusiasm, Lowry did as he was told, meeting, as usual, with the mockery of the street, since he had acquired an enormous Spanish hat, which caused outbreaks of mirth wherever he went. Burra had a good comprehension of Spanish by then, and he was intensely amused to hear someone

---

[2] A taropatch is an instrument descended from a Portuguese type of guitar, probably so named because it was popular with Hawaiian farm workers, who mostly worked in the taro fields. It had eight strings in four courses and was tuned like a ukulele, but was slightly larger. Outside Hawaii, it proved to be less popular than the ukulele, as it was harder to play; the principal manufacturer discontinued it in 1932. Lowry had played one since his schooldays.

remark, 'The big one is a German drunk, and the skinny one is queer', a comment which he promptly translated. It infuriated Lowry, as Burra no doubt guessed it would.

Burra often drew while he was talking; his path through life was littered with casual cartoons. One evening, he sketched a caricature of Lowry as a sombrero-wearing blimp, which the *padrona*'s son-in-law, who disliked Lowry intensely, grabbed and showed around. It made everybody laugh: Lowry, however, showed how susceptible he was to teasing by seizing the caricature, drawing a crude pipe in its mouth and tearing it up. He then turned on Burra. 'That was an unkind thing to do. The trouble with you is that people are too good to you.' 'Oh, you don't know half the things they say about me,' was Burra's deflating response, in his Mayfair cockney drawl.

Lowry, as usual, was drinking heavily. Evenings of more or less civilised conversation with the Richardses were interrupted by alcoholic harangues from Lowry, which annoyed Aiken, or sometimes Lowry disappeared entirely, so that Aiken was forced to co-opt Burra into helping him scour the cantinas for his delinquent protégé, which annoyed him even more.

But if life at the hotel was not always harmonious, there was a great deal in Granada to interest Burra. He, like Lowry, observed the wretched poverty in the streets, the cripples, the legless man propelling himself along on a stool. But there was more.

In the Albaicín – that crowded town – high whitewashed walls with narrow steep ways lead suddenly to a blind plaza with a latticed window and one green tree. There are ways whose straitness admits no vehicle and where one must stand against the wall to let the strings of donkeys go by. Streets and plazas have the air of something not secret, but not discussed. The eyeless streets (with windows looking inwards) are at once populous and furtive.

Burra loved it, with characteristic qualifications. He distrusted picturesqueness, and was not seduced by the aspects that struck either Lowry or Gertrude Bone. He wrote to Nash:

I don't realy know how I ever got here from Barcelona having got into the wrong train one & gone to Almeira & then failed to change it was all a dream the journey to Almeira I went by mistake was marvellous with mountains & ravines & lovely colour as for Granada its marvelous . . . its realy another Rye of course full of quaint old antiques & corners & imitation gypsys

Barcelona was lovely nothing but music halls and bars and cinemas . . . they did some lovely dancing with castanets however in daintie spanish costumes of black transparent net with diamonte embroidery (over the parts) . . . Conrad looks <u>worlds</u> better & so does la bonita Clarissa who whenever she moves out is attacked by millions of men who rush up and whisper 'guapa' in her ear or la chica bonita hermosa[3] however she bears it very well as for our old Lowry well known in every bar in town he looks flourishing & caused a riot in Ronda by appearing in a pale grey 50/-suit with a green stripe and a ten gallon Spanish hat.

Clarissa's memoirs confirm both the furore in Ronda and the flattering reaction she received from Spanish men.

The hotel, in those pre-air-conditioning days, had the usual disadvantages of the South. Burra commented, 'We have a romantic gypsy moon lighting up the old Alhambras fairy traceries I wouldn't have thought it possible that there could be so many flies as there are here the only place of escape is the cinema.' All the same, this letter ends:

a monster has just arrived here [picture of maniac in trilby with revolving eyes and goatee].
    Best love
    & wishes
    from Ed.
I dont want to leave
Spain not till
I must

Though it is clear from the Nash letter that Burra was not interested in them at the time, the arid, tawny landscape of southern Spain and the dusty, secretive buildings presenting a blank terracotta face to the world, with heavy iron grilles on the windows, sank deep into his mind. They came back to him a year or two later, when he started painting cityscapes as opposed to conversation pieces. The visit was also important for both Aiken and Lowry. Aiken wrote 'The Poet in Granada: Homage to Lorca'. García Lorca, in whom Aiken was interested, was

---

[3] 'Lovely . . . what a gorgeous, beautiful girl'.

the most significant contemporary poet of Granada, where his family had moved when he was eleven. Though Lorca himself was not there that spring, Ángel Barrios, a guitarist and Lorca's friend, ran a wineshop called El Polinario, where Aiken's party often went, and was happy to talk about him. Strongly identified as a man of the Left, Lorca was then embarking on his career as a dramatist. He would be murdered by Fascist partisans in Granada three years later.

Lowry, more momentously, met his future first wife, a petite, attractive and independent American ex-actress and would-be writer, Jan Gabrial. She arrived at the Carmona on 19 May, a day or two ahead of a boyfriend called Calef, a Syrian from Tangier who was eager to marry her. She observed that her fellow-guests included:

Two solid florid men at an adjoining table, one balding, a third man, smaller, nutlike; and a pallid 'madonna' whose dark hair, tightly pinned, lent her an aspect of enforced submissiveness . . . the madonna paused at my table to introduce herself as Clarissa Aiken and invited me to visit the gypsy caves with her. Later I'd learned that she'd been urged to do so by her husband.

The following day, she and Lowry visited the Generalife Gardens together. She was bowled over by Lowry's conversation; her diary records 'one of the gladdest, maddest mornings of my life . . . laughing so much as to be practically ill'. She was so fascinated by Lowry that the gentle Calef was given his marching orders, though she did not accept Lowry as her lover. She was only twenty-one, and while not precisely virginal, was scared stiff of pregnancy and cautious about committing herself to a full-blown affair. While Lowry yearned, Aiken was also attracted to Jan (he was habitually unfaithful to Clarissa), which increased the oedipal tension between the two men. However, Jan was only in Granada for a few days, after which she departed, as she had originally planned, for Seville. Lowry subsequently pursued her by letter, and they married the following year.

One of the things the quartet certainly did in Granada was to visit a bullfight; this is mentioned in *Ushant*, and confirmed by Burra: 'I went to a bull fight last Sunday my dear its gorgeous all the bulls gore everybody and do the bulls bleed yes sir and do the audience roar with laughter the costumes are lovely my favourite costume was vermilion trimmed with black lace . . .' Burra was wholly unsentimental about animals. A letter of Aiken's from his solo visit in 1926 gives a very full account of a bullfight, and also some context for Burra's reactions.

The audience an important factor – almost more than the bull. Takes sides, goads the bullfighters to take risks, boos and hisses, flings orangepeels, even cushions; the matadors become reckless, agitated, almost hysterical with excitement, especially if they have been having a bad run of luck.

That was fundamentally what interested Burra about the whole business. He made a drawing of a bullfight, which takes its viewpoint from the top of the arena, and focuses on the interactions of the excited spectators: the bull is a small and lonely figure in the distance, the cause, but not the subject. It is directly analogous to his drawings and paintings of stage-shows, which so often foreground the audience (such as *Musical Comedy, Barcelona*), or leave the drama out almost entirely.

He also painted a bullfight in 1933; a picture that is interesting and appalling at the same time, because it is completely static. The bull stands there, blank-eyed and foursquare as a toy, its shoulders stuck with banderillas, bleeding slightly from the nose, having apparently lost any kind of curiosity about its approaching death, while an ape-faced matador advances finickingly, sword extended. It depicts a moment of stasis under the blazing sun (the shadows of man, bull and picadors are black on the sand), from which all possible excitement has drained away. It is not even a painting about passive suffering, and it is a long way from Hemingway's 'moment of truth'. Perhaps it is telling a different truth. The picture evidences no sense of identification with either bull or man (or with the crowd; contrary to Burra's usual habit, one is not drawn into this picture by someone within it who is looking out).

The Spain visit terminated with a brief visit to Spanish Morocco. Relations between Lowry and Aiken had become so difficult that Aiken decided he could not bear to stay in Spain till the end of May, as originally planned. They all four went to Gibraltar, where Lowry remained, while the Aikens and Burra went over to North Africa, for a 'whirlwind look at Ceuta and Tetuan. He sulked, we sweltered.' It is a fair inference that Burra would rather have stayed in Spain, perhaps because he fell unexpectedly in love with Gibraltar; he wrote to Nash in 1934, 'how I envy you being in Marseilles and going to Gib my favourite town I don't know why but its lovely go the music store (union street) and buy me two nice Flamenco gramophone records and I will pay you back every penny.' This visit to Africa made no identifiable impact on Burra's work; there is nothing in his paintings specifically suggestive of Morocco except a painting of 1971 of whirling dervishes, and a pair of costume designs for Moorish servants (for *Carmen*, 1947), either or both of which may conceivably resurrect long-buried memories.

Burra's second visit to Spain was with Clover Pritchard a couple of years later. She had recently reappeared in his life, after three years of silence. The Hungarian count, Adam de Nagy, whom she had married in 1928, had proceeded to maroon her on his country estate near the Czech border, intercept her personal mail and prohibit her from writing to her friends (he was seriously unbalanced, and ultimately committed suicide). However, she had been permitted to write a letter to the *Morning Post* in defence of surrealism. Some time later she was in the garden making a snow statue of the Archduchess Maria Teresa of Austria when the servant who rode into town for the post appeared, and she was able to look through the mail before it was censored by her husband. She found a letter from Ed, Bar and Billy, who had read her statement in the paper, full of affection and making anxious enquiries about her welfare. She decided to walk out, strengthened by the knowledge that her parents were in Buda at the time, staying at the Hotel Gellert. Burra was the first of the friends to get a letter. 'Have just heard from Clover!' he wrote to Bar in spring 1931, 'who has left de Nagy & gone to live for the summer as its so cheap at Hotel St Gellert Szálló Buda P every letter and all her actions have apparently been spied on for years.'

The subsequent negotiations took some time. She returned to England in mid-1932, when she spent part of the summer with Burra and his parents at Springfield, and the two of them embarked on their joint project of learning Spanish. However, in the autumn of the same year, she went to Paris and began an affair with the poet Jules Romains, whom she had met at the French institute in London. Officially, she was his research assistant, and she did indeed spend time in the Bibliothèque Nationale making notes on his behalf. Thus, as Chappell observed drily, moving from the world of Ouida to that of Jean Rhys, though as he also noted, she got more fun out of it than the typical Rhys heroine – she had a natural taste for intrigue. Burra commented, 'she seems to be playing hide and seek in the shadier quarters of Paris from Madame Romains and enjoying it every moment'. He seems to be a little envious; 'I would like to go to Paris for a bit I must say and hang about in shady bistros keeping out of the <u>wifes way</u>.' It was the dramatic aspect that appealed to him. He went over to Paris to see Clover in April 1933, and met Jules Romains, whom he had admired as a writer for some years (Romains was at that time working on *Les Hommes de bonne volonté*).

The affair, however, was not lasting. It erupted into drama around the time Burra arrived: 'A scandal is about to burst shaking le tout Paris to its foundations as Madame Romains has discovered 3 of Clovers letters . . . C is expecting a heavily veiled visitor with a bottle of vitriol. I arrived to visit C and having been looked at suspiciously by the proprietor & spelling the name I was finally allowd up & [to] knock at the door . . .' By spring of 1935, it was definitely over. Burra, perhaps wanting to give Clover sympathy and a change of scene, suggested that he and she should visit Spain together. She describes what ensued:

'I know you'll like it', he said. 'Even better than France. It's much cheaper and the people are much nicer. You feel it as soon as you cross the frontier. They're not after your money all the time. And they're so much better looking.' But his main reason for going was to get away from the Jubilee celebrations of George V and Mary. 'If I hear the word Jubilee again, I'll be sick.'

They got the night-ferry at Newhaven, crossed to Dieppe and took the night-train to Barcelona, third-class. Burra did not believe in spending money on comfort, and in this case it led to an adventure.

As we sat in our corner seats of the night train to Barcelona, a most beautiful moonbeam of a young man got into our compartment after taking leave of an older, shady-looking gangster type who was giving him last instructions on the platform. Ed couldn't take his eyes off our fellow-traveller, whose pale-green skin and eyes, and suit to match made him murmur. 'Verde que te quiero verde', when the young man went into the corridor for a last mutter with his sinister friend . . . We soon stretched out along the seats on that long, hot night journey. The verdant beauty took off his shining patent-leather shoes and his black silk socked feet explored far up my side. A battle of tootsies ensued until we fell asleep. What a look of scorn he gave us in the early morning sunlight as he went off to shave. 'You can't have made the best of that heaven-sent opportunity,' Ed remarked as the moonbeam slid away into the crowded station.

It suggests something of Burra's attitude to his friends' sexual adventures. He liked to observe life imitating fiction. The remark Clover quotes is the first line of Lorca's 'Romance sonámbulo' ('green how much I want you green'), which had been published in 1928.

When they got to Barcelona, the hotel they were heading for, which they had seen advertised in *Paris-Soir*, turned out to be a flea-pit which Clover refused to enter. Burra insisted on staying, while she went off to the Gran Hotel on the other side of Piazza Colon. The first hotel was just as horrible as it had looked, so the next day they compromised on the Hotel Colon, opposite the Barrio Chino, Burra's main objective. This was not unlike the Vielle Ville of Marseilles, but was, if anything, more so. Just as in Marseilles, the buildings still conformed to the medieval street-plan, and it was one of the most densely populated urban areas in the world, insanitary high-rise slums with shafts of sunlight stabbing down into narrow, winding alleys. It was a major centre for Barcelona's sex industry, and a centre for entertainment more generally, exciting and dangerous: Burra had spent a little time there on his first visit to Spain before joining the Aikens at Granada, and had long wanted to go back. Clover refused to go there at night, but Burra did, insisting that he would be all right, on the grounds that he was too small and shabby-looking for anyone to bother about him.

Ed loved the tiny stages where nudes in diamanté jock straps pranced and sang in piercing voices. One night we heard a high Bloomsbury voice pipe from the row behind us, 'So much beyooteh in such a sordid little place.' This became one of Edward's favourite sayings.

At that point, if not before, it became clear that the PEN Club were holding their annual meeting in Spain; significant, since their President at the time was none other than Jules Romains. While Burra may have originally thought that Clover needed to be distracted and cheered up, it struck him that she might be even more invigorated by a little light vengeance. 'You should appear at the meeting, dearie, in a blond wig with a bottle of vitriol,' he suggested (economically recycling the vitriol joke he had already used in writing to Bar).

The plan was for them to spend a fortnight in Barcelona, then go down to Madrid. Burra must have been singularly gratified that fate permitted Clover at least a metaphoric vitriol-throw. Once arrived in the capital,

they went to Thomas Cook's to see if there was any mail, where Clover
found herself standing at the counter next to Romains and his new
mistress. He cut her dead, and she lost her temper. Dragging Burra, never
a swift mover, behind her, she gave chase down the Calle Alcala. Romains
and the girlfriend cast dignity to the four winds and unashamedly ran
for it, finally taking refuge in the Metro. Clover and Burra, meanwhile,
retired triumphantly to a café to catch their breath, where Burra drew a
caricature of 'Little Leggies' (as he christened him) and his girl bolting
down the entrance to the Metro, which they posted to Romain's publisher
in Paris. It must have made Clover feel a great deal better.

In Madrid, the shape of their days was to start with a visit to the
Prado, or alternatively browsing second-hand bookshops and stalls for
the writers they liked, the 'Generacion del '98', a grouping (or loose
affiliation) of writers, artists and thinkers who sought to address
Spain's problems of modernising in its own way by looking for purely
Spanish solutions. Their basic argument was that the modernism of
Paris or London was an inappropriate graft onto Spanish culture,
given 'the combination of popular mysticism and otherworldly
terrorism which still possesses one-third of our country'. Burra also
read a great deal of modern Spanish fiction as well as poetry and
comment. The inventory of his books includes a lot of both Ramón
Gómez de la Serna and Ramón del Valle-Inclán, significant Spanish
writers of the Thirties.

Burra's own explorations of the Barrio Chino and its Madrid equivalents were given focus by a book by the painter José Gutiérrez Solana,
La España Negra, 'which could be translated as "The Seamy Side of
Spain". Brothels, bullfights, doss-houses, the processions in Holy
Week, waxworks in a museum, slum carnival scenes, demolition of old
houses, beggars round braziers: subject matter that became very dear
to Ed on his return to Rye.' Stylistically, Solana's work has little or
nothing to say to Burra's. In terms of its intentions, it is a different
matter. Solana asserted, 'Painting is a magnificent art, not when it is
a reflection of nature, but when it attains realism.' He persistently
qualifies 'realism' with the adjective 'disquieting'. And if there is one
thing above all that Burra's painting evokes throughout his life, it is
disquietude; even the group of photographically accurate still lifes
which he painted in the Fifties exude a sense of being charged with
a potentially menacing life of their own. He paid careful attention to

Solanas's painting, as well as to his writing, though he seems not to have met him.

After the day's adventures with cafés, bookstalls and galleries, Clover and Burra would then to go to the cinema to rest their feet and recover, have dinner, and afterwards go to music-halls or the Circo Price, which had flamenco at irregular intervals. Burra reported:

I have just been to a flamenco singing competition at a place called the lirico Price realy Ive never seen anything like it I went in at 6.30 & came out half dead at 10.30 & it was still going on I left just after a wonderful old cook had shouted for an hour she must have been at least 60 with grey hair there was also a marvellous little boy aged about 10 in a red jersey accompanied by my new favourite Niño de Sambucar a guitar player to bring tears to your eyes its so beautiful.

Burra loved Spanish singers and dancers and the atmosphere of the clubs, which he painted and drew repeatedly. The chief monument of his time at the Circo Price is a painting of the singer La Niña de los Peines. Conrad Aiken, another enthusiast, observed the fine discrimination the aficionados brought to the dancing in Spanish *boîtes*.

Carmen Vargas is in many respects the best and most beautiful dancer I ever saw, the most seductive. Male audience loud in its comments, urging her with shouts to lift her skirts higher, hissing also when she did so if it were not done with sufficient subtlety and grace.

This can be seen in paintings such as Burra's *Flamenco Dancer* (1931): the white-clad danseuse, posed with the characteristically rump-out, shoulders-back stance of flamenco, is surrounded by a fascinated male audience whose absorbed expressions suggest connoisseurship rather than lust.

One figure to whom Burra devoted particular attention was the celebrated dancer, Pastora Rojas Monje. She was one of the great innovators in flamenco; her preference for the *bata de cola* ('tailed gown') was so persuasive that, early in the twentieth century, this style of tight gown with a train became the generally accepted costume, as it remains to this day. Similarly, the way she used her arms, raised commandingly above her head, became the model for subsequent dancers. She allegedly acquired her stage name of Pastora Imperio as a result of a comment by Don Jacinto Benavente, who, when he saw her, remarked, 'This girl is worth an empire.' She was a fine, fierce-looking creature in her younger days, but when Burra painted and drew her (*Madame Pastoria*, 1934–5) she was overweight, and showing every one of her forty-seven years; with dark bags under her eyes and deep grooves from her small nose to the corners of her mouth. But she had also, quite obviously, lost none of her power to charm; the potency of her stage presence is there in the picture – furthermore, in 1934, she triumphed in Falla's *El Amor Brujo*, which had been written for her in 1915.

While Burra's art was, on one level, nourished by the music-halls and flamenco clubs, it was also expanded by his academic study of paintings. Clover points to the particular importance of Goya to his artistic development.

At the Prado we spent a lot of time in the room where Goya's Black Paintings were very badly hung ... For Ed it was like entering the familiar world of his inmost, unspoken thoughts. As Goya had painted the gay, bright world of Madrid where he was court painter, so had Edward painted the gay, bright world of bars and music-halls of Paris and the Riviera of the Twenties and early Thirties. Then came the Napoleonic invasion of Spain and deafness after a serious illness to darken Goya's vision. The Spanish Civil War and increasing ill-health revealed the tragic sense of life in Ed that had long been latent in him. He sensed the Civil War in the air a year before it broke out in the summer of 1936.

Causey points out that Goya was not straightforwardly a chronicler of war, but a commentator on human nature in times of extreme disturbance, a stance that Burra shared.

John Rothenstein was the first to observe how important the war in Spain was to Burra.

The Spanish Civil War had an immediate and radical effect on Burra's art. From then on, it was characterised by a more solemn note, and tragedy upon a more exalted level became his constant theme.

The basic tendency of Burra's character was more saturnine than jovial, but up until 1936 he was quite a cheerful creature in his sardonic fashion. In the port towns of the southern Mediterranean, for example, what he tended to notice was humdrum domestic muddling along, flirtation, pretension, where more romantic contemporaries perceived a lawless landscape of vice and crime. This suggests a tendency to assume that people behave well rather than badly on the whole, even in difficult circumstances, natural to a man who was himself kindly, sensitive and the product of a very sheltered upbringing. Spain in the months before it slid into civil war was a revelation of the inherent horror of life, which, for Burra, was a glimpse into the abyss. It had suddenly become a place where people were dragged from their homes in the small hours, and when the corpses were found the following morning, nobody dared claim or identify them, let alone point a finger at the murderers. This went far beyond the banditry of Marseilles' *quartier privée*; to Burra it suggested a kind of collective insanity which shocked him to the core, precisely because of his liking and respect for the Spaniards as a people and the sense of affinity that he had with them.

Most English aesthetes thought of the war in Spain as a crusade; ghastly but necessary. When Nancy Cunard, passionately committed to the republican cause, canvassed the writers and poets of England, of the 147 responses she collected, 126 strongly supported the republic, while only five were for Franco and sixteen were neutral. She and John Banting were among the many English intellectuals who hastened to Spain to join the struggle.

Burra, Cunard and Banting were not mutually involved in the mid-Thirties, but the war in Spain created a major rift in Burra's personal circle all the same. Bar, in the summer of 1935, had two principal lovers: David Garnett, novelist, Bloomsburyite and founder of the Nonesuch Press, who was then unhappily married to an illustrator, Rachel (Ray) Marshall,[4] and Goronwy Rees, a strikingly good-looking left-wing Welsh writer and academic (whom his Oxford friend A.L. Rowse described as one of the 'deadly irresistibles'). In his autobiography, Rees gives an interesting snapshot of the impression that Bar created at thirty.

She had a sharp, almost microscopic painter's eye and was continually making me see things which otherwise I would have missed, so that with her, in the park, in the streets, in the Zoo, one always came home with a collection of *choses vues*, like the

---

[4] One of Garnett's novels was *Aspects of Love,* the basis for Andrew Lloyd Webber's musical of the same name.

hard brightly coloured objects which a magpie picks up for his nest. Her own flat was rather like just such a nest, filled with odd pieces of bric-à-brac that had taken her fancy, with paintings and drawings given her by her friends and cut-outs from magazines, and her own bright sharp eye and high clear voice had something which reminded one of a bird.

Rees at this time was Assistant Editor of *The Spectator*, but girlfriends apart, his personal life was dominated by his intense friendship with Guy Burgess, later revealed as being a Soviet spy (as indeed was Rees himself for a time, a fact he finally admitted on his deathbed).

Another friend of Burgess's was the Hon. Wogan Philipps. Like Rees, he was Welsh and charming. He was also the artist son of a ship-owner, a Communist and a future baron (eventually, the only Communist in the House of Lords, whose maiden speech called for its abolition), and he was attractive, sexy and amusing, though by no means an intellectual. His relationship with his first wife, the novelist Rosamond Lehmann, was under considerable strain in the early Thirties because the physical aftermath of the birth of their first child had left her unwilling to have sex with him.

Bar became friends with both Wogan and Rosamond. She was initially introduced into the Philipps ménage around 1932 by Julia Strachey (a member of the Bloomsbury set, as was Rosamond Lehmann), whom she was employing as a part-time secretary in her photographic studio. Rosamond commissioned portraits of both herself and Philipps. But as the summer of 1935 came to an end, Bar increasingly left Rees to his interminable debating sessions with Guy Burgess, and became sexually involved with Philipps. He, for his part, initially perceived their relationship as 'a cuddly friendship', a relief from the tensions of his marriage. In 1932–3, he had had an affair with Julia Strachey, and the wounded Rosamond had turned to Bar as her confidante, so she must have had some idea of what she was getting herself into.

Rosamond, a great beauty, took her husband's affair with Bar in her stride, because she did not perceive Bar as a serious rival (she had been far more upset about Julia). 'I never thought of such a perky little creature as a *femme fatale*,' she said to her biographer, Selina Hastings, somewhat condescendingly, looking back on the episode in old age. Moreover, she herself then embarked on an affair with Goronwy Rees. Even at the first shock of discovery, Rosamond wrote entirely amicably to Bar (a pure Bloomsbury letter, in its almost exaggeratedly civilised tone)[5]

I never meant to eavesdrop on the telephone. I was struggling to switch through to the studio, & suddenly heard your voice & thought, 'I'll just hang on till I can cut in with a word myself' – by way of a joke! Oh dear the joke was on me. I nearly fell through the floor. I'd no idea there was any 'situation' though often I'd thought it would be only natural if there were. Anything would be better than the present deadlock between W. & me – so I hope you and he – I don't know what I hope. The sad thing for me is he will choose people I'm fondest of which means they're lost to me ... I don't mean my affection for you could possibly change – but only it would be difficult to meet – at least I'd find it so.

But Bar, having entered into the affair light-heartedly, made the considerable mistake of falling deeply in love with Wogan, who for his part was engaged in that familiar riff on the old dance, the two-timer's two-step – which is to say, having initially been fascinated by Bar's generosity and emotional independence, he couldn't resist laying himself out to seduce her, only to retreat in panic when he was finally successful. Thus, when the Spanish Civil War broke out, Bar had been moving among strongly left-wing ideologues for a couple of years, was profoundly committed in that camp, and under considerable emotional strain.

Meanwhile, also in 1935, Clover, having got Jules Romains out of her system, had fallen in love with a Spaniard, Antonio Pertinez, whom she met in Madrid, where she was giving classes in English at the British Institute. Pertinez came from an old landed family with estates near Granada in a place called Gabía Grande, 'with 5,000 people and eighteenth-century plumbing'. Granada was reputed to have the most conservative oligarchy in Andalucía, of which the Pertinez family was a part. A story that Clover told Burra later, which he passed on, suggests as much:

She crept out to buy 2 oranges at the local store – Grannie was <u>dans toots ces états</u> when she came back, and said she had lowered the family as people would think

---

[5] Her last partner said to me, apropos of this letter, 'Bar had some blind and rather hard spots when it came to other women. I suppose you have to if you're having affairs with their stupid husbands.'

they couldn't afford servants. She ruled the roost with a rod of iron – sweet old thing.

Pertinez himself was a Republican politician, but no ideologue. According to his son, it was more a matter of the family's having deployed their several sons in useful professions for mutual advancement and support; Antonio merely happened to have drawn the card marked 'politics' rather than that of law or the Church; he was therefore at the liberal-reformist rather than the Communist end of Republican opinion. Antonio Ruiz Vilaplana, who was a member of the Burgos judiciary in 1936, describes the Republican party of an equally conservative part of Spain – Burgos – in terms that may shed light on Pertinez's political position.

There was, and had been for some time, a Republican party – conservative, needless to say . . . the president was a respectable bourgeois, of the city, very friendly with the bishop, and his wife was patroness of a number of pious Foundations, Missions and other charities. Burgos society was . . . by no means displeased to harbour such a party, which enabled them, in the hour of democratic triumph, to supply an element that, although republican, was yet not hostile to nor likely to attack in any way the ruling Catholic and social principles.

Pertinez was not a pillar of the Church, but he was more like this sketch than he was any kind of radical leftist. Burra thought well of him: 'Mdms man is charming & very respectable exactly like one of her drawings only greener with bags under each eye very funny he kills me.'

In the autumn, Clover and her fiancé returned to London for a time to stay with Bar in her Soho redoubt, and she made them very welcome.

Well. Madame has just left, having scavenged every dept at Barkers,[6] eaten all the kippers in Berwick St, & left a trail 6 ins deep of makeup and french papers all over Church St I think her man is madly attractive.

Clover and Pertinez then went back to Gabía Grande, where Burra joined them in June, and found the community so much to his taste

---

[6] A palatial Art Deco department store on Kensington High Street.

that he considered staying there. But when war was actually declared
in July 1936, Clover and Antonio, as well as Burra, hastily returned to
England – family legend has it, on a British Navy ship evacuating British
citizens, since Granada was one of the first places to fall to the
Nationalists. She was (just) pregnant – Edward Pertinez was born on
1 March 1937, and named after Burra, who was his godfather. The
young family settled, at the outset, with Clover's parents in High
Salvington, a satellite village bearing much the same relationship to
Worthing as Playden bore to Rye, and subsequently found a place of
their own on the Isle of Wight.

   Philipps, meanwhile, had convinced himself that he had to go to
Spain to support the International Brigade. Bar was so distraught that
she threatened to commit suicide if he left her, but he was adamant ('It
is because of my character, my fate, & I can't help it,' he declared, with
characteristic self-indulgence). Clover, for her part, was absolutely
enraged with both Bar and Philipps. The letters that she sent to Burra
from Madrid in 1935 before war actually broke out make it clear that,
from the point of view of a man such as Pertinez, whose principal
concern was with maintaining social stability, foreign Communists such
as Philipps were an unmitigated nuisance. 'Antonio had to become man
of all work at the local branch & is the only person capable of stepping
into the breach to help the new *governo* negotiate with the other left
parties to stop a mass demonstration of communists and syndics planned
for tomorrow the opening of carnival without carnage' . . . 'he strug-
gles with reds & sundries who are proving a bit troublesome to the
republican parties, then make out the repubs are traitors & when Oh
Oh walks into the assembly they sit in stony silence with shocked faces'.[7]

   The statements brought together by Nancy Cunard show that English
leftists saw the Spanish war as a curtain-raiser for the great international
battle between Socialism and Fascism, a fight of good against evil. But
not all Spaniards were so sure, or saw things in these terms. As V.S.
Pritchett discovered to his surprise, there were Spanish liberal-leftists
who thought Franco the least bad of the available options, and he even
enjoyed some support within the coalition of radical leftist parties known

---

[7] The nickname used here presumably derives from a music-hall song originally sung by Florrie
Ford, about an Italian ice-cream vendor, 'Oh, oh, Antonio' (1908). It may have been given him by
Burra, who loved music-hall songs.

as the Frente Popular. The Spanish intellectuals Clover and Burra had particularly involved themselves with, the Generacion del '98, were those who looked for Spanish solutions to Spanish problems. Within Spain, there were significant numbers of thinking people, by no means morally bankrupt, who perceived Franco as a least-bad Spanish solution. As his biographer, Jeremy Treglown, points out, V.S. Pritchett, a serious student of Spain, observed:

while 'the educated Spaniard was inevitably a revolutionary', ideas about revolution there were deeply bound up with, and complicated by, nationalism, religion, and tradition. The British Left were at best misled, Pritchett asserted, in regarding Spanish intellectuals 'as an Iberian branch of the Fabian society'.

Pertinez's politics were pragmatic rather than strongly ideological, and were arrived at as the result of intimate knowledge of his country and its inner life. Philipps was courageous, but not very bright, an unreflectingly loyal member of the Communist Party, and of an anti-Fascist Association of Writers for Intellectual Liberty, and he knew nothing whatsoever about Spain: neither he nor Bar spoke Spanish. He went for simplistic reasons, a victim of the 'easily-raised emotions of the ill-informed' on which Pritchett wrote so crisply.

The relationship between Bar and Clover became more and more tense. Bar wrote Burra a letter that, for once, casts aside camp and raillery, because she was at the end of her tether.

The breach is really on account of this bloody Spanish war. I know that is the bottom of the whole thing. She has lost no opportunity at sneering at W & showing dissaproval at him for going off there & whenever we meet she has let off a stream of abuse at the communists etc. it has upset me very much, as God knows I <u>hate</u> Wogan being there, & did everything I could to stop him . . . If he wasn't there I wouldn't care a fuck what anybody says or does, but when he is, I'm in such a state of worry & nerves I just can't take it. I suppose I should be saying all this to Clover, but I just can't bring myself to. Will you explain in a not too mocking manner, if the subject comes up again?

Burra was not good at dealing with strong emotion, as this letter hints. He had no real comprehension of the kind of love that makes you vulnerable; it is worth noting that Bar, who was devoted to him, did not trust him to get his tone right. His response to this letter was a colossal error of judgement. He received a letter from Clover, which seemed to him sufficiently explanatory of her point of view that he showed it to Bar. The result was catastrophic. Many years later, Bar wrote warningly to her then-lover, 'In future don't read any letters but those personally addressed to you. Do you know I didn't speak to Clover for 10 years on account of a letter she wrote to Edward which he showed me?'

Burra was caught between two proud, clever, passionate women, both of whom he loved dearly, who were personally committed on opposite sides. While he did not understand love in the exclusive sense of the word, he knew a good deal about loyalty, and for him to have taken sides with respect to the war meant choosing Bar or choosing Clover. He strongly disapproved of taking sides in any case; when Bumble and Gerald Corcoran broke up, he remained on the friendliest terms with both (as, indeed, they remained with one another). But even if his own closest friends had not been as entangled as they were, he disliked thinking in terms of abstract politics. He was far more interested in people than politics, in surfaces than in structures, and the whole thing was beyond him. The low-life interests expressed in his paintings of the Twenties were in dancing and drinking, entertainment, sometimes in edgy personal confrontations of one kind or another, never in thuggery of any sort.

Burra's parents' reaction may also provide a context for his own. They were afraid that this was the beginning of the end, as he told Aiken in a letter written not long after the outbreak of the war in Spain. In his reply, Aiken observes:

I was interested to hear that your mother was now beginning to consider Canada. Opinion is pretty general here now that wars and revolutions are absolutely inevitable in dear old europe, and that europe is an anachronism anyway, and will just have to destroy itself to make way for something a little more up-to-date. United states of Europe, soviet model. But I don't know, it looks just about as likely to me that germany and italy might turn the whole thing fascist . . .

There is no evidence that this is an attitude that Burra himself shared, but intense political gloom from his parents must have added to the force with which he rejected the entire issue.

The war had the effect of showing Burra how passionately he was opposed to violence, and, more surprisingly, how much he cared about religion – a subject that, like all other serious matters, he did not discuss. He told John Rothenstein:

One day when I was lunching with some Spanish friends . . . smoke kept blowing by the restaurant window. I asked where it came from. 'Oh, it's nothing', someone answered with a shade of impatience, 'it's only a church being burnt!' That made me feel sick. It was terrifying: constant strikes, churches on fire, and pent-up hatred everywhere: everybody knew that something appalling was just about to happen.

Between February and June that year, 160 churches were destroyed in Spain. Burra had always had a certain interest in the occult, and he believed strongly in the existence of a power of evil. He had a specific sense in 1936 that Spain was in the grip of a demonic force. Clover explicitly states that the powerful picture now known as *Blue Baby: Blitz over Britain* was painted in 1936 in immediate response to this feeling; it shows a colossal blue bird-headed demon with female breasts hovering over a devastated countryside in which tiny figures cower among the ruins of their homes.

It was in connection with this memory of the burning church that Burra told Rothenstein he was pro-Franco – though not to tell anyone. Rothenstein was duly shocked, and completely uncomprehending. The British Surrealist Group, with which Burra was affiliated, was actively left-wing and pro-republic, as were a variety of his closest personal friends. Wrestling with this conundrum, Rothenstein can only suggest that it was the deep anticlericalism of the republic that caused Burra to favour the other side, since he displayed a total absence of Fascist sympathies in any other context whatsoever. Indeed, he displayed positively anti-Fascist leanings, indicated for example when a doctor threatened to send him to a German sanatorium: 'I shall be soon on a trim German mountain top with a mass of brown shirts I shall pin up bits of Gringoire on pine trees showing up the regime in its true colours.[8]

[8] *Gringoire* was a French popular journal of politics and culture edited by Joseph Kessel, which became a pro-Nazi propaganda vehicle after the Occupation, but was not pro-Nazi when Burra wrote this in 1934.

However, it may simply be the case that Burra, far more informed about Spanish culture than most of those who expressed their opinions more freely than did he, was pro-Franco without being Fascist at all, and asked Rothenstein not to talk about it because he did not think such a position was comprehensible (indeed, Rothenstein's reaction shows that it was not). But liberalism, a conviction that people should be allowed to follow their own paths, was the position of men such as the philosopher Miguel de Unamuno, whom Clover and Burra both admired. It is as antipathetic to revolutionary Socialism as it is to Fascism: for such people, the political choices before them in 1936 were difficult indeed. One of the two Machado brothers, Manuel, supported Franco, and Unamuno initially veered towards him (though he then rejected him), and they were not the only Spanish liberals to do so.

Burra believed in people as individuals, and resisted any attempt to treat them as interchangeable units, which meant that he liked Communism no better than Fascism; in fact, he was that object of the scorn of both sides, a bourgeois individualist. He also had a sense, which he perhaps did not identify in himself until it was disturbed by his Republican acquaintances, that religious freedom was important, because it was, above all, individual. Burra was not attracted to Auden's work, but in this particular context, Auden may speak for them both.

On arriving in Barcelona, I found as I walked through the city that all the churches were closed and there was not a priest to be seen. To my astonishment, this discovery left me profoundly shocked and disturbed. The feeling was far too intense to be the result of a mere liberal dislike of intolerance, the notion that it is wrong to stop people from doing what they like, even if it is something silly like going to church. I could not escape acknowledging that, however I had consciously ignored and rejected the Church for sixteen years, the existence of churches and what went on in them had all the time been very important to me.

Burra's background was unemphatically Anglican, and he had no more time for organised religion than he had for organised anything else, but that does not mean that he did not have religious perceptions. It seems likely that he only got an inkling of what Christianity meant to him when he saw it under threat. Though Burra showed no especial zeal for church visiting when he was travelling, the only really distinguished building in Playden, where he lived, is a remarkably beautiful church built about 1190. He may have had an affection for the building, if not particularly for what went on there.

It is interesting in this context to find that Burra responded strongly to the 1947 Blake exhibition at the Tate. He shared Blake's unwillingness to be associated with any particular group or sect, his rejection of all dogma, including that of conventional religion, and his distaste for the industrial exploitation of his age. He was not drawn to Catholicism in the sense of being a potential convert, but he travelled along with it in some parts of his mind and art. He had a deep awareness of the existence of sin, and his interest in Catholic baroque art, as well as Spanish art more generally, meant that the formal tropes of Catholic art were available to him for organising his thoughts. In the Fifties, he produced a series of highly unconventional versions of traditional Christian subjects, such as a Coronation of the Virgin. More interestingly, a late painting about the rape of the English landscape (*Picking a Quarrel*) has, discreetly presiding, the Virgin of the Assumption, much as she would appear in an ex-voto.

War in the Sun (1938) is perhaps his most passionate statement about the war. Structurally, and in its handling of figures, and the impression of stasis that it shares with paintings such as Uccello's *Rout of San Romano*, it draws on serious study of the great painters of the Renaissance and baroque. Grey Gowrie, in the Sotheby's catalogue of paintings from Burra's estate sold after his death, emphasises its importance: 'One of the greatest paintings sold during my own seven years at Sotheby's was *War in the Sun* from the Walston collection. I remember ringing up all my friends and saying "we have a Spanish Civil War painting to hang beside *Guernica* or *The Weeping Woman*. You must come and see it".' It is a picture of extraordinary beauty, in the tawny colours of Spain; the eye is taken, above all, by heavy grilles, and it is only at a second glance that one sees that the middle foreground contains a tank.

Many of Burra's paintings of the late Thirties involve ruins; the rubble of destroyed buildings was one of the things that affected him strongly. Up to that point, his art had always been urban; he loved inner cities and ports, the complexities of civilisation. He was attracted to slums, to complex human life adapting and making do in decayed, uncared-for buildings, but he passionately loathed bombed-out ruins. The collapsed buildings in his Spanish paintings, with exhausted people crouching in the shadows, brutalised and bewildered, stand for the collapse of society, which has to run on consensus.

He also began to produce images of impersonal male power around this time, which, again, have connections to Renaissance and baroque art – the soldiers and torturers who flagellate Christ or torment martyrs. A powerful painting called *Beelzebub* (1937–8) expresses this principle of human evil; among the stones of a wrecked church, a busy group of thugs are energetically levering and destroying. The scene is dominated by a tall orange demon, in the hand-on-hip pose of an early modern aristocratic portrait, turning his head to look at the viewer; his face suffused by a grin of malignant idiocy. Spain, at its most self-defeating, witnessed by a man who loved it dearly.

IX

THE NEW FOUND LAND

AMERICA meant all sorts of things to Burra. He longed to go there from at least as early as 1929, when his diary entry for New Year's Day reads forlornly, 'worked drivelled about . . . wish I could go to Ammerica'. America was the point of origin of the music he most loved, black jazz, and of the majority of the films, good and bad, that were also part of the essential furniture of his mind. Overall, the sense he had of America was of a freer culture, where people could position themselves in the world on the basis of their abilities, and were less entrapped by an inflexible class-system.

In more than one respect, however, American society offered restrictions he was not accustomed to. Black/white relationships were quite different, something he discovered only gradually and up to a point. More obviously to him, when he first visited America, Prohibition was still in force, and though alcohol was not as important to Burra in the Thirties as it was later to become, the idea of lasting for an indefinite period without a drink was not an appealing one. His eventual arrival in the land of the free towards the end of 1933 – in the last year of Prohibition – on a ship which Bumble christened 'the American Tragedy', was not without incident. He travelled over with Sophie Fedorovitch; and according to Paul Nash:

Conrad [Aiken] met him at the Customs displaying the most awful mess of Woolworth underwear mixed up with paints and French and Spanish novelettes which was passed by the Customs officer, an enormous Irish Yank. But as Ed stooped to close up his bag, a large *bulge* in his hip pocket betrayed a considerable bottle of whisky. The officer leant over and without a word tapped the bottle with a pencil . . . But Ed didn't even straighten up, he leered round at the cop and said in that withering voice *it's a growth*. Conrad said the chap was completely broken, he just got very red and wandered away.

Burra was always hard to pin down on his travel plans, but when Aiken left Rye, Burra had vaguely indicated that he wanted to spend some time with him in Boston. Aiken, therefore, concerned that the pace of New York might come as a bit of a shock to his fragile young English friend, had (with uncharacteristic altruism) actually gone to New York to meet him, under the impression that Burra would be going home with him, and unaware that he was travelling with Sophie.

What in fact happened, according to Aiken, was that as they emerged from the customs shed, Burra was greeted by a liveried chauffeur. 'Are you Mr Burra? Come with me, sir, I've been sent to fetch you.' Without offering a word of explanation, Burra followed the man to a waiting limousine. Aiken, curious, pursued at a discreet distance, and was in time to observe a shadowy lady lounging in the back seat before Burra was whisked off. That was the last that Aiken heard from him for five weeks, according to Aiken's subsequent account – though the collection of Burra-Aiken letters now in the Huntington Library makes it clear that Burra did in fact give him a correspondence address some days later.

1933 was a year of travelling for Burra. Having spent the spring in Spain with the Aikens, he was in Marseilles and Martigues for part of the summer (catching up with Irene Hodgkins, among other things) and in the autumn he sailed for New York. Nash had visited New York in 1931, and loved it. He told Burra he must go, which he was eager to do, though concerned about how he was going to afford it: 'from the Nashs account you positively pay to move on the street'. Crossing the Atlantic by boat was a major enterprise, which took five days. It was less expensive during the winter season because of the risk of storms, which is why Burra went when he did, though the crippled state of his hands and feet (he didn't have a strong enough grip to save himself by grasping a hand-hold if he fell) meant that if the sea turned rough, he had to go to bed and stay there.

What finally made him commit himself was that Aiken was returning (temporarily) to Boston, which would give him somewhere to stay outside New York, while, at the same time, Frederick Ashton was going

over to choreograph and direct the dance element of Virgil Thomson
and Gertrude Stein's new opera, *Four Saints in Three Acts*. And above
all, he had acquired a friend in Harlem, where he most wanted to be.
One of the stories that circulated about Burra among his friends is that
this visit, though carefully planned on his part, took place entirely
without his family's knowledge. The canonical version of the story is
that of Rothenstein:

One evening he went out, telling his mother he was going into the garden. When
night came he had not returned. Nor was there any sign of him next day or for
many days. Then one evening, six months later, he walked into the house as though
he had just left it. It transpired that all this time he had been living in New York,
making drawings of Negro dives in Harlem. When questioned as to the truth of
this story, he admitted it was not entirely apocryphal.

The basic truth of the story, that he went to America without telling
his parents, is confirmed by Clarissa Aiken: 'Trailing Conrad on a
slower ship, Ed Burra had taken French leave of his family. His sister
was dismayed when I told her where he was.' It may be relevant that
the Burra parents' social circle was extremely anti-American. But,
although no letters to his mother survive from the trip, before long
he was writing to Anne, so it was certainly not the case that his family
heard nothing for six months. Friends, of course, knew all about it
from the start – Paul Nash wrote to Ruth Clark, 'Strange news from
Rye. Ed going to America on Friday and Conrad on Thursday! . . . Ed
dines with us at the Café [Royal] tomorrow so we shall hear all about
it then.'

Aiken was under the impression that the mysterious lady, whom he
can hardly have seen, was Nancy Cunard, but this cannot have been
the case. Although she and Burra were acquaintances, if not certainly
friends, her last, extremely public, descent on New York was in May
1932. She was back in Europe by the middle of August, and she spent
1933 in London. The car must have been sent by Olivia Wyndham,
Barbara Ker-Seymer's ex-lover: a person not unlike Nancy Cunard in
many ways; not least in her lifelong opposition to injustice, actual or
suspected. The lady in the back of the car was therefore either Olivia
or, even more probably, Sophie Fedorovitch, whom she had also invited
to stay. Burra tended to be one of the last off any train or boat, so Sophie

probably preceded him through customs, and she was not known to Aiken.

Olivia Wyndham dropped out of Bar's life at the end of 1929. She announced one day that she was going to New York for a month; could Bar carry on the business in her absence? She never returned; the kind of bad behaviour that Burra always rather admired, and approached, at least symbolically, in his occasional levanting from family life. The back-story was that she had fallen catastrophically in love with a distinguished black actress, Edna Thomas, who had come over to London to work in one of C.B. Cochran's 'Blackbirds' revues (as a *diseuse*; she could not sing, though she could put over a song superbly). Nearly thirty years later, Bar described Edna as 'the woman who made? ruined? my life', suggesting that her own feelings for Olivia had gone very deep.

According to Olivia's own somewhat bowdlerised account in an interview which she gave to a black newspaper in 1940, she visited America early in 1929, and was taken to a party given by A'Lelia Walker, the black heiress and salonnière, by the writer James (Jimmie) Stern, whom she had met on the SS *Olympic* going over – on arrival, both she and Stern had promptly immersed themselves in the society of the New York black intelligentsia. At A'Lelia's apartment she met Lloyd Thomas, and when they came over to England later the same year, the Thomases looked her up, and friendship ripened to the extent that when they went back, she went with them. In fact, she had embarked on an affair with Edna, but she was naturally not sharing this fact with the *New York Amsterdam News*.

Both women are described by Olivia's much younger half-brother Francis in a semi-fictionalised memoir. Edna Lloyd Thomas was 'a woman of enormous magnetism, great personal distinction, and knock-down charm'; still astonishingly beautiful in her late forties (she was born in 1885). She was a friend of Paul Robeson, and a veteran of Harlem's Lafayette Players who had also worked on Broadway, but her commercial success as an actress was hampered by her refusal to act maids, slaves or caricature 'nigger' parts of any kind, which kept her out of Hollywood (her only film credit is a bit-part in *A Streetcar Named Desire*, in which her light skin, straightish hair and relatively European looks allowed her to pass for Hispanic). Three years after Burra's visit, she reached probably the apogee of her career when she played Lady Macbeth in Orson Welles's fantastically successful all-black 'Voodoo

Macbeth' of 1936: in the Thirties, black actresses were not normally eligible for heavyweight classical parts.

What is extraordinary is not that Olivia fell in love with the beautiful and charismatic Edna, but that Edna succumbed to Olivia, who was physically and socially gauche. A Bright Young Person no more, she had lost interest in clothes or make-up, looked considerably older than she was, and was dowdy as only a blue-blooded English lady could be. 'Her manner was the reverse of effusive: dry, reserved, slightly governessy . . . she had a graceless, knock-kneed walk, which was none the less appealing in its suggestion of impetuous haste and eager welcome.' But there was a great sweetness about Olivia Wyndham. When she came back to England in 1939, her adolescent niece wrote in her diary, 'Mummy says she takes drugs and goes around with Negroes, but I don't care. I really like her.' She had a profoundly loving and loyal nature, and, like Nancy Cunard, she threw herself body, heart and soul into campaigning against racism.

On the other hand, for all Olivia's whole-hearted devotion, Edna must have found her domestically exasperating. 'If she had her way, my dear, she'd fill the place with the sweepings of the Harlem streets: drug fiends, pimps, prostitutes of *both* sexes! It's too hard on poor Edna, who has spent years struggling to establish a very highly regarded *salon* . . .' Edna, however, remained patient with Olivia, her social gaffes, her peculiar friends and even her continued addiction to heroin and alcohol. They were to love each other for the rest of their lives.

Almost immediately after following Edna home to Harlem, Olivia decided to spend the rest of her life in America. This is witnessed by the fact that on 23 April 1930 she married Howland Spencer, as the fourth of his five wives (and divorced him the following year). Spencer was an eccentric, extremely wealthy and very right-wing socialite. He had the misfortune also to be a distant cousin of Franklin D. Roosevelt, whom he loathed and insulted at every opportunity. Among his descriptions of the President was 'a swollen-headed nitwit with a Messiah complex and the brain of a boy scout'. In 1938, Spencer sold his estate, Krum Elbow, which had been in the Roosevelt family since it was granted to them by James II, to the black cult leader Father Divine, in order to annoy the Roosevelts, who were the immediate neighbours. Spencer's comment was, 'I've given him the first neighbor he's had in years, in Father Divine, who's not on relief.' He then moved to the

Bahamas, where he was granted an island for a rent of three pepper-corns by George VI, thus becoming a neighbour of Olivia's old friend 'Joe' Carstairs, the Queen of Whale Cay. Despite the five wives, Olivia's circle firmly believed Spencer to be homosexual, which suggests that this was probably a marriage of convenience to get her right of resi-dence in the US. Even leaving to one side their obvious sexual incom-patibility, given Spencer's politics, it seems unlikely that he and Olivia would ever have seen eye to eye on any issues whatsoever other than basic respect for black people as people. In any case, whatever social or sexual duties Spencer may have exacted during the months of their marriage, Olivia went back to Edna as soon as it was all over.

The home to which Olivia took Burra and Sophie was Apartment 2A, 1890 Seventh Avenue, in the depths of Harlem. One of its odder features was the continued presence therein of Edna's husband, Lloyd Thomas. By all accounts, he was an amiable waster, and the marriage had been for some time a marriage in name only, but they got along, and he gave Edna no reason to throw him out. However, in her new life as a Harlem habituée, Olivia achieved a bizarre kind of respectability as a born-again English lady. Her family home had been designed by Philip Webb and decorated by William Morris, and her brother, the heir, had allowed the family to take objects of sentimental value when he put the house up for rent in 1924. Olivia therefore took some of the furniture and the less valuable portraits over to Harlem (and perhaps also Burra's painting *Marriage*, which she bought for eighteen guineas in 1929), adding an incongruous top-dressing of pre-Raphaelite English country-house style to the décor of the flat. As if the massive trans-gressiveness of living in a *ménage à trois* in Harlem was somehow enough to be going on with, she took up dispensing Earl Grey tea, cucumber sandwiches and Gentleman's Relish to visitors.

However, Olivia continued to be a heroin addict, and though her half-brother was under the impression she had given up both other drugs and alcohol at Edna's urging, she fell off the wagon periodically, and in 1937 she went back to cocaine. She also continued to be friendly with Ruth Baldwin, as Burra promply discovered – 'There was a jolly cocktail party the other day at which Dame Baldwin appeared and did she get a turn when she saw me walk in if the empire state building had crept in on all fours she couldn't have had a worse shock.' The newfound respectability must have been liable to occasional implosions, since nothing and nobody could have made Ruth Baldwin respectable. She was addicted to heroin and cocaine, and also an alcoholic. In 1933, her short, loud life was already hastening towards its end: four years later, she collapsed at a Chelsea party and died of a drug overdose while her friends were listening to a boxing match on the radio.

Another frequent visitor to the Harlem flat was Nancy Cunard's great friend Iris Tree, who was married to Curtis Moffat, Olivia's erstwhile collaborator and mentor in photography. Like Ruth Baldwin, she was one of the more conspicuously badly behaved of the Bright Young People, but she was artier, more charming and less noisy than Ruth. She turned up in January 1934, 'much to Soph Soph's joy'.

Nancy Cunard has left a vivid sketch of the impression Harlem made on a Londoner in the early Thirties, an indication of how it might have struck Burra.

When I first saw it, at 7th Avenue, I thought of the Mile End Road – same long vista, same kind of little low houses with, at first sight, many indeterminate things out on the pavement in front of them, same amount of blowing dust, papers, litter. But no, the scale, to begin with, was different . . . the gleaming white and blond towers of down-town . . . are just visible like a mirage down the Harlem perspective . . . Harlem is romantic in its own right. And it is *hard* and strong; its noise, heat, cold, cries and colours are so. And the nostalgia is violent too; the eternal radio seeping through everything day and night, indoors and out, becomes somehow the personification of restlessness, desire, brooding.

It was the kind of place Burra really liked, blowing paper and all (which he represented, for example, in his *Harlem Scene*). Olivia's friend Jimmie Stern is another witness to the charm Harlem had for an upper-class Briton at that time: 'What do I (brought up in the British Isles) remember most vividly of that time and city? First, and without hesitation, the sensation of well-being. I have never felt so healthy, and seldom led a less healthy life. The sense of exhilaration gave one the feeling of dancing on air a few inches above the ground . . . it was in America, among Americans, in that gay, reckless, optimistic atmosphere, above all in the company of the Negro intelligentsia, that I began at last to break through the cement-like crust of my bourgeois British upbringing, to learn at last sometimes to utter an unhesitating Yes, where hitherto I would have withdrawn behind that cautious, instinctive, notorious No . . .' Burra, similarly, revelled in the atmosphere. He enjoyed the looks and style of black New Yorkers, and delightedly observed conversations and quarrels, sleazy hot-dog stands, luncheonettes, seafood bars, Jewish delis and uptown dives, filing details away in his extraordinary memory (he did not, there or ever, make *plein-air* sketches, or take photographs).

Harlem is like Walham green gone crazy we do a little shopping on 116th St every morning there are about 10 Woolworths of all sorts and a McRorys chainstore also 40 cinemas & Apollo burlesk featuring Paris in Harlem which I am plotting to go to but wont be allowed to I can see. It must be seen to be believed . . . Sophie and I go out and have breakfast at different quick lunches we hope to try the Arabian nights luncheonette tomorrow the food is delish 40000000 tons of hot dogs & hamburgers must be consumed in N.Y. daily as for the pies & sodas 2 minutes after arrival we were being treated to sodas in ye patio soda shoppie done up in the Mexican fashion . . .

American food habits had not yet crossed the Atlantic. More generally, in the mid-Thirties, England was yet to discover eating as a hobby. Burra ate little, but he ate with relish, and he particularly liked spicy and piquant dishes of all kinds. One painting of two men conversing outside a soul-food restaurant includes the sign in its window advertising 'fried hog maw' (pork tripe); one wonders if he tried it. The meals at Springfield followed the precepts of Mrs Beeton: kedgeree, brown Windsor soup, steak-and-kidney pie, fruit cake. Good of its kind; Burra's friends remarked on the niceness of the food at Springfield, but like all English food of its date, it was heavy and inclined to blandness. The cheap nourishment obtainable in the tea-shops and Lyons Corner Houses where Burra ate with his London friends was dull in the extreme: beans on toast, perhaps with a poached egg, rissoles, sandwiches of ham or meat-paste. Even if Burra didn't venture on fried hog maw, there was much to enjoy in Harlem. He particularly liked the seafood: '[I] live on a diet of fried shrimps and soft shell crabs washed down with a few clams': his *Oyster Bar, Harlem* presumably records a place of frequent resort.

Sophie was partly there because she had become fascinated by black dancing in venues such as the *Bal nègre* in Paris, and partly in order to give aid and comfort to Frederick Ashton, to whom she was devoted.

Ashton had been invited to choreograph Gertude Stein and Virgil Thomson's *Four Saints in Three Acts*, a seminal moment in the history of American modernism, which was to be staged with an all-black, therefore largely amateur, cast; a daunting prospect.

Ashton himself came over a couple of months later and stayed with Kirk Askew, a New York art dealer, and his beautiful wife Constance, an indefatigably hospitable couple who presided over a sort of intellectuals' salon from their brownstone on East 61st Street, entertaining almost every night (bathtub gin, delivered to the house in five-gallon jugs, flowed freely from six onwards, mixed with ginger ale). Askew himself dealt primarily in baroque paintings and drawings. He ran the 57th Street branch of Durlacher Brothers, the headquarters of which was in Bond Street in London, but he was keenly interested in contemporary art and the people who made it. Philip Johnson said unkindly, 'He collected people in the hopes that some of their distinction might rub off.' But he also conceded, 'Those rooms were just the crossroads of the world for several years.'

Burra, however, was not wholly impressed. 'Have only met one bevy of bogus so far at a dainty dinner party that Conrad Aiken asked me to they all sat round and listened to Bach and a terrific jew had such a charming pretty little french wife who had a school of the dance (in the Duncan Manner in the Catskill mountains) I was fascinated.' This sounds like the Askews all right (though Burra liked Constance Askew). But he was fundamentally more interested in the life of the street. During Prohibition (repeated in December 1933), Harlem's speakeasies were the centre of New York's nightlife. Burra was there for Prohibition's swansong. In the Twenties and Thirties, there were more than 125 places of entertainment of one sort or another clustered between 125th Street and 135th Street, and between Lenox and 7th Avenues, but with the repeal of Prohibition:

In one swift action, the clandestine speakeasies were unmasked for what they always had been: cramped subterranean *boîtes* where American attitudes toward elbow room – not to mention race – had been overturned in a renegade assault on propriety. Nightlife denizens could now go to larger, more comfortable clubs around the corner on 7th Ave. – Small's Paradise, the Ubangi – and drink to their hearts' content . . . Eventually, the Harlem music world scaled down to what it remains today: an active local scene patronised by uptown residents.

Burra, like John Banting (who wrote an essay for *Negro* on the superb dancers of Harlem), was fascinated by Harlem life, and staying with Olivia, he was well placed to see all that it had to offer. 'Olivia is such a figure in Harlem society you cant conceive,' he exclaimed. 'She seems to know all the neighbourhood.' Bar Ker-Seymer (who forgave her, and remained on friendly terms), reported in 1935:

Olivia, by the way, has been elected the only white member of the 'Sweep the Streets Clean' Harlem division! Rather an honour! The aim is to clean up Harlem but on the first meeting, Olivia as chairman, got up to make a speech & fell flat on her back under the table!

Through Edna and Olivia, Burra was introduced to the various pleasures of Harlem. 'Theres so much talent at the partys here that its more like non stop Variety,' he told Billy Chappell. 'We went to the Savoy dance Hall the other night you would go mad Ive never in my life seen such a display an enormous floor half dark ... Ive never seen such wonderful dancing.' The Savoy Ballroom, known as 'the Home of Happy Feet', occupied the entire block north of 140th Street on Lenox Avenue, and had a burnished maple dance-floor 200 feet by fifty. The customers vied with one another in spectacular and/or acrobatic routines, especially on Tuesday nights, which were set aside for serious Lindy Hoppers (a dance which took its name from Charles Lindbergh, after his pioneering solo flight across the Atlantic; it thus proclaimed itself as characterised by aerial acrobatics).

Burra's interest in black culture went back to his interest in jazz, established in his late teens, but was significantly enhanced by seeing black dancers of various kinds in London, where as early as 1926 he admired, and drew, Florence Mills in Lew Leslie's *Blackbirds*, and in the late Twenties regularly went to the black shows that C.B. Cochran mounted at the London Pavilion. He and Bar both socialised with black entertainers in London; Nora Holt, the model for Lasca Sartoris in *Nigger Heaven* (1926), was an acquaintance, and so was the cabaret singer Jimmie Daniels, who later, when he was the partner of Kenneth Macpherson, nominal husband of the lesbian heiress Bryher, became a very good friend of Bar's. Burra also sought out Paris venues where black dancers could be found, from Josephine Baker's *Revue nègre* to the anonymous amateurs of the *Bal nègre*.

He reports, in several letters, a surreal Harlem night out with Sophie, Olivia and the Thomases, which he evidently enjoyed immensely:

We went to an outrageous place called the theatrical grill a cellar done up to look like Napoleons tomb and lit in such a way that all the white people look like corpses. Ive never seen such faces the best gangster pictures are far outdone by the old original thing. The chief attracles of the cabarat was 'Gloria Swanson' a mountainous coal black nigger in a crepe de chine dress trimmed sequins who rushed about screaming Clappy weather, just cant keep my old arse together keeps runnin all the time etc and rush up to the table dragging his sequins up and disclosing a filthy dirty pair of pink silk panties how he managed I don't know no balls or anything else as far as I could see . . .

'Gloria Swanson' (né Winston), whom Burra sketched from memory in this letter and later drew, was the best-known female impersonator in Harlem (a title for which there was considerable competition at that time). He won a series of prizes at Chicago's drag-balls, and ran his own club in Chicago for a time before moving to New York around 1930. He took up a position in the Theatrical Grill, a popular cellar club on West 134th Street, where 'he reigned regally, entertaining with his "hail-fellow-well-met" freedom, so perfect a woman that frequently clients came and left never suspecting his true sex'. According to the anonymous gay Harlemite just quoted, 'Gloria' sang 'bawdy parodies', which agrees with Burra's witness (the song Burra quotes is a version of 'Stormy Weather', written for Cab Calloway and made popular by Ethel Waters, though many other singers covered it), but the rest of his memory suggests a somewhat more discreet performance than does Burra's description: '[he wore] net and sequins, velvet-trimmed evening-gown-skirts displaying with professional coyness a length of silk-clad limb'. But the most dedicated female impersonators went to painful lengths to tuck back and tape down their male organs in the interests of authenticity; Burra's observation suggests that having gone to all that trouble, 'Gloria' could not resist showing off the result.

As George Chauncey, historian of gay New York, has established, the Twenties and Thirties were not merely the heyday of Harlem entertainment in the general areas of purveying music, drugs and liquor, they were also the heyday of lesbian and gay clubs and performers. Drag-queens, 'Bulldaggers' and 'faggots' (the terms most commonly in use in black American parlance of the time) were a highly visible part of the Harlem community, particularly in the entertainment world; and the annual Harlem Hamilton Lodge no. 710 of the Grand United Order of Odd Fellows drag-ball drew literally hundreds of very odd fellows indeed, as well as thousands of spectators, many of them white, or straight, or both. Lesbians and gay men socialised openly, both amongst themselves and in mixed groups, which explains why Edna and Olivia took Burra to the Theatrical Grill (another great favourite of Olivia's was the openly lesbian Gladys Bentley's Mona's Club 440). It is also worth noticing Burra's delighted checking-off of 'real life' against the movies. The fact that lighting a room with red electric bulbs flatters a black clientele but has a deadening effect on white skins is an observation that he filed away for future reference, and came back to later in painting such as *Izzy Ort's*.

Burra stayed with the Thomases in Harlem till December, by which time he was getting restive. He loved Harlem, he was fond of Olivia and he liked the Thomases, but the flat was so dark that he couldn't paint, which he found increasingly frustrating. The sense of energy described so vividly by Jimmie Stern affected him also, but because of his basic lack of stamina, he found it impossible to sustain the degree of buzziness which the city demanded. 'It's a dream,' he told Clover, 'the only blemish is the apartment is dark as pitch and never sees the light of day so I cant properly work and what with rushing round the town all day in a permanent epileptic twitter I dont know what to do.'

Bidding farewell, not without relief, to Harlem, he went to Conrad Aiken in Boston for Christmas. This turned out to present problems of a quite different kind. Aiken was staying with his broker, who permitted a great deal of casual sex to go on in the house; this enraged Aiken (perhaps because he was not included, perhaps because of an atavistic rush of New England puritanism, or both); Burra himself was as indifferent as he had been to find himself staying in a *maison de passe* with Lucy Norton.

However, Aiken had left Rye, and Clarissa, in late September. By November, Clarissa was so bored and lonely in Jeakes' House that Margaret Nash suggested she went to London, which she did. She stayed in a staid Bloomsbury boarding-house for £2.5s, a week, two meals a day, gas fires extra. This was not exactly the high life, but the guests, as was usual in boarding-houses, ate together; and in a letter to the Nashes she happened to mention that she had spent an evening being harangued by a couple of humourless German students who had tried to convert her to Nazism.[1] Nash, in turn, mentioned her encounter to Burra, in the most casual fashion. 'This letter is rather boring but I am too rushed to think what there is to say. Clarissa is now on the Town that is she is ensconced in a boarding house or hostel or something surrounded by earnest male students – she steers in here occasionally . . . love to Conrad.' Both Englishmen thought Aiken's pathological jealousy was risible, and were inclined to applaud this miniature act of self-assertion, an attitude that was reflected in their correspondence (Nash's use of the phrase 'on the town', an eighteenth-century euphemism for having taken to prostitution, was a joke). Unfortunately, the result was no laughing matter for Clarissa, because Aiken got hold of the letter and exploded at the thought of his wife having unsupervised conversations with other men, however young and dull. Nash wrote crossly to Burra:

About a month ago I had a troubled letter from Clarissa asking if I had told Conrad she was on the town in a boarding house surrounded by earnest students or some balls like that. Believe me or not or believe her or not old Connie sent a <u>Cable</u>: I challenge your virtue stop hear you are on town stop living in boarding house stop surrounded by earnest students stop take next boat Boston Conrad.

There was, indeed, such a cable. Burra defended himself from the implication of deliberate mischief-making.

Yes dear your letter about Clarissa in a hostel arrived <u>in Boston</u> which was rather unfortunate as Conrad read it at once and at once developed a 6 foot spread of antlers. The man whos apartment he was living in a crazying ammerican was used as a perfect maison de passe which got on Conrads nerves. The subject is becoming a mania with C he enjoys every qualm Ime quite sure its so difficult being married to a mixture of Messalina and Manon like Clarissa is.

---

[1] It is worth remembering that Hitler had only become Chancellor in January of that year, and was not yet Führer – a sizeable sector of English opinion still regarded him as a statesman rather than a maniac.

With people such as Aiken whom he perceived as wallowing in emotionalism, Burra was inclined to discount the actual emotion (he announced the Aikens' return home with the words 'Othello & Desdemona Aiken are right this minute on the high seas', implying that he saw their behaviour as essentially histrionic, and disregarding the way Shakespeare's play actually ends). This was a blind spot of his, which stemmed from his very limited capacity for understanding emotions he had never experienced, above all, sexual jealousy.

Clarissa was then ordered to Boston in a second cable: 'close house board cat sail Boston ninth Laconia tourist returning Rye March'. She arrived to be greeted by a husband who was looking as stern and rockbound as the Massachussetts coastline, and the words, 'I sent for you in order to discuss divorce.' Looking back, Clarissa was inclined to blame Burra for Conrad's estrangement from her; it was one of the things that led her to see him as a mischief-maker. But the mischief was as much Paul Nash's as Burra's. In the days that followed, the relationship between the Aikens was patched up, for the time being, but the household cannot have been comfortable, and Burra did not stay long.

He returned to New York in January after his frigid New England Christmas, and established himself on 125 East 15th Street, which, like Harlem, greatly took his fancy. 'The East Side is lovely too a tangle of firescapes washing and fruit like a Berwick street that's burst all bounds everything here is more so.' If, for Burra, Harlem was jazz, dancing and the blues, the Lower East Side meant vaudeville performers such as Sophie Tucker, of whom he was also fond. Vaudeville was on its last legs; its epicentre, New York's Palace Theater, had gone over to movies only, with no live acts, in 1932. Some of the stars were still around, though sadly for Burra, Mae West had made it to Hollywood. Burlesque was also struggling; New York's great reformist Mayor, Fiorello LaGuardia, would close down the 'burley' houses in 1939. But it was still there for Burra, in 1933.

The great monument of Burra's interest in this aspect of American popular culture is his painting of Mae West. He adored Mae; and went to see *She Done Him Wrong* as soon as it came out. 'Mae Wests new pic is packing the paramount from 12 noon to 4 in the morning I am dieing to see it and prepared to beard a howling mob for Mae & pay 55 cents into the bargain ...' He was just as enthusiastic about *Belle of the Nineties* (an adaptation of her own, rather harder-edged play, and book, *The Constant Sinner*, toned down in line with Hollywood's recently introduced Hayes Code).

Despite all adverse criticism of meanies Mae West remains my favourite since seeing Belle of the 90's which I enjoyed more than anything Ive seen for a long time my favourite scene is when she stands draped in diamonte covered reinforced concrete with a variety of parrots feathers ammerican beauty roses & bats wings at the back and ends up waving an electric ice pudding in a cup as the statue of Liberty.

He once alleged that the only erection he ever experienced in his life occurred while watching Mae West. His image of her is not, however, based on the Statue of Liberty pose (though her ostrich-feather-trained dress is based on her costume in the film). He has her advancing triumphantly across a stage with hat, fan and train; she is holding the open fan horizontally in front of her torso so that her broad, swaying hips, groin and thighs and her glittering grin are the only elements that are clearly distinguishable. His Mae West is a woman whose personal glamour is being deployed with calculation, for her own ends; a 'monster', in Ed-speak.

Ashton, meanwhile, had turned up, to work on *Four Saints in Three Acts*. The premiere of his ballet *Les Rendezvous* (designed by Chappell) was in London on 5 December, and on the 6th he set off, steerage-class, for New York on the *Île de France*. He arrived on the 12th, to Sophie's relief; she was finding the Thompson/Wyndham ménage rather trying, not least because she couldn't stand Ruth Baldwin, who seems to have been a too-frequent visitor.

Ashton, however, had little time for his friends, even Sophie. He found that he had his work cut out for him. There were at that time no black, ballet-trained dancers, and to fulfil Virgil Thomson's requirements, Ashton needed to find six. 'We used to go to the Savoy Ballroom and pick out boys there who danced the Lindy Hop, or whatever it was at that time, marvellously, and ask them if they'd like to come and do it . . . at first they thought we were pulling their legs.' Teaching them was anything but easy. They were willing and talented, but the moves they knew were no substitute for a classical dancer's years of rigorous training. Virgil Thomson observed, 'they could dance like a house afire . . . but the muscular control involved in sticking your leg out at a right angle and holding it there . . . they knew nothing of that.' Thus Ashton had to junk most of his choreographic vocabulary. Also, dancing in the sense meant by the Lindy Hop was a matter of learning a number of moves and using them for brilliant improvisations. Some of the singers had been in revues, which helped, but the dancers had no training to help them memorise long sequences of steps, so they kept forgetting their parts.

One would get a whole scene set, and then one would come to lunch-time, and I'd say, Lets do it once more to make sure, and they would do it, and they would do it perfectly, and then come back after lunch, and I'd say, Now we'll go through Scene 2, and they'd never heard of Scene 2 and I'd have to start all over again . . . at the dress rehearsal . . . I was so tired by then, I came up on to the stage to give them my notes, and I started on the notes and I just burst into tears.

Burra was a sympathetic observer, and of course was reporting to Chappell: Chappell and Ashton had squabbled like fishwives for years, but they were genuinely attached to each other, and Chappell had a great regard for Ashton's ability. Burra told him: 'Madame A[shton] disappears up to Harlem at 9.30 each morning & returns a grey white shadow screaming for steak at about 6 each evening.' As they had done in Paris when Ashton and Chappell were with the Ballets Ida Rubinstein, Burra and Sophie formed part of a circle of supporters.

There were also nights out with Ashton, Sophie and a lesbian *grande dame*, the Duchesse de Clermont Tonnerre (one of the many lovers of Natalie Barney), who was also a friend of Gertrude Stein, Virgil Thomson and the Askews, and had come over from France to cheer on *Four Saints*. The group visited 'my favourite resort . . . an underground grave yard called the log cabin'. It was a discriminating choice. The house pianist was Willie 'The Lion' Smith, and the year before, the owner Jerry Preston had hired a waif of not quite seventeen as his new singer: her name was Billie Holiday. Burra also saw Bessie Smith at the Harlem Opera: for all that she was one of the greatest jazz singers of all time, he seems to have been more impressed than ecstatic.

Four Saints in Three Acts went up at the Avery Theater in the Wadsworth Athenaeum in Hartford, Connecticut, on 7 February 1934. The New Haven Railroad added extra parlour cars on the 7th and 8th, because it was the hottest ticket in, or rather out of, town: 'by Rolls-Royce, by airplane, by Pullman compartment and for all we know, by specially designed Cartier pogo sticks, the smart art enthusiasts coverged on Hartford,' one gossip-columnist enthused. Unfortunately, there were few hotels in Hartford, and the event coincided with a heavily attended bartenders' convention (the first since the end of Prohibition). It was snowing, and around zero; and every available bed, however unappealing, was in demand by the 299 avant-garde aesthetes and socialites that the theatre was capable of holding. The poet Bryher spent the night in a flop-house bunk more normally occupied by travelling salesmen and found, when she awoke in the morning, that the tip of her ear was frost-bitten.

Sophie was there somewhere too on that first night, initially anxious, then rejoicing, in the pandemonium of clapping and cheering that greeted the final curtain, the gradually appearing collaborators, Freddy Ashton stumbling on late from backstage, where he had presumably been weeping with relief and congratulating his dancers. Burra, who could not handle crowds and was probably worried about being out so late, was not; he reported to Nash in terms suggesting that he hadn't been there himself. But it was a runaway *succès fou*; so much so that many of the audience, when they had cheered themselves hoarse, began to cry. The show moved on to Broadway, and packed them in for six months; a stunning success for America's first major modernist theatrical event.

America and Spain between them taught Burra a great deal in the Thirties. His work in that decade still centred on interiors and street-scenes, but there was a new spaciousness in it: more architecture, a stronger sense of recession and less busy surfaces. While he had studied Goya and other Spanish artists profitably, he also learned from American painters, notably Edward Hopper, whose work was on show in the Museum of Modern Art when Burra was in New York. His later flower paintings suggest that he may also have studied Georgia O'Keeffe with some attention. Despite the impression given by his letters to his friends, he did not spend his entire time roaming from one dive to another. Apart from, of course, spending hours of almost every day painting and drawing, he took pains to inform himself about what was going on in the arts around him.

Paul Nash, when he visited America in 1931, made it somewhat tactlessly clear that he had no interest in American artists other than commercial cartoonists. 'From what I know of their work,' he said to James Thurber, *de haut en bas*, 'they are bringing up the rear of French modernism.' In an essay that he wrote on American painting, he contrived to notice absolutely nobody who is now considered important except Georgia O'Keeffe (who, in his view, made 'delightful feminine decorations'). Not so Burra. He went to exhibitions, and was concerned not only with the American scene, but with American responses to it. As Aiken phrased it: 'If the dear, pale, yellow-green, shadowless American landscape, lit everywhere by a blaze of light that was untamably indiscriminate, was different from that of Europe or England, did that necessarily make it unusably provincial or sterile? And the landscape of the American spirit, was that too so wholly without its native virtues and saliences, its clarities, its humilities and simplicities?' It was a subject he discussed endlessly with Burra, who profited from this lead.

Nash was, for good or ill, profoundly English, as Aiken himself recognised. 'He was the most English genius and the genius most conscious of English landscape painting, with all of its moods and tenses miraculously and calligraphically and lovingly caught by that all-seeing hawk's eye of his.' Nash himself, in his Unit One text, characterises the typical art of the English as manifesting 'a peculiar bright delicacy of choice of colours – somewhat cold but radiant and sharp in key' – which is to say, of course, the palette congenial to himself. By which token, Burra, with his penchant for deep, rich hues, was the least English of interwar English artists.

Rather awkwardly, Burra returned from America in March 1934 with a head full of images of Harlem and the Lower East Side, only to find that Unit One was definitely on, and he had to start frantically producing suitable abstracts, an episode discussed in Chapter V. But as the spring turned to summer, he found his energy-levels getting lower and lower, and his spleen began to swell painfully, giving him terrible backaches. He reported dejectedly to Bar in August, '. . . I got ill having eaten something the other day & had the Dr who at once said you have an enormous spleen & may have pernicious aneamia at any moment you must do someth so I said anyth but an operation dear so I am going to a specialist & I can see I shall have some horrible cure in nice german sanatorium.'

All his ills thus far had been put down to arthritis or rheumatic fever, but it cannot have been a great surprise to be diagnosed with pernicious anaemia, since his mother, whom he closely resembled, had also been diagnosed as a sufferer from this complaint many years previously. The diagnosis was depressing, since it put new barriers in the way of the life he wanted. His mother's life, spent oscillating between home and sanatoriums, taking care never to overstrain herself, had no appeal for him whatsoever.

Though the diagnosis was actually wrong, it represented a point where his heredity had finally caught up with him. Any kind of prolonged stress thereafter tended to produce complete collapse, attended by fever, jaundice, nausea, backache and strengthless exhaustion. The nice German sanatorium did not eventuate, probably because of the uncertain political situation. He was probably advised to take things easily, eat lightly but regularly, and certainly to stop drinking. None of which, of course, he did.

Burra was tempted back to America in January 1937, again by Conrad Aiken. His family life became notably duller in the late Thirties after his sister Anne married a cousin, John Francis Burra Huntley, on 14 October 1935. The Burra and Huntley families were long-term friends; there is a letter to Burra from his father written from Boxwell Court, which was John Huntley's parents' house at Tetbury, Gloucestershire, in 1924. However, it was a romantic rather than a practical marriage, and somewhat against her family's wishes. The couple were engaged for seven years, which suggests serious familial opposition. The marriage was eventually precipitated when John Huntley was offered a job in India. Her family expected Anne to go out there with him. Exceptionally close-knit as the Burras were, they were not at all happy about the prospect of losing her. But for some reason the job fell through, and the young couple went to live at Boxwell Court.

Huntley then failed to find alternative employment, which was also of course a concern, though of a different kind. Burra wrote to Anne from Boston in terms suggesting that she was putting a brave face on things: 'Dear A thankyou for yours and Ime sure you enjoy yourself studying the varying manifestations of mania round you at Boxwell it must be very interesting in a quiet way . . .' In another letter, '. . . life at Boxwell seems just like a novel you should write a book in your spare Time . . . you seem planted among the box wood for ever. I hope J gets a job.' Huntley finally found work in May 1937, managing a brewery in Guildford, and Anne was at last able to establish a home of her own.

Another reason for wanting to escape from England, besides avoiding listening to his parents fretting about Anne, was to get away from the media circus of Edward VIII's abdication in December 1936 and the subsequent coronation of George VI, which eventually took place in May 1937. The Burra parents were true-blue patriots, and doubtless there was a great deal of domestic huffing and puffing about that dreadful Mrs Simpson, with whom both Burra and Anne were fascinated – his letters to his sister from America all give her news of Wally, which was embargoed in Britain. 'The duchess of Windsor is in every paper Mexican or otherwise their every movement is carefully cronicled the Duchess seems to be turning into a dictator of fashion ... if I find anything particularly funny Ill send it.'

Conrad Aiken's marriage to Clarissa finally broke up in the course of 1936, partly because he had met another woman, a young painter called Mary Hoover. She was still only thirty (Aiken was forty-seven), but had studied in Fontainebleau, Munich and Madrid, and lived for a couple of years in the Balearic Islands in the Mediterranean. She was a considerably tougher proposition than her long-suffering predecessor.

Burra made a second significant contribution to the break-up of Aiken's second marriage, which, like his first (letting Aiken see Nash's letter about Clarissa in Bloomsbury), was probably quite inadvertent. Following a hint from Aiken, 'it would be fun to reappear a few years hence complete with the third Mrs Aiken, by gosh – and perhaps a child or two', Burra wrote to Clarissa (suggesting that he liked her rather better than she liked him), while she was crossing the Atlantic in 1936 to discuss divorce with Aiken, catching her up on where her husband seemed to have got to. 'I hear Conrad is expecting a happy event. It doesn't surprise me as I'm starting to get numb at the extremities owing to shocks over a long space of time & alcohol poisoning.' This letter reached Clarissa shortly after she arrived in America.

It was one of Burra's utter miscalculations; a point where he made trouble because the situation was completely outside his emotional range. That does not necessarily mean that his intention was malicious. He seems to have assumed that Clarissa would have been faintly pleased by the implication that Aiken was behaving no better towards Mary than he had towards her. He is certainly most unlikely to have known that in the course of Clarissa and Aiken's mutual reconciliation in Boston in the New Year of 1934, she had fallen pregnant, only to miscarry at three months, soon after their return to Rye, let alone that she had taken the loss of this baby extremely badly.

But in any case, he patently failed to understand that even without this additional twist, a childless ex-wife might well feel bitterly angry at such news, to judge by the detached tone of a letter to Paul Nash around this time, which similarly suggests that he was retailing gossip in good faith: 'I hear that Conrad is expecting a baby! Clarissa is burning she sent of[f] a filthy note to Mr & Mrs Mackechnie saying shes having a baby all I got was an abortion or words to that effect.' Robert and Margaret MacKechnie were more of Rye's many painters, and friends of Aiken's. As it happens, this rumoured pregnancy never resulted in a child; but since the news sent Clarissa into a frenzy of jealousy precisely when Aiken was trying to persuade her to divorce him, Burra undoubtedly made matters worse.

Aiken went to live with Mary Hoover in 17 Elwood Street, Charlestown, on Bunker Hill, across the Charles River from Boston, in 'a wonderful slum a stone's throw from the harbour . . . with a view of the Custom House tower from the back windows'. He tried to lure Burra over, promising him 'the cutest waterfront cafes you ever saw in your life, with such names as the Morning Glory, the Rainbow, Jack's, Charlie's, Jimmie's, Rocco's, and O'Neill's . . . this is where the navy yard is, hence large quantities of gobs, or what you would call jolly tars'.

Both Aikens were working for the Works Progress Administration at the time. While 90 per cent of the WPA's funding went to its enormous public-works programme, which primarily deployed unskilled workers on construction projects, it also addressed the specific problem of tiding America's artists over the Great Depression by instituting special programmes for writers, artists, theatre companies and musicians. Mary was on the Federal Artists' Project, Conrad on the Writers', and each of them got about $94 a month. As had been the case with Aiken's guardianship of Lowry, this sudden desire for Burra's company was therefore not entirely disinterested. He was to pay his share of household and food expenses, and the money would be extremely welcome.

Mary Hoover, soon to be Conrad Aiken's third wife, recalled seeing Burra for the first time, as he came off the transport steamer in

Charlestown, looking extremely ill: 'a slender small body with gnarled hands'. He was wearing a flapping overcoat with three missing buttons, and plimsolls, which he evidently perceived as sufficient to meet a New England winter. 'He had a small suitcase with him, but nothing in it except a roll of watercolour paintings and a few pairs of socks. There were no shorts, no shirts, no pyjamas.' The only other thing he had brought with him was a dose of 'some peculiar marine variety of flu', which kept him confined for a time.

As Mary explains:

We lived in an extremely 'pretty' inside, classic outside, brick house, built at the end of the seventeenth century, or earlier: small, four storeys, dormer windows . . . Ed was to have the south top dormer room for sleeping etc. and the north one for painting.

Not that it worked out like that. Burra annexed the dining-room, so that they had to eat in the kitchen, and adopted the downstairs lavatory as his bathroom. Aiken recalled:

The american scene and character . . . they had discussed this: Aiken and the Bassett, and Mary, and Edward while the gramophone squawked its 'Any Nuts, Hot Nuts', and Edward added one vermilion or purple cubicle after another to the infernal tiers of his opium den, his opium dream, in the chaos of shirts and shoes to which he had already reduced Mary's little front dining room.

Burra's washing gear, such as it was, was clearly in the downstairs bathroom (since the state of his hairbrush appalled Aiken's old Harvard friend, Gordon Bassett, when he nipped into the loo); the 'chaos of shirts and shoes' suggests that he was not only working, but sleeping down in the dining-room. And therefore that, even if he chose to give the impression that he was being bloody-minded, the problem with the cosy painter's nest lovingly created by Mary was that it was up three flights of stairs, and Burra was discreetly avoiding climbing stairs unless he absolutely had to. The sports shoes he was wearing when he arrived are another indication that he was having trouble with his feet, since he disliked such footwear: 'Theres something indescribably sordid about a tennis shoe – it reminds me of pimps & James Joyce & I don't know why.'

Unfortunately, his mobility problems arising from arthritis and rheumatic fever had been exacerbated late in 1932. He told Bar after a family holiday, 'I returned from bonnie Scotland with the worlds biggest bunion red hot and I can hardly walk now and had to hop about London on the way back in tortures.' A bunion is a very painful deformation of the big-toe joint, which warps the toe inwards: it can result from a number of causes, one of which is arthritis. After the joint has once given trouble in this way, it never entirely recovers, and the problem can easily flare up in times of stress thereafter. It was a particularly violent manifestation of the increasing deformation of Burra's feet, and meant that while most of the time he could walk perfectly well, he could not run, even in emergencies, and he was frequently unable to wear proper shoes.

The area where they lived struck Burra as 'an Irish ammerican midden of decayed grandeur parts are reminiscent of Bloomsbury'. Or, describing it to Paul Nash, as 'a remarkable slum in a labyrinth of tumbledown warehouses broken bottles saloons etc rather like the settings of early Charley Chaplin comedys & such inhabitants la sir.' In the evenings, the trio would walk across the Charlestown Bridge to Boston. Or rather, Aiken would stride ahead, with characteristic lack of concern for his companions, Burra would fall far behind and Mary would be in the middle, like a sheepdog would try and keep track of where Aiken was going, while at the same time trying to ensure that Burra did not get lost in the crowds. Aiken's total disregard for both Mary and himself may suggest why Burra found the ménage tiring. Another reason is suggested by a series of diary entries from his 1937 visit, which tells its own tale:

27 February ONeills
28 February ONeills
 1 March Silver Dollar
 2 March ONeills
 3 March Recuperating
 5 March ONeills
 7 March Finished Silver $
 9 March ONeills

As these entries suggest, though he greatly enjoyed drinking in saloons, he didn't quite have the Aikens' stamina. O'Neills was Aiken's favourite among the bars, partly because every fourth drink per person was on the house, and partly because of its colourful clientele. But they had other favourites. The Silver Dollar made a great impression on Burra: he described it for Paul Nash as follows.

The Silver Dollar Bar must be seen to be believed such a clientele of human debris interspersed with dwarfs, gangsters, marines, and hostesses fresh from the morgue. It has quite a Surrealist effect, especially a roller skating act on a floor 1ft 2inches which insisted on seizing hold of a member of the audience and swinging them round upside down. I got nervous I should be chosen for one of the lucky ones.

As the diary reveals, he finished a painting called *Silver Dollar* that March, presumably the one now called *Silver Dollar Bar*. Another bar that the trio frequented, which attracted Burra enough for him to paint it, was the strangely named Izzy Ort's.

Which particularly pleased Ed because it had a most unusual bar. Instead of the bar having mirror and bottles behind for the patrons to stare at their own faces, this one had – at a very slightly higher level – another group of imbibing customers, which made it very easy to lose one's identity and bring one into focus with the other's sins, or charms, as the case might be.

The art-critic Bryan Robertson, who also visited Izzy Ort's, noted its small, raised dance floor, and adds, 'It was not a vicious place, though considered disreputable by my Bostonian friends ... The clientèle was very mixed and the place had a kind of innocence ... the atmosphere was cheerful, uniquely American.' It is most probable that Izzy Ort's was also painted at this time, though both pictures are currently assigned to the Fifties. Matters are further muddled by an interview that Burra granted to the *Boston Herald* on 8 March 1937 (the day after his diary says 'finished Silver $'), in which the interviewer observed, 'The only work he has completed since coming to Boston six weeks ago . . . is a somewhat painfully exact reproduction of a night spent in one of the Hub's most garish honky-tonks. No imagination is needed to identify the buxom hostess, the negroid orchestra and entertainers, the barkeeps, the waiters, or the customers.' Unfortunately, this description matches the elements of the painting now known as *Izzy Ort's*, adding a further layer of confusion.

The Aikens suited Burra as hosts, at least when they didn't have too many other guests. He got on with Conrad Aiken, though he had no illusions about him, and almost certainly saw his best side. Aiken's self-absorption made for an absence of the fuss that Burra disliked more than anything, and he himself did not touch off any of Aiken's paranoias. Aiken's son John observed of his father in the Thirties, 'I think at this time Squidge, albeit a mere cat, may have been Conrad's favourite person; although Edward Burra, on account of his lack of emotional demand, must have been a close second.' As an artist, not a poet, Burra operated in a parallel creative world, and as a celibate of queer tendencies, he was detached from Aiken's roiling anxieties about his masculinity, and roused none of the insane competitiveness in the older man that contributed to wrecking his relationship with Lowry. He also liked Mary because she was naïve, generous-minded, optimistic and hospitable, though he probably did not like her paintings: Aiken reported on their first encounter, 'Ed is non-committal about Mary's [work] (as indeed about everything).' Burra could switch on English upper-class polite impenetrability when it suited him.

Whatever he thought of her painting, he certainly considered Mary a much more suitable wife for Aiken than Clarissa, and put his finger on an essential point: the hapless Clarissa's literary ambitions had caused nothing but trouble. 'Conrad is installed here among the debris of Charlestown with his new entended who is charming more suitable than Clarissa I should say & has her wits about her she paints so is not a rival literary creative entity.' In any case, Burra was conservative about hanging on to old friends, and stubborn about making new ones. At the Aikens, whatever his reservations may have been, there was familiarity, conversation on subjects he found interesting, and there was always plenty to drink.

X

MEXICO AND VENICE

Mexico

'I'VE never been even faintly curious about any northern country, but I've wanted, as long as I can remember, to go to Mexico and Venice,' Burra told John Rothenstein. W.H. Auden observed that the aesthetics of the Thirties pulled in two directions; there were those in love with the idea of the South, and those in love with the North. Burra and his friends were south-oriented; Auden the opposite, which is possibly one reason why Burra's circle disliked him, and made little cracks about 'vin audenaire'.

Around 1900, Guillaume Apollinaire became perhaps the first Western aesthete to interest himself in Mexico since the days of the Jesuits, but following on from Apollinaire's lead, the French surrealists of the Twenties became fascinated by pre-Columbian Mexican art, especially pottery and sculpture. Burra also acquired an interest in Mexican baroque, probably from Sacheverell Sitwell's seminal *Southern Baroque Art,* which was praised to the skies by Tom Driberg when it came out in 1924, and consequently much read in the circles within which Burra moved in London. He also owned *Three Centuries of Mexican Colonial Architecture*, and Rothenstein noticed images of Mexican churches among the detritus littering his studio floor. He was attracted by the highly accomplished Mexican caricaturist Miguel Covarrubias, who settled in the States and worked for *Vanity Fair*. Some of his own paintings of the Thirties, notably *John Deth* and his Harlem pictures, suggest that he studied Covarrubias to some purpose.

Burra's own Mexican adventure came about by happenstance, as the result of Conrad Aiken's chaotic emotional life. Aiken, as was mentioned at the end of the last chapter, divorced and remarried in 1937.

The word divorce has been bandied between us since late spring, and then things got acute after I crossed the Atlantic – really acute, so that divorce seemed to me the only way out – and while I was in that state of anger and despair I had to go and meet just the kind of woman I could fall in love with, and proceeded, quite unaware of what I was doing, to do so. And there I am, and there we are, blown to smithereens . . .

But Clarissa was not minded to be cooperative. The only solution, if Aiken and Mary were to marry, was for them to go to Mexico. The Republican government which took power at the Mexican revolution of 1910 was fiercely anti-Catholic, and as part of its programme of eradicating Catholic social conditioning, created the most liberal conditions for divorce then obtainable. As a temporary resident of Mexico, Aiken could divorce Clarissa unilaterally and then, after a month, remarry.

Burra had been with Aiken and Mary (then still Mary Hoover) since January 1937 as a paying guest. For four productive months he had been painting away in Mary's dining-room in Charlestown. But with his hosts thus driven by external circumstances to Mexico, he decided to go along. As he indicated to Rothenstein, he had been interested in South America for years; 'he threatens darkly to stay there,' said Aiken.

Mary Hoover was also professionally interested in Mexico. Like Aiken and Burra, she spoke Spanish, having worked with Luis Quintanilla on a set of murals at Madrid University. Since Diego Rivera was the most famous muralist working anywhere in the world at the time, she would certainly have been eager to see his work. American artists had started visiting Mexico in the Twenties. By the late Thirties there was a strong awareness among American modernist visual artists that very interesting work was being done there, enhanced by the considerable success in the US of Covarrubias and Rufino Tamayo. French artists who interested Burra were also interested in Mexico: André Breton, who visited Frida Kahlo and Diego Rivera in Mexico, came to the conclusion that the country and culture were in themselves naturally surreal, if there could be such a thing. No wonder Burra went along for the ride. He always preferred to travel in company, and would never have got to Mexico on his own. Also Aiken and Mary, for different reasons, promised to be stimulating companions.

The first problem turned out to be getting there. The Aikens had virtually no money; while Burra was habitually frugal, and not in the habit of spending money on personal comfort. He had budgeted carefully for his trip to the States; and in that pre-credit-card era, it was almost impossible for him to access more funds – though he sold a painting for $150 that spring, and his mother sent him some money in April, which will have given him a bit of a reserve. But he would not have wanted to travel separately from his friends. The three of them therefore set off for Mexico by train, day-coaches all the way.

Burra was used to travelling third-class about Europe, but the American experience was more than he had bargained for. Not that he expected it to be any fun; 'heaven knows what wild phantoms will emmerge at the other end with eyes stuck shut,' he wrote to his sister. But he had not, perhaps, quite taken on board the sheer size of America, and the amount of stamina that such a journey would require. Mary recalled:

At midnight, when stopped outside the Albany, New York station, the sleepy conductor roused us to tell us that if we wanted to go south to St Louis and Mexico, we'd have to change trains here and now and hurry, because this one was going West to Chicago. So, grabbing our luggage, we stumbled into the trainyard's pitch darkness, with just a few car windows lit to guide us, and in our usual duck procession careened past the terrifying, panting-to-start, gigantic engine, crossing just two feet in front of it, thanking the powers that help the helpless for every second it didn't start. Then there was the long exhausting walk alongside the waiting train on the other line until we found an open door to a coach, into whose horrid green plush seats we sank without a word.

Mary was young, strong, indefatigably optimistic, and in love. For Burra, who was none of these things except young, and was also semi-crippled, this must have been nightmarish.

With the dawn of the next day, the three travellers found themselves in an unfamiliar landscape of red earth and tobacco fields. When they got to St Louis with five hours to wait for the Mexico train and went to find some food, a superannuated burlesque theatre on the levee produced a quintessentially southern combination of rice, black-eyed peas, pork chops, sausage and collard greens. The next leg of the journey took them through Texas by night, a sinister panorama of derricks and spouting flames as the oil-wells burned off their surplus gas, to San Antonio, where they changed to a small train with a 'Jim Crow' car for black passengers (something neither Mary nor Burra had ever seen before, though Aiken, born in Savannah, would not have been surprised by it). From there they went to Laredo, where once more they had to change trains. It took three days and nights to get the length of America, slumped on a succession of dusty plush seats and dozing fitfully. Once over the border, they boarded the last of their trains at nightfall. It was scheduled to reach Mexico City at midnight of the following day.

The American trains had been anything but luxurious. The Mexican train dumped them into the Third World.

Baby pigs, baby humans, roosters, hens, dogs, and puppy dogs, peons, peasants of all ages, shapes and sizes, sitting on or lugging bags, baskets, aprons full of bread, sausages, beans, corn, dead and live rabbits, serapes, pottery, alparagatos, alparegos and everybody and everything that could yelling, laughing, screeching, crying at a pitch aimed to out-sound everyone and everything else. The seats, and their backs were slatted wood, so that everything small enough to crawl under or over, or in between never had such sport! Probably the only quiet things were the scorpions, tarantulas and viperos [*sic*].

With all this, the train whistled every time it crossed a path, however small; they could get no sleep at all. Burra, with no option but to stare out of the window, was entranced by the weird beauty of the Mexican landscape; the high, sharp mountains, the adobe villages with their small, squat pink churches. 'Never shall I forget,' said Aiken, 'the early morning landscape seen from the train, the little mudwalled pueblas, the prairie dogs, the one wolf, the Indians leaning timelessly on dead or dying walls. Gosh, the train ride was alone worth the agony.' But Burra, even more than the Aikens, arrived shattered. The journey was a taxing one by any standards; and he had no reserves of strength on which to draw. In addition, Mexico City is an extremely problematic place in which to recover strength, since it is sited on a high mountain plateau. Even the able-bodied, if they are unused to altitude, find themselves strangely exhausted by trying to get through an ordinary day at 7,000 feet. It is no place for the anaemic.

The trio were intending to stay briefly in the city, at the Hotel Canada, while the Aikens located a divorce lawyer. Having dropped off their luggage at the hotel, they went out, famished, to find some food at one in the morning. They found that Mexico, like Spain, was very much open for business at such an hour, and ordered tequila and some food, which unfortunately turned out to contain so much chilli that even Burra, who enjoyed spicy dishes, couldn't eat it. Aiken almost immediately became terribly ill, with the unfunny condition known as 'Montezuma's Revenge'. 'My insides came out of me in a steady and portentous stream, both ends, and I couldn't move for a week ... my heart began to achieve a *hum* rather than anything so discrete as a beat.' Mary in retrospect thought that in addition to his digestive problems, he might have suffered a mild heart attack adjusting to the altitude. She, of course, was therefore stuck in the hotel looking after him in the week or so that followed, but Burra, as soon as he had recovered a little, went out to explore.

He had been giving a lot of attention to the textures of decaying stonework since his first visit to Spain, and he adored Mexico City cathedral, both its crumbling pink exterior, crusted with sculpture, and the gloomy cavern within, lit with twinkling votive lights, gilded and decorated in high Mexican baroque taste. He seems also to have informed himself about recent Mexican art, and equally characteristically, investigated the world of Mexican popular entertainment. He described his findings in a long letter to his sister Anne:

However I got here I cannot imagine I never expected to reach such a queer place. 7000 feet high so as soon as you do anything you feel like a dead dog but lovely. The churches are wonderful & such simple piety Ive never seen people go to such a pitch of devotion they even kneel a good quarter of a mile round the cathedral reciting the rosary supported by a friend in pale pink crêpe[1] ... the dwarfs hunchbacks etc. here are worthy of Glasgow – to say nothing of other mysterious diseases I believe smallpox is very prevalent. Ive seen several pretty faces marked with little pits. I also read so in the paper, the markets are fascinating but how you would pack the things I don't know & they would be such a bore to carry the mere thought of any luggage makes me quite sick there a lot of curiosidades too ever so native enough to frighten you into a plumed serpent I cant buy anything Ive got more

[1] Religious observance was at that point proscribed in Mexico, but the government's hope that Catholicism would wither away was met by the fervent determination of many of the people that it should not.

than enough changing 4 times between here & Boston was enough for me in future I shall take a cegar box. Do not write here for I don't suppose we shall be here long at least I wont & I suppose between here & England letters will take at least a month – we went to a frightful revue at a fearsome building with a sort of coloured glass bruise on the top called Palacio le Bellas Artes precious little arte the safety curtain would be the envy of the paramount representing a view through a window made of mosaic of the mountain Popopopocapixl or something . . . it changes colours from sunset to dawn like a hangover the scene was supposed to be typically Mexican but never in my life have I seen anything so hideously monstrous. It took several days to get over the bad impression. there was a terrifying ballerina who appeared out of an aztec egg standing on a waffle supported by 4 Mexican charwomen in pale blue silk she then did a typical Mexican charleston on points there are several cabarets here full of typical Mexican hungarian sister acts. I wouldn't dare go the food is realy very curious indeed I suppose its Indian influence such pepper as allmost finished me off so you may imagine.

Burra was an adventurous eater, but Mexico – the original home of the chilli, which still uses more of them, more inventively, than anywhere else – was beyond him. By 'curious', he almost certainly means 'nasty'. Mexican food held little appeal for a Thirties English palate. To Graham Greene, who was there three years later, it was actively revolting, 'like the food you eat in a dream, tasteless in a positive way, so that the very absence of taste is repellent. All Mexican food is like that: if it isn't hot with sauces it's nothing at all.' Greene also qualifies Burra's tendency to see Mexico in terms of the familiar ('typical Mexican hungarian sister acts'), when he observes, 'Mexico City is older and less Central European than it appears at first – a baby alligator tied to a pail of water; a whole family of Indians eating their lunch on the sidewalk edge; railed off among the drug-stores and the tram-lines, near the cathedral, a portion of the Aztec temple Cortés destroyed.'

When Aiken was fit to travel, he phoned Malcolm Lowry, who had been living in Cuernavaca for the previous six months. Lowry was delighted to hear from him, and, as Aiken had clearly hoped and intended, invited him to stay. Though Lowry wanted to see Aiken again, Jan Gabrial, whom he had married in 1934, did not, and she was not in the least pleased. There was a lawyer in Cuernavaca who was prepared to take the Aikens' case, so the trio removed there. Cuernavaca is a resort-town in the mountains, about fifty miles from Mexico City and about 5,000 feet above sea-level (2,000 feet lower than the city itself), where those who could got away from the horrors of a metropolitan summer.

The town has a spectacular setting, under not one but two great volcanoes, Popocatépetl and Ixtaccihuatl. In the Thirties, it was a town of crumbling pink buildings, lush with bougainvillea, which, in order to keep out the heat, presented rather blank faces to the street, and it was perched on the edge of the *barranca*, a vast, tree-filled gorge. 'The fernlike trees were so interlaced across it that one thought of course it must be very shallow; only when one looked a second time did one glimpse – far below – and with a sudden contraction of the heart – tiny rocks and ripples in the filtered sunlight.' Its principal features include a substantial sixteenth-century Spanish colonial palace complex, built by Hernan Cortés and subsequently decorated with a set of frescoes by Diego Rivera, a tall sixteenth-century cathedral and an eighteenth-century formal Italian garden. But, although it possessed these amenities of a resort town for the wealthy, it was also, ominously, a drinker's paradise. Alcohol acts fast at high altitudes, tequila, habanera and pulque were cheap, and the *cantinas* were open from one day's dawn until the small hours of the next morning.

62 Calle Humboldt, which the Lowrys were renting, was set well back from the street on broad, lush, randomly planted grounds. It was a small, pretty, tile-roofed house with three bedrooms and a thirty foot veranda running along the back elevation with a breathtaking view of the volcanoes. 'In the evenings at twilight it was delightful to sit out there with one's drinks and look at the volcanoes and hear the humming of the insects from the garden below, and watch hummingbirds and just breathe the clear air,' Jan remembered. Though the rent was all of forty-four dollars a month, the amenities included a swimming-pool and three servants (dollars went a long way in Mexico, one reason why the Lowrys were there). There was a maid, Josefina, 'a tidy woman, always stiffly starched, her small face as crinkled as a nut', a gardener and a boy to run errands.

However, the Lowrys' home was not as paradisal, or even as comfortable, as this sounds. In Mary's memory, the Calle Humboldt was 'at the very bottom of a sinister walled, unpaved street', the Via Fernando il Catolico. The swimming-pool was small, 'about twelve feet by eight and ... covered in dead butterflies and various insects', though it was welcome in the heat; and the garden, albeit alive with dahlias, zinnias, petunias, limes and bananas, was a jungle. It also possessed an irrigation stream which ran along the edge of the garden by the house. Pablo, the gardener, knew nothing about plants and was 'allergic to energy'. He moved his girlfriend in, and worked haphazardly when he could be bothered, while the boy Eleodoro smoked pot, drank and fornicated.

The Lowrys had originally taken the house with their friend Alan Mondragon; but by the time the Aikens and Burra arrived, Mondragon had moved out. Unfortunately, he was the only Spanish speaker of the three. Jan had a few words, Lowry none. It is evident from between the lines of Jan's memoir that the servants as a group regarded the Lowrys as badly behaved rich gringo idiots, and that Josefina came to despise them (Lowry in particular) from the bottom of her heart. Her starched and tidy appearance did not in any sense imply that she was a hygienic housekeeper, and Jan, bohemian, unused to the tropics and almost without a language in common, was unable to get on top of the situation or even, perhaps, quite to realise the extent to which there was a situation to get on top of.

There were other, more visible, problems of a tropical kind. Rats, inevitably, 'something large and clumsy which clung to the roof tiles at night and coughed' and, more alarmingly, tarantulas and scorpions, which came through the roof tiles: Jan would go round with a long-handled feather duster last thing at night, 'carefully knocking the small brown scorpions from the walls and ceilings and stamping on them'. As the rainy season began in May, it became clear that the other thing that came through the pantiles in unlimited quantities was water; necessitating, at times, dining under individual umbrellas. But Jan loved her house, and Mexico; she and Lowry had a viable life together, his drinking was finally under control, and so she painted doors and made curtains and bedspreads, tokens of domestic happiness on a miniature budget.

When the Aikens and Burra arrived at 62 Calle Humboldt, where the Lowrys had lived since the previous November, Jan could not feel that Aiken had improved in the four years since she had last seen him.

He looked, in fact, at first sight, like a Midwestern banker . . . large, florid, balding. Yet he could transform two companions into a retinue, and his cold, arrogant, light-blue gaze above the ruddiness of his flesh displayed the decisive shrewdness of the Recording Angel . . . he now descended from the bus on heavy feet and turned to help a large girl with a withdrawn expression, and a tiny kernel of a man, like a shrunken bantam weight, who was carrying a duffel bag. In the tropical extravagance of the Mexican plaza, they resembled a seedy troupe forever touring the provinces.

Aiken was in a foul mood. He loathed Mexico, partly because he had been more or less ill since they arrived, but also because they had arrived in the middle of the rainy season. It poured most of the time that they were there, and the nights were split by apocalyptic thunderstorms.

When the Aikens appeared, Lowry gave up his twin-bedded room, which opened onto the veranda (as did the room originally Alan's, which Jan had appropriated; the Lowrys did not sleep together). Lowry therefore moved into the spare single room, and Burra slept on the veranda on a couch with a rustling cornhusk mattress; which was far from ideal since it gave him, and the two couples, no privacy, and if any of the other four moved about at night, they disturbed him. Since Aiken was still suffering to some extent from the runs, he presumably had to get up from time to time. Though the veranda was in itself an agreeable space with checkerboard tiles, and the small table and hard wooden chair essential to Burra's work (Lowry often wrote there), the arrangement put him in an awkward position, and he began to feel trapped. He made the best of the experience in a letter to his mother, in which any mention of his hosts is conspicuous by its absence.

I have moved from Mexico City to here which is much lower and boiling hot its the rainy season so rain every evening the house is quite nice rather like a Somerset Maugham house wonderful flowering shrubs etc. one has huge white trumpets upside down & gives off a strong scent at night rather like Harrods scent dept[2] scorpions we have found several whose bite is very poisonous also a frightful black spider with 3 red spots called a black widow poisonous too I have only seen one thank God they are not very large. very enervating the town is. a crumbling bit of old Spain the cathedral is Moorish unfortunately nobody is able to move. However I go to the town every day . . . There is an extraordinary view when not wreathed in the rainy season from the verandah here of Popacatapetle looking exactly like Fujiyama capped with eternal snows really fantastic at times. I came here by bus from Mexico City rattling & rushing over a precipitous route it finaly rises on the

[2] *Datura*, not then part of the English indoor gardener's repertory.

way to 10 000 ft but this is mercifully lower than Mexico City which is 7000 ft its very tireing ... all the best known little maladies of the tropics are very prevalent here such as dihorrea etc etc. The Emperor Maximilian had the palace here rather a pretty building fallen somewhat into decay with a covered terrace with a marvellous view of landscape & distant mountains. There are huge butterflies too one white one exactly like a white handkerchief.

Jan had managed to get Lowry's drinking under control in the months when they were alone together. But with Aiken in the house, he slid back into alcoholism. The atmosphere became very tense as relations between Jan and Aiken went from bad to worse. They had terrific battles about everything from politics to women's right to sexual fulfilment, the subtext of which was, of course, that they were fighting over Lowry. Her memoir barely mentions Burra (or Mary). She was so intensely aware of Aiken, 'that avid Greek chorus of one', as she bitterly calls him, that Burra, who was generally little trouble, must have been almost invisible to her. He and Mary were apparently very silent. Mary was perhaps out of her depth, while Burra's sharp tongue was inhibited by the circumstances. He was perfectly well aware that Lowry disliked him, and since it was Lowry's house they were staying in, his personal code of manners required that he should accommodate his host as far as possible and refrain from teasing. And for Burra, if Lowry could not be teased, there was very little that could be said to him. He had a certain respect for Lowry as a creative artist (which Lowry reciprocated), but they had nothing in common as people.

Aiken re-established his teacher–pupil relationship with Lowry, by setting him a series of blank-verse poetry exercises. They met at Karl's Café in central Cuernavaca around noon, when Lowry was more or less sober, to discuss the technicalities of verse. Lowry, who was far more concerned with developing his prose, then showed his Mephistophelian mentor the first draft of *Under the Volcano*. Aiken was genuinely impressed; and immediately sought to undermine his pupil. The two writers went back to their old game of using each other as copy, while accusing one another of plagiarism. Aiken, staring into the Lowrys' tangled garden, commented, 'I expect to see Rousseau riding out of there on a tiger', a remark that Lowry noted down for use in *Under the Volcano*, while Aiken's less-than-wonderful *A Heart for the Gods of Mexico* shows signs of his having read Lowry's draft.

Since they were living on a shoestring budget, the Aikens and Burra were more or less stuck in Cuernavaca, though they did take a bus to Taxco to look at the church there. They also went to the island of Janitzio (best known as the principal centre for the celebration of the Day of the Dead, though they were four months too early to witness this). Burra and Mary liked the newly erected colossal 120-foot statue of José María Morelos, a hero of the Mexican revolution after whom the district was named, fist raised on high: a sort of blocky, modernist Statue of Liberty. It was possible to climb up a winding spiral staircase inside the statue to the fist, though presumably Burra, on account of his sore feet, did not.

Life at Calle Humboldt was punctuated by domestic mishaps. The roof continued to leak; and Pablo the gardener contrived to block the irrigation stream so that it flooded the house one day. The watercourse was brought under control, but the flood seems to have disturbed the sanitary arrangements, since it is clear from the various accounts of the week that followed that the streamlet, though returned to its course, began to pick up sewage. Then the Lowrys' two adored cats, Chicharro and Xicottencatl, vanished; and on the night of 10 June limped back, poisoned, to die on the veranda. Lowry was sleeping off the previous night's tequila at the time, but Josefina, who had observed them creeping home (or, just conceivably, had poisoned them herself), tapped on Jan's door to wake her. Lowry was dead to the world, but Burra was always a light sleeper, and in any case was actually on the veranda when this drama got under way.

It is understandable that Jan does not include him in her written account of this piteous episode, but he must have been there as she grieved over her pets, offering what comfort he could. Burra did not keep animals himself, but he had a certain affinity with cats; when he was living on his own, he liked to watch them ('perfectly divine cats from the barn come over and hang about'), though he would not have dreamed of acquiring one. Burra's own stance towards the world was somewhat catlike, and cats often appear in his paintings as observers of the human comedy. Though he was not good at emotions, he was often surprisingly practical in emergencies, but there was nothing to be done for the poor creatures.

Jan, grief-stricken, let Josefina take the little bodies away so that Pablo could bury them; but when Lowry eventually awoke, he was appalled that she had not kept them so that he could say his goodbyes. Her decision seemed to him outrageously insensitive, and as he yelled at her, undone by grief, fury and a hangover, she could stand it no longer. It was the morning of her twenty-sixth birthday. She and Lowry had intended to go to Lake Pátzcuara in Michoacán that day anyway, to celebrate, so she went on her own. Lowry, as they parted at the bus station, gave her a little note apologising for his friends ('they compel me, too, to an inimical uneasy rhythm'), and promising that, once they were on their own again, things would be better.

Without the electric hostility between Jan and Aiken, the tension diminished. Mary and Burra painted (she was doing watercolours of flowers, he was working on a dead Christ; a response to the macabre splendours of Mexican Catholic art). Aiken got on with an article he was writing about William Faulkner. Lowry disappeared on a bender.

But Burra, though he continued to work with his habitual discipline, was beginning to reach the limits of his personal resilience. He and the Aikens had been at Calle Humboldt for just over a fortnight when Jan left, and though he continued to be fascinated by Mexico, between the domestic tension, the thunderstorms, possible livestock (including scorpions and black widow spiders) in his bed, and the stench of the irrigation canal, he could not get the rest he needed. He had had a long, wearing, virtually sleepless night, riven with appalling emotions. Like Aiken, he was suffering considerably from the altitude. But he was also becoming seriously undernourished, and he had terrible trouble with his digestion. The nightly drinking sessions had a cumulative effect, since tequila, let alone habanera and pulque, was hard on his fragile liver, and the food at Calle Humboldt was almost inedible. Capsicin literally burns the unaccustomed gut; and Burra had a delicate stomach in the first place. Aiken, in a letter written after Burra left, suggests there was also a problem with the water: 'The lawyer says the water is a <u>powerful cathartic</u>, full of sulphur from the volcano and some people (viz. yourself and me) never get used to it.'

But the problem with Josefina's food did not begin and end with chillies and sulphur. Jan remembered her as an adequate cook, though she produced stuffed peppers with monotonous regularity, but she had come to view her employers and their friends with utter contempt, and this seems to have been directly reflected in the food she prepared. With the mistress away, she was not prepared to bother herself at all. That afternoon, Mary looked into a pot on the stove, 'and saw a whole rabbit, ears, eyes, teeth, toenails, cotton-tail, all in its fur, slowly swirling in the barely simmering water.[3] When I asked Josefina why she didn't clean and skin it before she cooked it, she simply said "Very quick, very easy this way, all come off pronto in time for dinner."' Sickened, Mary beat a retreat.

After the siesta, the three of them went down the Via Fernando il Catolico to the Playa Centrale, where there was a bar, Charlie's Place, 'a little corner café with open stone arches and red covered tables', next to the bus station. Mary, unstrung by tequila, told the men about her encounter with Josefina's sodden rabbit. After a while they could see huge thunderheads of cloud building up, so they hastened back to Calle Humboldt before the storm broke; arriving just in time for a bolt of lightning to short out the electricity. They ate their dinner by candle-light, which made matters even worse, because they were more than usually keen to see what they were eating. The electricity came on again just before bedtime.

Lowry had not yet appeared. He eventually returned, very late and very drunk, in the middle of a thunderstorm. Trying to cross the garden in the pitch dark, he contrived to miss the little bridge and fall into the irrigation ditch; Aiken heard his cries and rescued him; the pair of them staggered back to the house – the veranda – stinking and plastered in excrement.

For all Burra's adventurousness, that and the rabbit finished him. He collapsed with dysentery; vomiting and purging so spectacularly that a doctor had to be sent for, storm or no storm; a version of the same syndrome that had afflicted Aiken in Mexico City. A fortnight later, he still showed no signs of mending, and even he was forced to admit defeat. He was feeling so dreadful he began seriously to think that he might die if he didn't get back to sea-level and edible food. It was a difficult decision: the Aikens could not leave Mexico unless they were prepared to give up the project of the divorce and remarriage, which they were not, and Burra was so frail he was afraid to travel alone. The Aikens wired Aiken's old college friend Gordon Bassett, with instructions to stand by in Boston. Towards the end of June, Burra took the key to the house in Charlestown, ordered a taxi to take him to Mexico City and boarded the Pullman to Laredo for the first leg of the daunting trip, by which time he was barely able to walk. He

[3] At 5,000 feet, water boils at about 95° C, which makes stewing problematic.

wrote to Anne, to whom he was generally franker than to anybody
else, from Boston.

I returned here alone very much the worse for wear for I had a terrible attack of
dysentry in Mexico where everything is of the dirtiest. Having gone on for 2 weeks
& no better & feeling like the wrath of God & looking a yellowish skeleton I finally
said I must leave so went off in a taxi for Cuernavaca to Mexico City this was quite
comfortable tho it had its bad moments in Mexico City of course no one knew anything
about anything but 1st class fare Mexicans being on a pinnacle of dishonesty far
outdoing any mere European manifestations however I got a ticket to Laredo the frontier and managed the journey pretty well. I went to Laredo pullman and day coach
on they are realy very comfortable air conditioned and you can go in the diner up
through Texas was a furnace at St Louis I waited 4 hours was mercifully air conditioned in the waiting rooms by that time I was beginning to develop rheumatism in
the feet so you may imagine I am now fairly crippled with it (for heavens sake don't
say so to Ma) but I think Ime getting on & the dysentry is pretty well done with of
course I should never have got over it in Mexico the filth in the kitchen was in the
realms of phantasy it was so terrific a pity because it is a wonderful place but so unfortunate Cortez didn't do a better job.

It was typical of Burra that even when at death's door, he did not indulge
himself with a first-class ticket. Despite his crippled state, he somehow
got himself to Boston and holed up in the little house at Charlestown,
where he phoned Gordon Bassett and begged for oysters.

Bassett went straight to the Union Oyster House, and got them to
open a dozen oysters and pack them in their deep shells flat in a box.
He carried them carefully over the bridge to Charlestown to Burra
who was, by this point, presumably starving, and desperate for something he could reliably keep down. Oysters might seem an eccentric
thing to want, but they are virtually fat-free. The request suggests
that he was sufficiently advanced in anaemia that his liver was not
functioning properly, and he was unable to digest fats, or complex
carbohydrates, or indeed, anything but the simplest foods. Bassett then
alerted the Aikens' Irish next-door neighbour, Mrs Curran. She helped
Mary with housekeeping, and she was fond of Burra, who was scrupulously polite, even in advanced debility. Bassett continued to visit with
oysters, but kindly Mrs Curran took over his day-to-day care and made
him Irish tea, which, he said to Mary subsequently, would have killed

or cured a dragon. He spent the next month in bed in Elwood Street recovering.

The Aikens returned from Mexico, married, around the beginning of August. Burra, who was still extremely frail, was desperate to get back to England as soon as possible, and the first boat out was a Holland–America line ship ('quite awful vintage 1910') called the *Scythia*, which docked at Southampton around the middle of the month. It was another purgatorial journey, third-class, though Burra was grateful to find that since the ship was not full, he had a cabin to himself. On the downside, 'my funeral nitch is two flights of stairs & 20 miles of rabbit warren from les waters [the lavatory] & with my feet my dear its quite a calvary when nature calls'.

When they got to England, he and the Aikens took the first train to Rye, where he arrived at Springfield without warning, emaciated, greenish-yellow with jaundice and looking half dead, wearing bedroom slippers because his feet were too swollen and tender for him to get a pair of shoes on, and reeking of Sloan's Liniment (a pungent mixture for alleviating rheumatic pain, which contains menthol, turpentine and capsicin). The Mexican adventure had done further permanent damage to his spleen and liver, but it had also been hard on his joints, which were worse than ever. He was so anaemic that he had to have a series of iron injections, and regular visits from a masseuse, Miss Wadcot, every three days or so into the New Year. He wrote to Nash, some time after his return, 'I take 15 iron pills a day and not a square inch sous le bas fond where there isnt the mark of a needle.'

The visit was brief, but important. 'I should never have left Boston Mass which suited me down to the ground not that Mexico isnt lovely if you can stand it,' he confessed to Chappell. It took him the rest of the year to recover his stamina and mobility. His friends came to visit, but he couldn't go out apart from occasional excursions when someone was able to put him in a car. However, Mexico strengthened and focused the new direction that he had taken after Spain, where the explosive tensions of a country about to slide into civil war focused his mind on violence and death. He was thus already attuned to the death-haunted religiosity of Mexico when he arrived there.

He was not the only English modernist to be interested by Mexican art. His fellow-Unit One member, Henry Moore, had been permanently reoriented as a sculptor by the limestone figure of the Mayan-Toltec rain-spirit Chacmool, discovered at the archaeological site of Chichén Itza. The figure reclines on its back with knees raised and head turned over the shoulder: Moore saw a plaster cast of it in Paris in 1925 and it set him on his lifelong series of reclining figure studies. Burra was also interested in pre-Columbian art, but even more in the Catholic baroque, in modern Mexican artists, and in folk art such as the sugar skulls produced for the Day of the Dead.

The painting he did at Cuernavaca is quite possibly lost (there is no 'slaughtered Christ', as Aiken describes it, among his known works). His most important Mexican painting, *Mexican Church*, was painted in Rye after his return: the composition is based on two postcards, one of a crucifix laid flat on an altar, viewed from the feet up, in Santa Catarina, Mexico City, the other showing the gilt reredos and tabernacle of the cathedral at Taxco. He had visited both churches; the postcards were to sharpen and focus his memory. He also produced an enormous pen, ink and wash drawing, best described by Mary Aiken, to whom he gave it, which recalls their hallucinatory trip across Mexico.

It is the landscape of that dawn we awakened to the sunrise glimmering through and over the mountains onto a village on the barren Mexican plateau below. The sky, mountains and village are at the top, and have an ominous feel about them. Then in the foreground is a large peasant woman, wrapped in a serape and ragged shawl, like a squatted Fate figure, stirring a large flat-lipped pot containing fleshy bones, set over a small fire. Her face is expressionless, as only an Indian's, or someone without hope, could be. Not glowering – merely being. Looking on, with a prayer in its piteous eyes that some morsel will, by an unhoped for good luck, come its way, is a mongrel bitch with great swollen dragging teats.

The unfortunate dog may be the same as the one Aiken noticed in Cuernavaca, 'a starved dog with a broken back, the hind quarters twisted, dragged itself crookedly to the little parapet of flowerpots by the entrance, and lay there, mutely begging. No attention was paid to it. The eyes, tender and trusting, beseeching, were enough to break one's heart; and when at last it gave up hope, and began to drag itself away, it heaved such a sigh of pure and beaten despair as ought rightly to have ended the world.' This huge drawing records the extraordinarily high horizon, and the way that the towns cling to the lower slopes of the great mountains; curiously, the alarmingly monumental figure of the Mexican woman is not, as Mary describes it, stirring her pot; her long dark arm is commandingly outflung, bisecting the painting, as if she is casting a spell.

Like the time spent in Mexico City, the sojourn in Cuernavaca had been uncomfortable, but not unstimulating. The American ambassador, who lived there, had commissioned Diego Rivera in 1929 to paint a set of murals in the town's principal monument, a grim, sixteenth-century fortress-palace built by Hernan Cortés. These showed a panorama of Mexican history, from the Spanish conquest to the liberation of the workers and peasants by the Mexican revolution. Mary Aiken would certainly have been interested since she had worked with Quintanilla, and quite clearly so was Burra. Rivera represents Spaniards in sixteenth-century armour confronting Indians in beaked masks derived from Aztec art. Burra had been interested in baroque soldiers for a few years, since his Spain trip, and he also had a liking for what he called bird-folk; bird-headed or masked people, who turned up often in his paintings both before and after Mexico. Rivera used the beaked Indians again in his paintings in the National Palace at Mexico City (1930–5), which Burra may also have seen.

He also informed himself about other Mexican artists. He had opportunities to see some of their work in Mexico City while Aiken was ill, and he also bought reproductions later. Some of the Mexican modern artists whose work has points in common with his own include Antonio Ruiz, who painted street-scenes not unlike Burra's Harlem conversation pieces; Frida Kahlo, whose work collapses the distinctions between high art and folk art, which may well have caught his attention; and Rufino Tamayo, since similarities between Burra's boldly coloured fruit and vegetable studies and those of Tamayo suggest that Burra was aware of him. The art-critic Edward Lucie-Smith has commented on the importance of the Mexican muralists as influences on his work (since Mary Aiken was trained in that tradition, they will certainly have talked about it, and he will have sought their work out), arguing for direct influence from José Clemente Orozco and Diego Rivera in Burra's work of the Forties and subsequently.

He was more certainly influenced by a graphic artist, José Guadalupe Posada (1852–1913), whom Rivera himself perceived as an influence. Posada's newspaper and magazine illustrations depicted firing squads and murders, and weirdly lively skeletons, riding bicycles, stepping out in dance-halls, preaching revolution. Burra certainly owned at least one of his little books, since he mentions coming across it in 1945, when it fitted with his mood very well.

After Mexico, Burra's work became more sombre. In the Twenties, he might have wanted to represent the Lowry ménage's self-indulgence and self-absorption, or the social comedy of a couple and their servants' attitude to them (a theme he treated in an early painting, *The Sisters*). A little later, he might have wanted to paint the garden – a painting of 1931 shows a commanding lady gesturing towards an onrushing tsunami of tropical jungle and parrots, which seems almost prescient. But he appears, in fact, chiefly to have been struck by the combination of playfulness with moral seriousness of Mexican baroque, and by the political seriousness of Rivera and Orozco's work. Religious painting, tragic painting. Mexico brought him up against the casual, appalling, interpersonal cruelties of the Third World, even more than the south of Spain had done, and strengthened his sense of the importance of religion – as a subject for art, and quite possibly as an aspect of life.

Burra had two phases of painting religious subjects, one in 1938–9, another in 1950–2. Clover, who was somewhat anticlerical, was inclined to be sarcastic about his post-Mexico paintings. 'Is it your mexican church that has attracted such a lot of attention? – you'll be getting fan-mail from Father Darcy before long and a specimen copy of the Tablet.[4] The first sequence of religious pictures, apart from *Mexican Church*, are *Holy Week, Seville*, which, like the Mexican picture, essentially addresses religion as a social phenomenon, and the *Vision of St Theresa* and the *Agony in the Garden*. These are both extremely strange pictures. The *Vision*, which is a pencil drawing heightened with wash, deliberately eschews the phallic symbolism of Bernini's famous sculpture and, indeed, of Teresa's actual vision; Burra leaves out the lance tipped with fire which the saint says was plunged into her bowels. The angel, like all Burra's angels, is a large and frightening figure, not, as Teresa described him, 'small of stature and most beautiful'. He seems to be holding a white-hot object, a burning heart perhaps, against the entranced saint's cheek. *Agony* focuses on the moment before Christ accepts his fate; powerful and sinewy, he is visibly striving with himself, hands knotted in indecision, while a grim, heavily muscled angel insistently proffers the cup that represents death on the cross.

---

[4] Father Martin D'Arcy, SJ, was one of the best-known Catholic apologists of his day, allegedly the model for Evelyn Waugh's 'Father Rothschild' in *Vile Bodies*.

Burra's angels perhaps owe less to conventional religious represen-tation than they do to the early, surrealist poetry of Rafael Alberti, above all *On the Angels* (*Sobre los Ángeles*, 1927–8), which presents a series of grimly alarming angels of anger, of death; angels who are cruel, even rabid. The poem 'The Two Angels', from a sequence within the collec-tion called *The Guest of the Mists* (*Huésped de las nieblas*), seems more explanatory of the 'St Teresa' drawing than the saint's actual vision.[5]

> O sword thrust in the shadows!
> Innumerable sparks
> Searing into my body
> Into my featherless wings
> Into that which nobody sees
> Life.
> You are burning me alive,
> Fly away from me now, dark
> Luzbel of the endings without dawns
> Of the wells without water.

Venice

In 1939, Burra was sufficiently recovered to go on his travels again, though to a less challenging destination. He went to Milan, Lombardy and Venice with his sister to look at art.

I heard from Mdme Huntley [Anne] who said she wishd to go to Venice for 10 days and asked me to come so I seized on the offer as I knew I should never get there otherwise as I cant get anywhere unless pushed . . . We have already been

[5] ¡Oh espadazo en las sombras!
Chispas múltiples,
Clavándose en mi cuerpo,
En mis alas sin plumas,
En lo que nadie ve,
Vida.
Me éstas quemando vivo.
Vuela ya de mí, oscuro
Luzbel de las conteras sin auroras,
De los pozos sin agua.
(translation by Peter Davidson and Nicola de la Peña)

told that Venice is full of fever mosquitoes too hot miasmas germans typhod enteric and ague Im taking a bottle of Dr J Collis Brownes chlorodyne[6] in case I entend to get in a 1^D steamer ploughing through the scum of old vegetables fish bones swollen cats abortions etc under the bridge of sighs.

He had wanted to see Venice for a long time; and he had admired Tiepolo since the Twenties. But as Causey observes, Tiepolo's *sprezzatura*, his light, bright colours, were, however enjoyable, no longer of real interest to Burra in the specific sense that they fed into his own art. In a sense, he visited Mexico and Venice in the wrong order – if he had got to Italy in the early Thirties, it might have made quite a difference, but after the cumulative effect upon him of Spain, the Spanish Civil War and Mexico, Venice was of relatively little use to him. The artist who above all fixed his attention and helped his work to develop at this time was Alessandro Magnasco, as Causey has also observed.

Magnasco's interests lay on the margins of society in groups of bandits, beggars and gypsies, monks and soldiers . . . like Burra's, Magnasco's subjects were alternately febrile and manic . . . his figures may be war-weary and disenchanted with life, but they exist in a world in which religion was obviously still a driving force, though, as with Burra, true faith borders both on sorcery and empty ritual.

As the news got grimmer and grimmer through the Thirties, it was Goya's series of etchings of *The Horrors of War*, Jacques Callot's *Miseries of War* series and Magnasco's alienated gypsies that fed his own preoccupations, not Tiepolo's exquisite girls and infinite late-summer skies of cerulean and Naples yellow. Burra experienced a significant exposure to Magnasco in Dublin before August 1937, most probably on the way back from Mexico, (though there is no direct evidence for when this visit took place, the letter in which he recalls it is absolutely datable by a reference to Clover's new baby): 'I like Dublin it has some of the most beautiful buildings Ive ever seen . . . & the Art Gallery has some wonderful treasures an "18th century Neapolitan collection" belonging to the Marquess of upsidedown consisting of Salvator Rosas Magnascos etc etc.'

Additionally, during his trip to Venice, he could have visited the

---

[6] A robust Victorian panacea which included tincture of cannabis, tincture of opium and chloroform, and continued to be marketed as a cure-all.

collection of the Venetian art-dealer Italico Brass, who owned about fifty Magnascos. Burra's interest in Magnasco is confirmed by another letter in which he explicitly claimed him as an influence.

Mr Minsky in the Listener is a regular sick. He tells me far more about what I've been copying than I do myself Crivelli & Ucello dearie Pierre Roy Berard I've seen about 1 Pierre Roy and another was an ad in Harpers. Ay shoud have thought a vague spirit of Magnasco was more to the pernt.

One specific Magnasco painting that is extraordinarily Burra-esque is *Il Furto Sacrilego:* this represents a baroque church with dramatically recessive perspective and a group of thieves assaulted by an active gang of skeletons who have come rushing out of their graves. It is in Milan, so it is just possible that Burra saw it in actuality (it was also reproduced in 1938 in a periodical he could have bought in Zwemmer's).

There was a Magnasco Society in England, founded in 1923, chiefly by Sacheverell and Osbert Sitwell and Tancred Borenius, which was part of the Twenties' revolt against nineteenth-century taste and values. It promoted seventeenth- and eighteenth-century Italian painting generally, not just Magnasco, but the important thing is that it looked above all for what was violent, excessive and indecorous in late-baroque art. The Magnasco Society was also linked with other aspects of the baroque in Thirties' England. As a decorative style, 'baroque' had definably queer overtones, inevitably so since it was championed by such leaders of fashion as Tom Driberg and Harold Acton.

William Gaunt's *Bandits in a Landscape* (1937) is a more academic manifestation of this interest in artistic developments after Caravaggio; and is a book that Burra almost certainly owned. It draws attention to the eighteenth-century painters of ruins, mostly in Rome, portraying people moving among crumbling buildings; to *capriccios*, which are landscapes informed by personal psychology – Gaunt specifically observes that 'the method had something in common with the present-day "surrealism"' – and to the wild and crazy paintings of Monsù Desiderio, of which a key example, the *Legend of St Augustine* (which could almost have been painted by Dalí), was straightforwardly available to Burra in the National Gallery in London. Whether or not Burra was interested in current debate about the baroque, he was certainly interested by Monsù Desiderio. He finally saw *Explosion in a Church*, which would have been particularly relevant to his work at the end of the Thirties, in 1952, when Francis Madan, who owned it, lent it to the National Gallery, and he was fascinated by it. But in the Thirties, he could have accessed a variety of late-baroque paintings by visiting Arthur Tooth & Sons, a gallery very familiar to him; when Gaunt was writing, for instance, they had Pannini's *Roman Ruins and Figures* and Ghisolfi's *Ruined Palace*); or by going to the various loan exhibitions held by the Magnasco Society at Thos. Agnew & Sons.

One of the few writers of the Thirties who made an explicit attempt to define the baroque was Peter Burra – a relative of the painter's, though not a very close one.[7] In 1930, he published an essay on the baroque in a quarterly called *Farrago* (which he edited). Burra was aware of *Farrago*, since two of his paintings are reproduced in the December issue of the same year, so he may well have seen this essay. In any case, whether he was interested in definitions or not, his paintings are created with reference to baroque art, and to the ongoing debate on the nature and value of baroque.

With respect to actual paintings, if one thinks of classical and baroque as opposed tendencies in art rather than period-markers, then much of what we think of as characteristic of Thirties' art in England is classical; refined, abstract, an art built up on principles of exclusion. Burra's art, by contrast, was baroque, in the various senses that it was eclectic, that it mixed high and low cultural references, that it was full of colour and incident, that it was more concerned with surfaces than structures and played games with perspective. The art-critic Marina Vaizey commented relatively recently, 'The fact that Burra can now be recognised for the original and powerful artist that he is . . . beyond the band of devoted collectors of his work, has a good deal to do with the 1980s rediscovery of the possibilities of richly-flavoured painting.' Even in the Thirties Osbert Lancaster recognised this, albeit rather backhandedly:

Burra, whether he knows it or not, is a traditionalist. His kinship . . . is with those anonymous masters who until a few years ago decorated merry-go-rounds and ice cream carts with the last genuine examples of baroque art in Europe.

[7] Peter James Salkeld Burra (1909–37), writer, critic, and Benjamin Britten's last major attachment before Peter Pears, was the twin brother of the singer and teacher Nell Moody, née Helen Pomfret Burra, whose name clearly identifies the siblings as members of the Pomfret/Curteis/Burra banking dynasty, though from a branch settled in Gloucestershire (probably descendants of James Salkeld Burra, Edward Burra's great-uncle).

This is implicitly belittling, implying that Burra's art is naïve, and therefore not art but decoration. But Burra's eye and taste were as educated as those of Paul Nash or Henry Moore, if not more so; he was very well read in both literature and art theory, and a serious student of older paintings; apart from Magnasco, his work signals a deep awareness of Bosch and Brueghel, Callot, Goya and El Greco, among many others. But his genuine kinship with baroque art, and the art of the French surrealists, for which Mexican art is in a sense a middle term, is shown by his openness to pop culture of all kinds from Mexican kitsch to Walt Disney, and by his refusal to acknowledge a hierarchy of high and low art forms. This is something that Thirties' England did not find easy to deal with; witnessed, for example, by Rothenstein's complete blindness to this aspect of his work.

XI

WAR

AT 11.15 on the night of 3 September 1939, Neville Chamberlain, then Prime Minister, told the people of England, 'We are now at war.' In the small hours of the following morning, the concept became abruptly real, as Britain was, for the first time, awakened by the wail of sirens. Whatever the result of the conflagration into which Europe was plunged in the last months of 1939, then unguessable, this announcement represented a crushing personal defeat for Chamberlain himself, the apostle of appeasement. Within a year, he was dead of cancer and chagrin.

Burra's last trip out of England before the war was the excursion to Milan and Lombardy which he made with his sister in July 1939. In the weeks that followed, he, along with everyone else, watched the government vacillate its reluctant way towards war. Burra's reaction was complex. In Spain, he had come to understand clearly how much he loathed and abhorred violence. But Hitler's determination to redraw the map of Europe seems to have left Burra certain that Germany must be resisted, in a way that he had not been with respect to the war in Spain.

Whether his parents shared this feeling is not certain. Osbert Lancaster observed that much of the English upper middle class in the interwar period was, without necessarily being anti-Jewish or pro-Hitler, very pro-German. Burra's mother was almost certainly among them. She was intensely musical, had studied opera in Dresden and continued to be passionately fond of opera (Wagner in particular) for the rest of her life, an interest she shared with her daughter. Lancaster says of his own regular interwar visits to the Salzburg Festival:

On looking back it sometimes occurs to me to wonder how far the widespread reluctance of the English upper classes to face German realities in the following years was due to these annual get-togethers . . . there can, I think, be small doubt that such contacts were largely responsible for one of the most widespread and dangerous illusions then current – namely, that the Bavarians and Austrians were kindly, sensitive peoples, the predestined and unwilling dupes of the brutal and callous Prussians.

Mrs Burra and Anne, like the Lancasters, went to German music-festivals, and even ventured a last visit to Dresden shortly before war broke out. Burra reported: 'Anne and mother have gone shakeing in their shoes (by air) to Germany! Where shortly we shall hear of them being driven thru the streets of Dresden with shaved heads and a placard "I spoke to a jew" on it.' It is obvious, however, that the Burras had no time at all for Hitler or his views. It may also be relevant that Anne told Andrew Stephenson, author of a thesis on Burra's painting, in an interview that the family had had business connections with Dresden before the First World War, which were then discontinued, which may suggest that Henry Burra was not of the pro-German party.

Burra himself showed little interest in German art other than that of left-wing contemporaries such as Georg Grosz and other artists covered by the German international art review *Der Querschnitt*, and for avant-garde photography. He never learned German, visited Germany or evidenced any enthusiasm for German music. But these were all aspects of his family culture, from which he distanced himself. His letters to his sister, and hers to him, exchange news about Wagner as well as films, though he never alludes to opera in any other context.

Clarissa Aiken once suffered through a senior Burra dinner-party with a collection of Indian Army colonels and their memsahibs, and reports its extremely right-wing and anti-American tone. 'Conrad winced through the table talk, which ranged from orchid-growing to Jew-baiting in Germany and the pernicious Hollywood influence . . . "I've never cared much for Margot Asquith" [an American], Mrs Burra said with birdlike gestures, "after seeing her paring her nails while in charge of the ices at a charity bazaar".' The Aikens vowed 'never again'.

Burra did not share his parents' social life ordinarily; it was only because the Aikens were there that he was sitting through such an evening himself. But they must have been difficult people to go through the war with, particularly his mother. Trudy Burra, like her son, was charming, attractive and wilful. She had been brought up with the expectation that she would always be waited upon; and her capacity to adjust to change was eroded by the fact that she was also 'delicate': unlike her son, she took the view that her health excused her from making any attempt whatsoever to take responsibility for herself. Henry Burra's grasp on other kinds of practicalities, however, is suggested by an undated letter that Burra wrote to Nash some time in the late Thirties.

Father has sold some fields apparently to make an airodrome & do the quainte olde folke burne? O Boye!! 'everyone' will leave 'everyone' is threatning to leave maybe if they disguise the airodrome as Haddon Hall & all the airplanes as sea mews it will be OK.

The Rye worthies may have been writing to the papers about 'eyesores', but the aerodrome was to see hard service in the years that followed. The RAF did not maintain a fighter group at Rye, but it sited an air-defence radar system there, which provided long-range early warning for the south coast and Channel.

One of the first signs that Britain was at war was the imposition of a blackout. Sylvia Townsend Warner observed in a letter to an American friend, 'It is indescribably moving to see that city [London] just quietly abandoning itself to darkness as if it were any country landscape ... the darkness falling, and the noise thinning out from a mass of sounds to individual sounds as though the night combed it.' It was obvious to both the British and German governments that if there were to be a war, it would be to a great extent a war in the air, and so blackout was one of the few aspects of the conflict for which the population was actually prepared. Detailed advice had been issued as early as July, and suitable material had been made available. What people found, however, when the blackout was actually enforced, was that the total absence of street-lights was disorienting, inconvenient, frightening and often dangerous. The government's preparations had unfortunately not included any attempt to stockpile torch-batteries, which were in very short supply.

The other early symptom of a wartime footing was the evacuation of children to the countryside, which began even before Chamberlain's announcement, on 1 September. At the outbreak of hostilities, the south coast was still perceived as 'the countryside' rather than – as it later became – virtually the front line. The Burras duly took in a group of evacuees, and, like many another middle-class household, discovered how different were the lives of the urban poor from their own. Both these experiences are reflected in a letter Burra wrote to Chappell at the beginning of the war, dated '1st <u>Triumphal</u> week <u>Shit</u>':

Nobody seems to have dared sing Keep the Home Fires burning – except me – Ime singing all the dear old hits – they don't seem to go down very well now . . . Mdm Ker-S couldnt keep away from her <u>infame reduit</u> Ive just heard from her she flashes her torch in the Blackout and surprises the strangest things going on. We've got some kiddies here 'Arry, Fred, Sheelah, Vera and Lily. Vera wets the bed we 'ad to buy some draws at Marx & Spencers (before they went up in price) Mother says she's got a weakness . . . The mothers are getting a bit restive for the dear old Elephant and Castle and feed the Kids on osborne biscuits & potted crab one was offered some <u>Fresh</u> vegetables the other day it nearly killed her poor woman she had to be brought round with a Japanese crab meat sandwich and some smiths crisps. Work parties are a cinch such fun making swabs to fill the cracks in the Maginot line & every 2nd person is an air warden. Thank God the theatres are shut for if Drury Lane was open I dread to think what sweet Ivor of old Novello would be thinking up with Mary Ellis as the spirit of Democracy including a real line Maginot real destruction of Warsaw the Derby Day 1914 and the Battle of Bunkers Hill . . .

Bed-wetting was a common response to the stress that children were under, and it also became clear to appalled hosts that a significant proportion of slum children were not potty-trained at all, but left to work out continence for themselves. Even *The Lancet* admitted: 'Somewhat unexpectedly, enuresis has proved to be one of the major menaces to the comfortable disposition of evacuated urban children . . . every morning, every window is full of bedding hung out to air.' It sounds as if the Burras responded more sensibly than many by buying rubber pants and refraining, as far as one can see, from blaming the unfortunate Vera.

The Burras' discovery of the terrible diet of the urban poor was matched in many middle-class households up and down the land, including that of Rosamond Lehmann and Wogan Philipps. Rosamond was in a nursing-home recovering from a miscarriage in the first week of the war, and so Philipps co-opted Bar, with whom he was still friendly, to help out. Rosamond returned home to find her husband and his ex-mistress struggling with eleven evacuees from the East End alongside Philipps' own Hugo and Sally. 'They were so miserable,' said Bar, looking back, 'they slept on the floor, and they peed everywhere and were sick, and they'd never cleaned their teeth in their lives. Rosamond got lovely meals for them, which they wouldn't eat because they wanted fish and chips.' But not long after her return, Rosamond spotted something which neither the inexperienced Bar nor her husband had noticed (Philipps, classically for a man of his generation, had spent little time with his own children): two of the evacuees showed symptoms of scarlet fever, which is violently infectious. Furious, and terrified, she bundled Hugo and Sally off, and, amid clouds of disinfectant fumes, arranged for the well evacuees to be sent away, and the ill ones to go to hospital. The Burras, fortunately, were spared any dramas of the kind.

Burra evidently added his limited strength to the sort of 'general usefulness' projects typical of the beginning of the war (such as making swabs). He also received a form from the Ministry of Labour, having been put by a committee of experts on a register of artists, which he duly filled in, detailing his fragile health ('rheumatism and an enlarged SPLEEN spleen sweatheart bigger then ever these days and distilling venom)', at which point any idea anyone may have had of making him an official war artist must have been shelved. He committed himself to what was later known as the Home Front, and refused to be driven out of Springfield. 'Not if I can help it my dear tooth and nail to the soil I am now look at the price of vegetables and fruit.' His personal preparation for the war was practical enough: buying up all the aspirin he could lay hands on, since it was the only effective medication for his sore joints.

Burra's interest in practical gardening became intense. Springfield had always had a kitchen garden and orchard – pre-war, it also had two gardeners. One remained with them until 1942, when he contracted whooping cough and had to give up work: he was probably Charles Boots, since a gardener of that name is left a legacy and the use of a cottage for his and his wife's lifetimes in Henry Burra's will. After 1942, Henry Burra had to keep the garden going himself, with help from his son when Edward was feeling strong enough. How much he could actually achieve, given his very poor health in the war years, his lack of stamina and half-crippled hands, is anybody's guess, but a well-maintained old-fashioned garden can soldier on semi-tended for a surprisingly long time with conscientious hoeing and raking. The pair of them scratched resolutely in the vegetable beds, doing their best.

Also, at some point during the war, the family seems to have taken up keeping chickens. This was a highly practical manoeuvre, as it turned out, since eggs became almost unobtainable – Aiken, on his post-war return to Rye, found things rather better than he had expected: 'only the egg eludes us save for a few that Ed steals from his hens'. In 1940, the government lifted all legal restrictions on keeping poultry (and rabbits) in domestic gardens. A supplementary hen-food called Balancer Meal was made available in exchange for surrendering the household's egg ration, but people with fewer than twenty hens could keep what the birds laid; so if the creatures could be cajoled into producing, then one might do rather well out of it. Springfield's established vegetable garden put quite a lot of hen-food potentially to hand, since hens happily eat old cabbage-stalks and potato-peelings, and above all enjoy the otherwise useless vegetables that caterpillars and grubs have got to first. However, finding the birds enough protein to keep them in laying condition would have been a struggle for the Burras, as for all amateur poultry-keepers of the period.

The months that followed September 1939 were subsequently known as the 'phoney war'. On the principle that although Hitler had done his best to avoid war with Britain, since he needed to concentrate on his eastern front, he was still likely to be a great deal better prepared than they were, Britons were braced for resistance. Unfortunately, nothing then proceeded to happen for quite some time. Fighting there was, but it was overseas, and censorship ensured that the public knew almost nothing of it. Meanwhile, Chamberlain hung on as Prime Minister, 'like a dirty old piece of chewing-gum clinging to a chair', promulgating his own state of denial about the war.

It became clear as the weeks went by that there was no immediate threat of invasion, and, at that stage, no aerial bombardment either. About 524,000 mothers with children under five had been evacuated in the first days of the war, but when no bombs eventuated, many of them started trickling home. By January 1940, only 65,000 were still where they had been billeted. When their mothers took Harry, Fred, Sheila, Vera and Lily back to the Elephant & Castle, as they did, they were following a general trend.

The ballet, with which Burra was much involved at this stage of his life, was fragmented by the war. When it broke out, the Vic-Wells Ballet was in Leeds, and was immediately disbanded. Ashton, Chappell and Robert Helpmann[1] went off to stay with Doris Langley Moore, an old friend of Burra and Chappell's, who was married to a rich man in Harrogate, a mere ten miles away, and they tried to work out what to do next. After the first shock was over, Chappell, flushed with patriotism, went into the army, becoming Gunner Chappell W.E. 979498. Once in, he was profoundly unhappy. In an essay he wrote about his experience in 1942, he says:

The life I lead in the army gives me nothing. My freedom is restricted, my privacy torn, my comfort abolished . . . army life lacks everything, particularly in a static unit. People do not realise it is worse for the spirit to be dreary than endangered; that boredom is worse than bombs.

His army career was boring and pointless to a quite unusual extent. He was also aware that it was destroying his future as a dancer, since the years were speeding by, and he couldn't stay in shape. Since he was unmathematical, he failed to master the basics of gunnery, which depends on calculation. However, some intelligent officer realised his immense gift for making something out of nothing, theatrically speaking, and put him to work as an entertainment organiser, talent-spotting among bored and anxious young men waiting to be sent on active service, and putting together amateur revues with a random cast of soldiers eked out with officers' wives and girls from the NAAFI.[2] As things turned out, Chappell saw no action at all other than that supplied by amateur dramatics, though in the second half of the war he served both in North Africa and in southern Italy. Burra experienced considerably more actual danger in his own home.

Meanwhile, what remained of the Sadlers Wells ballet re-formed as a touring company with two pianos, one played by Constant Lambert, the other by the rehearsal pianist, Hilda Gaunt, instead of an orchestra, and with Ashton as director. By 1940 the company was touring for

[1] Helpmann tipped up shortly before the war. He, Ashton and Chappell promptly became thick as thieves.

[2] The Navy, Army and Air Force Institutes, HM Forces' official trading organisation; one of the few institutions in a Forties' army camp that employed women.

ENSA (Entertainments National Service Association), and in May, as a propaganda exercise, they went to Holland, coinciding, unfortunately, with the German invasion. They returned in the straw-strewn hold of a cargo-ship under enemy fire (since the Germans were under the impression that it was carrying the Dutch Queen, Wilhelmina). But one by one, the stars disappeared; being young and very fit, they were naturally liable for army service. In June 1941, Ashton himself went into the RAF, where, like Chappell, he was both unhappy and inefficient. In the world of the ballet, the principal men who remained were Helpmann, who, since he had an Australian passport and could not be called up, continued to work with ENSA, and Constant Lambert, who was also safe from the army since, like Burra, he was a man who managed to achieve a great deal while being physically in very poor shape.

Burra's other friends began to scatter. Gerald Corcoran joined the army, and his marriage to Bumble started breaking up, due in part to the war. Burra notes in February 1940 that she was in a very brittle state of mind; and also that she stayed in London when her husband was posted to Wales. 'Bumble has been swept away like an autumn leaf and finally has shared a basement in St James Sqr or St James place with some woman from Paquin.[3] Sooner death than Aberystwyth . . .'

Clover vanished once more. She and Antonio returned to Spain just before the war, taking baby Edward with them. Franco had declared the end of the Spanish Civil War in April 1939, and they had decided to go back (Spain was neutral in the Second World War). They were taking a considerable risk: Antonio had after all been a Republican politician, a highly dangerous thing to have been in Franco's Spain. Something like two million former Republican politicians, soldiers and officials were imprisoned in the post-war period in vast camps – the official tariff for having served the republic was thirty years – and many were shot. For Pertinez, though, it was a question of weighing up different kinds of risk. If he stayed away for the duration of whatever reshufflings were occurring within the family in the post-war world, his share of whatever remained of the patrimony would almost certainly mysteriously disappear. There was also reason to think that the Pertinez family was sufficiently established within Granada to protect him – as indeed proved to be the case.

[3] Paquin was an established and very upmarket Paris fashion house, which had a branch in London from 1898.

But Burra was determined not to lose Clover again, as he had done during the bizarre episode of her Hungarian marriage. His pocket diaries for 1939 and 1940 do not survive, but that for 1941 does; and it indicates that he wrote to her faithfully every four or five days throughout the entire period. He also wrote regularly to his friends in the army, Chappell, Gerald Corcoran and Frederick Ashton: while his letters to Chappell were to a great extent relieving his own feelings, those to Corcoran focused on news of mutual friends, and letters to Ashton, whom he knew to be extremely unhappy, were designed to cheer him up.

Barbara Ker-Seymer stayed in London in the first year of the war, and joined the ARP (Air Raid Precautions department). Her ex-lover Olivia Wyndham returned to England shortly before the war, partly with the intention of seeking a cure for her addiction to heroin, and stayed on after war was declared to help with the first stages of the evacuation. But she was committed to America and to Edna; so she returned to the States, not without mixed feelings. Back in New York, she did what she could to shift public opinion towards American involvement, and as soon as America entered the war, she enlisted in the WAC (Women's Army Corps) and served with distinction as an army photographer. The only other member of Burra's circle to have a conventionally 'good war' was, surprisingly, Bunny Roger. Burra commented, 'I hear Bunny is an enormous success, & can do anything with the men & has been sent off to East Anglia to manage some. He & Miss Dietrich, dear, know <u>men</u>.' Later, he saw active service (his immaculate uniforms supplemented by a mauve chiffon scarf and full make-up), and served with conspicuous, and effective, bravery. 'Now that I have shot so many Nazis,' he is alleged to have said, 'Daddy must give me a mink coat.'

On 10 May 1940, as the Germans roared through Holland and Belgium towards the Channel, Winston Churchill became Prime Minister, and England finally acquired a government that believed in its own war. With the surrender of King Leopold of the Belgians on 28 May, the Germans reached the Channel. The evacuation of troops, mostly British, some French, from Dunkirk followed in the last days of May through to the early days of June – a logistical triumph which offset military defeat. After France fell on 17 June, Britain stood alone.

Conrad Aiken, back in the States, sent messages of gloom which completely misjudged the atmosphere in Britain itself: 'I can only hope you have been forcibly evacuated to clear the foreshore for military operations – it would be only sensible. Rye has been mentioned on the radio as "in the path" – I have a feeling that if we ever see the dear little place again, it will be <u>radically</u> changed. I feel to judge from all we hear on the wireless and in the papers that to write to you is practically like sending a letter to Atlantis – so sure are some people that this will be the end of England.'

But the fall of Chamberlain's government had been in the nick of time. It is hard to imagine anyone better able than Churchill was to cope with this series of catastrophes, and to articulate the resolute defiance that was the overriding mood of the time. A businessman in Accrington who went to his bank to withdraw his money in that terrible month asked, 'What shall we do when the Germans get here?' The deputy-manager answered him, 'Do? I'll tell you what we'll do. We'll get a gun and we'll shoot the buggers.' Burra's hatred of violence was profound; his own frailty and puniness would have made resistance to any normally constituted soldier virtually a joke, but if England had been invaded he would certainly have resisted. Everything that he says about the war suggests the extent to which he felt that it had forced him into a position against his own character, but there was nothing pacifist about him. In this, he was very characteristic of his generation.

If you have lived half your life's span without a passionate belief in anything, the bald discovery that you would honestly and in cold blood rather die when it came to it than be bossed about by a Nazi . . . that is something to have lived for.

So the novelist Margery Allingham, who seems on the whole to have been exhilarated by the discovery. Burra was not. He and Allingham were of an age; they had grown up deriding the true-blue certainties of the Edwardian era. It came as a bit of a shock to find patriotism and even an occasional moral certainty in the unvisited corners of one's own psyche, but it was not an uncommon discovery of the time. Stephen Spender's reaction was very similar.

Some artists retreated abroad. Auden and Isherwood went to America, as did Britten and Pears and – more within Burra's world – the dancers Anton Dolin, Alicia Markova and Michael Somes. Malcolm Lowry, who was in Vancouver when war broke out, stayed there. In 1936, Burra had seriously considered settling in Spain, but once war began, almost everything suggests that he was committed to England. The only thing that does not is a mysterious letter Aiken wrote to Lowry in December 1939: 'Ed writes that he may be coming over to Boston next month – if he can get here – so maybe we'll all be having a reunion.' This was still the period of the 'phoney war', when nobody yet had any sense of how successful the Luftwaffe would be in taking the war to Britain. Also, Burra's pictures were on show in the British pavilion at the New York World's Fair, but it would have been entirely uncharacteristic of him positively to seek out an exhibition of his own work. He said not a word about this to any of his English friends; if he did consider going abroad, he thought again.

During the war, Burra did a variety of work outside the house, without being able to take on anything very specific, since he could not predict how much energy he had available from day to day. Consequently, he did very basic jobs: 'I have been doleing out change and 2½d Tiffin at a canteen of unexampled squalor cups washed up in a thick velouté sauce I often think of taking a cupful home for braising Clara Carrot.'[4] Hot water was used as meanly as possible during the war, even when this militated against basic hygiene.

But the humdrum nature of Burra's wartime life mutated sharply into crisis in July 1940. Any possibility of a German invasion of Britain was dependent above all on mastery of the air. The 'phoney war' came to an abrupt end when the Battle of Britain began that month. From that point on, the experience of civilian life for Burra in Sussex, as for the residents of Essex and Kent, differed sharply from that of the rest of the country, because it was going on literally underneath the principal war zone.

To the civilian in the South East of England, the Battle of Britain meant vapour trails in the sky, the sound of aircraft engines, the frequent clatter of machine guns, followed by a hail of spent cartridge cases in the back garden, seven or even ten warnings a day, and the occasional crash as a bomb fell or an aircraft was shot out of the sky.

Life on the south coast could assume a sort of weird normality. A Sussex woman recalled lying sunbathing on her lawn in Lewes, watching the 'slim silver pencils of the Dorniers going over to bomb London'. But in the second half of 1940, 70,000 bombs fell on Kent; many must also

---

[4] Dr – not Clara – Carrot and Potato Pete were figures from Ministry of Food propaganda, intended to encourage people to eat more root vegetables.

have fallen on neighbouring Sussex. The novelist and poet Sylvia Townsend Warner (who was also living on the coast) noted, 'Gunfire light is quite different to lightning, it doesn't twitch, it just glares and goes, glares and goes.' If Burra's response to the war had overtones of hysteria at times, he had cause. 'All we have are air battles overhead with machine gunning swooping roaring and carrying on,' he wrote. Margery Allingham observed that 'from the ground you could only see the planes with great difficulty, for they flew very high. It was golden, glorious weather, and the world hummed with planes all day like bees in a lime tree . . . they looked like little white lice . . . they had an impersonal, transparent look at that distance.'

Paul Nash's response is well known. Though he was based in Oxford during the war, he produced canonical images of the Battle of Britain, and also of crashed aircraft, which became very much a feature of the south-coast landscape. In a *Punch* cartoon of September 1940, a yokel directed some visitors, 'Go down the lane past the Messerschmitt, bear left and keep on past the two Dorniers, then turn sharp right and it's just past the first Junkers.'

Burra had nothing to say about the war in the air. His art, up to that point, had always been dominated by the human figure, and he could do nothing with the abstract beauty of contrails against the sky; which 'hang about like bridal veils in long graceful festoons'. But Rye was swarming with soldiers, engaged in incomprehensible manoeuvres and leaping in and out of vehicles. 'Not <u>one step</u> do they ever walk. No wonder theres no transport. It's a miracle to me where all the petrol comes from I should think they wash in it.' His principal response to the war was a set of alarmingly diabolic pictures of impersonally hyperactive squaddies, with the muscles of baroque Titans and the meaningless energy of ants, which were praised by Wyndham Lewis, in one of the few remarks about his work that Burra cherished. 'I share Burra's emotions regarding war: when I see the purple bottoms of his military ruffians in athletic action against other stout though fiendish fellows, I recognise a brother.' As Gerald Corcoran observed, these were remarkable paintings because they called war itself into question: 'At the height of wartime propaganda, it was a very remarkable thing to paint a British soldier in this way.'

In August 1940, the Blitz on London began. Since those of Burra's friends who had not themselves been called up clung to their London homes like so many cats (notably Bar and Bumble, as well as many other people he cared about, such as Chappell's mother and sisters), he could do nothing but worry, and watch the skies. 'We have been very quiet the last day or two but for a vast hord pouring over yesterday morning & afternoon.' It was intensely stressful for anyone with an imagination, and for Burra, it was an unending nightmare. 'My mind I may add is never "taken off" anything unpleasant by <u>anything</u> – my skeletons are allways right there in my cupboard & no amount of false gaiety drink cinemas & what have you will remove them. I cant understand people who forget.'

It was not just the war in the air that worried him. The ancient bargain of the Cinque Ports, a disproportionately heavy commitment to naval defence, was still being paid by many families he knew, including his own. 'They say that quite a lot of shipping has been bombed & sunk I notice very little has been said on that subject but I think of it quite a lot' . . . 'I had a cousin went down on the Barham his poor wife knew all about it for months & wasn't allowed to say so everyone had been wondering why she was so quiet. I suppose theyl all go every one of my male relations, near ones, are in the navy.' Back in London, Billy Chappell's mother was bombed out, 'suddenly buried in a bookcase and a mass of lath & plaster', but none of Burra's group of close friends was either killed or wounded (though Bumble lost her brother, Bertie).

In summer 1940, Anne was in Wiltshire, where John Huntley was waiting to be mobilised.

Anne has turned into 'An Army Wife' . . . and has been sharing a house with other wives of officers in Wilts no one knows from day to day what any one else is going to do they are supposed to be going to France nobody knows when nobody knows how many people are sleeping in the house or what time the meals are.

By October, she was back at home, since her husband had been ordered overseas, and was doing a variety of war work. 'Very dutiful she is until death so to speak . . . ARP and the canteen where she listens to tall stories from the Irish Fusiliers and dispenses dough nuts bars of aero milk when they can get them and cups of tea À toute heure' . . . 'putting out incendiary bombs – driving an ambulance in raids & god knows what all'.

Rye was battered by bombs. 'We are in the middle of a fausse invasion it sounds like rush hour at the Elephant and Castle complete with dive bombers who suddenly come gliding down the road & brush the tree tops – we had a dressing station in the back yard they spent the night in the kitchen.' Springfield itself was never actually hit, but there were some very near misses.

There was a bit of a <u>degringolade</u> the day before yesterday evening which made the old home shiver like an ague[5] ... My back is racked with rheumatism and I have been unable to get a shoe on the right foot as the bunion joint has been suffering from a composite mixture of old broken chilblain and gout poor mans gout old dear don't mistake me ...

The rheumatic fever which he contracted in 1925 affected his back at that time, but it was only during the war that this particular problem resurfaced. More importantly, gout, one of the most painful of arthritic conditions, added itself to his mobility problems in the course of the war; and flared up periodically in later life. It occurs when the body produces more uric acid than the kidneys can dispose of. This forms needlelike crystals in connective tissue or in the space between two bones. The affected joint swells and becomes hot and agonisingly painful. Too much alcohol is implicated as a cause, as is taking too much aspirin; since Burra relied on aspirin to ease his sore joints, both were relevant at this stage of his life. After this first episode, Burra got gout from time to time in his bunion joint or his big toe, and sometimes in his heel: for instance, after imbibing five rounds of highly suspicious ersatz rum at the Swiss Hotel in 1942, he reported to Aiken that he 'had a big toe Sunday like a bright scarlet flaming red pepper'. On each occasion' the swelling lasted a few days during which he was completely immobilised, then went away, which is fairly typical.

A more continuous problem that Burra had during the war was his parents. They were too old to cope well with the sense of being constantly under threat, and they fretted and worried. 'Mumsie is getting a shade nervous,' he would report. 'Father flew in a fuss.' Burra, loather of fuss, was not invariably patient, since they sent him into a state of constant nervous irritation. 'Poor dear "mumsie" how she grumbles – shes so terrified she might have to do something for herself shes quite withering away, perhaps if they made their own bed? ... Ime a brute and so unsympathetic any grumbles I hear get nipped in the bud

[5] *Dégringolade*: things falling apart, or an occasion of sudden collapse.

... she must always go on as she has been accustomed to waited on hand and foot. How she is going to manage it in future I often wonder.'

It was only during the war that Burra took to referring to his mother as 'Mumsie'. When he was a child she was 'Mummy', in his teenage years and later he addressed and spoke of her as 'Mother'. 'Mumsie' sets a distance between them; it suggests that, far from participating sympathetically in his mother's feelings, he was coming to perceive her as a fully automated nagging machine. He commented unkindly that she was so afraid of bombs that she would only go out 'in her corn-flower hat sewn with flowers to represent pastureland seen from the air'. After a week of bombing that vaporised several entire houses in Rye, beside destroying a number of local landmarks, he responded to her twittering by asking her ironically, '"I wondered why the French gave in?" She was rather cross ...'

But Trudy Burra had reason to be nervous, since nothing whatever was safe, even staying at home, and any expedition, however basic, might take a sudden turn for the dramatic. On one occasion when he was coming home by train, Burra was nearly machine-gunned by a Messerschmidt which was strafing Rye station, and later in the war he also had a run-in with a V-2 even closer to home:

Well dearie what a whirl of Messerschmidt this evening they love it a little cloudy. About 8.15 as I was rounding the Velodrome Buffalo [the old drill hut in the garden] by the gate leading into the field. I heard a whistling bomb descending and held my head imagining I should be swept into the bamboo but it sounded about in the churchyard ... I was at the top of the hill and was reduced to crouching in the hedge – the lorry drivers fled like autumn leaves (falling early this year) & were all in hedges & ditches letting out a stream of fuck sod etc It's a sort of British Ave Maria each sod a pearl each fuck a prayer to twist a bugger by absence wrung Where will it all end may I be so bold as to enquire?

Where it very nearly did end was with Panzers in Mermaid Street. The German invasion plan, as finalised in August 1940, was that the attack group of the 9th Army was to leave from Le Havre and land in the Brighton-Worthing area of West Sussex, while the 16th Army was to leave from the Calais-Ostend-Antwerp area and land around Rye and at Bexhill-Eastbourne. There was not a lot to stop them; and the Ministry of Information's leaflet INF 13/219/2, on what to do in case of invasion (issued in spring 1941), had very little to suggest beyond: 'You will have to get into the safest place you can find, and stay there till the battle is over.'

There was no Battle of Rye in 1941, thanks to the prodigious efforts of the RAF. But, with the inevitable bathos of wartime, one drama of that year which loomed large on the Home Front was that the humble but irreplaceable onion vanished from the shops. The war produced a variety of unforeseen shortages. Matches, for example, after the fall of Norway in 1940, and batteries and alarm-clocks (both of which had largely been imported from the US). Similarly, market forces had so operated that the majority of onions eaten in Britain were actually grown in Brittany. The beginnings of the trade went back to the 1830s, but interwar, 1,500 'Onion Johnies' wearing striped jerseys and berets peddled – or pedalled – their wares in England, selling 9,000 tons of onions in a season from bicycles and wheelbarrows.

Thus, with the fall of France, suddenly there weren't any. Gardeners got busy in order to produce a crop the following year, but at least two nostalgic *Odes to an Onion* were written in 1941. Burra, with the resources of Springfield kitchen garden at his disposal, ensured that his friends did not go short if he could help it (even though his desire to provision his friends was at an angle to his parents' notions about disposing of their produce, and he sometimes had to resort to larceny, tiptoeing out at dawn with a basket and a trowel). He despatched onions about his circle: 'I sent 5 onions sewn up like an operation so may busy fingers that steal them rot away' . . . 'I am sending onions back in that tin I steal them at night *Voleurs d'oignons* by Jean Lorrain . . .'

Lovingly wrapped despatches of treats such as strawberries and asparagus were similarly distributed to those friends who remained in London. These would have been very welcome; vegetables were some-times so hard to get that 'Mrs Cohen will soon be appearing in a price-less necklace of potatoes having changed her emeralds for a bunch of pigeons eye radishes and a *lavaliere* of swedes' (this is not snide anti-Semitism, he means Denis Cohen the publisher's wife, Kathryn Hamill: the Cohens were still part of his social circle).

He also kept a beady eye on his friends' possible needs more gener-ally. 'Do you want any chocolate I notice quite a lot hereabouts . . . I hope you got 2 packs Craven A I sent. Plenty here if you want more . . . I hope you got 2 cauliflowers looking like a poitrine I had to tie them round with string as the top of the panier fleuri was getting like a thicket or Madame Colettes wig . . . you might send those two tins back if you fancy some currants & raspberries.'

He also despatched what news he could (letters were censored), and tried to keep Aiken informed about what was happening in Rye (Aiken still had Jeakes' House, which had been requisitioned as a base for fire-watchers). Aiken wrote, 'We heard last week that the [Henry] James house was gone – I hope it's not true.[6] And what else? I suppose we shall never know, despite your ingenious use of hippogriffs etc. . . . we get the most awful feeling here that a letter will never get to you fellows, or that England will suddenly disappear.'[7]

Another development of 1941 was that on 7 May Bar Ker-Seymer, who was then living in a cottage in Aldworth, Berkshire, which belonged to Rosamond Lehmann and Wogan Philipps, married her long-term suitor Humphrey Pease. Her relationship with Pease, then an investigator for Mass Observation, whom Chappell describes as 'a well liked drunken "man about town"', had begun, entirely frivolously on her part, in 1932. Looking back in conversation with Julie Kavanagh, she recalled, 'I remember saying to Fred [Ashton], "I really think it's time you had an affair with a woman", and he said "Well, I think it's high time you had an affair with a man". So one night we made a pact.'

She quite enjoyed the sex (more than Ashton did), but the experience failed to mellow her attitude towards the devoted Pease. She referred to him as 'The Trembling Stick', and was often unkind to him, but he persisted, and they went about together for years. 'He was a darling man. Very rich, and she treated him abominably,' said Chappell, long after. Barbara Roett's take was differently nuanced: 'Such a sweet and charming man, but completely inept.' A letter Bar wrote to a friend at the time implies that she married him essentially for financial reasons. Her photography business hit the rocks after the lease of her studio fell in; she was having trouble getting work, and her destructive relationship with Wogan Philipps, which ended only in 1939, had left her

---

[6] It wasn't true. The Garden Room, where James worked in the summer months, was destroyed in 1940, but Lamb House itself is still there.

[7] This seems to refer to the following letter, now in the Huntington Library: 'The Village fête went off fine several portents appeard – a Hippogrif was found screaming by the lych gate & several werewolves and vampires naild one had its teeth in the district nurse.' What it means, only Burra and Aiken knew.

emotionally exhausted. Pease's reliable affection combined with solvency seemed to offer some kind of solution.

It was a very peculiar marriage. She spent the honeymoon with her old friend the New Zealand avant-garde film-maker Len Lye, while Pease went to the races. But when they did finally get together as man and wife, she discovered that since they had first slept together, he had become sexually dependent upon a fetishistic scenario of the most depressing variety: in order to get any kind of rise out of him, she had to dress up as a nanny (starched apron, black lisle stockings, sensible shoes) and take charge. 'Master Humphrey, it's time for your bath!!' 'Oooo, Nanny, do I have to take *all* my clothes off?' Et cetera ... Fine if you like that sort of thing, but Bar was possessed both of a sense of proportion and a sense of humour.

Apart from the problems generated by Humphrey, Bar had further problems with accommodation at the end of 1941. Rosamond Lehmann wanted Diamond Cottage back to live in herself, and Bar needed a Berkshire base because of the work she was doing (she had joined Larkin and Company, a unit making instructional films for the armed services), so she took another cottage, at Amners Farm, Burghfield, near Reading. This caused her to see a lot of another old friend, a journalist called Betty Keen, who lived nearby and was also a friend of Burra's.

Bar's marriage ended abruptly, after exactly a year and a week. The reason cited in the divorce papers is non-consummation, which was not strictly speaking the case, but it was the quickest way of dissolving a marriage, and the nearest thing to a no-fault divorce then legally available. It was probably a mutually decided way out of a relationship both had decided was a false step, since she and Pease remained close, and he probably continued to support her to some extent. 'He enjoyed spending all his money on people for no good reason,' Chappell observed, rather sourly. Betty Keen had lunch with the pair in 1944, three years after the divorce, referring to them as 'Mr and Mrs Pease', so it is possible that even quite good friends did not realise that they were not still married. They were certainly still in touch thirty years later.

Bar found another home after the divorce, at 11 Fitzroy Street, a flat on top of the Cresset Press, and therefore almost certainly a loan or a peppercorn rental from the kindly Denis Cohen. Burra approved: 'I rather like Fitzroy Sq a very pretty garden in the middle surrounded by some lovely Palladian fronts and ruins.'

Burra read widely during the war, as did many. 'I can't get to the cinema somehow – I begin to wander and don't pay any attention,' he wrote in 1941. 'Reading doesn't fail me I find however.' Stephen Spender commented, 'Civilised values and activities acquired a kind of poignancy, because they were part of what we were fighting for.' Penguin's *New Writing*, edited by John Lehmann, sold 50,000 copies an issue. Burra read it, of course, and took *Horizon* (a new magazine, founded by Cyril Connolly in 1939 'to give writers a place to express themselves', which was required reading for anyone seriously interested in the contemporary arts) and kept up with new poetry. Aiken told him to take what books he liked from Jeake's House in 1940, where he picked up Jacobean playwrights and other seventeenth-century writers, along with modernist poetry (above all, Tourneur, Webster and T.S. Eliot). Aiken also sent over copies of *View*, *New Republic*, *Time* and other literary journals from the States.

Burra read an immense amount of verse of all description. The books he owned at the end of his life include not only new poetry of various kinds bought as it came out, but older poets as well. But in the war years it was the Jacobeans who meant as much to him as anyone: the lusher and weirder, the better. From Marlowe and Tourneur, he went to Greene, Shadwell and even Crashaw:

I payd a profitable visit to Masons Norman Rd & got a treat by Professor Saintsbury Elizabethan literature – the Prof puts all the poets in their proper places castigating 'excesses' Cyril Tourneur & Crashaw Crash is rather excessive & 'hysteric' at times nobodys ever excessive enough for me or sufficiently hysterical The strange think is how 'Frantick' the Elizabethans seem when compared to St Teresa Toiso de Molina Calderon Gongora Garcilaso de la Vega etc etc St Juan de la † Luis de Leon & Juana de la Cruz a mexican poetess dearie she rather reminds me of Emily Dickinson !!!!! but Viceregal not New England if you get what I mean? I must quote a little bit of Tourneur – considered 'attributed to the powerful but extravagant dramatist, Cyril Tourneur, who wrote this kind of thing –'

> 'From out the late a bridge ascends thereto,
> Whereon in female shape a serpent stands
> Who eyes her eye, or views her blue-vein'd brow,
> With sense-bereaving glozes she enchants,
> And when she sees a worldling blind that haunts

The pleasure that doth seem there to be found,
She soothes with leucrocutanized sound'
(the Radiogram in O'Neil's)[8]

... 'we could hardly end with anything further removed from the clear philosophy & the serene loveliness of the Faerie Queene' say Prof S. I think its wonderful I must say the quotes are worth the money alone Ill send it to you when I can be separated from it unless of course dearie Ay should be separated from it by Gods hand ... I should like Shadwells works A study of Crashaw has come out price 3 bricks Louisiana University by Professor Somebody and it sounds to me worth having – can you tell me why it is almost impossible to buy the greatest gems of English poetry exept in 2nd hand odd editions at an old clothes shop in Norman Rd?

While it is not cast in the language of literary criticism, this letter reveals something of the breadth and depth of Burra's reading, and of the powerful freshness and originality of his response to literature – his engagement with these writers is wholly independent of the critical consensus of his own day, which was very far from recognising that there could be such a thing as English Gongorism. More generally, the extensive series of letters to Aiken (long letters about every ten days through the war years) reveal that Burra, despite his offhand style and lack of formal education, was far more of an intellectual than most twentieth-century painters.

The continuous strain of coping with the war told on Burra's health, as well as on that of his parents. Because he was run down, his blood disease, spherocytosis, declared itself again, and as a result he suffered considerably from his spleen. 'I had a lift to London,' he told Conrad Aiken, 'it looked a shade depressing I thought perhaps it was me as I have a permanent hangover now. with no "fun" to be responsible for it. Spleen realy. only too real The spleen its not a literary figment I assure you its hard as a board.' As he implies, the notion of suffering from 'spleen' (used by eighteenth-century writers such as Pope to convey

[8] O'Neill's was a Charlestown bar well known to Aiken and Burra. 'Leucrocotanisèd' is a one-off word invented by Tourneur, meaning making a noise like a 'leucrota', a mythical creature described as 'the result of a mating between a hyena and a lioness. It has an extremely wide mouth, that stretches from one ear to the other, and only a single bone where teeth should be. Like the hyena, the leucrota can make sounds that resemble human speech.'

depression, melancholia, world-weariness and disgust) was by no means irrelevant as a description of his mental state, but in his case, it was based upon a cruel physical reality.

Anaemia, a lifelong problem which had last surfaced in Mexico, reappeared towards the end of 1941. According to his usual pattern, he also developed jaundice. His mother, who suffered from the same syndrome, also had jaundice, but transferred herself to a nursing-home in Birmingham. For once, he was fairly explicit about the state he was in. 'Thank God we have good fish here which I have poached and a 2 minute egg & Scotch porridge oats now & again Ive had such nausea.' He was very unwell for much of 1942. He gradually recovered from the jaundice, living mostly on boiled potatoes and porridge, though the anaemia was not easily shifted. He was very depressed, and felt trapped.

I am much better and a normal colour not that Ive been out but I may say Automne triste et monotone has been pouring with rain. Everyone in a teeny weeny little world is getting too much stuck together that's what it is. All those faces always watching never missing a thing in an unreal little world . . .

The war brought out everything he most loathed about Rye. Its smallness and smugness, the inhabitants' tendency to peep at neighbours' affairs, took on a new horror in the world of ARP wardens, 'Don't you know there's a war on?' and 'Is your journey really necessary?', which gave official licence to snoopers and busybodies of all descriptions. Travelling was very important to Burra, but his world had shrunk and become bipolar, Springfield and London, as it had been in his teens. When he did go to London, he stuck to a very small orbit. 'I revolve on my visits on an axis of Brewer St Windmill – Trocadero – Charing X Rd bomb crater.' When he did get away, it was intensely stressful, since he was moving from one war zone to another, and it was hard to keep his imagination under control. 'I see myself sitting for hours in the train with the line blocked as it often is.' He also confessed (to Chappell), 'I don't dare go away I feel there will be an invasion while Ime away and I shall never find anybody again! or the house will be reduced to Ashes.'

In terms of the actual conduct of the war, things improved in 1942. The Germans were defeated in North Africa and, crucially, at Stalingrad. As the Russians began their advance towards Berlin, Prague and Vienna in 1943, it was clear to the more thoughtful observers that the tide had turned against Germany, and that the defeat of Hitler was only a matter of time. But while there was a ray of ultimate hope which had not existed before, domestic life in Britain became grimmer and grimmer. Food and fuel were in very short supply, but so were crockery and furniture, both frequent casualties of bombing raids. Many house-wives, in the first flush of patriotism, surrendered their aluminium saucepans in 1940 to make Spitfires, and then wished they hadn't (though not my grandmother, I still have hers). Clothes rationing began in 1941, and from the onwards, clothing, household linen and, in time, almost all domestic items became virtually unobtainable.

Food rationing does not seem to have bothered the Burra household greatly. None of them were heavy eaters. One advantage of living in Rye was that they could get fish (which was never rationed, but for those not immediately contiguous to the sea, very hard to obtain); and with their own eggs and vegetables, they were far better off than most. On the other hand, they all drank, and Burra and his father smoked. Cigarettes were imported, and therefore only capriciously available. Wine was also a problem; wartime wine-drinkers and wine-merchants alike were drawing on the cellars they had accumulated pre-war, unable to replenish stocks. Supplies of beer were not equal to the demand: pubs sold what they had, put up a sign saying 'NO BEER' and waited for the next delivery. Spirits, though home-produced, were rationed (one bottle of gin or whisky every two months), and became increas-ingly strange as the war went on. 'We had some rum at Bergamots[9] which was Fire pure & simple pure spirit with 1^{D} worth of rum essence I only wish I had a private bottle but not very good for our ulcers.' In 1943, he wrote, 'they do say the whiskey isnt so much hooch as new & too new is raw.'

Rye was changing; the fussy, introverted little world of Tinkerbell Towne had been invaded by realities that could not be ignored. Aiken wrote, 'Rye, they do say, is spoiled. Gone tough, full of rape and violence, even murder; Canadian soldiers kicked to death by midlanders; chiefly because they get all the girls ... Ed writes more and more gloomily.' Burra, in fact, was exhausted by the continual tension; a temporary cessation of bombing just made him wonder what might happen next.

[9] Berlemont's, a French pub in Soho.

'We are simmering away here in a sort of fausse spring dentist waiting room atmosphere,' he wrote. 'Im always expecting a medusa head to burst out at me from the Bamboo.' He had given the idea of a Medusa head a new significance in a pre-war painting, *Medusa*, which shows a grand and terrible male figure, its body apparently scaled, and its upper lip eaten away by disease. He had seen such faces in southern ports in the Thirties. What he seems to be focusing on with this painting is that there are some kinds of ugliness so terrible that one cannot look away from them; corruption that becomes corrupting. The fact that Medusa has a sort of cloak of hanged men thrown over one shoulder suggests that the picture is one of the various statements about evil that came out of his experience of the Spanish Civil War.

Due to some energetic work on his behalf by Bumble, Burra had a major exhibition in the autumn of 1942 at Rex Nan Kivell's Redfern Gallery. He was not overwhelmed with gratitude. 'I have been talked and talked into a show at the Redfern. they frame pics & if sold I pay frames & they take 25 per cent. The whole thing makes me quite ill.' This was an extraordinarily generous deal, in fact, but he really was ill (anaemia and jaundice again), undergoing another series of iron-and-strychnine injections every three days, and too tired to think about it. 'Ive absorbed enough strychnine to convulse an army,' he observed, 'but it doesn't seem to convulse ME.'

He did not feel well enough to go up to London and see the exhibition. But he showed thirty-four pictures, including *Soldiers*, *Beelzebub*, *Torturers* and *War in the Sun* (briefly discussed in Chapter VIII), and his work was very respectfully received, even by those who disliked it, such as John Piper. Burra wrote to Mrs Chappell, 'I seem to have had quite a successful show at the Redfern Gallery from the reports my spies have sent in having overheard the most peculiar remarks.' His favourite was from Raymond Mortimer: 'I think it was him waild at Gnashy[10] at my exhib. "But theyre so <u>loud</u> " . . . Yes dear fearfully <u>loud</u> but everything is getting so <u>fraytefully</u> coarse and rough & we're all in it up to the neck.' But the critics responded to his new seriousness – this was the first time his post-Spain and post-Mexico pictures had been exhibited. Osbert Lancaster wrote in *The Observer*:

[10] Paul Nash.

Edward Burra ... is a serious artist working with serious themes ... in a war-racked South American landscape extravagant puppet figures such as have not appeared in European art since the death of Magnasco squeak and gibber among ruins of a high Renaissance grandeur. Over all there broods an atmosphere of sunny menace that recalls the Mexico of Graham Greene ... what Burra is trying to do, unless I'm very much mistaken, is not to select and record some single aspect of the modern tragedy ... but to digest it whole and transform it into something of permanent aesthetic significance.

In 1943, on 28 July, Anne Burra married again. Her first marriage, like Bumble's, had been a casualty of the war. Her second husband was Colin Ritchie, one of a family of Scottish Presbyterian great and good who had settled in Sussex in the nineteenth century while making their careers in London. The first Baron Ritchie had been Chancellor of the Exchequer, while the second became Chairman of the Port of London Authority, and a resident of Winchelsea in Sussex. The third Baron Ritchie, who succeeded his father in 1948, was Colin's older brother Kenneth. He made his career as a stockbroker, rising ultimately to becoming President of the Stock Exchange. He also lived in Sussex, in a house at Bosney, by Camber Sands, near Rye, and his great interest, outside his professional life, was lawn tennis: he was President of the Sussex Lawn Tennis Association. Anne had always been a keen tennis player, and presumably got to know the Ritchies through this common interest, since it was a family enthusiasm of theirs: Colin, the third brother, was excellent, good enough to play at Wimbledon from 1933 until after the war (as his younger brother Malcolm told me, adding, 'this was when tennis was genuinely amateur'). Colin and his sister Margaret were great friends of Anne's, and Burra frequently mentions them as visitors to Springfield in 1942.

According to Chappell, Colin Ritchie was 'very handsome, like a movie star almost'; an assessment corroborated by his younger brother: 'he was good looking and charming and possessed a marvellous sense of humour. He was really the darling of the family.' He was also a good golfer, played the piano, painted in watercolour and collected books: Anne, similarly, was a voracious reader, intensely musical and sketched, so it was a relationship based on a wide variety of mutual interests.

Despite his considerable gifts as an athlete, Colin Ritchie's life was affected by having caught rheumatic fever in childhood. One result of this was that he was not sent to public school, but to a small tutorial school, Brickwall, which was established in the ancient home of the Frewen family, the seventeenth-century Brickwall house in Northiam, not far from Rye. The school had a special agenda of helping dyslexic and dyspraxic children (a tradition that it still maintains, though it has since been refounded as Frewen College). After coming down from Oxford in the early Thirties, Ritchie was invited back to join the staff, and taught there all his life: the after-effects of rheumatic fever made him unfit for military service. After their marriage, Anne also worked at the school, where she taught English and maths. Like her brother's, her education, though largely informal, was surprisingly extensive, and she turned out to be an imaginative, inventive and effective teacher. 'It must be fun,' she used to say, which suggests a child-centred approach unusual in the Forties.

But Ritchie, albeit handsome and eligible, was not as lively a man as Anne might have been expected to choose. He did not, it seems, share what she had once referred to as her 'mad' side; the streak in an otherwise conventional personality which made her profoundly congenial to her brother. On the other hand, she and her new husband had plenty of interests in common. It is also possible that since her first marriage, a love-match achieved in the face of familial doubt, had ended in disaster, second time around she was more inclined to be pragmatic. Be that as it may, with her second choice, she embraced conventionality.

Burra, however, though he never directly criticised his sister's choice, clearly found Ritchie, and the life his sister shared with him, deadly boring. But Anne was 'mad' only north-north-west. She had been brought up in the expectation that she would take her place in Sussex society and, unlike her brother, she was perfectly happy to do so. The times were changing, and though she had received no training after school except nice girls' art-appreciation in Florence, she could have made a life as an independent woman (as Bar, for example, had done), but she was content to share a life bounded by home, Brickwall School and hobbies such as tennis. Ritchie was well liked by the Burra family other than Burra himself, though the amount of time Anne spent apart from him suggests that part of the recipe for the relationship was a degree of mutual detachment. The marriage was a contented, though not a passionate one, and childless.

The most exciting thing to happen to Burra himself in the last years of the war was a major ballet project in 1944, designs for *Miracle in the Gorbals*, choreographed by Robert Helpmann to a scenario by his lover, Michael Benthall. This was less a ballet than a dance-drama, a heavily allegorical weepie; set in a once-infamous slum area of Glasgow. Helpmann had to some extent moved into the space vacated by Ashton, then in the RAF, but since neither he nor any of the remaining male dancers were virtuosos, his creations relied for drama on his own gift for mime rather than on spectacular dancing. The narrative begins with the suicide of a young girl, who is resurrected through the healing power of a Christ-like Stranger. The Stranger is then murdered as a result of the incitement of the mob by a jealous and malignant Minister. The Stranger's movements were based on the paintings of El Greco, who was a surprisingly important influence on the art of the time. Paul Nash described him as 'the one master who seems to hold in his hands the secrets of the past and future of painting'. As a psychodrama – and even as a modern-dress ballet, the first English ballet to have a contemporary working-class setting – *Miracle* was perceived as strong stuff in its day. Helpmann presumably thought of Burra as designer because he had a unique ability to produce intensely dramatic images of people in cheap clothes, but the basic concept was far too sentimental for him to have much genuine sympathy with it.

The company, plus Burra, were hauled up to Glasgow in the middle of a wartime winter to do on-the-spot research. When Burra turned up at the hotel, squelching in from the discouraging Glaswegian rain in a shiny black mackintosh, he told a funny story about having fallen out of bed and having been unable to get up (presumably on the night sleeper from London); as he recounted his tale of yelling for help till someone noticed, everyone was in fits of laughter. Only afterwards did it strike Ninette de Valois that it could not have been in the least funny for him at the time. The Glasgow experience was useful to Burra personally, since it took him out of his tiny groove, which always had an invigorating effect. He painted a number of Glasgow pictures after his return home, such as *Gorbals Landscape*, with two women wrapped in shawls who have a conspiratorial air, set against a poverty-stricken landscape of brick tenements and railings, and he made a series of Glasgow drawings, comparable in their lack of sentiment with those of Joan Eardley, who was working-class Glasgow's principal chronicler.

Photographs and a model of the set survive, now in the Victoria and

Albert Museum, a sombre evocation of the Gorbals' vertiginous tenements, with belching factory chimneys in the distance. The drop-scene
was the hulk of a vessel under construction in the Clyde shipyards,
surrounded by cranes. The women of the Glasgow slums are not the
fantastical creatures of *Rio Grande*, but wear either aprons and shawls
or street-smart gear of the day, knee-length with padded shoulders, and
follow the suggestion made to him by Helpmann: 'I think some of the
girls should have terrible pompadours with dyed streaks in them – like
the girls in these terrible towns have their hair – bristling with celluloid barres and kirbigrips and with terrible Wedge shoes.' He reported
to Chappell from Springfield, after the first costume try-out.

Ive spent two days watching the Saddlers Wells infant school trying on a variety
of rags Theres one terrifying aged gutter midget queen type suddenly apeared in
a blue school cap. a very tight black and crimson lake striped football shirt & very
ragged plum shorts. Everybody roared he looked exactly like Caseys Court in Comic
Cuts[11] . . . I went to a rehersal too . . . in which Messia H'man was sweeping nobly
about being 'jostled' by members of the Caseys Court gang he was then surrounded
pushed over backwards & given a good sharp kick in the balls then a knee in the
stomach after that they all produced razors & slashed him in the face swept him
up & over & delivered 2 sharp pokes with broken bottles in the face then followed
a sort of descent de la croix copied from El Greco & a resurection and scotch jig
when it gets realy going it should brighten up the fans.

Though Helpmann's fancying himself as the Man of Sorrows cut very
little ice with Burra, he was immensely pleased that the first night was
a success. 'We had a lovely first night at the Gorbals youve no conception of how I enjoyed myself Everybody was disgusted They made a
very good job of it.'

   Another source of interest for Burra was the dancer who played the
'Official'. He was a beautiful and charismatic Italo-Swiss called David
Paltenghi. His father was the director of the Old Berkeley Hotel in
London, and expected his son to follow him, a hope that was disap-
pointed when Paltenghi decided that he wanted to be a dancer. As a

---

[11] 'The Casey Court Kids' was a strip in a weekly halfpenny comic called *Comic Cuts*, drawn by Tom
Browne – Burra's long-dead sister Betsy had loved *Comic Cuts*, but so did the teenaged Burra and
Chappell, who recalled that Burra particularly enjoyed 'Casey Court'.

very late starter, he could never hope to be a virtuoso, but he was splendid-looking, an excellent mime and had tremendous on-stage presence. Since male dancers were vanishing into the Forces or abroad, he was dancing principal roles with the London Ballet by 1940 (when he was only twenty-one) and the Sadler's Wells company by 1943. As a holder of a Swiss passport, he was not liable to call-up. Though Burra was wary of making new friends, he made an exception for David Paltenghi.

The ballet was a critical success: to the *Daily Express*, it was 'a sensational modern allegory, brilliantly executed and staged'; and Edwin Evans in *Time and Tide* said, 'I shall be surprised if this novel ballet does not turn out to be both a popular success and a landmark in the development of the art.' The *Glasgow Herald* singled out the set for favourable comment: 'Edward Burra's décor is a diversion for any eye, especially a Scot's one.'

It was also a great success when it toured (with ENSA; thus with the particular remit of entertaining serving troops): 'the ballet was an enormous success in Brussels, the dear boys particularly liked Gorbals Why of course they did so homely what with razors and fried fish its quite a breath of the old sod.' It is worth reminding oneself that this tour in January 1945 was the first time the English ballet had left Britain for five years. In Brussels, the actual battlefront was only seventy miles away; each night, 500 seats were reserved for men on forty-eight hours' leave from the front.

De Valois remembered having to take a dancer to hospital and waiting in Casualty; 'During that wait, a convoy of wounded men arrived from a field-hospital. It was a shock to see those men unloaded and laid out on all the available space on the floor and bench . . . it jerked me back to the madness of life at that moment.' There were four inches of snow on the ground, and no heating; in the circumstances, a miracle in a slum was resonant with the lived experience of the audience. In France, they played at the Marigny Theatre, mainly to US servicemen and women, but the ballet was attracting so much attention that the British Council arranged for them to give civilian performances at the Champs-Élysées Theatre, to capacity audiences. The Paris papers were impressed (though there were comments that the aesthetic was somewhat alien) and so were Parisian audiences.

Burra was evidently enough part of the ballet world to be welcome backstage; though he said to Bar, 'Ime rather <u>nervous</u> of backstage now dear having warmly congratulated the wrong person at the Gorbals preemiaire!' He went to see *Nocturne* a few weeks later (Ashton had been given some weeks' leave of absence to create it), and found Fonteyn 'beautiful, wonderfully distracted and romantic . . . behind the scenes, dearie, it was more distracted than romantic . . . Mrs Siddons and Mrs Bracegirdle or should it be the other way round [Ashton & Helpmann] standing washing in a minute dressing room like a couple of land mines waiting to go off. Mrs Brace G said, producing 2 grey rags, "please be more careful of the towels they cost coupons".' The contrast of backstage and frontstage had a great appeal for him, and he had been watching the jealous rivalry of Ashton and Helpmann with sardonic interest since Helpmann arrived in England in 1932.

By the later stages of the war, Burra had settled into a sort of grim endurance, like most of his compatriots. 'Everyones wearing thinner and thinner – either that or swollen up like a balloon – Do we look awful dearie everyone looks like kiddies to me except Bebe Daniels.'[12] Writing to Chappell's bombed-out mother, he confessed:

I wish it was all over Ime sure, to think its been going on 4 years I have lost all sense of anything at all and seem to exist in a sort of vacuum of timelessness since 1939.

One of the things that made matters notably worse is that in March 1944, because of the possibility of an invasion via Normandy, Rye became a restricted military area. Non-residents were obliged to leave the area of the south coast, and residents to remain within it; increasing Burra's sense of entrapment. Though he does seem to have been able to get to London when he needed to, no non-residents were allowed in. In the same month, he notes that for the first time there was no staff at Springfield at all. Rather unexpectedly for an upper-class man of his background, he could cook, as Mary Aiken discovered when he stayed with them in Boston in the Thirties. As the servants gave notice or were called up, he did more and more in the house. The household was,

---

[12] Daniels, a beautiful Texan film-actress, and her husband Ben Lyon, had chosen to spend the war years in Britain, where they starred in a long-running and much-loved radio comedy called *Hi, Gang!*

Burra averred, 'kept together by Mumsies grumbling she still manages to have breakfast in bed – the ghastly suffering of this war . . .'

The real suffering of the war, particularly in London, was considerably increased by the V-1s – unmanned rocket-bombs, known as doodlebugs – which arrived in June 1944. When the engine cut out, the explosion followed in five to fifteen seconds; Londoners (and inhabitants of the south coast) rapidly learned to remain blasé as long as the thing continued to make a noise, and to dive for cover when it stopped; 10,500 were launched, of which 2,400 got through to London – at the height of the attack, more then seventy a day – where they did a colossal amount of damage. Quite a few of the remaining 8,100, inevitably, landed in Sussex. A Civil Defence officer recalled what it was like to endure this form of attack.

We could hear the oncoming doodle bug behind us chugging like a motor bike, in front of us on a rise to the left we saw two semi-detached houses. A man was digging in a garden alongside, a little boy was running up the garden path towards the house . . . at the doorway was a woman beckoning him to hurry indoors . . . there was a loud explosion, a mushroom cloud of dust. Everything went up; no houses, no man, no mother and no boy. We picked up three dustbins full of pieces out of the rubble. The only way to identify where they were was the dampening dust and the cloud of flies.

From Rye, Burra could see doodlebugs clattering across the sky, with flame jetting from their tails. Sometimes they were closer at hand, such as the one that came down in Playden. The V-2s, which appeared in September 1944, were even worse, because supersonic; thus the actual explosion happened before the sound caught up with them and they seemed to come out of nowhere. Bizarrely, the government tried to suppress the fact of their existence; the 'burst gas main' excuse became so threadbare as to be a joke; as Burra sarcastically observed, having gone up to town for the first night of *Miracle in the Gorbals*, 'there are quite a few gas mains going off I suppose it must be the pipes wearing thin'.

Burra was surprisingly productive through the war years, considering the state he was in. Apart from his designs for *Miracle in the Gorbals*, he continued to paint, though brushes, paper and paint were not always easy to get, especially vermilion. 'Ive got quite a lot of paper (if it isn't blown up) Vermilion water colour has suddenly risen to 3/6 a tube as its used to rub gun barrels! Lechertier Barbe [his colourists] tells me Cadmium red 2/- & all the other colours havent gone up at all & brushes – Ive layd in a little stock as "Oh we cant get anymore russian sable" they say.' He had a lucky find in 1943: 'Water color brushes are getting a shade "difficult" I went into Reeves a shop I loathe and discovered a whole consignement just arrived. The old man said they hadnt had any for months as they were all bought up by the forces who were takeing to sketching etc in their spare time.' His favoured paper was Whatman Antique, in the largest size they produced, though if he was feeling mean, he would paint on any old stuff off the studio floor.

What comes out above all in Burra's wartime letters is his profound loyalty to his friends (and to his parents, for all that they drove him mad), and also his basic strength of character. He did not flee to America, claim the privileges of an invalid or artist status, or start drinking himself to death. Within the limits of what was physically possible for him, he did his bit; he did public-service work of a more or less menial nature, and looked after his parents, house and garden. More than ever, he acted as a clearing-house of information between his friends, and he also bombarded them with concrete, well-thought-out tokens of love and concern. He did not complain. 'If I think Ive got enough cigarettes & sausages 35 per cent meat 999 per cent Elizabeth Ardens under arm paste for 3 days ahead Ime fine.' Cigarettes were a problem for so inveterate a smoker, but even those he would give away.

Another thing that comes out in his wartime letters – perhaps because of the equal chance that either he or his correspondent might be dead before the letter reached its destination – was an uncharacteristic frankness. He wrote in February 1940, 'I would like to see Freds new piece it sounds very good any thing to do with the powers of evil dearie. Ime a great believer in them.' This was *Dante Sonata*, at the New Theatre, St Martin's Lane, the first wartime ballet.

It was one of Ashton's finest moments, perceived by many contemporaries at the time as the greatest ballet England had yet produced; though it did not stand up to revival. The anonymous dance critic of *New Writing* commented that *Dante Sonata* 'shows a profounder and more dynamic reaction to the conflicting forces at war than any of the war pictures hanging in the National Gallery'. It is one of the peculiarities of ballet that it can address the mood of a moment so completely that a work can be both immensely important and completely ephemeral.

Vaughan sums up: 'What one mostly remembers from *Dante Sonata* are its images of shame and suffering, turmoil and torment.' Though the two groups who struggle for supremacy were identified in second and subsequent performances as the Children of Light and Children of Darkness, neither side 'wins'; the ballet refuses to become an allegory for the war. A contemporary critic commented, 'Most of us feel that the world is too much for us, and we would give anything to be able to roll on the floor and tear our hair and scream. *Dante Sonata* does it for us.' Burra would have enjoyed that, and the ballet's lack of a simple resolution. Though the war brought out a latent Englishness in him, flag-wagging made him sick.

The war caused him to look both into himself and at others, and what he found there was darkness, as he had done in the run-up to the Spanish Civil War. In another revealing letter, he says, 'Dearest B. Fiendish did you say dear? I reach such a pitch of venom & spleen that I find myself falling back from myself. I think such wicked thoughts & fly in such black rages I fear sometimes I may meet "somebody" when I go out of an evening to have a look at the barrage if any in the kitchen garden . . .'

His Scottish nanny is at the back of this, and James Hogg's *Confessions of a Justified Sinner*, where this notion of somehow calling up a demon in one's own form ultimately comes from. There was a huge amount of anger in Burra, going back to the frustrations and miseries of his sickly babyhood. In the war, it rose to a point where it nearly overwhelmed him. 'The very sight of peoples faces sickens me Ive got no pity it realy is terrible sometimes Ime quite frightened at myself I think such awful things I get in such paroxysms of impotent venom I feel it must poison the atmosphere.' Some of Burra's paintings suggest that he sometimes thought of himself as a small stinging thing; acutely aware of his meagre size and physical helplessness, but full of malice; a scorpion, perhaps (such as *The Ham* (1931), the principal subject of which is menaced by a tiny creature mad with wrath). But anger is less paralysing than despair, which in the circumstances was the alternative.

Another thing that comes out of the wartime correspondence is how important Billy Chappell was to him. Letters to Billy are the lightning conductor for everything he did not say aloud. 'Im taking up my pen for Sundays venom, dearie, it relieves me' . . . '[I] do hope a whacking whistling double distilled Vitriol 1000 ton Molotov bread basket hits them fair & square That's how I feel charitable & full of mothers milk turned to Eiffel

tower lemonade & citric acid burns to the bone acts like a charm . . .' He
did not write quite like this to anyone else, even Bar or Clover.

Bar was also worn down by the war. She married again on 31 March
1945. Her tone, imparting this news to Burra, suggests something of
the weariness that was almost universal in Britain that year.

I got married to young John Rhodes who recently came back from Holland, he is
very nice, very domesticated, and a wonderful character (so important!).

I hastened to inform Mrs Chappell & told her if she wanted to let of [*sic*] a
stream of abuse & invective to you, to mind and put the right address on the envelope this time.

She and Billy were mutually estranged as the war progressed (though
not so much so as to stop writing letters, clearly). Miserable himself,
he felt that she was not pulling her weight, having neither gone into
the services nor undertaken specific war-work. 'He generally delivers
me a lecture about being a waster,' she wrote. But her mother died in
October 1945, and he wrote to say he was sorry. 'I had a letter from
Billy, who has quite changed his tune on hearing of my mother's death,
a little tribulation wins him round in no time. You must have written
and told him.' After that, fences were mended.

Many of Burra's paintings from later in the war express a sense of
desolation. He made a series of paintings of post-cultivation landscapes,
land that has gone back to scrub woodland and brambles, littered with
broken wheels. As a gardener, battling the encroaching weeds at
Springfield, he knew how fast rampant wilderness takes over, and how
hard it is to eradicate. These pictures are statements about loss and
damage, civilisation in retreat.

His art was changed, and darkened. The soldiers he painted were
not people, they were fearful embodiments of destruction. Like Ashton
in *Dante Sonata*, he was primarily conscious of the depersonalisation
and brutalisation that turned boys into interchangeable moving parts.
There is no doubt that Burra considered the war one which needed to
be fought, but he had a strong sense of what it cost; the loss and damage
it wrought. Burra in the Twenties and early Thirties was often impish;
and there was a great deal of comedy in his work. From the late Thirties
onwards, that is no longer true.

When the end of the war came, he was too exhausted, physically and emotionally, to rejoice. Nor, for those of a thoughtful disposition, was there much to rejoice at. He was among those who saw the atomic bomb as a terrifying development rather than a solution, and he was at his lowest in August 1945, writing four days after the surrender of Japan, less than a fortnight after the *Enola Gay* and *Bockscar* dropped their bombs on Hiroshima and Nagasaki:

I've given up dearie & never go out and can scarcely speak I dread going to London & put it off and cant see anyone very neurotic it seems to me but now everything is all over except the ATOMS HE! HE! I realy feel like <u>death</u> and I cant go on I suppose if I was to go away somewhere a long way off for a change it might do me good but you cant get away from <u>yourself</u> for long I find that spectre will always rise up at you . . .

What rose up, in the end, was his own indomitable spirit. Paul Nash ended the war in a nursing home, and died in 1946. Burra, though he was exhausted by the war, survived. Because his general level of vitality was so low, it took him a long time to recover. But he toughed it out in his own way; he was changed, and certainly damaged, by the war, but he was not defeated.

XII

RUINS IN A LANDSCAPE

POST-WAR recovery was a long, slow business. On a personal level, Burra was in a state of total exhaustion in 1945. He was forty years old, anaemic, intermittently crippled, emotionally drained and almost without energy. For those who were marooned in various corners of Europe and beyond, desperate to get home, the end of war was a cause for true rejoicing, tempered by the frustrating slowness with which the army released them. For those at home, while it is hard to underestimate relief at the basic fact that nobody was dropping bombs on them any more, the war dribbled to an agonisingly long, slow close. Rye nights were still rocked by explosions long after VE Day, because the beaches were mined. Denton Welch visited Camber Sands, a famous beauty spot by Rye, in 1946, and was repelled: 'The surroundings were so disgusting, both in themselves and because they were shelled and bomb-blasted, and the sea was so far away, so monotonously vast and flat, that we sat on the beach for a minute, then scuttled away.'

In the last months of the war, as the government dared to admit to itself that it seemed to be winning, the blackout was gradually lifted, but only to the extent of a 'dim-out'. 'Half-lighting' became legal at dusk from Sunday, 17 December 1944: 'Windows, other than skylights, need be curtained only sufficiently to prevent objects inside the building from being distinguishable from outside.' The blackout was not abolished inland till 24 April 1945, and for those, like Burra, who lived less than five miles from the coast, it was not abolished till 10 May, ten days after Hitler's suicide. Burra wrote crisply to Chappell, still fretting in Naples four months after the Germans had surrendered in Italy: 'Don't take on so dearie everybody is sick of waiting in queues no cigarettes nothing to drink & no clothes . . . youll soon be cowering over your gas ring & a pot of old tea I daresay.'

Chappell had good reason to feel ill used, as it happened. He had been put to work in Italy organising amateur concerts and shows to keep the troops happy while they awaited demobilisation, and made himself so useful that, as he finally discovered, the army neglected for an entire year to inform him that he himself was entitled to go.

The sense of a desperate collective effort which had kept many people going began to evaporate after VE Day, but in the months that followed there was no immediate chance of setting about the regeneration of society or the economy, and very little amelioration of individual lives. The country was virtually bankrupt. Post-war, domestic life continued to be extremely difficult, and at times even worse than during the actual hostilities. The winter of 1946/7 was one of the harshest for many years, and coal was in extremely short supply. While the war had seen rationing of meat, sugar, fats, cheese, eggs and tea, the immediate post-war period saw even more basic foodstuffs join them. Bread and flour rationing came into force on 21 July 1946 (and lasted until 1948), while even potatoes were rationed in 1947. Much of Europe was on the verge of famine, as was India, then embroiled in the civil war that preceded independence. Much British – and American – wheat was being used to avert actual starvation abroad, leaving little to go round at home.

In England, petrol rationing continued until 1950, clothes rationing until 1949 and food rationing did not finally end until 1954. Despite the respect and admiration which most of the nation felt for Churchill as a wartime leader, a Labour Prime Minister, Clement Attlee, was brought in with a colossal majority on a tide of national determination that in order to justify the sufferings of the war, they must become the birth-pangs of a new and fairer Britain. Attlee found himself setting about the creation of a Welfare State in a drab, grey and infinitely depressing world of rubble, bomb-craters and shortages. Stephen Spender noted in his journal, just after the war, that he 'had a strong feeling of the complete rotting away of England . . . in this damp cold weather, after the fog, a lot of London had this horrible sweetish-sour odour'.

As Spender implies, housing was no small aspect of the post-war crisis. The best part of a million homes had been either eradicated or damaged beyond repair; and not only did the families who had lived in them need to be rehoused, there were the cohorts of those who had married during the war, who were hoping finally to set up home together. The shortage of the basic raw materials for building made catering for these legitimate needs agonisingly slow. Burra reflected, apropos of Chappell's mother, who had been bombed out of her London flat in Great Ormond Street:

I had a dirge from your poor mother . . . all she longed for was a home of her own but my dear it seems absolutely impossible for people to find homes of their own or anybody elses. They are taking empty houses in Rye & poking famillys into them & the mayor raised a stink by saying people should put people in their spare rooms.

Thus Chappell's first problem, when he finally managed to escape from the army, was finding somewhere to live, and also somewhere for his mother to live. He had no money, and neither had she. But as he was mooching despondently about London, he suddenly found himself face to face with Lord Ritchie – that is, Kenneth Ritchie, the older brother of Anne Burra's recently acquired husband Colin. Lord Ritchie, as Chappell put it, had been 'very much a night club person about town' before the war, and he and Chappell were old acquaintances, entirely independent of the recently forged link between the Ritchies and the Burras. They exchanged news, and Chappell was amazed to hear Ritchie say that he was looking for a tenant. He was senior partner of a stockbroking firm, Richardson & Glover, by then, so a man of considerable means, and he maintained both a family home at Bosney, by Camber Sands, presided over by his wife, and a house in Thurloe Square, opposite the Victoria and Albert Museum. But he only wanted the drawing-room floor for himself, since the house was basically a pied-á-terre for when he needed to be in London. A housekeeper lived in the basement with her husband, who was the Square gardener, but upstairs was vacant. He preferred to have somebody he knew as a tenant, he explained, and never advertised. He thereupon offered Chappell the top two floors of no. 40 at a moderate rent, which he was delighted to accept, and he and his mother moved in (they lived there together till she died suddenly in 1952: thereafter he lived there alone).

Once he had sorted out somewhere to live, the other question on Chappell's mind was what to do next. He was forty-one and in no shape to resume a career as a dancer, so he decided to capitalise on his knowl-edge of, and interest in, costume, and open a theatrical dressmakers and design business in Bruton Place, W1. It was a type of venture he had considered before – in 1937, he and Bunny Roger had seriously considered starting a dressmaking establishment together, but shortly before the shop doors opened in Great Newport Street, Bunny suddenly decided to go it alone, and it opened as Neil Roger, not Roger & Chappell. The general poverty-strickenness of the times is suggested by a letter that Burra wrote to him: 'I was wondering if you would like some nice useful thing for the house as you are opening house & Ime sure you want some dish cloths and Ive got some coupons . . .' But the letter went on to say that Burra was reading and enjoying *Ulysses*, and was signed 'Blessed mother Mary Anycock' (a perversion of the name of a seventeenth-century saint, Margaret Mary Alacoque), which suggests that he was beginning to cheer up.

The artists started trickling home. Ashton was back with the ballet, overweight, unfit, but impatient to realise some of the ideas he had been gestating throughout his unhappy sojourn in the RAF. 'Fred is thinking he's going to make his debut with Cesar Francks Variations & décor by Sophie & then hopes to do Don Juan as a grand piece du fin du monde. Roger Furse is doing some superb pieces for Helpman . . .' Burra reported, ending rather sour-grapeishly, 'Everybodys so glamourous except me.'

He was probably cross about *Don Juan* moving down Ashton's list, since he and Ashton had been discussing it for years, and he had done some preliminary design work as early as March 1945. In the event, when *Don Juan* finally got off the drawing-board, Ashton did indeed ask him to design it, but that was not to be until 1948. Meanwhile, the César Franck ballet to which he had turned his energies, called *Symphonic Variations*, was an acknowledged masterpiece with designs by Sophie Fedorovitch, which has stood the test of time (unlike *Don Juan*) to become one of the Royal Ballet's signature works.

Burra's first post-war opportunity as a designer came in the course of 1946, when he was asked to take on Bizet's *Carmen*; the first real opera to be staged since the beginning of the war. During the Second World War, the Royal Opera House had done duty as a Mecca ballroom, and there was a distinct chance that it would remain a dance-hall after the war. But after lengthy negotiations, the music publishers Boosey & Hawkes acquired the lease of the building from the Morleys (who owned Mecca) before they turned it into the biggest bingo-hall in Britain. Ninette de Valois's Sadler's Wells Ballet was invited to become the resident ballet company; a move that sent de Valois into a state of panic, lest their entire repertory turn out to be swamped by their enormous new stage. 'It could be likened to a crazy nightmare, wherein I might be given Buckingham Palace, a few dusters, and told to get on with the spring cleaning . . .' But they reopened the Opera House on 20 February 1946, with the largest-scale ballet in their repertory, *The Sleeping Beauty*, in a sumptuous new production designed by Oliver Messel, with Margot Fonteyn as Aurora, and Helpmann doubling as the Prince and the Bad Fairy.

There was no ready-made opera company in London suitable for transfer to the Royal Opera House, but David Webster, the new General Administrator, with his music director Karl Rankl, immediately began to build a resident opera company. In December 1946 they shared their first production, *The Fairy Queen*, with the ballet company, and on 29 April 1948, the new Covent Garden Opera Company mounted its first solo production, *Carmen*, directed by Peter Brook (then a tyro of twenty-three), with Karl Rankl as conductor.

Burra's fascination with flamenco dancers and Spanish low-life made him a natural choice of designer, but he was more than pleased to have been asked. He took the whole thing immensely seriously. Rather than producing the over-the-top colourful designs that might have been expected of him, he drew on his memories of the Spanish poor in the Thirties, and produced a rather low-key set of costumes in an unusually muted tonality leaning on brown and ochre. Costumes, of course, were a difficulty. Even the Royal Opera House had to work within a quota of coupons, which militated against extravagance. Some of the surviving designs have swatches of material attached, suggesting that Burra was overseeing the work conscientiously, and in detail. He was not wholly delighted with the production side; he wrote to Chappell in December:

I saw act I of Carmen the set I mean, it couldn't have been worse painted (unless I had done it with a tooth brush to please the head mistress when she was asleep like the story in Little folks 1912 or so) but from the 10th row youd never notice any of the little nuances and from anyway further just a lovely far away dream There is a dainty tower at the back the very image of the Empire state without King Kong . . .

And in 1946, he got out of his tiny Rye-Charing Cross-Rye orbit for the first time in six years (apart from the Glasgow adventure). Conrad and Mary Aiken had returned to Rye in November 1945. They found Jeakes' House distressingly derelict.

The house is dreadfully shabby and run down, dreadfully defaced by the Philistine firefighters – nails driven in everywhere . . . no scrap of paint is left on stairs or floors, where hobnailed feet kicked and trampled . . . a temporary ceiling of asbestos paper showers the kitchen floor with Little Nell snow whenever the wind blows.

Nobody at the time recognised asbestos as a health hazard; this state of affairs was merely perceived as a depressing nuisance. But Burra turned up to greet them with a half bottle of rum, and they were so pleased to see one another that the three of them decided to go to the Lake District together.

Aiken had intensely enjoyed the time he spent there during his first visit to England in 1908, and wanted to share it with his wife and Burra. By 1945, Burra's travels abroad had been fairly extensive, but there is little to suggest that, apart from his therapeutic visits to Bath, he had seen much of England itself other than from the windows of trains going to Scotland to visit outlying bits of his mother's family. The visit to the Lakes gave him an English landscape very different from that of Sussex: harsher, barer, and more magnificent. He was more interested by it than he had anticipated, and it perhaps helped to set him off in a new direction, landscape, which was to concern him more and more in the Fifties and Sixties.

Another new venture was a foray into designing for the films. The Redfern Gallery show in 1942 had been a critical success, but had only made him £121. Though he had two exhibitions at the Leicester in 1947 and 1949, his actual earnings in and after the war were almost entirely from design work of one kind or another, and he probably thought of himself as primarily a designer, professionally speaking. Accordingly, he agreed to do some work for the Rank Organisation in 1948:

Well dearie here lies a mere hulk of poor Edward Burra the darling of our crew.[1] As what with designing the death trap & spies parlor in the cellars of Doomesday Grange for Highbury Studios a hacking cough with phlegm on the side & an attack of my old complaint which commenced with a quartern ague lasting half an hour I couldnt

[1] A reference to Charles Dibdin's song 'Tom Bowling' (1789).

keep still for a minute & chattered all the time, I realy am half crazy. I keep getting telegrams from Highbury and go trailing off with a paper bag containing a very dirty cigarette tin containing some frowsy mumbled old tubes of mud & one or two cleaned up brushes & pencils & proceed to put in & take out spiders webs, chandeliers put in archs all in five minutes & straight off, only somebody with no scruples & completely insensitive could ever do it. however I enjoy it very much.

The Highbury Studios were used by the Rank Organisation, one of the biggest British film companies, from 1945 to 1960 (when the building was finally pulled down). In a subsequent letter, he explained, 'The film I was doing was a blood curdling 2nd feature called "a peice of cake".'

This was something of a milestone in the ignoble history of terrible films. It came about because J. Arthur Rank was keen to bring new talent into British cinema, and approached Cyril Fletcher and his wife Betty Astell, established music-hall troupers, to star in a comedy called *The Venus Touch*, ultimately based on a book by F. Anstey (itself a version of a story that had been doing the rounds since the twelfth century). Unfortunately, it was then discovered that Mary Pickford had long since acquired the rights and refused to release them.[2] Meanwhile, Rank had issued contracts to Fletcher and Astell for six weeks of work. After a great deal of shouting and waving of contracts, Betty Astell declared she would find a story herself, and did.

Like Anstey, she dusted off a venerable plot: a household visited by an apparently benign magician who seems at first simply to shower his hosts with all they need or want (a wish-fulfilling fantasy of off-ration food, drink and new clothes). But this benefactor gradually reveals his demonic nature and gets his victims into more and more trouble. The producer, John Croydon, wrote the screenplay from Betty's scenario, while time ticked away, since there were only six weeks available for the whole project from start to finish. The result was, inevitably, hastily written, underrehearsed and done on the cheap. Somewhere along the way, John Croydon came up with the idea of involving Burra; presumably because he had seen some of his work.

[2] Thus reminded of her property, she sold her rights to Leicester Cowan at Universal, who made *One Touch of Venus* (1948), starring Ava Gardner as the goddess. Anstey is better remembered for *Vice Versa* (in which father and son swap bodies and roles), which was also made into a film and has spawned many imitations.

His contribution was considerable. In the final dénouement of the film, Cyril pursues Betty, abducted by their demonic guest, to Doomsday Hall, and when he walks through the door, he walks into Burra's imagination. Burra produced a series of splendid designs, vertiginously tilting corridors, a gallery of tiny caves with overtones of Piranesi, and a demon's lair burgeoning with strange rubbery forms.

The set gives the impression that Burra rather enjoyed the work, but his letters to Aiken show that it was also a considerable strain, because of his health and the constraint on time. He became suspicious of the Rank Organisation's terms of engagement. 'Corcoran tells us they are notoriously crooked – very slippery & wont pay unless they are threatened by Corcoran ... I was supposed to have got 250£ I have got a contract thank God.' But Burra was not good at contracts, and it seems most unlikely that the document was looked-over by Corcoran, since Cyril Fletcher records ingenuously, 'some of [the] designs were offered to us at the end of the picture for most reasonable sums, like £50 or so' – Corcoran would not have left the actual artwork at Croydon's disposal, and it sounds very much as if Croydon, who had overspent his budget, made a spirited attempt to raise the money to pay Burra off by flogging his paintings to the cast. Burra may have got paid in the end (though there is no evidence in his papers that he did), but pursuing and badgering reluctant debtors takes a lot of energy. The experience put him off any further involvement with films.

His next project was in partnership with Ashton, who in 1948 finally got round to mounting his Don Juan ballet (the ballet, incidentally, settled accounts swiftly and meticulously). Ashton's first thoughts were to base it on Zorrilla's play, *Don Juan Tenorio*; mistrustful of his grasp of Spanish, he asked Burra for a précis. He got, in return, an enthusiastic, four-page, unpunctuated sentence: 'It starts off during carnival with mascaras [maracas] etc. ...' The précis then became somewhat intertwined with Burra's inner visions: 'The next scene is the pantheon and Don J arrives the statues come to life an entire dinner table laden with deaths heads hourglasses vipers twined tumblers of boiling blood abortions in aspic etc whirls out of a tomb ...' Clearly, it would not do; while the scenario might work as the basis for a future painting, it was not a sketch for a ballet.

Burra then sent an alternative sketch of his own, focused on Don Juan, Doña Ines (in Zorrilla's play, Ines has a role similar to Donna Anna in

Mozart's version) and her father; which Ashton also ignored, in favour of a stripped-down rendering of the classic version. Burra was, if anything, pleased. He commented to Bumble, 'Its what I hoped he would do instead of cooking up some crazy plot.' Burra's own thoughts about Don Juan seemed to be revealed by a series of unfinished watercolours, several of them numbered, perhaps conceptualised as designs for drop-curtains, or perhaps just pictorial responses to the story. The one labelled 1 shows the Don with Doña Ines and her distraught father under a skull-faced moon, while no. 4 represents the statue of the Commendatore advancing on the aghast Don as he sits at dinner – others, unnumbered and more abstract in concept, focus on the statue of the Commendatore.

Ashton, for his part, was very impressed by Burra's complete absence of ego over the whole project; he found that if he made the slightest suggestion that anything might be changed, Burra was happy to junk his designs and create alternatives. There were at least three set projects, completely different, before the final design was arrived at. Ashton's concept was to produce a very abstract version, and Burra met him by paring away Spanish details and producing a rather minimalist set depicting a partially ruined viaduct, related to his painterly preoccupation of the time, ruined buildings.

Despite his exhaustion, he was again very conscientious about overseeing the realisation of his work: 'Ive been at Covent Gdn screaming abuse in the stalls arranging Don Juan & tearing snoods off the girls heads. The show was being lit by Michael Benthall who did it very well. & they managed to paint an edge of brick work round my holes at the back however I stopped them painting the whole set a shade darker. Mrs Glock did a very good job she paints scenery very well also the costumes were beautifully made & I was very pleased with them!'

In Ashton's version, the Don encounters and embraces six of his former loves, only to find that he himself has attracted the attention of 'La Morte Amoureuse' (Fonteyn), a relationship oddly parallel to that of Orphée and Death in Cocteau's 1950 film (and perhaps drawing on Cocteau's earlier stage version, also called *Orphée*, which was produced at the Théâtre des Arts in June 1926, and in London in 1928, where Bar and Paul Nash certainly saw it, and Burra and/or Ashton may have seen it also). For most of the ballet, the Don divides his attentions between La Morte and seducing a 'Young Wife' (Moira Shearer) until the kiss of La Morte finally kills him. The ballet was not a success.

Critics pointed to its lack of lyricism and passion; and *The Times* complained that Ashton spent most of his time devising 'novel ways of transporting the female body . . . a sure sign of strain'.

Burra was at the first night, which was a disaster, as he told Aiken: 'on the opening night Margot Fonteyne as la morte amoureuse? is supposed to appear to Don J in a hole at the back, needless to say up dashed Don J but morte amoureuse failed to jell in her hole as the laytes had fused HAHAHA poor Margot also slipped & her knee was the size of a balloon.' She had torn a ligament, and had to be replaced by the glamorous, but less charismatic, Violetta Elvin, which cannot have helped.

The ballet's principal problem, however, was Helpmann. Ashton's inspiration for the figure of the Don was a flamenco artist called Luisillo from Carmen Amaya's gypsy troupe, then in London, who danced with his partner Teresa 'like two fierce and beautiful birds lovemaking'. Even Arnold Haskell, who was inclined to disapprove of 'music-hall', said of him, 'his combination of fire, rhythm and absolutely classical precision are altogether incredible'. It was unfortunate, therefore, that Ashton was not in a position to kidnap Luisillo, since there was nothing in Helpmann's own character that he could draw on to realise such a conception. Wary of Helpmann's technical limitations, Ashton did not give him much to do as a dancer, and since the projection of intense heterosexual glamour was not precisely suited to his gifts, he was unable to carry off the role by sheer acting. The result was 'a glum static figure, who even when the swelling music demands some virtuoso dancing, can do no more than run futilely across the stage'. As Cyril Beaumont unkindly pointed out, Helpmann spent most of the ballet carrying women about, looking bored to tears. Burra designed some very beautiful costumes for the principal danseuses, and had a great deal of fun with striped, *commedia dell'arte*-style garments for the Carnival sequence – he also gave several of the revellers beaked masks, which, though they obviously relate to Venetian carnival masks, are also a feature of several of his paintings, harking back to the Aztec warriors in beaked masks he had seen in Rivera's murals in Mexico.

When the war ended, Burra was no longer young. He was in dreadful shape physically, but also he had lost his early interest in human interaction, either low-life or high-society, and his enhanced sense of the tragedy and futility of human endeavour had led him away from satire. Rothenstein recalled a conversation he had with Burra after the war. 'David Low [the cartoonist] said to me that something of the satire had gone out of his caricatures, when the world had become so horrific a place. "What", he had asked, "can a satirist do with Auschwitz?" "I entirely agree", Burra said. "so many appalling things happen that one's response diminishes. Still," he added, "everything *looks* meancing."' For Burra, everything always would. His sense of the essential horror of the world had strengthened in the war years to the extent that it never really left him.

More generally, the world of English art was at a low ebb by 1945, despite the enlightened patronage that appointed artists such as Paul Nash, Henry Moore and Eric Ravilious as official war artists, and the creation of CEMA (Council for the Encouragement of Music and the Arts), which later became the Arts Council. Bryan Robertson, who did as much as anyone to turn the situation round when he became director of the Whitechapel Gallery in 1951 as a twenty-seven-year-old *Wunderkind*, observed:

In 1945 ... our artists had a merely local reputation. Our closed and empty museums were in the charge of caretakers. There had not been a big new book or a major exhibition since 1939, and for our knowledge of Paris and New York, we relied on censored letters and clandestine copies of reviews printed by hand in the French provinces.

Burra, like everyone else, had been thrown on his own resources. The trends of his work in the immediate post-war period are a greatly increased interest in both still life and landscape, and a revival of his 'birdfolk'. *Birdmen and Pots* of 1946 shows figures in beaked masks with something of the spry, disengaged interest of birds, with a table full of pots and jugs whose forms echo those of the figures. Birds in paintings are often symbols of freedom – as they are, for example, in the work of Paul Nash – but the birds Burra painted are almost never on the wing. In actual life, he loved birds, put out food for them and observed them with care, but their symbolic role in his paintings allies them with his wartime soldiers: they are mechanical beings, shorn of the human individuality that had once interested him above all else.

It may be relevant that there had been chickens at Springfield during the war. A small flock of birds one feeds and observes regularly reveals itself as a miniature society which, to a sensitive observer preoccupied with evil, offers a nightmarish caricature of human interaction.

One rapidly learns to perceive individual quirks of personality in a group of chickens, but they are not endearing. They are intensely hierarchical, and they persecute weaklings. However well they are treated, an injured bird who is bleeding sometimes provokes a cannibalistic reaction in her fellows, who peck her to death and eat her. The figures in *Birdmen and Pots* have a fowl-like air of slightly menacing, bright-eyed, rapacious interest: they are also all making the sign against the evil eye.

The most significant new development in Burra's art post-war is the landscape with figures, which focuses more on the landscape than the figure, who is often seen from behind or with a face in shadow. These paintings have a clear relationship to late-baroque *capriccios* and ruin-pictures. The emotional energy is generated by the scene as a whole and not by the figures, who are either passive or introverted. *Rye Landscape with Figure* (1947) is an extensive panorama of Rye, with a curiously sinister slinking figure in the foreground, in fact based on the man who had been the keeper at Springfield, Dick Mills; looking over his shoulder, but refusing communication. Burra also painted the harbour at Hastings. In contrast to his soldier pictures of five years previously, the human figures in this study seem to be going about their business with dreamlike leisure, and the main figure is collapsed and lassitudinous.

While the paintings of this period suggest Burra's depression and lack of energy, there was one feature of his life as he moved into his forties which was a very positive development: a renewed closeness with his surviving sister, Anne. They had been very fond of one another as children, but as young adults their lives drifted apart because their interests and their respective circles of friends were so different. But the family reunited in the late Forties. Anne was still living in Northiam and working at Brickwall School, and she and Colin went to Scotland together every year, but they also began to spend a certain amount of time in Playden.

In 1948, the Ritchies made themselves a little private flat in the attics of Springfield Lodge (out of the old servants' quarters; the Burras, like everybody else in the upper middle class, found it impossible to replace their pre-war staff; though Frederick Rose, who had joined the staff of Springfield as a teenager, returned to the household after the war, and looked after both the older Burras through to their deaths). However, Anne was also often there by herself. This suggests that she had decided she

needed to keep an eye on her parents' ménage, and wanted to spend more
time with her own family than her husband did – though this did not, as
far as anyone records, generate friction. The flatlet had two bedrooms, but
its approach to a kitchen and bathroom was 'a Belling cooker behind a
rare old tapisserie reeking of sausages ... unfortunately theres no water
up here but a cold tap that once its turned on you cant turn off' – a detail
that tells one something important about servants' lives pre-war. Burra
himself was increasingly conscious that Springfield had outlived its time.
'Its sad about this house as it could realy be made very nice in flats.'

Anne's commitment to Springfield in its decline seems to signal a new
closeness between brother and sister. The Burras would not be the first
or last siblings to be drawn together by the mutual problem of coping with
querulous, ageing and ailing parents; but in addition, Anne must have
become increasingly conscious of how frail her brother himself had become,
since she started taking him off for little holidays. The first such trip was
in 1947, when the two of them went to Ireland together.

Burra first got interested in the west of Ireland when he was coming
back from his disastrous visit to Mexico in August 1937, and the *Scythia*
paused momentarily at Galway before docking in Southampton. Burra did
not get off, but he was fascinated by what he saw from the deck. He wrote
to Nash soon after he returned, '... I wish to go to the West of Ireland
now leaving Galway Bay where 200 got off for a squint at the ould sod
we passed by the coast & its quite lovely terrific towering rocks black with
vitreous green and grey mountains & not a soul & beautiful sandy bays.'

Ireland remained neutral during the Second World War, but in the
battle for independence, and the period that preceded it, the grandiose
homes of the Protestant ascendancy were mostly abandoned, if not actually burned to the ground, and the parlous state of the Irish economy
through the nineteenth century and into the twentieth ensured that little,
if anything, was repaired, painted or renewed. Burra in the Forties could
probably not have borne anywhere offensively prosperous-looking, but
Ireland was certainly not that. On the other hand, its ruinous aspect was
gently crumbling rather than the patchy devastation to which he was
accustomed, since Irish cities had not been shelled. The grand railings
that are so characteristic of the Dublin townscape still graced the streets,
as they do to this day, whereas those of London and Rye had gone for
scrap. It is easy to see why Burra wanted to go to Ireland, and also why
his family would have seen this as the most positive impulse he had shown

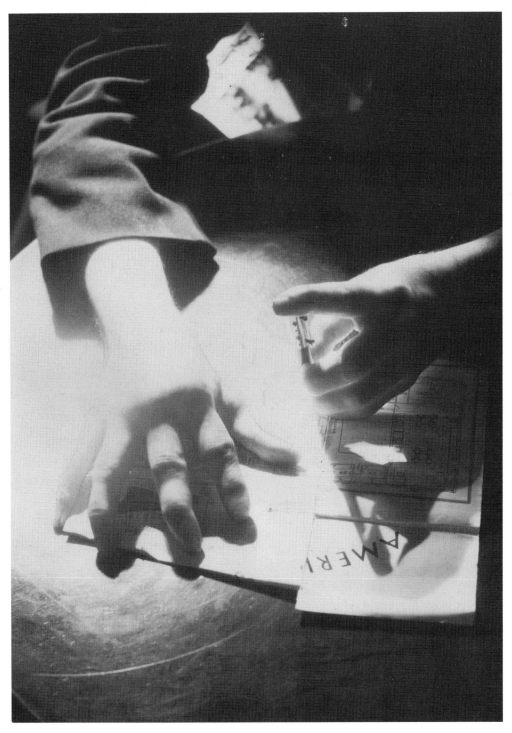

Burra's hands when he was 28, photographed by Barbara Ker-Seymer for
Unit 1: The Modern Movement in English Architecture, Painting and Sculpture, 1934.

The dancer Arthur Mahoney
in Flamenco costume.

Bumble on holiday
in the South of France.

Bar wearing her white matelot
trousers, with Clover (c. 1930).

Sophie Fedorovitch, Marty Mann and Bar on
Princess Murat's yacht (Violette Vanderbilt Murat
was a lesbian with many friends in the arts).

Burra in America, at his one-man show at
Springfield Museum of Art, Massachussetts.
Two of his paintings, 'Opium Dream' and
'The Torturers', hang behind him.

Edna Lloyd Thomas,
Burra's hostess in Harlem, in 1936.

Burra and Billy Chappell in Fitzroy Square
during the war (after 1942).

Anne Burra during the war.

Billy Chappell in his living room on Thurloe Square in the Sixties.

Bumble at home.

Burra, Bar and David Paltenghi in the Mandrake Club in the Fifties.

Burra with Mary Aiken at Rock Harbour,
Orleans, Cape Cod, 1955.

Conrad Aiken.

Bar and Barbara Roett on holiday in Venice.

Gerald Corcoran in later life.

John Banting in Hastings,
late Sixties.

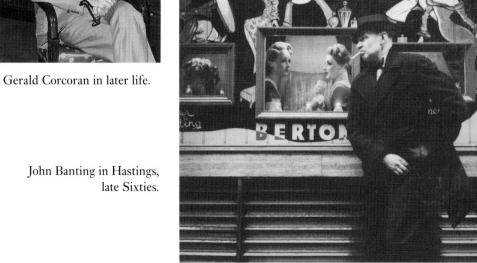

Burra painting (c. 1970).

since the end of the war, and why Anne wanted to make it possible for
him.

The 1947 trip very nearly failed to happen – Burra forgot his passport,
and discovered this only after turning up at Holyhead at five-thirty in the
morning 'after a perfect death rattle in the Irish mail in which everybody
ended up upside down with their feet poked in each others eyes & grey in
the face.' He had to go all the way back to Rye, and then back to Holyhead,
where of course he had missed his boat. But as usual, once launched on
his travels, he was not easily discouraged or defeated, and when he got
there, Galway offered much to entertain him, despite a bus strike. Anne
and he were intending to travel about the country on local bus services,
taking things as they came. But for a time, the strike kept them from making
the expeditions they had intended, so he sat down and wrote letters.

this hotel looks as if it was full of commercial travellers very middle class and
priests with familys. Of course if you want to drink yourself into the grave at the
double & who doesn't you just must come here. its an alcoholics '<u>must</u>' for Ive
never seen so much Powers & Jamiesons whiskey together in one place & you can
swill non stop & I also find 2 doubles set you up quite nicely so Ime wondering if
they dont add a bit of water in Old England . . . I find plenty to occupy myself in
monster study and staring at huge pots of jam bars of Dutch & Danish chocolate
etc and realy lovely Aran tweed in large bales. theres a sort of off white type fairly
smoothish that Ime sure youd be mad about. I believe you could take away a length
without it being torn off you . . . A high tearing Atlantic gale is now whistling
through the seminaries, convents, retreats for the fallen, St Mary Magdalenes
laundry & Loyolas pension lunchs & dinners . . .

Whisky, chocolate, and so forth were either on ration or unobtainable
in England, and alcohol had become more important to him during the
war years. He eyed the whisky thoughtfully, but unfortunately he had
discovered that 'they simply remove it at the customs'; though he would
have been allowed to take Chappell a length of tweed, and probably did.
He wrote to Aiken from Cork, where he and Anne spent a week in April
1948 exploring Bantry Bay, Limerick and Kinsale, in a slightly more
elevated mode.

Weve been to Limerick in a bus yesterday starting in a sort of green pea dripping
thunderclap the windows of the bus were invisible & there was a thick fog at a

yard but when we reached Lim it got lovely & realy I must say L is wonderful. lovely 18th century houses & doorways & stone greek temples etc. Im afraid however that some of the loveliest 18th century houses are tenements of such a pitch of degringolade, digne de Mrs Kirby & inhabited by crones who vanish into portals smoothed shiny by layers of crasse. many are too far gone & are falling down. as are many of the warehouses glowering down on the Shannon with their hollow windows. it's the colour thats so beautiful and wonderful sort of brownish pink.

In September he and Anne returned to Ireland and went to Dublin, Sligo and Galway. All the letters from these various visits suggest that he responded strongly to the landscape and to the shabby charm of Irish cities. He wrote from Galway to Paul Nash during his second visit of 1948:

There are no lack of ruins here I must say Ireland is one of the most beautiful countries Ive ever seen. Galway is lovely and full of crumbling warehouses and the harbour is a sight such beautiful colours it really is extraordinary.

He enjoyed the atmosphere of Ireland, in both senses: the pace and quality of life on the one hand, and the pure and lovely light on the other. He seems always to have felt at ease in Catholic countries; and to have enjoyed the social and public manifestations of religion. As a great believer in demons, he perhaps liked to feel that there was plenty of holy water about. He was particularly delighted by Dublin, as he wrote to Conrad Aiken after his return to England:

The city is really lovely it's the light I think for the sun suddenly bursts forth in the middle of storm clouds and whirling wrack and the effect on the 18th century facades is lovely also the banks of the Liffey when well <u>lit</u> (?)[3] are beautiful & the river & Howth head away in the distance in golden aureate glow with the Dublin gasworks & electricity combine in the background looking so serene and romantic it was like a soothing syrup. Another thing is that nobody seems to care in Dublin whether its pouring or what happens nor do they look so cross. They also like to talk. I don't think theyre so hag-ridden over there . . .

---

[3] Burra's question mark (probably to signal double-entendre: when the banks have adequate lighting they look beautiful; they also seem beautiful to an onlooker who is drunk ('well lit')).

Ireland was good for him. 'I must say I feel very much better as I was getting so hagridden & in such a state of nerves I scarcely knew what to do. & this place is good for the nerves very relaxing.' It gave him the kind of social interaction he most liked – Burra was not antisocial, though he gave that impression to people who were trying to pin him down. Chappell commented, 'He's a very gregarious person by nature but certain people irritate him, you know, he slides out, he's a great slider-outer.' He particularly liked sitting in pubs, slightly, though not very, drunk, and the genial Irish habit of including total strangers in general conversation suited him very well.

The Irish experience was a genuine renewal of his spirits; it brought back his interest in life. He made several paintings of Dublin: the shawled women and eighteenth-century houses; a few motor cars contesting the wide streets with donkey-carts. Unlike the tragic landscapes with broken wheels he had painted during the war, his Irish townscapes suggest a modest sense of hope and renewal. The grand houses of the Protestant ascendancy may have become slum tenements, but slums are inhabited by people. This is regeneration, not degeneration; a new life, that of the indigenous Irish, established in buildings intended for a life of a quite different kind. A good thought to take forward into the Fifties.

In 1950, Burra undertook another major ballet commission, *Don Quixote*, for Ninette de Valois. It was an indirect testimony to the success of his *Don Juan* and *Carmen* designs; he was evidently perceived as having a particular affinity with Spain. He was still very far from recovered from the attrition of the Forties: as he said to Aiken, 'Im in a permanent boiling rage which bursts out now and again when I dont have fits of depression & apathy. I was just thinking how drab they all looked the other day in London when I was down for Don Quixote everyone looked as if theyd had a mud dip.' Nonetheless, he rose to the challenge of the ballet, a strange, ambitious concept, which aimed to present the Don as more of a tragic than a comic figure.

It derived from a score with a complex history. Harold Rubin, who acquired the Arts Theatre Club in Great Newport Street near Leicester Square, with the declared purpose of creating a permanent home for ballet and a social club for dancers, came into contact with a distinguished Catalan composer called Roberto Gerhard, who had ended up as a fellow of King's College, Cambridge, after the fall of Barcelona left him stranded in exile. In 1940, Gerhard was working out a scenario from Cervantes's novel, and creating a ballet score, which achieved a temporary realisation when it was played on the radio in 1940. Rubin, impressed, acquired the score, and wanted to produce it as a ballet, but was forced by the exigencies of the war to wind up his company.

Sadler's Wells Ballet became interested in the score in 1949, initially as a project for Robert Helpmann, and the ballet was duly entered into the production schedule for February 1950. Helpmann, however, was involved with producing his first opera (*Madame Butterfly* at Covent Garden, January 1950) and did not have time to choreograph it. De Valois therefore took on the project herself, since the premiere had already been announced (it seems to have been an example of poor liaison between the opera and ballet sides of Covent Garden). It was, however, Helpmann, with whom Burra had worked on *Miracle in the Gorbals*, who talked him into it: 'I do hope so much you will do it, dear Ed,' he wrote coaxingly. 'I cannot think of another designer who could do it as well.'

The music and décor were very much admired; but the ballet was probably overambitious, and was certainly inaccessible. Kathrine Sorley Walker, the chronicler of Ninette de Valois's work, writes:

The finished article was one of the most subtle, tantalising, difficult and elusive ballets I have seen. At first sight it looked dry to the point of aridity, totally reticent, theatrically disappointing. By the end of the second performance, I was filled with admiration. In my contemporary notes, I wrote of its slow and dignified movement, the half comic touches, the refined inflections of mime and reflections of the score, and the way effects were built up by sparse and economic means.

Walker pays tribute to the effect of Burra's work on the project.

There were five scenes, all enhanced by superb costumes, sets and drop curtains by Edward Burra in predominantly orange, red and dark coffee colours . . . an initial drop curtain of the dreaming head of Don Quixote surrounded by his visionary characters recalled in its atmospheric power the same designer's curtain of a ship in the slips of a builder's yard for Miracle in the Gorbals . . . another act drop, a near view of Quixote and Sancho Panza on horse and mule, preceded scene 2, the wayside inn.

Scene three had a backdrop of windmills. There are black-and-white photographs of three of the five drop-curtains in the Tate, from which it is clear that Burra was using Salvador Dalí's work as a reference point.

Unfortunately, for all the excellence of Burra's work, acknowledged by everyone who commented on it at all, the ballet was a dud of a particularly exasperating kind. Fonteyn was 'fascinating' in the dual role of Dulcinea and a gypsy girl. Helpmann as Don Quixote, concealed beneath a crust of make-up and false hair, mimed his way through as best he could, but the score, though musically brilliant, did the choreographer no favours. 'De Valois did not have the long danceable sections of music that could have involved her in the development of solos and *pas de deux* or virtuoso *enchaînements*,' Walker explains. Another problem was the stage. Covent Garden and the Metropolitan Opera House, the two venues where the ballet was performed, are very large. De Valois herself felt that her choreography would have had more of an effect in the relatively intimate context of Sadler's Wells – in other words, she had failed to adjust her unconscious assumptions about the relationship of the work to the audience so as to fill the grand space of Covent Garden. *Don Quixote* was the first ballet she had personally choreographed since the move to the Opera House and, as it turned out, it was the last.

The London critics were on the whole kind about *Don Quixote*, and some were positively enthusiastic, but audiences did not enjoy it. They found it too intellectual, too much a story told in mime rather than a ballet, and they refused to be educated into appreciating it. *Don Quixote* was included in the Royal Ballet's US tour of 1950/1 to see if it would work in America. But American audiences disliked it even more than the English had, and so it was dropped from the repertory, a failure. Walker loyally suggests that 'there is some ground for thinking that on both sides of the Atlantic it was well ahead of its time', which may be the case, though it clearly laboured under serious difficulties from the start.

XIII

STILL LIFE

THE principal signal, both internally and to the world, that Britannia had finally dusted herself off after the war was the Festival of Britain in 1951. The first post-war trade fair, *Britain Can Make It*, in 1946, had been, domestically speaking, as much annoying as inspirational. New, stylish, modern goods of all kinds were shown to a fascinated but frustrated audience – frustrated, since everything they saw was for export only, and unobtainable. Throughout the Forties, almost nothing in the way of manufactured goods was available for home consumption because of the colossal foreign debt which Britain had racked up in the course of the war, mostly to America, but also to several countries of the Commonwealth. Export was absolutely crucial to national solvency; and the citizenry just had to put up with shortages.

Post-war Britain enjoyed full employment, but had almost nothing to spend its money on. The longed-for smart clothes, fridges, washing-machines and cars were all vanishing overseas, bringing in dollars; rationing remained in force, and currency restrictions kept everyone at home. One result was a golden age for entertainment – people were even buying pictures.

Chappell, who had been compelled to close his shop, because so many people owed him money, and he could afford neither to carry £2,000 worth of bad debts nor to pursue those responsible in the courts, was forced back on the theatre as a profession in the Fifties. In the middle of 1950, he landed a role in a sophisticated farce called *The Little Hut*, translated from the French original by Nancy Mitford, directed by Peter Brook and designed by Oliver Messel. The star was Robert Morley, and Chappell played a monkey (it was set on a desert island). Funny and slightly risqué, it hit the taste of the moment so accurately that it ran for 1,261 performances at the Lyric, and did wonders for his personal balance of payments.

In 1951, the Festival of Britain marked a change of direction in British culture. After all those years of make-do and moral exhortation, it was conceived of as 'something to give Britain a lift', above all, as entertainment; with fireworks, dancing and a funfair. There were also exhibitions, including one from the Arts Council, *Sixty Paintings for '51*. Burra was amongst those commissioned to produce a large picture on a theme of the artist's choice, which, for no very obvious reason, resulted in his extremely strange Caravaggesque *Judith and Holofernes*.

Judith and Holofernes signalled a curious phase in Burra's output at the beginning of the Fifties. He produced a series of intensely emotional biblical pictures strongly referential to the art of the sixteenth century – Caravaggio and El Greco in particular – as well as to his time in Mexico (and also to Bosch; particularly the latter's wonderful *Christ Crowned with Thorns* in the National Gallery, acquired in 1932, which surrounds Jesus with four sharply differentiated grotesque figures, and even more, to the solid mass of faces in Bosch's *Christ Carrying the Cross* in the Musée des Beaux-Arts in Ghent, which Burra cannot have seen other than in reproduction). Another artist whose attitude to religion as expressed in painting may be relevant to this group of Burra's works is the Belgian James Ensor, especially *Christ's Entry into Brussels* (1889).

These paintings were shown at the first exhibition Burra had with the Lefevre Gallery: it was a widely noticed success, and was the point at which his life really began to straighten out, since thereafter he exhibited with the Lefevre more or less bianually. His biblical paintings seem to have shocked and disturbed a number of contemporary critics, because of their violence and their radically unconventional depiction of Christ, though they also impressed them. They are above all about religion as a social phenomenon: Burra situates a smouldering, shamanic, often intimidating Christ among hundreds of people; fighting to throw their palms before him, to bring him the sick to be healed, or even, in *The Expulsion of the Moneylenders*, to escape from him. They are among the most peopled paintings Burra ever produced; and unlike the 'soldiers' pictures, they are full of individuals. In *The Coronation of the Virgin*, a powerful, thick-muscled Christ who seems to be sitting casually on a step is crowning his diminutive mother with careful, rather awkward hands as if he is afraid he might hurt her, but the most vivid faces are the Three Marys in the foreground, who seem to be undergoing a surprising range of private emotion, from (it seems to me, at any rate) chagrin to glutinous sentimentality via dour satisfaction. The Apostles have turned their backs on this glorious event and are arguing like members of the Left Book Club, as if they disapprove of the whole thing. On the other hand, the middle ground is occupied by the angelic chorus, who are swinging like the orchestra of the Savoy Ballroom; unlike the Apostles, they are evidently right behind the enterprise, and making as much noise as they possibly can with many trumpets and an isolated guitar. There are many ways of reading this painting, some of them theological. Its first owner was Michael Benthall, the librettist of *Miracle in the Gorbals*.

Burra's attitude to Christianity remains wholly unknowable. When he was asked in interview, 'Would you say you'd ever been a religious person?' his reply was interestingly nuanced. 'I wouldn't say so in a churchy sense. No, perhaps not.' Clearly, he did not want to talk about his inner life, but both his work and his letters indicate that he was, in some sense of that word, 'religious', though it would not be legitimate to assume that he was therefore a Christian. Catholic baroque art provided a series of reference points for expressing passionate emotion, which he explored for a while in this period, then dropped. These paintings are theatrical in two senses: they draw on a Caravaggesque idiom of expressive gesture derived from Burra's serious study of late-baroque art, and they also draw – as do other of his works, such as *Figures in a Landscape* (1937–9) – on the ballet; the long, shapely, tights-clad male legs that appear in many of his Forties' and Fifties' paintings evoke the Italian Renaissance up to a point, but to at least as great an extent they evoke the physical expressionism of abstract ballets such as *Dante Sonata* and *Symphonic Variations*: in his *Expulsion*, moneylenders tumble and roll down the steps of the Temple like so many coins, just as they might have done in a ballet.

There is a considerable amount of evidence for Burra's interest in the occult, which went well beyond his liking for H.P. Lovecraft and other writers of the kind, and strengthened in later life. Among the books in his cottage at the time of his death were a seventeenth-century mystical work he had picked up somewhere, Jacob Boehme's *The Three Principles of the Divine Essence* (published in 1648), and a fair selection of nineteenth- and twentieth-century work on magic, such as P.-L. Jacob, *Curiosités des sciences occultes* (1902) and Eliphas Lévi's *Transcendental Magic* (1855). In the Seventies, he bought reprints of other nineteenth-century occultist classics, Edward Bulwer Lytton's *Zanoni* (1971) and *A Strange Story* (1973), and Papus's *The Tarot of the Bohemians* (1972). He also owned Alan Mercier's *Les Sources esotériques et occultes de la poésie symboliste* (1969) and Charles Williams's *Witchcraft*. These acquisitions suggest that ideas of spirits, powers and demons active in the world were of continued interest and importance to him, though there is nothing to suggest that he either practised any form of magic or belonged to any kind of organisation such as the Order of the Golden Dawn. (He had a certain interest in Aleister Crowley, whom he regarded as 'an eccentric of the first class', but saw him as essentially a comic figure. Also, his lifetime allergy to organisations of any kind would in any case militate against this possibility.)

On a more trivial level, Burra was superstitious. Nearly all his surviving diaries contain a pressed four-leafed clover, suggesting that finding one was an annual ritual. On one occasion, after an excursion had gone disastrously wrong, he noted that he had put on a ring with a death's-head he bought in Toulon, which had perhaps not been wise: 'Theres something not quite legitimate about that ring. I think it brings ill luck.' He continued to tell his fortune with ordinary playing cards from time to time throughout his life (his diaries suggest that he may have habitually done so at New Year), though there is nothing to indicate that he mastered the Tarot.

Even were it not for this evidence of his continued interest in occultism, it seems moderately certain on the basis of his work that, whether or not he believed in anything remotely resembling an Anglican (or Catholic) idea of God, Burra believed, in some sense of that complex word, in demons, and also in *genii loci*, *numina*, spirits of place. He was open to the possibility of the supernatural, for example, in a garden in Yorkshire that took his fancy, 'huge trees & grass which is what I like. dead still & foggy, & rather dim, I must say if I had been alone & it had been my garden, I should find it a shade eerie – one expects something'. This receptivity is evidenced by many pictures, including *After the Market Closed* – probably Chapel Market in Islington – in which a couple of burly men are carrying away a dismantled stall, accompanied by a demonic Topsy-like figure who is keeping pace with them; and by

Snowdonia no. 2, in which the bleak, hunched shoulder of the mountain reveals a cold face of cloud, while a diaphanous blue frost-giant moves across, or through, the landscape. Not all Burra's empty landscapes are as unpeopled as they first seem; they have an inner life, and birds and demons move in them.

This may also relate to his liking for the paintings of Bosch and Brueghel – I am thinking in particular of Bosch's contemplative *St Anthony*, who sits musing by a stream, lost in deep thought, while a grotesque little demon does its puppylike best to attract his attention (this painting is in the Prado; Burra will have seen it). Burra's personal beliefs and emotions could not be accommodated more than temporarily by the tropes of baroque Christian art, but it is less true to say that he stopped painting religious pictures than it is to say that he developed a personal vocabulary for expressing his sense of the numinous, which increasingly, as he got older, was expressed through places rather than people. George Melly commented about his late work, 'All that strangeness has now sunk into landscape.'

In this, Burra was completely at odds with the trend of English painting. Bryan Robertson observed in 1965:

A younger generation has turned its back, in recent years, on the English landscape tradition, believing that the very nature of 'typically English' landscape painting is evocative of a dated nostalgia, a digression from the basic problems of modern art.

Burra's English landscapes owe something to early-nineteenth-century predecessors such as Henri Fuseli and John Sell Cotman, just as his paintings of orchard trees draw on Samuel Palmer, but they are among his most disturbing works. He did not, in any sentimental sense of the word, love nature. He opened his eyes and mind to it until he was so overwhelmed by the beauty and horror of the world that he had to paint to bring his reactions under control. The landscapes are neither dated nor complacent. Rather than being nostalgic, they suggest an environmental awareness significantly ahead of his time, which is also witnessed in his letters. 'All the wild life & birds have been conscientiously poisond by sprays, why everyone isnt beginning to wither & turn dry I don't know – it realy is satanic, they are trying to do something about it I saw in the Observer today – I never eat anything without running it under the tap – partridges & pheasants are suffering, I hope some chemical manufacturer drops dead from a stewed pigeon."[1] His choice of adjectives is significant; he may not have believed in God, but he certainly believed in Satan.

Robertson implies that the landscape was 'a digression'; no subject for art, because it was something that could be taken for granted. Modern man existed in an urban environment, and 'basic problems' were psychological, interpersonal or abstract. Burra's discarded wheels, brambles and demons state obliquely that landscape was not a digression at all; that beside the outer and inner lives of people in cities, there was an additional and serious problem that was clamouring for reconsideration with increasing urgency: the relationship of man and nature. Burra's landscapes are landscapes under threat.

In tune with the overall mood of the time, Burra's life began to open up again in the Fifties. He resumed regular visits to Paris, and in August 1950 went to Tours with Anne, their cousin Eleanor Brodrick (herself a second cousin, but also the wife of their first cousin, Willie) and her daughter Jill, who was Anne's god-daughter. He still had very little energy. Before he left, he wrote to Chappell, 'If I had strength I would stay in Paris on the way back but I cant be bothered to find a hotel or alter my ticket. its terrible but its true now I just don't care really whether I come or go.' He enjoyed it once he got there, but the letters suggest that he is living within new limitations. 'The others went to chattoos [châteaux] & I went and layd down . . . Spent a night in Paris at the Terminus Est. [i.e. the station hotel] rather above my station but I couldnt struggle on it was one mass of Americans & world-waize motor bus tours setting off . . .' A year or so later, when Anne was planning another trip, he commented, 'A. has got some hotel in Bayonne . . . I hope it's a good one as Im tired of walk ups in all their unbridled scruffiness . . .' He was changed from the pre-war Burra who had been content with the first flea-pit to come along.

It is, however, clear that his sense of humour and his zest for life began to return. He spent a week or so in Paris with a couple of friends in 1950, which was a tremendous success: the letter he wrote to Aiken suggests that he was more genuinely cheerful than he had been in years.

---

[1] Rachel Carson's *Silent Spring* (1962) set in motion a new sensitivity to the impact of chemicals on the ecosystem, but this letter was written in 1961.

... Ayme told that its 'fashionable' for intelectuals to gather at the Rotonde &
Coupole in Montparnasse after dinner unfortunately I never can get that far we
finaly ended up in a kind of rendezvous for Tarts & had a lovely time we couldn't
leave. they kept walking by outside very fast with a very hautaine air & after
whirling past 2 or 3 times whirled into the Bar and had coffee. it was exactly
like a smart cocktail party only all the guests were very well behaved – especialy an aged broken down queen with a beard and a green & gold lamé turban
& gold earrings an[d] a sort of Intelectuals tweed suit the whole had obviously
been slept in for the last 6 months as they were engrained in filth, sandals, &
very dirty barefeet. he kissed all the girls wrists & carried on an espiégle conversation. a few gentlemen came in but nobody seemed to care – they were realy
wonderful. We all feel much better from the food which is excellent and have
found 2 or 3 restaurants. One very good Italian one called Chez Alexandre in
the Rue des Canettes a little street off the Place St Sulpice that's the one I like
the best.

Good restaurants, after a decade of substitution, stodge and ersatz this-
and-that, had an enlivening effect. Clover thought that the trip had
done him the world of good; she wrote to Aiken, 'I don't think you
need worry about him . . . he walked for miles in Paris, and was revived
by the food.'

He went to Barcelona in 1952 with Bar Ker-Seymer, his last visit to
Spain. His diaries suggest that they were doing much as he had always
done in Spain, and going to cafés and flamenco bars: he also discovered tapas bars; ideal for a man with a tiny appetite who liked to drink:
'Have been feeling very well on a diet of Amer Picon[2] & fried octopus
& beer . . . I have a private beer parlor with small plates of fried egg
plant sardines octopi etc right in the street with a billiard saloon at the
back I find I never want to eat' – a bone of contention, inevitably, with
Bar, who thought good dinners one of the points of going on holiday,
but the only cause of friction in what was otherwise a very happy couple
of weeks. He was beginning to plan, and to look forward to things: 'I
particularly want to visit Rome & Naples having never been,' he wrote
in 1951.

However, plans of various kinds were temporarily shelved in the
interests of the major domestic development of the Fifties, which was

[2] A bitter orange and gentian-flavoured drink, not unlike Campari.

that the Burras gave up Springfield Lodge. Burra wrote to Margaret Nash (whom he had fallen out of touch with after Paul's death in 1946), catching her up with the news: she was, by then, living in Oxford.

The duckie old town of Rye looks exactly the same & we are moving down there sometime if everybody doesn't fall dead first. Poor Father is so decrepit he realy loves poking around Rye High St buying sardines or something & he cant garden up here any more & realy the whole place is too big. I don't see myself living there somehow well we had many happy times in Iden & Rye . . . our house in Rye is where Dickie & Zendra or whatever her name was house was, that peice got bombed & theyve been allowed to put the houses up again more or less its where that nice little Wesleyan chappel was realy fixed – the shell of that & a gorgeous view & East wind as you know.

Margaret Nash was saddened: '[I] cannot believe that you are going to sell your lovely Springfield house with its Firbank conservatory and easy Victorian comfort.' But though washing-machines and vacuum cleaners were being made, they were not obtainable, and a house designed for a high-Victorian lifestyle could only be made comfortable by a platoon of servants maintaining the infrastructure. The Burras could no longer afford eight servants, and without them, Springfield was getting shabbier, dirtier and sadder by the week. Only the faithful Frederick Rose returned to work for the Burras after the war, which made the household unsustainable. Even the house itself was starting to crumble due to lack of maintenance; shortly before they finally left, Burra commented that, 'the mess and dirt are beyond all praise. I found all the plaster had fallen in in my book cupboards'.

They finally moved to Chapel House in Rye in the spring of 1953, when Henry Burra was eighty-two, taking Frederick as their only living-in servant (there was also a charlady to do rough work (Phyllis) and a cook (Mrs Smith) at their new establishment, but these ladies only came in during the day). Chapel House was much smaller than Springfield. While the Burras were by no means poverty-stricken, they still needed to retrench. The cost of living had risen sixfold since the First World War, putting a strain on anyone who lived on income from capital, since return on investment was by no means keeping pace with the rise in the retail price index, the cost of labour and increased taxation. The crisis point for England's landowning aristocracy, such as the family of Burra's friend Olivia Wyndham, came after the First World War, when land values plummeted – thus Olivia's brother, like many other owners of great houses, was forced to sell Clouds in the Twenties. But for families such as the Burras who were afloat, financially speaking, on the proceeds of banking rather than large-scale landowning, crisis was staved off until after the Second World War. Since the Burras were not extravagant and their money was intelligently invested, they were better off than many of their kind. But Burra's own anxiety about establishing himself professionally in the interwar period must be related to the fact that by the Fifties his parents, let alone he himself, seemed to be at some genuine risk of outliving their wealth. It is clear that Henry and Trudy Burra worried a good deal, certain, as were many other members of their class, that the world they knew and understood had collapsed around them; afraid for their future. More realistic than many, they sold the only home Henry Burra had ever known, and made the best of things.

Their new establishment was a mannerly red-brick house, next to the fourteenth-century Ypres Tower, and off the secluded square behind St Mary's Church, in one of the quietest, yet most picturesque corners of Rye. It was not, however, conveniently located, from Burra's point of view. It was handy for the High Street where his father loved to potter, so therefore it was at the highest point of the town, a walk down-or up-hill to and from the station, and all the approaches were cobbled: not easy to walk on even for the able-bodied. One of the few things to be said for it, perhaps, from his point of view, was that there was a pub, the Ypres Inn, only a minute or two away, albeit down a steep flight of stairs.

As Burra told Margaret Nash, the great point of the house was its spectacular view out, across the old walls of Rye and over the River Rother and Romney Marsh. The great disadvantage was the corollary: an exposed position that made it very vulnerable to the wind. It was far more comfortable than the old house had become, though: Burra told Aiken it was 'very comfortable & warm. I can actualy take my clothes off in the bathroom.' But at the same time, the first real sou'wester of autumn suggested that it was not very solidly built, and that there were problems in store: 'this place up here was like being outside in the gale everything was suspended in mid air'. Burra, unfortunately, was enormously sensitive to draughts, because of his rheumatic joints, and always acutely aware of the prevailing wind.

He was not at all pleased to be living in Rye, though he passively accepted his parents' choice of Chapel House. He seems to have realised how much he loved the garden at Playden at the point where he lost it, to judge from his remarks about the Chapel House garden, 'a lovesome spot consisting of coke logs & mud. the soil is wonderful consisting of pipe stems old teeth & oyster shells to the depth of 1 foot', with a couple of old buddleias struggling back to life. There was a combination of inertia and protectiveness involved in his attitude. On the one hand, he didn't want to think about organising any kind of alternative life for himself. On the other, he knew how much looking-after his parents needed, and having stuck with them so long, he was beginning to feel that he had to see them out.

His dislike of Rye itself, however, was real, frequently and vigorously expressed: 'ducky little TinkerBell towne is like an itsy bitsy morgue quayte <u>dead</u> – its like Horror Comics – I am TOT – I come from the land of the living dead . . .[3] While 'TinkerBell towne' might be thought to have some affectionate overtones, the new name he coined for it after the move, 'Fort Dung Box', had none. On the other hand, the vast skies and flat landscape that were opened up by Chapel House were something to enjoy, and gave him a purchase on other wide, flat landscapes, such as that of the Cambridgeshire fens, which he painted in the decade that followed. Burra's painting *Ramparts* shows that he was susceptible to this at least: Clover noticed as much. 'Ed seems much better and has done a lot of very good paintings, with the new view from Chapel House creeping in behind the bar clients.'

Burra managed to dodge the actual process of moving, or at least settling in, because he went to America for the summer of 1953. In the same letter to Margaret Nash quoted earlier, he says, 'I heard from Conrad the other day, they want me to come in see them in Brewster Mass – & I would love to go but how unless they put up a bond of 400$ you cant take any money & you arent allowed to land without $400 I believe . . . Im so depressed about it as I so much want to go & people dont last forever . . .' It suggests that some of his resilience had returned, and with it, a desire for new adventures. Also, that he was very fond of Aiken, then sixty-three. As we know, his pocket diary suggests that throughout the war he wrote faithfully to Aiken about every ten days; this must have

[3] TOT: German for 'dead'.

strengthened a friendship which, over the years, had become very important to them both. He and Mary were also very fond of one another.

Draconian currency restrictions were a major problem for post-war travellers from England: Burra could not take more than £100 out of the country, while the US required incomers to have visible means of support. It was managed somehow. Burra had some money in a dollar account with the Second National Bank of Boston, which he had set up in the States in the late Thirties, from selling a few pictures in America. There may have been more in it than he thought.

As usual with the Aikens, elaborate financial negotiations were involved; rendered still more intricate by the fact that on some previous occasion he had evidently lent them money: Mary Aiken wrote, 'Dear Ed we're serious about your coming here but we're broke as usual. If one of us were to come over presently, i.e. within the next 2 months, will you come back & stay for as long as may be? This is a move we actually can't afford to make – but as we figure that the passage for one of us would about pay back what we owe you – bless your heart, dearie . . . Notion is that you will be able to pay us some such small stipend as is necessary out of Scudder etc. for food drink and chicanery. It will be small & can be arranged "to suit" . . .' Scudder was the Scudder, Stevens & Clark Fund, which seems to have been where the Boston bank invested Burra's money, and such arrangements were a necessary aspect of dealing with the Aikens at all; he paid up quite cheerfully. Though cautious, Burra was by no means ungenerous.

The Aikens had acquired a rambling house at West Brewster on Cape Cod in 1940, which they called '41 Doors'. It had a wonderful site. Aiken described it as 'on the north side of the cape, high up, and with a distant view of the sea . . . there are lovely trees round about . . . and a cranberry bog, twenty feet below, which in spring becomes a pond. The house sits there among the spruces as if it had been there a thousand years . . . the country is as simpatico as any I've seen, rolling, wooded, with cleared patches, and far views to the sea, marshy as it approaches sea level, then fine broad sand beaches.' In its relation to the sea, it was not unlike Rye. And Burra had a bedroom with a card-table, where he could work in peace. But he was not very interested in landscape at that particular moment, and nothing in his work directly reflects this location.

It is not quite clear what he was working on at Brewster. Andrew

Causey, in his definitive catalogue of Burra's work, suggests that this visit stirred memories of his bar-hopping visit to Boston in 1937, causing him to start work on a series of paintings of sailors in bars, which harked back to his interest in low-life places of entertainment of some twenty years previously, since Mary Aiken identified a photograph of Burra working on *Silver Dollar Bar*, with the half-finished painting draped over his little table, as taken at '41 Doors'. However, the background is not very specific (basically just a sash window and a blank wall), and the painting is securely dated to March 1937 by Burra's pocket diary for that year, so perhaps the easiest explanation is that Mary mistook a '41 Doors' window for one at 17 Elwood Street. It is probable, therefore, that the stylistically similar *Izzy Ort's* was also painted in 1937.

Another of the great pluses of retreating for that particular summer to '41 Doors', apart from avoiding the inevitably tiresome and pottering process of his elderly parents' re-establishing their life in a new house, arguing about the arrangement of the furniture and developing a new daily routine, was escaping the coronation of Queen Elizabeth (he had contrived to be in America, similarly, for the coronation of George VI). The whole 'Land of Hope and Glory' side of Englishness, to which his parents subscribed, infuriated him, and he is never known to have had a good word to say about the monarchy, or any of their attachments other than Mrs Wallis Simpson, whom he enjoyed, since she was a very good class of 'monster'. But although he was glad to be out of England, he started to get restive in Massachusetts. He began to see the sorts of things that he saw in Sussex, only more so: 'Its Hastings realy, the figures dearie! I don't know how they dare parade themselves about with the most terrible gams & hanging bottoms of Babylon in very tight shorts – no wonder theyve got Bums after a double egg peanut mayonnaise 3 decker jumbo sandwich & a Barrel of milk . . .'

'41 Doors' started to get him down. 'I don't want to see a soul as if I see anymore strange people I shall scream – Im beginning to be unable to keep a polite interested face. Conrad of course is ready for anybody . . .' Part of his problem was his intense dislike of being forced to make conversation with the many friends of the Aikens who passed through '41 Doors'. 'I prefer drinking in a saloon I loathe drinking at home unless its people I know very well & dont have to make an effort,' he confessed to his sister. In mid-August, he fled the Aikens and moved to Boston by himself, to a rented room in Haviland Street, 'a basement overlooking the N.Y. Central tracks'. It was a flea-pit, but welcoming: 'everybody in the basement kept their doors firmly open & by the time I got in they were all drinking beer & drunk so asked me in so I never got to bed till about 3 or 4 sometimes . . . You havent seen life till you've lived in a basement the landlady remarked – she was always très digne untill she fell down on the floor.'

When not enjoying Boston-Irish hospitality in Haviland Street, he renewed his acquaintance with Boston bars; 'the Novelty Bar was very good on Washington St if you ever go to Boston its full of sailors, petty gangsters, aged whores and queens wrangling over the sailors like gulls over something that's been thrown off a boat and a Hill Billy orch magnified into an earthquake'.

One bar painting, *Tropical Bar Scene*, definitely does date to this visit, of a bar with a décor of tropical landscapes. In this same letter (to Chappell) he mentions, 'I went to the Hi Hat to hear the Errol Garner Trio, very grand & mostly coloured – with smart colored society ladies sipping pint tumblers of I don't know what quite; & Bourbons.' The painting may therefore be of the Hi Hat; it certainly represents a rather smart club with a mostly-black clientele, and Burra may well have been drawn to the Hi Hat on more than one occasion, since the legendary clarinettist Charlie 'Bird' Parker was playing there in the early Fifties.

The Aikens acquired a toehold in New York in the 1950s, a cold-water, one-room, walk-up flat, at 332 East 33rd Street, known to them as the Slumlet. Burra went back to America again in January 1955; not precisely to stay with the Aikens, but to spend time with them, which he found more manageable. He rented a room nearby, on 21st Street near Gramercy Park, so that when he had finished his day's work, he could go over to the Slumlet and drink with the Aikens for the evening. But there was, once more, the problem of having been able to bring very little money, and he was proposing to stay in America for quite some time. After a while, he left the Aikens in New York and returned to Boston, where he rented a room at 41 Anderson Street, in the unsmart bit of Beacon Hill, from a Latvian lady with twenty cats. He liked it there, and found he could work. Above all, 'there are no temptations as in NY to stay out boozing till 4 AM in Moriartys Tavern – where the money goes dearie'. It cost only nine dollars a week and had rudimentary cooking facilities and a fridge, so he could cater for himself, and drink jug wine. He described it more fully to Chappell, some time in March. 'It gets more & more like Zazu Pitts in "Greed" behind a barricade of gallon jars of california claret (type) & empty instant coffee jars & old sardine tins.'

In April, he took a train up to Washington, and joined the Aikens there. Aiken had been Poetry Consultant to the Library of Congress from 1949 to 1952, and they had a house in South Capitol Street, two blocks away from the Capitol, with a well-lit spare bedroom big enough to hold a worktable. Burra was starting to work on flower-paintings at that time, so as well as visiting the National and Freer Galleries, he visited the Botanical Museum. All of these were within walking distance of the Aikens' house.

After Washington, the trio went back to Boston, to the city at first. He wrote to his mother, from 93 Revere Street, in May:

Its been terribly hot and Im back in Boston again on a very noisy corner and was sorry to leave Washington which I thought was lovely with plenty of trees – I think I may eventualy sell some pictures & have sold 2 one of flowers which could have been sold several times – which is rather annoying. There was a very good notice in the Boston Sunday Herald I sent to Gerald. We drove back from Washington in the very old baby Austin which broke down just outside New York & had to be dragged to a sort of ash heap where we took a taxi! ... I don't have any frig in this room so I cant keep anything – butter wouldn't exist a moment otherwise its very nice & not quite such a slum as Anderson St was. I think we are going to Brewster next week I never seem to stop moving & gradualy leave everything behind. I shall get home with nothing at all!

The show he mentions in this letter was at a commercial gallery, the Swetzoff, at Newbury Street, Boston, in April 1955. It was a critical success, though it was intensely annoying to have Hyman Swetzoff tell him that he could have sold the only flower-painting forty times over, since Burra could get no more money out of England, and was desperate for dollars. The deal they had agreed was the usual one, that Burra should pay for mounting, and Swetzoff would take a normal agent's fee of one-third. 'I impressed on him I had no money so he'd better sell something dearie or the mounts wont get payd for,' Burra said.

Gerald Corcoran, had he been consulted, would not have been pleased. When Burra told him about it, he advised, with remarkable

moderation, that Burra needed to 'mind out', since Swetzoff was a slippery customer, and also that he should ensure that Swetzoff charged
the same as the Lefevre for pictures of a comparable size and state of
finish. A caveat that Burra, inevitably, ignored: 'Realy what I want is
some money – almost any money.' Also, he liked Swetzoff, an obvious
rogue, but an appealing one.

The result, as always when Burra attempted to do business for
himself, was a mess. Two pictures were sold and two were on approval
by the time the exhibition closed. There is no indication that Burra ever
paid the framing bill; conversely, three months later, Swetzoff showed
no signs of settling up, and was not to be found. Moreover, when Burra
decided simply to take the remaining pictures away, he discovered that
Swetzoff, without consultation, had had them mounted on heavy card.
As usual with Burra's work, most of the pictures were extremely large,
and he was completely unable to transport them (he carried his paintings about in a roll, another reason why he preferred watercolour to
oil). Bundled together, they made a daunting object: 'the package which
is about 5 feet by 4 feet is very heavy – I can't pick it up, & you know
I'm strong,' said Mary Aiken. The pictures had to be abandoned in
America when Burra sailed on 2 October, and once back in England,
he did nothing about getting them shipped. Swetzoff's elusiveness
would have made this quite difficult, unless a friend had waded in on
his behalf (as Bumble, for example, had retrieved unsold pictures from
the Redfern for him in 1942), but in any case, there was always a strong
element of 'out of sight, out of mind' with Burra. He was never very
interested in what happened to his work: a picture which the Tate considered buying in the early Forties, but didn't, was simply left lying about
there because he failed to retrieve it, and was only found when a private
customer wanted to buy it in 1944 and John Rothenstein instituted a
search for the thing.

Burra seems never to have seen any money from Swetzoff – his 1956
letters to Aiken are punctuated with variations on 'Ive heard no more
from Swetz'. After a while, he stops mentioning him. Swetzoff was
murdered in 1959, and when Aiken returned to Boston in 1961, he instituted an investigation and found that the pictures were still in the gallery
basement. When he told Burra, the latter replied, 'Can you keep the
pictures Swetz has – ? I clean forgot about them.' So there, in the
Aikens' Newbury Street flat, they remained until 1974, when Mary,

then a widow, set about the complex business of getting the paintings, which by then were very valuable, shipped to the Lefevre.

Burra's close friends were middle-aged as the Fifties opened; and since they had been a talented bunch to start with, they picked themselves up after the war and were successful in one direction or another. They were very much the people they had always been, if not more so: Bar inclined to be bossy, Clover to self-dramatise, Chappell to moan, and Bumble to be a whirl of efficiency. After *The Little Hut*, Chappell reinvented himself as a versatile director and producer of revues, musicals and plays (so perhaps his wartime misadventures came in useful in the long run). His first venture was *The Lyric Revue* in 1951, but he went on to direct and/or produce a series of other revues through the Fifties and into the Sixties, as well as a variety of drama, from Sheridan's *The Rivals* and Gluck's *Alceste* to Wolf Mankowitz's *Expresso Bongo*. He also devised shows and wrote libretti; one such venture was a 'nostalgia' show, *Fieldings Music Hall*, which he devised and produced at the Gaiety Bar, Prince Charles Theatre, in 1964.

Bar Ker-Seymer's second marriage fared no better than her first. She produced a late-born son, Max Humphrey Lionel Ewart Rhodes, in 1947 (his second name confirms that she and Humphrey Pease had remained good friends). In the same year, she withdrew completely from both photography and film work. But two years later, Burra and the Rhodes family went to France together, and in the course of the holiday John Rhodes walked out, leaving Bar distraught. No letter written at the time survives from the principals, but a common friend, Betty Keen, wrote to Burra afterwards.

Barbara told me the whole business in a letter and I was so horrified I've not known what to say so haven't replied although I must tonight. It was so awful happening on your holiday like that and such a shock for Bar. Oh dear, oh dear. She said you had helped such a lot and if you hadn't been along she'd probably have jumped into the Channel. It must have been a hideous business for everyone.

When they got home, Bar retreated for a time to Conygar, the Welsh home of Emily ('Micky') Hahn, an American writer and journalist and long-term stalwart of the *New Yorker*, who had been a friend of hers – and Burra's – since 1930. The question of what she was going to do next, and how she was going to manage life as a single parent, was answered by a visit to America in 1950, where she was struck by a new post-war concept, the launderette. She immediately grasped the basic point that washing services were going to be an essential aspect of the new servantless world, so in 1951 she co-opted her mother's quondam maid, Lily, embarked on life as a businesswoman and opened one of the first launderettes in London, at Victoria (it was not the very first, which opened in May 1949). The machines were supplied by Bendix; and the venture was a success, so she opened a second in Horseferry Road: her firm was known as Ker-Seymer's Westminster Launderettes.

Bumble continued to design for the theatre and for films, very successfully, and also became a non-executive director of Marks & Spencer. She began working intermittently for Warner Bros as well as for London theatres, and in 1952 her design work for *Pickwick Papers* was shortlisted for an Oscar. She dressed Judy Garland on a number of occasions, and designed the women's costumes for *The Prince and the Showgirl* (the beaded white dress she designed for Marilyn Monroe was recently sold for $62,500). Incidentally, Chappell was also involved in this film, as dance arranger (he 'is going to teach her [Monroe] some 1911 dance steps. they should study early Chaplin comedies,' Burra remarked); an indication that the friends continued to look out for one another.

Doris Langley Moore's marriage, like Bumble's, was a casualty of the war (she divorced in 1942), but also like that of Bumble, and to some extent Chappell, her career flowered out of the passionate interest in clothes that the group had shared in the Twenties. She made herself the world expert on the history of fashion, and did some work in film and theatre. She designed *The African Queen* (1951) and wrote a scenario for an Ashton ballet, *The Quest* (based on Spenser's *Faerie Queene*, and not British ballet's finest hour). She also wrote a great deal, and in 1955 founded the world's first museum of costume. Burra saw little of her, but she kept in touch with Bumble and Chappell, whose professional concerns were much more closely linked with her own.

Clover, meanwhile, continued to live in Spain and to work for the British Council, while Antonio made some money, though not much, from his share of the family estate. She also kept on with her literary life; she translated a variety of books from and into Spanish, and edited a collection of V.S. Pritchett's short stories in 1958 (and had an affair with him in the early Sixties). They were not at all well off; and she could not afford to buy English books, so until she came back to England in the Sixties, Burra regularly sent her books and literary papers. Clover and Antonio kept Edward in Spain with them until he was ten, then sent him to school in England, first to a prep school, Windlesham, and then to Bryanston (where Max also went in due course). Whenever possible, Clover came over to spend time with him, but the school fees were a struggle for her, and she was very dependent on her friends and family to look after Edward in the holidays. Apart from calling on her mother and aunts, she also leaned on her old friends: she mended fences with Bar, who often had Edward at Easter, and in the summers he went to the Burras.

Burra quite liked having someone in his workroom as long as they didn't try and talk to him. Back in the early Twenties, when Chappell was visiting Springfield, he would sit in the studio for hours while Burra painted, leafing through the magazines and putting on records. Later on, several of Burra's letters invite close friends such as Barbara and Marty to 'come and watch me work'. He would certainly not have been deflected from painting by the presence of a teenager, and he liked being read to. Since the younger Edward's French was very good, Burra used to get the boy to read him *romans policiers*, such as the Maigret stories, supplying, every now and then, the meaning of the words that his godson didn't understand, and incidentally revealing a deep and wide knowledge of French argot.

Among Burra's writer friends, Conrad Aiken continued to be married to Mary Aiken and to go on much as before, bibulous, compulsively unfaithful and permanently broke, though entirely in America – the Aikens sold Jeakes' House soon after the war. Burra was a regular correspondent and occasional visitor. Lucy Norton became increasingly well known as a translator, and Anthony Powell became a noted establishment novelist with his twelve-volume *Dance to the Music of Time*, but both dropped out of Burra's life. Among the relatively few painters he knew, Paul Nash, his principal mentor, had died in 1946, but when a painter friend of his own generation, the surrealist John Banting, settled in Rye in 1956 with a hard-drinking boyfriend called Jim, Banting and Burra started seeing a lot of each other.

Ashton, of course, was established as British ballet's most distinguished choreographer, and was becoming more and more famous. But in 1953, his friend and muse Sophie Fedorovitch died in a domestic accident, to universal shock and regret, gassed by a malfunctioning

boiler. Another friend from the world of ballet, Constant Lambert, died
in 1951 (of alcoholism combined with undiagnosed diabetes mellitus),
an occasion that was marked by a BBC retrospective. Burra did not
watch it, but his comment was characteristic.

Bar said all the old ghosts Billy Fred etc. on the Constant Lambert programme
looked a 100! & the camera had enormous close ups of Billy, very trying. Bobbie
[Helpmann] kept as far away as poss.

He had no illusions about eternal youth. Clover noted of him, 'he hated
Peter Pan and the current craze for not wanting to grow up'. He wrote
to Chappell during the war that Bar had told him she had been looking
at old photographs, and found them depressing. He added, 'Your telling
me As for old letters dearie "Aparitions" I call them I wish I had the
strength to destroy them all but they might be of use "Historical" value
as a guide to the horrors of the 20's and 30's.'

He was also blankly uninterested in his own past. If he was confronted
with one of his own paintings, he would scrutinise it carefully, and sometimes a detail would make him laugh: the quality of his reactions
suggested that he had forgotten his work so completely that he felt it
had nothing to do with him. It was the same with the letters; in 1972,
Bar showed him some that she had kept, and as she told John Rothenstein
afterwards, '[he was] in fits of laughter the other evening over them as
though they had been written by someone else!' The stories, and perhaps
the writing, struck him as funny, but did not evoke memory. The fact
that so many letters survive is more a testimony to inertia than anything
else, since when he moved house (or rather, was moved), the contents
of his studios were shovelled into crates, unsorted, in the faint hope
that he would eventually decide what he wanted to keep.

One person who became very much part of Burra's life in the Fifties
was David Paltenghi, whom he met over *Miracle in the Gorbals*, in which
Paltenghi had danced the 'Official'. In terms of his stage presence, he
was a classic *danseur noble*, virile and splendid, but, as Arnold Haskell
observed, he was also highly intelligent. He was keen to try his hand
as a choreographer, an opportunity that Rambert was able to offer him
when he rejoined her company as a guest artist in 1950 (he had danced
with it before joining the Sadler's Wells Ballet in 1941). He created five
ballets for her in 1950 and 1951. *Canterbury Prologue*, based on Chaucer's

Canterbury Tales, was the last of these, a commission from the Arts Council for the Canterbury Festival. The subject might seem to call for shawms and crumhorns, but in fact *Canterbury Prologue* had music by the modern English composer Peter Racine Fricker, whose style was chromatic and contrapuntal, in the mode of Schoenberg and Bartók.

Paltenghi asked Burra to design *Canterbury Prologue*, which he agreed to do. Paltenghi wrote emotionally, 'I am so happy and proud we shall do this work together. I promise you Edward that I shall put all I have into it's success.' However, looking back on his work in her autobiography, Rambert thought that although Paltenghi had good ideas, his talent as a producer was not matched by any great gift for choreography. Burra was happy to work with him because he liked the younger man enormously, but he refused to go and see the result. Perhaps he had his doubts, and certainly the music was not his thing, but in any case, it was a very hot summer.

Mama Tilda & Anne went to Canterbury yesterday in a sort of Central American Jungle sweat bath. to see the wife of Canterbury Bath & came back stricken they obviously thought it terrible. The music was very modair style I gather. David P keeps ringing up & trying to make me go over & Im behaving very badly and saying Im out or away. Im so busy & feel so tired I cant have both and I don't care not realy.

What he must mean by 'I cant have both' is that if he went to Canterbury there would be a period of recovery in which he was too tired to paint, and there was never any doubt where his priorities lay. 'Tilda' (Mrs Matilda Loeb) was a rather wearing German friend of his mother's – '[she] never stops murmuring compulsively about thousands of caracters perfectly charming men & people etc whose names Im sort of beginning to know when they turn up in the flood ... she drives poor mother out of her mind.'

Despite Burra's lack of enthusiasm for the *Canterbury Prologue*, he had a special feeling for Paltenghi, another in the series of glamorous men who moved Burra in some way throughout his life. When Chappell was asked about Burra's sexual life, on two separate occasions, his first reaction was 'No idea, he'd never have told anyone.' His second was to mention David Paltenghi. Burra was visibly devoted to Paltenghi: Chappell, who had been observing Burra all his life, thought that he had never seen his friend's emotions so near the surface, and Paltenghi adored and admired the painter in return. They liked to be together, and to sit leaning against one another like small children, enjoying the first and simplest pleasure of the flesh, proximity.

Sadly, by the Fifties, Paltenghi's life was veering out of control. He developed gout in his thirties, which put paid to his dancing career, though he began a new and successful life in film and television, as director, producer, sometimes actor. Due perhaps to frustration, he also became a very heavy drinker, to an extent that made Burra's own occasional excesses seem downright moderate, and in 1961 died of a stroke. 'Its a terrible loss he used to manage to revivify everybody in the most extraordinary way,' said Burra sadly. Like Conrad Aiken, and later John Banting, he was one of the people who provoked Burra into drinking more himself, since associating with Paltenghi created a context in which keeping up was the only thing to do; whatever the cost. '3 days was my limit,' he confessed, 'by that time if gin was brought within 1 ft of me I gagged.'

Paltenghi brought Burra into his own, rather younger, social circle, which included a sculptor called Barbara Roett and her then-lover, a half African, half English medical student called Geoffrey Dove. Paltenghi (dressed, most inappropriately, as a monk) took Burra along to a fancy-dress party, also attended by Barbara and Geoffrey Dove (Barbara was a missionary – in a pot – and Dove was a cannibal). Barbara spotted Burra across the room, 'I thought he had a marvellous face, especially his nose, very attractive and sensible and amused.' She was rather tongue-tied at that stage of her life, so she sent Dove over to chat Burra up on her behalf. The two men got on immediately, and subsequently Barbara Roett and Dove invited Burra to a dinner-party. He brought Bar, with whom, as usual, he was staying, along with him.

This encounter was the point from which Bar's roller-coaster private life began to straighten out. Like Burra, she was greatly taken with Geoffrey Dove, but, more importantly, she and Barbara Roett were drawn together. In 1953, Bar ended a serious affair with Allan Morrison, a distinguished black journalist whom she had first met in 1944 when he was over in Europe reporting for *Stars & Stripes* – though they were in love, and he was fond of Max, the relationship had no future, for geographical reasons; he needed to live in New York because of his work (he wrote for *Ebony* after the war), she needed to be in London, so by mutual agreement they reluctantly bowed to the realities of their situation. She then embarked upon a relationship with Barbara Roett, who had given up on trying to make a living from sculpture and had become an interior designer (though she prefers the term 'carpenter'). When they moved in together, they were twenty-five and forty-nine respectively, and Max was five.[4] In 1955, Bar divorced Rhodes for desertion (he was living abroad by then), and changed Max's name and her own to Ker-Seymer. The two Barbaras were together for about thirty-five years, until Bar Ker-Seymer's eventual death in 1993.

Burra's feelings for Paltenghi complicated Bar's life considerably. She was trying to juggle the demands of her business and the care of her young son, but Burra was increasingly inclined to use his London weekends to get plastered in Soho with David Paltenghi, whereupon he would roll up at Bar's house, quite unaware of the extent to which he was being a nuisance. An evening that Bar reported to the other Bar, then in America, suggests the kinds of problem he could create (the 'Carmen' who is mentioned was her au pair).

Ed has been staying, with disasterous effect on my peace of mind, however Carmen has become very adept at finding new hiding places for the drink. One evening, just in time, we had managed to conceal everything except about 2 ins of Brandy, which David knew about anyway, so it was no good hiding. That was drunk in no time and David was getting a bit restless. I was trying to keep Ed reasonably sober as we had to attend a first night. Suddenly there was a ring at the flat door and there on the threshold was a very cheerful man from the wine society bearing in his arms a crate containing my whole months supply! Quick as a flash C and I pushed him out & up the back stairs into her room. He was very puzzled but we just made it. Carmen has been trying to find me someone for the holidays. She had decided on the ideal girl but after a night when David passed out on the floor, and Ed took a pillow and settled down for the night beside him (like Siamese twins, they refused to be parted) Carmen came to me and said she had decided this particular girl wouldn't do as she was 'Too narrow of the mind!' . . . the Agencies are inundated with desperate Mothers in the same predicament as me, and not a girl to be found anywhere.

[4] Barbara Roett had some difficulty at first in persuading Bar's friends to take the relationship entirely seriously. When Goronwy Rees came to stay in 1957, after he was hounded out of Aberystwyth, she was incensed to find that he had got into bed with Bar as of right. Bar's family treasures included a head of Napoleon by Canova. Barbara threatened to brain him with it, and he scuttled off to sleep elsewhere.

At that point (1954), Burra had been weekending with Bar for twenty-eight years. He tested her loyalty severely from time to time (losing a working mother holiday-cover for her seven-year-old is a pretty severe test by anyone's standards), but she remained his staunch and faithful friend.

Bar's life was strangely involved with alcoholics, for a woman who was herself a moderate social drinker. But she seems to have understood that quite a few of her friends, from Olivia and Marty through to Paltenghi, Banting and Patricia Highsmith, were driven by demons from which she was free. It was also very much the way of bohemians of her generation not to sit in judgement, but to take people as you found them. At any rate, she was endlessly tolerant and patient with all of them, as she was with Burra, who was a binge-drinker rather than an alcoholic, but unfortunately did much of his bingeing under her roof.

One of Burra's projects in the late Fifties, which was uncharacteristically nostalgic and backward-looking, was another theatre design. He was asked to take on a musical by Langston Hughes called *Simply Heavenly*, set in a Harlem bar; the plot, such as it was, dealt with the misadventures of Jess Semple, who is trying to get divorced and marry his girlfriend, while being distracted along the way by another girl. The best of the music, however, goes to another barroom habitué, Miss Mamie, a confirmed spinster, who is being pursued by a watermelon vendor. It was directed by Laurence Harvey, and Burra enjoyed himself. It was a long time since he had been to Harlem, but his memories were very happy ones, and it was a part of his past he was glad to revisit.

[I have been] very busy trying to arange one set containing 2 bedrooms a Bar Lenox Avenue 2 parallel streets disapearing in a vista, a panorama of Harlem a stoop, & a lobby – so I have plenty to work on. I went to an audition at the Victoria Palace, the West Indians were very insulted at being asked to speak in a 'murkan' accent! I left them to it now Mr H is in Paris looking for a girl I only hope a 'murkan'.

If it was a 'Miss Mamie' whom Harvey was looking for, the part was eventually taken by the excellent, and American, Bertice Reading, who had been working in England since 1955. But although a recent revival was successful and well received, suggesting there is nothing wrong with the play itself, the original production seems to have lacked sparkle.

Burra's own work, however, was much appreciated, not least for its impressive grasp of stagecraft. Clover wrote from Madrid, 'We've had a p.c. from Jimmy [Daniels] saying that Bar and Bum went to the first night of Simply Heavenly and the only things they cited were the costumes and décor – what a pity it isn't a better show.' This is borne out by an anonymous review in Burra's cuttings file: 'If I mention the designer Edward Burra before the author, it is because his revelation of bedrooms at different levels, a street scene and a bar where all the characters meet seemed to contribute more to the evening.'

The pattern of Burra's social life began to change post-war. Afternoon drinking clubs became increasingly a part of his life when he was on the loose in London. English licensing laws were strict in the Fifties. Pubs stopped serving at two-thirty, shut at three and did not reopen till seven, but the law was bendable by means of private-club licences, which allowed afternoon or after-hours drinking (which is how Burra was able to arrive more or less drunk at Bar's house in the early evening, as he frequently did). These were very different institutions from the 'gentleman's clubs' of Piccadilly, which he would not have been seen dead in.

The Mandrake Club in Dean Street, Soho, was one of his haunts. Jennifer Mortimer recalls it, and post-war Soho:

My first glimpse in the fifties proved to be rather disappointing; it was late evening, grey, and scarred by bomb damage. The signs of austerity had a firm grip. The streets were ill lit (good for some) and assorted ladies of the night smoked in doorways and gathered on corners . . . we turned into a shabby and seedy alleyway with rickety old houses grim with neglect . . . we crossed to the other side of the street and entered a dark doorway . . . suddenly light, guitar music, laughter and the aroma of delicious cooking assaulted our senses. I was immediately lost to the heady jollity which engulfed us. It was the Mandrake Club. Officially a chess club, it also embraced art students from nearby St Martins, actors, writers, painters, performers, and of course very serious chess players, and possibly some gangsters. Waitresses swirled about in their voluminous skirts on layers of petticoats with shoes laced up to the knees serving food and drink.

The patron of the Mandrake was Boris Watson, ex-proprietor of the pre-war Café An', and the club expressed his own passion for chess, which was by no means a gimmick; quite a lot of the floor-space was given over to tables with chessboards. There is nothing to suggest that Burra had the slightest interest in chess, or any other game, so he presumably went there for the general ambience.

The Colony Club Room, also known as Muriel's after its manager, a formidable lesbian called Muriel Belcher, was another Soho drinking club much favoured by artists – it was Francis Bacon's home from home – which Burra visited once in a while, but with his usual distaste for the obvious, he was much fonder of the Mandrake and the Stooge.

Im usually being a recluse in the Duke of Wellington Wardour St Done up in early Midevil Denham style nobody goes there Im so busy listening to other peoples conversations I never can leave till 2.30 when I move to 'The Stooge'.

Burra was often referred to as a 'recluse' by journalists, basically because he didn't go to his own exhibitions; though as he says later in the same letter, in his most 'Edwardian tart' mode, 'Aye have quayte a social layfe in may fashion dearie – & its got to be may fashion or no social layfe.' This basically meant clubs; he hated parties of all descriptions, and though he enjoyed good food, long, shapeless afternoons smoking, drinking and watching the world go by were more his style. He was by no means inevitably plastered at the end of these sessions; Denby Richards, who was also a habitué of post-war Soho, recalls him as a moderate imbiber by local standards. As well as the drinking clubs, he liked Porte, an Italian café in Old Compton Street, where one could sit for hours undisturbed with a cup of coffee and the papers. He noticed, and appreciated, in 1954 that suddenly, 'the whole of London is bristling with Espresso coffee machines Italian made so you can get wonderful coffee everywhere instead of a mysterious Beverage it's a nice change'.

However, one of his companions during these London afternoons was Dylan Thomas, a drinker of quite a different stamp; Richards used to see them together. They may have been introduced by John Banting, whom Dylan met towards the end of the war, when both men were working with the documentary film-maker Donald Taylor, or they may simply have gravitated towards one another out of mutual interest. Thomas was also a friend of Barbara Ker-Seymer's, and he and Burra certainly knew one another by 1943. Thereafter, they were periodically to be found together in the Swiss Hotel, which was one of Thomas's haunts. Burra was a long-term admirer of Thomas's verse: he was writing excitedly about the poems to Conrad Aiken as early as 1940, responding to Thomas's third (1939) collection, *The Map of Love*:

I bought the Map of Love and why I didnt do it befor I dont know but I was afraid of a disapointment. Its wonderful – can it be a <u>real</u> poet dearie? AudenspenderlieshMcNeesh[5] – who I allways maintain arent 'poets' at all should retire to their proper status – Dylan Thomas to me to be in the grand tradish as you might say in No. 2 'I make this in a warring absence when' rather reminds me of you in places!? Should we <u>admire</u> him? Does he toe the party layne? I havent seen the prose yet Have you got 'portrait of the artist as a young dog' from an examination of the few notices Ive seen it sounds very good rather frivolous Ime afraid some notices were rather <u>patronising</u> I don't think Dylan can be a 'serious' artist do you?

Burra was always, having suffered himself, inclined to dismiss the opinions of critics, and he bought all Thomas's collections as they came out. He perhaps liked the man for some of the same reasons that he liked Aiken himself, whom he missed: both were difficult and gifted, alcoholics, but people with whom really interesting conversation was possible.

Having discovered *Ulysses* at the end of the Forties, another of his great pleasures in the Fifties was Joyce's heir apparent, Samuel Beckett, a writer who became very important to him. Clover introduced him to *Molloy* in 1951–2, and thereafter he read everything of Beckett's as it came out. 'He saw himself in those tramps. Beckett expressed what he had always felt about life: "a long, muddy ditch along which one crawls with another tramp behind trying to stick a tin-opener up one's arse".' The essential nihilism of Beckett suited his mood, or one of his moods. He liked *The Unnamable*, the idea of living in a jar; 'All I want is a jar big enough.' He produced a number of paintings of large, inhabited teapots and coffee pots which may have been sparked by Beckett. In other moods, however, he also took to the crude final-frontier-conquering optimism of *Astounding Science Fiction*, and letters to Chappell (who shared this taste) were sprinkled with references to space-opera and sword & sorcery.

His next venture in terms of actual painting was unexpected. Between 1955 and 1957 he struck out in a completely new direction, and produced a series of still lifes which are barely recognisable as his. In contrast to his habit of a lifetime, these were painted from life with meticulous,

[5] A composite 'modernist poet' running together W.H. Auden, Stephen Spender, Cecil Day-Lewis and Louis MacNeice.

hyper-realist accuracy and without the expressive distortion so characteristic of his work. In *The Blue Striped Shirt*, the soft texture of the
striped cotton is contrasted with the high glaze of a Worcester tureen in
a manner that represents a technical *tour de force*: nobody else would have
attempted, let alone succeeded, in doing this in watercolour rather than
oil paint. At least three of these paintings involved (different) wicker
baskets, and they also all included vessels tilted forwards to display the
interior.

In the same period, he made a number of semi-abstract flower paintings; while the blooms are botanically identifiable, they are significantly
simplified, and above all characterised by a blazing, saturated intensity of
colour which gives them a disquieting liveliness – they are like flowers
from a dream, or seen under the influence of drugs; other paintings, of
garden and orchard scenes, evoke Samuel Palmer's *The Magic Apple Tree*.
Burra began experimenting with flower-painting from 1955, and returned
to flowers periodically for a number of years. These pictures were always
good sellers, which meant that the Corcorans encouraged him to work
in this vein, though he sometimes jibbed: in 1974, when he had got rather
bored with them, he wrote, 'They are pestering me to do Flowers – and
I thought of a nice bunch of plastic like they have in pubs.'

The death of Burra's father at the end of 1957 marked the end of
an epoch for the family. He was eighty-eight, and had been failing for
some months; Trudy, at the time, was in the grip of Asian flu, and intermittently delirious. Burra did his best to look after both of them, and
wrote to Chappell on Boxing Day, in a tone somewhere between defiance and numb despair:

thanks to anti biotics and moussec papa seems to be still living as of writing . . .
Mama is in the last stages of asiatic cholera . . . the countess Ritchie has got a nose
like a scarlet door knob that admits no air whatever . . . so things have not been
very gai . . .

I humbly & proudly suggest getting larger & larger & shorter & shorter &
blonder & blonder as the glorious years roll bye on the widest of all wide screens
. . .

Burra and his father seem never to have been close. However maddening
Burra found her at times, Trudy emerges from his letters (and her own)
with a rounded, human personality. Though Henry Burra was no

authoritarian, the Edwardian separation of the *paterfamilias* from his family seems to be reflected in the Burra household. There are no surviving adult letters exchanged between Burra and his father; no mention in letters to others of pursuits that they had in common, other than gardening during the war. The only hint of anything stirring beneath the blank surface of the relationship is that for Burra's twenty-fifth birthday, his father gave him a copy of *Moll Flanders* – presumably for its riotous depictions of London low-life. Otherwise, Henry Burra paid the bills, sat on committees, allowed his wife to rule the roost, fathered four children, saw two of them die and outlived the world he understood. Whatever he may have wanted, or thought, he seems to have kept it to himself.

When it finally came to it, at the New Year, Burra observed his father's gentle, old man's death with detached pity, and without sentiment.

I must say the dieing didnt seem unduly to put out Father, I stayd up from about 2 on on his last night & he had some trouble breathing & had some whiskey & hed all his wits about him. The next morning he was asking what he was having for breakfast & lunch! & became unconscious about 9.30 or so & didn't realy know anybody – breathing quite peaceful & drank a few spoonfuls from time to time & died at 2.15. it was as if bubbles rose from the bottom of a stagnant pond. I was dreading the funeral but it went off very nicely in Playden church & a lovely after-noon. As Ide had 4 double whiskies, I couldn't think why everybody looked so glum.

XIV

FLOWER POWER

BURRA went into the Sixties rather tottery. He had mumps in the spring of 1959, complicated, as usual, by another flare-up of spherocytosis-induced anaemia. Mumps is a particularly dangerous disease for men who catch it as adults, since a quarter to a third experience swelling of one or both testicles, which is painful and may cause sterility. But Burra had no active sexual life, and was not the slightest concerned about his capacity to sire children. More to the point, he had never confused his creative impulses with his virility. Veteran of many illnesses and no stranger to physical pain, he refused to be perturbed.

Am out of the clink which I was in such a state of boredom I nearly died (not of anemia) I soon picked up after the blood transfusion which took 4 hours ... As for the mumps – everyone was furious as I felt absolutely nothing at all my face was a x between the late Sydney Greenstreet & Charles Laughton ... I even had a swollen ball – that 'they say' is too awful not for me ... but of course by that time I was in full spate with a temp of 102 an enormous spleen and a swollen liver – the Dr from the hospital was struck dumb.

Burra was accustomed to having his strangely enlarged spleen treated as a wonder of medical science whenever he fell into the hands of doctors; as far as he was concerned, it made a change for them to be prodding his testicles instead, a matter for his own peculiar gallows humour.

He only had a spleen at all out of bloody-mindedness. The fact that it had swollen in the first place was a consequence of spherocytosis. It first gave trouble in 1934, as he told Bar: 'I got ill having eaten something the other day & had the Dr who at once said you have an enormous spleen

& may have pernicious aneamia at any moment you must do someth so I said anyth but an operation dear so I am going to a specialist.' The medical wisdom of the Twenties decreed that the spleen was an organ, like the appendix and the tonsils, that you were better off without, if it showed the slightest sign of misbehaviour. The specialist told him to have his spleen removed, and his mother sent him to London with the money for the operation. However, when he got to London, he stood up the surgeon and spent the money on getting himself tattooed in the Waterloo Road. The tattoo was on his left shoulder; a ferocious Chinese mask with a dagger. For no very obvious reason, Burra was fiercely and irrationally opposed to the idea of undergoing an operation of any kind, and successfully avoided the experience (apart from losing some teeth) until he broke his hip late in life.

In his case, unfortunately, the medical wisdom of the time was correct. Removing his spleen would have given him something far more like a normal life. It was the deformed red blood cells getting trapped in his spleen that caused the anaemia and jaundice which intermittently made his life a misery. Without it, there would have been nowhere for the cells to get stuck, and they would have functioned more like normal ones. The other problem with keeping his spleen was that if it swelled too much, it gave him agonising backache. He could deal with pain, but there was also a risk that if he had a bad fall while it was swollen, it might rupture, which is potentially fatal.

Thus he was very unwell at the beginning of the Sixties. Mumps he could take in his stride, but the anaemia was far more serious, and it remained a major problem for him throughout the decade. In the first half of the Sixties in particular, his red blood-cell count was sometimes so low that he could barely move. In 1961 he wrote, 'My blood count hasn't gone up as it ought so the Dr has produced some kind of Swedish iron injection guaranteed non carcinoginious in rats. I had one yesterday and felt I'd been kicked in the arse by a mule.' Another anaemic episode in 1963 laid him low for three months.

Each of the series of major illnesses he suffered in the course of his life did damage, from which he soldiered on without ever quite making a full recovery. As time went by, his friends, led by his sister Anne, Bar and Billy Chappell, entered upon the most benign of conspiracies, to keep Ed on the road, happy and productive, without ever forcing him to admit, to himself or anybody else, how frail and dependent he was becoming.

One acquisition of the Sixties was a doctor he really trusted. Not, unfortunately, his own doctor at home in Rye, but Barbara Roett's ex-lover, who remained a good friend of both Bars. Dr Geoffrey Dove was large, handsome and charming, with an interestingly chequered past. His first degree was in geology, from the Royal School of Mines, where he also became a runner of near-Olympic standard. He went out to Africa as a geologist with a mining company, and a serious accident plunged him seventy-five feet down a mine-shaft, leaving him paralysed from the waist down – temporarily, as it turned out. He gradually regained his mobility (though he always walked with a limp), but decided to give up his original profession and retrained as a doctor. He was partial to a drink, and he had personal experience of long-term pain; both these aspects allowed him to establish more of a friendly rapport with Burra than any medic had previously achieved.

But there was more to it than that. Burra loved him. Dove was one of the splendid, genial, attractive men that Burra fell for periodically throughout his life, and he became Burra's informal (and very tactful) adviser on the management of his health. Burra wrote to him both with gossip, as he did with all his friends, and with information about his physical woes, which he seldom mentioned to others. Thus he wrote to Dove in January 1963 about the misery he experienced that winter (the worst for almost a century), 'The NE wind has been my greatest X to bear as once that starts theres nothing to do but set the house on fire & lay down in it & even then the wind would blow the flames away from you.' Chapel House was not well built and, perched up on the ramparts of Rye, it was a wind-trap.

His father's death left Trudy Burra well provided for. Clearly, money had never been discussed between the parents, since she was anxious about her future after her husband's death: it was some time before she knew how she stood. Even four or five months after his father's death, Burra was writing to Aiken, 'I cant leave poor mother quite yet as she hasn't yet found out about the moolah & doesn't yet know if she can yet die in the manner to which she has been accustomed (!) I [am] fully prepared for the hospital and the gutter but then I have been terribly coarsened by my proceedings.' In fact, as befitted the scion of a banking family, Henry Burra had created a family trust with Anne, her cousin Austin Blomfield, and a solicitor with the splendidly implausible name of Waltheof Tooth as the trustees – though not Burra himself. As his father was well aware, he had no patience with business and did not understand money.

Trudy Burra feared and dreaded death duties – the almost superstitious fear of a woman who had never had to think about where her income came from – but the main purpose of a family trust was to avoid them. The major disposition of Henry Burra's property was within the terms of the settlement he had made on his marriage, essentially, provision for his wife and any future children. The residuary estate was held in trust for Burra and his sister in equal shares. Both sets of provisions were intended to ensure that money remained within the family. Despite Trudy's fears, there was a fair amount of it, much of it in property: three houses in Rye, of which Chapel House, then valued at £6,000, was the most valuable, two cottages and a substantial house (The Hooks) in Playden, opposite Springfield, which had previously been inhabited by Henry Burra's unmarried sister Denise ('Aunt Denny'), plus £39,663 in stocks. The total value of the estate held by the Trust was £55,646. Given the enormous rise in the value of property since the Fifties, it is hard to make this meaningful, but the residuary estate of which Burra had half had a net value of £5,859 (about £90,000 today). Property was then nothing like as significant as it is now. But at its most basic, if the stocks were safe and highly conservative, yielding an average 3 per cent, then Mrs Burra had a basic annual income of £1,200 from stocks, plus either rental value from five houses or the capacity to cash them in if she needed more capital.

Burra himself, if he left his inheritance in the bank, had also acquired a minute income of about £150 a year. He probably felt no richer, though, since the money was not straightforwardly his to spend, but only yielded income. In any case, it made little difference. There were times in the Thirties and Forties when he had been agonisingly short of money – he was earning very little, and his father seems to have discontinued his allowance once he was fully adult. But by 1960 he was earning more than he needed, since there was nothing much he wanted to spend money on. As far as he was concerned, his private income might as well not have existed.

Despite the chronic tiredness that was the principal symptom of his anaemia, Burra doggedly continued to paint, and his professional life became more and more upmarket. From 1952 onwards, due to the continued support of Gerald Corcoran, he had a one-man show at the

Lefevre Gallery more or less every other year. Thanks to the Corcorans, Rothenstein and his own talent, he had become a well-known painter whose work was represented in national collections, without his needing to do anything about it. The establishment began to make room for him. Clover recalled that in 1961:

The Royal Academy rang him up when I was staying with him at Chapel House . . . He was painting in his top-floor room that had yellowing pages of *The Times* pasted over the windows when the light was too strong. Frederick, the manservant, shouted from below: 'The Royal Academy on the phone, Mr Edward.' 'Tell them to fuck off, I'm busy,' Ed shouted back. They rang again next morning. The same reply was bowdlerised to them by Frederick. 'They want me to go and get my medal,' Ed said, 'and have lunch. I wouldn't mind being an ARA [Associate of the Royal Academy] if I didn't have to do that.' But they were adamant and so was Ed . . . he only accepted a CBE when told it could be sent to him.

This was not so much arrogance as exhaustion. 'I just cant be bothered to move the Academy gets very busy & tried to make me come to lunch on the 28th [May] but I put it off till June 18th I wish they would leave me alone I don't want their horrible old Academy having done without it 40 odd years.' In fact, his blood count was so low his doctor had forbidden him to go to London, saying that if caught any kind of infection, it might kill him. He was feeling no better in June. Going to Hastings to see a film left him so tired that he had to go to bed at half past nine. He could not realistically undertake a trip to London just then, and he was not prepared to explain why, so he put them off again. Permanently, in the event.

Burra often gave the impression of being difficult to long-suffering souls such as institutional secretaries. Some of this was genuinely to do with preferring to pursue his own course, or with agreeing to things when he was drunk and then forgetting about them. His letters suggest, though, that he was habitually rather courteous and obliging, but that he often did not have the energy to cope with demands that a man in normal health would have had no trouble with at all. Thus he might agree to something, and then become enraged and sulky when it turned out to be a bit more than he could cope with. But he absolutely refused to start using his very genuine debility as any kind of excuse or explanation. He had spent his entire life defying his health, and insisting on living to the full in his own way, and he much preferred giving the impression that he was a bloody-minded and amnesiac drunk, which had the advantage of keeping people off his back. Bar scolded him in 1967, 'I'm so sorry about that terrible aneamia attack. Needless to say you do nothing about these impending attacks, such as having B.12 injections or taking iron or something. I'm sure you needn't have them so badly.' This might have been the case, but paradoxically, Burra seems to have regarded occasional crippling bouts of illness as part of the price he paid for having a life. His mother had allowed her health to become her hobby: because of his deep affinity with her, he was aware of the danger of turning into a version of her as he got older. Managing himself in the way that Bar suggests would have been a kind of admission of defeat.

In one respect, Burra's life began opening out in the Sixties. With the invention and commercial development of high-speed hovercrafts, the amount of cross-Channel ferry traffic increased enormously, a particular benefit to those who lived on the south coast. One of the new minor pleasures of Burra's life subsequently was nipping over to Boulogne on a day trip for a French lunch with his sister, but work was as important to him as ever. 'If I don't work I can hardly have the force to get up and stay in bed reading till 10.30.' Painting was necessary to him; when he was working on a painting, he was focused and could cope with his life, and even enjoyed it in his own way. Enforced breaks, whether periods in hospital or even holidays, not only made him more and more anxious and unhappy, but he began to find them actively stressful.

He also did not drink – or more precisely, did not get drunk – at home, only when he considered himself on holiday. 'Bumble asked me to stay a few days ... & I couldn't face it. I shall only start drinking again if I go to London, out of desperation & here Im not tempted to except on a day trip to Boolong & the next day I didn't feel very good.' Permanently tired as he was, the relentlessness of never-had-it-so-good London was beginning to get him down. 'Oxford strasse & all the Bright (dead) lights in the West End <u>depress me</u>! to such a state that I must be drunk then I feel quite cheerful – for a <u>time</u>.'

He fell out with Barbara Ker-Seymer briefly in 1962 because they had a date to meet at a cinema, he got blind drunk in the Capacannina Club with the manager of Wheeler's Restaurant and inadvertently stood her up. He was generally courteous about keeping appointments, but he had always guarded his independence, his right to disappear. It was hard for him to acknowledge that he could not ask quite as much of his friends as he had of his parents, whom he had, on occasion, left wondering what had happened to him for weeks at a time. Or, equally unpalatable, that he had reached a stage in life in which failing to turn up would cause people to start worrying and wonder if they should ring the police or the hospitals.

The estrangement with Bar did not last long. He had of course been a regular visitor to the first house she shared with Barbara Roett and Max, which was in Marylebone, but in 1963 the family moved to Islington, to a house just off Upper Street, which he liked enormously. It is one of an elegant terrace of small, gracefully proportioned eighteenth-century town-houses in dark brick, where he could lie on a convenient sofa in the drawing-room looking out of the back window. Islington rapidly became his favourite part of London. 'It will probably be ruined & made terribly quainty dainty wee before you can say knife at present its strictly Non U & working & pubs full of ladies pickled in years of Guiness & gin & very scruffy and a wonderful market open all Sunday morning' . . . 'I go and stay the week end . . . & spend a happy Sunday morning in Chapel Market & surrounding Bars full of crones & Irish men – and various members of the "oldest North London criminal families" conspiring in corners – sometimes they even dance' (this is probably represented in *The Juke Box*, 1964–5). His idea of bliss was 'ruminating for hours in Wards Irish House drinking double bells with an occasional pint of guiness! What I realy enjoy doing & then going to the cinema & having egg & chips after.'

He had loved films since the Twenties: Max Ker-Seymer remembers him particularly liking cowboy movies, but he also became passionately fond of Hammer horror films.

Have been going to nothing but Horror pictures! Mostly made by Hammer films in Technicolour with 'real' sets & a very gothic 'Rasputin the mad monk' 'The Reptile' 2 stories freely adapted from H.P. Lovecraft! Freida Jackson held forth in a very high class English accent from a 4 poster bed heavily (& happily) hung with thick crêpe & suddenly burst out with an axe & a completely discomposed face made of foam rubber and attacked the heroin. She realy gave me quite a turn – it was called the Light from beyond Space & the plants in the conservatory began to strangle people as nameless things were carefully preserved in the cellar: Dracula & Fu Manchu & one about Zombies by Boris Karloff dear old soul I have a mania for these things.

Burra was a long-term devotee of horror fiction, which typically sets up an idyllic, or at least ordinary, *mise en scène* and subverts it, a notion basic to his world-view. He always preferred schlock to art-house films, the worse the better.

The films did not filter directly into his painting, but he produced a number of pub pictures in later life. *The Boozer*, painted in the 1970s, may be an Islington picture, *The Agricultural Arms* certainly is. These were the first interiors he had painted for a considerable time. His old interest in social interaction had returned, though with a difference. The clientele are often sharply observed, but they tend to be transparent, superimposed on one another like drifting shadows, or revenants (or even, Eliot's 'crowd flowing over London Bridge', in *The Waste Land*). The observation of detail in *The Boozer* (bumfreezer jackets, carcoats, denim suits, girls with little knitted hats over long hair; 1974 bang on the button) is as particular as ever, but it is the fact of people congregating, amicably coexisting, that is the focus and not the people themselves. He explained this as a function of increasing age. 'Don't you find as you get older, you start seeing through everything?' A letter he wrote to John Banting from an unsmart hotel in rural Herefordshire may also shed light on this aspect of his work. 'What I like about this part is its rather <u>run down</u> & everyone looks like real people for realy in the Souse East & Tinker Belle part of England people arent quite real to me.' Like Bosch and Brueghel, whom he admired, he had a tendency to visualise metaphor; to paint, for example, a romantic girl 'with stars in her eyes' as a girl with stars for eyes (in *Izzy Ort's*).

He continued to travel widely within England, with Anne, or Chappell, or both, and from 1965 developed a particular attachment to Harrogate. Clover retired from the British Council in 1960, and came back to a pied-á-terre in Islington, near Bar, though Antonio continued to be involved with the family estates at Gabía Grande until 1965, when, as she explained to Conrad Aiken (with whom she was very friendly): 'the state of Spain may bring Antonio over, penniless, as in 1936, he is holding out there on our savings and his gambling at poker and on the Market, but agriculture has collapsed'. She added, 'I'm waiting for us to know if Edward's nylon firm, which has been taken over by ICI, is going to be moved to Harrogate from Knightsbridge. If it is, I'll have to go with him, let this flat and get one in the North – I feel like Mrs Gaskell! Ed Burra hopes we shall go up there as he'd like to stay with us, he says the South is getting unbearably smug and overcrowded.' This indeed all turned out as projected, and the Pertinez family lived together in Harrogate until 1971. Burra was a frequent visitor. He loved the town, and he found the flat comfortable, since Antonio Pertinez shared his views on the importance of being properly warm. He also got on well with Antonio himself, who much preferred speaking Spanish to English and was consequently always pleased to see Burra.

Sometimes he went up on the train by himself, sometimes Anne took him up – she was a dauntless driver, who would do Rye to Harrogate in a day. Edward Pertinez had a car, so with one or the other as chauffeur, Burra explored northern England. On all these travels, he absorbed and responded to the English countryside. He did not sketch on site. His normal practice was to sit in the car and study the scene intently, and once at home, to work up a distillation of the landscape that had most interested him, from memory. His primary reference points for landscape painting were the Romantics; the names that crop up in his letters are Blake, Fuseli and John Martin rather than Paul Nash, or English water-colourists such as Cotman. His treatment of skies, for example, owes something to the watercolours of Blake and Fuseli. He became particularly fond of the bare, bleak landscape of the Yorkshire moors.

When he was at home, he succumbed to some extent to the latest contribution to the sapping of the nation's moral fibre, which was television, though like much of his generation, he never switched allegiance from radio. Once he was living on his own, he owned a transistor, but did not acquire a TV. Television was first broadcast in 1936 (service was suspended during the war, and resumed in 1946), but the medium did not really achieve lift-off until the mid-Fifties. Burra's parents, like many other Britons, seem to have first encountered television at the coronation of Elizabeth II (in 1953). They certainly watched it: 'Mama said the show was wonderful on Teevey you might have been right in the abbey,' Burra noted from Boston. Since he could only paint by natural light, evenings were in any case waste time for him.

At the beginning of the Sixties, his mother acquired a set of her own, which lived in her room, and for the first year he showed mild symptoms of becoming an addict. As a connoisseur of schlock, he found that the programmes' lack of sophistication did not necessarily render them unenjoyable. He commented to Chappell, 'we had part of yr revue' (*Living for Pleasure*, directed by Chappell, which was on at the Garrick) 'on the TV on Tuesday I must say it made the rest of the programmes look like the Biggleswade womens Institute Christmas concert party'. But he enjoyed some of the offerings in his own sardonic way; he was intensely amused, for example, by *Madame Butterfly* with the great – and large – Australian soprano Joan Hammond as Cio-Cio-San; 'one of the funniest things Ive ever seen', though as he recognised himself, his amusement was 'rather unfair realy as at a safe distance – say in Covent Gdn she wouldn't have looked to bad but nothing is spared on TV'.

The medium was too new for the production side to have quite grasped that opera-singers in close-up can look very strange indeed, but Burra, inevitably, was not prepared to shut his eyes or cooperate with good intentions. His mother was seriously interested in opera, so it is to be hoped that he did not infuriate her by rolling about in hysterics. His laughter, fortunately, was almost soundless, like his screams (he screamed often, a Twenties mannerism). But he rapidly became bored with the whole thing, since by 1967 he was writing, 'Thank God I don't have to look at it as its in her room.' He loathed milieux, public or private, where the television was on all the time. Non-stop TV was his only problem with the Pertinez household, fond though he was of them. The only programme there is any kind of evidence for his watching after he was living on his own is *Poldark* – the word appears in large letters in his 1975 diary (it went out in October that year). The attraction was probably less the drama than the ravishing Cornish scenery – he loved Cornwall, and painted it often – so perhaps he took the trouble to go round to Anne's to watch it.

One of the things that he came to enjoy once more as his zest for life returned was fashion. His interests as a painter had moved on from recording the passing scene, but his observation of day-to-day quiddities was as lively as ever. After nearly two whole decades of austerity and make-do, the young had finally broken out in style, and he appreciated it enormously. He had enjoyed the mad little hats of the Thirties, but he also adored the beehives and backcombing of 1959, and avidly collected extreme examples, just as he had done in his younger days – 'I saw one seated in the 2 magots [the café Les Deux Magots, in Paris] that was at least 2 feet high next to a hair do in brightest ginger orange.' Bar Ker-Seymer, always stylish, acquired a black nylon fur beehive hat while they were on holiday together in Paris. In the early Sixties, women's fashion was still ladylike: bouffant, lacquered hair, panty girdles, knee-length pencil skirts and stiletto heels added up to a look which was chic and sophisticated, but restrictive.

Interested though he was in women's fashion, Burra was even more appreciative and observant of what was worn by men (he made a painting called _Zoot Suits_, for example, in 1948, current whereabouts unknown). He was fascinated by a suit that Desmond Corcoran was flaunting in 1962:

Desmond appeared in a very sharp suit for work at the galleries! Digne de Bunny. with a very long double waistcoat with buttons in a V & very high at the neck. it was beautifully made but he must have drugged the Tailor to have induced him to produce anything so oo tray it looked very nice.

In the early Sixties, men's fashions were beginning to change profoundly. For the whole of Burra's lifetime, gentlemen's bespoke suits had been highly conservative garments made to be worn for decades; and only lesser breeds, such as cads, spivs and queers, sought to attract attention by their dress. Desmond Corcoran's fab gear presaged a change of attitude; the 'Peacock Revolution' was under way.

It is worth noting that Burra's reference point is Bunny Roger, part of the gang of friends who had gone to Toulon together in the early Thirties. Roger continued to see a lot of Bumble, Bar and Billy Chappell, though he and Burra met only occasionally. By the early Sixties, he had become a director of Hardy Amies, and was one of the few oldies to be considered genuinely cool by the fashionable young. Thus Andrew Loog Oldham:

Bunny was unapproachably aloof but I learnt enough from him by just looking. He paid meticulous attention to every detail of his appearance. Everything he did was a piss-take and a celebration. He looked almost sixty but he used to prance about in the most amazing three-piece chalk-striped suits. His jackets were so tightly waisted that they flared out like a skirt. The trousers were tighter than drainpipes and his shirts had high, rounded, stiff starched collars. His lips were permanently pursed, and he always wore a grey bowler hat, pearl tiepin, make-up, eyeliner and a carnation.

Bunny's self-presentation in his indefinitely extended middle age was as overtly queer as that of Quentin Crisp. 'Where are your pearls?' a taxi driver jeered, watching him powdering his nose in the back of the cab. 'Never with tweeds,' was the crisp response.[1] In Burra's generation, extreme dandyism was an essentially homosexual phenomenon, but the real point of Desmond Corcoran's new suit is that by 1962 hip tailoring could be sported by a heterosexual member of the professional classes during working hours, which marks a significant change in men's attitudes to themselves.

Another great feature of the Sixties was moral panics. Burra's take on one such, the Profumo affair (1961), was characteristically sensible.

What a squawk dearie because Mr Profumo has been to bed with the same tart as an attache at the Russian embassy! ... Im sorry for La Belle Keeler who seems to be chased from pillar to post never a moments peace poor thing West Indians shooting through the door Mr Profumo Dr Boyd and all ...

At the time, the English press was writing about Christine Keeler as if she was the whore of Babylon. As her solicitors pointed out, 'Those who speak of her without charity seem to take no account of her youth nor of the fact that since the age of fifteen her manifest immaturity has been consistently exploited by a so-called adult society.' But Burra was never to be caught up in any hysteria not generated by himself.

One problem that loomed larger as he got older was that the diminished liver function which went along with his anaemia made it hard for him to recover from the drinking bouts which were part of his life. Sometimes he got drunk because he felt like it, or out of depression, or in order to fortify himself for dealing with strangers, but often, as had been the case with his relationship with David Paltenghi, his motivation was more complex.

John Banting re-entered Burra's life when they were both in their sixties. They had first encountered each other around 1925, when they were both surrealists interested in black culture, and since Banting was gay, good-looking, interested in ballet and based in Paris, they must have bumped into each other repeatedly in Select, the Dôme, the bars of the rue de Lappe and at parties. They were close enough in the late Twenties/early Thirties for Banting to paint Burra's portrait (it is now

---

[1] No real lady of the Edwardian era wore pearls (suitable for town) with tweeds (country). Quite impossibly vulgar.

in the National Portrait Gallery), but in the intervening decades their paths diverged. However, when the lease of his London flat ran out in 1956, the chronically impecunious Banting moved into a disused small house, 62 Church Square, Rye, which belonged to a friend, and where sooner or later he must have bumped into Burra, since it was just round the corner from Chapel House. When that lease also ran out, he moved to Hastings, where he settled in 1965.

Banting had remained friendly with Bar Ker-Seymer, with whom he had also once been close: when she set up her photographic studio in Bond Street after Olivia Wyndham had deserted her for Edna Lloyd Thomas at the end of 1929, it was Banting who decorated it. When Banting's beloved friend Nancy Cunard died in 1965, he wrote to Bar to see if she had photographs or negatives. She did not, and wrote regretfully, 'Unfortunately all my negatives got lost what with the war and one thing and another. I have got one print of Nancy in woollen anklets and a turban lying prone on a piece of corrugated iron.' But after that, they resumed correspondence and saw one another quite often.

Banting was something of a mess by the Sixties; and living on an annual allowance from a rich boyfriend of his youth (perhaps Edward Sackville-West). George Melly comments, 'By that time whiskey had destroyed his ability to offer anything beyond scribbles.' His archive in the Tate includes a pathetic collection of autobiographic fragments, many of them written in the third person, as if by a journalist 'visiting Mr Banting at home'. Much of this material was manifestly written when he was extremely drunk, and it makes painful reading. His main interest other than alcohol seems to have been plants. His flat was full of them, and they are often discussed between himself, Bar and Burra. He lived with a remarkably silent boyfriend called Jim or Jimbo, who was generally believed to be Glaswegian, but was eventually discovered to be an ex-fisherman from Devon. 'John remained a surrealist in spirit,' says Melly. 'Ed Burra and John used to roam Hastings Old Town together.'

It was impossible to spend any time in John and Jim's company without getting plastered, since they were both alcoholics. Bar pleaded with Banting to be more responsible towards Burra, probably in 1965.

I get a bit alarmed when I hear that you have been on the bash together as he is not in the best of health, to say the least of it, and drink in large quantities is <u>fatal</u>, however he does seem to be a bit more careful these days, since his Mother has been so ill.

Expecting Banting to police Burra's drinking was wholly unrealistic. Burra himself found Banting's drinking a problem, fond though he was of him. 'Friday I went out with Banting and Jim we ended up at the Pipemakers Arms which had an extension till midnight . . . the next day I was a wreck as usual & that evening John rang up and said do come round and have a few Bloody Marys I was so horrified at the idea I screamed NO NO I really cannot spend my life feeling ghastly all the time & I suspect J gets "bored" & just wants company. he can talk to me and no holds barred!' Banting became very dependent on Burra for emotional support, and received it. In one of his last letters he wrote, 'Dear Ed you are my consolation in this wilderness'.

As Burra was too essentially kindly to say, Banting was living in the past, which made him saddening company. One of the casualties of the generation of the Bright Young People, he had a lifelong tropism towards the beautiful and doomed. In his sixties, addled by booze and unable to paint, he was dimly aware that his place in history was as an ubiquitous 'friend of' – friend of Brian Howard and Harold Acton, and thus connected with the Eton-and-Oxford set, who, as a good Communist, he despised while remaining susceptible to their glamour;[2] friend of Nancy Cunard, of Dolly Wilde, of Dylan Thomas, of any number of golden lads and lasses whose self-destructive instincts brought them to disaster. Brian Howard died in his arms, and he was central to getting people together for Howard's collage biography (*Portrait of a Failure*) put together by Marie-Jacqueline Lancaster, which was published in 1968.

Burra himself was either bored or distressed by looking back. There can have been few people as intelligent who have ever existed more entirely in the present. He wrote rather sadly to Banting, 'Oh these memories down Memory Lane, theyre all very well in small quantities but not be heaped on as one goes on.' He kept old letters – he kept everything – but refused to reread them. His basic self-discipline never failed him, and he was essentially forward-looking. Unlike Banting, once the hangovers started interfering with his work, he began throttling

[2] Both aspects are represented in his *Blue Book of Conversation* (1946).

back, though the 'out of body' sensation of being moderately drunk was far too important to him for him ever to stop entirely.

However, when he was away from home, he added Banting to his collection of regular correspondents, which must have been somewhat easier at times than actually being in his company. Despite his often-expressed dislike of talking about 'Fart', he did, in fact, like to talk about painting and painters, but only with fellow-practitioners who knew what he was talking about. It was intellectualising about painting that bored him. He comments, for example, 'I think Dubuffet paints with a wonderful technique – very meticulous, et d'un gout exquis. Despite sinister remarks re "modern painters" we are asked to admire & who copy graffitti! By the Pres of the Royal Acad Sir Wheeler Dealer (now retired) you need as much technique to copy graffitti as a horses arse as Ellen Terry said to Irving' (he often drops into French when writing to Banting).

Burra's pattern of travel changed in the Sixties. He never caught up with the concept of travelling by air, and all his visits to America were by boat. The only time he was ever on a plane was in 1971, when the art critic Barrie Sturt-Penrose suggested that the two of them pay an impromptu visit to Belfast. The plane was just about to take off when Penrose became violently ill, and he and Burra had to be unloaded so that he could be taken to hospital (he turned out to have kidney-stones). But since getting across the Channel had become so fast and simple by the mid-Sixties, Burra extended his European travels, crossing from Dover to Calais and taking trains onwards from there.

He went to the Netherlands and Belgium for the only time in 1964. He adored Rotterdam (which is not only Europe's biggest port, but has a wonderful art museum with several paintings by Bosch, and much else to interest him); but inevitably, having absorbed the contents of the Museum Boijmans van Beuningen, he gravitated to the dockside bars. Having visited the Pub Maewest (a name that was bound to attract him) and the Golden Gate:

I went to another one I don't know the name which had the drunkest people in it Ive seen since I left Avenue B. & a screaming queen who flew in a rage with his Boy friend. a very neat young man in a smart overcoat & a hairdo, & suddenly bellowed in English Get OUT! And denounce me if you DARE!! No one took any notice at all ... by that time everyone was being treated to Beers by a blue grey figure who had obviously been on the bar for days as he had quite a patina! I

couldnt think why I was surrounded by glasses. I then retired in fairly good order
... the Hague ... I very much liked & it has some eccentrics I noted of the first
water – they are getting rather <u>rare</u>.

He did, of course, also visit all the great art museums in Amsterdam
and The Hague; and was intrigued by the modernist flavour of Dutch
post-war rebuilding, which was far more architecturally daring than the
English approach to the same problem.

In September 1965, Burra went back to Florence, where he had not
been since 1927, and stayed with American friends who were in the habit
of taking a summer flat there, the novelist Jennings Rice and his wife Marie,
whom he had met via the Aikens; Rice was one of his regular correspondents from the war years onwards. He enjoyed this enormously (not least
because Marie Rice was a superb cook in the Italian mode), and repeated
the visit in the following year. The Florence trips gave rise to one of Burra's
most beautiful paintings, a view of the bridges over the Arno. He did not
quite have the stamina for a third visit; 'the traffic and the noise is something terrible I think let alone crowds of milling visitors'. He made a thorough and careful inspection of the Uffizi collection during his 1966 visit,
but found it almost too much for him. 'I was trodden on & mangled trying
to get into an elevator in the Uffizi by about 20,0000 Amurkan young ladies.
it must have been one of those Finishing schools they nearly finished me.
I took refuge up about 4000 marbel stairs the pix are at the Top and you
can perfectly well see all the (unpopular) pictures which nobody dreams
of looking at – no time my dear. I got to everything in the end.'

He was surprised, and pleased, in June 1967 to find his liking for
Italy reciprocated: he received a letter saying that he had won the
Marzotto prize of three million lire. The prize was awarded by a large
Italian textile group, as a piece of arts sponsorship, which they described
as 'un momento di vivace ed intelligente mondanità'.[3] 'Well dearie I
was surprised,' he wrote, 'as I never thought they gave prizes to anything
that wasnt "abstract" & the size of the Front of Warner bros – disgusting
isnt it? ...' This prize was for a painting called *The Fates*, which he
had forgotten about (actually, a very powerful painting from 1937).
Communications went adrift because he was travelling for quite a bit
of the early part of the year, entirely in England, and the letter they

[3] 'A moment of lively and informed worldliness'.

sent to him was not forwarded. He eventually discovered from reading the *Daily Telegraph* that he was supposed to be receiving the prize in Valdagno that very day. The Marzotto prize was awarded for the last time the following year, and an exhibition was toured, which he saw at the Royal College of Art; noting, again, the judges' unfashionable liking for figurative painters.

Burra's own art of the Sixties develops themes he had begun to explore in the previous decade. There is a good deal of landscape, and some still lifes. Another theme was violence, abhorrent to his own nature, but an aspect of human life he had been thinking about since the war. *The Straw Man* (1963) is a particularly important painting in this respect; a group of tough, working-class men are kicking a straw-stuffed dummy with all their force; a scene both sinister and pointless, rendered more so by a mother and child who are walking past unperturbed, and two other men in conversation. It is the figures' obvious delight in their own strength that gives the image its curious viciousness. It harks back to earlier pictures such as *Riot* (1948–50), an onrushing, red-hued crowd lit by flaming torches, a scene which represents one of Burra's personal nightmares, since he loathed being in any kind of a crowd at any time.

Burra is generally perceived as a satirist; a benigner version of Georg Grosz. But very few, if any, of his pictures of the Sixties and Seventies have any satiric component whatsoever, and few seem to me even playful. Most are lyric or melancholy, a few mystical, some ugly and disturbing. But 'satire', in the Sixties, became a dominant cultural mode, as it has remained: it has little, if any, power to shock. *That Was the Week that Was* did not discomfit its audience, and did not expect to, it was too cool for that. *Private Eye* was similarly, to borrow a phrase of Simon Armitage's, on a prejudice-confirming mission. Sixties' satirists became, as they have remained, licensed jesters. No wonder that Burra went somewhere else.

One London art event of the mid-Sixties he seems (unusually) rather sorry to have missed is the Marcel Duchamp retrospective at the Tate in 1966, which was a major occasion: the old guard of English surrealists turned up en masse for a private view and dinner. Banting went, because his old friend Julian Trevelyan had given him his private view card, and stayed with Bar; he knew Duchamp from 1930, a year in which he would have been both attractive and full of promise. They had some conversation, perhaps saddening for both; Banting knew no-one else in the room. Burra wrote, 'I'm glad you made it to the Fish Fry (and Chianti) I seem to have gone to Harrogate at the <u>wrong</u> moment – when I got back I found a p view card, to be played on the phonograph.'

Another thing that emerges from Burra's letters of the mid-Sixties is that he was increasingly involved with his own domestic life, though Frederick Rose remained the principal organiser of Chapel House, with the assistance of a cleaner and cook who came in during the day: Edward Pertinez, who was very intimate with the household, is clear that it was Frederick who kept the place going. He looked after Burra's mother, who was demanding and difficult, and indeed, after Burra himself, but so tactfully that Burra was unaware of it, and did not resent it, though he normally loathed being interfered with. However, cooking devolved to Burra at least some of the time: Mrs Smith did lunch, but if Frederick was not available, and as Trudy Burra always had her breakfast in bed, someone had to do it for her, and someone had to make supper. 'Over a week after you left,' Burra wrote to Chappell, '2 lbs of the sausages were unearthed in the Fridge! Even I didn't dare eat them I wish Ide known – they must have thought I was saving them for my little gathering of Dark Things on the Gibbet marsh.'[4] Another letter to Chappell similarly bears witness both to an avid reading of H.P. Lovecraft and his imitators, and to Burra's increasing domestication: 'Thank you so much for the lovely shirt Ive been wearing it ever since. Its such nice stuff and I must wash it soon. I like the colour I have a tendancy to DARK creatures of the DARK and crocodile people buried for countless eons of unrecorded time and mysteriously appearing in a small colony in the Bronx.'

His sister, despite her commitments in Northiam, spent a lot of time in Chapel House, as Trudy Burra got more and more tottery. Anne's husband Colin Ritchie was also the product of a loving and united family, and from 1964 Burra often mentions Colin's brother, Kenneth, Lord Ritchie, who also lived in the Rye area, at Bosney on Camber Sands. He had cancer of the throat in 1963, and his wife Joan died in the same year, so he began to spend more time with his brother and Anne. They all came to the Burras for Christmas lunch at Chapel House

---

[4] The Gibbet Marsh is an area down by the River Rother, under the windows of Chapel House.

in 1964, which was not an unmixed success, since he had undergone an operation for the cancer in September and had had to learn to talk in whispers, which Burra found rather difficult. 'I cant hear him very well as Ime deaf & used to howling all the time but I should soon get used to it anyway I think its marvelous & he looks much better & Im sorry to have to say, younger and <u>slimmer</u>, having been removed from the late Lady J's cuisine.' Burra became rather deaf in the Sixties (as did Bar), something that increased his difficulty in dealing with crowds and strangers.

Despite practical problems, relations between Burra and his sister's family were civil. He was fond of Ken Ritchie, and comments that Anne and Colin are going off for a holiday together in Devonshire, adding casually, 'I wouldn't mind going down there.' He assumes he would be welcome, and he seems to have been right. However, Bar was under the impression that Burra tolerated rather than appreciated his brother-in-law: 'I don't think Ed cares for Colin . . . very much as he is a terrible hypochondriac which is a thing Ed hates, being a silent sufferer himself.' Conversely, though Ritchie himself was a heavy drinker and smoker, which at least eased one possible area of tension, Burra was far too bohemian in his habits of life for his brother-in-law; and also, too flippant in his modes of speech; when for example, he referred to Brickwall School as 'Narkover Academy' (from the surreal world of 'Beachcomber'), he would not have intended to give offence, but may well have done so. This may explain why Anne tended to take Burra off on his own. It is noticeable that the dozens of surviving postcards Anne sent to her brother were always signed 'A', never 'A & C'. There is only one in the whole of the Tate's collection which is addressed to Burra by his brother-in-law, and it supports Bar's observation by being a litany of complaint: 'A most unfortunate Hol. First A and now me with ghastly colds . . .'

Trudy Burra had a life of her own, post-widowhood; she had her own circle of friends (or, as in the case of Mrs Loeb, mentioned in the previous chapter, at the very least, of people she had known for a long time). However, Edward Pertinez felt that she had taken the death of her husband very badly. Though he might find himself staying for weeks at a time during the summer holidays, she was, to him, a remote figure who lived withdrawn in her own world: he saw more of Anne, who did not live in the house, than of Trudy, who did. But she was a determined and assiduous keeper-up of family ties. Chappell commented, 'to me the countryside round Rye is mostly populated by the cousins and the in-laws of the Burras. I do not know and have never attempted to find out the exact numbers of the regiment.' Burra kept up with them to some extent, particularly his Brodrick cousins, but his mother, as 'Aunt Trudy', was a conspicuous nodal point within a large extended family. After her major collapse in the autumn of 1964, he observed, with respect to that Christmas, 'Everybody thinks they will tire mummie & havent dragged along all their terrible children & so on to see Aunt Trudy who just *loves* to see them' – it is a fair assumption that before that, they did.

One important new friend Burra made in the Sixties was Francis Bacon. Burra had hugely admired Bacon's retrospective in 1961. John Banting introduced them in 1962, as Burra mentions in a letter to Conrad Aiken; after which they spent a lot of time together boozing in the Colony Room and other Soho haunts. They had a good deal in common: both patrician in background and queer in foreground, much of an age (Bacon was two years younger), stubbornly individual. Both heavy drinkers, indifferent to comfort, painting as if their lives depended on it in a compost of junk and pinned-up postcards (Bacon's studio is now on view, since it has been transported in its entirety to the Hugh Lane Gallery in Dublin). Grey Gowrie observes, 'In the annals of British modern art, only Francis Bacon, perhaps, revealed his own personality as forcefully in all his work as Burra. Both were thoroughly uncompromising artists with a shared indifference to the fate of their paintings once these were complete. Burra was even more extreme in this regard than Bacon, who would at least attend important exhibitions of his own.'

Another, quite different, new friend he acquired was a woman called Monica Wodehouse, who simply rang the bell at Chapel House one day in 1960 while her lover Scott cowered behind the garden wall, expecting to hear the door slammed in her face. Normally, Burra fiercely resented such intrusions from total strangers, but something about her took his fancy, and he invited them in. In the course of conversation, he discovered that her mother had been a dancer in Paris, and Mistinguett's understudy, and that Scott worked in films. He wrote to Monica regularly for the rest of his life, and they saw each other once in a while and had a good scream. Part of her charm for him was her energy and spirit; another part was that Barbara disapproved of her. His circle, in their fifties and sixties, was becoming more and more establishment; and whereas he was patient of this with respect to his sister and brother-in-law, he was inclined to feel that some of his friends needed shaking up a bit. 'Mrs R [Bar Ker-Seymer] does not approve of M realy. Mrs R is becoming terribly Boorgwah in her old age. its those relations in Summerset or wherever Flower shows & wimmins institutes & that – Blood will out.'

Apart from reminiscing about the *monstres sacrés* of Twenties' Paris with Monica, Burra occasionally found himself interacting with contemporary stars when he was out and about with Bumble Dawson, who worked for Warner Bros. Back in 1945, he had enjoyed finding himself, in her company, having lunch with Laurence Olivier and his wife Vivien Leigh, and she continued periodically to take him with her into the curious world of international celebs. No longer professionally interested in 'monsters', he found them tiring.

Im supposed to be staying with Bumble this coming weekend and be dragged round to a lot of people that I dont know and dont care anyway, but I hope to see the Corcoran family at Sunday lunch time with luck! She always seems to have dreadful people to do with the film buisness, very rude and boring, very often, but I suppose she keeps 'in' with all the monsters.

He dodged at least as many of Bumble's invitations as he accepted, and infinitely preferred staying with the two Bars in Islington. He did not, however, enjoy the company of another of their regular guests, the novelist Patricia Highsmith, who met the Bars on holiday in the South of France in 1966 and regarded Bar Ker-Seymer thereafter as one of her closest friends. Highsmith was an extremely difficult woman, obsessive and self-tormenting, and a very heavy drinker, even by Burra's standards. 'Perhaps Pats liver is turning to rock,' he suggested to Bar. 'I don't know how she keeps it up I must say I couldn't do it.' He did rather like to rub into her that Highsmith behaved even worse than he did. She could also be very aggressive, which he really could not handle, so when she was staying in Charlton Place, as she did in January/February 1969 (she was in London for the launch of *The Tremor of Forgery*), he preferred to stay away.

Thus, in February 1969, his London visit was to the Corcorans rather than to the two Bars. Gerald and Phyl Corcoran had remained on excellent terms with Bumble, and took Burra to her birthday party, along with a particularly spirited daughter of the shires called Lady Sarah Ponsonby. Lady Sarah made a good thing out of producing distressingly lifelike paintings of racehorses in action: she had the immense virtue of treating her work as a straightforwardly commercial enterprise and not taking herself too seriously. She had arrived at the Corcorans' already stoned and with her hat over one eye, and had offered a reefer around: Burra accepted with alacrity and took to her enormously, so by the time they set out, they were all in fits of giggles. It was a very smart party: Bunny Roger was there, 'looking wonderful in black', then, 'suddenly I noticed a tiny person in white with a huge bright red vagabond hat. Judy Garland who was murmuring on a sofa She soon manoevered herself into our little circle, she was fascinated by Ponsonby.'

Judy Garland and Bumble had been acquainted at least since 1962, when Bumble dressed her for her last film (*The Lonely Stage/I Could Go On Singing*), and according to Burra, she had coped well with the diva's mood-swings: 'one moment you can do anything with her & the next she becomes terribly grand! However she seems to be very nice, they seem to get on well.' A few weeks later, when Burra was staying with Bumble for a weekend, she had a lunch party for Judy Garland and the singer Johnny 'Cry Guy' Ray,[5] which was on the whole a success, though the celebs arrived an hour and a half late. Since Burra had spent the interval placidly drinking gin and ruminating, as he was always happy to do, he had barely noticed.

The following evening, Bumble and Burra went to a private screening of the Warner Bros. film of *The Madwoman of Chaillot* at Jack Warner's private theatre, where they encountered, among others, Princess Margaret and the then-Leader of the Opposition, soon to be Prime Minister.

As we were sitting there having been given a drink who should materialise but a phosphorescent very buttoned up little person who looked lit up from inside accompanied by a young man in a duffle coat Margaret & Tony! Bumble did a backward

[5] Johnny Ray was an American rhythm 'n' blues singer famed for his emotional delivery, a major teen idol of the period. He was another tormented individual, an alcoholic and a closet homosexual.

curtsey into my gin & then after a bit of standing up the picture began – befor that I said how do you do to a surly pudding face that I suddenly realised was Mr Heath! Goodness knows why I should say how do you do to him . . .

Burra seems to have enjoyed the evening only up to a point, and didn't like the film itself, an adaptation of Giraudoux's play starring Katharine Hepburn, 'no more mad than Mrs Golder Meyer & all far too clean'.

He was interested, as who would not be, to meet stars of the magnitude of Judy Garland and Vivien Leigh, but fragile, vulnerable women did not appeal to him. The women who had attracted him as a painter, such as Mae West and Pastor Imperia, had been the ones with the self-confidence of tigers. Nonetheless, Bar got the impression that he got rather friendly with Judy Garland, and said so to John Banting – 'they have met two or three times lately,' he told James Stern in April, 'I would like to see them cackling away over a bottle of whisky.' Burra's life had involved a considerable experience of troubled and drug-addled souls; and he generated no emotional static of his own. He might have been good for Judy Garland, but the relationship was abruptly severed when she died in a London hotel on 22 June that year, 1969, of a drug overdose.

Even if he did get attached to Judy Garland, Sarah Ponsonby was a still more welcome acquaintance. Cannabis first entered Burra's life in 1950, when he encountered a couple of reefer-smoking black nightclub performers who were friends of Bar's and felt sufficiently venturesome to try some. He quite liked it. 'You seem to be able to buy any quantities in London,' he wrote to Aiken, 'I had one and found it rather a pleasant effect Im afraid, "smoothing" – they taste like Dr Blossers cigarettes for the toobs to me' (thereafter, he often referred to reefers as 'asthma cigarettes'). Since cannabis was not readily available in the circles in which he moved in the Fifties, he did not pursue the experience. But in the Sixties there was much more of it about, and he began to realise how much he enjoyed it. 'I feel absolutely nothing <u>at all</u> I said Oh nothing . . . till I suddenly burst out in fits of laughter every time I looked at anyone . . . Its much better than drink – you dont get a Hangover.'

Cannabis made Burra silly. Left to himself, he was an essentially serious, even sombre, man in late middle age, often – perhaps always – in pain, very aware of the dark side of things, and above and beyond that, when he was not actually painting, he was subject to fits of nervous irritation and anxiety. The boy who had shrieked with laughter in the Velodrome Buffalo was lost forty-odd years in the past. But getting stoned sometimes led him to recapture the innocent hysteria of his teens, an unalloyed pleasure. Sarah Ponsonby was extremely generous with her supplies. He wrote to Banting a couple of years later: 'I had dinner with Desmond & Judith Corcoran whilst at Bumbles. Miss Ponsonby floated in after – floated was the word, stoned outa sight and she rolled 2 reefers 5 feet long I had a real good fit of giggles it was wonderful. She asked Bumble and myself down to her commune in Worcestershire I can imagine . . . I wish I had some reefers 5 feet long she can roll them beautifully too.'[6]

In 1966, Mary Quant chopped six inches off the skirts she was selling at Bazaar, her boutique in the King's Road, and the Swinging Sixties began. Burra's circle was middle-aged. His principal contact with the world of the young and hip was Bar Ker-Seymer's teenaged son Max, who had been born in 1947 and was thus at an ideal age to get the most out of London's sudden efflorescence of teenage style.

Just befor I left Islington Max arrived & I heard what I imagined was Blind Boy Williamson mixed with little Richard, or rhythm & Blues going on in the kitchen – definitely I thought from Birmingham – it was his group, they realy were very good. It would be rather funny if he had a career rushing from Odeon to Odeon in a mini bus – followed by a howling mob they had cut a disc.

By Birmingham, he means Birmingham, Alabama, a great centre for Black R&B. It was a scene that must have been duplicated in a great many kitchens in 1965. Like most such ventures, the disc plummeted into oblivion; and Max 'the Mod' Ker-Seymer's main impact on pop history seems to be his passionate and eloquent devotion to The Who, as they were before they were spoiled by success.

One difference that Burra perceived between the new generation of teenagers and his friends when young was that they struck him as alarmingly trusting. 'When I left Max was refusing to get up & laying in bed waiting for the Ting a ling a ling from his agent who was supposed to be

---

[6] Desmond had married Judith Keppel in 1964: they divorced in 1980. A woman of great resourcefulness, she achieved considerable fame twenty years later when she became the first person to hit the jackpot on *Who Wants to Be a Millionaire?* in 2000.

getting "them" a job. They seem to me to live in a sort of myth world. I never could. I never ever believed anybody.' However, Burra's memory was letting him down; he had forgotten that, at twenty-two, he had passively entrusted the development of his career to Paul Nash to a quite extraordinary extent, and Nash had not failed him.

Apart from liking the dope and quite liking the music, some aspects of Sixties' culture were very much to Burra's taste. It was a great age of satire, which meshed with his generally sardonic take on life. He had long enjoyed French satirical journalism such as the long-established *Le Canard Enchainé*, and he became a regular reader of *Private Eye* (launched in 1961) and also of the underground papers *Oz* and the *International Times* (the former the object of a High Court trial for obscenity in 1971, the latter frequently raided by the police). 'When he comes to visit, he buys every known underground paper he can find, and the more hostile and subversive the better,' Bar told John Rothenstein. He also read American underground papers sent over by the Aikens, and followed *Flook* in the *Daily Mail*, which was drawn by 'Trog' (Wally Fawkes), but came to be written by a variety of hands, including George Melly and Humphrey Lyttelton, and consequently morphed from a strip for children into left-wing contemporary political satire strangely lodged in an otherwise right-wing paper read by such people as Burra's mother.

The children of the Sixties are often presented as an uniquely irreverent generation in stylish revolt against the stuffy certainties of their parents. From the point of view of Burra, born in 1905, the new generation of youthful hedonists simply reminded him of the way he and his friends had lived forty years earlier. One significant difference is that in the Sixties, a good few cultural innovators were actual teenagers, whereas interwar there were few genuine *enfants terribles* other than some of the dancers. However, another respect in which the scene was all too reminiscent of the world of the Bright Young People was its insularity: 'The small band of achievers, the swingers' heroes and heroines, were less than fifty individuals. They were all to be found in the same places, eddying around each other in a gavotte of mutual and exclusive congratulation. The rest were mere sightseers.' Much the same could have been said of the bohemians, partygoers and Chelsea Arts Club habitués of the Twenties.

More young people were having sex at an earlier age (though not as many as the Sunday papers imagined), but since Burra had nothing against fornication, and was not in the least jealous of the new opportunities open to the young (a regrettably common reaction among men of his generation), this did not bother him in the slightest. The Wolfenden Committee legalised homosexuality in 1967, which caused various outbreaks of moral panic about moral fibre (weakening of) and 'danger to the virile manhood of this country', but since many of Burra's friends, male and female, had been living in gay relationships for anything up to forty years, he was, again, underwhelmed.

Miniskirts were not news to him, either. Bar's knees had been on public view in 1926, when she had also worn her hair in an Eton crop; for anyone who had moved in arty circles in the Twenties, the Sassoon bobs and tiny straight-up-and-down dresses of 1966 were no more than a variation on a pre-existing theme. Moreover, the drugs scene was comparatively tame: the classic Sixties' drugs were handfuls of uppers and downers, plus cannabis; the druggier friends of Burra's youth, such as Olivia Wyndham, Brenda Dean Paul and Ruth Baldwin, had used heroin, cocaine, or both, along with staggering quantities of alcohol.

He visited the King's Road out of curiosity in 1967, with the two Bars, and returned many times to admire the view.

We went to the Chelsea Potter in the Swinging K Rd at lunch all Booteeks & Beatneeks layabouts etc & miniskirts. but not the _thigh_ dearie _that_ is very often anything but mini especially in white stockings its quite fascinating almost like Montparnasse in the 20ies!

While benignly intrigued, he was, as always, observant of the gulf between intention and result. 'The bigger the leg the minnier the skirt!' The teenagers of the Forties and Fifties were slender, because sugar and fats were on ration. By 1967 – since their mothers, products of the war years, tended to think of sugars and fats as desirable 'energy foods' rather than, as women have come to do more recently, as 'empty calories' – a good few young women were rather less Twiggy-like than the mode required, especially if they ventured on white stockings. I am old enough to remember the effect that Burra noticed, of plump white knees twinkling beneath pelmetlike skirts.

What was newest about the Sixties look was not short hair on girls, but long hair on men; a phenomenon that has been subjected to a good deal of semiological analysis. Burra, however, does not seem to have found it either wonderful or alarming. Relatively few of his paintings of the Sixties and Seventies involved the human figure in any case, but he showed no interest in long-haired men. He let his own wispy locks grow long and lank in the Seventies, which looked absolutely terrible, but that was because he realised he could now get away with not going to the barber, and he couldn't be bothered. Sixties' manes, of course, were perceived as so significant that *Hair* was the name given to 'the American tribal love-rock musical', one of the iconic shows of the era. It opened in London – one day after the formal abolition of theatre censorship – on 27 September 1968. Burra went, and found it on the whole tame, a bit sweet and earnest.

We actually went to 'Hair' I really rather enjoyed it very jolly & very moralistic I thought . . . somebody said Fuck but as everyone is always saying Fuck its lost its cherry as you might say.

The only aspect of youth culture that Burra greeted with positive enthusiasm was the increasing use, and hence availability, of cannabis. He never experimented with acid, though he was not against it on principle. 'Such a pity its not legal as it would do far less harm than alcohol,' he commented. His only censorious remark in connection with drugs was not focused on the evils of abuse. Charlie Watts of the Stones said that he never really saw anything until he took acid, and Burra seems to have found it sad that it took LSD to persuade someone to open his eyes to 'natural objects trees & trunks etc People don't see a thing I believe, they never look at anything realy, People in the train never look they give me the creeps.'

Burra himself observed as if every look might be his last. 'He sat very still,' Chappell remembered, 'and his face appeared completely impassive. He might, I thought, have been staring at a blank wall, until I saw the intensity of his gaze. I do not remember Edward ever making any sort of note: not even the faintest scribble; yet weeks, even months later, the shapes, the tones; the actual atmosphere; and the colour of the clouded skies looming above those moors, hills and valleys he had looked at so intently, would appear on paper.'

Pop Art is a defining aspect of the Sixties as a cultural phenomenon; the art of Warhol, Roy Lichtenstein, R.B. Kitaj. In the Twenties the surrealist movement, and Burra, in so far as he was a part of it, had engaged very fully with popular culture, and Burra himself had been intensively involved with the consideration of street style, particularly black style. By the later Sixties he was no longer at all interested in such themes himself, and his past involvement with them meant that he was not very 'sent' by the Young Turks of the art world. Works such as Michael Andrews's *Colony Room* conversation piece, or his *All Night Long*, which Bryan Robertson describes as having an 'element of orgy, element of nightmare, elements of a stylised "good time" and elements of fugitive deep feeling', could be seen as lineally descended from Burra's work of the early Thirties, but Burra's own attention was elsewhere by then.

However, Burra was aware of a variety of younger artists' work, and broadly sympathetic to it. 'I went to the young contemprys at the Tate with Bar we enjoyed it very much – I like to see a lot of Bright colour. All done with the most perfect meticulous technique – no botching about' (this was in 1967). The work of Robert Rauschenberg (who, in the Fifties, had been part of a neo-Dada movement in America) was exhibited at the Whitechapel Gallery in 1964 and Burra responded strongly to it. The Whitechapel Gallery in the East End, headed by Bryan Robertson, was perhaps the most forward-looking art venue in London in the Sixties, and Burra kept an eye on what was going on there. He did not care for Allen Jones, 'horrid pictures of huge legs in High heels', but one younger English artist he admired without quali-fication was David Hockney. 'Ide rather like to meet Hockney his paint-ings at that huge POPFART show were very good and one wonderful portrait – not very POP it seemed to me'[7] (an assessment that squares, incidentally, with that of Hockney himself, who disassociated himself firmly from Pop Art: 'I've always despised the idea of pop,' he said firmly). Burra was immensely pleased when Hockney was given a major exhibition at the Louvre; 'English painter given large exhibition in Paris! Mercy gawde . . .' As he very well understood, for the French to admit that England had produced a major painter was an important moment in the coming-of-age of the London art scene. It seems to be one of the few moments when Burra was demonstrably proud to be English.

At the beginning of 1968, Billy Chappell, who had been renting a weekend cottage at Newchurch in the middle of Romney Marsh for a peppercorn since 1964 (it belonged to the poet and publisher Erica Marx, another friend from the circle of Nancy Cunard), took Pump

---

[7] He is referring to the major Pop Art exhibition at the Hayward Gallery, 1969.

Cottage in Rye, which belonged to Kenneth Ritchie, instead. Though he was often away, abroad or in London, working on one production or another, thereafter he was at least periodically available to keep an eye on his oldest friend.

Burra needed his friends more than ever in those months, since his mother was going into her final decline. She had eaten very little for years, and for the last six months of her life more or less lived on Farrah's peppermint lumps, which Clover faithfully posted down from Harrogate, four tins at a time. As with a previous collapse which she suffered in the autumn of 1964, she was very hard on the indispensable Frederick. Burra wrote in January:

We are staggering on here at the rate of heaven knows what a week about 50£ or more – on night nurses and day nurses – A[nne] is almost at her wits end. Frederick is busy biteing everybodys head off – as hes never not answering mumsies bell & emptying the commode.

The situation had nowhere to go but down; and Frederick, under too much pressure to keep up his usual standard of discreet unobtrusiveness, became more and more irritating. 'I had lunch with Anne today we had a small (stinking) chicken which tasted very good cooked by Auntie Fredrick, who just adores to cook and boss about and snap everybody's head off – doing "too much" of course.' Mrs Burra lingered on till 14 May, too ill to live, and too tough to die. 'We live on Junkie time,' Burra wrote, 'the pills are like clockwork.' It was a miserable and stressful five months, and by the time his mother breathed her last, Burra himself was too drained to feel much. He wrote to Chappell:

I was in a terrible way when she was first very ill 3 years ago? & I got Anne back from Scotland as I thought she was dieing, and its been hanging like a bomb ever since. She realy was in such a state of misery & discomfort & half doped. Im glad shes dead & its all over.

Chappell says that the only time he ever saw Burra weep was after the death of his mother. But the question, perhaps, is what he was weeping for. They had been extremely close, especially during his childhood and adolescence; she was a personality, strong-willed, intelligent, funny and musical. Yet for thirty years she allowed herself to become a burden upon those who cared about her, anxious and complaining, without even the mitigation of getting any fun out of it. Burra understood from the inside the energy lapses, the anaemic episodes and the genuine debility which encouraged her to become so helplessly dependent. Children often judge their parents harshly for what they have most in common: he was inclined to be hard on her. But beyond that, it was not her death that needed mourning, so much as the waste of nearly half of her life.

His friends promptly rallied. The Bars offered their support without hesitation. '... Needless to say your friends are all most concerned about your future, what is to be done about the house, where you will live, etc. I expect Ann will arrange everything, but do count on Bar and I if there are any unpleasant removal or transport jobs to be done. We feel that you must be spared as much as possible.' But he took a long time to recover from his bereavement, and as always, psychological stress had immediate physical effects and brought on his anaemia. Bar was very worried about him. In 1969, she wrote to James Stern:

I agree with you about this last show of Ed's. Poor creature, he was so upset about his mother's death and he has been very ill himself all this time. I am amazed that he has even been able to hold a brush. When he is upset his paintings get very hostile. According to John Russell his paintings are like the neighbours in 'a delicate Balance' who are possessed of 'an overwhelming and inexplicable fear'. I don't know what the 'evident terror' in his paintings is caused by, probably fear of death in slow stages. He is terrified of not keeping going, and yet courts disaster by drinking himself to death.

However, though his state of mind was obviously important, the big question facing Burra and his friends was the practical one of what on earth he was going to do next. He was finally entirely responsible for himself – and for Frederick.

One thing that he was by no means short of, since the family trust had devolved to himself and Anne, was money, and so one of his first considerations was pensioning off Frederick in a decent and suitable manner. Gerald Corcoran, who combined his role as Burra's dealer with that of his financial adviser, told him, 'As things stand at the moment you could buy a cottage for Frederick, a small annuity for him and an annuity for yourself and still have something left over.' This he did, at least with respect to Frederick. He also had money from his mother – she left her entire personal estate (£7,581), as distinct from the family trust, to her son, apart from £500 to Frederick, not because she did not value her daughter, but because she thought her son needed it more. In terms of the way the Burras thought, that made sorting out Frederick his problem rather than Anne's.

Bar took the occasion to speak with the frankness of a lifelong friend and suggest that he do something similar for Billy.

I am so glad to hear that you will buy Frederick a house. You will never regret it and he will be grateful for life . . . with a roof over his head and an annuity Frederick will be all set for a peaceful old age with no further worries. I do hope it all comes off. I gave away more than half of what I had and I really don't miss it as I live off an overdraft. I haven't known what it is like to have any actual money in my account for over thirty years. As for poor Billy, he is in a constant state of worry about his overdraft as he has no capital to fall back on. You could give him an annuity and never notice the difference, as what is going to happen is that the government is going to claim nearly all the money you have when you die. The money could be used to give happiness and a little security to someone when they are still alive. I suppose you will never speak to me again for saying all this, but it does seem to me a terrible waste to leave money doing nothing in the bank when it could be working for you and doing good.

As usual with Burra and practical matters, inertia won out; Bar was complaining years later that he hadn't got around to making a will (and he never did). But he did not forget about Billy.

Frederick wrote formally (to 'Mr Edward and Mrs Ritchie') the following April, with the news that he had been up to Springfield to scatter Mrs Burra's ashes, in terms which indicate that for all that he was the perfect butler in company, the employer-servant relationship was not one in which he felt it necessary to pretend to Jeeves-like impassivity. They had been through a lot together.

I walked quietly over to Playden and met Mr Ellis [the quondam gamekeeper] at Springfield we made our way down the once beautiful garden, now unbelievably neglected & full of desolation, in the lower orchard the daffodils were just in bloom & strangely it looked rather as it used to do, near the old fountain facing the temple we scattered the ashes of your mother. Rather a sad duty, & the last possible thing I could do for her.

I had become very attached to her over the long period of time I had been with you all & especially during her long illness. I have missed her terribly, although she had at times not been very kind to me especially when Da was alive, the recent frustrations and getting things settled and cleared have helped me forget her many faults which sadly we all of us have more than our share. I forgive her everything. A small farewell to you both. I would much rather it be like this, very many thanks for your help & for so much that will prove to be most useful, very acceptable and truly appreciated.

    Frederick

Frederick continued to write long, newsy letters to Burra for the rest of the latter's life, and to receive them. He considered retiring to the house Burra had bought for him, but he was too much in the habit of working, so he took another job as a live-in servant, and kept Burra up to date with exactly what he thought of his new employers – not much, on the whole.

Finally, Burra was on his own. 'I hate houses,' he wrote to Conrad Aiken, '& don't care about them at all or furniture or dinky all atomic kitchens or anything like that <u>at all</u>. nor do I care for this horrid little Beautee spot now becoming a kind of overblown gift shoppe with pottery plaques with the name of the house on every sweet little place all the old inhabitants have moved or moved themselves to council estates on the outskirts so the centre is completely given over to gyfterie and other forms of perversion.' Little though he relished the prospect of moving house, he was determined to get out of Rye.

XV

GETTING QUIETLY PISSED

BURRA professed not to have any kind of aesthetic views about houses, despite having inhabited upper-middle-class homes of taste all his life. He declared, 'I plan to retire to a modern Bungalow with a picture window with nylon lace curtains criss cross across it . . . not in Tinker Belle Towne. I always thought those windows would be good for a studio.' When the light was too bright for him in Springfield or Chapel House, he pasted newspaper across the panes, or rigged up an old sheet. Nets would have done the job nicely. Since he was not worried about looking for anything attractive, the principal question was: where?

Not Rye. Apart from its overweening picturesqueness, which had annoyed him all his adult life, there were simply too many people in Rye by 1968. Burra had always disliked being in a crowd, but this distaste strengthened to detestation in later life. In the late Sixties and early Seventies, Rye in summer was a popular tourist destination, full of people on Pontin's holidays milling around High Street and Mermaid Street (there was a huge Pontin's holiday camp at Camber Sands). It was hard, even frightening, for the elderly Burra, especially when he was burdened by a shopping-bag, to struggle through bovine crowds of people milling about with nothing much to do. The old part of Rye has narrow eighteenth-century pavements, and he could not cope with being forced onto the cobbles: due to his arthritic feet and ankles, he could not walk on an irregular surface. His decreasing mobility also made the sheer steepness of the streets at the top of the town very difficult for him. Bar observed, 'It must be about the worst place in England for walking about. All those cobblestones, apart from anything else.' By the same token, though regular visits to London were essential, he could not envisage living there, because the pace of life was too fast.

The place he liked best was Harrogate, where the Pertinez family lived, but it was too far from London, where most of his other favourite people were. He quite liked the look of Brighton. But his principal motive was negative: he was desperate to get away from Chapel House, which was really his mother's home rather than his, and, above all, was perched on one of Rye's highest points, scoured by the east wind he loathed, surrounded by street after street of cobbles, and freezing cold – it had turned out to be catastrophically expensive to heat. Unfortunately, the house hung on the market, since it needed a lot doing to it, and also, the thought of househunting filled him with horror.

But amongst the property which Burra and his sister had inherited from their father were a couple of gardeners' cottages at Playden, which had once been staff cottages attached to Springfield. One of them was occupied for life by Mrs Nellie Boot, the widow of an erstwhile gardener, the other, slightly larger, was vacant. He told Aiken early in 1968, 'I think of takeing over one of the gardeners cottages & living in it! the lavatory is by the kitchen door & no bath but a nice garden & the house is in quite good order & a fire place in every room. Newish too not far from the Peace & Plenty! anyway it isn't in Rye – thats the main thing. Ther seemed to be a room I could work in.'

The Springfield cottages are attractive little square houses, not particularly cottagey, with gardens. Their main drawback is that they front onto the main road, and are set only a few feet back from it. Even in 1968, when Burra was still weighing up advantages and disadvantages, he noted sardonically that 'the traffic [was] like a quiet day on 23rd street cross town [in New York] only noisier and faster now, strangely enough you don't hear a sound at the back'. Another factor was that in 1968 Anne and Colin retired to Playden, to a house on a new estate called Fair Meadow ('wot we used to call the Hilly Fields & was a short cut over it from the Kings Head to Rye!'). Thus, if Burra moved to Playden, he would have his sister just around the corner. He would not have admitted that that was a consideration, but it probably was.

Burra vacillated between the cottage and a new-build house on an estate not far away, and eventually moved to the cottage late in 1969. Before he could move in, it needed a new cement floor, a new kitchen and bathroom, and central heating, all of which took some time to complete. Even without having to househunt, the move exhausted and depressed him. By his sixties, any kind of stress brought on his anaemia and left him prostrate. Both Bars helped out, but the bulk of the organisation was done by Anne and Frederick. Once he was settled, he had a genuine sense of escape and relief. 'This is very comfortable with plenty of hot water & warm & easy to turn on some heat for a while, and it's a relief to be out of dear little Rye which is already crowded with people gapeing & crazed with boredom.'

He felt no sentiment, positive or negative, about going back to where he started from, slightly to his own surprise. 'Its very odd,' he confessed, 'it doesn't seem realy to make that much difference to me where I am if I can work but havent done any of that the last 3 or 4 weeks Anne & Frederick have been wonderful. I get so fractious & tired I don't know what Im doing & am a complete blank I cant remember anything or where Ive put anything down.' He never expressed the slightest curiosity about the new inhabitants of Springfield. The only comment he ever made on his declension from the big house to a servants' cottage was in 1975, in a letter to Bar apropos of some old Springfield Lodge writing paper, which he had found and was using: 'hope you notice the frightfull fall in my <u>living standards</u>? From Springfield <u>Court</u> they now call it to 2 Springfield Cotts? I love it when people keep talking about living standards – they <u>must</u> be kept-up – your ass.'

He was briefly tempted to a surrealist décor: 'They sent me 2 huge books of the most hideous wall papers Ive ever seen in my life. some of them I was almost tempted to have for a joke most were a sort of Westwickham cum Stock Brockers Boudoir made over public house style. I did rather Fancy a dado of hunting hats & whips.' His eventual scheme was straightforward, if not conventional, and used paint, not paper. The sitting-room had vermilion walls, dark bright-blue curtains and white woodwork; there were a few nice pieces of old furniture from his parents' house, despite his assertion (to Aiken) that 'Ive got the horror of anything but an orange crate.' What pleased him most about the house were its nice new, oil-fired hot-water and central heating system, and the 'daylight' strip-lighting that had been installed, which enabled him to work in low light conditions for the first time ever. Five years later, he had still not unpacked all the book boxes. He installed a telephone, somewhat reluctantly. 'Anne said she would never have a moments peace & be dead with worry if I didn't ... It doesn't worry me not having a phone.' He moaned on one occasion, 'I wish the telephone was torn out by the roots.'

Within weeks, he was using his elegant new living-room as a depot-cum-studio, and living almost entirely in the kitchen. As he became more affluent, he could not resist buying clothes, which after a while were everywhere, five deep on all the hooks, overflowing the chairs, competing for space with the books, papers and letters, which, as throughout his life, were filed on the nearest flat surface.

Burra had always loved clothes. He had been a dandy in his teens, and though he owned very few clothes in the Thirties, that was because he was living on an allowance and saving his money for books and travelling. But according to Chappell, once clothes became obtainable again after the war, he would visit redoubts of old-fashioned men's tailoring such as Simpson's and Aquascutum and emerge with elegant jackets and beautiful blazers, though what he actually wore from day to day were tartan shirts, corduroys or jeans and thick sweaters. On his deformed feet he wore what he called 'sand-shoes', a kind of rubber-soled plimsoll, which he bought in Lillywhites sports shop in Regent Street. He took to wearing these in the Forties and Fifties when his feet were particularly bad (from their resemblance to boxing shoes, David Paltenghi dubbed him 'The Champ', after Wallace Beery's character in the 1931 film of the same name). Though he had once cared a great deal about shoes, by the Seventies he wore his plimsolls almost all the time, since they were the only footwear he could still walk in.

Though he did wash his clothes, he never ironed anything. He would probably not have done so in any case, on the grounds that it was a waste of time, but in his later sixties he could not stand with any comfort for more than a few minutes. From his fifties onwards, standing made his feet and ankles swell, and he avoided doing so if at all possible. The shirt and trousers, therefore, were generally crumpled, and so, though cleanish and expensively dressed, he conveyed an overall impression of scruffiness.

Alexandra Stanciow, a relative of the Corcorans, recalls dining with Burra and the Corcoran family at the Mirabelle (then one of the smartest restaurants in London) in the Seventies. Burra looked, on the whole, like a tramp, and had donned an old-fashioned double-cuff shirt, worn without links so the cuffs flapped like the Mad Hatter's. Presumably, even if he had been able to find a pair of cufflinks, he would not have been able to do them up due to his twisted fingers. The service was extraordinarily slow and poor. 'It's because of me, dearie,' Burra said; it was evidently a reaction he was accustomed to. Even apart from his clothes, he was an odd-looking old fellow by 1970. George Melly recalled:

The face with its sharp small features and network of fine lines, the hair whispy and approximately combed, the teeth a disaster area, the eyes alert and yet curiously abstracted, the arthritic hand . . . wrapped around a glass which would have fallen if held between the fingers.

His teeth were indeed a disaster area. They were decay-prone and irregular all his life, and inevitably became heavily nicotine-stained. They gave him a great deal of trouble, and he lost several over the years, though never enough to require dentures. His hands were profoundly deformed by his sixties, wasted and twisted, with swollen joints at wrist and knuckles; he could move them with immense precision, but he had almost no grip. He liked to wear big junk-jewellery rings, of which he had a fair collection, which emphasised the grotesque shape of his fingers.

However, quite apart from his general appearance of dilapidation, Burra's tendency to use his eyes as if he was, literally, a camera must on occasion have conveyed the impression that he was stoned, if not worse. He made publicans and headwaiters nervous: 'They don't quite approve of me – I always ask why? & they get very up tight. Quite sober too but difficult to place & all the pubs in the West End are getting paranoid over hippies & drug takers.' On another occasion he remarked, having caught a glimpse of himself in a mirror, 'No wonder they wouldn't serve me – what I looked like – methylated spirit in person.' He observed his own physical appearance in the same way that he observed everything else: accurately, without pity and without the slightest impulse to interfere.

Barbara Roett once answered the door in Islington to find Burra standing between two policemen – 'two young silly fellows; Ed looking tired and bored'. He had been trying to effect an entry to the house, they explained; in fact, scratching at the front-door lock with his key (turning keys was something he found quite difficult), and he had struck them as such a suspicious-looking character they were not prepared to accept his explanation that he was legitimately in possession of the key because he was staying there. He was not even indignant – he never was, she said.

He was by no means immobilised in the Seventies. Some of the time he could walk, and took pleasure in walking, but periodically arthritis, gout or even corns grounded him, and he could only get about if Anne took him in her car. Normally, though, his erratic, stalking progress moved him about quite briskly, and he could walk more easily than he could stand still.

He continued to drink (and to smoke cannabis from time to time) in the Seventies. His friendship with the permanently sodden Banting perhaps pushed him a bit further in this direction than he might otherwise have gone. He found it increasingly stressful to visit anywhere he hadn't been before, or to meet people he did not already know well, and needed whisky to calm himself down. Being somewhere he couldn't get a drink if he wanted one made him nervous. He wrote to John Banting, certain to sympathise on this issue, about one of the less successful of his little trips with his sister:

Anne wanted to go away for 3 days . . . finaly rang up & said Ive been very excentric & taken rooms at Letchworth . . . Letch is hell – the first garden suburb all lovely trees & very genteel & not a sign of anywhere to DR-NK. I dont scarcely dare write it, having received a flood of abuse from Miss K.S. about my behaviour on Whit M[onday]! when I arived unconscious and spilt the milk so to speak. we got to a very nice hotel in bloody Letchworth who knew nothing about us so sent us off to another horrible place looking too 'Temperance' that put me into a screaming state of combined paranoia & claustrophobia & persecution mania etc so off we went to some little place rather more seedy, called Boston, where I had an antiente chamber looking on to a grave yard. I was fully expecting the Brides of Dracula.

What he means by 'a flood of abuse' is that Barbara screamed at him for getting dead drunk, because she was afraid that, with his liver in the state it was, he would drop dead. Or, of course, get mugged, or fall under a car. She was not much of a drinker herself ('she says she cant get drunk but she hasn't realy tried "keep pegging away" as they used to say in my school report,' Burra commented). She also disliked dealing with him when he was unduly plastered. The two Bars' house in Charlton Place was quite his favourite place to stay in London, so she attempted from time to time to keep his drinking under control by saying that she wouldn't have him back if he didn't behave himself. She suggested that if he felt compelled to take the edge off things, he should smoke cannabis instead, since it seemed to her less physically damaging for him. He regarded this, inevitably, as the heinous crime of making a fuss. The tantrum in Letchworth makes it clear that he was capable of making a sizeable amount of fuss himself.

However, the occasion for this reading of the riot act, which annoyed him so much, was one of the most epic boozing sessions he ever engaged in:

I suppose I must have put away a great deal of gin to become quite unconscious. I thought it was lovely driving back from Putney laying on my back & looking at the sky & waving my arms about. it seems I was still doing it when I arrived at Charlton P but I knew nothing about it at all till I found I was going to bed & being given a nembie by Billy![1]

That is to say, he had got drunk in Putney with their common friend Geoffrey Dove: not for the first time, or the last. But the Putney bender was something very out of the way, and seems actually to have frightened him. His diary entries tell their own tale:

31 May went out with Geoffrey . . . drank myself unconscious
1 June felt like glass
      returned [home]
2 June back ache
3 June back ache J[ohn Banting] called up
4 June back ache
5 June better

When he subsequently wrote to Bar from his room overlooking the graveyard, he was as apologetic as he ever got. 'Im sorry your upset you always did tell me I had a good instinct of self preservation but that depended on how ill I felt, this time I didn't feel the least ill, Just divine, so I had no pres[entiment, i.e. warning] – afterwards I had a terrible Backache for days from an enlarged spleen now gone, in a very quaint old Hostellerie in I'm not sure where, Bedfordshire? I suspect after 5 double scotches you must be angry but I feel much better.' He might

---

[1] Nembutal (pentobarbital) is a barbiturate, used as a tranquilliser.

have shrugged off concerns about his health, but losing four days' work was for him a serious matter, and he was not at all anxious to repeat the experience.

Despite the boozing (it is worth observing that it is often in the context of seeing John Banting, or in letters to him, that there are details about getting drunk, a claiming of common ground), and although Burra was taking on being an independent householder for the first time in his life at the age of sixty-four, his life at Springfield Cottages settled rapidly into a disciplined routine. He slept very little, a lifelong habit. His working hours began at eight or eight-thirty. He worked for four hours or so at a stretch, and took a break when he got tired and had some lunch, did a little housework, wrote letters or pottered. He had a rest in the afternoon, during which he read, and if he had the energy, he then went back to work, thanks to his new daylight strip-lighting. There was a daily rhythm.

Mrs Smith, who had cleaned Chapel House, came to the cottage twice a week, under strict instructions to put everything back on the floor where she found it once she had finished. When he needed anything, Anne took him up the road in her car to do his shopping. There is no shop in Playden, and Burra preferred Peasmarsh to Rye, despite Rye's more upmarket shops, because Peasmarsh was less crowded, more or less on the flat, and had a supermarket where he could get what he needed in one place. In addition, Anne could drive him virtually to the door. He did his own cooking, and even a little gardening (though Anne did the lion's share of this also).

She commented in an interview, 'He likes his garden very much. He is very interested really in vegetable growing though it's me has to do most of the hard work . . . but he loves all these sort of pot plants and all the little bits there you can see he can do quite easily – and he's really got green fingers, Edward, anything he puts in grows.' He had started growing vegetables during the war, and since Springfield Cottages had a sizeable garden (Chapel House did not), he went back to growing some of his own, particularly broad beans and mangetout, which were relatively hard to get in shops in the Seventies.

The garden did tend to get away from him; he complained after the dry summer of 1972, 'The garden is in a terrible state B'd Beans eaten by black fly and a mass of weeds – teeny pots. dried up when they ought to have been rained on. realy I cant cope with it. a pity for you could

grow a lot in it if you gave up your entire life and worked all day. anyhow
it looks pretty I must say in its wylde waye.' He was very taken the
following year by the flowers on his Brussels sprouts, which had bolted,
and he was also fond of his yellow lupins, which he painted more than
once. He had geraniums in the windows, though his small front garden
was full of dock and brambles left to rampage ('an outrage to metroland',
he said, not without satisfaction), and letters, particularly to Chappell,
give updates on individual cherished favourites, lilies in particular, which
were carefully watched from first bud to final glory.

In 1970, the Conservative government led by Ted Heath threw down
a challenge to the labour unions and, as a result, the early Seventies
were plagued by strikes. Soon after Burra's first venture into independent living, there was a refuse collectors' strike, by which he was
quite unperturbed. He wrote to Chappell, 'Are you going back to
Thurloe [Chappell's attic flat in Kenneth Ritchie's house in South
Kensington] or don't you dare! I hope your not knee deep in sewage &
head over heels in crap. The only things in my dustbin are empty
½ Haig bottles & tins of evaporated milk – otherwise I burn, & the rats
bats starlings and other waylde creatures not dead from chemicals finish
off the rest.' He developed his own way of living in harmony with
nature. 'Ive got a very happy familly of rats live in the deep tangled
wylde woode in the back yard quite a thiket. they carry away my old
fish bones & bones of any sort and they are never more seen so everything is as neat as a new pin.'

While striking bin-men were not a big problem for him, like the rest
of the country he was massively inconvenienced by the 1973 oil crisis
(he had put oil-fired heating into the cottage), which was complicated
by the miners' working to rule. Fuel stocks ran so low that in the New
Year that followed, Heath introduced the Three-Day Week, and the citizenry found themselves plagued by power-cuts and driven back onto
using candles. In 1970, when the electricity workers' union threatened
a week-long strike in January, Burra had bought a 'Beatrice' one-burner
camping stove as a domestic insurance policy, which enabled him to
make a hot meal during a power-cut on more than one occasion in the
years that followed. It became Blessed Beatrice in a number of letters,
in sardonic reference to Rossetti's painting of *Beata Beatrix*. In response
to the 1973 crisis, he acquired (at Anne's suggestion) a more elaborate
'Aladdin' paraffin stove, which would heat as well as cook. It went on

fire the first time he used it – he burned his face and hand carrying the blazing object out of the cottage – but thereafter it behaved, and he learned how to cook on it, though he needed Anne's help with it. 'The old Aladdin is going along fine – I am quite unable to turn it on, & make it Blue, as my fingers are too twisted to turn the handle & its too stiff – Anne puts it on in the afternoon.'

There were also train strikes in the Seventies, which were more of a genuine inconvenience for him, but by his late sixties he was often glad of an excuse not to go to London. As long as he was able to do things at his own pace, he was resourceful, and seldom put out; whether by the unavailability of sugar, bread shortages or even the toilet-paper famine of 1973. He reverted back to his mentality of the war years. 'What other treasures have you been offered this week in the way of meat whiskey etc etc?' he asked Chappell. 'Anything useful?'

As well as the daily rhythms of life at Springfield Cottages, there was also, as there had been all his life, a larger rhythm. About every three weeks, strikes and his health permitting, he went to London and spent a couple of nights with Barbaras Ker-Seymer and Roett in Islington, with Chappell in his attic flat in Kensington, or with Gerald Corcoran and his second wife Phyl in Chelsea. In between, Anne and, when he was in Rye, Chappell, kept an eye on him.

Burra was cherished and looked after in his old age, while managing to avoid acquiring any kind of live-in carer. Mrs Smith did basic cleaning, but Bar, Billy, Clover, the Corcorans and Bumble quite evidently continued to assume (it was never even discussed) that supporting Ed in various ways so that he could go on working was part of their overall task in life. Just as importantly, his sister Anne subscribed absolutely to the view that he must be not only encouraged, but facilitated to do as he wished. It was, in very large measure, she who enabled him to travel, live and work as he pleased. Sibling affection is probably the single most underrated type of relationship in contemporary society, but when brothers and sisters are close, they can be very close indeed.

Landscape was the enduring pleasure and principal theme of his late work. Anne had plenty of leisure in her retirement, and she got rather bored with Fair Meadow. 'A isnt a very homey buddy,' Burra commented. 'I dont think she cares a fig realy – she is like me.' Several times a year, she took him off for short motoring holidays to look at new places, sometimes accompanied by Chappell, when he had time, experiences that fed directly back into Burra's painting. Chappell was also indispensable. By 1971, he and Burra had known one another for fifty years, during which time they seem never to have quarrelled. Their dependence was mutual: Burra's practical need for his friend was intense, but for his own part, Chappell wrote, 'I get smoothed out at 2 Springfield cott.' When he had two successive operations on blocked leg veins in the Seventies, it was Bar who looked after him when he came out of hospital, but it was Burra who paid at least part of the bill. Though sex was not an aspect of their relationship, many marriages have been shorter and have involved less mutual commitment.

One of the great entertainments of Burra's later life was cooking, which he had done sporadically for years, but now discovered as a real interest, shared with Chappell, who also loved to cook. Chappell's food reached print in a volume of Beryl Reid's reminiscences and recipes, which includes a chapter called 'Billy Chappell and His Magic Ways': 'Billy is always so inventive with what he calls his "cheats" and his "False this and False that" which always turn out so successfully . . .' Chappell's is the food of Ambrose Heath or thereabouts, a domestication of interwar smart but inexpensive dining. The recipes Beryl highlights include Tongue with Madeira Sauce, Zabaglione, and Stuffed Tomatoes (stuffed with grapefruit, tuna fish, anchovy and Hellman's mayonnaise; a mixture with a very Thirties' flavour).

Burra's food was more robust, and had no pretensions towards smartness whatsoever. 'I got a hand of pork & trotter the other day for 40p very good too.' 'I had a marvellous peice of Skate I fried, dredged in flour with some of that mysterious herb of Annas . . . the sorrel I made into soup.' He was fond of vegetables all his life, though never a vegetarian – Chappell, at one of his first visits to Springfield Lodge in his teens, was surprised and abashed to find his new friend passing up the succulent steak-and-kidney pudding which he himself was eyeing hungrily, and making himself a salad. John Aiken (son of Conrad) observed that Burra 'was a connoisseur – and excellent cook – of vegetables, and mostly preferred his own cooking to that of his friends.' However, he was also fond of meat: he particularly liked inexpensive cuts, and often bought breast of lamb or shin of beef. He was very partial to fish, his staple whenever he was afflicted with anaemia, and shopped for it with care: one good reason to go to Dungeness, which he liked to do when someone was visiting with a car, was to buy fresh-caught fish. When he was taken out, 'he liked good-value meals in side-street pubs with atmosphere, liver-sausage sandwiches or fish and chips in cafés with a raffish clientele'. On more upmarket occasions, he was clear about his preferences. 'I love the Savoy Grill. proper style that is and very good cooking never messed up and exactly what it should be.' He also, perversely, liked the ultra-establishment Simpson's in the Strand.

I know those Italian restaurants pitch dark & no room to move and very expensive in SOHO & elsewhere – I hate them realy for those prices you could have gone to Les Jardins de Gourmets & much better & not much more expensive. The best bargain is 'Simpsons' strange as it may seem tho theyre very particular about ties, twice they lent me one (always either Eton or the Horseguards) you should see the clients, expense acounts business they might be terrified of you if you didnt wear a tie . . .

Burra never wore a tie, though he did own at least one, and sometimes remembered to pocket it when he was expecting to be taken somewhere smart. He occasionally mentions being taken to Chinese and Indian restaurants and enjoying it, but his basic taste had reverted to plain, old-fashioned English cooking – food his parents would have enjoyed.

He was highly quality-conscious. He would not buy battery chickens – for gastronomic rather than ethical reasons, since he had no sentimentality about animals – and he did without, unless Chappell brought him a free-range one from London. The chickens he could buy locally seemed to him to have come from 'Farmers Horror Farm they have a very old faded taste of dead fat that's died of some horrible desease & exude a horrible yellow grease. & theres no escape from them in our little rural super.' Though supermarkets were a great convenience to him since he got so tired, he had a conscience about using them: 'Very nice vegetables these Sainsburys veg very good quality but I feel I ought to support the stalls in Berwick St especialy one I buy sprouts etc from.'

His cooking was surprisingly perfectionist. 'I find my legs are better since Ive given up making white sauce. Fatal to me, not fatal to eat but standing stareing & stirring it! if I keep my legs up all the time they are much less swollen.' This was after an accident, when he was particularly frail, but clearly, white sauce to Burra was proper béchamel, à la Elizabeth David, who says severely in *Mediterranean Food*, 'The sauce should cook very slowly for 15 or 20 minutes . . . this precaution is frequently omitted by English cooks.' He was temperamentally disinclined to slap things together any old how. If he could not stand up long enough to make white sauce properly, he would not make it at all.

He continued, as he always had, to read a great deal in his sixties, and his taste remained adventurous and extremely eclectic (he picked up new serious fiction, particularly American, as it came out: *The Dharma Bums*, *Catch-22* and *One Flew over the Cuckoo's Nest* are among the works he bought in the year of publication, and he was also reading Louis-Ferdinand Céline, whom he admired greatly, Yukio Mishima, Flann O'Brien and quite a lot of history). Though he frequently claimed not to be interested in 'personalities', he read a surprising number of biographies.

Alongside all this serious reading, one of the passions of his later years was sword and sorcery. The same Burra who had responded to the stream-of-consciousness fantasy of *Fantômas* and *Les Vampires* when young was equally gripped in his old age by the world of strangely underdressed nubile priestesses, giant broadswords, antediluvian lizard kings, lost empires and tidal waves; an erupting vocabulary of motifs from the uncensored unconscious with a built-in appeal for someone whose receptivity was trained on Twenties surrealist theory (it is relevant that the writings of H.P. Lovecraft, one of the founding fathers of the genre, were directly inspired by his nightmares). Leaving to one side, of course, that you can simply enjoy the stuff because it is wild, weird and grand, providing that you leave your sense of humour behind the door.

He and Chappell avidly collected and read Robert E. Howard's 'Conan the Barbarian' series and Lin Carter's 'Thongor of Lemuria' books, both published from 1965, while Burra, at least, had been reading the works of H.P. Lovecraft and his heirs since someone sent him a volume of Lovecraft's stories during the war. It was an interest that increased over time, partly perhaps because it was something he could talk about with the absolutely indispensable Chappell, partly because he found sword and sorcery genuinely addictive: 'its like a vice realy it gets you'.

In 1971, Burra was made a CBE in the Birthday Honours list, an honour that he accepted, since, after some argument, they agreed to send him the medal in the post without his having to go to the Palace.

The letter offering him the honour arrived, fortuitously, when John Banting was with him: Banting wrote a letter of acceptance, and got Burra to sign it. It was represented to him by his friends that it might help to keep publicans from throwing him out.

His art, once more, underwent an expansion in the Seventies. Much of his late painting was landscape, into which he infuses an extraordinary impression of vastness and strangeness. These late landscapes are overwhelming, and minimally marked by human habitation. Typically, though, he saw what was in front of him. On a motoring holiday, what one sees above all is miles and miles of grey tarmac stretching into the distance. By 1970, the motorways were a powerful new feature in the English landscape, though one that most people interested in landscape contrive to edit out. There was a vast amount of traffic on Britain's roads. As early as 1961, the busiest section of the A1 was carrying more than 50,000 vehicles a day, about one in five of which were lorries. At peak times there were regular queues of traffic up to five miles long. Motorways had to come, and did. The first sections of the M1 went down in 1958/9, followed by a rapid proliferation of fast roads snaking in all directions.

One important subject Burra took on, therefore, was motorways. A few of his earlier road-paintings are celebratory – there is a sense of romance, freedom and adventure in the ribbon of road snaking over deserted countryside, as in the early Shell posters (he himself had once designed a Shell poster, though it was not used); as Causey observed, he 'had always been interested in the emotional potency of perspective'. Those he did in the Seventies are anything but optimistic.

The art-critic Christopher Neve sums up the peculiar effect of these paintings, extending Causey's basic observation: 'What gives the pictures their emotional potency is their raking depth to the horizon, their roller-coaster perspective ... By 1960 he could do almost anything with perspective ... he watched the countryside as though craving extremes, and painted it as though something terrible were about to happen ... if he played up the awesome, the flawed and threatening, we can see the accuracy of it sticking up through the pelt of fields and moors whenever we look.'

The drama of the great arterial roads' impact on the landcape appealed to Burra, but most of the pictures of the Seventies show the motorways as hostile intrusions into the landscape: the bulleting vehicles images of unthinking mechanical energy, like the soldiers he painted during the war. A sub-group of paintings are even stranger: the huge mechanical diggers of the construction industry are portrayed as independently motivated carnivorous dinosaurs, snapping at each other and at the landscape with mindless hostility and greed. The oddest of these images, *Machines Quarrelling*, has within it a tiny apotheosis of Nuestra Señora de Guadalupe, who seems to be a sad witness to the rage of the machines; though she gives the whole image the flavour of an ex-voto, calling into question where, if anywhere, a miracle might be seen to be under way.

When he was questioned in an interview, he was characteristically unhelpful. 'They just please me for some reason . . . I'm rather attracted by the trucks. Grinding their way through everything.' Like most of what he said to interviewers, this was less than the whole truth. He was strongly aware of the destruction being wrought upon the fabric of England, and saddened by it: he wrote to an American friend, for example, 'I went away to Kings Lynn & Boston not Mass, Lincs, which I like lovely buildings all quietly crumbling under 20 ton trucks roaring by – if you want to see any England hurry, befor a tin box is erected on the rubble containing a Fyne Fayre supermarket.'

Burra was one of the first painters to call England's love-affair with the car into question. Many of his paintings of the later Sixties and Seventies suggest that the massive shift to road-freight and personal car-ownership, which characterises the Sixties, was already giving rise to serious problems. There were three million more private cars on the roads at the end of the Sixties than there had been at the beginning, and much though Burra enjoyed his motoring holidays with his sister, he was a train- and bus-user at heart. There is, in his work and writing from the early Sixties onwards, a distinctly ecological streak (he was also reading books such as E.F. Schumacher's *Small is Beautiful*). The post-war world struck him as profligate. The children of the Sixties could swing all they liked as far as he was concerned, but he was less enthusiastic about the brave new world's addiction to personal comfort and convenience – above all, to the new assumption that everyone should aspire to own a car: 'What annoys me is that in the midst of all these traffic blocks you see one person in each car, which seems rather uneconomical.'

His attitude to the built environment mellowed in his later years.

Though Rye continued to infuriate him, his comment that Bath city council was 'busy ruining the goose that lays the golden eggs ... by destroying irreplaceable 18th century buildings' was shrewd and rather ahead of his time; it also suggests that he was more responsive to 'beautee spots' than he made out. Just as he admired beautiful men who were not conscious of their beauty, he responded strongly to places that were architecturally distinguished, but not prinked out as showplaces, towns such as Boston (Lincs.), King's Lynn and Dublin.

Nobody who lived through the war could be really antagonistic to new building, but whereas he was, at various times in his life, fascinated by the streetscapes of inner-city slums in Marseilles, Harlem, Glasgow and Dublin, he made no images of the new housing that was springing up everywhere, and he clearly had enormous reservations about the way townscapes were changing. Pylons, cooling-towers and bridges all interested him, but not the new shopping centres and tower blocks. Writing of two of the Sixties' most notorious creators of concrete Gulags, he commented, '... I wonder how many perfectly nice Town centres T Dan Smith & Alderman Cunningham have managed to completely kill stone dead & dehumanise between them? They should be imprisoned in Tescos for Life & never allowed out.' As early as 1950 he had ceased to love London; by the Seventies, he did not even like it. His ideal town by then was Harrogate, because it was smallish, and life was lived with a certain decorum; and perhaps, above all, because there were not hordes of people.

Burra was persuaded into a couple of minor professional adventures alongside his painting in the course of 1971. When he visited Burra in order to interview him in spring of that year, the journalist and critic Barrie Sturt-Penrose found the old blocks that Burra had made under Paul Nash's tuition in 1929 among the detritus of his studio floor. According to Clover, who was furious, what then happened was that 'Barry Penrose ... made Ed drunk & ransacked the cottage, finding these woodcuts now on exhibition in London & some rather battered but beautiful drawings that Ed in his cups let go at £20 a piece: they'd fetch about £500 each I expect when they're exhibited in the autumn – but Ed says the Lefevre can't grumble as Gerald hasn't bothered to find out what was in the cupboards when Ed moved into the cottage.' She clearly felt that Penrose had been opportunistic and exploitative, as did the Corcorans, though Burra himself was indifferent: 'Desmond & Mr Postan of the Hamett Gallery are very agitated, & D says he could make 3000£ out of them – <u>WHO</u> was going to do anything about them? I never thought they were any good anyway – & no one else moved a finger till Mr P picked them up so why should anyone complain?'

Penrose took the blocks to Eric Gill's printer, who cleaned the blocks up and printed off an edition, which was published by Alexander Postan in collaboration with *The Observer*, Penrose's employer. Then followed the most difficult aspect of the entire enterprise: persuading Burra to sign them. Burra disliked signing his work; many of his paintings are signed only with a stamp. His signature is drawn rather than written, with little resemblance to the fluid script of his letters. There were nine woodcuts, and forty-five copies of each. He agreed to initial them, but writing EB 405 times began to bore him, and some of them ended up signed 'E. Balls' or 'E. Fuck'.

Burra was only very faintly interested in being brought face to face with work he had done more than forty years earlier: 'very posh they look,' he remarked of the new edition. To Banting, he was sharper: 'I had a letter from Nan Kivel [of the Redfern Gallery] about some of those bloody old prints. He has the First Edition! (HA HA) he proudly says printed & very badly done by yours truly & where did the old sod get them from? Its wonderful how the vultures gather isnt it?' Burra had a poor memory for the minutiae of his own life. Rex Nan Kivell had bought a set of his engravings when they were first exhibited at the Redfern in 1929.

The success of the woodcut enterprise emboldened Postan to try and persuade Burra into making some new prints. 'Mr Alexander Postan has left us some copper plates for etchings & says hes going to print them so we're doing a few prints! I don't particularly want to realy,' Burra wrote in the autumn of 1971. Copperplate etching is not physically tiring to do in the way that woodblock engraving is, but this letter suggests he regarded the etchings as a chore rather than an opportunity.

They were completed in the summer of 1972. 'Postan came down today and I gave him 2 engravings (itchings dear) he plots to publish in a portfolio of 3 & sell them separately we hope to make some money.' The third 'itching' did eventually materialise. One is called 'Drag Queen', a fashion shoot with a topless, yet androgynous model whose attire is strangely suggestive of the Folies of 1929 or so, despite the up-to-date hairdo, while the figure on the right is a reworking of a peculiarly sinister danseuse who features in a drawing that was used for the front cover of a ballet-magazine called *Covent Garden Books* in 1948. The second, 'Mrs Pot', is of one of the bizarrely spooky Teapot Gods (with baleful eyes peering from beneath the lid) that he had also been painting in 1948; and the third, 'Wednesday night', is an anecdotal image of a very rough-looking rock 'n' roll singer belting out a song in a crowded pub, probably based on one of his nights out with John Banting: it is like a more developed version of the sort of drawings he did in his letters. All three suggest that Burra was not reaching out for new ideas, and his heart was not in the enterprise. A letter he wrote to Bar suggests that he was also nursing a sense of injury over the deal: 'Alexander Postan is coming tomorrow with some more prints for me to sign for my charity – Alexander P's new Alpha Romeo . . . A and a friend came down & I signed 500 00 prints' (225, in fact). Mike Goldmark of the Uppingham Gallery told me that, as with the woodblocks, some distinctly wayward signatures resulted.

Another new acquaintance whom Burra made in the early Seventies was George Melly, who, like Francis Bacon, was introduced to him by John Banting. Melly was one of the more notable Soho personalities of the era: an *Observer* columnist, a practising anarchist and lecturer on surrealist art, who also wrote the words for *Flook* and sang in the style of Bessie Smith. His band, which came to be known as George Melly and the Feetwarmers (and which included Wally Fawkes, the artist for *Flook*, on clarinet) developed an enthusiastic following, which included Burra on one occasion.

Yesterday I went to a cabaret at a caravan sight at Bo Peep Hastings to hear George Melly with John & Jim and various members of the Melly family . . . all the kiddies were up & in the amusement arcade till a good ½ past midnight dressed in skin tight pink knickers with a coat made of rags & stockings with rings round them. I never got back till about 1.30 & then I was in such a state I boild a peice of bacon & never went to bed till between 2.30 and 3!

Melly, for his part, greatly respected Burra as a painter (and as a person).

I had admired his work ever since, during my naval training, I had discovered it in one of the 'Penguin Modern Painters' series in the middle forties. Later, during the sixties, my wife and I had bought a picture from one of his bi-annual exhibitions ... I was apprehensive of our meeting. I'd heard he could be dismissive if he didn't take to you ... our destination was a club attached to a caravan park where I was to sing and which John, who had accompanied me there before, thought Ed would appreciate.

As Burra indicates, it was a somewhat surreal evening. 'The clientele, dressed up to the nines, were prosperous East-Enders who looked as though they'd done well in scrap metal or second-hand cars, and they exuded a slightly dodgy bonhomie.' John Banting painted a set of toes onto the front end of a pair of dark-blue gym-shoes, à la Magritte, to wear in honour of the occasion.

But the contact was just in time, for John Banting, after a lifetime of alcohol abuse, was finally falling to bits. Burra reported:

I went to see John this afternoon at St Helens Hospital where he was being ministered to by belle negresses and is having an operation on Tuesday next for the rehabilitation of his arse which will be combined with his cock and he says its distinctly Picasso cum Heath Robinson it frightens me all right ... hes been having trouble at that end for 18 months or more past & I hope when this is all over with will be better! If it doesn't finish him off but I don't think it will.

Banting's life had taken a belated turn for the better a few months before. After decades of eclipse, he had a show at the Hamet in December 1971, cheered on by both Bar and Burra, who was partly responsible. When John Rothenstein and Barrie Sturt-Penrose came to see Burra earlier that year, as he told Bar, 'I put them all onto J. Banting who I hope may get a exhibition & loves having people Barrie P & Mr Postan from the Hamet Gallery & the boss of the H Gallery too & is having a wonderful time with it all hes very social of course.' The exhibition was a success. Bar went to the private view, and took Burra with her to a later viewing, by which time Banting had sold twenty-eight paintings; she counted. But this renaissance came in time to assure a future Banting did not have, and there could in any case have been no follow-up since he could no longer paint. He never recovered from his operation and died at the end of January 1972.

Melly and Burra, however, remained mildly friendly for a time; very much on Burra's terms.

Once I and the diamond butterfly girl went, by appointment, to pick him up in her car. We knocked at the door of his cottage and nothing happened. We knocked again. Finally a grubby curtain was raised an inch or two and an eye was revealed. The curtain was lowered. Several minutes passed. Were we to go away? Had he changed his mind? We waited uncertainly and then, just as we were about to call it a day, he appeared from the back of his cottage, greeting us with apparent surprise. It was extremely, and I believe deliberately, disconcerting.

In the early Seventies, the Tate began to lay plans for a Burra retrospective. Once the process got under way, someone, in the course of this, came up with the thought that it would also be an idea to make a film of Burra, and there was a preliminary discussion between Bar and a producer friend of hers. She wrote to Banting, 'I saw Anne Balfour-Fraser and she said the Arts Council are not releasing the money for Ed's film until 1972, so I told her they had better hurry up, as Ed will either be dead, or so eccentric that he won't allow anyone to go near him!' She also did her best to soften up Burra himself.

Miss Balfour-Fraser who produces those marvellous films on paint<u>ings</u> (not 'ers') wishes to meet you with a view to making a film of some of your paintings. I said I was sure that would be OK as long as there was no talk of Fart and you didn't have to do anything yourself.

She presumably had her fingers crossed behind her back at the time; or at least hoped that Ed could look after himself (as, in his own curious fashion, he could).

In 1972, Peter and Carole Smith were finally commissioned to make a filmed television interview of Burra for the Arts Council. No project could have been less to his taste. He liked the camera crew as people, and indeed liked the Smiths. 'Im very fond of them, and they've been very good realy,' he admitted. But he hated performing, and felt he had been misled at the start. 'When they started talking of this film, I thought it would be just the paintings & perhaps a photo or two of me, little did I know it was to be a quaynte personality sketch.' He complained bitterly to everyone he knew, including John Banting:

Talking of empty bottles and old shit & that all. There are a young man, a director & cameraman called Peter Smith, & a sort of lady producer I've only seen once called Taylor Balfour or Balfour something & friend of Bars I think who wants to do a film of my Paintings (<u>Paintings</u> I was told and of course it wouldn't bother me) rather a nice young man – he came down yesterday or the day before to interview me on my past life the Chelsea P the Royal College & when this and when that & what date this & if I shat etc & this & that & done no good as I cant remember <u>a thing</u>, ever, or any date So he didn't get very much, some of it on tape worm I believe & then said he would interview Bar Clover Billy and you maybe & was about to get onto Sir F Ashton & I can imagine Freds face. so I put him off that A HOPE! I realy became almost unconscious with boredom then said they would make the film in Sept perhaps, & come down here & photograph me washing a shirt etc – drinking dearie till Im dead drunk & abusive more like – with 3 cameramen & god knows what all. & what may I enquire has all that crap to do with Painting?

His complete lack of interest in his own past made him a formidable prospect as an interviewee. However, as he freely admitted, he took advantage of being prevented from painting to get high, and stay high for days. 'I love to be stoned. It quite prevents one from doing any work so I can rarely be really stoned except when the film was being made what else was there to do.' Despite questions anodyne enough for an interview with a member of the royal family, Burra looks as if he is being interrogated: he also keeps looking away from the camera, yawns and screws his face up. The dialogue that resulted is somewhere between Harold Pinter and Samuel Beckett. 'I must babble something, mustn't I?' he enquired, acidly, in response to the simplest of questions. 'Do you think it's bad to pry?' asks Carole Smith, in desperation. 'It may not be bad to pry, but some people don't like being pried *on*. [pause] Do they? [pause] No.' He was resentful of the entire process.

Having been photographed cooking 4 sausages from the butchers for myself and Bars lunch I was asked to sit down & eat them being photographed of course so I firmly refused to & they had to be satisfied with 2 bites. why we shouldn't have lunch in peace I don't know.

Marina Vaizey commented that 'Burra, amid some giggling, gave away absolutely nothing', but the film has its moments. Towards the end, Carole Smith asks him why he thinks people go to see his pictures.

'They try to improve themselves, dear.'

'Do you think they improve themselves by looking at your pictures?'

Burra, gradually overcome by wheezing chuckles, eventually gets out, 'Oh yes, don't you think so?'

'How do they improve themselves by looking at your pictures?' she asks, patiently.

'I *don't know*!' – collapsing into almost silent laughter.

Many years later, Peter Smith put together, as a historical record, all his interview footage of Burra (now in the British Film Institute). What this suggests is that Burra rapidly developed a perversely good sense of when the film was about to run out, and made his own entertainment. After an hour and a half of parrying questions of every description, he began of his own accord to talk about Modigliani with some animation (he did genuinely have a feeling for Modigliani; in his 1929 diary, he records going to an exhibition of his work, 'most beautiful things I've seen for years'). Just as he was getting into his stride, the tape ran out: off-camera, the unfortunate Peter Smith may be heard actually emitting a sharp scream of frustration.

Once it was all over, Burra was prepared to find the experience more or less funny.

Having just completed Super Market Susie retitled Mrs Wiggs of the cabbage patch, for Vitagraph I don't want to go anywhere and would like to do some <u>painting</u>! . . . youl thrill to Susie trapped in a flood of flaming Mazola and a human vampire in the cellars of blazing Tescos – Sob at Mrs Wiggs watering 3 dead geraniums, shudder at the flames of hate! . . . be horrified at Susie Wiggs dragged through scenes of unspeakable vayce & degradation in the lowest dens of harrow Rd by the notorious George Melly . . .

The Smiths had set up an evening with Melly at a drag-show; their last meeting. It was not at all the kind of place Burra would have sought out, or that he went to in the ordinary way; he preferred boring pubs where nothing happened. He grumbled, 'I have been brow beaten into coming up on Monday to go to some Fucking pub in the Harrow Rd', though once he was there, he mildly enjoyed it: 'Miss Phyllis Monkman in a pink negligée & a huge blond wig looking like Louie the Ritz with delirium tremens & a giantess in green with a slit in her dress trimmed with green carpet – the audience was quite innaresting too.' Melly recalled, 'It was as tawdry as he'd hoped and he got on immediately with the artistes, none of whom had the least idea who he was ... we drank a great deal and parted in the street outside, he apparently sober, me extremely drunk. "Goodnight, dearie. You *are* in a state", were his parting, and for me final words.' It is worth observing that he broke off contact with George Melly at that point, as if he felt exploited in an unacceptable way.

He actually behaved better than he thought he did. Peter Smith, writing to thank Anne for all her efforts behind the scenes, said, 'In fact, he seemed incredibly patient throughout the filming.' From the first, he had taken a personal liking to Peter and Carole Smith, despite his reluctance to perform. After all the fuss had died down, he evidently thought of them as friends. He often mentions them in letters to Bar in the months, and years, that followed; he kept in touch with them to the end of his life, followed their professional careers, and was pleased when they had a baby – he even went to see it.

The Tate retrospective itself he found an equally depressing prospect. Some light on his lack of enthusiasm is shed by his correspondence. He seems, for some unknown reason, to have been certain that there would be a retrospective for his sixtieth birthday – that is, in 1965 – since in February of that year he evidently advanced it as a reason for not visiting America that autumn. 'I'd forgotten your Giant Retrospective was scheduled for Fall Production, though I must say it's un<u>like</u> you to stay around for it,' wrote Aiken. His surprise is understandable: the implication is that, most uncharacteristically, Burra allowed himself to invest emotionally in the idea of a major exhibition. His hopes were raised again in 1968, on the evidence of a letter from Gerald Corcoran to Norman Reid, Director of the Tate: 'He is delighted to accept your invitation to have a retrospective exhibition of his work at the Tate Gallery in 1973–4. I am, of course, also very glad because I know he was very upset when the idea of holding this exhibition in 1968 was dropped.'

After two bitter disappointments, Burra had talked himself out of wanting such a thing, so when it actually happened, it just reminded him of the sense of rejection he had felt in the Thirties and made him angry.

Nobody ever looked at those early drawings of mine except to say nasty things if possible so I gave up doing them its realy very funny except all I feel is a strong urge to vomit & I don't want to see any of the fucking crap . . . I suppose if theres a horrible exhibition at the Tate they will have a horrible dinner (by candle light!) I realy shall have to be away or sick or dead I can imagine what that will be like.

He wrote more temperately, but no more enthusiastically, to Conrad Aiken. 'They have suddenly put my apothosis at the Tate next year instead of 2 yrs on so I get consultations which mean nothing to me as I dont know where any of the pictures are & don't care anyway. it might have been FUNNE 20 years ago – but now, No. not much. Mrs Rhodes tells me that some people would be in bliss – the last one was how they should be hung, and I said you hang them anyway you like honey – !'

Inevitably, as the exhibition approached, people kept bothering him. 'That girl from the Tate who came down here (by train) dragging a portfolio that would have held Venus & Adonis by Titian at the least, & containing one teeny photomontage or something Ide done 40 yrs ago & they wanted to know something about it, wants me to go out to dinner on Monday 27th & discuss about pictures for the exhibition, & what there is to discuss anymore, I can't <u>think</u>.' He wrote to Chappell in 1973, 'I thought of coming up this W.e [weekend] maybe but I just collapse. and I dread all the terrible horrors being brewd up over this Tate affair – surely they have everything they want by now but me and they can leave me alone. its like a night mare to me – very wrong Im sure but there it is.'

Barbara Ker-Seymer finally persuaded him to visit it, something he was shy about. 'What for?' he asked. 'I've seen all the paintings. I know them.' She pointed out that it would be only courteous to Michael Compton, who had mounted the exhibition; on which basis, he agreed to go.

We were in the Tate and approaching the entrance to his exhibition, when Edward paused and started to dig in his pocket. I asked him what he was doing and he said, rather crossly, 'I haven't got a ticket.' I told him he didn't need a ticket, and he said, 'You have to buy a ticket to get in. It says so.' I said, 'Ed, you are the artist, you painted all these pictures. You don't have to pay to see your own paintings' . . . Edward was still rather dubious but passed in without any notice being taken of him. He walked straight through the exhibition almost without pausing or appearing to look right or left . . . saying as he left 'Very nice', and made off in the direction of the exhibition of Paul Nash's photographs.

One of Burra's more endearing features was that despite his wayward-ness, he would do things out of politeness, sometimes against his better judgement. He liked the Smiths, and he could see perfectly well that the documentary mattered to them, so he put up with it. Similarly, when he was caught by a journalist from the local paper, he was too polite just to say no:

A strange voice I took for a wrong number slightly Home Counties cokney announced 'I am the Hastings Observer' what do you think of modern man? I was just trying to get a peice of boiled beef out of a saucepan & drinking the Demon Rum when the phone rang so wasnt feeling very like modern man & burst into hysterics of laughter at the thought & said it would take me a month to think about m.m.[modern man] we're doing a series they said! & were quite stuffy. I then thought up one or two thoughts that wouldn't be in the H.O. not suitable . . . Theres no such thing as modern man theres a 'thing' called a CONSOOMER.

He confessed, 'I hate to answer the telephone for fear its something I cant think up an excuse fast enough to get out of.' One of the few post-Seventies' developments which I am certain that he would have liked is the answerphone, though he would probably never have picked up the messages.

However, one thing which genuinely delighted him in his old age was finding that public taste had finally caught up with his art. For many years, he had been accustomed to the sort of comments recorded by Clarissa Aiken, when she was in charge of an exhibition of art that included his work; 'Revolting . . . look at that limb in *Two Women*, like a sausage . . .', 'any child could have done better . . .' He was inured to never being understood. Quite suddenly, he found that ordinary people enjoyed his work, and although he was almost always stonily indifferent to appraisal by professional art critics and art journalists, he was touched by it.

I had a very sweet letter from Mrs E. Toft 20 Victoria Rd Haworth Keighley Yorks. saying I watched your exhib on Thurs night I realy enjoyed the paintings my daughter who is 8 years old thought you very nice it is the first time I have ever wrote to anyone in my life like this But I just have to say to you thank you for ½ an hr of yr wonderful work yrs faithfully Mrs Toft. She must have meant it.

He mentions 'a fan letter from a Bus driver post marked Stoke Newington but unfortunately not signed & no address'; he would clearly have replied to this communication if he could. He was also pleased, and surprised, to find that the TV film meant that all kinds of people suddenly knew who he was. It had apparently not occurred to him that people might actually watch it.

On the way to the Trafalgar a young gentleman told me he had just seen my film & liked it! which brightned me up as I felt I lookd like a derelict meths drinker with assorted bags etc. on the way to the crypt. I went and had a drink at the Trafalgar & the other barmaid asked after my arthritis! I thought it very kind quite a change from the BUMS RUSH.

It was the only kind of fame that seemed to mean much to him. Friendly recognition; the kindness of strangers.

XVI

EMPTY BOTTLES AND OLD SHIT

BURRA was slowing down as he approached seventy. He was very tired. The Royal College of Art offered him an honorary degree in 1975, which he refused. Their regretful letter in reply survives: hoping that 'it will give you some sense of pleasure that your work should be so greatly appreciated, particularly by the younger generation here, that the Council and Senate should have decided unanimously to offer you the highest honour the college can bestow'. But he was past caring about such things, and it was more than he could cope with.

His mind was intensely active, but his behaviour, to those who did not know him intimately, seemed increasingly eccentric. His response to the new was as fresh as ever, but he could only digest what he saw at his own pace, which was much slower than most people's. It was not that he could absorb less, but that he needed to ruminate. After one holiday with his sister, when they had ended up staying in a different place every night (the Cairngorms, Perth, North Berwick and Ripon), he wrote to Bar, 'I must say I find one night stands very tireing. I like to be left in places for 2 or 3 days otherwise I realy begin to see double, & dont know where I am, & when I arive I feel so exhausted I cant go out & begin boozing out of a tooth glass.' It was not a question of the travelling as such, since Anne made all the arrangements and he needed to do nothing except sit in the car. It was partly that any social occasion involving strangers, even checking into a hotel, was slightly stressful for him, but mostly that he was unable just to let the landscape scroll by. He observed with such intensity that he needed time for his impressions to settle.

These holidays, however, were central to his work. He and Anne

occasionally visited recognised beauty-spots, but more often they went
to remote places, the remoter and more old-fashioned, the better. He
wrote to Banting from 'another gloom box in Herefordshire' in terms
which make it quite clear what he liked about the deep provinces, and
why.

What I like about this part is its rather <u>run down</u> & everyone looks like real people
for realy in the Souse East & Tinker Belle part of England people arent quite real
to me. I suppose theres not so much money about and absolutely not a bit of Fart
– not a mausoleum or sketching class for 50 miles around. There was a dinner last
night in here for 100 farmers & freemasons husbands & wives & by 11.30 it was
Bedlam, they started off very smart in long dresses & Tux & ended like a demonstration with nerve gas & broken bottles at the University of Tuscaloosa.

The downside of visiting areas as remote as Lincolnshire, rural East
Anglia and Herefordshire in the Seventies was that the hotels could be
quite horrible; and Burra became a connoisseur of the provincial would-
be smart – 'they rivet me in a dreadful way'. 'The posh hotels food is
nearly always awful and of an unheard of pretention & bogusness,' he
observed to Bar, out of bitter experience. 'Sole plastique à la Cream
Marienbad turns out to be a small peice of <u>lemon</u> sole or plaice covered
in mash pots at side & the whole coverd in white paste – helpd on by
2 v old potato chips and sweet corn if you dont notice and they get it
on your plate so after picking at 4 mouthfuls of <u>genuine Fish</u> you do
leave rather a lot on the side to everyones surprise . . . but if you must
have prayvate toilets & bawthes you must suffer for it in some way its
only fair.'

Similarly, the décor sometimes achieved levels of kitsch which made
hiding in one's room boozing out of a toothglass seem only reasonable.
'The hotel in Kings Lynn had about 5 bars in it and chips with everything in the Buccaneer Bar & Poachers Grill lit with wagon wheels stuck
with candles made of plastic parchment.' Fortunately, Anne shared his
sense of humour about such things, and his pleasure in ironic observation. In any case, as long as he had some whisky to fall back on, he was
good-humoured and uncomplaining.

The real point, in any case, was the long hours spent sitting in the
car, with the landscape unscrolling before him. He was particularly
drawn to the barer and bleaker areas of Britain, and he liked upland

moors, areas such as North Yorkshire and the North Pennines; landscapes where, superficially, there was not a lot going on. As he stared out of the car, he absorbed the palette of colours; the characteristic shapes, the feel, or mood, of the place. Something would bring a landscape's particular qualities into focus for him; the shape of a folding valley, perhaps, the way the light fell on the line of a hill, the shape of a road snaking across undulant terrain, or the curiously different, brighter green of a sheepfold in upland moors . . . 'He would say, "Let's stop here", suddenly to Anne, and he'd look and look and look and not say anything,' Chappell remembered. In letters, it is occasionally possible to see a landscape taking hold of him: 'Ebbw Vale must be seen to be believed. Like a boiling cauldron with a giant steel plant bang in the centre just befor you enter there is a deep sort of orange umber mountain with huge dark mauve stripes pouring down the sides! what on earth that could have been I never found out.'

He sometimes took notes, presumably in his hotel room, since Anne, Clover and Chappell are all adamant that he never sketched *plein-air*. These are very rough drawings indeed, on the sort of child's sketch-pads that could be bought at Woolworth's or a stationer's, using purple felt-tip or blue biro (he rather liked both for writing letters, so they were to hand). But he took no note of colours, he was able to remember them. After a day in the car, he was exhausted because his mind was full of what he had seen; the process of digestion was already under way, and parts of his mind were already starting to occupy themselves with technical issues of interpretation. Weeks or months later, this mass of very detailed impressions was distilled into another enormous watercolour.

However tired he got, painting was always necessary to Burra. One of the very few glimpses into his mind which he permitted to Peter and Carole Smith was that he absolutely had to work. 'I think you ought to work, to paint, otherwise if you don't do enough painting, what's the point of it all.' What he did not reveal directly was that, as much as or more than it had ever been, painting was compulsive. In the last year of his life he wrote to Bar, 'I am between paintings so am in a dreadful way. I hate being between so will start anything no wonder they get odd sometimes.' It is impossible really to know what he meant by being 'in a dreadful way'. It is possible to guess, though, that unless he tamed and exorcised his sensory impressions by getting them onto paper, they started to overwhelm him; that he was subject to nightmarish states of hyperaesthesia. If he didn't paint, he drank, because it was a way of dulling things down.

Barbara Roett told me that his attitude to his own work, once it had left the house, was completely detached. He didn't remember doing it, or associate it with himself in any way: 'He would point at something and go into peals of laughter.' He was genuinely pleased and interested by the idea of seeing again the paintings that had inadvertently got left in Boston in the Fifties. 'I'm quite overcome,' he said, looking at the photographs of paintings he had completely forgotten, brought to him by John Aiken. 'I'm going to *study* these.' That was the week before his final illness.

The note of dislike for London which begins to appear in his letters in the mid-Sixties intensified in his last years. When he was sixty-eight he wrote, 'I had a little note from Beatrice Dawson. I dread it. Asking me if I could be induced to stay & I don't want to I realy <u>dread</u> coming to London the only place I can bear at all is Charlton P [the two Barbaras' house in Islington] maybe in the good old summer tyme I shall feel more like it – I don't like staying with people realy I prefer the Grand Hotel Harrogate listening to monsters & mooning over double scotch that or assorted derelicts in Liverpool St Buffet.' Yet staying with people had been a very large part of his life. But he had to make an effort to respond, even with his oldest friends, and it was getting harder for him. In another letter he said, 'I can only think if I stand still & stare four hours in the kitchen or sit in a gloomy un done up pub <u>if</u> I can find one.' He liked, or rather needed, to contemplate. One word which often appears in his late letters is 'whirl', because most people moved too fast for him. 'We whirled at such a rate round the Lake district It all seems mixed up & run in to each other,' he complained. '<u>They</u>' (he said approvingly, of the Corcoran household) 'are very lazy & don't whirl madly about all over London never drawing breath!'

His early interest in earning money left him after the war, since there were almost no expensive things he still wanted to do. In 1958, he came to an arrangement with the Lefevre by which they virtually became his bankers. They sent him a cheque for £500 twice a year, which covered his expenses, and he left the surplus to pile up. The amount he got from them rose over time in line with inflation and his increased earnings, but an end-of-tax-year account which survives from 1974 shows that Gerald Corcoran had just paid £12,791.41 to the Inland Revenue on Burra's behalf, which left £39,025.52 of the painter's money in the care of the Lefevre. There is some reason to think that his half-yearly dole was, at that point, £1,900. All this, of course, was his own money earned from painting, nothing to do with the money that reposed in the family trust, which he never thought about, and perhaps did not quite understand to exist. He was therefore quite correct in saying, 'Ive got plenty of money (worthless paper) to go on for some time & anything more if there would be anything more will be removed by the Inland Rev & VAT and a wealth tax Im sure.'

He was right about that, too: 1974 was the great era of surtax; in 1973, Denis Healey was reported as promising to 'tax the rich till the pips squeak', and there was an 80 per cent tax on earnings above £4,000. From a tax point of view, life was particularly difficult for someone who earned large sums intermittently – the natural state of affairs for a painter who had biennial exhibitions – far more so than it is now. Seventies' tax-law was relatively inelastic: it assumed that people lived either on salary or on unearned income, and was not well adjusted to dealing with oddities such as creative artists.

Burra did not understand anything at all about tax, and refused to learn. Maths had been one of his worst subjects at school, and as an adult, he was practically innumerate. Tax, and money more generally, frightened and upset him, as well as making him angry. 'Just had another bullying demand for over £2000£ this time, having just payd £3000, and I don't know whats been sold <u>if</u> anything and Im getting desparate Ive sent it all to the accountant – I don't <u>have</u> any expenses to <u>claw back</u>,' he wrote, furious. 'Such a queer "business" with no expenses – it's a bloody Fucking racket & if anybody thinks Im going to vote they can stuff themselves.' Basically, he left his accountant and the Lefevre Gallery to sort it out between them, while Gerald Corcoran patiently attempted to ensure that Burra did at least set his expenses against tax:

1) How much do you think you spend a year on paper, watercolours, etc? I should think about £250 would cover it.
2) How often do you come up to London per year and for how many days? I would say twenty five times a year for four days each time. I would claim £10 per day.
3) How often do you go to Harrogate? What is the fare?

4)   When did you go to Florence and for how long? You could, I think, without
      any trouble, claim £20 per day for these trips.

Still less did Burra understand VAT, introduced in Britain in
November 1972. What is more, he didn't want to, and was not prepared
to try. Unfortunately, his taxable turnover was above the threshold, so
he found himself liable. He was enraged, to begin with, to find himself
thought of as a manufacturer, partly because the paintings were, to him,
by-products of his compulsive need to paint rather than an end in themselves. 'Great "business" I run,' he complained. '"Novelties" & "Gyftes"
– plastic cunts made into salt pepper & mustard in different shades, a
very good line and that's not the ½.' A hapless official was sent to try
and explain his situation to him, a most unenviable task. 'The VAT man
told me I was registered as a business. They send me a paper every
quarter I dont understand a world of it [if] I dont fill in what Ive sold!
during the ¼ (French letters & DILDOES with a real Dimond Drip)
they will "assess me" & if I dont pay send in the Bailifs – I said I didnt
care if they did. Very nice man I may say but I wonder if they ever
dream how ordinary people live & havent a clew about Fartists of any
sort. not a clew. I don't know what I sell ever.'
     Unfortunately, the complications of tax meant that the more Burra
sold, the more of a problem he created for himself. They also ensured
that he got very little enjoyment out of his money. As he perceived it,
he was 'taxed' by the Lefevre, since the gallery took one-third of the
gross profit, which was a standard rate at the time (it would now be
considered modest). He also had to pay for the framing, which was
similarly standard practice, though this has never stopped anyone feeling
ill used. The tax-man then gouged what was left, and now suddenly the
VAT man wanted a cut as well. After a Lefevre exhibition, he wrote
sarcastically, 'over a thousand pounds went to VAT so after 33 ⅓ per
cent & those frames I make a fortune & far exceed the Soshulcontrack
dont I?'[1] As he understood it, he was taxed and taxed and taxed, to the
point where he worried that there wasn't enough left to live on. It all
made him *feel* poor, even though he wasn't by any possible objective
measurement.

---

[1] The 'Social Contract' was a great phrase of the time; it was much bandied about when Labour
was seeking – successfully – a return to office in 1974.

He became increasingly peculiar about money. Barbara Roett observed that he was mean to Bar, whom he thought of as a business-woman, therefore prosperous, which she was not – 'Ed can get his hand into his pocket, but he can't get it out again,' Bar used drily to comment. Literally so: his small crumpled claw would descend slowly and fumblingly into his pocket, and stick there, as he visibly changed his mind. Yet he once asked Barbara Roett herself, apropos of nothing, while staring out of the window in Islington, 'Do you want some money?' – he could understand that she might be short of money because she was young, whereas he refused to understand that Bar's unhesitating hospi-tality arose from bottomless generosity rather than financial security. The offer was an indication, she thought, of affection. Similarly, John Aiken, Conrad's son, noted that Burra never played the host in restau-rants, 'but from time to time would slip a large banknote into one's hand, saying for example, "that'll pay for a few brussels sprouts"'. For himself, his way of life was frugal; he had a good sense of how much he needed to get through a year, and he no longer wanted to travel beyond Britain because he hadn't the energy. And there was no point in saving for his old age since he was enough of a realist to know that he would not have one.

It is so often the case that the final turning-point of someone's life is a fall. It seems as if the jolt to an elderly body has effects far beyond the directly physical repercussions of a broken bone; it starts the clock ticking on the final countdown. Burra's body at sixty-nine was more like that of a man in his eighties. Chappell's account of what happened when Burra fell in October 1974 and was taken unconscious to hospital is both horrific and funny.

Anne went to meet her brother off the London train at five, but when he was not on the expected train or either of the two that followed it, she rang Bar, who rang Chappell. Some time later, St Thomas's Hospital rang Bar, with whom Burra had been staying, to say that he was in casu-alty. Bar then alerted Geoffrey Dove; and Barbara Roett remembers Dove ringing the hospital, saying urgently, 'Don't touch him, don't touch him, nobody touch him!' He was afraid that if a consultant saw Burra, he might schedule an immediate operation to remove his spleen, and he was convinced that although a splenectomy would have been a good idea in the Thirties when Burra was very much younger and fitter, at his age and in his generally debilitated state, such an operation would probably kill him. Dove joined Bar and Chappell at Islington, and the three of them set out for St Thomas's, where they found Burra, still in casualty.

He was wearing a cotton hospital shift tied with tapes and staring with guarded hostility from a tilted stretcher bed stuck in a corner: his face incredibly wan, his hair standing up every which way, his bony arms tangled over his head . . . and a mauve lump the size of a hen's egg just above one eye.

Shaking with mixed emotions – relief at finding him; terror at finding him in such circumstances – we burst into hysterical jabbering. 'For heaven's sake, Ed! What *have* you been doing? *Why* didn't you make them ring before? They said you have been here since four-thirty.'

Ed's baleful expression told us we were guilty of what was to him the unforgivable crime of 'Making a Fuss'. His reply was not only a flat statement of fact. It was delivered with deliberate complacency. 'I was dead *drunk*', he said . . .

A young nurse standing a few feet away looked round. It was abundantly clear from her expression that she regarded each one of us with suspicion. She was in the middle of counting what turned out to be one thousand and nine hundred pounds in twenty pound notes which Edward had been carrying in his inside breast pocket.

The money was presumably one of his half-yearly doles from the Lefevre. He also possessed a battered plastic carrier bag, 'to which he had obviously clung as though it contained the Koh-i-noor. Its actual contents, we discovered later, were two pounds of scrag end of lamb purchased from the butcher near Raymond's Revue Bar.'

His friends were relieved to find that the damage was apparently superficial. When the X-ray came back, it revealed that no bones were broken, and though the hospital kept Burra under observation that night, when Dove arrived to check up on him the following day, he was able to persuade the hospital to release Burra to Charlton Place. His injuries were certainly painful: he confessed to Monica Wodehouse that 'my ribs and shoulder were terrible & as I also had a frightful cough every time I coughed it was like being stabbed'.

By January, he was writing to Clover that he was better. The only problems were that the episode brought on his anaemia again, as almost any physical setback did by then, and that even after three months he was still having trouble sleeping. 'I feel much better in fact normal I think due to "Oravite" vitamins that Geoffrey gave me & Ive been taking them since the accident . . . I still take Johns nembies (1 at night) as I don't sleep but now & again if I don't & <u>lay awake</u> thinking horrors. N's are the only thing that seem to be quite natural like the real thing.' 'John' here may be John Banting, who had been dead for two years by then: in a letter written in the last months of his life, he was nagging Burra to get his doctor to prescribe him Nembutal, and may have pressed a supply upon him. A barbiturate such as Nembutal is quite unsuitable for a heavy drinker, and so Burra's doctor gave him Mogadon, which had disastrous effects. 'It sounds like the Beast in Revelations and acts like him after going off into abstract nightmares I awoke & got up to piss but found I had no balance at all and couldnt walk straight. However I managed – and slept all the rest of the night. Never again.' Sleep problems aside, there seemed to be no reason for Burra not to make a full recovery. But in retrospect, Chappell saw him declining from that point on.

The tenderness of Chappell's love for Burra comes through his last memories. How clear his friend is in his mind, six years after his death. Usually only lovers or parents write like this, so aware of the other's physical presence and well-being. After Burra's accident:

I noticed his face seemed smaller – paler. Not actually marked, but as though its outline had been redrawn by a slightly shaky hand. After two or three whiskies, the faintest pink glow appeared on his cheekbones and the extreme tip of his deli-cate nose.

The visits to London became fewer and far less energetic. He seemed relieved rather than resentful (as one had known him before) at the close watch his friends kept on his comings and goings. He was met at the station and taken to the home-ward train again at the end of his visit. I would catch sight of him when I went to meet him and see him moving (as slowly and deliberately as a snail) among the trailing figures of the last passengers to alight; a duffle bag hung over his shoulder. I felt a surge of affection as I watched him approach so slowly and painfully, and we embraced when he passed the barrier (who are those two dotty old men kissing each other? They must be foreigners).

Burra started to be more of a worry to his friends after the accident. It limited his life considerably, because he was so frightened of falling again that it slowed him down, both literally and psychologically. He admitted to Clover, 'I find London a bit of a trial as I walk about an inch a mile reeling about & don't dare go by bus I'm terrified of falling over Ive not tried the tube.' Bar started to find him rather difficult to manage. He wrote in June 1975, 'I havent seen Bar but Ive "heard" quite a lot as we write I think shes terrified to have me to stay without Nurse Chappell.' Chappell was becoming indispensable to him, though he did not actually move into 2 Springfield Cottages. Burra valued his privacy to the point of obsession.

He recovered sufficiently to be disenchanted by politics. 'As soon as I he[a]r MORLS mentioned I begin to shudder – everything to do with the present govt is strongly MORL even Lady Forkbender is MORL not like Christine Keeler.'[2] 1975 was the last, increasingly peculiar, year of Harold Wilson's government; in which his secretary, Marcia Williams, whom he had ennobled as Lady Falkender, played a curiously dominant role, and Westminster had become 'a strange world of backstabbing and personal viciousness'. Burra commented acidly, 'Louis le Harold 15th Wilson so dixhuitieme don't you think? Ennobleant ses vielles Tourtes?'[3] Life went back to a sort of normality, but on a quietly diminished level. He continued to go and stay with the Barbaras, but he did less and less. 'I don't ever go out further than Chapel Market & the Duke of Pisspot when Im in Islington & never get up till 11! It is a rest from washing cooking shopping painting – even that! I get stuffed in a cab & go & see Gerald at the Gallery & then I go back to the bottle & read Sci-Fi. There realy are quite a few things Ide like to see but its all Too much.'

Kenneth Ritchie, Anne's brother-in-law, was dying in the course of 1975, of cancer; Burra wrote in August, 'Now he's in St Helens Hospital Ore having had a hemorage from the arse. said to be from the liver – "They" don't say anything – nor do "they" know anything – more than "les medecins de Moliere" if you ask me. I realy think Ken shows spirit.' He was transferred to King Edward VII's Hospital for Officers in September, and in October died there. Colin Ritchie thus became fourth Baron Ritchie of Dundee, in succession to his two older brothers, and Anne became Lady Ritchie. Though he was fond of Kenneth, Burra

---

[2] This substitution of Forkbender for Falkender refers to the Israeli psychic Uri Geller, seen bending cutlery by the power of mind alone on the Dimbleby show in 1973: *Private Eye*, to which Burra was devoted, used to refer to her thus.

[3] 'Ennobling his old tarts'.

did not attend either his memorial service at St Martin-in-the-Fields or Colin's subsequent investiture in Westminster Abbey.

One minor embarrassment which resulted from the death of Kenneth Ritchie was that he was discovered to be discreetly homosexual. Chappell, describing how he came to live in Thurloe Square to an interviewer in the Nineties, explained that he had got to know Kenneth Ritchie pre-war because he was 'very much a night-club person about town'. A phrase which suggests at least the possibility that they had met in clubs that Chappell himself frequented, and therefore that Chappell, at least, was quite well aware of his tastes (it might also explain why Ritchie liked to hand-pick his tenants). Chappell was promptly drafted in: 'Mrs Chappell left with Colin & Anne (in Kens new Rover) for Thurloe P where they are examining papers – 5 copies of "HIM", "MAN" Gay Liberation monthly &c several copies were found at Bosney & smuggled out for fear they should be discovered by Mrs Grimgore whilst cleaning up.'

But the principal fall-out, as far as Burra was concerned, from the demise of Kenneth Ritchie was that at the end of 1975 Billy Chappell had to leave not only Pump Cottage in Rye, which was Ritchie's property, but his flat in Thurloe Square. He was one of three tenants there; Ritchie had used only the first floor as his London pied-à-terre, with a housekeeper and her family in the basement, someone else on the second floor, and Chappell on the third and fourth. 'A & Colin are going up to morrow to see lawyers and try & get poor old Donald or Ronald or whatever his name is to <u>leave</u> – where to, I can't think,' Burra wrote (Donald/Ronald was the second-floor tenant). 'When Mrs Baker [the housekeeper] & co. leave there won't be anybody to do the hot water etc.' Chappell's tenancy was an agreement between friends, but in any case, the 1974 Rent Act maintained the principle established by post-war legislation on property, of protecting sitting tenants. As long as there were no improvements to the flat, rents remained fixed at what they had been when the tenancy began, and tenants had the right to remain indefinitely.

Colin and Anne (who were principal beneficiaries; they got 42 per cent of Kenneth's estate) wanted to sell the house; but the relations between Burra, Chappell and the Ritchies were such that this had to be a matter for mutual negotiation. It seemed to Burra that the only thing to do was to act on sustained nagging from both Bar and Anne, and buy Chappell a place of his own.

. . . we have been looking about for a little residence for Billy the Ritchies ought to pay not me I think for <u>alternative accommodation</u> as Colin said if the house had sitting tenants they could only get £15.000 but if it was empty £40.000 however I don't mind paying & am pleased to do so. For <u>something</u> must be done I realy do think.

Chappell, meanwhile, moved to a ground-floor flat with garden, part of a house belonging to Alexander Grant, a principal dancer with the Royal Ballet, who left the country that year for a seven-year stint as Director of the National Ballet of Canada. Meanwhile, the usual suspects – Anne, the Bars and Chappell himself – started looking for somewhere suitable and affordable. 'Im afraid I shall never be able to afford a large enough house to hold all the Chappell relics,' Burra worried. 'I can afford up to 12 or 13 thousand but not more realy.' He was horrified to discover how the price of houses had risen, even in the few years since he had been looking for a new home himself.

They ended up finding a modest house in Rye in the spring of 1976; one of a terrace of attractive early-nineteenth-century bay-windowed brick cottages in a street called Rope Walk, very handy for the station (Chappell's London base continued to be Alexander Grant's garden flat). The house needed some work: '. . . the builders will soon be attacking Ropewalk I expect heaven knows what they are up to as no one goes near the place! Hes got the key – I have no interest in houses realy.' The renovations sprang the usual problems, and by the time Chappell was able to move in, everyone was sick of it. 'Well dear Mrs Chappell says if any one else writes & says its positively no trouble whatever to move she is going to scream stamp and hit people . . . I think Cyril has finished painting & then I was informed by her ladyship that a "piece of the ceiling" had come down in the Bow window! So I hope the builder will see to it.'

One interesting aspect of this gift was that Chappell was apparently unaware of it at the time. When he was interviewed about his life in the early Nineties, his version of events was, 'originally Edward saw the house, and said, "do you want the house?" and he paid the rent. Of course, I was rather broke at the time.' Chappell had never had any money. As a dancer, he had been ludicrously badly paid, and his post-war career as a director and designer had never been particularly lucrative. Further, his working future was not looking very promising, because his work was beginning to seem rather old-fashioned, and he had nothing in the way of pension. Burra, perhaps, feared that giving Chappell a house would damage the friendship, which was of the greatest importance to him, or perhaps he was just embarrassed. In either case, Chappell genuinely seems not to have realised that Burra had bought the house for him. The facts of the matter only unravelled when Burra died – intestate, since he had quite typically not got round to making a will. But that meant everything went to his sister, who acted as Burra had, of course, trusted her to, and gave the house to Chappell. 'When it became Anne's property she said, "Well, I don't want it, I'm going to give it to you."'

But the muddle may have arisen for quite different reasons, since Burra had other things on his mind than Chappell's finer feelings as the spring went on. In May 1976, while the builders were still at work on 23 Rope Walk, he fell over again, this time while sober. He stumbled over a picturesque, deep, eighteenth-century doorstep while coming out of a shop in Rye High Street, and crashed to the pavement. There was no handrail; perhaps it had been a casualty of the wartime salvage drive. Thus it might be said that Tinkerbell Towne did for him in the end. He broke his leg and hip, and his recovery was lengthy and very painful. He spent a week in hospital (the hospital in Hastings in which Banting died) and three weeks in a Hastings nursing home, St Augustine's, by which time he could move about with a Zimmer walking frame, whereupon he was released to the care of his sister at 5 Fair Meadow.

I realy felt if I didn't get out of that home I should kill myself being deadly depressed from about 200000 anti Biotics didn't help at all.

His depression was not eased by malnourishment, since he found the food at St Augustine's inedible. Clover wrote urgently, 'You <u>must have some proper food</u> a cold buffet could be laid on without hurting their feelings – surely – even if only Tomatoes, a bottle of olive oil, a few lemons, some "lazy garlic" in a false plastic head you shake out finely powdered, for dressing. Some good cheese & biscuits, a tin of tongue or lamb's tongues, hard boiled eggs (very good with dressing) a lettuce. Tins of tunny fish or crab . . . besides antibiotics, I think it's the lack of good food depressing you most.'

He was initially very glad to get out of the nursing home, but staying with the Ritchies was not that much of an improvement. The overall shock to his system set off his anaemia, since he mentions living on porridge, Ambrosia creamed rice and a little fish. But apart from that, he did not feel comfortable or welcome. 'Wimbledon we have which I don't mind & a quarrel every evening which comes on as soon as my Lord has had one too many. He gets very techy! Its very odd realy as otherwise he behaves very well & is very kind.'

Though Burra was clearly trying to give credit where credit was due, he and his brother-in-law were fundamentally incompatible. Also, Burra was not at his most adaptable. He was very depressed, longing to get back to the work without which his life made no sense to him; loathing the pain he was in and the hideous Zimmer frame, and bored out of his mind. But even if he had not been so fretful, he was inevitably a disruptive presence in a more conventional household. 'Everything is so spotless and neat and nice and gracious I hardly knew where to put out a cig,' he complained, after going there for Christmas lunch one year. Ritchie came to dislike him intensely during this enforced stay, which distressed Anne greatly.

Another reason why Burra longed for home was that he did not share the household's taste in food, dictated in part by the fact that Anne did not enjoy cooking, and in part by Ritchie, who wore dentures by the Seventies and had difficulty chewing. The household's diet involved far more ready-prepared food than Burra was used to. In the main, Anne had to cater for him separately, because of his jaundice, but a very unhappy letter to Chappell suggests his claustrophobia and sense of entrapment.

Here we are sulking away (after the 5th gin) . . . I had a sole yesterday it was very good – 'they' had pies from the swiss pie shop – so if you come down in the morning you might – get a couple of soles or a couple of skate peices! . . . Well I realy don't think we are very happy here but theres nothing I can do about it. Hope to see you Thursday – & I have been walking without the machine – I can walk into the kitchen & bedroom & lavatory etc. How I hate being 'dependent' and having it thrown at my head at intervals.

Burra went home as soon as he possibly could, still in considerable pain. The table and chairs in the kitchen were shifted round to give him a series of things to cling on to as he moved about, and Bar Roett had the good idea of moving his bed down to the studio, for which he was grateful. By that time, Colin did not even want Anne to go and see him, so she had to slip out discreetly, not taking the car. 'A will walk down, thereby obviating paranoia-hysteria which goes on full outside here at intervals with a vengeance – your right I cant face those happy evenings theyre too much. I dont care for such behaviour. He couldn't possibly have been kinder & nicer when A was away in Summerset. It realy is weird.' Burra was no stranger to nervous irritation, but he was used to being loved. He found Ritchie's reaction to him incomprehensible.

The summer of 1976 was extraordinarily hot; but although Burra normally enjoyed the heat, he was past taking pleasure in it. He was also profoundly grieved by the death of Bumble Dawson in June. 'I am unable to write about it,' was all he said (she had recovered magnificently from a terrible car accident in 1975, but then died of a heart attack). His body began slowly to heal: by the beginning of July he could report, 'I have been trying to walk alone & almost can. leaning on the furniture.' However, in mid-August, he was still dependent on the Zimmer and still in pain from day to day, but above all, glad to have escaped from 5 Fair Meadow.

I must say I like to buy my own things & Im thankful to be back here & doing a bit of painting too I don't believe its ever going to rain again – & the country is Bright yellow! Like gamboge & chrome! very beautiful in a way.

John Aiken took him to Stone Cliff, in Sussex. 'Though no more than two hundred feet high, it forms an impressive ridge . . . normally a rich green . . . it was in the great British drought of 1976 burnt to a wonderful range of shades of gold and warm brown. I like to think that my pointing this out to Ed as we drove past it, not many months before his death, inspired him to paint it.' Yellow was a favourite colour of his; and this was his last completed painting. The house, however, was beyond him (many of his last letters are dated from 'The Shambles'), and he was even prepared to admit his dependence.

Ive been meaning to write but have been swamped in riseing tides of rubbish and old bottles & dirty clothes. I think Billy is coming down tomorrow & he wont stand for it, nurse Chappell will soon have it ship shape (I only hope).

Two months later, he was dead. Chappell records the onset of his final illness. He had been working on Sheridan's *The Rivals* in Dublin, and as soon as he returned, went to see Burra in Playden.

At the dead end of September I spent my last weekend with him. Everything appeared more or less as usual until on Sunday he excused himself and retired to bed. Later, I heard him vomiting in the bathroom. Over-respectful (as we had always been) of each other's privacy I waited till I knew he was back in bed before I ventured into his room. He was on the bed; ashen faced, fully dressed, looking drained of all energy. I enquired tentatively if he wanted something to drink. He refused saying he felt terribly sick. I brought him a bowl and retired to the kitchen; later to my room.

Neither of us slept. I lay listening. He vomited on and off all night. No ordinary sickness; only dark, stinking water. I would take the bowl, empty it, rinse it and return it to him. Towards daylight he slept a little; I was thoroughly alarmed by the time Anne arrived.

'He's very unwell,' I said, and told her about the sickness. I returned to my work in London full of forebodings. When I rang that evening Anne told me he had been taken to the hospital. I never saw him again.

Burra died on 22 October, in the hospital in Hastings. Anne described his last few days in a letter to Barbara, written the day after the funeral.

I couldn't really speak yesterday and there wasn't much chance to tell you about Edward's last fearful week and perhaps you don't really want to know in which case read no further.

I do think St Helen's hospital behaved rather cruelly to him on the last Friday by not telling me earlier how ill he had become so that I didn't see him till he was almost unconscious. When I reached him in the E Sussex hospital he just murmured 'I'm dying' & then I think lost consciousness.

A very kind clergyman appeared soon after then from visiting someone in the next bed, he took one look & said 'I see how it is' & gave him a blessing. After all that along came some sort of a surgeon creature blithely telling me that they were trying to resuscitate Ed in order to operate on the bowel which would probably mean removing the spleen. I asked if Ed had given permission for this which took the surgeon back a bit & he had to admit that of course Ed was much too ill to be able to do such a thing. I then felt really trapped knowing that Ed couldn't possibly recover <u>properly</u> with or without the operation & that he would much rather die than have one. Soon after this he was taken into Intensive Care where the sister had no illusions about his condition – she and the matron were kindness itself – I must truly say I was thankful when he finally gave in and died – he could <u>never</u> have fully recovered & I felt he would have been pleased to have cheated the surgeon!

That is why I nearly fainted when on Monday morning a post mortem was suggested, asked for in fact, but I wouldn't give permission – it sounds as though I was against all surgeons which is far from the case but Ed as you know had a sort of dread & prejudice.

Thank you very much for your letter and for all your help and kindness.

Everything in Burra's letters confirms Anne's instincts. She knew her brother better than anyone. Burra was only ever prepared to live on his own terms; and he several times expressed his extreme distrust and suspicion of surgery. His death certificate gives bowel obstruction, bronchopneumonia and hereditary spherocytosis as the causes of death. Presumably it was the pneumonia that actually killed him.

As his shattered friends kept telling one another, he had done amazingly well. 'People have been expecting me to die for fifty years,' he said in an *Observer* interview in 1971, truthfully. He responded sharply when Rothenstein spoke to him of his uncertain health, 'Nonsense. I have the constitution of a mule. Otherwise, how could I have made it for so *long*?' One truth balances the other; he lived in a state of chronic debility which would have flattened a lesser man, but he was also remarkably tough. Having never been well in his life, he knew how to manage himself.

Many platitudes might be offered at this point. Given his essential strength, of mind, if not of body, if he had refrained from taking inappropriate risks, smoked less, not inhaled ('I draw deep in,' he said), just said no, refused to go to Mexico, observed guidelines, eschewed getting blind drunk in the Capacannina Club with the manager of Wheeler's, let well-intentioned people run his life for him, been frightened of more things, he might have lived longer. But he passed the Bible's three score and ten, if only just, and the living that he did in that time was real and on his own terms.

Despite his fragile body, he insisted on his right to experience. He complained very little, and whined not at all. He made a variety of practical demands on his friends, but almost no emotional demands. He lived in a way that filled his mind with images, memories, nightmares

and random associations while allowing him the intellectual and physical control that translated this internal world into ever larger and more
beautiful pictures. His contempt for his physical health was that of a
man who was recklessly consuming himself in passionate observation.
Only an extraordinary will kept him going till he was seventy-one.

As solitary celibates go, his was hardly a life without love. His relationships were unorthodox, but they were enduring; he was not the
single most important person in anybody's life except his sister's, and
perhaps Billy Chappell's, but he was one of the three most important
to a good half dozen. Of Anne, there is no real doubt. Chappell remarked,
'Edward was her be-all and end-all. Her poor husband never got a look-
in.' And Chappell himself, though he had a variety of lovers in the
course of his life, seems never to have found anybody else quite so interesting as he found Burra. Bar thought that for Burra, that was probably enough; that he was happy in his own way. She remarked, 'I think
he led a very vicarious life. He . . . we . . . were all passionately interested in films. And I don't think in a way he was really concerned with
first hand relationships – in spite of all the people he knew, the friends
who always surrounded him . . . Edward's letters were always full of
detail . . . but not much about how he felt.' But he was intensely loyal,
and inspired intense loyalty. He got the kind of love that suited him.

He could be maddening, even to those who loved him best. He was
wayward, unpredictably reserved, sometimes demanding; he had blind
spots, notably about money; he developed 'things' about people, or
places; he preferred to seem rude or bloody-minded than to admit weakness; sometimes he *was* rude or bloody-minded. For someone brought
up to be an English gentleman (and, to a surprising extent, going along
with his parents' notions by and large), he did amazingly few things
just because other people thought he should, any more than did Francis
Bacon or Derek Jarman, other original-minded queers who were the
products of essentially similar backgrounds. David Dickinson, who was
a child growing up in Chapel Square when Burra lived there, aware of
him not as a painter, but as a strange and singular grown-up unlike any
other, wrote to me, 'Years later when I met Owen's line, "the low sly
lives before the fauns" I thought of Ed Burra. He was before the fauns.
And the queer thing is one knew he was special.'

As a painter, the element of his work which surprises the most is his
extraordinarily vigorous capacity for reinventing himself. Burra kept

having new ideas into his last year of life, and he never degenerated into delivering the expected. Some elderly painters go on embarrassingly cranking out versions of stuff once perceived as dangerously avant-garde, unaware that things have moved on. Others, even more embarrassingly, bolt on a random selection of borrowings from whatever is new without really adjusting their mentality. Neither of these is remotely true of Burra. He is as much of a concentrated intelligence, with as much to say, in 1976 as he had been in 1926. Naturally, what he has to say is different, and if he had survived into his eighties, it would have been different again.

George Melly once asked the philosopher A.J. Ayer to define genius. He said, 'A genius is someone who alters, however radically, however slightly, our perception of reality.' Burra certainly did that: Bumble remarked, 'After you had seen a drawing by him you saw those people all over the streets. Everyone looked like his strange view of them.' But what people mean by 'Burra-esque' is his work from 1926 to 1937; when his work was dominated by social comment, or social satire; the iconic images of sailors, dockside barmaids, black street life, which *are* 'Burra' to most people. William Feaver, in the Lefevre centenary catalogue, says, 'He would have given cosmetic surgery a good going over. Forever Burra: those narrowed eyes and fake grins when the skin's pulled tight behind the ears.'

Not necessarily. Feaver is thinking of the Toulon smart set paintings of the Twenties, the sailors in bars, and the 'monsters', Mae West & co., whom Burra was painting in the Thirties. While the weeny, vulnerable-looking child-women who were fashion icons in the Sixties and Seventies were not Burra's cup of tea, if he had still been interested in painting 'monsters', the era was not short on grotesques. He was strongly drawn to Janis Joplin, whom he admired as a singer, and pitied, 'one of the damned, poor thing', but it never occurred to him to paint her. There were also the new media personalities and celebrities, there was the ever-flamboyant drag-queen Danny La Rue, holding court in his club in Hanover Square from 1964, 'the notorious George Melly', and the denizens of the Colony Room.

But Burra's high-camp low-life had been ground-breaking, even shocking, in the Twenties. To have continued painting in that vein at a time when nobody, not even Mrs Mary Whitehouse, was shocked or disturbed by Mr La Rue would have made him a sort of court jester, a

Beryl Cook for the thinking classes. He would have had an eager audience if he had been content to be Burra-esque, but he was not, though it was obvious in his later years that he would have profited mightily from so doing: Barbara Ker-Seymer commented sadly in 1971 to John Banting, apropos of his Hamet Gallery exhibition, that buyers were jostling for the opportunity to buy the Thirties' paintings, but 'none of them will look at Ed's beautiful landscapes'. Both his implicit questioning of motorways and all they implied, and his highly individual mystical streak, made him an uncomfortable presence in the have-it-all Seventies.

Being disquieting was part of his mission in life. His work of the Thirties was perceived as disturbingly weird by a variety of contemporaries. Even in 1942, the critic Raymond Mortimer reeled out of Burra's wartime exhibition in the Redfern Gallery, wailing 'They're so *loud*.' Bryan Robertson was eventually so convinced of Burra's importance that he wrote a book about him (in 1979), but in his large-scale survey of British art published in 1965 Burra is not even mentioned, a censorship by silence that is a testimony to the genuine difficulty which he presented to the critical establishment in his lifetime (similarly, he is not mentioned in H.J. Paris's *English Water Colour Painters* (1945) – though Paris subsequently wrote to Burra with abject apologies for omitting him).

It is worth remembering that at a time when English art was almost wholly dominated by abstraction and landscape – the Thirties – Burra painted highly individualised people against city backgrounds. At a time – the Sixties – when art was dominated either by abstraction or by the human figure, variously treated, he turned to landscape. 'He saw and painted the related but utterly unobvious; and only artists and children have the imagination and courage to do that.' His motto was 'la minoria siempre' ('always side with the minority') and he lived up to it: he spent his life jumping off bandwagons. He was not always easy company, but he saw through his own eyes, and never through anyone else's.

NOTES

MANUSCRIPT sources for Burra's life are listed as follows: material in the Hyman Kreitman study collection in Tate Britain is referred to with the prefix TGA, with its section, box and item number. Material in the Huntington Library, San Marino, California, is from their Aiken collection, calendared under AIK: the letters are divided into groups by sender and receiver, but the items are not individually numbered. Material headed SCRO is from the Sussex County Record Office, Lewes; anything headed NLA is from the National Art Library (in the Victoria and Albert Museum). The Lefevre Gallery's letters collections are not calendared, and are therefore referred to only under 'Lefevre' with the sender and receiver, and the known, or inferential, date of the letter.

NB: nomenclature has presented a certain problem. The subject of a biography is most properly referred to by his surname; this convention has been adopted. Most of Burra's women friends, however, changed their surnames at least once; and switching between Clover Pritchard, Clover de Nagy and Clover Pertinez, for example, in different chapters is calculated to irritate more readers than it enlightens; however, after 1927, no contemporary would have referred to her as Pritchard. I have therefore referred to Burra's women friends by their first names.

Abbreviations are as follows:

AB	Anne Burra
AIK	Aiken Collection, Huntington Library
Aiken Letters	Joseph Killorin (ed.), *Selected Letters of Conrad Aiken* (New Haven & London: Yale UP, 1978)
BB	Betsy Burra
BC	Billy (William) Chappell

BD	Bumble (Beatrice) Dawson
BFI	British Film Institute
BKS	Barbara Ker-Seymer (Pease, Rhodes)
BR	Birdie (Florence) Rushbury
CA	Conrad Aiken
Causey, *Burra*	Andrew Causey, *Edward Burra: Complete Catalogue* (London: Phaidon, 1985)
CP	Clover Pritchard (de Nagy, Pertinez)
EB	Edward Burra
EB Remembered	William Chappell, *Edward Burra: A Painter Remembered by his Friends* (London: André Deutsch, 1982)
GC	Gerald Corcoran
Hayward catalogue	*Edward Burra: Hayward Gallery, London, 1 August – 29 September, 1985* (London: Arts Council of Great Britain, 1985)
JB	John Banting
Kavanagh, *Ashton*	Julie Kavanagh, *Secret Muses: The Life of Frederick Ashton* (London: Faber & Faber, 1996)
Lefevre	Burra archival collection, Lefevre Fine Art Ltd, 31 Bruton Street, London W1J 6QS
MA	Mary Hoover Aiken
MN	Margaret Nash
MW	Monica Wodehouse
NLA	National Art Library
PN	Paul Nash
Rothenstein, *Burra*	John Rothenstein, *Edward Burra* (Harmondsworth: Penguin, 1945)
SCRO	Sussex County Record Office
SF	Sophie Fedorovitch
SL	Seymour Lawrence
Stephenson, *Burra*	Andrew Stephenson, *The Work of Edward Burra, 1919–1936: Content and Imagery* (Edinburgh University D. Phil., 1988)
TGA	Tate Gallery Archive
WD	William Chappell, *Well Dearie, the Letters of Edward Burra* (London: Gordon Fraser, 1985)
WP	Wogan Phillips

Preface

XI   Burra: 'I don't know . . .':   TGA 2002/1.4, transcripts made from Arts Council
                                            film.

XIII   'Bring a psychiatrist   Bragg/Bacon, BBC film for the *South Bank Show*, 1985.
       and we'll find out':   Rothenstein in *EB Remembered*, p. 46.
XIV   irritation at documentary: *WD*, p. 191.
XIV   'Edward's personality':   Chappell, *EB Remembered*, p. 36.
XIV   a letter by George Bernard   Maisie Ward, *Gilbert Keith*
       Shaw: *Chesterton* (London: Sheed & Ward, 1944).

I.   Rye

1   description of gardens: Roger Cardinal, *The Landscape Vision of Paul Nash*
                                            (London: Reaktion, 1989), p. 16, 'elsewhere he
                                            seems struck by the eeriness of white statuary
                                            gleaming within clumps of deep shadow, finding
                                            several instances of such effects in gardens like that
                                            of Springfield near Rye in Suffolk'.

2   Rothenstein notes Burra's interest: Rothenstein in *EB Remembered*, p. 45.
3   'everything crumbling away . . .': TGA 2002/1.4, transcripts made from Arts Council
                                            film.

3   'a perfectly English look':   William Chappell, 'A Painter's Childhood Home',
                                            Interiors, April 1982, pp. 51–4.

3   a stuffed barn owl: Clarissa M. Lorenz, *Lorelei Two: My Life with Conrad
                                            Aiken* (Athens: University of Georgia Press, 1983),
                                            p. 113.

3   hall and staircase: Rothenstein, *Burra*, p. 9.
3   Burra's aesthetic: Chappell, *EB Remembered*, describes the incredible
                                            mess and muddle Burra generated around himself
                                            by his absolute and total indifference to cleanliness,
                                            order or comfort (p. 29): the 'sociological, autobi-
                                            ographical, geological strata'.

3   Robert Burra's descendants: Anne Ritchie in *EB Remembered*, p. 15.
5   'The library at Springfield . . .': Clover in *EB Remembered*, p. 79.
6   'Physically . . .':   Chappell, *EB Remembered*, p. 36.
6   Henry and Trudy's characters: Chappell, National Sound Archive tape 1897A.
6   American friend's profligacy with   *WD*, p. 10, 20 March 1973; *WD*, p. 210, 1975, 'I
       heating and lighting: somehow got innarupted by . . . Mrs Mary Augusta
                                            Aiken a very old friend of mine who has taken a
                                            cardboard plastic olde worlde Fyre Trappe upper
                                            very slippery wooden ladder in Ye Mynt Rye! and
                                            being American promptly turned every electrical
                                            appliance full on in every room of the house! talk
                                            of conserving energy dearie and I don't dare dream
                                            of the electricity Bill.'

6   1926 Christmas decorations: TGA 974.2.2.13, EB to BKS, 28 December 1926 (also
                                            following quotation).

7   Miss Isabella McCallum: There is a drawing in Causey, *Burra*, and another in

the Sotheby's catalogue, 3 June 2002, no. 211 (illustrated).

8   a lifelong attempt to look   Anne Ritchie in *EB Remembered*, p. 19.
     steadily at horror:

8   the Chelsea Palace variety   Causey, *Burra*, no. 117.
     theatre in the King's Road:

8   'The popular music . . .':   Osbert Lancaster, *All Done from Memory* (London: John Murray, 1953), p. 14.

8   cartoon identified as a *Peg's Paper*   *WD*, p. 28.
     illustration:

9   'Well dear . . .':   *WD*, p. 38.

9   'One of the things . . .':   Agatha Christie, *An Autobiography* (London: William Collins Sons & Co., 1977), p. 28.

9   'The library . . .':   Clover Pertinez in *EB Remembered*, p. 79.

10   'for sheer pleasure . . .':   Lancaster, *Memory*, p. 31.

11   Edward's constitution: There is a photograph of Burra at five or so with his sister Anne in *EB Remembered*, p. 18.

12   'I went to bed . . .'   TGA 974.2.2.46, EB to BKS, ? 1927/8.

14   'Écrivez moi une carte postale . . .':   TGA 939.2.4, Father to EB, April 1913 and 1 July 1914.

14   Sweets by post: Anne Ritchie in *EB Remembered*, p. 16.

14   Trudy's communications   TGA 939.2.4, Mother to EB, 6 October 1927, from
     with her son: Higham House, Robertsbridge, Sussex.

15   '17 October 1915':   *WD*, p. 11.

15   'he's really a terribly bad writer!':   *WD*, p. 161.

16   'Though pain be stark and bitter':   Maisie Ward, *Gilbert Keith Chesterton* (London: Sheed & Ward, 1944), p. 381.

16   'Dearest Daddie':   *WD*, p. 11.

17   this perception contains a   Samuel Hynes, *The Auden Generation: Literature and*
     substantial measure of truth: *Politics in England in the 1930s* (London: Faber & Faber, 1976), p. 329; Cyril Connolly, *The Enemies of Promise* (1938).

17   'the early ending of his   Rothenstein, *Burra*, p. 9.
     formal education':

18   life as an onlooker: Causey, *Burra*, no. 13.

19   a fribbling amateur and celebrity: Philip Hoare, *Serious Pleasures: The Life of Stephen Tennant* (London: Penguin, 1990).

19   'It's no good asking':   Chappell, National Sound Archive tape F 1896B.

19   'Anne was able to . . .':   *WD*, p. 32.

20   'Our parents . . . tide was high':   Anne Ritchie in *EB Remembered*, p. 16.

21   'suffragette, post-impressionist   E.F. Benson, *Mapp and Lucia* (London: Hutchinson,
     artist . . .':   1922), p. 27.

22   'au reservoir':   *WD*, p. 39. Burra re-encountered these late in his life, having forgotten them; his comment was, 'another perfect period peice. He has a sharp eye!' *WD*, p. 210.

22   eating in the kitchen with the servants: Lorenz, *Lorelei Two*, p. 113.

22   'Miss Mapp had sent':   Benson, *Mapp and Lucia*, p. 121.

23   'I have also visited . . .':   *WD*, p. 32 (1926).

23   friends with Nash: *WD*, p. 28 (1925).

23 Nash's fascination with American cartoonists: — Paul Nash, 'American Humorous Draughtsmen', *Week-End Review*, 8 August 1931.

23 'I went to see Paul N . . .': — TGA 2.2.52, EB to BKS, 27 February 1928.

24 'Well, I'd describe it as a pleasant din': — James King, *Interior Landscapes: A Life of Paul Nash* (London: Weidenfeld & Nicolson, 1987), p. 91.

24 Conrad Aiken in Rye: — Nash and Aiken met by chance, and became friends, Nash then brought Burra to Aiken's attention. Conrad Aiken, *Ushant* (New York: Duell, Sloan and Pearce; Boston; Little, Brown and Company, 1952), p. 278.

24 'Paul Nash, artist . . .': — *Aiken Letters*, p. 174, 25 April 1931.

24 'the variety of [Rye's] characters': — Aiken, *Ushant*, p. 251.

24 'couldn't walk a step . . .': — TGA 974.2.2.45, EB to BKS, ? 1927.

25 'Just as the modern Italian . . .': — Paul Nash, *Room and Book* (London: Soncino Press, 1932), pp. 27–8.

25 'He made no effort . . .': — Lorenz, *Lorelei Two*, pp. 8–9.

25 'If the town itself . . .': — Aiken, *Ushant*, p. 251.

26 'kept up Conrad's spirits . . .': — Lorenz, *Lorelei Two*, p. 147.

26 'The conversation at supper . . .': — John Aiken, Jane Aiken Hodge and Joan Aiken, *Conrad Aiken, Our Father* (Rye: Anthony Neville, 1989), p. 52.

26 'chewed the fat . . .': — *Aiken Letters*, p. 227, 1939.

27 'Ime reading a book by D.H. Lawrence . . .' — *WD*, p. 21.

27 'Tony, all beaming . . .': — *Aiken Letters*, p. 227, 1939.

27 'that astonishing pair . . .': — Aiken, *Ushant*, p. 252.

28 'Miss W is very funny . . .': — TGA 70.50.2049, EB to Margaret Nash, from Springfield.

28 'the antiente town . . .': — *WD*, p. 74.

28 'Sooner or later . . .': — Aiken, *Ushant*, p. 253.

28 'Anne is having her beau . . .': — TGA 974.2.2.58, EB to BKS, 22 August 1928.

28 'We are having a jolly lot . . .': — TGA 974.2.2.13, EB to BKS, 28 December 1926.

29 'Mummy got quite annoyed . . .': — TGA 939.1.4, AB to EB, 26 January 1930. She and her mother are at Cap Hotel, Bordighera, EB is at Springfield.

29 'We have such a jolly deb staying . . .': — TGA 974.2.2.22, EB to BKS, 15 June 1927.

30 'Betsy is going to . . .': — TGA 939.2.1, EB to AB, 25 January 1926.

30 'Anne has been to a jolly dance . . .': — TGA 2.2.24, EB to BKS, 19 July 1927.

30 'as for Clovers toes!': — TGA 974.2.2.112, EB to BKS, 25 August 1934.

30 homosexuals and murderers: — Aiken, *Ushant*, p. 252: 'Mrs Q, whom everyone thought to be a murderess, but who had miraculously got off, came down to [Rye] at once, after the trial, as a matter of course.'

30 'That Victorian house . . .': — Aiken, *Ushant*, p. 255.

31 'The walls are covered . . .': — Rothenstein, *Burra*, p. 9; *EB Remembered*, p. 29: Billy Chappell's description. Possibly he came to prefer the privacy and withdrawal represented by going up to the top of the house, or even to relish the implication of being the Creature in the Attic. Or more practically, was it Nanny's old room?

31 'The only time . . .':   Chappell, National Sound Archive tape 1897A.

32 'Painting is of course a sort of drug':   Rothenstein, *Tate Gallery Retrospective Catalogue*, p. 92 (letter to Chappell, c.1945.)

II. London

33 'we . . . could not bear   Anne Ritchie in *EB Remembered*, p. 16.

34 'I was only allowed . . .':   *EB Remembered*, p. 16.

34 'The Zepp raid':   *EB Remembered*, p. 20.

35 'resembling Monte Carlo':   *EB Remembered*, p. 17.

36 'Dear Edward':   *WD*, p. 12.

36 'Darlin Sis':   *WD*, p. 13.

37 'new cook is a jolly girl':   *WD*, p. 13.

37 'convention itself':   TGA 939.1.4, AB to EB, 26 January 1930. She and Ma were at Cap Hotel, Bordighera.

38 'the very model . . .':   *Flower of Cities: A Book of London. Studies and Sketches by Twenty-Two Authors* (London: Max Parrish, 1949), p. 172.

38 Al Stewart on Elvaston Place: 'Elvaston Place', first released as the B-side of the single 'News from Spain' (1970).

38 'Nothing will induce me to stay . . .':   TGA 974.2.2.39, EB to BKS, 20 December 1927.

39 Darnton Road: Chappell interview, National Sound Archive tape F1897A.

40 'We have a trying uncle . . .':   TGA 939.2.4, BC to EB, 24 July 1924.

41 'Oh her hubbie . . .':   *WD*, p. 31.

41 'I knew the hideous secret . . .':   TGA 974.2.2.39, EB to BKS, 20 December 1927.

41 'talking nonsense by the hour . . .':   Barbara Ker-Seymer interview, quoted by Kavanagh, *Ashton*, p. 83.

41 'We were very juvenile':   TGA 2002/1.4, transcripts made from BBC film.

42 'was out with a party . . . I should have gone':   TGA 939.2.4, BC to EB, 6 October 1927.

42 Chappell's masturbation: Kavanagh, *Ashton*, p. 24.

43 'Painters would be more in evidence . . .':   Anthony Powell, *Messengers of Day* (New York: Holt, Rinehart and Winston, 1978), p. 34.

43 'sexual infantilism . . .':   Goronwy Rees, *A Chapter of Accidents* (London: Chatto & Windus, 1972), p. 92.

44 Barbara Ker-Seymer: Chappell interview, National Sound Archive tape F1896B.

44 passion for film: Barbara Ker-Seymer interview, quoted by Kavanagh, *Ashton*, p. 82.

44 declaiming subtitles: Chappell, *EB Remembered*, p. 31, and TGA 974.2.2.42, EB to BKS, summer 1927 (from a film starring Lya de Putti).

44 'We spoke the same language':   Barbara Ker-Seymer interview, quoted by Kavanagh, *Ashton*, p. 82.

45 *Sporting Sketches*:   Macdonald Hastings, *Diane: A Victorian* (London: Michael Joseph, 1974).

45 dying only in 1946:   Hastings, *Diane*, pp. 40–1.

45 Caroline Creyke's interests: And, possibly, other women: a poem she published called 'Alone by the Sea' hints that she was once attracted to another girl (Hastings, *Diane*, p. 135).

45 'painted, sang, & was clever':   Hastings, *Diane*, p. 115.

45 Ker-Seymers in Park Lane: Hastings, *Diane*, pp. 221–3.

45 'Every time I read your address . . .':   TGA 779.1.345, BKS to JB, 9 December 1970.

46 'I've done my painful duty . . .':   Redacted by Barbara Roett, interview, 3 September 2006.

46 'where the fly-blown   Christopher Isherwood, *Lions and Shadows* (London:
    respectability . . .':   Hogarth Press, 1938), p. 58. The house was 26 Gledstanes Road, West Kensington, W16.

46 Barbara Ker-Seymer and   Marie-Jacqueline Lancaster, *Brian Howard: Portrait*
    Brian Howard: *of a Failure* (London: Timewell Press, 2005), p. 136.

46 'I do think a bunch of feathers . . .':   TGA 974.2.2.21, EB to BKS, 31 May 1927.

47 they rapidly became friends: Clover Pertinez in *EB Remembered*, p. 73.

47 Burra and beautiful clothes: Chappell, *EB Remembered*, p. 111.

47 Henry Moore on Burra's circle: Bryan Robertson, *A Sense of Place: The Paintings of Paul Nash and Edward Burra* (New York: Grey Art Gallery, New York University, 1982), p. 13.

47 'You know dear . . .':   *WD*, p. 38.

48 'Dearest Ed . . .':   TGA 939.2.4, BC to EB, undated, but 5/6 April 1929, from 35 Darnton Road.

48 'this evening she has . . .':   TGA 974.2.2.9, EB to BKS, 28 July 1926.

48 Burra's clothes: 974.2.2.77, EB to BKS, 29 August 1929.

48 events at Chelsea Arts Club Ball: *WD*, p. 64.

49 'some nice cockle shells':   *WD*, p. 43.

49 Fishnet Annie: *WD*, p. 43.

49 'it was a perfect dream . . .':   *WD*, p. 42.

49 Chappell on the foursome: Chappell in *WD*, p. 15.

50 'God rot the tea club':   *WD*, p. 15.

50 'an elderly but game Edwardian   Melly in *EB Remembered*, p. 8.
    tart . . .':

51 Goronwy Rees on Ker-Seymer: Selina Hastings, *Rosamond Lehmann* (London: Vintage, 2003), p. 148; Rees, *Chapter of Accidents*, p. 129.

51 'To hear them talk theoretically . . .':   Richard Aldington, *Death of a Hero* (London: Chatto & Windus, 1929), p. 24.

51 '[Ed] always made you feel . . .':   TGA 2002/1.4, transcripts made from BBC film.

51 'wrote most frivolously to me . . .':   Julie Kavanagh, review of *Well, Dearie*, drawing on interview with Bar Ker-Seymer (from a cutting in the Burra archive).

52 'mind you watch out . . .':   *WD*, p. 34, EB to BKS, January 1927, from 148 rue Vaugirard.

52 'Have you ever . . . ?':   Powell, *Messengers of Day*, p. 157.

52 Hermione Baddeley's rudeness: Chappell in *EB Remembered*, p. 36, notes, 'the only time I saw him weep was after the death of his mother'.

53 erections: Kavanagh, *Ashton*, p. 85.

53 Burra's problem standing: *WD*, p. 62.

53	Pritchard on Burra's pain:	Rothenstein in *EB Remembered*, p. 77.
53	'My wish affair . . .':	TGA 939.1.1, EB pocket diary for 1929.
54	'I love to be stoned . . .':	*WD*, p. 196.
54	heroin addicts:	Marek Kohn, *Dope Girls: The Birth of the British Drug Underground* (London: Lawrence & Wishart, 1992), pp. 120–49.
55	'I . . . had never heard . . .':	John Lucas, *The Radical Twenties: Writing, Politics, and Culture* (New Brunswick, NJ: Rutgers University Press, 1999), p. 127; Hubert Nicholson, *Half My Days and Nights: A Memoir of the 1920s and 30s* (London: Autolycus Publications, 1993), p. 64.
55	'I Guess He Will Tonight':	*WD*, p. 54. The first poem in Cecil Day Lewis's *Transitional Poems* quotes Sophie Tucker.
56	'. . . And I'm gonna buy . . .':	*WD*, p. 134.
56	'die Ruth Baldwin yellow . . .':	*WD*, p. 87.
56	photo of Nils Asther on a postcard:	*WD*, pp. 56–7.
56	'If you want to get . . .':	*WD*, p. 71, August 1929.
57	'these ten-inch bakelite records . . .':	'Into the Groove', *Tate Etc.* 2 (2004), http://213.121. 208.204/ tateetc/issue2/behindthecurtain.htm
57	'I'm serious about my work . . .':	TGA 2002/1.4, transcripts made from BBC film.
57	modernism in 1926:	'Only from about the year 1926 did the features of the post-war world begin clearly to emerge – from about that date one began slowly to realise that the intellectual and artistic output of the last seven years had been rather the last efforts of an old world, than the struggles of a new.' T.S. Eliot, 'Last Words', *Criterion* 18 (1939), p. 271.
58	'We called normal men . . .':	Kavanagh, *Ashton*, p. 84.
58	Betjeman's, Waugh's, and the Sitwells' rudeness:	Lucas, *The Radical Twenties*, p. 41.
58	'at that time there was . . .':	George Orwell, *The Road to Wigan Pier* (London: Gollancz, 1937), pp. 170–1.
58	Burra's six-month 'disappearance':	Rothenstein, *Burra*, p. 7.
58	'I should like to draw all day':	*WD*, p. 24.
59	student assignment:	Causey, *Burra*, p. 10.
59	'He was a wonderful draughtsman . . .':	John Aiken in *EB Remembered*, p. 52.
59	'The process of drawing . . .':	Michael Ayrton, 'The Art of Drawing', in Michael Ayrton, *The Rudiments of Paradise: Various Essays on Various Arts* (London: Secker & Warburg, 1971), pp. 169–70.
59	'I'm not at all sure . . .':	*WD*, p. 16.
60	'There were a lot of serious students . . .':	Interview, in Kavanagh, *Ashton*, p. 82.
60	Chappell on Burra's energy:	Chappell, National Sound Archives tape 897A.
60	'We would sit side by side . . .':	Michael Rothenstein, National Sound Archive tape C466/02/01–05.

61 'went with the Rushbury . . .': TGA 939.2.4, BC to EB, 23 December 1924.
61 'I hear you have been luring . . .': Lefevre, EB to Florence Rushbury, 1924.

III. Moving On

62 drawing a single eye: Christopher Neve, *Unquiet Landscape: Places and Ideas in 20th century English Painting* (London: Faber & Faber, 1990), p. 118.

62 'In those days . . .': Rothenstein, *Burra*, pp. 11–12.
63 'The small figure . . .': Rothenstein, *Burra*, pp. 11–12.
63 Lucy Norton's passion for ballet: Sue Bradbury, 'Lucy Norton' (obituary), *The Independent*, 18 July 1989.
63 'he thought . . .': *WD*, p. 28.
63 'she took three books . . .': TGA 974.2.1.13, BKS to EB, some time in summer 1927.
64 'Billy has once more . . .': TGA 974.2.1.25, BKS to EB, 17 February 1928.
64 'They are not such bad little things . . .': TGA 939.2.4, BC to EB, 6 October 1927.
65 '[it] makes . . .': *The Technique of the Love Affair, by a gentlewoman*, ed. Norrie Epstein (Edison, NJ: Castle Books, 2002, first published 1928), p. vii.

66 'What is this . . . ?': TGA 974.2.2.3, EB to BKS, summer 1926.
66 'Do you mean to say . . . ?': TGA 974.2.1.8, BKS to EB, 27 August 1926.
66 'I am so glad . . .': TGA 974.2.2.11, EB to BKS, 9 September 1926.
67 'My <u>dear</u>': TGA 974.2.2.13, EB to BKS, 28 December 1926.
67 Hodgkins became increasingly annoyed: TGA 974.2.2.28, EB to BKS, 6 September 1927: she is at the Pier Hotel, Sea View, Isle of Wight.
67 'By the way': TGA 974.2.1.11, BKS to EB, 14 January 1927.
67 'Barbara spends her time . . .': TGA 939.2.4, BC to EB, 3 June 1928, from 35 Darnton Road.
67 'Well dear, what have you . . . ?': TGA 974.2.2.15, EB to BKS, 6 February 1927.
68 'Have you heard anything . . . ?': *WD*, p. 40.
68 'Dennis is in search . . .': TGA 974.2.1.37, BKS to EB, 31 October 1928.
69 'He liked to spend . . .': Chappell, in National Sound Archive tape 2630A.
69 thoughtfulness which touched her deeply: TGA 939.2.4, BC to EB, 14 July 1927, from 35 Darnton Road.
69 'Dearest Ed . . .': TGA 974.2.1.1, BKS to EB, 16 September 1925.
69 'She was a plump . . .': Chappell, *EB Remembered*, p. 65.
69 '. . . oh my dear . . .': TGA 974.2.1.12, BKS to EB, 25 January 1927.
70 'Dear Ba Ba . . .': *WD*, p. 39.
70 Nash sharing anxieties: Anthony Bertram, *Paul Nash: The Portrait of an Artist* (London: Faber & Faber, 1955), p. 225.
70 Burra's manner with Nash: Bertram, *Paul Nash*, p. 303.
71 'Dear Ed . . .': TGA 939.2.4, BB to EB, 13 May 1927, presumably from The Links, Meads, Eastbourne.
71 He used to work over her drawings: Anne Ritchie in *EB Remembered*, p. 27.
72 'Well dear . . .': *WD*, p. 69.
72 'I did get a letter . . .': TGA 939.2.4, BC to EB, 19 August 1929, from c/o

		Matheson Lang Co., 'Jew Süss', King's Theatre, Glasgow.
72	a predictable imbroglio:	Marek Kohn, *Dope Girls: The Birth of the British Drug Underground* (London: Granta Books, 1992), p. 117.
73	'I'm so sorry ...':	TGA 974.2.1.42, BKS to EB, must be mid-August 1929.
73	'Well dearie':	TGA 974.2.2.77, EB to BKS, 29 August 1929.
74	He sat by her bed:	Chappell in National Sound Archive tape 1897A.
75	talking him into becoming a dancer:	Chappell in Clement Crisp, Anya Sainsbury and Peter Williams (eds), *Fifty Years of the Ballet Rambert* (London: Scolar Press, 1976), pp. 38–41.
75	'I approached the inevitable ...':	Chappell in Crisp et al., *Fifty Years*, p. 39.
75	new relationships:	Kavanagh, *Ashton*, pp. 159, 252.
76	she could not afford to buy a bed:	Simon Fleet, 'Sophie Fedorovitch, a Biographical Sketch', tipped into *Sophie Fedorovitch: Tributes and Attributes* (London: privately printed, 1955), pp. 5–6.
76	'I also visited ...':	John Rothenstein, *Edward Burra* (London: The Tate Gallery, 1973), p. 88.
77	'Sophie says ...':	TGA 974.2.2.96, EB to BKS, 23 August 1932.
77	'quiet, calm and deliberate ...':	Chappell, in Crisp et al., *Fifty Years*, p. 40.
77	'my dear I adore ...':	TGA 974.2.2.40, EB to BKS, some time in 1927.
77	Wyndhams at Clouds:	Caroline Dakers, *Clouds: The Biography of an English Country House* (New Haven & London: Yale University Press, 1993), p. 202.
78	snakes twined round her arms and neck:	Kavanagh, *Ashton*, p. 85.
78	'She was invited ...':	Val Williams, *Women Photographers* (London: Virago, 1986), p. 99 (interview with Barbara Ker-Seymer).
78	Olivia Wyndham's photographic subjects:	*WD*, p. 54: Burra was looking at her photographs. The Beaton portraits are in the National Portrait Gallery.
79	*Vile Bodies*:	Evelyn Waugh, *Vile Bodies* (London: Chapman & Hall, 1930), p. 123.
79	'part of the cultural archaeology ...':	By John Pearson, in *The Sitwells: A Family's Biography* (New York, 1978).
79	Cedric Morris writhing on the gravel:	TGA 974.2.1.31, BKS to EB, 4 June 1928.
80	'As no one ...':	*WD*, p. 59.
80	'have never even heard ...':	Diana Souhami, *Wild Girls: Paris, Sappho and Art* (London: Phoenix, 2004), p. 162.
80	'Of course says Birdie ...':	TGA 974.2.2.27, EB to BKS, 27 August 1927.
80	'Are you going to ... ?':	TGA 974.2.2.51, EB to BKS, 1928.
81	'Ed was rather quiet ...':	TGA 2002/1.4, transcripts made from BBC film.
81	'Did B tell you ... ?':	TGA 2.2.24, EB to BKS, 19 July 1927.
81	'Bugger Heaven ...':	TGA 939.2.4, BC to EB, 14 July 1927, from 35 Darnton Road; see Marie-Jaqueline Lancaster, *Brian Howard: Portrait of a Failure* (London: Timewell Press, 2005), p. 158.

81	one of the first society ladies to parade a black boyfriend:	Joan Schenkar, *Truly Wilde* (London: Virago, 2000), p. 138.
81	'I had been at Olivias . . .':	TGA 939.2.4, BC to EB, undated, but 5/6 April 1929, from 35 Darnton Road; Lancaster, *Brian Howard*, p. 161.
82	'desgusting I call it . . .':	TGA 974.2.2.33, EB to BKS, 28 October 1927.
82	'Lady Aimée Bureaux . . .':	TGA 974.2.2.8, EB to BC, c/o the Ballet Club: no date, inferentially dated from the fact that Billy was twenty in September 1927.
83	'My dear I have been . . .':	TGA 974.2.1.54, BKS to EB, 18 September 1928.
83	'an unprincipled . . .':	Rose Collis, *Colonel Barker's Monstrous Regiment* (London: Virago, 2002), pp. 177–9.
83	'and to think . . .':	TGA 939.2.8, Florence Rushbury to BC, Sunday, i.e. March 1929.
83	Barbara's pocket diary:	TGA 974.1.
83	'I'm having three jolly days . . .':	TGA 974.2.1.34, BKS to EB, 2 February 1929, from Tickerage Mill, Blackboys, near Uckfield, Sussex.
83	'yes dear I shant . . .':	TGA 974.2.2.71, EB to BKS, 12 February 1929.
83	'I must go home . . .':	TGA 974.2.1.40, BKS to EB, 2 August 1929, from 19 King's Road, Sloane Square.
83	'Sometimes a great butch lady . . .':	Kavanagh, *Ashton*, p. 84.
84	'I saw dainty':	*WD*, p. 55.
84	'Ruth took drugs':	Kate Summerscale, *The Queen of Whale Cay* (London: Fourth Estate, 1997), pp. 78–9.
84	She was a big girl:	Summerscale, *The Queen of Whale Cay*, p. 78.
84	'It was not enough . . .':	Humphrey Carpenter, *The Brideshead Generation* (London: Weidenfeld & Nicolson, 1989), p. 291.
84	'Babs went out . . .':	TGA 974.2.3.6, EB to BC, 1 August 1929.
84	She 'was never mistress of her camera . . .':	Cecil Beaton and Gail Buckland, *The Magic Image* (London: Weidenfeld & Nicolson, 1975).
85	Bar's studio:	Kavanagh, *Ashton*, p. 134.
85	'a sharply radical portraitist . . .':	Kavanagh, *Ashton*, p. 135.
85	'Burra's extraordinary fantasies . . .':	Nash, 'Photography and Modern Art' (1932), *Writings on Art*, p. 77.
86	1932 photograph:	TGA 974.5.4, p. 24, no. 9, 'Paris, 1932'.
86	'Brian at one time announced . . .':	Lancaster, *Brian Howard*, p. 136.
86	'making her subjects appear . . .':	Williams, *Women Photographers*, pp. 100–1.
87	also a friend of Burra's:	TGA 974.2.2.53, EB to BKS, 22 March 1928.
87	'Non-serious amateurism . . .':	Williams, *Women Photographers*, p. 99.
87	'It seemed to me . . .':	Quoted on the National Portrait Gallery website.
87	'How about coming up . . . ?':	TGA 974.2.1.47, BKS to EB, end of December 1930 or January 1931.
87	'at least 5 times life size':	TGA 974.2.2.79, EB to BKS, 28 January 1930.
87	Bar started working as a fashion photographer:	One such photograph, of the androgynous Nancy Morris (sister of Cedric Morris), is illustrated by Williams, p. 101.
88	'a tough American woman . . .':	From an autobiography which he published under the

pseudonym 'Robert Hutton', *Of Those Alone* (London: Sidgwick & Jackson, 1958),pp. 144–5.

88 'have just heard . . .': TGA 972.2.2.198, EB to BKS, undated.

88 'Am so sorry about Condé . . .': TGA 974.2.3.19, EB to Marty Mann, January 1933.

88 'I feel it best . . .': TGA 974.2.2.403, Dolly Wilde to BKS, 30 March 1932.

88 a new life as Director of the National Council on Alcoholism: Sally Brown and David R. Brown, *A Biography of Mrs Marty Mann* (Hazelden: Center City, Minnesota, 2001), pp. 71–7.

88 'I thought more than once . . .': TGA 974.2.2.306, Marty Mann to BKS, 25 August 1956. The comment quoted in a footnote is from TGA 974.2.1.132, BKS to B. Roett, 10 October 1954.

89 Burra and Powell's friendship: Powell, *Messengers of Day*, p. 126.

89 'Thanks for your interesting letter': TGA 974.2.2.38, EB to BKS, 12 December 1927.

89 'well at last I've seen Billy's new piece . . .': TGA 974.2.1.31, BKS to EB, 4 June 1928.

90 mingling of avant-garde students: Carpenter, *Brideshead Generation*, p. 78.

90 the parties Morris and Lett threw: Kavanagh, *Ashton*, p. 109.

90 Clover Pritchard vanishes: *WD*, p. 72.

91 'she had become identical . . .': *WD*, p. 72.

91 'Dearest Snooks': TGA 939.2.4, Mother to EB, 6 October 1927, from Higham House, Robertsbridge, Sussex.

92 'the most dissipated men I ever saw': TGA 974.2.2.17, EB to BKS, 8 March 1927.

92 'a feeling that the covers . . .' Causey in Hayward catalogue, p. 37.

92 some familiarity with 1890s painters: See Philippe Jullian, *Dreamers of Decadence* (London: Phaidon, 1974), fig. 58, Delville's *Trésor de Satan*, and fig. 127, Frédéric, *Le Torrent*.

93 'last night was a blizzard . . .': TGA 8913.13, EB to SL, 30 December, 1962, from Chapel House.

93 '. . . there was such an Ammerican sailor . . .': *WD*, pp. 35, 31.

93 'You can't camp . . .': Quoted in Ian Gregson, 'Camp's Out', *Poetry Review*, 86: 3 (Autumn 1996), p. 15.

93 'but what can one say to these people?': Samuel Hynes, *The Auden Generation: Literature and Politics in England in the 1930s* (London: Faber & Faber, 1976), p. 278.

94 Humphrey Jennings' hygiene: A revelation gleaned from a 'mass observation' piece of diary-keeping. Kevin Jackson, *Humphrey Jennings* (London: Picador, 2004), p. 170.

94 '[I hope] you are having baths . . .': NLA 86.x.25, Burra 1, PN to EB, 30 January 1927.

94 'the lower orders': *WD*, p. 31, 'what my granma must be like I cannot <u>think</u> for at the best of times she fears a revolution & Lives in mortal terror what she must be like what she must be like . . .

94 'Burra's primary interest . . .': Causey, *Burra*, p. 9.

95 'Most of us didn't even know . . .': Christopher Isherwood, *Lions and Shadows* (London: Hogarth Press, 1938), p. 110.

95 'we all volenteered': TGA 974.2.1.4, BKS to EB, 17 May 1926.

95 Burra's sense of common ground: Hynes, *The Auden Generation*, p. 274.

95	'he treated everybody with equal contempt':	Interview, 15 June 2006.
95	'I fly in a rage . . .':	Huntington Library, AIK 2197–2380, EB to CA, 11 November 1941.
95	almost Swiftian:	*WD*, p. 28.
96	'was very handy for ladies on the game . . .':	Stephenson, *Burra*, p. 195, quoting letters written to him by Clover and Bar.
96	'What other artist . . . ?':	Rothenstein, *Burra*, p. 13.
96	'if it hadn't been for Steinlen . . .':	Stephenson, *Burra*, p. 71 (from an interview, 23 July 1982).
97	'Don't you <u>adore</u> . . . ?':	TGA 974.2.2.45, EB to BKS, ? 1927 (*WD*, p. 59).
97	modernist art's preoccupation with the city:	Eric Hobsbawm, *Age of Extremes* (London: Michael Joseph, 1994), pp. 289–91.
98	young people rolling in the gutters:	Hynes, *The Auden Generation*, p. 44.
98	'Burra's concept of modern life . . .':	Causey, *Burra*, p. 14.
99	'Artists are continually enlarging our conception of the beautiful . . .':	Rothenstein, *Burra*, pp. 13–14.
99	Nash called Burra the modern Hogarth:	NLA 86.X.29, Margaret Nash memoir of Paul Nash, p. 43.

IV.   Finishing Schools

101	popular children's book:	Johanna Spyri, *Heidi* [1880], ch. 23.
101	'Bordighera is famous for its floriculture . . .':	Quotations from Karl Baedeker, *Northern Italy: Handbook for Travellers* (Leipzig, etc.: Karl Baedeker, 1906), pp. 104–6.
101	developers supplemented the native flora:	Mary Blume, *Côte d'Azur: Inventing the French Riviera* (London: Thames & Hudson, 1992), p. 38.
102	'The sea will be choppy . . .':	Lefevre, EB to BR, February 1925.
103	'When the sick people arrive . . .':	Frederic Lees, *Wanderings on the Italian Riviera* (Boston: Little, Brown & Co., 1913), pp. 34–5.
104	'I had a nurse at Bawdi . . .':	Lefevre, EB to BR, c.July 1925.
105	'We came back . . .':	*WD*, p. 16.
106	'I still hobble . . .':	*WD*, p. 21.
106	'I cant walk properly yet . . .':	Lefevre, EB to BR, c.July 1925.
106	'How are you old man . . .':	Lefevre, Trudy Burra to EB, at 10 Pulteney Street, Bath.
106	'Anna departs for Italia on the 25th . . .':	*WD*, p. 22.
107	teenage brides of art:	*WD*, pp. 18–19.
107	Severini's one-man exhibition:	Causey, *Burra*, p. 20.
107	'I returned from London . . .':	TGA 939.2.1, EB to AB, 22 April 1926, to Miss Anne Burra, Villa Donatello, Viale Principe Amedeo, Florence. Postcard.
108	Burra quoting Baudelaire:	Causey, *Burra*, p. 13.
108	English artists and surrealism in French periodicals:	Charles Harrison, *English Art and Modernism, 1900–1939* (New Haven & London: Yale University Press, 1994), p. 298.
109	'At war with bourgeois culture . . .':	Frederick Brown, *An Impersonation of Angels: A*

	Biography of Jean Cocteau (London: Longman's, 1986), p. 178.
110 Nancy Cunard and Aragon's affair:	Anne Chisholm, *Nancy Cunard* (London: Sidgwick & Jackson, 1979), pp. 103–4.
110 'I have again heard from the Rushbury . . .':	*WD*, p. 21.
110 'Studios meublés . . .':	TGA 939.2.4, BR to EB, 8 July 1925, from Hôtel des États-Unis, blvd de Montparnasse, Paris, to c/o Miss Godolphin, 10 Pulteney St, Bath.
110 'You do write me lovely news . . .':	Lefevre, BC to EB, August 1925.
110 'has always seemed to me . . .':	Natalie Barney, *Souvenirs indiscrets* (Paris: Flammarion, 1960), p. 21.
111 'I have been back in Paris . . .':	TGA 939.2.4, BR to EB, 8 July 1925.
111 'by all odds the most interesting place . . .':	John Glassco, *Memoirs of Montparnasse* (Oxford: Oxford University Press, 1995), p. 253.
111 'the café du dome is so awful . . .':	Lefevre, EB to BR, January 1927.
111 'Well dear hear am I . . .':	TGA 974.2.2.88, EB to BKS, 17 May 1931, from Le Dôme.
112 Monsieur made Welsh rarebit:	Glassco, *Memoirs of Montparnasse*, p. 14.
112 'my sort of Irish brother':	Chisholm, *Nancy Cunard*, p. 243.
112 locales for encountering the marvellous:	Louise Tythacott, *Surrealism and the Exotic* (London: Routledge, 2003), p. 32.
113 avid collectors of the débris of popular culture:	Tythacott, *Surrealism*, p. 42.
113 'We went down to Billy's little cottage . . .':	TGA 779.1.337, BKS to JB, undated, but 1964–9.
113 theorists of modern art who rejected the importance of drawing:	Harrison, *English Art*, p. 22.
113 'among the younger artists . . .':	Harrison, *English Art*, p. 83.
113 Mistinguett's costumes:	Phyllis Rose, *Jazz Cleopatra: Josephine Baker in Her Time* (London: Chatto & Windus, 1990), p. 91.
114 Paris music-hall entered its golden age in the Twenties:	Rose, *Jazz Cleopatra*, pp. 92–5.
114 enthusiasm for *négritude*:	Brown, *Impersonation of Angels*, p. 162.
114 'Chic Paris had not turned out . . .':	Rose, *Jazz Cleopatra*, p. 18.
115 'makes us revert to the ape . . .':	Rose, *Jazz Cleopatra*, pp. 31, 33.
115 'tall, vital . . .':	Rose, *Jazz Cleopatra*, p. 101.
115 modernists' and surrealists' interest in black culture:	Tythacott, *Surrealism and the Exotic*, pp. 109–27.
116 African motifs influence on Twenties Art Deco:	Petrine Archer-Straw, *Negrophilia: Avant-Garde Paris and Black Culture in the 1920s* (London: Thames & Hudson, 2000), pp. 74–8.
116 'But I *ain't* African':	Chisholm, *Nancy Cunard*, p. 170.
116 *Le Pompier des Folies Bergères*:	*The Fireman of the Folies-Bergère*, 1928, 8 mins. Directed by Joé Francys and Max Obal, with Claire Rommer and Josephine Baker among the bevy of semi-nude dancers who star in the hallucinations of a drunken fireman (on DVD from Kino International Corp.).

116 'You know what will people think . . .':   Lefevre, EB to BR, January 1927, from Hôtel Paris New York, 148 rue Vaugirard.

117 Burra and Lucy's reaction to nocturnal sounds: Sue Bradbury, 'Lucy Norton' (obituary), *The Independent*, 18 July 1989.

117 '. . . you should see the suite . . .':   TGA 974.2.2.16, EB to BKS, 7 March 1927, from Hôtel Paris New York.

117 'havent yet got over the looks':   TGA 974.2.2.15, EB to BKS 6 February 1927

117 'of course they think you and Lucy are lovers . . .':   TGA 939.2.4, BC to EB, 14 January 1927.

118 'Lucy went twice . . .':   EB to BR, January 1927, from Hotel Paris New York.

118 he and Chappell had already met Morris and Lett: *WD*, p. 35.

118 'When we were in Paris . . .':   TGA 974.2.2.43, EB to BKS, some time in summer 1927.

118 'I am beginning to fear . . .':   TGA 974.2.2.15, EB to BKS, 6 February 1927, from Café du Dôme.

118 Burra's admiration for Cocteau: Causey, *Burra*, p. 19.

118 'the work of Jean Cocteau . . .':   William Wiser, *The Crazy Years: Paris in the Twenties* (London: Thames & Hudson, 1983), p. 134.

119 Cocteau's influence on Burra's art: Cocteau's 'Au Bar', illustrated by William Wiser in *The Crazy Years*, p. 21, is very like one of Burra's drawings of parties.

119 'Perhaps more than any other single figure . . .':   Andrew Causey in *Edward Burra: Hayward Gallery, London* (London: Arts Council, 1985), p. 37.

119 'My new occupation':   TGA 795.2, EB to PN, 19 May 1931.

119 Burra's admiration for Wyndham Lewis: Noel Riley Fitch, *Sylvia Beach and the Lost Generation* (New York & London: W.W. Norton & Co., 1983), p. 286.

V.   Art and Craft

120 Watts and Holman Hunt could demand high fees: Caroline Dakers, *Clouds: The Biography of a Country House* (London & New Haven: Yale University Press 1993), p. 26.

120 Nash notes public view of Royal Academy 'Art' and Modern Art: Nash, 'Art and the English Press' (1933), in Andrew Causey (ed.), *Paul Nash's Writings on Art* (Oxford: Oxford University Press, 2000), p. 101.

120 Osbert Lancaster dates 'Vogue : Regency' to late Thirties   Osbert Lancaster, *Homes Sweet Homes* (London: John Murray, 1939), p. 74.

121 'Boy, it's tough to be Modern!'   TGA 939.2.4, PN to EB, around 1934, from Marseilles.

121 'highbrow culture and lowbrow sex . . .':   Stephen Spender, 'Road of books and vices', *The Independent Magazine*, 18 November 1989, pp. 75, 78.

121 Cyril Beaumont sold books on the ballet: Cyril Beaumont, *Bookseller at the Ballet* (London: C.W. Beaumont, 1975).

121 Burra read *The Anarchist*:   *WD*, p. 177.

121 'Henderson was short, rotund . . .'   Reg Groves, *The Balham Group: How British Trotskyism Began* (London: Pluto Press, 1974), p. 45.

122 Henderson published David Bomberg's *Russian Ballet*: — Ian Norrie, *Mumby's Publishing and Bookselling in the Twentieth Century* (London: Bell & Hyman, 1982), p. 76.

122 Zwemmer's importance for British artists: — Nigel Vaux Halliday, *More than a Bookshop: Zwemmer's and Art in the 20th Century* (London: Philip Wilson Publishers, 1991).

122 'The determined neglect of modern art . . .': — Halliday, *More than a Bookshop*, p. 38.

122 'the gradual dwindling of interest in all matters known as 'art' . . .': — Nash, 'Art and the English Press' (1933), in Causey (ed.), *Writings on Art*, p. 101.

123 'that liberty to browse along the shelves . . .': — Halliday, *More than a Bookshop*, p. 13. Second quotation is William Johnstone, ibid.

123 'paintings by Tiepolo, Signorelli, Magnasco . . .': — Rothenstein, *Burra*, p. 9.

123 Burra browsed Zwemmer's foreign art journals: — Halliday, *More than a Bookshop*, p. 44.

123 'No. 78 Charing Cross Road . . .': — Halliday, *More than a Bookshop*, p. 52.

124 Leicester and Independent Galleries promote modern European art: — Cecil Porter, *Six Decades at the Leicester Galleries, London, as seen by the press* (London: Ernest, Brown & Phillips, 1964).

124 Leicester exhibits Matisse, Picasso, Cézanne and Van Gogh: — Halliday, *More than a Bookshop*, p. 38.

124 'not only in the artistic world . . .': — Dakers, *Clouds*, p. 222.

124 Mayor Gallery became the home for Unit One: — Halliday, *More than a Bookshop*, p. 115.

124 'Yours and the Mayor Gallery [are] the only two places . . .': — Quoted in Halliday, *More than a Bookshop*, p. 15.

124 Adelphi shows British Modernists: — Halliday, *More than a Bookshop*, p. 38.

124 Lefevre Galleries and Arthur Tooth & Sons follow trends: — Halliday, *More than a Bookshop*, p. 87.

125 Burra's first commission: — Julia Ramos (the Rushburys' daughter), pers. comm.

125 Burra complains in letter that commercial galleries take a commission: — Lefevre, EB to BR, July 1924, from 73 Belsize Park Gardens.

126 Bumble admitted to Henry Tonks' painting class at Slade: — TGA 974.2.2.36, EB to BKS, 6 October 1927.

126 'Bumble and me had such a time . . .': — *WD*, p. 40.

126 'You are not forgotten! . . .': — TGA 939.2.4, Hugh Blaker to EB, 9 January 1928.

126 'Mother and Father went & Mother said . . .': — *WD*, p. 40.

126 'Mrs Burra took umbrage': — Clarissa M. Lorenz, *Lorelei Two: My Life with Conrad Aiken* (Athens: University of Georgia Press, 1983), p. 203.

127 'A strange old person called Mrs Dew Smith . . .': — TGA 974.2.2.37, EB to BKS, 9 December 1927.

127 'My pics may be shown to Dottie . . .': — TGA 974.2.2.29, EB to BKS, 18 September 1927.

127 'If the Leicester galleries dont like my interesting little drawings . . .': — TGA 975.3, EB to PN, autumn 1928.

127 Freddy Mayor exhibits Burra's   Mayor's recollection, in TGA 2002/1.4, transcripts
     paintings; they don't sell: made from BBC film.

127 'My dear . . . <u>what</u> do you think   Julia Ramos, pers. comm.
     arrived on Saterday . . .':

127 'I am doing a show with   TGA 974.2.2.71, EB to BKS, 12 February 1929.
     "Ethelbert W . . .':

128 Burra earns £144.7s.0d from   TGA 939.2.4, from Ernest Brown & Phillips, Leicester
     Leicester show: Galleries, 1 June 1929.

128 Burra sells 'Portrait' through Rye   TGA 939.2.4, Rye Art Club to EB, 7 July 1929.
     Art Club:

128 'Lucy [Norton] was so charming . . .':   *WD*, p. 51.

128 'Its awful the poverty that strikes . . .': *WD*, p. 61.

129 'I wrote back . . .':   *WD*, p. 61, EB to BC.

128 '[He] only really understood cash . . .': Chappell in *EB Remembered*, p. 66.

129 'Ed was very unrealistic about   Barbara Roett, interview, 3 September 2006.
     money . . .':

129 'He is as nearly indifferent as an   Rothenstein, *Burra*, p. 7.
     artist . . .':

130 'He did not give them titles until   Rothenstein in *EB Remembered*, p. 46.
     their exhibition was planned . . .':

130 'Started Dollys Party':   TGA 939.1.1, EB pocket diary for 1929.

130 'We've got fifteen of them up in our   *Aiken Letters*, p. 214.
     queer cellar-salon . . .':

130 'I'me so busy doing a cover design   NLA 86 X 27, Simon 7, 8 July 1931.
     for The Buggers . . .':

131 Burra designs a poster for the   Sold by Anthony D'Offay in 1980.
     Olympia Horse Show:

131 Crawfords commission and reject   TGA 974.2.2.46, EB to BKS, ? 1927/8.
     car advertising designs:

131 Shell and London Transport   See *The Shell Poster Book* (London: Hamish Hamilton,
     commission and reject design   1992).
     adverts:

131 Shell uses many avant-garde artists   James King, *Interior Landscapes: A Life of Paul Nash*
                                                  (London: Weidenfeld & Nicolson, 1987), p. 112.

131 'Thank you for your postcard . . .':   TGA 939.2.4, Christian Brown, London Transport
                                                  publicity officer, to EB, 9 July 1936.

132 Burra's design for the Underground: It is now in the Tate Gallery archive: Causey, no. 51.

132 'the textile merchants have agreed   NLA 86 X 25, Burra 5, 7–8 November 1933.
     to pay you £10 . . .':

132 'We are going to have a little   TGA 939.2.4, M. Fordham, Beauty Editor of *Vogue*,
     exhibition . . .':   to EB, 29 April 1936.

132 Lucy Norton spends summer holiday Lefevre, EB to BR, 18 August 1927.
     with Madge Garland:

132 'You may keep the drawings . . .':   TGA 974.2.3.19, EB to Marty Mann, January 1933.

133 'possessed control over a small   Anthony Powell, *Messengers of Day* (New York: Holt,
     printing press':   Rinehart and Winston, 1978), p. 175.

133 Burra's Firbank commission: David Gascoyne interviews, National Sound Archive,
                                                  C466/03, tape 4, side A.

133 'It remains to be seen chicks . . .':	*WD*, p. 122.
133 'I'm terribly shocked to hear about the foul behaviour . . .':	TGA 771.5.3, illustrated letter, Paul Nash to EB, undated (1942).
133 Burra's frontispiece for C.F. Ramuz's *The Triumph of Death*:	Hayward catalogue, pp. 152–3.
134 Burra's trouble in getting paid:	TGA 974.2.2.132, EB to BKS, 26 February 1973.
134 'I also heard a plaint . . .':	Huntington Library AIK 3940–3942, EB to CA, 25 December 1966.
135 'from time to time he contributes . . .':	Rothenstein, *Burra*, p. 7.
135 'Have been to 2 gallerys – Levys – I was too 'literary . . .':	*WD*, p. 82.
135 Julien Levy Gallery's Parisian focus:	Steven Watson, *Prepare for Saints: Gertrude Stein, Virgil Thomson, and the Mainstreaming of American Modernism* (Los Angeles & London: University of California Press, 1998), p. 149.
135 Burra in dialogue with Brook Street Art Gallery:	TGA 939.2.4, the Director, Brook Street Art Gallery, to EB.
136 'the nutty professor . . .':	TGA 974.2.2.125, EB to BKS, 11 April 1972.
136 'a disabled painter':	TGA 779.1.327, BKS to JB.
136 Nash offers to teach Burra how to make woodcuts:	TGA 974.2.2.50, EB to BKS, 21 February 1928.
137 'you mustnt enjoy the actual peenting . . .':	*WD*, pp. 175–6, EB to CP, 8 February 1968.
137 'the dangerous seduction of skilfulness':	Nash, 'Woodcut Patterns' (1927) in Causey (ed.), *Writings on Art*, p. 52.
137 Burra's attempts using woodcut:	Reproduced in Hayward catalogue, p. 144. In the 1971 reprint, this was retitled *Woman with a Tray*.
137 'The tool has to be held in such a way . . .':	R.J. Beedham, *Wood Engraving* (London: Ditchling Press, 1921), ch. 4.
138 'I'm sure nothing short of dragging the front door off . . .':	TGA 974.2.1.26, BKS to EB, 24 February 1928.
138 Gibbings shows Burra's woodcuts to Redfern Gallery's director:	Hayward catalogue, pp. 144–5.
138 Nan Kivell keeps a set of woodcuts:	TGA 779.1.98, EB to JB.
138 Burra and Nash work together on collages:	Causey, *Burra*, no. 66.
138 'We never bother to paint in this part now . . .':	*WD*, p. 57. Painting: Causey, *Burra*, no. 62.
139 'I always say you can't expect publicity . . .':	TGA 939.2.4, PN to EB, around 1934, from Marseilles.
139 'I was late to ask you to send some work . . .':	TGA 939.2.4, SF to EB, January 1931.
139 'Many thanks for sending me the review . . .':	TGA 939.2.5, William Rothenstein to Miss Blomfield, 14 January 1931, from the Royal College of Art. Miss Blomfield was probably a relative, via his aunt Anne's marriage to the architect Reginald Blomfield.
140 'Why you ever said you were 24 . . .':	TGA 939.2.4, BC to EB, 23 April 1929, from 72 blvd de Montparnasse (Hôtel St Brieuc).

140 'I sacrificed myself . . .':	TGA 939.2.4, PN to EB, around 1934.
140 'If you do it you do it . . .':	TGA 2002/1.4, transcripts made from Arts Council film.
140 'Just Bad Feeling, Surrealist Says . . .':	Interview reproduced in Hayward catalogue, pp. 64–6.
140 'Dearie can I come on Monday . . .':	TGA 974.2.2.87, EB to BKS, 26 February 1931.
141 'I didn't like being told . . .':	Hayward catalogue, p. 12.
141 'There are, I think, a few of your paintings in America . . .':	TGA 939.2.4, Alfred Barr, from MOMA, to EB, 27 August 1936.
142 'Thank you for your letter dearie . . .':	TGA 972.2.2.93, EB to BKS, 2 January 1932.
142 'though as persons . . .':	Paul Nash, letter to *The Times*, 12 June 1933.
143 'My Inertia received a rude jolt . . .':	TGA 974.2.2.110, EB to BKS, 13 March 1934.
144 Lancaster's review of Burra's work as too narrative for Unit One:	Osbert Lancaster, 'The Chosen Eleven', *The Architectural Review* 75 (451) (June 1934), pp. 211–12.
144 *South West Wind:*	In Hayward catalogue, pl. 10.
144 Burra's painting, *Sea Urchins:*	It is probably *Chestnuts*, which appears in a list of the year's paintings in an undated notebook, apparently from c.1937/8, TGA 939.1.15.
145 Cooper and Read write Burra's personal statement for Unit One:	King, *Interior Landscapes*, p. 174.
145 'you never heard what I've got to say . . .':	TGA 939.2.4, PN to EB, 1934.
145 'The Unit I Book . . .':	TGA 795.10, EB to PN, 10 April 1934.
145 'working class subjects of all kinds . . .':	Francis Wheen, *Tom Driberg: His Life and Indiscretions* (London: Chatto & Windus, 1990), pp. 132–4.
145 Burra's possible contribution to Artists International:	TGA 771.1.3.
145 'Today, when the capitalist system . . .':	The manifesto was quoted in *The Studio*, December 1934.
146 'The press, unable to appreciate . . .':	Herbert Read, 'Surrealism and the Romantic Principle', in *The Philosophy of Art* (London: Faber & Faber, 1964), p. 105.
146 'Among artists and intellectuals especially . . .':	*International Surrealist Bulletin* 4 (London: Zwemmer, 1936), p. 8.
146 'The validity of theory . . .':	*International Surrealist Bulletin* 4, p. 9.
147 *Saturday Market:*	Causey, *Burra*, no. 87.
147 Chappell reminisces about the glamorous Corcoran:	Chappell, National Sound Archive tape 2630A.
148 'the great Dawson Corcoran button consortium . . .':	TGA 795.11, EB to PN, undated, from 13a Market Street.
148 Corcoran buys *Dancing Cows:*	Causey, *Burra*, no. 46; Chappell, *EB Remembered*, p. 66.
148 Corcoran acts as Burra's agent:	*WD*, p. 106, EB to BC, 1940.
148 Corcoran becomes chairman and owner of Alex Reid and Lefevre:	Details from Alex Corcoran, pers. comm.
148 'those . . . shows in Bruton Street . . .':	Christopher Neve, *Unquiet Landscape: Places and Ideas in 20th Century English Painting* (London: Faber & Faber, 1990), p. 120.

149 'Mr Burra is good fun . . .': *Truth*, 1 June 1932 (from Burra's cuttings file, TGA 939.8.3).

149 'I was so sorry about Gerald Corcoran . . .': TGA 939.2.4, Rex Nan Kivell to EB, 6 February 1947, from the Redfern Gallery.

149 'I was informed they made 200£ . . .': TGA 974.2.2.14, EB to BKS, 1944.

149 'Gerald and Desmond knew exactly how to handle him . . .': Chappell, National Sound Archive tape 2630A.

149 Burra defends Corcoran to John Banting: TGA 8429.12, letter from John Banting to James Stern, 1970.

150 'Bar says she wants to buy that picture of Falmouth . . .': *WD*, p. 211, EB to BC, 14 March 1976.

VI. The Warm South

151 'I think of going to Toulon . . .': Paul Fussell, *Abroad* (Oxford: Oxford University Press, 1980), pp. 9–23, and letter in Lefevre.

151 'One couldn't ask him where he was going . . .': Anne Ritchie, TGA 2002/1.4, transcripts made from Arts Council film.

151 'Where are you going, Ed?': Barbara Roett, interview, 3 September 2006.

151 'Do not fuss . . .': *WD*, p. 37.

152 agonies with a wisdom tooth cut short trip: TGA 939.2.4, Lucy Norton to EB, 25 March 1927, from Hôtel Paris New York.

152 'there is no known type of stopping . . .': Lefevre, EB to BR, 1929.

152 'a pleasant little port . . .': Tristram Hillier, *Leda and the Goose* (London, New York & Toronto: Longmans, Green & Co., 1954), p. 76.

152 'If you could see the jolly men . . .': *WD*, p. 36 (also following quotation).

153 'Everyone walks about with drawing books . . .': TGA 974.2.2.30, EB to BKS, 24 September 1927, from Hôtel Cendrillon, Cassis.

153 Marseilles as what Burra had dreamed of: *WD*, p. 38.

153 'I hear you are going to Marseilles . . .': TGA 974.2.1.13, BKS to EB, summer 1927.

153 Burra read Claude McKay's *Banjo:* TGA 974.2.2.78, EB to BKS, 30 October 1929.

153 'from a café table at the Cannebière . . .': Hillier, *Leda and the Goose*, p. 81.

154 'As I write I am surrounded . . .': Richard Shead, *Constant Lambert* (London: Simon Publications, 1973), pp. 78–9.

155 'Ed and I went up to the red light district . . .': Letter from BKS to Andrew Stephenson, 30 May 1984, quoted in Stephenson, *Burra*, p. 154.

155 Edward Wadsworth's drawings and painting of Vielle Ville: Jonathan Black, *Edward Wadsworth: the Complete Paintings and Drawings* (London: Philip Wilson, 2005), pp. 58–63.

156 'Toulon was not concerned with the tourist trade . . .': Stella Bowen, *Drawn from Life* (London: Virago, 1984), pp. 136–7.

156 'Toulon was a great naval port . . .': Mary Blume, *Côte d'Azur: Inventing the French Riviera* (London: Thames & Hudson, 1992), p. 105.

157 'Nothing can be pleasanter . . .':   NLA 86.X 27, Withers 52, PN to Percy Withers, 11
                                            April 1930.

157 'The boys who had turned the   Stephen Spender, *World within World* (London:
    deepest mahogany . . .':   Hamish Hamilton, 1951), p. 107.

158 'Everybody else was black . . .':   Chappell interview, Kavanagh, *Ashton*, p. 137.

158 'A girl must either accept to   Sibylle Bedford, *A Compass Error* (London: Virago,
    dance . . .':   1984), p. 114.

158 Cocteau at the Hôtel de la   Frederick Brown, *An Impersonation of Angels: A
    Rade in 1930:   Biography of Jean Cocteau* (London: Longman's,
                                            1986), pp. 303–5.

159 'Les photographes sont   TGA 974.2.2.220, Jean Desbordes (friend of Jean
    splendides . . .':   Cocteau) to BKS, 8 October 1931, from Toulon.

159 'Burra never sunbathed   Anthony Powell, *Messengers of Day* (New York: Holt,
    (then the rage) . . .':   Rinehart and Winston, 1978), pp. 156–7.

160 'there stood a group of   Hillier, *Leda and the Goose*, p. 96.
    old friends . . .':

160 Chappell describes a glamorous   Chappell, National Sound Archive tape F1896B.
    blond pirate:

160 Powell leaves the dance: Michael Barber, *Anthony Powell: A Life* (London:
                                            Duckworth, 2005), p. 90.

160 'dancing to the music of   Hillier, *Leda and the Goose*, p. 96.
    accordions . . .':

160 'I'm leaving tomorrow . . .':   Powell, *Messengers of Day*, pp. 158–9.

161 Hodgkins moves to Gascony with   Hillier, *Leda and the Goose*, p. 99.
    Hillier when she falls pregnant:

161 Doris Langley Moore persuades   Hillier, *Leda and the Goose*, p. 99.
    Hodgkins to marry Hillier:

161 'Tall and slim, clothed in a   Hillier, *Leda and the Goose*, pp. 122–3.
    singlet . . .':

161 South African poet, Roy Campbell: Samuel Hynes, *The Auden Generation: Literature and
                                            Politics in England in the 1930s* (London: Faber &
                                            Faber, 1976), p. 121.

161 'Did Madame H bring the   974.2.2.84, EB to BKS, summer 1931.
    kiddies? . . .':

162 'In the restaurant were two men':   TGA 974.2.3.9, EB to BC, autumn 1933.

162 'You need never go home to see   *WD*, p. 78.
    your friends . . .':

162 Burra draws cowboys for Corcoran's   Chappell, 'Burra and the Corcorans' in *EB Remembered*,
    son Desmond: p. 67.

162 'I sent Varley & Prentis . . .':   TGA 934.2.3.11, EB to BC, March/April 1936, from
                                            the Hotel Aragon, Madrid.

163 Kathryn Hamill's work in *ABC of*   Andrew Wilson, *Beautiful Shadow, A Life of Patricia
    the Theatre: Highsmith* (London: Bloomsbury, 2004), pp. 155–6.

163 'not content with a bandage . . .':   *WD*, p. 57.

163 'To make an even number . . .':   Anthony Bertram, *Paul Nash: The Portrait of an Artist*
                                            (London: Faber & Faber, 1955), p. 146.

164 'Hey dey here we are in Toulon . . .': *WD*, p. 62.

164 'jamais plus, jamais plus . . .':   Bertram, *Paul Nash*, p. 146.

164 'Mrs N was not at the cot ...':   *WD*, p. 35.
164 'Toulon is quite famous for bad ...': Bertram, *Paul Nash*, p. 147.
164 'wasted in cafés in this glorious   NLA 86.X 27, Withers 52, PN to Percy Withers, 11
     country':   April 1930.
165 'I remember Paul telling me   TGA 7615.1.17, Ruth Clark to Anthony Bertram,
     afterwards ...':   1951.
165 'Paul ... became really   NLA 86.X.29, Margaret Nash memoir of Paul Nash,
     interested ...':   p. 43.

VII. Ballet

166 'Dolin sent me a photograph ...':   TGA 939.2.4, BC to EB, 23 December 1924.
166 Susie Salaman worked for   She designed and choreographed *The Tale of a Lamb*
     Marie Rambert: in 1929, *Our Lady's Juggler* in 1930 and eight other
                                          ballets. Clement Crisp et al., *Fifty Years of the Ballet
                                          Rambert* (London: Scolar Press, 1976), p. 60.
166 distinguished artists design   Nash designed J.M. Barrie's play with ballet, *The Truth
     English ballets: about the Russian Dancers* (1920).
167 Chappell and Ashton dance at Covent Kavanagh, *Ashton*, p. 88.
     Garden for the Royal Opera:
167 'It became Mim's showpiece ...':   Kavanagh, *Ashton*, p. 89.
167 'Elle a la souplesse du serpent ...': V. Svétlow [pseud. for V. Ivchenko], *Le Ballet
                                          contemporain*, trans. M.D. Calvocoressi (St Peters-
                                          burg: Golicke and Willborg, 1912), p. 78.
167 'thin, frail and brittle as blown glass': William Chapell, *Fonteyn: Impressions of a Ballerina*
                                          (London: Spring Books, 1950).
168 Nijinska accepts Chappell into the   Kavanagh, *Ashton*, p. 96.
     company to please Ashton:
168 Nijinska aware of Ashton's potential: Kavanagh, *Ashton*, p. 93.
168 'I'd not done very much ...':   Chappell, National Sound Archive tape 1897A.
168 'her efficiency is overwhelming ...': Kavanagh, *Ashton*, pp. 91–2.
168 Nijinska throws music at Chappell: Kavanagh, *Ashton*, p. 97.
168 'We are all in the pink ...':   *WD*, p. 49.
168 Ashton and Chappell paid   David Vaughan, *Frederick Ashton and his Ballets*, 2nd
     meagre wage: edn (London: Dance Books, 1999), p. 26.
169 'What our Ballerina will look like ...': TGA 974.2.2.59, EB to BKS, 6 October 1928.
169 'The only person who hasn't payed   TGA 974.2.2.61, EB to BKS, 10 October 1928.
     for Freddie ...':
169 'someone told him how a friend ...': TGA 939.2.4, BC to EB, 8 January 1929, from Bristol
                                          and Majestic Hotels, Monaco, Monte Carlo.
169 'Jolly Carline ...':   TGA 974.2.2.59, EB to BKS, 6 October 1928, from
                                          Hôtel St Brieuc, Montparnasse, on paper stolen
                                          from the Café du Dôme.
170 'There is the sweetest little   *WD*, p. 48, EB to BKS, 19 October 1928.
     Ammerican creature ...':
170 'He was not only wonderful   Kavanagh, *Ashton*, p. 101.
     looking ...':
170 'Arthur & Billie open in pullman   Kavanagh, *Ashton*, p. 101.
     porter suits ...':

171 Barbara Roett suggests Burra susceptible to magnificence: Barbara Roett, interview, 3 September 2006.

171 1929 diary: TGA 939.1.1.

171 'You'd never have known . . .': Chappell, National Sound Archive tape 1897A.

171 'If it ends as its begun my dear . . .': Kavanagh, *Ashton*, p. 98.

172 Burra's painting of Ashton: Kavanagh, *Ashton*, p. 98.

172 Bar prefers John Banting's portrait of Billy: TGA 779.1.348, BKS to JB, 12 October 1971.

172 Aniseed lifesavers: TGA 974.2.2.103 EB, to BKS, undated [May 1929].

172 'He was a neat, elegant dancer . . .': *WD*, p. 61.

172 'I adore him whatever you say . . .': TGA 974.2.2.81, EB to BKS, March 1930.

173 'Fred used to bully . . .': Kavanagh, *Ashton*, p. 98.

173 'I got a shock . . .': TGA 974.2.1.48, BKS to CP and EB, spring/summer 1935.

173 'The loveliest thing about the dancing . . .': TGA 974.2.2.218, BC to BKS, 16 October 1928.

173 'heavy men . . .': TGA 974.2.2.218, BC to BKS, 16 October 1928, from Hôtel St Brieuc; John Glassco, *Memoirs of Montparnasse* (Oxford: Oxford University Press, 1995), p. 45.

173 'We went to the Rue de Lappe . . .': *WD*, p. 46.

174 'corrugated-iron drill hall . . .': Chappell, *EB Remembered*, p. 33.

174 the attractions of Rue Blomet: Billy Klüver and Julie Martin, *Kiki's Paris: Artists and Lovers, 1900–1930* (New York: Harry N. Abrams, 1989), p. 152.

174 'two short gliding steps . . .': 'The Biguine of the French Antilles', in Nancy Cunard (ed.), *Negro: An Anthology* (London: Wishart & Co., 1934), p. 401.

174 'The real truth . . .': *WD*, p. 51.

175 'If Fred & Billy . . .': Kavanagh, *Ashton*, p. 100.

175 'All the work . . .': Ashton interview with Don MacDonagh, *Ballet Review* 3.4 (1970).

175 'the effect was that . . .': *Week-End Review*, vol. 4, no. 72, 25 July 1931.

175 'now everyone has left . . .': TGA 939.2.4, BC to EB, 8 January 1929, from Bristol and Majestic Hotels, Monaco, Monte Carlo.

175 'a limited dancer': Mary Clarke, *The Sadler's Wells Ballet: A History and an Appreciation* (London: Adam & Charles Black, 1955), p. 122.

176 'As the faun . . .': Peter Brinson, 'William Chappell' (obituary), *The Independent*, 4 January 1994.

176 'Did I tell you . . .': *WD*, p. 71.

177 buying linen: Kavanagh, *Ashton*, p. 111.

177 'fan letter': *WD*, p. 73.

177 'there has been no attempt . . .': Vaughan, *Ashton and his Ballets*, p. 149.

178 Mr Cochran: TGA 939.1.1.

178 the project was quietly dropped: Kathrine Sorley Walker, 'The Camargo Society', *Dance Chronicle* 18.1 (1995), 1–114, p. 11.

178 Chappell's costumes: Illustrated in Judith Chazin-Bennahum, *The Ballets*

	of Anthony Tudor: Studies in Psyche and Satire (New York & Oxford: Oxford University Press, 1994), p. 35.
178	Burra's costume drawing	Sotheby's, Works from the Estate of Edward Burra, Lady Ritchie of Dundee and Associated Owners (London, 3 July, 2002), p. 64 (no. 285).
179	'It is absolutely nonsense':	Keynes-Lopokova letters, quoted by Kavanagh, Ashton, p. 138.
179	'The buzz of surprise . . .':	Ashton in EB Remembered, p. 61.
180	'skin-tight bodices . . .':	David Vaughan, Frederick Ashton and his Ballets, 2nd edn (London: Dance Books, 1999), pp. 67–8.
180	'a big flower . . .':	Kavanagh, Ashton, p. 141.
180	'Baclanova is a rare old gem . . .':	WD, p. 70.
180	Peggy Hookham's crush on Chappell:	Meredith Daneman, Margot Fonteyn (London: Viking, 2004), p. 79
180	The first Barabau:	Reba Adler, 'Two Versions of Barabau', Dance Chronicle 4.4 (1981), 347–73.
180	dropped out of the repertory:	S.L. Grigoriev, The Diaghilev Ballets (London: Constable, 1953), p. 212.
180	'Barabau, Barabau . . .':	Kathrine Sorley Walker, Ninette de Valois: Idealist without Illusions (London: Hamish Hamilton, 1987).
181	'Barabau is the most successful . . .':	Arnold Haskell, Dancing Round the World (London: Victor Gollancz, 1937), p. 290.
181	studies for the 'opium' ballet:	Reproduced in Jill Anne Bowden, 'British Artists and the Ballet: The James L. Gordon Collection', Dancing Times (November 1995), pp. 137–46.
181	'A West-End Opium Den':	Illustrated in Marek Kohn, Dope Girls: The Birth of the British Drug Underground (London: Granta Books, 1992), p. 89.

VIII.   Spain

182	books on Spanish Baroque sculpture:	Rothenstein, Burra, p. 15. Among his books when he died were Nadine Daniloff and Georges Pillement, La sculpture baroque espagnole (Paris: Albin Michel, 1944) and Otto Schubert, Geschichte des Barock in Spanien (Esslingen: Paul Neff, 1908).
182	random lists of words in Spanish:	TGA 939.1.16.
182	'a mis soledades voy . . .':	Clover Pertinez in EB Remembered, p. 74.
183	a personal motto:	Clover Pertinez in EB Remembered, p. 75.
183	'an impatience of backwardness . . .':	Gertrude Bone, Days in Old Spain (London: Readers Union, 1942, first published 1937).
183	'Spain: stinks . . .':	Aiken Letters, 111–15.
183	'Ashen and orange fields . . .':	Bone, Days in Old Spain, p. 59.
184	'The translucent light . . .':	Tristram Hillier, Leda and the Goose (London, New York & Toronto: Longmans, Green & Co., 1954), p. 139.
184	'My trip to Spain . . .':	Aiken Letters, p. 200.

184 Lowry's father paying Aiken   Clarissa M. Lorenz, *Lorelei Two: My Life with Conrad Aiken* (Athens: University of Georgia Press, 1983), p. 84.

184 'bottle-a-day bard . . .':   Jan Gabrial, *Inside the Volcano: My Life with Malcolm Lowry* (New York: St Martin's Press, 1947 p. 125.

184 wrestling-match: *Aiken Letters*, pp. 153–5.

185 Lowry was also there: *Aiken Letters*, p. 174.

185 Lowry's damaged personality: Gordon Bowker, *Pursued by Furies: A Life of Malcolm Lowry* (London: HarperCollins, 1993), pp. 97–8.

185 Aiken studied Spanish at Harvard: Conrad Aiken, *Ushant* (New York: Duell, Sloan and Pearce; Boston: Little, Brown and Company, 1952), p. 207.

186 Clarissa's unhappiness and   Lorenz, *Lorelei Two*, p. 172.
     Burra's observation:

186 Burra's tooth comment: Lorenz, *Lorelei Two*, p. 195.

186 'A daintie "colony" . . .':   *WD*, p. 77.

186 route from Tilbury to Granada: Bone, *Days in Old Spain*, p. 34.

186 Pension Carmona: Bowker, *Pursued by Furies*, p. 150.

187 'Weather permitting . . .':   Lorenz, *Lorelei Two*, p. 151.

187 'A legless man . . .':   Bowker, *Pursued by Furies*, p. 150.

187 Lowry and the Richards: Bowker, *Pursued by Furies*, p. 151.

187 'a travel-weary, shabby figure . . .':   Lorenz, *Lorelei Two*, p. 155.

188 'Lowry, and Burra and Aiken . . .':   Aiken, *Ushant*, p. 296.

189 'The big one is a German drunk':   Lorenz, *Lorelei Two*, p. 159.

189 'In the Albaicín':   Bone, *Days in Old Spain*, p. 34.

189 'I don't realy know . . .':   TGA 792.12, EB to PN, from Pension Carmona, Alhambra.

190 'We have a romantic gypsy . . .':   TGA 974.2.2.105, EB to BKS, from Pension Carmona.

191 Lowry met his future first wife: Her own account of this is given in Gabrial, *Inside the Volcano*, pp. 3–4.

191 'Two solid florid men . . .':   Gabrial, *Inside the Volcano*, p. 3.

191 bullfight mentioned in *Ushant*:   Aiken, *Ushant*, p. 359.

191 'I went to a bull fight . . .':   *WD*, p. 90.

192 'The audience an important factor':   *Aiken Letters*, p. 115.

192 a drawing of a bullfight: Causey, *Burra*, no. 59.

192 foregrounds in stage-show works: Causey, *Burra*, no. 66.

192 1933 bullfight painting: Causey, *Burra*, no. 93.

192 'whirlwind look at Ceuta . . .':   Lorenz, *Lorelei Two*, p. 158.

192 'how I envy you . . .':   TGA 795.11, EB to PN, spring 1934.

193 'Have just heard from Clover!':   TGA 974.2.2.108, EB to BKS, spring 1932.

193 Clover in the Bibliothèque Nationale: TGA 939.2.4, CP to EB, 20 March 1933, from Hôtel de la Paix, 29 quai d' Anjou, Île St-Louis, Paris.

193 'she seems to be playing . . .':   *WD*, p. 87.

193 'I would like to go to Paris . . .':   *WD*, p. 89.

194 'A scandal is about to burst . . .':   TGA 974.2.2.104, EB to BKS, 9 April 1933, from Hôtel du Brabant, rue des Petits Hotels.

194 'I know you'll like it':   Clover Pertinez in *EB Remembered*, p. 75.

196 the 'Generacion del '98': José Luis Barrio-Garay, *José Gutiérrez Solana: Paintings and Writings* (Lewisburg, PA: Bucknell University Press, 1976), p. 41.

196 'the combination of popular mysticism . . .': Barrio-Garay, *Gutiérrez Solana*, p. 50.

196 *La España Negra*: Clover Pertinez in *EB Remembered*, p. 81.

196 'Painting is a magnificent art . . .': Barrio-Garay, *Gutiérrez Solana*, p. 18.

197 'I have just been to . . .': *WD*, p. 93.

197 painting of La Nina de los Peines: *WD*, p. 179.

197 *Flamenco Dancer* (1931): Causey, *Burra*, no. 81.

198 'This girl is worth an empire': Sotheby's, *Works from the Estate of Edward Burra, Lady Ritchie of Dundee and Associated Owners* (London, 3 July 2002), p. 38. In 1964, Burra mentions encountering his 'old painting of La Nina de los Peines at the Circo Price' at Desmond Corcoran's (*WD*, p. 179); the face is a good fit.

198 depiction of Pastora Rojas Monje in *Madame Pastoria*: Causey, *Burra*, no. 115.

198 'At the Prado . . .': Clover Pertinez in *EB Remembered*, p. 80.

198 Causey points out: Causey, *Burra*, p. 45.

198 'The Spanish Civil War . . .': Rothenstein, *Burra*, p. 15.

199 horror in Spain before Civil War: Ruiz Vilaplana, *Burgos Justice: A Year's Experience of Nationalist Spain* (London: Constable & Co., 1938), pp. 34–44.

199 Cunard's poll: Anne Chisholm, *Nancy Cunard* (London: Sidgwick & Jackson, 1979), p. 241.

199 description of Goronwy Rees: Selina Hastings, *Rosamond Lehmann* (London: Vintage, 2002), p. 177.

199 'She had a sharp . . .': Goronway Rees, *A Chapter of Accidents* (London: Chatto & Windus, 1972), p. 128.

200 Rosamond commissioned portraits: Her portrait was reproduced in *The Bookman*, December 1934, p. 172.

200 'a cuddly friendship': Hastings, *Rosamond Lehmann*, p. 171; letter WP to BKS in the Tate.

200 Rosamond turns to Bar as confidante: Hastings, *Rosamond Lehmann*, p. 154.

200 'I never thought of such . . .': Hastings, *Rosamond Lehmann*, p. 176.

201 'I never meant to eavesdrop . . .': TGA 974.2.2.302, Rosamond Lehmann to BKS, 22 March 1936.

201 'with 5,000 people . . .': Edward Pertinez, interview, 15 June 2006.

201 'She crept out . . .': *WD*, p. 168, EB to MW, 19 November 1965.

202 'There was, and had been . . .': Vilaplana, *Burgos Justice*, pp. 9–10.

202 'Mdms man is charming . . .': *WD*, p. 92.

202 'Well. Madame has just left . . .': TGA 974.2.1.51, BKS to EB, 16 October 1935, from Church St.

203 'It is because of my character . . .': TGA 974.2.2.37, WP to BKS, 22 March 1937, from Section Sanitaire, 14e Brigade International, Spain.

203 'Antonio had to become . . .': TGA 939.2.4, CP to EB, 28 February 1935, from

		Spain to Point Hill, Rye, Sussex, and February 1935, from Café Royal, Granada, to Point Hill.
203	left-wing support for Franco:	Jeremy Treglown, *V.S. Pritchett: A Working Life* (London: Pimlico, 2005), p. 73, quoting V.S. Pritchett, 'The Passing of Spanish Liberalism', *The Spectator*, 11 December 1936.
204	'while "the educated Spaniard ..."':	Treglown, *V.S. Pritchett*, p. 69, quoting Pritchett in the *New Statesman*, 24 August 1934.
204	'easily-raised emotions ...':	Hastings, *Rosamond Lehmann*, p. 188; Pritchett, 'Tendencies of the Modern Novel: V. Spain', *Fortnightly Review*, February 1934, p. 207.
204	'The breach is really ...':	TGA 974.2.1.60, BKS to EB, 13 October 1937.
205	'In future don't read any letters ...':	TGA 974.2.1.137, BKS to Bar Roett, 8 March 1956.
205	'I was interested to hear ...':	*Aiken Letters*, CA to EB, 1936, p. 210.
206	'One day when I was lunching':	Rothenstein, *Burra*, p. 15.
206	160 churches were destroyed in Spain:	Fernando Díaz Plaia, *La Guerra de España en sus documentos* (Barcelona, 1966), p. 16.
206	Clover on *Blue Baby*:	Clover Pertinez in *EB Remembered*, p. 82. Paul Nash wrote to Burra after the Redfern Gallery exhibition (1942) saying that he had suggested to Sir Kenneth Clark that 'quite a few should go to cheer things up among the War artists at the National Gallery. There was a flying blue monster I thought very suitable. It's almost my favourite' (quoted in *EB Remembered*, p. 66). It ended up in the Imperial War Museum: it is probably the painting identified in the Redfern catalogue as *The Spectre* (not illustrated).
206	Rothenstein on Burra's pro-Franco attitude:	Rothenstein in *EB Remembered*, pp. 45–6.
206	'I shall be soon ...':	TGA 974.2.3, EB to CP, August 1934.
207	Miguel de Unamuno and difficult political choices:	V.S. Pritchett, 'Miguel de Unamuno', *The Spectator*, 28 February 1936, and 'The Passing of Spanish Liberalism' *The Spectator*, 11 December 1936.
207	'On arriving in Barcelona ...':	W.H. Auden, in the Dean of New York (ed.), *Modern Canterbury Pilgrims*, (London: Mowbray, 1956), p. 41.
208	Burra and Blake:	Sotheby's, *Works*, p. 70.
208	'One of the greatest paintings ...':	Sotheby's, *Works*, p. 1.
209	*Beelzebub*:	Causey, *Burra*, no. 138.

IX.   The New Found Land

210	worked drivelled about ...':	TGA 939.1.1, EB pocket diary for 1929.
210	'the American Tragedy':	TGA 795.4, EB to PN, en route to NY.
210	'Conrad [Aiken] met him ...':	NLA 86.X.26, Clark 7 b–c, PN to Ruth Clark, September/October 1933.
211	Burra-Aiken letters in Huntington Library:	Aiken in *EB Remembered*, p. 98.
211	'from the Nashs account ...':	TGA 974.2.3.19, EB to Marty Mann, January 1933.

211 Burra's state during voyage: TGA 974.2.3, EB to CP, July 1937.

212 'One evening he went out . . .':   Rothenstein, *Burra*, p. 172.

212 'Trailing Conrad on a slower   Clarissa M. Lorenz, *Lorelei Two: My Life with Conrad*
     ship . . .':   *Aiken* (Athens: University of Georgia Press, 1983),
                                           p. 172.

212 parents' anti-American circle: Lorenz, *Lorelei Two*, pp. 112–13.

212 'Strange news from Rye . . .':   NLA 86.X.26, Clark 6, PN to Ruth Clark, September
                                           1933.

212 Nancy Cunard's movements,   Anne Chisholm, *Nancy Cunard* (London: Sidgwick &
     May 1932–1933:   Jackson, 1979), pp. 194–206.

213 'the woman who . . .':   TGA 974.2.1.134, BKS to Bar Roett, January/February
                                           1956.

213 interview in a black   'From the Brilliance of Mayfair to —— She
     newspaper in 1940:   Renounced British Tradition for her Negro
                                           Friends', *New York Amsterdam News*, June 1940
                                           (press-cutting in a scrapbook belonging to Barbara
                                           Ker-Seymer, now in the Tate. The *New York
                                           Amsterdam News*, founded in 1909, was one of the
                                           most significant papers produced by and for the
                                           black community in the US).

213 'a woman of enormous   Francis Wyndham, *Mrs Henderson and Other Stories*
     magnetism . . .':   (London: Jonathan Cape, 1985), p. 68.

213 Edna Lloyd Thomas in Welles'   Steven Watson, *Prepare for Saints: Gertrude Stein,
     Macbeth: Virgil Thomson, and the Mainstreaming of American
                                           Modernism* (Los Angeles & London: University of
                                           California Press, 1998), p. 313.

214 'Her manner was the reverse . . .': Wyndham, *Mrs Henderson*, p. 73.

214 'Mummy says . . .':   Joan Wyndham, *Love Lessons: A Wartime Diary*
                                           (London: Heinemann, 1985).

214 'If she had her way . . .':   Wyndham, *Mrs Henderson*, p. 70: Wyndham
                                           represents Edna Thomas as 'Ruby Richards'. On
                                           the Harlem salons, see Aberghani & Sandra L.
                                           West, *Encyclopedia of the Harlem Renaissance* (New
                                           York: Checkmate Books, 2003), pp. 292–3.

214 'I've given him . . .':   'Howland Spencer Praises Divine's Work at Krum
                                           Elbow', *The Poughkeepsie Star-Enterprise*, 18
                                           September 1939.

215 Olivia's Earl Grey tea,   Kavanagh, *Ashton*, p. 165.
     cucumber sandwiches:

215 Olivia and drugs: TGA 974.2.1.59, BKS to EB, 30 September 1937.

215 'There was a jolly cocktail party . . .': John Rothenstein, *Edward Burra* (London: The Tate
                                           Gallery, 1973), p. 89.

216 Ruth Baldwin's death: Kate Summerscale, *The Queen of Whale Cay*
                                           (London: Fourth Estate, 1997), pp. 78–9, 152.

216 'much to Soph Soph's joy':   TGA 974.2.2.109, EB to BKS, 8 January 1934. See
                                           Iris Tree, in Simon Fleet (ed.), *Sophie Fedorovitch:
                                           Tributes and Attributes* (London: privately printed,
                                           1955), p. 14.

216 'When I first saw it . . .': Nancy Cunard, *Negro: An Anthology* (London: Wishart & Co., 1934), p. 67.

216 *Harlem Scene*: Causey, *Burra*, no. 114.

216 'What do I . . .': Miles Huddleston, *James Stern: A Life in Letters, 1904–1993* (Norwich: Michael Russell, 2002), pp. 40–1.

217 'Harlem is like Walham green': *WD*, p. 83.

217 painting of two men outside soul food restaurant: Causey, *Burra*, no. 109.

217 '[I] live on a diet . . .': Huntington Library, AIK 2197–2380, EB to CA, 1890 7th Ave, appart. 2a, NYC.

217 Sophie and dancing at the Bal Nègre: Tree, in Simon Fleet (ed.), *Sophie Fedorovitch*, p. 14. On the rue de Lappe, see *WD*, p. 51.

218 Askews' salon: Watson, *Prepare for Saints* p. 187.

218 'Those rooms were just . . .': Watson, *Prepare for Saints*, pp. 189, 190. Aberghani & West, *Encyclopedia of the Harlem Renaissance*, p. 295.

218 Burra liked Constance Askew: Rothenstein, *Edward Burra*, p. 89.

218 more interested in life of the street: Kavanagh, *Ashton*, p. 164.

218 speakeasies as centre of New York night-life: Arnold Shaw, *Let's Dance: Popular Music in the 1930s* (New York & London: Oxford University Press, 1998), p. 39.

218 'In one swift action . . .': David Freeland, 'The Rise and Fall of the Original Swing Street', *New York Press* 18, issue 46 (2006) http://www.newyorkpress.com

219 'Olivia, by the way . . .': TGA 974.2.1.48, BKS to CP and EB, spring/summer 1935.

219 'Theres so much talent . . .': *WD*, p. 84.

219 Lindy Hoppers: Causey, *Burra*, no. 120.

219 Burra at London black shows: Causey, *Burra*, p. 56.

219 Jimmie Daniels and Bar: TGA 974.2.1.41, BKS to EB, 2 August 1929; TGA 974.2.1.50, BKS to EB, August 1935.

220 'We went to an outrageous place': *WD*, pp. 79–80.

220 '[he wore] net and sequins . . .': George Chauncey, *Gay New York: Gender, Urban Culture, and the Making of the Gay Male World, 1890–1940* (New York: BasicBooks, 1994), p. 251.

221 Harlem Hamilton Lodge ball: Chauncey, *Gay New York*, p. 245; Watson, *Prepare for Saints*, p. 68.

221 Olivia's affection for Club 440: She says so in the 1940 interview cited earlier.

221 'It's a dream': TGA 974.2.3, EB to CP, October 1933.

221 Clarissa in boarding-house: Lorenz, *Lorelei Two*, p. 174.

222 'This letter is rather boring . . .': NLA 86X25, Burra 5, PN to EB, 7–8 November 1933.

222 'About a month ago . . .': NLA 86X25, Burra 7, PN to EB, 9 February 1934.

222 'Yes dear your letter . . .': TGA 795.8, EB to PN, presumably February 1934, from Springfield.

223 'Othello & Desdemona Aiken . . .': James King, *Interior Landscapes: A Life of Paul Nash* (London: Weidenfeld & Nicolson, 1987), EB to PN, March 1934.

223 'close house board . . .':   Lorenz, *Lorelei Two*, p. 177.

223 'The East Side is lovely . . .':   *WD*, p. 84.

223 'Mae Wests new pic . . .':   *WD*, p. 79.

224 'Despite all adverse criticism . . .':   *WD*, p. 89.

224 erection: Kavanagh, *Ashton*, p. 85, 'when asked if he had ever had an erection, he admitted only to a very slight one while watching a Mae West film'.

224 Ashton in London for *Les Rendezvous*:   David Vaughan, *Frederick Ashton and his Ballets*, 2nd edn (London: Dance Books, 1999), p. 95.

224 'We used to go to the Savoy Ballroom . . .':   Vaughan, *Ashton and his Ballets*, p. 97.

224 'they could dance . . .':   Watson, *Prepare for Saints*, p. 252.

225 'One would get a whole scene set . . .':   Vaughan, *Ashton and his Ballets*, p. 101.

225 'my favourite resort . . .':   *WD*, p. 86.

225 Burra sees Bessie Smith: *WD*, p. 87.

225 First night of *Four Saints in Three Acts*:   Kavanagh, *Ashton*, p. 172.

226 Burra reported to Nash: TGA 795.8.

226 crying audience: Watson, *Prepare for Saints*, pp. 265–80.

227 'From what I know of their work':   Anthony Bertram, *Paul Nash: The Portrait of an Artist* (London: Faber & Faber, 1955), p. 172.

227 'delightful feminine decorations':   Andrew Causey (ed.), *Paul Nash's Writings on Art*, (Oxford: Oxford University Press, 2000), p. 63.

227 'If the dear, pale . . .':   Aiken, *Ushant*, p. 136.

227 'He was the most . . .':   *Aiken Letters*, p. 275.

227 'a peculiar bright delicacy . . .':   Roger Cardinal, *The Landscape Vision of Paul Nash* (London: Reaktion, 1989), p. 76.

227 '. . . I got ill . . .':   TGA 974.2.2.112, EB to BKS, 25 August 1934.

228 '. . . life at Boxwell . . .':   TGA 939.2.1, EB to AB, 21 February, second letter February, from 17 Elwood St, Charlestown, Massachusetts.

229 'The duchess of Windsor . . .':   TGA 939.2.1, EB to AB, 29 June 1937, from 17 Elwood St.

229 Mary Hoover's travels: Charles C. Eldredge, *Tales from the Easel* (Athens: University of Georgia Press, 2004), p. 74.

229 'it would be fun to reappear . . .':   Aiken, *Letters*, p. 211.

229 'I hear Conrad is expecting . . .':   Lorenz, *Lorelei Two*, p. 215.

230 'I hear that Conrad is expecting a baby!':   TGA 795 36, EB to PN, 25 December 1936.

230 'the cutest waterfront cafes . . .':   Aiken, *Letters*, pp. 209, 211.

231 'He had a small suitcase . . .':   January 1937, Mary Aiken in *EB Remembered*, p. 84.

231 'The american scene . . .':   Aiken, *Ushant*, p. 289.

231 'Theres something indescribably sordid . . .':   Lefevre, EB to BD, Springfield (wartime), undated.

232 'I returned from bonnie Scotland . . .':   TGA 974.2.2.85, EB to BKS, late in 1932.

232 'an Irish ammerican midden . . .':   *WD*, p. 94.

232 'a remarkable slum . . .':   TGA 795.5, EB to PN, from 17 Elwood St.

232 diary entries: TGA 939.1.3.

232 O'Neills was Aiken's favourite: Aiken in *EB Remembered*, p. 85.

233 'The Silver Dollar Bar . . .': TGA 795.5, EB to PN, from 17 Elwood St.

233 'Which particularly pleased Ed . . .': Aiken in *EB Remembered*, p. 86.

233 'It was not a vicious place . . .': Robertson, introduction to Lefevre catalogue, *Edward Burra: Paintings from America* (London: Lefevre Gallery, 1980), p. 2.

233 'The only work . . .': Rosenau, reprinted in Hayward catalogue, p. 66, cross-referenced with TGA 939.2.1, EB to AB, 8 March 1937.

234 'I think at this time Squidge . . .': John Aiken, Jane Aiken Hodge and Joan Aiken, *Conrad Aiken, our father* (Rye: Anthony Neville, 1989), p. 24.

234 'Ed is non-committal . . .': *Aiken Letters*, p. 214.

234 'Conrad is installed here . . .': TGA 795.5, EB to PN, from 17 Elwood St.

X. Mexico and Venice

235 'I've never been . . .': Rothenstein, *Burra*, p. 12.

235 'vin audenaire': Peter Davidson, *The Idea of North* (London: Reaktion, 2005), pp. 83–4; Clover Pertinez in *EB Remembered*, p. 80.

235 surrealists' fascination with pre-Columbian Mexican art: Louise Tythacott, *Surrealism and the Exotic* (London & New York: Routledge), p. 175.

235 Rothenstein noticed images of Mexican churches: Rothenstein, *EB Remembered*, p. 45; *Three Centuries of Mexican Colonial Architecture* (Mexico City: Mexican Government Department of Education, 1933).

236 'The word divorce': *Aiken Letters*, p. 212.

236 'he threatens darkly to stay there': *Aiken Letters*, p. 215.

236 Mary Hoover's professional interest in Mexico: *Aiken Letters*, p. 216.

236 awareness among American artists of interesting work: Kurz Heinzelman, *The Covarrubias Circle* (Austin: University of Texas Press, 2004), p. 65.

236 Breton on the intrinsic surrealism of Mexico: Tythacott, *Surrealism and the Exotic*, p. 175.

237 details of Burra's travelling funds: TGA 939.2.1, EB to AB, 27 February 1937, from 17 Elwood St, and TGA 939.2.1, EB to Trudy Burra, April 1937, from 17 Elwood St.

237 'heaven knows . . .': TGA 939.2.1, EB to AB, 11 May 1937, from 17 Elwood St.

237 'At midnight . . .': Mary Aiken in *EB Remembered*, p. 88.

238 travelling via Laredo: A picture in the Redfern Gallery retrospective exhibition of 1942 was identified as *Texas Bar*; possibly identical with *Figure in a Café* (1936, Causey, no. 127). If it is a memory of Texas, then it is a memorial of this journey.

238 'Baby pigs, baby humans . . .': Mary Aiken in *EB Remembered*, p. 90.

238 'Never shall I forget': *Aiken Letters*, p. 216.

239 'My insides came out . . .': *Aiken Letters*, p. 216.

239 'However I got here ...': TGA 939.2.1, EB to AB, May 1937, c/o Wells Fargo Express, Av. Madero, Mexico D. F.

240 'like the food you eat in a dream ...': Graham Greene, *The Lawless Roads* (Harmondsworth: Penguin, 1939), pp. 34–5.

240 'Mexico City is older ...': Greene, *Lawless Roads*, pp. 69–70.

241 spectacular setting of Cuernavaca: Gordon Bowker, *Pursued by Furies: A Life of Malcolm Lowry* (London: HarperCollins, 1993), p. 207.

241 'The fernlike trees ...': Conrad Aiken, *A Heart for the Gods of Mexico* [1939], in *The Collected Novels of Conrad Aiken* (New York, Chicago & San Francisco: Holt, Rinehart and Winston, 1964), p. 464.

241 'In the evenings at twilight ...': Bowker, *Pursued by Furies*, p. 207.

241 staff at 62 Calle Humboldt: Jan Gabrial, *Inside the Volcano: My Life with Malcolm Lowry* (New York: St Martin's Press), pp. 104–5.

241 'at the very bottom ...': Mary Aiken in *EB Remembered*, p. 93.

241 'about twelve feet by eight ...': Arthur Calder-Marshall, *Malcolm Lowry Remembered* (London: Ariel Books, 1985), p. 111.

242 'carefully knocking ...': Gabrial, *Inside the Volcano*, pp. 113, 117.

242 dining under individual umbrellas: Gabrial, *Inside the Volcano*, p. 128.

242 'He looked, in fact ...': Gabrial, *Inside the Volcano*, p. 127.

243 Aiken was still suffering from the runs: Gabrial, *Inside the Volcano*, p. 126.

243 he began to feel trapped: Mary Aiken in *EB Remembered*, p. 93.

243 I have moved from Mexico City: TGA 939.2.2, EB to Trudy Burra, May? 1937, from c/o Lowry, Calle Humboldt 62, Cuernavaca, Morelos.

244 They had terrific battles: Bowker, *Pursued by Furies*, p. 215.

244 'that avid Greek chorus ...': Gabrial, *Inside the Volcano*, p. 129.

244 Burra and Lowry having nothing in common: Gabrial, *Inside the Volcano*, p. 128: 'the others never saying much anyhow'.

244 They met at Karl's Café: *Aiken Letters*, p. 306.

244 'I expect to see Rousseau ...': Bowker, *Pursued by Furies*, p. 216.

245 a winding spiral staircase: Gabrial, *Inside the Volcano*, p. 141.

245 'perfectly divine cats ...': Lefevre, EB to BC, New Year letter, 1972.

246 'they compel me ...': Gabrial, *Inside the Volcano*, p. 130.

246 'The lawyer says ...': TGA 771.1.2, CA to EB, 29 June 1937, from Cuernavaca.

246 Josefina's contempt: Gabrial, *Inside the Volcano*, p. 145.

246 'and saw a whole rabbit ...': Mary Aiken in *EB Remembered*, p. 93.

247 'a little corner café ...': Aiken, *A Heart for the Gods of Mexico*, p. 464.

247 Burra boards Pullman to Laredo: Conrad Aiken, *Ushant* (New York: Duell, Sloan and Pearce; Boston: Little, Brown and Company, 1952), p. 350.

248 'I returned here alone ...': TGA 939.2.1, EB to AB, 29 June 1937, from 17 Elwood St.

249 'my funeral nitch ...': *WD*, p. 97.

249 'I take 15 iron pills a day ...': *Aiken Letters*, p. 219, TGA 792.18, EB to PN, Thursday 12 August 1937, from Springfield.

249 'I should never have left . . .':　'quite awful . . . ', *WD*, p. 97; 'if you can stand it . . .', *WD*, p. 98.

250 *Mexican Church*:　Causey, *Burra*, p. 146.

250 'It is the landscape . . .':　Mary Aiken in *EB Remembered*, p. 92. Illustrated in *Edward Burra: Drawings from the 1920s and 1930s* (London: Lefevre Gallery, 1993), p. 62.

250 'a starved dog . . .':　Aiken, *A Heart for the Gods of Mexico*, p. 465.

251 Lucie-Smith on the importance of Mexican muralists:　Edward Lucie-Smith, *Art and Artists* 12 (1977), 4–10, p. 9. See Alma M. Reed, *The Mexican Muralists* (New York: Crown Publishing Ltd, 1960).

251 Burra possessing one of Posada's books:　*WD*, p. 126.

252 'Is it your mexican church . . .':　TGA 771.1.8, CP to EB, 23 November 1942, from Gabía Grande, Granada.

253 'I heard from Mdme Huntley . . .':　TGA 974.2.2.113, EB to BKS, summer (pre-war) 1939.

254 'Magnasco's interests . . .':　Causey, *Burra*, p. 66.

254 'I like Dublin . . .':　Lefevre, EB to BC, after August 1937.

255 Italico Brass, who owned about fifty Magnascos:　Denys Sutton, 'La vie en rose', *Apollo* (May 1972).

255 'Mr Minsky in the Listener . . .':　*WD*, p. 118 (1942).

255 *Il Furto Sacrilego*:　*Alessandro Magnasco, 1667–1749* (Milan: Electa, 1996), pp. 220–1.

255 reproduction in 1938 periodical:　B. Geiger, 'Beitrag zu Magnasco', *Pantheon* (September 1938).

255 Gaunt observes:　William Gaunt, *Bandits in a Landscape* (London: The Studio Ltd, 1937), p. 73 and *passim*.

255 Burra finally saw *Explosion in a Church*:　*WD*, p. 138; Félix Sluys, *Didier Barra et François de Nome, dits Monsù Desiderio* (Paris: Editions du Minotaure, 1961), p. 108.

256 paintings at Arthur Tooth & Sons:　Gaunt, *Bandits in a Landscape*, p. 102.

256 'The fact that Burra . . .':　Marina Vaizey, 'Art: Life at the edge of surrealism', *The Times*, 18 August 1985.

256 'Burra, whether he knows it or not . . .':　Osbert Lancaster, 'The Chosen Eleven', *Architectural Review* 74 [451], June 1934, pp. 211–12.

XI. War

259 'On looking back . . .':　Osbert Lancaster, *With an Eye to the Future* (London: Century, 1986), p. 99.

259 'Anne and mother . . .':　TGA 974.2.2.199, EB to BKS, undated.

259 Anne told Andrew Stephenson in an interview:　Stephenson, *Burra*, p. 127, n.93, interview with Anne Ritchie, 30 November 1982.

259 'Conrad winced . . .':　Clarissa M. Lorenz, *Lorelei Two: My Life with Conrad Aiken* (Athens: University of Georgia Press, 1983), p. 113.

260 'Father has sold some fields . . .':　TGA 795.13, EB to PN, from Springfield.

260 'It is indescribably moving . . .':　William Maxwell (ed.), *The Letters of Sylvia Townsend Warner* (New York: Viking, 1983), p. 61.

260 advice had been issued as early
as July:

Norman Longmate, *How We Lived Then: A History of Everyday Life During the Second World War* (London: Hutchinson, 1971), p. 35.

260 government forgets torch-batteries:

Longmate, *How We Lived Then*, p. 41–2.

261 'Nobody seems to have dared . . .':

WD, p. 103.

261 'Somewhat unexpectedly . . .':

Longmate, *How We Lived Then*, p. 52.

262 Rosamond makes arrangements
for evacuees:

Selina Hastings, *Rosamond Lehmann* (London: Vintage, 2002), p. 200.

262 Burra receives form from the
Ministry of Labour:

WD, p. 104.

262 'Not if I can help . . .':

Longmate, *How We Lived Then*, p. 111.

262 Burra's interest in practical
gardening:

Huntington Library, AIK 2197–2380, EB to CA, 14 December 1942.

263 'only the egg eludes . . .':

Aiken Letters, p. 267.

263 Balancer Meal exchange:

Longmate, *How We Lived Then*, p. 232.

263 censorship:

Margery Allingham, *The Oaken Heart* (London: Michael Joseph, 1941), p. 133.

263 'like a dirty old piece . . .':

Longmate, *How We Lived Then*, p. 101.

263 Only 65,000 were still where they
had been billeted:

Longmate, *How We Lived Then*, p. 58.

264 'The life I lead . . .':

'The Sky Makes Me Hate It', *Penguin New Writing* 13 (April–June 1942), p. 14.

264 Chappell as entertainment organiser:

Chappell, National Sound Archive tape 2628A.

265 return voyage in under-fire
cargo-ship:

Ninette de Valois, *Come, Dance with Me* (London: Hamish Hamilton, 1957), pp. 136–9.

265 'sooner death than Aberystwyth':

WD, p. 111.

265 punishment of Spanish
Republican politicians:

Hugh Thomas, *The Spanish Civil War*, revised edn (London: Penguin, 1965), p. 923.

266 Burra's wartime letters:

Kavanagh, *Ashton*, p. 277.

266 Olivia Wyndham's wartime
movements:

Francis Wyndham, *Mrs Henderson and Other Stories* (London: Jonathan Cape, 1985), pp. 82–3. Her niece Joan Wyndham met her during this trip.

266 'I hear Bunny . . .':

Lefevre, EB to GC, probably 1941.

266 '"Now that I have shot so many . . ."':

Raleigh Trevelyan, 'Neil (Bunny) Roger', *New Dictionary of National Biography*.

266 'I can only hope . . .':

TGA 771.1.3, CA to EB, 22 July 1940.

267 'What shall we do . . . ?':

Longmate, *How We Lived Then*, p. 105.

267 'If you have lived . . .':

Allingham, *The Oaken Heart*, p. 69.

267 Spender's reaction was very similar:

Spender, 'September Journal [1939]', in *The Thirties and After* (London: Fontana, 1978), p. 102.

268 'Ed writes . . .':

Aiken Letters, p. 239.

268 'I have been doleing out . . .':

WD, p. 109; Longmate, *How We Lived Then*, p. 153.

268 'To the civilian . . .'

Longmate, *How We Lived Then*, p. 114.

268 'slim silver pencils . . .':

Longmate, *How We Lived Then*, p. 115.

269 'Gunfire light . . .':

Maxwell (ed.), *The Letters of Sylvia Townsend Warner*, p. 62.

269 'All we have . . .':

WD, p. 108.

269 'from the ground . . .': Allingham, *The Oaken Heart*, p. 228.

269 'Go down the lane . . .': Longmate, *How We Lived Then*, p. 116.

269 'hang about like bridal veils . . .': Allingham, *The Oaken Heart*, p. 245.

269 'Not <u>one step</u> . . .': Burra in *EB Remembered*, p. 106.

269 'I share Burra's emotions . . .': Wyndham Lewis, 'The London Art Galleries', *The Listener*, 9 June 1949.

269 'At the height: TGA 2002/1.4, transcripts made from BBC film.

270 'We have been very quiet . . .': *WD*, p. 108.

270 'My mind I may add . . .': Lefevre, EB to BC, 4 July, probably 1940.

270 'They say that quite a lot . . .': *WD*, p. 114, and Lefevre, EB to BC.

270 'I had a cousin . . .': *WD*, p. 112.

270 'suddenly buried in a bookcase . . .': *WD*, p. 115.

270 'Anne has turned into . . .': *WD*, p. 105.

270 'Very dutiful she is . . .': *WD*, p. 111; Lefevre, EB to BC, 4 July, probably 1940.

270 'We are in the middle . . .': Lefevre, EB to BD, Springfield, wartime, undated.

271 'There was a bit of a degringolade . . .': *WD*, p. 113.

271 'had a big toe Sunday . . .': Huntington Library, AIK 2197–2380, EB to CA, 18 June 1942.

271 'Mumsie is getting a shade nervous': *WD*, p. 108.

271 'Father flew in a fuss': *WD*, p. 111.

271 'Poor dear "mumsie" . . .': Huntington Library, AIK 2197–2380, EB to CA, 16 February 1942.

272 He commented unkindly: Lefevre, EB to BC, 4 July, probably 1940.

272 '"I wondered why . . ."': Burra letter in *EB Remembered*, p. 101.

272 'Well dearie what a whirl . . .': *WD*, p. 110.

273 'You will have to . . .': Marion Yass, *This is Your War: Home Front Propaganda in the Second World War* (London: HMSO, 1983), pp. 34–5.

273 selling 9,000 tons of onions: Philip Delves Broughton, 'French Onion Johnnies wobble back into limelight', filed 23 August 2003, http://www.telegraph.co.uk

273 two nostalgic *Odes to an Onion* were written: Longmate, *How We Lived Then*, p. 144.

273 'I sent 5 onions . . .': *WD*, p. 114.

273 'I am sending onions back . . .': *WD*, p. 120.

273 'Mrs Cohen will soon be appearing . . .': *WD*, p. 111.

273 'Do you want any chocolate . . .': *WD*, p. 112–3, 116.

274 'We heard last week . . .': *Aiken Letters*, p. 248 (7 September 1940). Burra letter, Huntington Library, AIK 2197–2380, EB to CA, 12 August 1940.

274 'I remember saying to Fred . . .': Kavanagh, *Ashton*, p. 156.

274 'The Trembling Stick': Kavanagh, *Ashton*, p. 159.

274 'He was a darling man': Chappell, National Sound Archive tape 2630A.

275 'Master Humphrey, it's time . . .': Barbara Roett interview, 3 September 2006.

275 Bar's sense of proportion and humour: Barbara Roett interview, 3 September 2006.

275 Bar joins Larkin and Company: Val Williams, *Women Photographers* (London: Virago, 1986), p. 103.

275 divorce papers: TGA 974.3, BKS divorce papers, 14 May 1942.

275 'Mr and Mrs Pease':   TGA 939.2.4, Betty Keen to EB, 30 October 1944, from 5/157 Old Church Street, London SW3.

275 'I rather like Fitzroy Sq . . .':   Huntington Library, AIK 2197–2380, EB to CA, 14 May 1943.

276 'I can't get to the cinema . . .':   Lefevre, EB to BC, wartime, undated.

276 'Civilised values and activities . . .':   Stephen Spender, *The Thirties and After* (London: Fontana, 1978), p. 91.

276 *New Writing* selling 50,000:   Alan Jenkins, *The Thirties* (London: William Heinemann with Book Club Associates, 1976), p. 184.

276 'I payd a profitable visit . . .':   Huntington Library, AIK 2197–2380, EB to CA, 12 August 1940.

277 'it looked a shade depressing . . .':   Huntington Library, AIK 2197–2380, EB to CA, 7 December 1941.

278 mother's jaundice: *WD*, p. 116.

278 'Thank God we have good fish':   *WD*, p. 116.

278 'I am much better':   *WD*, p. 119.

278 'I revolve on my visits . . .':   Burra in *EB Remembered*, p. 108.

278 'I see myself . . .':   *WD*, p. 108.

278 'I don't dare . . .':   *WD*, p. 109.

279 'We had some rum . . .':   *WD*, pp. 113–14, 1940.

279 'they do say the whiskey . . .':   *WD*, p. 121.

279 'Rye, they do say . . .':   *Aiken Letters*, p. 259 (12 February 1942).

280 'Im always expecting . . .':   Lefevre, EB to BC, 1942.

280 'I have been talked . . .':   *WD*, p. 119, EB to BC late autumn 1942.

280 'Ive absorbed enough strychnine . . .':   Lefevre, EB to GC, from Springfield, wartime, undated.

280 John Piper's reception of exhibition: John Piper, 'Edward Burra at the Redfern', *The Spectator*, 4 December 1942.

280 'I seem to have had quite . . .':   *WD*, p. 120, EB to Mrs Chappell.

280 'I think it was him . . .':   Huntington Library, AIK 2197–2380, EB to CA, 9 January 1942.

281 'Edward Burra . . .':   *The Observer*, 29 November 1942

281 'very handsome, like a movie star . . .':   Chappell, National Sound Archive tape 2630B.

281 'he was good looking . . .':   Letter from Lord Ritchie, 10 September 2006.

282 re-founded as Frewen College: Edward Pertinez interview, 15 June 2006.

282 'It must be fun':   Letter from Lord Ritchie, 9 September 2006.

283 based on the paintings of El Greco: Arnold Haskell, *Miracle in the Gorbals* (Edinburgh: Albyn Press, 1946), p. 21.

283 'the one master . . .':   'Back to the Sources', in *Week-end Review*, 7 February 1931.

283 Ninette de Valois hindsight: Ninette de Valois in *EB Remembered*, p. 62.

283 Glasgow drawings: Causey, *Burra*, no. 166, and drawings nos 67, 68, 70.

284 'I think some . . .':   TGA 939.2.4, R. Helpmann to EB, 28 June 1944, from New Theatre, St Martin's Lane.

284 'Ive spent two days . . .'   *WD*, p. 123, 20 October 1944

284 'We had a lovely . . .':   *WD*, p. 124.
284 David Paltenghi: Biographical details supplied by Pamela Darnley-
                                            Smith (David Paltenghi's widow), 19 March 2007.
285 'Edward Burra's décor . . .':   Quotations from Haskell, *Miracle in the Gorbals*, pp.
                                            30–1.
285 'the ballet was an enormous   *WD*, p. 125.
    success . . .':
285 'During that wait . . .':   de Valois, *Come, Dance with Me*, p. 159.
286 'Ime rather nervous . . .':   TGA 974.2.2.115, EB to BKS, December 1944.
286 'please be more careful . . .':   Kavanagh, *Ashton*, p. 301.
286 'Everyones wearing thinner . . .':   *WD*, p. 124.
286 'I wish it was all over . . .':   *WD*, p. 120.
286 Burra the cook: Aiken in *EB Remembered*, p. 85.
287 'kept together by Mumsies . . .':   *WD*, p. 123.
287 10,500 V-Is were launched: Longmate, *How We Lived Then*, p. 491.
287 'We could hear the oncoming   Stanley Rothwell, *Lambeth at War* (London: SE1
    doodle bug . . .':   People's History Project, 1981).
287 'there are quite a few gas mains . . .': *WD*, p. 124.
287 'Ive got quite a lot of paper . . .':   Burra in *EB Remembered*, p. 106.
288 A lucky find: Huntington Library, AIK 2197–2380, EB to CA, 14
                                            May 1943.
288 No complaints: *WD*, p. 110.
288 Uncharacteristic frankness: *WD*, p. 105.
288 *Dante Sonata:*   Arnold Haskell, *Ballet – to Poland* (London: Adam &
                                            Charles Black, 1940), p. 79.
288 'profounder and more dynamic':   'Dance Critic', 'English Ballet in Wartime', *The
                                            Penguin New Writing* 13, April–June 1942, p. 110.
288 Immensely important, and   David Vaughan, *Frederick Ashton and his Ballets*, 2nd
    completely ephemeral: edn (London: Dance Books, 1999), pp. 179–80.
289 'Most of us feel':   P.W. Manchester, *Vic-Wells: A Ballet Progress*
                                            (London: Victor Gollancz, 1946), pp. 45–6.
289 'Fiendish did you say dear?':   Burra, in *EB Remembered*, p. 102.
289 'I think such awful things . . .':   Hayward catalogue, p. 11.
289 'Im taking up my pen':   Burra in *EB Remembered*, p. 104.
289 'That's how I feel . . .':   *WD*, p. 110.
290 'I got married':   TGA 974.2.1.66, BKS to EB, 1945.
290 'being a waster':   TGA 974.2.1.63, BKS to EB, 22 May 1944, from 11
                                            Fitzroy St, W1.
290 Bar's mother's death: TGA 974.2.1.68, BKS to EB, October 1945.
291 'ATOMS HE! HE!':   *WD*, p. 127.

XII.   Ruins in a Landscape

292 the beaches were mined: *WD*, p. 129.
292 Camber Sands: *The Denton Welch Journals*, ed. Jocelyn Brooke
                                            (London: Hamish Hamilton, 1952), p. 228.
292 'Don't take on so dearie':   *WD*, p. 128.
293 Chappell demobilised: Chappell, National Sound Archive tape 2638A.

293 'horrible sweetish-sour odour': Stephen Spender, *The Thirties and After* (London: Fontana, 1978), quoting his journal for 1953, p. 175.

293 Housing shortage: *WD*, p. 127. *WD*, p. 107, mentions that Mrs Chappell and Honor Blair were living together in Great Ormond Street in 1940.

294 Chappell's flat: Chappell, National Sound Archive tape 2628A.

295 Bunny's new business: Lefevre, BKS to EB, 6 July 1937.

295 'Ive got some coupons . . .': *WD*, p. 129.

295 Artists return home: *WD*, p. 128.

295 Cross about *Don Juan*: *WD*, p. 125.

295 *Symphonic Variations*: David Vaughan, *Frederick Ashton and his Ballets*, 2nd edn (London: Dance Books, 1999), pp. 205–9.

296 'It could be likened to a crazy nightmare': Ninette de Valois, *Come, Dance with Me* (London: Hamish Hamilton, 1957), pp. 166–7.

296 Burra's designs: James Hyman Fine Arts, *Edward Burra: Stage and Cabaret*, 21 January–7 March 2003.

296 'it couldn't have been worse painted': *WD*, p. 129.

297 'The house is dreadfully shabby': *Aiken Letters*, p. 267.

297 1942 show: Huntington Library, AIK 2197–2380, EB to CA [spring 1943].

298 'however I enjoy it very much': Huntington Library, AIK 2197–2380, EB to CA [1948].

298 the ignoble history of terrible films: Cyril Fletcher, *Nice One, Cyril* (London: Barrie & Jenkins, 1978), pp. 135–6.

299 'I have a contract thank God': Huntington Library, AIK 2197–2380, EB to CA [late summer 1948].

299 a spirited attempt to raise the money: Fletcher, *Nice One, Cyril*, p. 137.

299 'It starts off during carnival': Kavanagh, *Ashton*, p. 362.

300 'instead of cooking up some crazy plot': Kavanagh, *Ashton*, p. 362.

300 Burra's own thoughts: Four of the seven are illustrated in the Hayward catalogue, nos. 140 1–vii, p. 153, where they are conjecturally linked with Burra's cover art for a book called *The Triumph of Death*.

300 Burra's absence of ego: Three are illustrated in Sotheby's *Works from the Estate of Edward Burra, Lady Ritchie of Dundee and Associated Owners* (London, 3 July 2002), nos 274, 275 and 279.

300 '. . . I was very pleased with them!': Huntington Library, AIK 2197–2380, EB to CA, undated, but after 25 November 1948.

300 Ashton's version: Frederick Brown, *An Impersonation of Angels: A Biography of Jean Cocteau* (London: Longman's, 1986), pp. 263–4; TGA 974.2.1.26, BKS to EB, 7 April 1928.

301 '. . . a sure sign of strain': Vaughan, *Ashton and his Ballets*, p. 228.

301 '. . . the opening night . . .': Huntington Library, AIK 2197–2380, EB to CA, undated, but after 25 November 1948.

301 Luisillo: Keith Money, *Margot Assoluta* (London: Fair Prospect, 2000), p. 66.

301 '... altogether incredible':   *The Ballet Annual* 3 (1949), p. 30. Teresa and Luisillo
                                      made a great impression: they are sketched on p.
                                      33, and photographed on pp. 95 and 99.

301 'a glum static figure ...':   P.W. Manchester, *Dance News*, November 1953.

301 bored to tears: Kavanagh, *Ashton*, p. 363.

301 beautiful costumes: Causey, *Burra*, nos 168, 169, 170, 171, all painted in
                                      1946.

302 'everything *looks* menacing':   Rothenstein in *EB Remembered*, p. 47.

302 'our artists had a merely   Bryan Robertson and John Russell, *Private View: The
     local reputation':   Lively World of British Art* (London: Thomas
                                      Nelson, 1965), p. 6.

303 Burra and Anne: *WD* (note by Chappell), p. 107.

304 Springfield has outlived its time: *WD*, p. 134.

305 'an alcoholic's "must"'   *WD*, p. 131.

305 'We've been to Limerick':   Huntington Library, AIK 2197–2380, EB to CA, from
                                      Cork, April 1948.

306 'Ireland is one of the most beautiful   Hayward catalogue, p. 127.
     countries ...':

306 'I don't think they're so hag-ridden   Hayward catalogue, p. 126.
     over there ...':

307 Ireland was good for him: Huntington Library, AIK 2197–2380, EB to CA
                                      undated, from Cork, thus April 1948.

307 '... a very gregarious person   TGA 2002/1.4, transcripts made from Arts Council
     by nature ...':   film.

307 depression & apathy: Huntington Library, AIK 2197–2380, EB to CA, 15
                                      January 1950.

307 Harold Rubin: 'Dance Critic', 'English Ballet in Wartime', *Penguin
                                      New Writing* 13, p. 110.

308 'I cannot think of another designer   TGA 939.2.4, R. Helpmann to EB, 8 August 1949, re
     who could do it so well':   *Don Quixote*.

308 'filled with admiration':   Kathrine Sorley Walker, *Ninette de Valois: Idealist
                                      without Illusions* (London: Hamish Hamilton,
                                      1987), p. 256.

308 '... atmospheric power ...':   Walker, *Ninette de Valois*, p. 256.

309 the ballet was a dud: Meredith Daneman, *Margot Fonteyn* (London:
                                      Viking, 2004), p. 253.

309 '... it was well ahead of its time':   Walker, *Ninette de Valois*, pp. 260–1.

XIII. Still Life

310 Chappell forced to close his shop: Lefevre, BC to EB, 11 July 1950, from 40 Thurloe Sq.

311 the Festival of Britain: Peter Hennessy, *Never Again: Britain 1945–1951*
                                      (London: Vintage, 1992), p. 425.

312 Burra's attitude to Christianity: TGA 2002/1.4, transcripts made from Arts Council
                                      film.

313 he was superstitious: TGA 974.2.2.122, EB to BKS, 30 December 1971.

313 '... a shade eerie ...':   Lefevre, EB to BC [1967], from Queen's Close.

314 'all that strangeness':   TGA 2002/1.4, transcripts made from Arts Council
                                      film.

314 'A younger generation . . .': Bryan Robertson and John Russell, *Private View: The Lively World of British Art* (London: Thomas Nelson, 1965), p. 49.

314 '. . . I never eat anything without running it under the tap . . .': Huntington Library, AIK 3940–3942, EB to CA, 28 May 1961.

315 'If I had strength': *WD*, pp. 134–5.

315 '. . . rather above my station . . .': *WD*, p. 135.

315 '. . . Im tired of walk ups in all their unbridled scruffiness . . .': *WD*, p. 136.

316 '. . . "fashionable" for intelectuals . . .': Huntington Library, AIK 3940–3942, EB to CA, from Hôtel Lavoisier, rue Lavoisier, Paris.

316 '. . . revived by the food': Huntington Library, AIK 1422–1438 (1438), CP to CA, 28 December 1950, Madrid.

316 '. . . a bone of contention . . .': Huntington Library, AIK 3940–3942, EB to CA, undated.

316 beginning to plan: Huntington Library, AIK 3940–3942, EB to CA, from Springfield, 16 August 1951.

317 'The duckie old town of Rye . . .': TGA 90.50.2051, EB to MN.

317 Margaret Nash was saddened: TGA 70.50.2052, MN to EB, 19 February 1952.

317 '. . . all the plaster had fallen in my book cupboards': Huntington Library, AIK 3940–3942, EB to CA, undated [spring 1953].

318 Henry and Trudy Burra worried a good deal: Compare Harold Nicolson's lament in his diary, 'the world as I know it has only a few more hours to run', quoted in David Cannadine, *Aspects of Aristocracy: Grandeur and Decline in Modern Britain* (New Haven: Yale University Press, 1994), pp. 231–2.

318 the house: Huntington Library, AIK 3940–3942, EB to CA, 10 November 1953.

319 '. . . old teeth & oyster shells . . .': Huntington Library, AIK 3940–3942, EB to CA, 10 November 1953, and AIK 2381–2391, EB to MA, 14 December 1943, both from Chapel House.

319 '. . . I come from the land of the living dead . . .': *WD*, p. 145.

319 'Ed seems much better . . .': Huntington Library, AIK 1422–1438 (1425), CP to CA, 4 [September 1953] from Hillcrest, Gorse Lane, High Salvington.

320 '. . . for food drink and chicanery': TGA 939.2.4, MA to EB, 16 January 1950.

320 a wonderful site: *Aiken Letters*, pp. 246, 247.

320 he could work in peace: Mary Aiken, *EB Remembered*, p. 95.

320 not quite clear what he was working on: Hayward catalogue, p. 70.

321 'Its Hastings realy': *WD*, p. 141.

321 '. . . intense dislike of being forced to make conversation . . .': *WD*, p. 139.

322 a flea-pit, but welcoming: TGA 939.2.1, AB to EB, summer 1953.

322 'the Novelty Bar was very good on Washington St.': *WD*, p. 140.

322 'there are no temptations . . .': *WD*, p. 140.

323 '... like Zazu Pitts in "Greed" ...': *WD*, p. 139, Huntington Library, AIK 3940–3942, EB to CA, undated, from 41 Anderson St, Boston, Massachusetts.

323 '... back in Boston again ...': TGA 939.2.2, EB to Ma, 28 May 1955, from 93 Revere St, Boston.

323 '... he'd better sell something dearie ...': Huntington Library, AIK 3940–3942, EB to CA, undated, from 41 Anderson St, Beacon Hill, Boston [February?].

324 'Realy what I want is some money ...': Huntington Library, AIK 3940–3942, EB to CA, undated, from 41 Anderson St.

324 '... I <u>can't</u> pick it up, & you know I'm strong': TGA 939.2.4, MA to EB, 22 February 1975.

324 'out of sight, out of mind' with Burra: TGA 939.2.4, John Rothenstein to EB, 17 August 1944.

325 Bar Ker-Seymer's withdrawal: Val Williams, *Women Photographers* (London: Virago, 1986), p. 103.

325 '... a hideous business for everyone': TGA 939.4, Betty Keen to EB, from Idaho Springs, Colorado.

325 Retreat to Conygar: Ken Cuthbertson, *Nobody Said Not to Go* (New York: Faber & Faber, 1998), p. 317.

326 opened one of the first launderettes in London: Alan Bennett, *Untold Stories* (London: Faber & Faber with Profile Books, 2005), p. 199.

326 '... 1911 dance steps': Huntington Library AIK 3940–3942 EB to CA, 4 August 1956.

326 Clover: V.S. Pritchett, *Selected Short Stories*, chosen, with an introduction, by Mrs Clover Pertinez (Madrid: Alhambra Series of English Literature, 1958).

327 Edward Pertinez: Edward Pertinez, interview, 15 June 2006.

328 '... all the old ghosts ...': *WD*, p. 136.

328 'he hated Peter Pan ...': Clover Pertinez in *EB Remembered*, p. 74.

328 'Your telling me As for old letters dearie ...': *WD*, p. 122.

328 '[he was] in fits of laughter ...': TGA 8726.4.41, BKS to J. Rothenstein, 2 March 1972.

328 Arnold Haskell on David Paltenghi's intelligence: Arnold Haskell, *Ballet* (Harmondsworth: Penguin, 1938), p. 190.

328 *Canterbury Prologue*: Information from Julian Paltenghi, pers. comm.

329 'I am so happy and proud ...': TGA 939.2.4, David Paltenghi to EB, 22 February 1951.

329 Paltenghi as a choreographer: Marie Rambert, *Quicksilver, an Autobiography* (London: Macmillan, 1972), p. 190.

329 'Mama Tilda & Anne went to Canterbury ...': *WD*, p. 136, EB to CP, 1951.

329 '[she] never stops murmuring compulsively ...': *WD*, p. 158.

329 Burra and Paltenghi's close relationship: National Sound Archive tape 1897A.

330 'Its a terrible loss . . .':   Huntington Library, AIK 3940–3942, EB to CA, 7 February 1961 (next quotation is also from this letter).

330 'I thought he had a marvellous face . . .':   Barbara Roett, TGA 2002/1.4, transcripts made from Arts Council film.

331 Allan Morrison: TGA 974.2.2.307, Allan Morrison to BKS, 3 October 1953.

331 'Ed has been staying . . .':   TGA 974.2.1.132, BKS to B. Roett, 10 October 1954, from 11 Fitzroy Sq.

332 '[I have been] very busy . . .':   WD, p. 142.

332 'We've had a p.c. from Jimmy [Daniels] . . .':   TGA 939.2.4, CP to EB, 24 May 1958, from Madrid to Chapel House.

333 'My first glimpse in the fifties . . .':   Jennifer Mortimer, 'First Impressions of Soho', Soho Clarion 117 (Summer 2004), p. 8.

334 'Im usually being a recluse . . .':   WD, p. 137.

334 Denby Richards' recollection of Burra in Soho: Denby Richards, telephone interview, 9 April 2006.

334 'the whole of London is bristling . . .':   Huntington Library, AIK 3940–3942, EB to CA, 5 November 1954.

334 John Banting and Dylan Thomas work with Donald Taylor: Andrew Lycett, Dylan Thomas: A New Life (London: Weidenfeld & Nicolson, 2003), pp. 240–4.

335 'I bought the Map of Love . . .':   Huntington Library, AIK 2197–2380, EB to CA, July 1940.

335 Burra buys all of Thomas' collections: EB to CA, 9 January 1942. Copies of Thomas's successive collections were in his library at the time of his death.

335 'He saw himself in those tramps . . .':   Clover Pertinez in EB Remembered, p. 77.

335 'All I want is a jar big enough':   Causey, Burra, p. 74.

336 'They are pestering me to do Flowers . . .':   WD, p. 204, EB to CP, 3 or 4 August 1974.

336 'thanks to anti biotics and moussec . . .':   WD, p. 143.

337 Burra's father gives him a copy of Moll Flanders: TGA 939.1.1, EB pocket diary for 1929 (29 March).

337 Henry Burra's death: Huntington Library, AIK 3940–3942, EB to CA January 1958

XIV.   Flower Power

338 'Am out of the clink . . .':   WD, p. 144.

338 'I got ill having eaten something . . .':   TGA 974.2.2.112, EB to BKS, 25 August 1934.

339 Burra buys tattoo with operation money: Hayward catalogue, p. 63.

339 tattoo: a ferocious Chinese mask with a dagger: Sotheby's, Works from the Estate of Edward Burra, Lady Ritchie of Dundee and Associated Owners (London, 3 July 2002), p. 49. Photograph (1934) by Barbara Ker-Seymer.

339 'My blood count hasn't gone up as it ought . . .':   WD, p. 148.

340 Dr Geoffrey Dove: Obituary, *Update* [Journal of the Royal School of Mines Association, part of Imperial College] 15, autumn 2002.

340 'The NE wind has been my greatest X . . .': TGA 974.2.3.17, EB to Geoffrey Dove, 8 January 1963.

340 'I cant leave poor mother quite yet . . .': Huntington Library, AIK 3940–3942, EB to CA [spring 1958].

342 'The Royal Academy rang him up . . .': Clover Pertinez in *EB Remembered*, p. 78.

342 'I just cant be bothered to move the Academy . . .': *WD*, p. 147.

342 Burra's dangerously low blood count: *WD*, p. 158, EB to BC, 11 April 1963.

343 'I'm so sorry about that terrible aneamia attack . . .': TGA 974.2.1.94, BKS to EB, 23 September 1967.

343 'If I don't work I can hardly have the force . . .': *WD*, p. 137.

343 'Bumble asked me to stay a few days . . .': *WD*, p. 149.

343 'Oxford strasse & all the Bright (dead) lights . . .': *WD*, p. 156.

343 Burra falls out with Barbara Ker-Seymer: *WD*, p. 152.

344 'It will probably be ruined & made terribly quainty dainty . . .': Huntington Library, AIK 2197–2380, EB to CA, 17 December 1964; *WD*, p. 169; Causey, *Burra*, no. 305.

344 'ruminating for hours in Wards Irish House . . .': *WD*, p. 189.

344 'Have been going to nothing but Horror pictures! . . .': TGA 8913.14, EB to Seymour Lawrence, 17 August 1966.

345 'Don't you find as you get older . . .': Chappell, *EB Remembered*, p. 117.

345 'What I like about this part . . .': TGA 779.1.100, EB to JB.

345 'the state of Spain may bring Antonio over . . .': Huntington Library, AIK 1434, CP to CA, 25 February [1965], from Flat 2, 42 Queensbury St.

346 Romantics as primary reference-points of landscape painting: Causey, *Burra*, p. 68.

346 'Mama said the show was wonderful . . .': *WD*, p. 141.

346 Burra could only paint by natural light: John Rothenstein, *Edward Burra* (London: Tate Gallery, 1973), p. 26; SCRO 8503, EB to CP, 2 January 1970.

347 'on the TV on Tuesday . . .': *WD*, p. 143.

347 'Thank God I don't have to look at it . . .': SCRO 8503, EB to CP, 15 June 1967.

347 'I saw one seated in the 2 magots . . .': *WD*, p. 145.

348 'Desmond appeared in a very sharp suit . . .': *WD*, p. 152.

348 profound change in men's fashion: 'The garment industry threw itself headlong into revolution for reasons of its own: the counterculture merely happened along at precisely the right time with what the industry believed to be the right

attitudes toward clothing and the right palate of looks.' Thomas Frank, *The Conquest of Cool: Business Culture, Counterculture, and the Rise of Hip Consumerism* (Chicago: University of Chicago Press, 1997), p. 186.

348 'Bunny was unapproachably aloof ...': Andrew Loog Oldham, *Stoned: A memoir of London in the 1960s* (London: Vintage, 2001), p. 126.

348 'Where are your pearls?': Raleigh Trevelyan, 'Neil (Bunny) Roger', *New Dictionary of National Biography*.

349 'What a squawk dearie ...': *WD*, p. 148.

349 'Those who speak of her without charity ...': Brian Masters, *The Swinging Sixties* (London: Constable, 1985), p. 98.

350 Banting moves to Hastings: From autobiographical notes made by Banting. TGA 779.5.14.

350 'Unfortunately all my negatives got lost ...': TGA 779.1.327, BKS to JB, no date, but after the death of Nancy Cunard.

350 'By that time whiskey had destroyed his ability ...': George Melly, *Slowing Down* (London: Viking, 2005), p. 103.

350 'I get a bit alarmed ...': TGA 779.1.324, BKS to JB, no date.

351 'Friday I went out ...': *WD*, p. 163.

351 'Dear Ed you are my consolation ...': TGA 939.2.4, JB to EB, 19 January 1972.

351 'Oh these memories down Memory Lane ...': TGA 779.1.107, EB to JB, V (Venice?), AM.

352 'I think Dubuffet paints with a wonderful technique ...': TGA 779.1.96, EB to JB (probably 1966).

352 Barrie Sturt-Penrose violently ill on plane: TGA 974.2.2.122, EB to BKS, 30 December 1971.

352 'I went to another one ...': *WD*, pp. 162–3.

353 'the traffic and the noise is something terrible ...': *WD*, p. 177.

353 'I was trodden on & mangled ...': TGA 8913.15, EB to SL, 25 November 1966.

353 Burra hears of the Marzotto prize ceremony: *WD*, p. 174.

353 'Well dearie I was surprised ...': SCRO 8503, EB to CP, 15 June 1967, she was at 14 Queen's Close, Queen's Road, Harrogate.

354 the judges' unfashionable liking for figurative painters: *WD*, p. 177.

355 'I'm glad you made it to the Fish Fry ...': TGA 779.1.67, EB to JB, c.23 June 1966.

355 'Thank you so much for the lovely shirt ...': *WD*, p. 161.

355 Kenneth, Lord Ritchie of Bosney on Camber Sands: *WD*, p. 165.

356 'I cant hear him very well ...': *WD*, p. 165.

356 'I wouldn't mind ...': *WD*, p. 158.

356 'I don't think Ed cares for Colin ...': TGA 779.1.336, BKS to JB.

356 Edward Pertinez sees Trudy as a remote figure: Interview, 15 June 2006.

357 'to me the countryside round Rye . . .': Chappell, *EB Remembered*, p. 109

357 'Everybody thinks they will tire WD, p. 166.
mummie . . .':

357 Burra admires Bacon's retrospective Causey, *Burra*, p. 71.
in 1961:

357 Banting introduces Burra and Bacon: EB to CA, 14 June 1962.

357 Francis Bacon's studio now on view: John Edwards and Perry Ogden, *7 Reece Mews: Francis Bacon's Studio* (London: Thames & Hudson, 2001).

357 'In the annals of British Grey Gowrie in Sotheby's, *Works from the Estate of Edward Burra, Lady Ritchie of Dundee and Associated Owners* (London, 3 July 2002), p. 11.
modern art . . .':

358 'Mrs R [Bar Ker-Seymer] does not WD, p. 199.
approve . . .':

358 Burra lunches with Laurence Olivier WD, p. 125.
and Vivien Leigh:

358 'Im supposed to be staying with TGA 779.1.93, EB to JB (must be January 1972).
Bumble . . .':

358 Burra often dodges Bumble's WD, p. 173.
invitations:

358 'Perhaps Pats liver is turning TGA 974.2.2.134, EB to BKS, ? autumn 1971.
to rock . . .':

358 Patricia Highsmith in London for Andrew Wilson, *Beautiful Shadow: A life of Patricia Highsmith* (London: Bloomsbury, 2003), p. 291.
The Tremor of Forgery:

358 Burra avoiding Patricia Highsmith: WD, p. 180, EB to CP, 1 February 1969.

359 'looking wonderful in black . . .': WD, p. 179.

359 'one moment you can do anything WD, p. 155.
with her . . .':

359 'As we were sitting there . . .': WD, p. 180.

360 'they have met two or three times TGA 8429.3, JB to James Stern, 10 April 1969.
lately . . .':

360 'You seem to be able to buy any Huntington Library, AIK 3940–3942, EB to CA, from Springfield.
quantities in London . . .':

360 'I feel absolutely nothing at all . . .': Huntington Library, AIK 3940–3942, EB to CA, February 1969.

361 'I had dinner with Desmond & TGA 779.1.94, EB to JB.
Judith Corcoran . . .':

361 Max Ker-Seymer's passionate http://www.thewho.org/tales/max.htm
devotion to The Who:

361 'When I left Max was refusing to WD, p. 172.
get up . . .':

362 'When he comes to visit . . .': TGA 8726.4.41, BKS to J. Rothenstein, 2 March 1972.

362 'The small band of achievers . . .': Masters *Swinging Sixties*, p. 15.

363 Burra unconcerned by the sexual 1 November 1968, WD, p. 178. Though Dominic Sandbrook, *White Heat* (London: Little, Brown, 2006), pp. 466–71, points out that for the vast majority 'the sexual revolution of the sixties was little more than an illusion'.
revolution of the sixties:

363 'danger to the virile manhood . . .': Masters, *Swinging Sixties*, p. 108.

363 'We went to the Chelsea Potter . . .': 1967, *WD*, p. 172.

363 'The bigger the leg . . .': TGA 779.1.73, EB to JB, 30 January 1967.

364 'We actually went to "Hair"': *WD*, p. 178.

364 'Such a pity its not legal . . .': *WD*, p. 176.

364 'natural objects trees & trunks . . .': *WD*, p. 176.

364 'He sat very still . . .': Chappell, *EB Remembered*, p. 112.

365 'element of orgy . . .': Bryan Robertson and John Russell, *Private View: The Lively World of British Art* (London: Thomas Nelson, 1965), p. 262.

365 'I went to the young contemprys . . .': *WD*, p. 172.

365 Burra responds strongly to Robert Rauschenberg's work: *WD*, p. 161.

365 'horrid pictures of huge legs . . .': *WD*, p. 179.

365 'Ide rather like to meet Hockney . . .': *WD*, p. 181.

365 'I've always despised the idea of pop': Quoted in Sandbrook, *White Heat*, p. 70.

365 'English painter given large exhibition . . .': TGA 974.2.2.126, EB to BKS, May/June 1972.

366 'We are staggering on here . . .': SCRO 8503, EP to CP, Christmas Eve 1967.

366 'We live on Junkie time . . .': SCRO 8503, EP to CP, Christmas Eve 1967.

366 'I was in a terrible way . . .': *WD*, p. 177.

367 '. . . Needless to say your friends . . .': TGA 974.2.1.97, BKS to EB, 16 May 1968.

367 'I agree with you about this last show . . .': TGA 8429.25, BKS to James Stern, 14 April 1969.

367 'As things stand at the moment . . .': TGA 939.2.4, GC to EB, addressed to Chapel House, Gungarden, Rye, Sussex.

368 'I am so glad to hear . . .': TGA 974.2.1.95, BKS to EB, 19 August 1968, from 34 Charlton Place.

368 'I walked quietly over to Playden': TGA 939.2.4, Frederick Rose to EB and AB, 2 April 1969.

369 'I hate houses . . .': *WD*, p. 177.

XV. Getting Quietly Pissed

370 'I plan to retire to a modern Bungalow . . .': *WD*, p. 178.

370 'It must be about the worst place . . .': TGA 974.2.1.120, BKS to EB, 19 October 1976.

371 Chapel House expensive to heat: Huntington Library, AIK 2197–2380, EB to CA, 5 December 1969.

371 'I think of takeing over . . .': Huntington Library, AIK 3940–3942, EB to CA, 19 May 1968.

371 'the traffic [was] like a quiet day on 23rd street . . .': Huntington Library, AIK 3940–3942, EB to CA, October 1968.

371 'wot we used to call the Hilly Fields . . .': Huntington Library, AIK 3940–3942, EB to CA, 19 May 1968.

372 'This is very comfortable . . .': *WD*, p. 183.

372 'Its very odd . . .': TGA 974.2.2.120, EB to BKS.

372 'hope you notice the frightfull fall . . .': TGA 974.2.2.178, EB to BKS, undated, on Springfield paper.

372 'They sent me 2 huge books . . .': Huntington Library, AIK 3940–3942, EB to CA, Christmas 1968.

372 'Ive got the horror of anything . . .': Causey, *Burra*, p. 74; EB to CA, 19 May 1966.

372 the house at Springfield: *WD*, p. 202.

372 'Anne said she would never have a moments peace . . .': *WD*, p. 182.

373 'I wish the telephone . . .': *WD*, p. 149.

373 David Paltenghi dubs Burra 'The Champ': Interview, Pamela Darnley-Smith, 19 March 2007.

374 'The face with its sharp small features . . .': Melly in *EB Remembered*, pp. 8–9.

374 'They dont quite <u>approve</u> of me . . .': *WD*, p. 194.

374 'No wonder they wouldn't serve me . . .': TGA 974.2.2.181, EB to BKS, Christmas-ish, but undated and year uncertain.

374 'two young silly fellows . . .': Barbara Roett, interview, 3 September 2006.

375 'Anne wanted to go away for 3 days . . .': TGA 779.1.99, EB to JB, from University Arms Hotel, Cambridge (1972).

375 'she says she cant get drunk . . .': *WD*, p. 195, EB to CA.

375 Barbara's dislike of Burra's drunkenness: TGA 779.1.103, EB to JB.

376 Barbara suggests Burra smokes cannabis: TGA 974.2.1.109, BKS to EB, 20 February, probably 1970.

376 'I suppose I must have put away . . .': TGA 779.1.103, EB to JB, June 1971.

376 'Im sorry your upset . . .': TGA 974.2.2.121, EB to BKS, June 1971.

377 'He likes his garden very much . . .': TGA 2002/1.4, transcripts of interviews made for Arts Council film.

377 'The garden is in a terrible state . . .': TGA 974.2.2.126, EB to BKS, May/June 1972.

378 'Are you going back to Thurloe . . .': *WD*, p. 186.

378 'Ive got a very happy family . . .': TGA 974.2.2.185, EB to BKS, 20 August 1975.

379 'The old Aladdin is going along fine . . .': TGA 974.2.2.138, EB to BKS [1973].

379 'What other treasures . . .': *WD*, p. 205.

379 importance of sibling affection: Two professional psychologists, Stephen B. Bank and Michael D. Kahn (*The Sibling Bond* (New York: Basic Books, 1982), pp. 4–5), comment that their professional training had given them so little help with sibling relationships that they found themselves 'in a foreign country without a map'. Their research, however, suggests that the emotional relationships between siblings are of enormous personal significance even in modern America, which is probably the least kin-conscious society in the world.

379 'A isnt a very homey buddy . . .': Huntington Library, AIK 3940–3942, EB to CA, 19 May 1968.

380 'I get smoothed out at 2 Springfield cott . . .': Lefevre, BC to EB, 31 January 1972, from Thurloe Sq.

380 Chappell's operations partly paid for by Burra: Lefevre, BC to EB, 21 April 1970.

380 'Billy is always so inventive . . .':   Beryl Reid, *Beryl, Food and Friends* (London: Ebury Press, 1987), pp. 127–42, 138.

380 'I got a hand of pork . . .':   *WD*, p. 188.

380 'I had a marvellous peice of Skate . . .':   *WD*, p. 181.

380 'was a connoisseur . . .':   John Aiken in *EB Remembered*, p. 52.

381 'he liked good-value meals . . .':   Aiken in *EB Remembered*, p. 52.

381 'I love the Savoy Grill . . .':   *WD*, p. 195.

381 'I know those Italian restaurants . . .':   TGA 779.1.100, EB to JB. (1970).

381 'Farmers Horror Farm . . .':   TGA 974.2.2.123, EB to BKS, late autumn/winter 1971.

381 'I find my legs are better . . .':   *WD*, p. 207.

381 'The sauce should cook very slowly . . .':   Elizabeth David, *A Book of Mediterranean Food* (London: John Lehmann, 1950), p. 187.

382 'its like a vice realy it gets you':   *WD*, p. 194.

383 Banting writes Burra's CBE acceptance letter: John Rothenstein, *Edward Burra* (London: Tate Gallery, 1973), p. 35.

383 'had always been interested . . .':   Causey, *Burra*, p. 78.

383 'What gives the pictures . . .':   Christopher Neve, *Unquiet Landscape: Places and Ideas in 20th century English Painting* (London: Faber & Faber, 1990), pp. 122–3.

384 'They just please me for some reason . . .':   TGA 2002/1.4, transcripts made from Arts Council film.

384 'I went away to Kings Lynn . . .':   TGA 8913.14, EB to SL, 17 August 1966.

384 'What annoys me is that in the midst . . .':   Huntington Library, AIK 3940–3942, EB to CA, 16 October 1961.

385 'busy ruining the goose that lays the golden eggs . . .':   *WD*, pp. 289–90.

385 '. . . I wonder how many . . .':   TGA 974.2.2.187, EB to BKS, undated.

385 'Barry Penrose . . . made Ed drunk . . .':   Huntington Library, AIK 1422–1438 (1437), CP to CA, 8 August 1971, from 14 Queen's Close, Harrogate.

386 'Desmond & Mr Postan . . .':   TGA 974.2.2.121, EB to BKS, May 1971.

386 Burra signs some woodcuts E. Balls: Barrie Sturt-Penrose, *The Observer*, 25 July 1971.

386 'very posh they look':   *WD*, p. 186.

386 'I had a letter from Nan Kivel . . .':   TGA 779.1.98, EB to JB.

386 'Mr Alexander Postan . . .':   *WD*, p. 188.

386 'Postan came down today . . .':   *WD*, p. 193.

387 'Alexander Postan is coming tomorrow . . .':   TGA 974.2.2.123, EB to BKS, late autumn/winter 1971.

387 'Yesterday I went to a cabaret . . .':   *WD*, p. 188.

387 'I had admired his work ever since . . .':   Melly in *EB Remembered*, p. 9.

388 Banting paints toes on his shoes: *WD*, p. 189.

388 'I went to see John this afternoon . . .':   *WD*, p. 189.

388 'I put them all onto J. Banting . . .':   *WD*, p. 186.

388 Banting sold twenty-eight paintings: TGA 779.1.349, BKS to JB, December 1971.

389 'Once I and the diamond butterfly girl . . .':   Melly in *EB Remembered*, p. 10.

389 'I saw Anne Balfour-Fraser . . .':   TGA 779.1.348, BKS to JB, 12 October (1971).

389 'Miss Balfour-Fraser . . .':   TGA 974.2.1.108, BKS to EB, undated.

389 'Im very fond of them . . .':   *WD*, p. 195.

389 'Talking of empty bottles . . .':   TGA 779.1.106, EB to JB, presumably end January 1972.

390 'I love to be stoned . . .':   *WD*, p. 193.

390 'I must babble something, mustn't I?':   Peter K. Smith (dir.), *Edward Burra: The Complete Interviews* [1972], 1982.

390 'Do you think it's bad to pry? . . .':   Smith (dir.), *Edward Burra*.

390 'Having been photographed cooking 4 sausages . . .':   *WD*, p. 190.

391 'They try to improve themselves, dear . . .':   Aiken in *EB Remembered*, p. 51.

391 'most beautiful things I've seen for years':   TGA 939.1.1, EB pocket diary for 1929, 28 March.

391 Peter Smith's frustration: Smith (dir.), *Edward Burra*.

391 'Having just completed Super Market Susie . . .':   *WD*, p. 191.

391 'I have been brow beaten . . .':   *WD*, p. 190.

391 'Miss Phyllis Monkman . . .':   Lefevre, EB to BC, 28 April 1972.

392 'It was as tawdry as he'd hoped . . .':   Melly in *EB Remembered*, p. 11.

392 'In fact, he seemed incredibly patient . . .':   TGA 939.4.5, Peter Smith to AB, 30 April 1972, letterhead of Balfour Films, 76 Brewer St London W1.

392 Burra finds Tate retrospective depressing: *WD*, p. 189.

392 'I'd forgotten your Giant Retrospective . . .':   *Aiken Letters*, p. 319, CA to EB, 20 February 1965.

392 'He is delighted to accept your invitation . . .':   TGA 939.2.4, GC to Norman Reid, 28 July 1971.

393 'Nobody ever looked at those early drawings . . .':   *WD*, p. 289, EB to CP.

393 'They have suddenly . . .':   *WD*, p. 194.

393 'That girl from the Tate . . .':   TGA 974.2.2.124, EB to BKS, late June/July 1972.

393 'I thought of coming up this W.e . . .':   *WD*, p. 196.

393 'We were in the Tate . . .':   Ker-Seymer in *EB Remembered*, p. 70.

394 'A strange voice I took for a wrong number . . .':   TGA 779.1.107, EB to JB.

394 'I hate to answer the telephone . . .':   *WD*, p. 199.

394 'Revolting . . . look at that limb . . .':   Clarissa M. Lorenz, *Lorelei Two: My Life with Conrad Aiken* (Athens: University of Georgia Press, 1983), p. 202.

394 'I had a very sweet letter from Mrs E. Toft . . .':   *WD*, p. 197.

395 'a fan letter from a Bus driver . . .':   *WD*, p. 167.

395 'On the way to the Trafalgar . . .':   TGA 974.2.2.138, EB to BKS, 1973.

XVI. Empty Bottles and Old Shit

396 'it will give you some sense ...': TGA 939.2.4, from Royal College of Art, 13 January 1975.

396 'I must say I find one night stands ...': TGA 974.2.2.136, EB to BKS, 8 July 1973.

397 'another gloom box in Herefordshire ...': TGA 779.1.100, EB to JB, 1970.

397 'they rivet me in a dreadful way': WD, p. 184, EB to BC, 1970.

397 'Sole plastique à la Cream Marienbad ...': TGA 974.2.2.125, EB to BKS, 11 April 1972.

397 'The hotel in Kings Lynn had about 5 bars ...': TGA 8913.14, EB to SL, 17 August 1966.

398 'Ebbw Vale must be seen to be believed ...': Huntington Library, AIK 3940–3942, EB to CA, 1 May 1971. He painted it later in 1971 (Causey, Burra, no. 374).

398 'I think you ought to work ...': TGA 2002/1.4, transcripts made from Arts Council film.

398 'I am between paintings ...': TGA 974.2.2.182, EB to BKS.

399 'He would point at something ...': Barbara Roett, interview, 3 September 2006.

399 'I'm quite overcome ...': John Aiken in EB Remembered, p. 53.

399 'I had a little note from Beatrice Dawson ...': WD, p. 201.

399 'I can only think if I stand ...': WD, p. 181.

399 'We whirled at such a rate round the Lake district ...': WD, pp. 197, 183.

400 'I've got plenty of money ...': WD, p. 202.

400 'Just had another bullying demand': TGA 974.2.2.140, EB to BKS, 7 February 1974.

400 'How much do you think you spend a year ...': TGA 939.2.4, GC to EB.

401 'Great "business" I run ...': WD, p. 202, EB to WC, 15 February 1974.

401 'The VAT man ...': TGA 974.2.2.188, EB to BKS, undated, but 1974.

401 'over a thousand pounds ...': WD, p. 207, EB to BC, 16 June 1975.

402 Barbara Roett sees Burra's monetary offer as affection: Barbara Roett, interview, 3 September 2006.

402 'but from time to time ...': John Aiken in EB Remembered, p. 52.

403 Burra in casualty: Chappell, EB Remembered, p. 114.

403 'my ribs and shoulder were terrible ...': WD, pp. 205–6, EB to MW, 22 October 1974.

403 'I feel much better ...': SCRO 8503, EP to CP, January 1975.

404 'It sounds like the Beast in Revelations ...': TGA 974.2.2.175, EB to BKS, around this time.

404 'I noticed his face seemed smaller ...': Chappell, EB Remembered, p. 116.

405 'I find London a bit of a trial ...': SCRO 8503, EP to CP, 2 February 1975.

405 'I havent seen Bar ...': WD, p. 207.

405 'As soon as I he[a]r MORLS mentioned ...': WD, p. 208.

405 'a strange world of backstabbing ...': Illtyd Harrington, Camden New Journal, 26 June 2003.

405 'Louis le Harold 15th Wilson . . .':   SCRO 8503, EP to CP, 24 February 1975, from London.

405 'I don't ever go out further than Chapel Market . . .':   *WD*, p. 211.

405 'Now he's in St Helens Hospital . . .':   *WD*, pp. 208–9.

406 'Mrs Chappell left with Colin & Anne . . .':   TGA 974.2.2.177, EB to BKS, probably end of 1974.

406 'A & Colin are going up to morrow . . .':   TGA 974.2.2.176, EB to BKS, end of 1974.

407 '. . . we have been looking about . . .':   TGA 974.2.2.163, EB to BKS, 4 January 1976.

407 'Im afraid I shall never be able . . .':   TGA 974.2.2.176, EB to BKS, undated but early 1976.

407 '. . . the builders will soon be attacking Ropewalk . . .':   TGA 974.2.2.166, EB to BKS, 1 July 1976.

407 'Well dear Mrs Chappell . . .':   TGA 974.2.2.170, EB to BKS, probably early September 1976.

408 'When it became Anne's property . . .':   Chappell, National Sound Archive tape 2630B.

408 'I realy felt if I didn't get out . . .':   *WD* p. 211.

408 'You must have some proper food . . .':   Lefevre, CP to EB, 10 June 1976.

409 'Wimbledon we have . . .':   TGA 974.2.2.180, EB to BKS.

409 'Everything is so spotless and neat . . .':   TGA 974.2.2.122, EB to BKS, 30 December 1971.

409 Anne's distress at Ritchie's dislike for Burra: Letter from Lord Ritchie, 10 September 2006.

409 'Here we are sulking away . . .':   Lefevre, EB to BC.

410 'A will walk down . . .':   Lefevre, EB to BC.

410 'I have been trying to walk alone . . .':   TGA 974.2.2.166, EB to BKS, 1 July 1976, and TGA 974.2.2.180, EB to BKS.

410 'Though no more than two hundred feet high . . .':   Aiken in *EB Remembered*, p. 53.

410 'Ive been meaning to write . . .':   *WD*, p. 213.

411 'At the dead end of September . . .':   He says August, but other data suggest September.

411 Burra's death: TGA 939.7.10.

412 'Nonsense. I have the constitution of a mule . . .':   John Rothenstein, *Edward Burra* (London: Tate Gallery, 1973), p. 11.

412 'I draw deep in':   TGA 974.2.2.202, EB to BKS, undated but January 1972.

413 'Edward was her be-all and end-all . . .':   Chappell, National Sound Archive tape 2630B.

413 'I think he led a very vicarious life . . .':   TGA 2002/1.4, transcripts made from Arts Council film.

414 'A genius . . .':   George Melly, *Slowing Down* (London: Viking, 2005), p. 208.

414 'After you had seen a drawing . . .':   TGA 2002/1.4, transcripts from Arts Council film.

414 'He would have given cosmetic surgery . . .':   *Edward Burra: A Centenary Exhibition* (London: Lefevre Fine Art, 2005), p. 9.

414 'one of the damned, poor thing':   TGA 974.2.2.148, EB to BKS, 17 November 1974.

415 'none of them will look at Ed's beautiful landscapes':   TGA 779.1.348, BKS to JB, 12 October 1971.

415 'They're so *loud*':   *WD*, p. 198.

415 Burra omitted from H.J. Paris's *English Water Colour Painters:*   *WD*, p. 129.

415 'He saw and painted the related . . .':   Christopher Neve, *Unquiet Landscape: Places and Ideas in 20th century English Painting* (London: Faber & Faber, 1990), p. 124.

TIMELINE OF THE LIFE
OF EDWARD BURRA

1905   Edward John Burra born.

1909   Anne Petronill Burra born.

1914   Sent to prep school, Northaw Place, Potters Bar, Herts. Frequently ill.

1916   Elizabeth Mary (Betsy) Burra born.

1917   Pneumonia: sent home from school. The end of Burra's formal education. Went to Bath for arthritis treatment at least once between 1917 and 1920.

1920   Visited Switzerland with his mother.

1921   Took art lessons with Miss Bradley in Rye.

1921–3   Chelsea Polytechnic, where he studied life drawing, illustration and measured architectural drawing.

1922   Designed a poster for the Olympia Horse Show.

1923–5   Royal College of Art. His drawing tutors were Randolph Schwabe and Raymond Coxon.

1923   November: William Roberts exhibition at Chenil Gallery: Burra went with his friend Clover Pritchard and was greatly impressed.

1924   Redfern Gallery show of the work of students from the Royal College of Art, including Burra.

1925   March: went to Bordighera with his mother, had rheumatic fever.

        July: recuperated in Bath.

        Summer: met Paul Nash.

        October: in Paris with his friend Billy Chappell, staying in

Montparnasse under the chaperonage of Henry and Florence Rushbury.

1926   Late April: family visit to his sister Anne in Florence (they also visited Siena). On the way home, Burra stopped off in Paris on his own. He was home by July.

1927   January to March: visited Paris again with Lucy Norton and Sophie Fedorovitch. Sophie painted a picture of him (lost).

June: ill again; painted Springfield views since he was not going out.

August: Hugh Blaker introduced Burra to Oliver Brown of the Leicester Galleries.

September: went to Cassis and Marseilles with Billy Chappell. Home in October.

November: death of Burra's grandmother, Cecile Robertson-Luxford.

December: exhibited at the New English Art Club, probably encouraged by Nash.

1928   February: Nash offered to teach Burra wood engraving.

May: commissioned by Crawfords to do advertising designs for motor-cars, which were subsequently rejected.

June: exhibited at the New English Art Club again.

September: visited Toulon with Chappell, Irene Hodgkins, Bar Ker-Seymer, Brian Howard, Anthony Powell.

October to December: in Paris with Chappell, Frederick Ashton, Sophie Fedorovitch, Cedric Morris, Arthur Lett-Haines, Arthur Mahoney, John Banting.

1929   March: enormously impressed by Modigliani exhibition.

April: first one-man exhibition at the Leicester Galleries in London.

May: in Paris with Chappell, Frederick Ashton, Sophie Fedorovitch, Arthur Mahoney and Birger Bartholin; home at beginning of June.

14 August: Paul Nash drew garden buildings at Springfield.

26 August: Betsy Burra died of meningitis.

September: Burra and his mother went to Scotland.

October: exhibited with the London Group.

Burra's woodblock prints shown at the Society of Wood-Engravers' exhibition at the Redfern Gallery in this year.

1930   January: started making collages with Paul Nash.

February to April: travelling in France with Paul and Margaret Nash, Ruth Clark: Paris (including a visit to Léonce Rosenberg's gallery), Toulon, Cassis, Nice, Cros de Cagnes.

November: visited Scotland.

Exhibited with the London Group again.

December: the Nashes moved to New House, Rye.

Later in this year Burra edited a review, on the evidence of a letter from William Rothenstein, who saw it in January 1931.

1931   January: introduced to Conrad Aiken, who had settled in Rye the previous year, by Paul Nash.

End February: visited Marseilles.

May: visited Paris again, going about with Birger Bartholin and Sophie Fedorovitch, shifting from Montparnasse, the scene of previous visits, to Pigalle. Went back to Toulon at end of May.

August: to Toulon with Chappell and Bar. Irene Hodgkins paid a visit to Cassis to catch up with old friends, but missed Burra. Cocteau, Desbordes, Gide, Maurois and Tchelitchew were also all at the Hôtel du Port, Toulon.

Summer: Paul Nash proposed to Cassell that Burra illustrate a de luxe edition of Aiken's *John Deth*, but the project did not come off.

October: exhibited in *Recent Developments in British Painting*, Arthur Tooth & Sons (with John Armstrong, Paul Nash, Edward Wadsworth, Ben Nicholson).

1932   May/June: showed some 'decorative objects' (painted trays) at the Zwemmer Gallery.

June: second one-man exhibition at the Leicester Galleries.

Illustrated Humbert Wolfe's *ABC of the Theatre* for the Cresset Press.

Burra's work included in an exhibition of British art at the Hamburg Kunstverein.

Made uncredited costume designs for Anthony Tudor's ballet *Lysistrata* (Ballet Rambert).

Autumn: designed the sets and costumes for Frederick Ashton's ballet *Rio Grande* (first performance 29 November, Savoy Theatre).

1933   Ashton and Burra began planning an opium dream ballet, which came to nothing.

Late March to early April: in Paris with Clover Pertinez, met Jules Romains, who was working on *Les Hommes de bonne volonté*.

April to May: first visit to Spain, starting at Barcelona, then joining the Aikens and Malcolm Lowry in Granada.

End May: visit with Aikens to Spanish Morocco, returning to England by sea from Gibraltar via Lisbon.

Work by Burra included in College Art Association International.

Worked on textile designs with the encouragement of Paul Nash, and sold one ('Pimentos') to an unidentified firm.

Early autumn: Burra went to Marseilles and on to Martigues to see Hodgkins.

Late September: went to New York with Sophie Fedorovitch. Stayed with Olivia Wyndham and Edna Lloyd Thomas in Harlem till December, and also at their country home, Sandy Hook, Connecticut.

October: Burra's work included in the *Art Now* exhibition at the Mayor Gallery and illustrated in Herbert Read's accompanying book.

Christmas: Boston (with the Aikens).

1934   January: returned to New York, Lower East Side. Visited Picasso exhibition at the Wadsworth Athenaeum.

February: returned to England.

Well represented at the 'Unit One' exhibition at the Mayor Gallery in London (and provincial tour).

August: diagnosed as suffering from pernicious anaemia.

Made advertising designs for Shell-Mex and London Transport (unused).

1935   Bar moved to Church Street.

Spring: visited Barcelona and then Madrid with Clover. Spent time in dance and strip clubs in the Barrio Chino district of Barcelona. When in Madrid, studied Goya's Black paintings.

Work included in *Exposition internationale d'Art Moderne* (Brussels).

July: returned to England because his father was ill.

14 October: Anne Burra married John Francis Burra Huntley.

1936   Designed sets and costumes for Ninette de Valois's ballet *Barabau* at Sadler's Wells Theatre.

April: went to Spain again with Clover.

June: represented in the *International Surrealist Exhibition* in London and signed the statement by the English Surrealist Group which appears in the *International Surrealist Bulletin* no. 4.

18 July: Spanish Civil War broke out. Burra and Clover returned to England, and Clover married Antonio Pertinez.

December: exhibited in *Fantastic Art, Dada, Surrealism* at the Museum of Modern Art, New York, and was represented in the accompanying book.

1937   January: went to America and stayed in Charlestown with Conrad Aiken and Mary Hoover. Visited *Fantastic Art, Dada, Surrealism*, which was on tour at the Springfield Museum of Art, Massachusetts.

April: in New York, staying in Brooklyn with Jennings and Marie Rice.

May: one-man show, Springfield Museum of Art, Massachusetts.

May: by train to Mexico with the Aikens. Spent time in Mexico City, then went to Cuernavaca to stay with Malcolm Lowry. Also visited Janitzio and Taxco. Went down with dysentery.

Included in the surrealist section of the Artists International Association exhibition, *Unity of Artists for Peace, Democracy and Cultural Development*.

Late June: returned to Charlestown, extremely ill.

July: home to Rye with severely restricted mobility. Treated with massage and iron and strychnine injections.

July: exhibited with Artists International.

September: travelling in Cornwall.

November/December: exhibited in the Oxford Arts Club.

1938   Exhibited in the *International Surrealist Exhibition* at the Galerie des Beaux-Arts in Paris.

July: visited Dublin and the west of Ireland.

Exhibited at the Pump Room, Bath, *Exhibition of Watercolours, etchings, woodcuts, lithos etc. by contemporary artists.*

A one-man show at the Matthiesen Gallery was planned, but did not take place.

1939   Summer: visited Milan, Lombard cities and Venice with his sister Anne.

3 September: war declared.

October: included in *Contemporary British Art* in the British Pavilion at the New York World's Fair (and North American tour).

1940   Suffered from rheumatism, chilblains and gout.

June: included in *Surrealism Today* at the Zwemmer Gallery.

1941   October: anaemia and jaundice.

1942   October: very ill with anaemia and jaundice: received iron and strychnine injections.

November/December: exhibition at the Redfern Gallery, London.

December: working on designs for the jacket of Salvador de Madariaga, *Heart of Jade* (Collins), not used.

1943   May: afflicted with tinnitus and water on the knee.

28 July: Anne married Colin Ritchie.

1944   June: designed sets and costumes for Robert Helpmann's ballet *Miracle in the Gorbals*.

1945   Publication of John Rothenstein, *Burra*, in the Penguin Modern Painters series.

1946   Stayed at Grasmere in the Lake District with the Aikens.

Cover art for Routledge edition of *The Triumph of Death* by C.F. Ramuz.

1947   Spring: designed sets and costumes for Bizet's *Carmen* at the Royal Opera House.

June to July: one-man exhibition, Leicester Galleries.

Visited Dublin, Galway, with his sister Anne.

1948   April: visited Cork with Anne.

September: visited Dublin and Galway again, and also Sligo, with Anne.

Summer: worked on the set for *A Piece of Cake* for the Rank Organisation at the Highbury Studios.

November: designed set and costumes for Ashton's ballet *Don Juan*.

Illustrated Poe, *The Tell-Tale Heart*, Mark Twain, *The*

Adventures of Huckleberry Finn and Laurie Lee, *The Voyage of Magellan*.

Visited New York, Boston, Brewster on Cape Cod, with the Aikens.

1949 One-man exhibition at the Leicester Galleries, London.

1950 February: designed sets and costumes for De Valois's ballet *Don Quixote*.

August: visited Paris, Tours, Avignon, Orange and Nîmes with Anne, Eleanor and Jill Brodrick (cousins).

October: visited Paris with Rye friend Peggy Webb.

1951 Designed set and costumes for David Paltenghi's ballet, *Canterbury Prologue*.

Visited Bayonne and Biarritz with Anne.

Included in the Arts Council Festival of Britain exhibition, *Sixty Paintings for '51*.

1952 March: first exhibition at the Lefevre Gallery in London, biblical subjects.

July: visited Paris with Clover.

July to August: visited Barcelona with Bar.

October: Aiken returned to Rye and persuaded Burra to revisit America.

1953 April: visited Boston, then went to stay with the Aikens at Brewster, Massachusetts.

July: the Burra household left Springfield for Chapel House, Rye.

October: Burra returned from America.

1954 February: in hospital for a blood transfusion.

July: visited Paris with Bar for a jazz festival.

1955 January: retrospective one-man exhibition at the Magdalene Sothmann Gallery, Amsterdam.

17 January: arrived in New York and stayed first at East 21st Street, then at 41 Anderson Street, Beacon Hill, Boston.

April: one-man show of new work at the Lefevre.

April: stayed in Washington with the Aikens. In third week of May returned to Boston to 93 Revere Street.

May: one-man show, Swetzoff Gallery, 66 Huntington Avenue, Boston.

September: met Clover in Paris.

1956   April: anaemia attack, threatened with blood transfusion. Father ill, apparently with lung cancer.

October: one-man exhibition at Museum of Art, Rhode Island School of Design, Providence.

1957   Burra included in *Critic's Choice: 1957 selection by Nevile Wallis*.

February: to Paris with David Paltenghi.

May: visited Oxford, where he was interested in the botanical gardens.

May: exhibited flowers and still lifes at the Lefevre.

October: pictures included in *Contemporary British Art* exhibition in Paris.

October: went to Paris with Clover for a week.

31 December: Burra's father died.

1958   March: Burra designed set, drop and poster for Langston Hughes, *Simply Heavenly*.

Oxford University Press began discussing Bible drawings for their *Illustrated Old Testament*.

May: visited Oxford.

September: visited Dieppe with John Banting.

1959   February: had mumps and anaemia.

April: visited Salisbury and Longleat with Anne.

October: visited Dieppe with Banting.

October: visited Paris with Clover.

One-man exhibition at the Lefevre Gallery.

November: *Three Contemporary English Artists* exhibition, with Derrick Greaves and Hubert Dalwood, Whitworth Art Gallery, Manchester University.

1961   July: one-man exhibition at the Lefevre Gallery.

August: visited Paris with Bar, particularly interested by Gustave Moreau at the Louvre.

September: trip to Boulogne with his cousins.

1962   June: impressed by Francis Bacon exhibition at the Tate.

July: exhibited six pictures at Battle.

August: visited Ely with Anne.

Visited Ireland with Anne.

Took a number of day trips to Boulogne with Anne and other relatives.

1963 Refused an ARA offered by the Royal Academy of Arts.
April: one-man exhibition at the Lefevre.
April to June: suffered anaemia and nausea.

1964 April: visited Holland with Anne, went to Boijmans Museum and Rotterdam docks, Mauritshuis and Rijksmuseum.
Met Francis Bacon via John Banting.
September: Trudy Burra thought to be dying.

1965 Visited Norwich with Anne, returned via Cambridge and visited the Fitzwilliam.
May: one-man exhibition at the Lefevre Gallery.
Exhibited in *The English Eye*, Marlborough-Gerson Gallery, New York.
August: visited Florence, stayed with Jennings and Marie Rice.
November: 'fascinated' by the William Roberts exhibition at the Tate.
Worked on contributions to the *Oxford Illustrated Old Testament* (Book of Judith, Daniel, the Three Holy Children and Zachariah).

1966 Visited Lincoln, Boston and King's Lynn with Anne.
September: revisited Florence in third and fourth weeks of the month, stayed with Jennings and Marie Rice.
First approach from the Tate about the retrospective eventually held in 1973.

1967 January: enjoyed *Young Contemporaries* at the Tate.
February: impressed by Millais exhibition at the Royal Academy.
April: visited Peterborough, Norwich and the north Norfolk coast with Anne, came back via Bury St Edmunds.
May: one-man exhibition at the Lefevre.
June: visited Clover Pertinez in Harrogate, trip to Fountains Abbey.
June: won the Marzotto prize.
August: further visit to the Pertinez household in Harrogate, went with them to Rievaulx and the Bowes Museum at Barnard Castle.

1968 March: visited the Welsh border country and Wye Valley with Clover.
Billy Chappell moved to Pump Cottage, Rye.

May: death of Burra's mother.

September: visited Clover at Harrogate.

1969   Moved from Chapel House to 2 Springfield Cottages, a gardener's cottage next to his former home, Springfield Lodge, at Playden, near Rye.

Visited Rochester, the Peak District, Bath and Salisbury with Anne. Had gout.

April: one-man exhibition at the Lefevre.

March: travelled in Kent, visited Rochester and admired the oil refineries in the Thames estuary.

July: visited Buxton and the Peak District, Hayfield and Glossop, the Blue John cavern, Chatsworth and Haddon Hall with Anne and Billy.

October: a second exhibition, of drawings, at the Lefevre.

November: to Llanthony, Hay-on-Wye, Brecon, Bath and Salisbury with Anne.

November: visited Dieppe with Banting.

1970   January: visited Dieppe with Banting.

May: visited Norwich, Blakeney, Blickling and Yarmouth with Anne.

August: visited Penzance with Anne.

October: went with Anne to Oxford and the Welsh border country.

1971   March: visited Bath and admired the costume museum, and then went on to south Wales. Liked Newport, Ebbw Vale and the Valleys.

April: showed new work at the Lefevre Gallery.

May: visited Canterbury.

June: Awarded a CBE in the Birthday Honours list. Visited East Anglia: Letchworth, Boston and Cambridge with Anne.

July: showed early woodcuts at the Treadwell Gallery in London.

September: to Dieppe with John Banting.

October: visited Cheltenham, Chester, Liverpool and Harlech with Anne.

October: Hamet Gallery exhibition, drawings of the Twenties and Thirties.

1972　January: John Banting died.

Visited north Yorkshire and Northumberland with Anne.

1973　April: visited the Lake District with Anne and Billy, back via Buxton.

May: Edward Burra retrospective of 143 of his pictures at the Tate Gallery.

May: new work at the Lefevre Gallery.

June: travelled in the south-east with Anne, ending up in the Blue Boar, Cambridge.

July: visited Boston, Lincs, Grassington and Cambridge with Anne.

September: visited Tavistock and Dartmoor with Anne.

1974　May: visited North Yorkshire with Anne, Northumberland (Lindisfarne and Warkworth Castle) and then went on to Scotland to the Cairngorms.

October: fell during a visit to London and was badly bruised.

1975　January: visited Canterbury, Isle of Grain, oil refinery with Bar.

April: visited Falmouth, the Lizard, Penzance, Land's End and Salisbury with Anne.

May: showed new work at the Lefevre.

September: Kenneth Ritchie died and was succeeded as Lord Ritchie of Dundee by Colin Ritchie.

December: Mary Aiken visited Rye and stayed till New Year.

1976　February: gastric flu.

May: fell in Rye, broke a leg and cracked a hip.

Late September: taken to Hastings hospital with a blocked bowel, where he died on 22 October, aged seventy-one.

THANKS AND ACKNOWLEDGEMENTS

AMONG the many people who have contributed in one way or another to this biography, I should like to thank Gauvin Bailey, Fanny Baldwin, Janet Barnes, Andrew Biswell, Sally and David Brown, Pat Brückmann, Ann Caesar, Andrew Causey, Alexander Corcoran, Desmond Corcoran, Eddy Coulson, Neil Curtis, Pamela Darnley-Smith, Peter Davidson, Nicola and Juan de la Peña y Montezuma, David Dickinson, Kathleen Dickson, Ann Dillon, Elizabeth Elliot, Mike Goldmark, Aoife Goodman, Selina Hastings, Jane Aiken Hodge, Merlin Holland, Bernard Horrocks, Arnold Hunt, Julie Kavanagh, Pat Kavanagh, Max Ker-Seymer, Andrew Losowsky, Dan McCannell, Jill Macdonald, Paula Maclean, Leanne Mahoney, David Man, Sarah Money, Denny Nicol, Julian Paltenghi, Juliette Paton, Edward Pertinez, Alan Powers, Jane Pritchard, Lucy Quarry, Julia Ramos, Simon Rees, Barbara Roett, Denby Richards, Lauren Rigby, Lord Ritchie of Dundee, Hugh Robertson, Alison Saunders, Joan Schenkar, Tom Shakespeare, Alexandra and Johnny Stanciow, Francis Stevenson, Winifred Stevenson, Lady St Johnston, Chris Whittick and Val Williams.

In particular, both Edward Pertinez and Barbara Roett allowed me to interview them at length about Edward Burra and his circle, and both made me greatly valued gifts: Edward Pertinez gave me a portrait photograph of his mother, Clover, and Barbara Roett made me the talismanic present of one of Burra's much-chewed paintbrushes. Nobody who has read Julie Kavanagh's biography of Ashton will be unaware of how much I owe to her intimate, insider's knowledge of the ballet world, and above all to the interviews that she extracted from a number of Burra's friends who had died by the time I embarked on this book. Equally, I am greatly indebted to Andrew Causey for his pioneering catalogue of Burra's work, as well as for his personal assistance and his generous loan of a number of Burra's exhibition catalogues.

I have also received the most generous help and cooperation from librarians and archivists at Lewes County Record Office, the Huntington Library, San Marino, CA, the British Library, the British Film Institute, the Arts Council England, the National Art Library, the Royal Opera House, Rye Art Gallery, Edinburgh Museum of Modern Art, the British Library, the Society of Authors, the National Portrait Gallery, the National Sound Archive, the Theatre Museum and the National Monuments Record. I am grateful above all to Tate Britain, which holds the great bulk of the archival material relating to Burra's life and work. The reading-room staff have, without exception, been understanding about my need to get though enormous amounts of data with maximum speed and efficiency, and they have been geniality itself about accommodating me. Dominic Persad and Lucy Scrivener, on the photographic side, have been helpful to an extent that deserves separate acknowledgement.

Equally, Alexander and Desmond Corcoran and the staff of the Lefevre Gallery have done everything possible to facilitate this work. Not only did Desmond Corcoran allow me to interview him, and lend me photographs, but they both answered questions and gave me access to their own collection of Burra letters and much other archival material associated with the painter that they hold (which includes most of the letters used in the printed collection of Burra's correspondence, *Well, Dearie*). They also let me see their unique collection of printed material connected with the painter, and their great albums of photographs of every work by Burra they know to exist.

Like all biographers, I owe a special debt to the copyright holders who have given me permission to quote from unpublished material. In many cases, they have also been very generous with their time and property, they have consented to interviews, answered letters or lent me irreplaceable family photographs. First of all, with respect to Edward Burra and his immediate family, I must thank Mrs Denny Nicol and other surviving Burra family members, as well as Alexander and Desmond Corcoran, his literary executors. I am also particularly grateful to the Arts Council England for permission to cite transcripts from interviews with Edward Burra and his friends, made by Balfour Films on behalf of the Arts Council in 1973, Tate Britain for Paul Nash, Jane Aiken Hodge for Conrad and Mary Aiken, Max Ker-Seymer for Barbara Ker-Seymer, Edward Pertinez for Clover Pertinez, Julia Ramos for Florence Rushbury, Merlin Holland for Dolly Wilde, and the Society of Authors as the literary representatives of Rosamond Lehmann.

Every effort has been made to contact copyright holders, though in one or two cases these remain elusive.

INDEX